Church and Theology in the Nineteenth Century

Church and Theology in the Nineteenth Century

Ferdinand Christian Baur

EDITED BY
Peter C. Hodgson

TRANSLATED BY
Robert F. Brown and Peter C. Hodgson

CASCADE *Books* · Eugene, Oregon

CHURCH AND THEOLOGY IN THE NINETEENTH CENTURY

Copyright © 2018 Peter C. Hodgson and Robert F. Brown. All rights reserved. Except for brief quotations in critical publications or reviews, no part of this book may be reproduced in any manner without prior written permission from the publisher. Write: Permissions, Wipf and Stock Publishers, 199 W. 8th Ave., Suite 3, Eugene, OR 97401.

Cascade Books
An Imprint of Wipf and Stock Publishers
199 W. 8th Ave., Suite 3
Eugene, OR 97401

www.wipfandstock.com

PAPERBACK ISBN: 978-1-5326-3231-0
HARDCOVER ISBN: 978-1-5326-3233-4
EBOOK ISBN: 978-1-5326-3232-7

Cataloguing-in-Publication data:

Names: Baur, Ferdinand Christian, author. | Hodgson, Peter C., editor and translator. | Robert F. Brown, translator.

Title: Church and theology in the nineteenth century / Ferdinand Christian Baur ; edited by Peter C. Hodgson ; translated by Robert F. Brown and Peter C. Hodgson.

Description: Eugene, OR: Cascade Books, 2018. | Includes bibliographical references and index.

Identifiers: ISBN 978-1-5326-3231-0 (paperback). | ISBN 978-1-5326-3233-4 (hardcover). | ISBN 978-1-5326-3232-7 (ebook).

Subjects: LCSH: Church history—19th century. | Theology—History. | Theology, Doctrinal—History.

Classification: BT21.2 B29 2018 (print) | BT21.2 (epub).

Manufactured in the U.S.A.   MARCH 12, 2018

A translation of Ferdinand Christian Baur, *Kirchengeschichte des neunzehnten Jahrhunderts*, edited by Eduard Zeller (Tübingen: Verlag und Druck von L. Fr. Fues, 1862).

Contents

Editor's Foreword   xiii

Introduction   1

PART ONE:
From the Beginning of the Nineteenth Century to 1815

1. Introduction   9
   Survey of Political Events   9
   Germany under Napoleon; the Wars of Liberation   12

2. History of the Catholic Church   17
   Secularization in Germany   17
   The Napoleonic Concordat   21
   The Situation of the Protestants under Napoleon   22
   The Condition of the Catholic Church in Germany   24
   History of the Papacy: Pius VII up to His Imprisonment   26
   Pius VII in France; the Council of Paris; Further Negotiations   29
   The Pope's Return to Rome   35

3. History of the Protestant Church   36
   Introduction   36
   The Protestant Literature   38
   Herder   38
   Schiller and Goethe   42
   The Romantics   48
   German Philosophy: Kant   52
   Fichte   60
   Schelling   68

Jacobi	73
Schleiermacher: *Soliloquies, Speeches on Religion, Christmas Eve*	77
General Condition of Theology: Dogmatics	87
Daub, *Theologumena*	89
Rationalistic Exegesis: Venturini, Paulus	90
New Testament Criticism: Eichhorn, Schleiermacher	94
Historical Theology: Planck, Marheineke	95
Theological Journals	97

PART TWO: From 1815 to 1830

1. Introduction	101
Political Conditions	101
Ecclesiastical Developments	105
2. History of the Catholic Church	107
The Papacy: The Restoration Politics of Pius VII	107
Success in Italy, Spain, and France	109
Affairs in Germany	110
Other Matters in the Reign of Pius VII	112
Leo XII and Pius VIII	113
The Fortunes of the Jesuit Order after Its Suspension	114
The Generals of the Jesuit Order since Its Reinstatement	116
The Jesuits in Italy, Spain, and Portugal	117
The Jesuits in Austria, Bavaria, and Elsewhere in Germany	119
The Jesuits in France	121
The Relations between Protestants and Catholics in France	125
The Catholic Church in Belgium	129
The Catholic Church in Italy, Spain, and Portugal	131
The Catholics of Ireland	133
The Catholic Church in Bavaria	134
The Catholic Church in Prussia	136
The Ecclesiastical Provinces of the Upper Rhine	137
Switzerland	140
The Trends of the Times: Advocates and Struggles	140
3. History of the Protestant Church	144
Ecclesiastical Conditions Linked to Political Conditions	144

Negotiations Concerning Ecclesiastical Conditions in Prussia   145
The Ecclesiastical System in Southern Germany   148
Church Ritual in Prussia   149
Celebration of the Jubilee of the Reformation;
   Harms, Ammon, and Schleiermacher   154
The Union; Introducing It in Prussia   158
The Union in Baden, the Palatinate, and Nassau   161
Further Deliberations and Disciplinary Measures for Promoting the
   Union in Prussia   162
Dogmatic Alignments: Rationalism and Supernaturalism   165
The Standpoint of Schleiermacher's *Glaubenslehre*   172
The *Glaubenslehre*'s Position on Belief in Miracles   174
Its Teaching about Sin and Redemption   178
The Christology of the *Glaubenslehre*   183
The Pantheism of the *Glaubenslehre*   190
The *Glaubenslehre*'s Relation to Church Teaching   191
The Internal Coherence and Historical Significance of the
   Glaubenslehre   194
De Wette's Philosophy of Religion and Dogmatics   198
De Wette and Schleiermacher   202
The Nature of Dogmatics at That Time   204
Marheineke   205
New Testament Criticism: Gieseler and Bretschneider   207
Church History: Neander   209
Theological Orientations and Their Publications;
   the *Evangelische Kirchenzeitung*   211

PART THREE: From 1830 to Most Recent Times

1. Introduction: Political Conditions   221

2. History of the Catholic Church   226
   A. The Papacy   226
      Gregory XVI; Unrest in the Papal States; Reaction   226
      The First Years in the Reign of Pius IX   230
      The Year 1848; Retreat of the Papists; the Roman Republic   234
      Pius IX and the Papacy after 1849   239
   B. The Most Recent History of the Jesuits   242

The Jesuits in France under Louis Philippe	242
The Jesuits in Switzerland; the *Sonderbund* War	247
The Fate of the Jesuit Order since 1848	250
C. The Conflicts between Rome and Germany Prior to 1848	252
The Controversy about Mixed Marriages:	
The State of Affairs up until 1837	253
Droste-Vischering and Dunin	255
The Controversy Resolved in Prussia	258
Assessment of the Issues in the Controversy	259
The Controversy about Mixed Marriages in Württemberg	262
Hermesianism and Its Condemnation	262
Bautain	268
The Philosophy of Günther and Its Condemnation	270
German-Catholicism: The Sacred Tunic	272
Ronge and Czerski	274
The Further History of German-Catholicism Prior to 1848	277
German-Catholicism since 1848	282
The Assessment of German-Catholicism	284
D. Möhler's *Symbolik* and the Protestant Response	287
Möhler's *Symbolik*	287
The Protestant Response; the Significance of the Dispute	290
The State of Catholic Theology Today	295
The Dogma of the Immaculate Conception	296
E. The Most Recent Conflicts of the Catholic Church	
with the Government of States	298
The German Episcopacy in 1848	299
The Catholic Church in Austria; the Concordat;	
The Position of the Protestants	299
The Church Controversy in Baden	304
The Württemberg Concordat and the Baden Concordat	307
F. Concluding Remarks	311
Spain, Portugal, and Italy	311
France	313
Switzerland	314
3. The History of the Protestant Church	316
A. The History of Theology	316
Hegel: The General Character of His System	316

Hegel's *Philosophy of Religion*	319
The Hegelian School and "Positive Philosophy"	324
Strauss's *Life of Jesus*	328
The Opponents of Strauss: Steudel, Hengstenberg, Tholuck, and Others	333
The Moderate Faction: Ullmann, Neander, and Others	338
Weisse and the Hegelians	343
Strauss's *Streitschriften* and "Vergängliches und Bleibendes"	347
A Look Backward at the Straussian Movement	349
The Ecclesiastical Reaction	350
Schelling in Berlin; Neander	352
Bruno Bauer	355
The *Deutsche Jahrbücher*	358
Feuerbach	359
Baur and the Tübingen School	363
Dogmatic Theology: Nitzsch, Twesten, Marheineke, and Others	368
Strauss's *Glaubenslehre*	371
Mediating Theology; A More Modern Supernaturalism	374
Rothe, Fichte, and Weisse	377
The Union Theology	379
The Orthodox Theologians: Hofmann and the Erlangen Group; and Baumgarten	381
Historical Theology	385
Biblical Exegesis	386
Old Testament Theology: Hengstenberg	389
Ecclesiastical and Theological Journals: *Theologische Studien und Kritiken, Evangelische Kirchenzeitung*, and Others	393
B. Ecclesiastical Affairs	398
The Union and the Traditional Lutherans in Prussia	398
The Bishopric in Jerusalem	404
Arrangements for a System of Governance in Prussia; The Protestant Conference; the 1846 General Synod	407
The Protestant Friends	417
Discussion of the Matter in Print; The Protesting Theologians and the *Evangelische Kirchenzeitung*	419
Free Congregations	423
The Charter of 30 March 1847	424

The Dismissal of Uhlich	425
The Growth and the Suppression of the Free Congregations	427
Deliberations about a Synodal System of Governance	429
The Protestant High Consistory in Berlin	430
The Union and Lutheranism in Prussia	432
Stahl on the Union	435
More on the History of Ecclesiastical Conditions	441
The Union in the Palatinate	442
A Further Attempt at Union: The Gustavus Adolphus Foundation	445
The Eisenach Conferences	447
The Protestant Church Congress	448
The Home Mission	454
The Protestant Alliance	455
The Current State of the Protestant Church: High Church Attitudes and Science	457
Orthodoxy and Pietism	462
The Neo-Lutheran Concept of the Sacraments	463
The "Theology of Established Facts"	466
The Pneumatic Interpretation of Scripture	467
Concluding Thoughts	468

Appendix 471

1. Protestantism in the German Catholic States and Countries Other Than Germany	471
In Bavaria	471
In Austria	473
In France	474
In Switzerland	479
In England: Puseyism (The Oxford Movement)	480
2. The Sects of Most Recent Times within the Catholic Church and within the Protestant Church	485
The New French Church	485
The Saint-Simonians	485
Irvingism	489
The Plymouth Brethren	494

The Württemberg Sects: The Harmonists, the Michelians,
the Pregizerians, and the Adult Baptizers   495

Index of Persons   499
Index of Subjects   507

Editor's Foreword

Ferdinand Christian Baur (1792–1860) began publishing a five-volume history of the Christian Church in 1853. The first volume was called *Das Christenthum und die christliche Kirche der drei ersten Jahrhunderte* (Tübingen, 1853). A second, revised and expanded edition appeared in 1860, the year of Baur's death; and a third edition, identical with the second, in 1863, published under the title *Kirchengeschichte der drei ersten Jahrhunderte*. It was the latter edition that was translated into English by Allan Menzies as *The Church History of the First Three Centuries*, 2 vols. (London and Edinburgh, 1878–79). The new title, imposed by the editors to provide uniformity for the series as a whole, unfortunately obscured the fact that Baur initially distinguished between "Christianity" as the original phenomenon and "the Christian Church" as what emerged from that phenomenon. We intend to provide a new translation of this first volume, using the second edition of 1860, and restoring its original title.

In 1859 Baur published the second volume, *Die christliche Kirche vom Anfang des vierten bis zum Endes des sechsten Jahrhunderts in den Hauptmomenten ihrer Entwicklung* (The Christian Church from the Beginning of the Fourth Century to the End of the Sixth Century in the Major Moments of Its Development). He himself prepared the manuscript of the third volume for publication but died before it could appear, so it was brought out by his son Ferdinand Friedrich Baur in 1861 as *Die christliche Kirche des Mittelalters in den Hauptmomenten ihre Entwicklung* (The Christian Church of the Middle Ages).

Manuscripts remained for two additional volumes of the church history. Ferdinand Friedrich Baur edited the fourth volume, which appeared in 1863 as *Kirchengeschichte der neueren Zeit, von der Reformation bis zum Ende des achtzehnten Jahrhunderts* (Modern Church History, from the Reformation to the End of the Eighteenth Century). Initially this was the end of the series, and it was not until 1850, twenty-three years after he first lectured on modern church history, that Baur made the nineteenth century a separate topic for lectures, beginning with the year 1800 and continuing up through the 1850s. Baur's son-in-law, Eduard Zeller, edited the various lecture manuscripts and published them in 1862 (Tübingen) as *Kirchengeschichte des neunzehnten Jahrhunderts* (Church History of the Nineteenth Century). He created a unique document; it and the first volume are considered the most important contributions in Baur's vast undertaking (which runs to over 2,600 printed pages).

Zeller had access to lecture manuscripts with many improvements and additions made along the way, as well as to student transcripts of Baur's lectures, which he used to rightly order the later additions.[1] The Baur Papers in the University of Tübingen Library contain a lecture manuscript for nineteenth century church history (Mh II 166 l), which runs to 248 pages. Heinz Liebing, editor of the reprint edition in 1970, examined this manuscript and discovered that additional pages have been interleaved into the original 248 pages, so that the full length is 380 pages. Thus there are two levels to the finished product: the original manuscript used in 1850, and the many additions made to it by Baur on the occasion of subsequent lectures, which continued through 1859–60. Zeller reported in his preface to the first edition that he only tried to put the various additions into their proper locations, and here and there made small stylistic improvements that any author would want for a published work. He provided supplementary information in footnotes only for the years 1860–61, and clearly marked these supplements as editorial. Liebing concludes that Zeller produced an authentic, reliable published version of his father-in-law's lectures. Only a German critical edition could determine any progression in Baur's point of view during the 1850s, and such has never been undertaken.

Baur regarded himself as a contemporary of the six decades from 1800 to 1860, in which he became a participant from about 1830 onwards. His work was viewed after his death as both a *Darstellung* (presentation, portrayal) and a *Quelle* (source).[2] Liebing says it is the initial source of a history of effects (*Wirkungsgeschichte*) that by 1970 had lasted more than a century, and, we may add, continue into our own time. We can consider the work most helpfully as a "participant history."

As a participant history the book has uneven qualities. It provides extraordinary insights into Baur's theological (and philosophical) predecessors and contemporaries in Germany. He gives critical accounts of Herder,

---

1. For information in this and the next paragraph I rely on the editorial introduction by Heinz Liebing to the reprint of this volume in *Ausgewählte Werke in Einzelausgaben*, ed. Klaus Scholder, 5 vols. (Stuttgart–Bad Cannstatt, 1963–75), vol. 4 (1970), vii–xxiii. Zeller published a second edition fifteen years later, in 1877, to which he added a new preface and more editorial notes on recent literature, but made no changes in Baur's text. The first volume of Baur's church history (*Das Christenthum und die christliche Kirche*) is reprinted in *Ausgewählte Werke*, vol. 3 (1966), ed. Ulrich Wickert.

2. See Zeller's preface to the 1877 edition (Leipzig), x.

Goethe, Schiller, Kant, Fichte, Schelling, Schleiermacher, Hegel, Möhler, Marheineke, Daub, Strauss, Feuerbach, and other seminal thinkers for modern theology. We are calling the book *Church and Theology in the Nineteenth Century* because Baur says in his introduction that, as we approach more closely our own time, "we cannot consider the changes in outer church life without finding their true and authentic ground in the prevailing theological views and orientations, in the revolution that religious and dogmatic consciousness underwent in one aspect or another in different epochs; and such a revolution is itself in turn conditioned by everything that defines the political, scientific, and intellectual character of an age." He announced his lectures for the first time in 1850 as "Most Recent History of Christian Theology and the Church from the Beginning of the Nineteenth Century to the Present"; and for the final time in 1859–60 as "Most Recent Church History Since the Beginning of the Nineteenth Century, with Particular Attention to the Development of Theology."[3] So the lectures were intended from the beginning as a history of the church *and theology*, and they link together political, cultural, ecclesiastical, and theological developments. Large portions of the work are devoted to the details of Catholic and Protestant church history (mostly in Germany and France) in each of the three main periods, and these details may seem uninteresting to us. But they put to rest the myth that Baur constructed history a priori and paid little attention to empirical details. Also the three periods (1800–1815, 1815–1830, 1830–1860)[4] are not proportioned equally, and Baur's interest focuses most intently on his own time (and place). Only in the Appendix is any significant mention made of developments in the United Kingdom, and America is left out completely. While these restrictions indeed seem parochial, English-speaking readers will gain information on events and figures about which they knew nothing previously, and Baur describes religious beliefs and practices with which we are analogously familiar from our own time and place.

For each of his major studies, whether in New Testament, history of religion, history of dogma, or church history, Baur wrote extensive critical introductions that trace the history of the discipline in question up to his own time. In the case of the church history, he published a separate book,

---

3. See Ulrich Köpf, "Ferdinand Christian Baur and David Friedrich Strauss," in *Ferdinand Christian Baur and the History of Early Christianity*, ed. Martin Bauspiess, Christof Landmesser, and David Lincicum, trans. R. F. Brown and P. C. Hodgson (Oxford, 2017), 34 n. 247. German edition: *Ferdinand Christian Baur und die Geschichte des frühen Christentums* (Tübingen, 2014).

4. The three periods, marked by political turning points, are characterized as those of revolution, restoration, and attempts at the mediation of antitheses, but this tells us little about the actual contents.

Die Epochen der kirchlichen Geschichtsschreibung (1852), translated as *The Epochs of Church Historiography*.⁵ At the beginning of the concluding chapter, Baur writes:

> It has long been acknowledged that the historian can be equal to his task only in so far as he transposes himself into the objective reality of the subject matter itself, free from the bias of subjective views and interests, whatever they may be, so that instead of making history a reflection of his own subjectivity, he may be simply a mirror for the perception of historical phenomena in their true and real form.⁶

What is the "objective reality of the subject matter itself"? According to Baur, it is the matrix formed by the intermeshing of the "idea" of the phenomenon in question and the historical material in which the idea actualizes itself. For the Christian church, this idea is the principle of Christianity itself--the idea of divine-human union-and-unity (*Einheit*) in Christ and in Christian consciousness through the ages. Baur goes on to say that, in even the most recent treatments of the history of the Christian church,

> the idea still hovers indefinitely and at a great distance over the manifestations to which it must be related. It is not yet strong and vital enough to penetrate and vivify the historical material, as the soul animates the body, or to become, through such an organic unity, the moving principle of the entire series of manifestations in which the history of the Christian church takes its course. Or should there still be any doubt as to whether the history of the Christian church is the movement of the idea of the church, and therefore consists of something more than a succession of changes following one another at random? If it is right to speak of an idea of the church, then that idea, like any other, must possess within itself the living impulse to go out from itself and to become actualized in a series of manifestations that can only be regarded as various aspects of the relation that exists generally between idea and manifestation.⁷

---

5. In *Ferdinand Christian Baur: On the Writing of Church History*, ed. and trans. P. C. Hodgson (New York and Oxford, 1968), 41–257.

6. Ibid., 241.

7. Ibid., 241–42. See also 244. Significant is Baur's footnoted reference in the middle of this passage to Friedrich Schelling's "brilliant ideas" about the advance from a pragmatic to a "universal" or "absolute" standpoint in the writing of history. He quotes from Schelling's *Vorlesungen über die Methode des akademischen Studium* (Stuttgart and Tübingen, 1803), 213 ff.; ET: *On University Studies*, trans. E. S. Morgan, ed. Norbert Guterman (Athens, OH, 1966). See especially lecture 10, "On the Study of History and Jurisprudence," from which Baur's quotations are taken (ET 104–7). Baur was

The various periods in the history of the church can be distinguished in terms of the primary historical forms by which the idea manifests itself--whether in the form of dogma, as in the ancient church; or in the form of ecclesiastical hierarchy, as in the Middle Ages; or in the form of faith and subjectivity, as in the churches of the Reformation. Each of these forms is present in all ages, but their peculiar mixture determines the character of each age. In the Enlightenment of the eighteenth century, subjectivity came to the fore, but the task of the nineteenth century was to find ways to mediate this newly-found subjectivity with the objectivity of God and history, and to do so without regressing into traditional forms of doctrine and belief. Despite the great achievements of Schleiermacher and Hegel in the first third of the century, from Baur's perspective the second third (c. 1835 to 1860) failed miserably at this task. The conservative reaction to Strauss's *Life Jesus* set scientific theology back by at least a generation. Baur shows how both the Catholic and Lutheran Churches, under pressure from modernity, became increasingly entrenched in reactionary stances.

In discussing J. G. Fichte's view of the relationship between philosophy and history, Baur makes the following revealing comment:

> What would the metaphysical truth be without its historical mediation, if it did not actualize itself in the consciousness of humanity by appearing in history, and doing so not merely in scattered individuals but in the organic nexus of historical development, thus emerging out of the abstract region of philosophy into the concrete life of religion, and becoming part of the collective consciousness of a religious and ecclesial community? And what, on the other hand, would the historical aspect be—everything that has objectified itself in such a broad scope in the history of humanity and has been incorporated into human consciousness—how subjective and contingent would it be in all its external objectivity if it could not also be grasped in its true objectivity, and thus in the final analysis as a metaphysical truth grounded in the essence of God himself? Thus it is always a matter here of the vital conjunction of the two opposed aspects, the metaphysical and the historical; but for Fichte himself, the two sides still remain in an unmediated, abstract dichotomy.[8]

This is one of Baur's few methodological remarks in the text. The volume as a whole bears testimony to both the fruitfulness and the ultimate failure of his vision. Baur was the greatest historical theologian of

---

influenced by Schelling before his first encounter with Hegel.

8. See below, p. 64.

the nineteenth century. He conceived of history as a theological discipline grounded in the idea of God's self-mediation (which constitutes history as such), and of theology as a historical discipline committed to the unbiased research of historical science (*Wissenschaft*). Holding these two aspects together proved eventually to be an impossible task because the two disciplines retreated from each other—history into a strictly empirical method, and theology into a confessional stance. Whether the failure was built into the vision, or came about as a result of intellectual and moral weakness, is a question that still engages us today. Historical reality is indeed often resistant to rational truth, and facts have distorted ideals into demonic caricatures, as the twentieth century bears tragic witness. So we have become suspicious of overarching historical visions; but without some sense of the purpose and direction of history it is difficult to make sense of life. We turn back to figures like Baur for guidance.[9]

❀

The present volume builds on the trajectory of our recent translations of Baur's *History of Christian Dogma* (Oxford University Press, 2014) and *Lectures on New Testament Theology* (Oxford University Press, 2016); and prior to Baur, our translation of new editions of several of Hegel's Berlin lectures (philosophy of religion, history of philosophy, philosophy of world history, philosophy of art, proofs of the existence of God). We are grateful to Oxford for publishing an English edition of the collection of essays cited in n. 3, *Ferdinand Christian Baur and the History of Early Christianity* (2017). This book contains fifteen essays by contemporary scholars and a bibliography of works by and about Baur. Wipf and Stock Publishers is continuing with further translations of Baur. *Church and Theology in the Nineteenth Century* (volume 5 of the church history) is the first volume to appear, and it will be followed by *Christianity and the Christian Church of the First Three Centuries* (volume 1 of the church history).

We have introduced subheadings into the text from the table of contents, and have broken up Baur's long paragraphs into shorter ones. The book has three types of footnotes. Editorial notes are the most common, providing background information on names, movements, and events, and

---

9. For further discussion, see *Baur and the History of Early Christianity* (n. 3), and Peter C. Hodgson, *The Formation of Historical Theology: A Study of Ferdinand Christian Baur* (New York, 1966; reprint Minneapolis, 2007). See also Baur's own analysis of "Baur and the Tübingen School," which focuses on his contribution to New Testament studies, in the present volume, pp. 363–68.

they are not indicated as such unless added to a Baur note or a Zeller note. Baur's own notes are marked as [*Baur*] and occur infrequently; sometimes information provided in the text is moved to the notes where it is more suitable [*Baur, in the text*]. Eduard Zeller added his own notes [*Zeller*], sometimes to provide clarification but more often to add information about events occurring in the two years between Baur's death and the publication of the work. Some of these notes are quite lengthy, and we abbreviate them because our focus is on what Baur thought, not Zeller.

What Baur thought is always interesting, and he had an amazing grasp of historical details spanning nineteen centuries from Christian beginnings right up to his own time, together with a sense of how everything fits together in a tragicomic story. But he did not draw facile conclusions. The book ends (prior to the Appendix) on a rather gloomy note about the dominance of authoritarian, conservative factions and expresses only a modest hope for "a freer and more rational outlook."

Introduction

No special justification is required if I separate the most recent church history from general church history and make it the subject of its own lectures. Not only is the material church history has to work with and to present so extensive and abundant that it becomes increasingly difficult to complete the whole in unbroken continuity up to the present in the brief time we can allot to it; but also the most recent period demands a different kind of treatment from what came before.

The closer we come to the present, the more familiar is the ground on which history plays out. For this reason, the presentation must dig more deeply into details and develop more precisely the connection between events rather than merely present what is already known; and the nature of the case itself obliges us to do so. The closer we are to events, and the more we witness the historical process unfolding before our own eyes, everything appears to be more closely and thoroughly intertwined. The events and the processes cannot be separated, so that when something catches our eye we are increasingly led beyond it and always attend to something else if we are to form a clear representation of the thing at hand. Especially in the arena of the most recent history, we must not be satisfied with the merely outward aspect of events. Deficient as our knowledge remains in many cases, so much that automatically impacts us allows us to see more deeply into the inner connections of events, into their effective causes, into the motives and interests of active agents. The entire spirit of the age is still directly felt afresh in our own day, and it alone ultimately enables us to explain why the most important circumstances all in fact transpired and took the exact form that they have.

For this very reason—because the closer we stand to the theater of history the more everything is seen to be more tightly and vitally interconnected—I also believe that the topic of these lectures has to be expressly described as not just ecclesiastical matters but also theological matters. As a rule, the more precisely we delve into the nexus of causes and effects, the more we are pointed back from the external to the internal. So too we cannot consider the changes in outer church life without finding their true and authentic ground in the prevailing theological views and orientations, in the revolution that religious and dogmatic consciousness underwent in one aspect or another in different epochs; and such a revolution is itself in turn conditioned by everything that defines the political, scientific, and intellectual character of an age. Such an inner and deeper connection is found in every age, but in none more so than in the most recent times, when ecclesiastical matters are conditioned by the general course of development and character of the present day. If there was once an age in which the whole of world history was basically church history, having its dominant center and principle of movement in church history,[1] now it is very much the opposite. If we wanted to take the ecclesiastical and theological aspects purely by themselves and separate them from everything else, from political and scientific matters, from everything that belongs to modern culture, then it would be impossible to provide a vital and concrete perception of them. Precisely this is the most distinctive characteristic of the most recent period in the arena of the church—that people everywhere see themselves being in a freer and broader sphere in which the particular can be rightly grasped and conceptualized only by looking at the whole. The principal task of such a presentation must be never to lose sight of this universal aspect. If our task only involves one special topic, that topic is actually only the specific point from which we must be oriented to the spirit and character of the age in general.

We can say that the general topic of these lectures is the most recent church history. But what are we dealing with under the heading of "most recent"? What does it examine? The concept of "most recent" is an especially relative one. We can ascribe a shorter or a longer period of time to the most recent history. If we say that the most recent history is the history of "the present," that too is a very fluid concept. We also need not limit the present in which we live in such a way that we cannot go further back and include much that has a closer or a more distant relation to the present, in order to gain a clearer picture of the conditions of the immediate present. But there must always be a very prominent turning point from which we start out in order to arrive at what lies closest to us in the present.

This point can be defined differently depending on the point of view and purpose that one brings to bear in such a presentation. The latest historian writing on the topic of the most recent church history, C. Schwarz in *Zur Geschichte der neuesten Theologie* (1856),[2] specifies this point as the year

---

1. The period of the Middle Ages.
2. Carl Schwarz, *Zur Geschichte der neuesten Theologie*, 2nd ed. (Leipzig, 1856).

1835, in which Strauss's *Leben Jesu*[3] appears. The history of the most recent theology is the history of the last twenty years. Here it is evident that this most recent period is fixed as it is because the presentation is restricted to purely theological matters. But if we combine the theological with the ecclesiastical, or make the latter the principal object of investigation, we cannot remain at this point in time.

In his *Kirchengeschichte der neuesten Zeit* (1855), Gieseler[4] goes back to 1814. The year 1814 designates a highly important turning point in political affairs, but what significance does it have for ecclesiastical matters? Gieseler makes the following claim also with respect to the church: the mighty hand of God was so obviously at work benefiting people in Napoleon's downfall that it was bound to move them to acknowledge and praise God. The eighteenth century's lack of faith completely disappeared in the purifying fire of this event, and faith and piety rose up with new power. The sovereigns too have openly stated how "God is our only help and he alone has helped us," and they have provided their people with shining examples of humility before God and of inner piety. Thus it appears that a new age has begun for religion and the church too. Only two difficulties remain to be overcome. People no longer adhere strongly to the confessional doctrines of the church, and numerous reforms are needed in church institutions and ordinances. But these ecclesiastical conditions are closely connected with political circumstances. So the political views of the rulers of the states have also affected their treatment of the affairs of the church. In addition, peoples' opinions about church affairs have likewise been influenced by the prevailing political views.[5]

This is the way the great turning point of the year 1814 is comprehended from a perspective that is edifying in purely religious or practical terms. Its significance for the ecclesiastical dimension is that people could again be Christian, religious, church-going, right-believing. But is this not merely a passing mood of the time? And if it is not that but something more lasting, is not the change introduced by it grasped far too externally if it is seen to be due only to feeling grateful for liberation from French domination and to the example of the piety of sovereigns? But that does not say very much, since in general the piety and religiosity of peoples change periodically, sometimes increasing and sometimes decreasing. Nor is it an apt characterization of the further course of the period beginning with this turning point to view it in terms of the opposition between the two parties, the liberals and the

3. See below, pp. 328–33.

4. Johann Karl Ludwig Gieseler, *Kirchengeschichte der neuesten Zeit* (Darmstadt, 1855) (vol. 5 of his *Lehrbuch der Kirchengeschichte*, 1842–57).

5. [Baur] Gieseler, *Kirchengeschichte*, 9ff.

absolutists. This opposition basically is seen throughout church history with various modifications; and in theology the opposition between views and orientations continues without change for long after 1814. Hence the mood occasioned by the year 1814 and the events at that time are accorded far too great an importance as to their effect on the church and theology. If we choose to date the most recent church history from the year 1814, then the period beginning with that year must be seen from the same perspective by which it is considered in a political framework. In terms of its political character, it is generally described as the period of the Restoration.[6] This designation is also very appropriate for its ecclesiastical and theological aspects, and the term "restoration" gives us a perspective from which the various orientations that emerge in this period can be integrated.

But if we speak about a restoration, a return to earlier conditions, then we must know not only what is to be restored but also why people look back so enthusiastically to conditions and circumstances that are no longer viable, why principles and outlooks are to be revived that public opinion has already more or less clearly rejected. The reason can only be found in the whole series of changes that took place in the preceding period. Hence we must go back to these changes. Restoration cannot be understood apart from the negative element that its positive features wish to replace. In political history the portrayal of the restoration period requires at least looking back to the time of Napoleonic rule. In church history we must go back even further if we want to regard the more recent period as that of a restoration. This is because the changes with which the restoration is concerned are not as forceful and evident as those in the political arena. But in order not to reach back too far beyond the time that is regarded as belonging to the present, and to keep as much as possible to the same perspective for political and ecclesiastical issues, it is appropriate to fix the beginning of the century [as the starting point for the first period].[7] This is the time span (1800–1815) during which, in political affairs, Napoleonic hegemony took its course and came to an end with his downfall. It is also the time during which the most important changes occurred for the church (and here we are looking mainly at the Catholic Church). So overall we see the entire period caught up in

---

6. The Bourbon Restoration was the period in French history following the fall of Napoleon in 1814 until the July Revolution of 1830. The brothers of the executed Bourbon king Louis XVI reigned in highly conservative fashion, and the effects of the restoration of the French monarchy were felt throughout Europe.

7. Baur traces the period of the revolution in theological consciousness (the Enlightenment) back to about the middle of the eighteenth century, so that in its full extent the first period runs from c. 1750 to 1815. See his *Kirchengeschichte der neueren Zeit, von der Reformation bis zum Ende des achtzehnten Jahrhunderts*, ed. F. F. Baur (Tübingen, 1863).

continuous, deep-seated change that disrupts all the public affairs of the existing order and completely reshapes everything. In the intellectual realm, to which theology is closely related, there were also such astonishing shifts in viewpoints and systems that the phenomena in this area have shown a similarly revolutionary character. The more important, the more forceful, and the more consequential these changes were, the unavoidable reaction that arose against them is hardly surprising.

The reversal in political conditions cleared the way; but the deeper and more universal ground was that two opposing principles were locked in unresolved conflict with each other—the principle of the old traditions, and that of the ideas stirring a new age. Since the reaction in the political arena was the first to emerge and to play its major role on this stage, we can name the period stemming from this source with the political term "restoration period" (1815–30). People wanted to restore as much as possible what the previous age had torn down or reshaped. This was successful in various connections, but always only up to a certain point, because resistance had to be reckoned with that thwarted a complete return to the old times. Where it succeeded, the restoration was therefore always only an apparent one. In fact there was a struggle between opposing orientations and aspirations, a seesawing struggle between two principles in which at intervals each one in turn was able to fight back against, and suppress, the other side.

This became more characteristic of the situation beginning in 1830. The principle that was strongly restrained during the period of the restoration became more energetic on various issues, and it is not surprising that it finally and decisively prevailed. This is the main distinction to be made between the two periods into which the timeframe beginning in 1815 falls. The period of restoration lasts only as long as neither of the two principles in conflict with each other, and thus bound together, is decisively able to free itself from the other. The principle of restoration not only asserts itself, but its unabated attempts to gain more ground are not without success. This state of ever shifting circumstances took a new turn in 1830.[8] The political revolution of this year signaled a new and far-reaching popular movement in which the consciousness of the times became distinctly recognizable. Thus the struggle between restoration and anti-restoration entered a new

---

8. The July Revolution of 1830 removed the Bourbons from the French throne and initiated a period of more moderate government. This had repercussions especially in Belgium and southern Europe, but the German rulers, after initial disturbances (culminating in a liberal festival at Hambach in 1832), were able to quell any significant changes (the Six Acts of June 1832), and Prussia remained aligned with Austria and Russia in an alliance of the status quo. The first English Reform Bill passed Parliament in June 1832.

phase in which the two sides made it a matter of principle. Previously concerned to balance out the two principles and to have them mutually accommodating, now people wanted nothing further to do with an arrangement in which each side was limited by the other. The consciousness of the age became increasingly clear that each of the two principles could only be maintained with complete consistency. Thus the time dating from 1830 can only be designated as the period in which, on the one hand, each of the two principles is, conceptually, on the verge of quickly shifting into the other; and, on the other hand, each strives at least as much to separate and distance itself from the other as far as possible, and to achieve full validity in its own sphere. This tendency of the time is so characteristic that it is visible not just in the political realm but as well in familiar phenomena in the ecclesiastical and theological spheres.

In this way we have briefly indicated the general perspectives from which the period lying before us will be treated, in three parts. Many issues from the second part extend over into the third part, and the farther away we move from the year 1830, the more that year no longer seems so significant as a turning point, in light of what follows. But still the events of 1830 were important enough in themselves, and if they did not have as rapid an impact in the political arena as initially had been assumed, nonetheless the contemporary phenomena in the ecclesiastical and theological realms were clear harbingers of a new epoch. In establishing a timeframe for the final period—although in this case the distinction is still more fluid, and becomes clearer and more definite as time goes on—we should certainly not hesitate to maintain the indicated perspectives in order to grasp the periods in their characteristic differences.[9]

---

9. [*Heinz Liebing reports (p. xvi of his preface to the reprint edition, see Editor's Foreword, n. 1) that the following, concluding paragraph of the Introduction is written in Eduard Zeller's hand. It is uncertain whether Zeller composed it himself or (which seems more likely, given the first-person reference) copied it from a lost notation by Baur.*] Regarding the literature, it is evident that very little has been written about a period that belongs completely to the present age. We mention Gieseler's *Neueste Kirchengeschichte von 1814 bis auf die Gegenwart*, edited from his papers by Redepenning in 1855 [see n. 4]. It forms the fifth volume of Gieseler's large work on church history. Gieseler's treatment differs from mine in two respects: first, as indicated, he dates the most recent church history from the year 1814; and second, he does not devote equal attention to the theological aspect alongside the merely ecclesiastical, and does not sufficiently identify the principle at work in theology, and its connection with the general culture of the time. Gieseler's work contains a great deal of special material, especially on the political side; but the general perspective and the elements in terms of which the various periods are characteristically distinguished are too little evident. Thus he organizes the whole only in terms of the series of individual countries.

PART ONE

*From the Beginning of the
Nineteenth Century to 1815*

1

Introduction

Survey of Political Events

The beginning of Part One takes us back to the turbulent times during which the French Revolution completed its course. Since from its beginning it was a world-shattering event, it was the center of gravity of all political movements of the European states. The torrent, which had powerfully and perilously swollen the stream of revolutionary sentiment, had begun to recede, and more fixed points in the newly forming order of things already had begun to emerge amid the widespread destruction and confusion of the previously existing order. By the first days of the new century, a man stood at the pinnacle of power in France. This was a man who managed to forge the chaotically confused elements in France together and to amplify the power delivered into his hands from the revolution, which he would use to determine the fate of Europe for years to come. After he became the First Consul of the French Republic, in 1799, Napoleon Bonaparte (1769–1821) demonstrated the great organizing talent that set him apart. Because of him France became a newly organized state, rejuvenated with powers nourished by the revolution. Thus he now exerted the greatest influence on the whole of a Europe crumbling as the result of the revolution, and he effected the most important changes in political affairs and all related matters. The entire period of Napoleonic domination involves a series of events that, to an ever greater extent, caused everything to be torn loose from its old footings and the foundations of a new structure to be laid on the wreckage of the old.

The first important event of this period was the peace concluded between the French Republic and the German emperor at Lunéville in February 1801, as a result of the victory of the French at the Battle of Marengo.[1] This treaty separated the left bank of the Rhine from Germany and joined it to France, and this brought about a series of changes that were of great importance in the ecclesiastical realm as well. This was the beginning of the dissolution of the German imperial regime as it had existed since early times. Its complete dissolution came about a few years later.[2] While France became a united monarchy by the transformation of the Republic into a hereditary empire,[3] as seemed to befit the needs of the nation, everything that happened in Germany since the Peace of Lunéville showed ever more clearly how little the decaying and collapsing system of the old aristocracy and monarchy had aroused resistance to itself, whereas resistance seemed ever more necessary the more power the new rulers seized. The new coalition formed against France in 1805 came to an end, following the Battle of Austerlitz, with the Peace of Pressburg concluded in December of that year. That treaty considerably diminished the power of Austria and also cut loose from German imperial authority a number of German imperial princes—the electors of Bavaria, Württemberg, and Baden, who were elevated to being kings. Thus at the beginning of 1806 the German emperor saw that it was necessary for him to dissolve the empire and relinquish the German throne.

What happened to Austria in 1805 with the Battle of Austerlitz, happened to Prussia in 1806 with the Battle of Jena. Prussia, so resplendent in its ancient glory as a significant state, all at once became a minor territory. Under the name of the Confederation of the Rhine, to which the Electorate of Saxony (elevated to a kingdom) and the newly erected Kingdom of Westphalia (ruled by a French prince) belonged, the greater part of Germany became a French province. The mighty French Empire, constantly and rapidly expanding, and utilizing all the instruments of power and politics, attained its long-sought goal of a universal European monarchy. The pressure on the general atmosphere at that time quickly became so great that Austria hoped to shake off the yoke of foreign domination by the great exertions it made in

1. The battle was fought between France and Austria in northern Italy, and the "German emperor" who signed the treaty was the Holy Roman Emperor Francis II.

2. Since its formation in the early Middle Ages, the Holy Roman Empire was a confederation of most of the countries in central Europe. It was predominantly German speaking, but included the Low Countries, the Kingdom of Burgundy, the Kingdom of Bohemia, and territories in northern Italy as well. The emperor was crowned by the pope after a selection usually by German prince-electors. The last emperor, Francis II, dissolved the Empire in 1806 after the creation of the Confederation of the Rhine by Napoleon.

3. Napoleon was named emperor of the French in 1804, a post he retained until his defeat in 1814, and briefly regained in 1815 before his final deposition.

1809. These efforts just served to entrench opinions about the omnipotence of its foreign domination. The peace newly concluded in Vienna, which joined the new French dynasty with the old Habsburg dynasty through family ties, just seemed to establish a new guarantee for the continuing existence of the French monarchy.[4]

The extent to which the peoples and states of Europe—with the exception of the English who were protected by their insular situation, and the tenacious resistance of the Spanish religious fanaticism—were under French control, and how little these apparently independent peoples were able to resist the force of necessity and so joined in campaigns of conquest, we see in 1812 when the French emperor turned against the emperor of Russia, with whom he previously had been on friendly terms, in order to expand his universal monarchy in this direction too. As he explained in his war manifesto, Napoleon supposed that, in the war for which he himself was responsible, Russia would simply be meeting its fate. But the menacing fate now fell upon the bold [would-be] conqueror himself. The burning of Moscow, and the deadly harshness of the Russian winter on the withdrawing army, brought a sudden reversal: the extraordinary events could be seen to herald the cry for liberation from the oppression of foreign domination.[5] In Prussia there had long been a secret, calculated plan, relying on both moral energy and political shrewdness. Now it suddenly and powerfully came out into the open, and the heroic uprising of the entire people directly shows that now they faced an entirely different opponent than in the days of the catastrophe at Jena. To be sure, victory over a military power as well organized as the French required many bloody battles with varying outcomes; but by the end of 1813 things had gone so far that now the whole of Europe was allied against France, whereas the previous year it had taken the field with France. Despite the valiant resistance that the united armies met with in France, the empire could not endure. It collapsed to such a degree that Napoleon had to abdicate and withdraw from the stage.

What was scarcely thought possible now happened: the exiled Bourbons again mounted the French throne and claimed their hereditary rights to it. But in a short while the contrast between the new rule and the

---

4. At the Treaty of Schönbrunn in 1809, Austria lost a fifth of its population but survived as a state. The next year the childless Napoleon divorced Empress Joséphine and married the Austrian archduchess Marie Louise, who bore him a son in 1811.

5. Napoleon invaded Russia in the summer of 1812. The Russian forces kept drawing back to Moscow, where they finally gave battle. The French won but at a tremendous cost, and their morale was broken. After Moscow was burned rather than surrendered to the French as a winter haven, the French army withdrew in a disastrous retreat. Conflicts continued throughout 1813 with all the allied powers until France was worn down; and in April 1814 Napoleon abdicated.

previous one was felt so deeply, and the sympathy of the French nation for the emperor who had elevated France to the highest level of its power and glory was so strong, that he only needed to reappear in order to topple the Bourbon throne once again. The whole of France fell to Napoleon with new enthusiasm when in 1815 he landed on the French coast with a few comrades from the island of Elba. While the monarchs assembled in Vienna, to divide the spoils of their conquests, were deeply involved in their diplomatic negotiations, which became ever more complex because of their discrepant interests, the destiny of Europe had to be decided once again by force of arms. The Battle of Waterloo finally put an end to Napoleon's domination.[6] The negotiations of the Second Treaty of Paris and the acts of the reopened Congress of Vienna lay the foundation of a new political system, which in particular established the internal circumstances of Germany as they still are today.[7]

Germany under Napoleon; The Wars of Liberation

If we survey this time frame, we can rightly say that there is no period of history with such a great reordering of circumstances as in this short span of fifteen years, and with one world-historical event following upon another. What the French Revolution meant for France, the revolution proceeding from Napoleonic rule meant for the lands to which it extended, especially for Germany. If the French Revolution was the most decisive break with the past and its traditions, with a system that had become outdated in all its forms, then the same thing was supposed to happen in other lands too. We see the old forms collapsing everywhere. It is as though a mighty storm blew across the whole of Europe, bringing down everything lacking the power to withstand it. Initially we can see in this entire period only the caprice and forceful dominion of a bold conqueror, who allowed nothing to stand in the way of pursuing his plans ever further. But it would be very one-sided

---

6. Napoleon returned to Paris to rule for a hundred days before he was defeated at Waterloo by the combined forces of Britain, Prussia, Austria, and Russia. The British exiled him to the island of St. Helena off the coast of West Africa, and he never escaped again.

7. The Congress of Vienna founded the German Confederation, a loose league of 39 sovereign states. The permanent presidency of the Confederation was given to the Austrian emperor, thus sidelining the claim of Prussian dominance. The Revolutions of 1848 agitated for unity and freedom in the German states. But it was not until Bismarck became minister-president of Prussia in 1862 (two years after Baur's death), followed by the Austro-Prussian War, that the process began of establishing the German Empire, uniting all the scattered parts of Germany except Austria under Prussian hegemony in 1871.

just to stop at this point; rather things must be viewed from the standpoint of a historical process through which the states and peoples of Europe had to pass in order to enter a new period of their political and intellectual development. Progress does not always occur on the smooth and peaceful path of gradual inner development; there are also times of revolution when, once people recognize what the times call for, they must attain it, albeit only through struggle and force. When the whole system of the old aristocracy and monarchy became an unbearable weight, the French nation disburdened itself of it by means of a movement that merits the name of revolution, if any movement does.

Other lands too, especially Germany, found themselves in a similar condition. They plodded along in the most cumbersome way with forms that had become antiquated and that therefore maintained their coherence through longstanding convention, but lacked any inner vital power. The entire system of German imperial government was antiquated, decaying and withered. Just one example is that the relationship of the imperial leader to the imperial princes was lacking in any inner sense of purpose and stability. When we compare Germany with France, the great difference, however, is that in Germany people had not yet properly felt all the deficiencies and shortcomings from which they suffered. People deceived themselves about their own condition and hoped that a thorough remedy of the affliction might bring something better; but they believed that the old, worn-out diplomatic artifices of a dishonest, morally disreputable politics would provide the remedy. We can only imagine how deluded people were if they believed, not only in Prussia but also the other German lands, that a state such as Prussia, with its self-proud aristocracy, its rigid bureaucratic mechanisms, its outmoded traditions from a time on whose dead capital people drew without having the spark of its spirit within them, could take on an opponent such as Napoleon.[8] People in Germany first had to come to a realization about themselves, to a clear awareness of what was lacking in all the circumstances of the life of the people and the state—of what could happen only through such experiences as had occurred in the most palpable way over a series of years. We can now look back on the entire period of French domination—during which Germany was not only robbed of its political and national independence, but also became inwardly alienated and

---

8. Prussia and Austria were ruled at this time by two reactionary sovereigns, Frederick William III and Francis II, who attempted to maintain the status quo of "enlightened absolutism." These states crumbled under French attack, and a German longing for national identity was awakened in the aftermath, fostered in part by the great literary and philosophical thinkers who now made Germany the center of the intellectual universe.

torn apart—with the feeling of deepest shame and humility. But this was the necessary path by which Germany could emerge from the old unhealthy circumstances and rise up, inwardly strengthened with fresh moral energy.

Seen from without, the time of French domination was, for Germany and the lands on which the pressure weighed most heavily, simply a period of oppression; but viewed more closely, at bottom it was a conflict of the old and new, a conflict between two opposed principles, one of which had a national, popular origin, while the other rested on the system of ancient legitimacy and dynastic interests. The first of these principles was represented by the French nation. However one may judge the revolution in other respects, France attained a national strength and moral energy through the revolution that placed it far above other nations. By contrast, the other principle was represented by those states that were incapable of any vigorous resistance. From this we can see how completely the authority of the state had withered when it concentrated all its power in a monarchy based only on its absolute right and unconnected to any vital ties to the people. The result of the struggle between the two principles in the period before us shows very clearly the intrinsic tendency of the new age that began with the French Revolution: to replace the old traditional regime with a genuinely popular rule arising out of the self-consciousness of the people, and the extent to which this age has its distinctive center of gravity only where a people and state become aware of and assert their national interests. Nothing shows this more clearly than the final result of the struggle between these two principles during the period we are examining. Napoleonic domination, which far exceeded its natural limits, had to collapse as soon as it disowned the source from which it had emerged, and assumed a despotic character that was essentially no different than the old monarchy—as soon as what originally had been a purely national power believed it was able to maintain itself by destroying the national status of other peoples in the most violent fashion. In doing so, it awakened the adversary to which it would succumb. What toppled Napoleon is neither the misfortune of the Russian campaign, nor the courage of the opposing armies and commanders, nor the politics and diplomacy of the cabinets. Even when we attribute the greatest importance to all these contributory causes, in the final analysis what destroyed Napoleon is nothing other than the popular interests that initiated the resistance against him, the hatred that foreign domination evoked when aroused German national consciousness felt itself vulnerable under the pressure of foreign rule.

The sole means by which the legitimate monarchs, so deeply humiliated by the revolutionary upstart, could rise up against him and once again claim their lost power, was by appealing to the people. "To my people!" rang the words of the king of Prussia, words that first signaled the great struggle for liberation on the part of the German nation; and the powerful uprising of the nation, which immediately followed this appeal, proved that it just expressed what already had prepared and developed itself in the self-consciousness of the people, and now became living reality. A recent writer, the author of *Der deutsche Protestantismus*, rightly asks:

> It has been a long time since we heard these words! All the authorities of the spiritual and worldly hierarchy have long forgotten or lost sight of them! Why were they first spoken by a king? Once again there is official recognition of the existence of a people, of a unity in which all the artificial and natural social distinctions come together as entirely one. The detached leadership we have had until now, the achievement and result of our political development since the Reformation, has now turned back again to the deepest and most immediate foundation on which every state rests, and did not hide the fact that it rests on the same foundation. Is this not an admission that the political form of the eighteenth century, enlightened absolutism, has come to its end? That its material and spiritual means do not suffice to answer adequately the great question of whether it should exist at all? Did this admission not set aside everything previously regarded as valid and constitute a revolution?[9]

It was indeed a revolution—that great upsurge of the German nation in the noteworthy year of 1813.[10] Now that the people understood themselves for the first time as a nation, they stood on the same ground as the French in the days of their first revolution, but with the great difference that what the French attained, in the heat of passion and with all the aberrations of revolutionary excess, became for the Germans, in the school of hard experience, an achievement resting on moral energy. Thus it was not so much a political revolution as a moral rebirth of the nation. Except that the revolution of course also had to proceed further beyond the point to which the nation had arisen. This too was possible, while facing certain obstacles. What we have initially established to be the result of the world-historical process in the period before us—through the French Revolution and in direct or indirect association with it—is the revitalization of national self-consciousness. The same principle that we first encounter in the political and national

---

9. Karl Bernhard Hundeshagen, *Der deutsche Protestantismus, seine Vergangenheit und seine heutigen Lebensfragen* (3rd ed., Frankfurt am Main, 1850), 124. Baur quotes from p. 118 of an earlier edition. Just prior to this passage Hundeshagen refers to the words of the king, "To my people!"

10. In the autumn of 1813, Napoleon's armies were defeated and withdrew from Germany, allowing the German states to be liberated from French occupation.

arena—this return into self, this direct self-awareness as originative element or principle on which all else rests—we will recognize in other areas too as the distinctive tendency of the new age.

2

History of the Catholic Church

Secularization in Germany

We begin with the Catholic Church since the political events during this time period had the most direct influence on it. The major territorial adjustments that occurred in Germany as a consequence of the Treaty of Lunéville placed the Catholic Church in Germany in an entirely different position. At that time, Germany was still made up of ecclesiastical territories of every description from the most extensive to the smallest, including ecclesiastical electorates and principalities, archbishoprics and bishoprics, abbeys and priories, chapters and monasteries, and so on. These ecclesiastical territories together formed a not insignificant set of lands standing under the direct sovereignty of the [Holy Roman] Empire. This set of lands came back from the hands of its ecclesiastical holders into secular control because this seemed to be the best way, under procedures already set up by the Peace of Westphalia [in 1648], to compensate the hereditary rulers for their losses. The German Empire had already agreed at the Congress of Rastatt[1] to cede the left bank of the Rhine River, and it established the principle that the estates should be compensated for any losses by the distribution of ecclesiastical holdings on the right bank of the Rhine. This formed the basis for the Treaty of Lunéville, which the emperor signed for himself and the empire, and which the empire formally recognized. After Austria and France had agreed upon all matters at Lunéville, the Reichstag in Regensburg was

---

1. The Second Congress of Rastatt (1797–99) was intended to negotiate a peace between the French Republic and the Holy Roman Empire, and to compensate those princes whose lands on the left bank of the Rhine had been seized by the French during the War of the First Coalition. The Congress was interrupted by the War of the Second Coalition, but the negotiations begun there were resumed after the Treaty of Lunéville in 1801, with the recognition that any compensation plan should be based on the secularization of the ecclesiastical states of the empire.

occupied, from February to September 1801, with the question as to how the empire should express its endorsement of the partition. To this end, a commission or a so-called imperial delegation was established, which would only become effective nine months later when the several princes had worked things out among themselves in Paris, where Talleyrand[2] was operating a virtual marketplace in German territories. France had already concluded a secret agreement with Russia in October 1801 for the same purpose, the distribution of existing ecclesiastical holdings. These two countries took the matter completely into their own hands, under the pretext that two such wholly disinterested powers as France and Russia should be the ones to offer remediation and provide the empire with a strictly neutral plan for reparations.

In a joint statement from the French and Russian governments, Russia recognized all of the concessions that the German princes had previously gained in Paris, through begging or bribery. The two powers presented this document to the Reichstag in June of 1802, with the demand that it be respected. After deliberations, the Reichstag adopted the so-called Final Recess (*Reichsdeputationsrecess*)[3] on 25 February 1803. As a result, the office of ecclesiastical prince was abolished; the only such prince who continued in office was the then Coadjutor of Mainz, who was in fact an archbishop and remained a member of the imperial estate and a secular prince. As the imperial chancellor he was a prince elector and, as the Lord of Aschaffenburg and Regensburg, he retained 24 square miles and 82,000 subjects out of the 171 square miles and 350,000 subjects from the previous electorate of Mainz; and, as before, he had a million thalers in revenue. Karl Theodor von Dalberg[4] held this office at that time. He enjoyed the favor of Napoleon and, because of his humanity, his culture, his love of the arts and sciences, which he generously supported, he had many personal qualities that added further distinction to his high position.

Even after the old German imperial constitution had become completely obsolete, this ecclesiastical prince retained his title and now, as

2. Charles Maurice de Talleyrand-Périgord (1754–1838) was a bishop, politician, and diplomat, who served as foreign minister under Napoleon. In order to consolidate French gains, he opposed Napoleon's later military adventures. In 1814 he took charge of the restoration of the Bourbon monarchy, and at the Congress of Vienna negotiated a favorable settlement for France.

3. This law secularized nearly 70 ecclesiastical states and abolished 45 imperial cities to compensate German princes for territories west of the Rhine that had been annexed to France.

4. Karl Theodor Anton Maria von Dalberg (1744–1817) was archbishop-elector of Mainz, arch-chancellor of the Holy Roman Empire, and afterwards the only prince-primate of the Napoleonic Confederation of the Rhine and grand duke of Frankfurt.

prince primate, became a member, and the presiding officer, of the Rhine Confederation. His metropolitan or archbishopric authority encompassed all of Catholic Germany with the exception of Austrian and Prussian lands. Since the metropolitan rights of Mainz had been ceded to the episcopal see in Regensburg, a metropolitan chapter had to be set up in Regensburg. The first step in this direction was taken by the elector/arch-chancellor in early 1805 when he was in Paris, with a statement to Napoleon and a proposal to the pope regarding the organization of the metropolitan chapter. A papal bull of 4 February 1805 referring to it was communicated to the two cathedral chapters of Mainz and Regensburg that were supposed to be joined into the new metropolitan chapter. But ensuing events prevented the plan from being carried out. After his return [from France] to Rome, the pope chose not to go further in this matter, even though the prince-primate pursued his plan until 1809. In Germany the secular authority of the pope was abolished in 1809, as well as the last vestiges of the former imperial constitution, the spiritual authority still linked to secular power. The states of the primate were converted into the grand duchy of Frankfurt.

Thus, during this entire period, the [power of the] Catholic Church in Germany was being progressively vitiated. With the loss of the ecclesiastical electorates, Catholicism lost its most important political strongholds, and its political power essentially ceased to exist. The principle of secularization was so far reaching that the church passed entirely into the hands of the state. At the time of the Final Recess, things had already reached the point where legislation provided that all the properties of bishoprics and monasteries in the former as well as the new political dominions, properties of the Catholic Church and those of the Lutherans, now stood freely and completely at the disposal of the respective secular sovereigns, for the purpose of easing their finances. The church for its part hardly raised any objection to this, and the pope himself was in no position to do more than lament these changes. By the time he protested at the Congress of Vienna they were an accomplished fact, and the force of political events was far too overwhelming for ecclesiastical interests to succeed in making their case. The ecclesiastical electorates attracted emigrants from, and supporters of, the old monarchy, and, as the hotbed of conspiracies and intrigue against the republic, they were all the more susceptible to legitimate conquest.

The storm of political revolution quickly achieved what would have been much more difficult to attain by reforming the church. Although secularization was accomplished by purely political and worldly interests, people in fact expressed, and brought to general attention, the fact that the essence of religion and Christianity rests not on external political power but rather is completely independent of it. And because Catholicism divested itself of these impure material elements of its existence—despite the fact that the force of external circumstances brought about this act of self-divestment, which allowed it to become a less encumbered spiritual power—it took a significant step in the direction of Protestantism.

Externally, the two confessions now stood in an equal relationship to each other. The provisions of the Peace of Westphalia, with reservations intended to favor the Catholic religion, had become meaningless. The terms of the Peace of Lunéville had given the Catholic Church in Germany an essentially different structure. Not only had it suffered significant material losses but also it was left in a condition that required reorganization. The shifts in political boundaries had consequences for the church: old ties had been severed and new ones had to be established. In particular, the peculiar situation arose that Catholic regions now stood under the rule of Protestant princes. After the dissolution of the imperial federation, the power of the princes in relation to the church and the ecclesiastical situation of their states was limited only by the acts of the Rhine Confederation. These acts indeed insured that Catholics were entitled to their own church system of governance, but at the same time it was left to the provincial rulers to regulate its implementation, to stipulate what seemed necessary to guarantee their newly granted sovereignty and enforce the principles established for governing their states, and to establish unity and cohesiveness in the forms of governance.

It was quite foreseeable that many conflicts with the principles of Catholicism could arise. This was especially the case for the new kingdom of Württemberg and the two grand duchies of Darmstadt and Baden. By the end of 1807 the royal government of Württemberg and a papal nuncio were negotiating a concordat, but soon afterwards it was revealed that the negotiations had broken off. The peculiar difficulties of these new conditions led one of the most respected Protestant theologians of the day to discuss this matter in a book devoted to the question.[5] His book examined the different points under consideration, and the essential principles and views of both parties, with the utmost care and fairness. But the complexity of political developments during this period meant that all the apparently needed changes must await a calmer time.

---

5. [*Baur, in the text*] Gottlieb Jakob Planck, *Betrachtungen über die neuesten Veränderungen in dem Zustand der deutsche katholischen Kirche und besonders über die Concordate zwischen protestantischen Souverains und dem Römische Stuhl, welcher dadurch veranlasst werden möchten* (Hanover, 1808).

The Napoleonic Concordat

However, a very important concordat had already been signed at the beginning of this period, in the country that provided the first powerful impetus for all these changes. Napoleon concluded this concordat with the pope during the first years of his consulate. He put an end to revolution and anarchy, and established unity and order, calm and deliberation, as the basis for the state; and he clearly demonstrated his talent for governing by his attempt to eradicate all traces of the extreme aberrations in religious and church matters too that the revolution had left in its wake.

Even though, as is commonly claimed, he may have only been following the basic tenets of politics, he still also recognized that religion and Christianity satisfied an essential requirement of human nature, too important to ignore if states were to remain stable. We can compare in this regard the speech given by the privy councilor Portalis on behalf of the government on 15th Germinal X (5 April 1802), when the concordat of 16th Messidor IX (15 July 1801) was presented to the legislative authority.[6] This speech developed the reasons for reestablishing worship and for the new church law. It answered the principal question—Do people need religion? Is it a general human need?—and it did so in such a way that those who understand religion not just from a purely political point of view could be in complete agreement. Although the national synod gathered in Paris in 1801 failed to arrive at a satisfactory conclusion, in that same year Joseph Bonaparte and Cardinal Consalvi concluded a concordat that the pope approved on 15 July 1801. Its main points were as a follows: Catholicism is the religion of the majority of the French population; the properties of the church will not be returned, but the state will assume responsibility for supporting the church in a suitable fashion; both priests loyal to the government and those who sought asylum abroad will relinquish their offices but can be reappointed; the bishoprics will be organized in accord with political divisions, but with consideration given to the earlier episcopal sees; the First Consul will appoint the ten archbishops and fifty bishops of France, and the pope will grant them their canonical status; priests will be appointed by the bishops; the First Consul retains the same prerogatives the former government had; the pope is the sovereign of the Papal States and head of the church. To this end, Napoleon provided through constitutional laws that the publication of

---

6. The concordat of 1801 was an agreement between Napoleon and Pope Pius VII. It remained in effect until 1905 and solidified the Catholic Church as the majority church in France, with most of its civil rights restored (but not the lands and endowments confiscated during the revolution). Jean-Étienne-Marie Portalis (1746–1807) became the minister of public worship under Napoleon. Also, see p. 245, n. 24.

papal decrees is subject to the approval of the government, that the Privy Council can take action against the abuse of spiritual power, and that teachers at the seminaries are to observe the four articles of the Gallican clergy.[7]

The inauguration of the concordat was celebrated at Easter in 1802, and it still forms the basis for the governance of the French Catholic Church. The concordat with the Italian Republic in 1803 was quite similar. Although the concordat did not entirely satisfy the pope, and the constitutional laws even less so, the reestablishment of Catholicism and its formal recognition as the prevailing state religion provided a firm basis for church matters; and supporters of the old church could, despite some misgivings, take comfort in the fact that Catholicism had emerged in this form from the storms of a revolution that had proscribed all religion and publicly proclaimed atheism.

The Situation of the Protestants under Napoleon

At the same time, the concordat provided the occasion for considering the relationship between Protestants and the state. Protestants believed they had been overlooked when the concordat was made public; they thought its first article violated religious freedom, the legal basis for which they had long sought and first achieved in the Revolution. The constitution of 22 August 1795 guaranteed freedom of religion by stating that no law-abiding persons could be prevented from practicing their religion. Since the concordat raised concerns among Protestants, the privy council presented to the First Consul, in March 1802, a report meant to satisfy non-Catholics. It stated that, since the concordat has determined necessary matters with respect to Catholics in France, it is also appropriate to establish the civic and political conditions for adherents of the other religions as well. It said that the first article of the concordat, which explains that the Roman Catholic apostolic religion is the religion of the majority of French citizens, could lead to abuses that must be avoided. The will of the majority is controlling for the minority when it is a matter of civic and political institutions and the law. There can be no dispute about this; the minority must acquiesce to the majority. The practice of worship, however, its customary exercise and teachings, is a matter of individual free will and free choice. A state cannot survive without uniform laws; but the fact that it can survive without religious practice, or with different religious practices, gives the individual the right to choose this or that religious practice, or none at all. The statement

---

7. These four articles, adopted in 1682 but later revoked, placed limits on the authority of the pope and defined the Gallican position, favored by Napoleon, as opposed to that of the Ultramontanes (see n. 17).

that the majority of the French people confess Catholicism does not give this religion either civil or political preeminence. The reason for saying this is simply because this issue [of a Catholic majority] is the first one the concordat addressed. The other religious organizations will enjoy equal rights with Catholicism.

Protestantism constitutes a significant presence in the French Republic, and for this reason it warrants protection. It has other claims to consideration and favorable treatment as well. Its adherents established the first liberal principles of government and have promoted ethical behavior, philosophy, the arts and sciences. During these times they have rallied behind the flag of freedom, and remain loyal to it. Thus it is the duty of the government to protect the peaceful gathering of this enlightened and high-minded minority, which assembles in commendable witness to Christ. Apart from the salaries and pensions of priests [which are paid by the state], Protestants enjoy the same rights that have been secured for Catholics under the concordat.

Immediately after this report, all provisions that restricted freedom of worship were nullified; and the privilege to worship freely, albeit only within churches, was placed under the protection of local authorities. In April 1802 the legislative authority enacted into law the articles relevant to Protestant worship. In keeping with the original statutes of both Protestant churches, the law guaranteed complete equality of Reformed clergy, with clergy as chairmen of the consistories and special synods, while it acknowledged that the Lutherans could, in addition to consistories, have clerical inspectors and general consistories under lay leadership. The only change to the old governance of the French Reformed Church was the requirement that it replace its completely independent consistories, colloquia, and provincial and national synods with two tribunals subject to the government, as well as other restrictions. The administrative forms of the new state did not harmonize well with the earlier structures of the church. Every consistorial and synodical decision, even regarding matters of faith, had to be approved by the government before it could be published. The equal standing of the pastors seemed compromised by a permanent presidency; elders were chosen from among the most wealthy; the privileges of the consistories were expanded; the synods were restricted; congregations no longer elected their pastors and elders; French citizenship was now required of pastors; and they had to conduct their studies in a French seminary. In September 1808 a theological faculty was established in Montauban, in addition to the one in Geneva, to train Reformed clergy; in May 1803 an academy and seminary had already been established in Strasbourg to train Lutheran clergy. This made three theological seminaries for Protestant France, which encompassed three million souls, 63 Lutheran consistorial churches with 521 pastors, and 127 Reformed consistorial churches and 19 chapels, with 651 pastors.

On the whole, Protestants were in a very favorable position under Napoleon's rule. On numerous occasions the emperor demonstrated his good will toward them; he said that he considered them to be his best subjects. At his coronation he spoke to the consistorial presidents of the Reformed Church gathered there, stating that he was happy to see the assembled pastors of the Reformed Church of France, and was using this opportunity to tell them how pleased he has been with the favorable reports about the loyalty and uprightness of the pastors and members of the various Protestant confessions. He let it be known that his intention and firm decision was to protect their religious freedom; that the rule of law stops where the unbounded rule of conscience begins; that the law and the prince may do nothing contrary to freedom [of conscience]; that these principles are both his own and the nation's; and should any of his successors be misled into breaking the oath that he has given, let him be cursed by the people and be justly branded with the epithet "Nero."

There is no reason to doubt the genuineness of Napoleon's pronouncement acknowledging the principle of religious freedom. Those who were particularly knowledgeable about the ecclesiastical situation of France in that time praise how well the two Protestant confessions behaved toward each other, and also how the Catholics behaved toward the Protestants. The mutual understanding existing between Catholic and Protestant clergy was said to be extremely cordial. Enlightened Catholics behaved as though they wished to atone for the injustice visited earlier upon Protestants. Even the French National Institute gave surprising evidence of the great progress Protestant ideas were making in France when it announced an essay contest regarding the influence of Luther's Reformation on the political situation of the different states in Europe and on the advance of enlightenment. In April 1802, the prize was awarded to a Catholic, Charles de Villers,[8] who answered the question favorably with respect to Protestant interests.

The Condition of the Catholic Church in Germany

It was a direct consequence of the Revolution that in France these more liberal views and principles became predominant. In Germany too such ideas had to be acknowledged. The changed political circumstances required

---

8. Charles de Villers (1765–1815) was a French philosopher who translated Kant and, from 1797, lived with Dorothea von Schlözer (a prominent German intellectual) and her husband in a *ménage à trios* in Göttingen, where de Villers taught philosophy.

different premises than those still based on the Peace of Westphalia. Since, following the Treaty of Lunéville, all German states now consisted of large numbers of Catholics and Protestants, the previous laws governing unequal rights in individual states were no longer tenable. The Rhine Confederation had already pronounced that Catholics and Protestants were guaranteed the same civil rights. Thus, barring exceptional circumstances, it should not have mattered at all, in civil and political affairs, whether a person professed to be a Catholic or a Protestant. The *aequalitas exacta mutuaque* (complete and reciprocal equality), which the Peace of Westphalia guaranteed only *in abstracto*—that is, only insofar as the two religious communities in themselves, taken as a whole, were considered equal [before the law]—should also be considered valid *in concreto*, that is, for the concrete relations among individuals.

Denial of equality for Catholics in a state such as Württemberg, where only Lutheran Protestants had enjoyed civil liberties, was now no longer possible. During the first year of Friedrich's reign as king,[9] the religious edict of 15 October 1806 appeared and marked a new era in the history of the church in Württemberg. In order to guarantee subjects free and unfettered practice of their religion throughout the kingdom, no matter to which of the already recognized religious groups they belonged, the edict established a number of provisions expressing the spirit of genuine Christianity. They rested on the principle that confessional differences should not justify any inequality before the law. Similar decrees were needed in other states of the Rhine Confederation. It was first of all this policy that removed barriers previously preventing a closer association of members of different confessions. Also the general consciousness of the times no longer supported these barriers.

At no other time did the particularism of the confessions count for so little. Given the general upheaval and the many changes already made, people had become rather indifferent to the positive element in religion; in keeping with the times, political matters were of such prominence that religious and ecclesiastical affairs gained less attention. The heads of the Catholic clergy found themselves under pressure; the entire character of an epoch in which education and enlightenment were valued did not sit well with views and principles that appeared to stem only from the obscurantist centuries of the Middle Ages. The humane views of respected Catholics

---

9. Friedrich Wilhelm Karl von Württemberg (1781–1864) was duke, elector, and the first king of Württemberg (elevated to the throne by Napoleon on 1 January 1806). Soon thereafter, Württemberg seceded from the Holy Roman Empire and joined the Rhine Confederation.

such as Dalberg, Wessenberg, Sailer, Werkmeister,[10] and others evidenced a broad range of learning and tolerance of other confessions. Following their lead, Catholic and Protestant clergy in Germany and France got along well with one another. The theological literature of the time reflected the same spirit. A number of important scholarly works clearly show the influence of the general culture and education at this time, including its influence on the Catholic Church. Works such as Jahn's "Introduction to the Bible" and Hug's "Introduction to the New Testament"[11] provide admirable examples of not only basic erudition but also the liberal views of their authors. Although these writers make clear their allegiance to the principles of their church, they present these principles in a milder form, and take care to avoid anything that might be particularly offensive to Protestants. For example, Hug's "Introduction" is a work that could as easily have been written by a Protestant theologian, and would occupy a quite respectable place in Protestant literature. Even contemporary textbooks on dogma almost entirely lacked earlier polemics. Dogmatic theologians sought to base their church's systematic thought on a general philosophy of religion, and were thus inclined to turn to the reigning philosophical systems, namely those of Kant and Schelling, by utilizing them in presenting their own system, both as a whole and as a set of individual dogmas, where such philosophies seemed particularly suited to this approach.

It is remarkable, especially if one considers that a wholly different spirit would soon become dominant, how the Catholicism of that time desired to move beyond its former authoritarian constraints and, instead of holding fast to its particularity, to follow the general trend of the intellectual climate.

History of the Papacy: Pius VII up to His Imprisonment

There is scarcely a period in the history of the papacy so rich in developments as the first decade and a half of our own century. The lengthy papacies of Pius VI (1775–99) and Pius VII (1800–1823) appear well-suited to demonstrate, in a series of rapidly changing events and practical experiences,

---

10. On Dalberg, see n. 4. Ignaz Heinrich von Wessenberg (1774–1860) was a liberal Catholic, administrator of the Diocese of Constance, and advocate of a German National Church. Johann Michael von Sailer (1751–1832) was bishop of Regensburg. Benedict Maria von Werkmeister (1745–1823) was a Catholic theologian in Württemberg.

11. Johann Jahn (1750–1816) was a Catholic biblical scholar who taught in Vienna. He wrote an *Einleitung ins Alte Testament* (1792). Johann Leonhard Hug (1765–1846) taught in Freiburg. His *Einleitung in die Schriften des Neuen Testaments* was first published in 1808.

all the things that could quickly befall the papacy, so as to enhance it or humiliate it.

In 1799, at a conclave of thirty-five cardinals in Venice, Cardinal Chiaramonti was elected pope as Pius VII.[12] He remained in Venice for a period before his installation in Rome in 1800. In the first years of his reign, before the papacy barely revived its spirits, it encountered in rapid succession a number of crucially important events that seemed to augur poorly for it: Bonaparte's return from Egypt, the fall of the Directory, the introduction of the Consulate, the victory at Marengo, the French dominance in Italy, and the Peace of Lunéville. Soon, however, the hero of the revolution, whose hand came to hold all the power in the Republic, found it expedient to consider how religion and the church might assist in reconciling public opinion with the revolution and securing a firm basis for his rule. The aforementioned concordat was the result of these efforts to link political interests with ecclesiastical ambitions. With this, the papacy at least regained secure footing in France. It suddenly appeared that things had returned to the day of Pepin,[13] the old ruler of the Franks who received his crown from the hands of the pope, when Pius VII came over the Alps at the end of 1804 to Paris (a city still for the most part paying homage to atheism and the religion of reason), accompanied by all the trappings of his high office, to set the emperor's crown on the new ruler, and to consecrate the founding father of a new dynasty with his priestly blessing.

The splendid opportunities that seemed to open up for the papacy with the acknowledgment of its spiritual power had drawn Pius to Paris; but he soon saw that recollections of the Carolingian era, and of Charlemagne—whose example increasingly inspired the new emperor—served quite different purposes. Each new step taken by the bold strongman was a new setback for the pope and loosened ancient ecclesiastical ties. From the start of 1808, the emperor's demands grew ever more far-reaching. The Papal States, the only entity in Italy that had not yet become a French province, remain a far too inept obstacle to his plans there. The French military had already reached the Quirinal Palace [in Rome]; one bastion after the other, one province after the other, was wrested from the pope, who could only lament the violence he suffered. On 17 May an imperial decree was signed,

---

12. Barnaba Niccolò Maria Luigi Chiaramonti (1742–1823), a Benedictine monk from a noble family, reigned as pope from 1800 until his death. He was in his sixties during his ordeal with Napoleon. In 2007, the process began of canonizing him as a saint. Apropos of sainthood, note Baur's remark at the end of this chapter. The detailed discussion illustrates the contentious struggle over the papacy's secular authority.

13. Pepin the Short (c. 714–68), son of Charles Martel, king of the Franks from 751 until his death.

apparently quite by design, at the imperial headquarters in Vienna, and it was announced in Rome on 10 June 1809. According to it, the Papal States were to be incorporated into the French Empire, ending the temporal rule of the pope forever. In the legal rationale accompanying the decree, the emperor accorded himself the same privilege that Charlemagne once invoked, that of granting the popes territory and subjects. These endowments were made to the Roman bishops as feudal estates only to benefit Christianity but not the enemies of the Catholic religion (namely, the English with whom the pope did not wish to go to war). Reference was also made to the disputes that constantly arose out of the mingling of spiritual and temporal powers. Rome was declared to be an imperial free city; palaces for the ruling pope were to be constructed in Rome, Paris, and several other cities of the Empire; two million francs of income were to be guaranteed to him; and the costs of the College of Cardinals and the Congregation for the Propagation of the Faith were to be covered by the state budget.

After this decree was announced—which Rome had long anticipated and to which it had readied a response—the pope released a manifesto as a formal address that was posted and distributed everywhere. This official statement urged Romans and all of Christendom, in the strongest terms, to witness this sacrilege against the church. Its opening words echoed the famous opening of Cicero's Catiline Orations:[14] *Adunque sono adempite le tenebrose trame dei nemici della sede apostolica!* ("The enemies of the Apostolic See have fulfilled their dark plots!"). The pope did not wish to announce immediately the excommunication that had already been prepared, but was persuaded to do so the following day. It appeared in the form of a papal bull that banned the planners, executors, and promoters of the expropriation of Rome and the Papal States. The ban specifically mentioned Napoleon. When the pope refused to retract the excommunication and rejected all entreaties, he was removed from Rome by military force in early July, and taken, via Florence and Genoa, first to Grenoble and then to Savona [in northern Italy near the French border], where he was held prisoner under harsh conditions. The ongoing attempts to negotiate with the pope remained fruitless.

---

14. These orations were given by Marcus Tullius Cicero in 63 BC, exposing the plot of Lucius Sergius Catilina to overthrow the Roman government. The opening lines: "When, O Catiline, do you mean to cease abusing our patience? How long is that madness or yours still to mock us? When is there to be an end to that unbridled audacity of yours, swaggering about as it does now?"

Pius VII in France; the Council of Paris; Further Negotiations

The emperor's greatest embarrassment came when the pope refused to invest the bishops Napoleon had appointed with canonical offices. As a consequence, twenty-seven dioceses lacked bishops recognized by the pope. The chapters had, either freely or under duress, given the bishops capacity to act as chapter administrators and thereby serve their new dioceses at least in that capacity. This was, however, only a provisional measure, and it encountered considerable resistance. Members of the chapters refused to obey, and the pope demanded that these bishops not be recognized as chapter vicars. When the emperor learned of these machinations, he had the pope guarded even more closely. More importantly, he was induced to carry out an idea he had had in mind for some time. He would convene a council, either to bring the pope into acquiescence or to render him dispensable, by setting the higher authority of the assembled church over against the pope's authority. To this end, he had already seated a clerical commission consisting of several prelates and clergy, whom he charged with discussing all the issues that the plan for a council might raise. It was to convene on the same day as the baptism of the king of Rome, 9 June 1811, but did not meet until the 16th. The emperor agreed with the suggestion of the most enlightened members of the Council—the archbishop of Tours, Louis Mathias de Barral; the bishop of Nantes, Jean-Baptiste Duvoisin; the bishop of Trier, Charles Mannay, among others—to send a deputation to Savona to take a conciliatory step before the opening of the council.

The deputation consisting of these three bishops would come not in the name of the emperor but rather represent a large number of the bishops gathered in Paris who wished, prior to the council, to reach an understanding with the pope. They generally regretted the situation in which the French church found itself in face of the pope's refusal to grant the canonical appointments, and they considered it an abuse of papal powers. For they viewed his refusal as stemming from his decision to use this prerogative as a weapon in his quarrel with the emperor. The emperor himself took the matter so seriously because it placed in question the concordat's very survival. The three prelates sent to Savona were charged with demanding a proviso according to which the pope would be bound to approve the investiture within three months, provided he had no objections to the worthiness of the appointees. After expiration of the three-month period, the metropolitan, or in his absence the elder prelate of the ecclesiastical province, would be empowered to make the canonical investiture. The emperor also gave the emissaries the additional charge that, if the pope were sufficiently amenable, they could also negotiate about the future situation of the papacy per se. The provisions were to be that the pope could freely choose to reside in Rome, Avignon, or Paris, or in all three in turn; funds in the amount of two million francs were to be his; and the salaries of the cardinals and the minister for ecclesiastical government would come from the imperial treasury. Moreover, the pope would have the right to receive emissaries from all the worldly powers and in turn to send his representatives to them, and he would be entirely unhindered in his administration of church matters. Everything that might contribute to the prosperity, glory, and spread of Catholicism would be done. The sole condition was that, if the pope chose to stay in Rome, he would have to take the same oath to the emperor as that sworn to by all the prelates of the Empire. Should he prefer to reside in Avignon, he only need swear to undertake nothing counter to the principles contained in the 1682 declaration.[15]

After lengthy negotiations in Savona with the emperor's envoys, the pope finally agreed to draw up a statement, which he would leave unsigned, containing the following provisions: (1) his agreement, for this one time, to invest the twenty-seven prelates, but indeed without the formula *motu proprio* (at his own initiative) that would make it seem he had chosen them himself rather than just confirmed those selected by imperial authority; (2) the obligation for the Holy See to invest, within six months, the prelates named by the secular sovereign, failing which the metropolitan would count as empowered by the pope to install them in the pope's name; (3) as soon as the pope would be free and together with his cardinals, his readiness to listen to any suggestions regarding the future position of the Holy See. Subsequently the pope reneged on this last point.

The emperor was satisfied with the results of this delegation, at least in believing he got what he wanted with regard to the canonical investiture. Now it would all depend on what the council would say about this. Although the council feared the emperor's power, dissatisfaction with his government was certainly present. The assembly was large enough to overcome the timidity of individuals and to amplify the overall mood. The unfortunate plight of the pope weighed heavily on the entire assembly. In one of the early meetings, a respected prelate, Dessole, Bishop of Chambéry, expressed the opinion that the bishops gathered in the council were not able to deliberate as members of the church while its head, the honorable Pius VII, remained locked up. He proposed that the entire assembly should move to Saint-Cloud[16] to demand of the emperor that he first of all set Pius

---

15. The Four Gallican Articles. See n. 7.
16. A western suburb of Paris where Napoleon's *coup d'état* overthrew the French

VII free. The ensuing commotion was so great that Cardinal Fesch, the emperor's uncle and archbishop of Lyon, who chaired the meeting, could only counter the step the assembly threatened to take by declaring the session adjourned. The emperor took this news very badly and refused to accept the message replying to the emperor's peremptory and presumptuous communication. After such preliminaries, including also the exclusion of the non-invested prelates, the council moved to debating the main question, which was, for the time being, referred to a commission. The commission first took up the agreement made at Savona, but immediately took issue with the fact that the pope had not signed the note sent to them. They claimed that such a document was invalid and had perhaps been obtained from the pope through false pretenses, or else simply because he was held prisoner. Hence, it was best to proceed as though there had been no discussion with the pope. The question was whether the council was competent to decide the matter on its own, a question that was vehemently disputed. Those who supported the competence of the council, such as Duvoisin, emphasized that this is admittedly an extreme emergency, and in such an exceptional case any church should have its own internal mechanism for dealing with it. The metropolitan should of necessity receive his former authority to install bishops if an overriding [secular] power happens to separate them from the pope for years, and so on. Nonetheless, the vote to thus empower the council failed. The emperor was extremely vexed, and the following day the commission repealed its decision once it realized the danger to which it had exposed the church. Of course the pope's situation was unfortunate, but this could best be remedied by the council inserting itself between the pope and the emperor. The means for doing so was found in the note from Savona approved by the pope; changing it into a decree of the council would convert it into a law of the state, and it was thanks to the pope that a solution was provided for rescuing the church from a pitfall. The commission accepted this proposal, made by Duvoisin. The declaration of Savona was converted into a decree of the council, but the stipulation was attached that its validity was dependent on approval by the Holy Father, thereby providing the endorsement that the original document lacked.

This solution, however, once again resulted in ambiguity. It did not restore the principle of canonical investiture, and it nullified the authority of the council, making everything dependent on a second action by the pope. When the commission presented its (very one-sided and revised) report to the assembly, it caused great unrest anew. Partisans of the government said

---

Directory in 1799. The emperor must have been in residence in the palace there at that time.

that to declare the council incompetent was to put the entire matter once again in the hands of the pope. Their opponents responded that, even if the council were competent, its decisions required papal approval. While some members spoke of the pope's almighty power, others brought up the bull of excommunication, which, judging from its impact, must simply be considered a murderous attack, a work of anarchy. Hearing this, the archbishop of Bordeaux stormed into the midst of the assembly and threw the Acts of the Council of Trent on the table, with the words: You are claiming that princes cannot be excommunicated, and then you condemn the church that has so ordered it. Cardinal Fesch was only able to end the tumultuous scene by delaying any vote. But it never came to a vote because the emperor found these scenes reason enough to dissolve the council and have the leaders of the opposition (the bishop of Tournay, the bishop of Troyes, and the bishop of Ghent [Prince de Broglie]) arrested and brought to Vincennes.

After the council was dissolved, the participants were convinced individually to approve a decree stating that the period for filling the vacant episcopal sees should be limited to one year, after which the metropolitan would be empowered to install those clergy already nominated. A clause with a new remedy regarding the pope was added to the decree: the proviso that, should he not agree, the council would make an independent decision to submit the decree to a new vote and send it to the emperor, so that it might become a law of the state. Of the 110 members, 85 signed the decree, whereupon the dissolved council was once again assembled to consider the documents for approval, with a positive outcome no longer in doubt. To gain approval from the pope, a new deputation consisting of bishops and archbishops was sent, with the emperor's consent, to Savona. Upon presentation by the deputation, the pope approved the decree anew and promised to install the twenty-seven new prelates without delay. The emperor presented the decree to the state council and had it incorporated into the state legal code. However, the brief in which the pope had given his decision contained Ultramontane teachings,[17] so the emperor passed it on to a commission of the state council to check it for agreement with the principles of the Four Gallican Articles of 1682.

Thus the emperor achieved his intention but only through force; and he encountered resistance, both from the assembled clergy and from public opinion, which showed significant sympathy for the plight of the pope, a resistance the emperor could scarcely overlook. The war with Russia followed immediately thereafter. As much as these events apparently had to

---

17. The Ultramontanes emphasized papal authority over temporal as well as spiritual affairs. See p. 123, n. 30.

take attention away from everything else, the catastrophic Russian campaign made it very clear to him that the negotiations with the pope needed to be resumed at the point at which they had broken off before the war. The situation he now found himself in seriously motivated him to smooth over, as much as possible, his quarrel with the pope that had been turning minds against him.

Meanwhile, during the summer of 1812, the pope was removed from Savona to Fontainebleau to prevent the English from abducting him. He remained a captive but was treated differently than before. He lived in the same quarters he had occupied during the emperor's coronation, and he was now shown all due consideration and honor. On the second day after the emperor returned to Paris from Russia on 18 December, he wrote the pope to express both his pleasure at having him so near and his wish to visit him. A few weeks later, on 19 January, the emperor came to Fontainebleau and paid the pope a surprise visit, during which, after ceremonial greetings, they at once began to discuss very serious matters.

From the outset, the emperor destroyed the pope's hope of returning someday to Rome; his only choice was between Avignon and Paris. It would be best for him to choose Paris, but if he were to choose Avignon, he would enjoy complete freedom, receive emissaries from all the worldly powers, have recompense of two million francs for properties of the Papal States that had already been sold, and be given back all unsold properties to be managed by his representatives. To accommodate the pope, the bishoprics belonging to Rome were to be reestablished, and the pope would appoint the bishops. In addition, he would be allowed to make the appointments in ten dioceses in either Italy or France to enable him to reward officers in his government. Hence, to the fullest extent possible, the pope was to be granted an independent existence in keeping with his standing. However, he must renounce his worldly power. To convince the pope of the necessity of doing so, the emperor employed all his persuasive power. He made the case to the pope that separating spiritual and temporal power, and relinquishing the latter, was part of the unavoidable revolution of the age. The influence and everlasting permanence of religion have nothing to do with temporal matters. So much has happened in the previous twenty years that has never been seen before. The temporal power of the pope is among those many things that must pass away. We should see the special favor of providence in the fact that providence uses as its instrument a sovereign who is so favorably disposed toward the Catholic religion as the emperor is, and who will show even more favor toward the church than Charlemagne did. The pope was so impressed that he could not resist, and the only thing remaining was to find a formula weighing least heavily on his papal consciousness.

The emperor also knew how to address this matter. He was satisfied that the document did not mention either Rome's renunciation of power or having Avignon as the papal seat; rather it spoke of the independent existence of the Holy Father and the free exercise of his pontifical power in the bosom of the French Empire. It was expressed simply as follows: His Holiness will exercise the pontificate in France and in the Kingdom of Italy in the very same way and form as his predecessors. This was followed by the aforementioned conditions regarding the rights and income of the pope. The terms already stated in the pope's brief were retained for the canonical investiture of those bishops named by the crown—that the investiture should occur within the six months after their nomination by the temporal power, and, should that not happen, the eldest prelate of the province should be authorized to perform the withheld or delayed installation. To soothe the pope's conscience, the following clause was added: the Holy Father agrees with these stipulations with a view to the current situation of the church, and with confidence inspired by his majesty, the emperor, that he will bring his powerful patronage to bear on the many concerns of the church during these times. In that form, the concordat was to have the binding power of a treaty but not be published until the cardinals had been apprised of it; as natural and indispensable counselors of the church, they were entitled to register their opinion. This document was signed by both the emperor and the pope on 25 January 1812.

The emperor took great pains to convince the pope of his good will, and in the same vein he freed those cardinals remaining in custody, known as the "black cardinals," and brought them back to Paris. But this proof of his favor nevertheless turned out badly. Scarcely had the black cardinals received access to Fontainebleau than the pope, who until then had remained cheerful and contented, became gloomy. Only now did he recognize what he had done when he saw how unwary he had been: to surrender the temporal power of the papacy, to unleash a monstrous revolution in the church from his position of complete power, to relinquish St. Peter's patrimony (which was not his to give away)—and all of this was unnecessary because Napoleon was nearing his downfall. The pope had been tricked about the state of affairs in Europe, and he ought not to be bound by such a devious and forcible act. One can only imagine the pope's distress upon realizing this. Since public retraction was not possible, he decided to remain quiet and await further developments. Thus the true state of affairs remained unclear. The emperor announced everywhere that a concordat with the pope had been concluded, that he was free, that he would soon choose the place from which he would exercise papal power, and that all the difficulties of the church had been resolved. But the message from the other side said that this was all lies, that the pope had agreed to nothing. A rumor even went around at that time that the emperor had badly mistreated the venerable old man, had even dragged him around the floor by his white hair—all of which has been shown to be untrue.

The Pope's Return to Rome

The situation remained unchanged until the fall of Napoleon's empire. After the allies invaded France in January 1814, Napoleon gave the order to return the pope to Rome. This did not happen immediately; it was not until March that he was handed over to the Austrian troops in Italy. His festive return to Rome took place on 24 May 1814. Thus the papacy had faced a period of the greatest challenges and deepest humiliation, and it seemed to be closer than ever to complete collapse. But now the little ship of Peter could safely return to its harbor from the storms of a revolution so harrowing and far-reaching. The sympathy awakened everywhere for the aged head of the church—during this long period of his resistance to the feared ruler, whose raw power had not shied away from what was holy—proved advantageous to the papacy as it sought, beneath the remnants of its ancient power, to recover what it had lost and set upright again the seat that had been overturned. This became the task of the next period.

The admiration with which the pope's behavior is generally viewed during this period is exaggerated. He certainly endured his plight with resignation and dignity, but it is undeniable that his steadfastness did not face all the trials that earlier popes underwent. One praises him too much if one ignores the fact that he repeatedly made concessions he himself later regretted. We might excuse this due to his circumstances and his advanced age; but where human weakness is undeniable we do not see the halo of a saint.

3

History of the Protestant Church

Introduction

If the history of the Protestant Church had to be limited, in the time period with which we are concerned, to what is specifically ecclesiastical, then the dearth of historical material would be an embarrassment. Just as we look in vain for ecclesiastical movements and events that were of sufficient historical importance to deserve our attention, so too we look in vain for phenomena in the field of scientific theology that were of deeper significance. We could have just called attention to how indifferent and negative this period was toward everything positive, how lukewarm it was in its Protestant convictions, how indifferent it was to everything having to do with the church. Upon closer inspection, however, we see immediately how contrary it would be to the concept of Protestantism if we confine ourselves here to "church" in the narrower sense.

The period of which we are speaking here is distinguished by the fact that in it the intellectual life of the German nation underwent a new and splendid revival. Exceptional minds, such as are rarely found together in such numbers within a brief time span, enriched the affairs of the nation with the most important products of their creative genius. With a series of philosophers, among whom the names of Kant, Fichte, and Schelling each designated an independent stage of development, philosophy went through a new and highly remarkable period; with poets such as Schiller and Goethe, poetry experienced a new classical age; with so many other distinguished persons, whose names only need to be mentioned to indicate their national significance, new avenues of original intellectual endeavor opened up in the most diverse directions. As revolutionary as the immediately preceding period had been, and as politically turbulent as those times were, the widespread, great convulsion experienced at this time appears to have increasingly aroused and awakened intellectual forces at their deepest foundations and in their most creative activity. These forces made conquests in the intellectual arena comparable to so much that happened at that time in wholly different arenas, in the theater of warfare and politics. No other period of the modern age was so productive, so rich in fruitful ideas, so grasped by a movement that penetrated so deeply and extended so broadly.

Since from our standpoint we can only draw distinctions between Catholicism and Protestantism, if we now ask how all this is related to the Protestant Church, it must appear as highly significant that all those heroic figures who were the major leaders of this great intellectual movement belonged to the Protestant Church. To be sure, this is merely a superficial observation, but closely related to it is the idea that there must be an inner connection of this phenomenon with the essence and principle of Protestantism. The spirit of the age ruptures the bonds that previously restrained and confined it; it clears a new path of progress in the various fields of intellectual endeavor; it creates a new world struggling for freedom and independence; its entire endeavor consists in grasping itself based on itself, by going deeply into itself in order to come to full consciousness of itself and to know itself as free and absolute power over everything. This is nothing other than a return to the Protestant principle, which now for the first time frees itself from its bondage in order to become in actuality what it is in itself. Protestantism in its innermost nature is the principle of autonomy,[1] of liberation and withdrawal from everything in which the self-conscious spirit does not recognize its own nature and is unable to know itself as being at one with itself. Thus, where we must recognize this tendency as the common characteristic at the basis of a series of phenomena, we rightly assert that it can have emerged only on the soil of the Protestant principle and is essentially conditioned by this principle itself. For this reason a history of the Protestant Church in this period has the task of also drawing these phenomena into the sphere of its consideration. They too have a closer connection to Protestantism.

When the common characteristics of an entire series of phenomena decisively create a specific form of consciousness, then the religious aspect can hardly be missing as an essential element. Thus the consciousness of every age is also related to Christianity in some specific way. Depending on its general characteristics, the whole outlook of an age must be shaped

---

1. Autonomy is certainly central to the Protestant principle as Baur sees it. But he recognizes in other contexts that this is also a principle of theonomy—not of the heteronomy by which it has been bound in the past—because the liberated self finds itself in the closest communion with the ground of its being, absolute spirit or God. He calls this theonomous autonomy "faith." See p. 293, n. 71.

by Christianity in one way or another. So it is always important to grasp this kind of view, expressing itself as the consciousness of the times, on the basis of the essential nature of Protestantism as one element in the historical development of our times.

The Protestant Literature

When we classify the various phenomena that we are to view in these terms, we can place at the head those whose works, by and large, have a universal character; next are the ones in which philosophy has taken its specific course of development, and they include figures who have a more particular relation to religion and Christianity without in fact specifically being theologians. If we identify these two groups by the names of the persons who were the major leaders of these movements, then Herder, Goethe and Schiller, as well as Schlegel, comprise one group; another is made up of the philosophers Kant, Fichte, Schelling, and Jacobi; and Schleiermacher has a place of his own.

Herder

Among the persons who, as major leaders of the intellectual movement, are the chief representatives of the period starting at the beginning of the century, Herder[2] rightly stands out. Since he died in 1803, only the final years of his life belong to the nineteenth century; but if there was ever an outstanding man of his time who left the imprint of his spirit on the newly beginning century by his entire life and activity, it was Herder. He was one of the most multifaceted, comprehensive, and innovative thinkers, who, like few others, stimulated and enlivened people in the most diverse spheres. He was a poet, philosopher, historian, theologian, preacher, practicing minister, pedagogue; and taken as a whole, we would completely misjudge him if we were to view his knowledge and activity, extending to so many subjects, as

---

2. Johann Gottfried Herder (1744–1803) was a philosopher, theologian, poet, and literary critic, who embodied the ideals of the Enlightenment and Romanticism. A student of Kant in Königsberg, and a protégé of Hamann, he was a clergyman, teacher, and writer who moved to Paris, Strasbourg, and finally Weimar. A prolific and enormously influential author, he is best known for his *Treatise on the Origin of Language* (1772), *On the Spirit of Hebrew Poetry* (1782–83), *God: Some Conversations* (1787), and *Ideas on the Philosophy of the History of Humanity* (1784–91). Of the many collections in English, see *Herder: Philosophical Writings*, ed. Desmond M. Clarke and Michael N. Forster (Cambridge, 2007), and *Against Pure Reason: Writings on Religion, Language, and History*, ed. and trans. Marcia Bunge (Minneapolis, 1993).

being merely that of a superficial dilettante lacking focus. He is best known for addressing, with all his passion and his essential energy, each topic he took up. He knew how to penetrate to the heart of all matters and to grasp them in the deepest roots of their own existence and actual life principles. However diverse the spheres of his intellectual activity and operations, we always find the same originality of spirit by which he united everything into a harmonious whole.

If his writings sometimes lack thorough exposition, are incomplete, deficient in fuller questioning, or fail to carry through with an idea, and sometimes lead to rigidity, apparent contradictions, and assertions that prove to be off the mark, farfetched, or overconfident, the whole nevertheless remains of value despite its particular shortcomings. There are always new insights to be gained from him, original ideas that shed new light on what is under consideration. In intellectual productivity he ranked well below a poet such as Goethe, and in acuteness and consistency of thought well below a philosopher such as Kant; but in contrast he had a much greater receptivity, the capacity to place himself into, and live within, the most diverse intellectual and national forms of the life of peoples in all ages, to take them up into his feeling and soul in all his intellectual individuality, and to reproduce them from it. Kant said of him very appropriately: "It is as though his genius did not simply harvest ideas from the broad fields of the sciences and arts in order to communicate them more effectively; rather he transformed them by a certain law of assimilation into his distinctive and specific way of thinking."[3] To whatever he assimilated in this way and reproduced from within, he gave the distinctive mark of his own mode of perception, a concrete and vital form conducive to becoming a stimulating and fruitful contribution to the general consciousness of his time.

Herder called poetry, philosophy, and history—the three lamps that illuminate the nations, sects, and peoples—a sacred triangle. Poetry elevates people by its pleasant, sensual presentation of things that transcends division and narrow-mindedness; philosophy lends people firm, enduring principles; and if further maxims are needed, history will not fail to provide them. The unity of these three areas that thoroughly meld in him constitutes the distinctiveness of Herder's worldview, as it is illustrated especially by his *Ideen zur Philosophie der Geschichte der Menschheit*.[4] He designated its distinctive principle by the word "humanity" (*Humanität*), which he

---

3. Immanuel Kant, review of J. G. Herder, *Ideen zur Geschichte der Philosophie der Menschheit* (1785). *Akademie Ausgabe der Schriften von Immanuel Kant* (1912), 8:45.

4. First published in 1790–94 in Karlsruhe in 4 vols. Translated as *Reflections on the Philosophy of the History of Mankind*, abridged edition by Frank E. Manuel (Chicago, 1968).

emphasized more strongly than any other term and used constantly. He is justly called a priest of humanity, a priest of the genuinely human. The concept "humanity" expresses the significance that Herder has for modernity. Humanity was for him the highest achievement to which human beings could aspire—their unity with God, the truly divine-human. In it he saw the character of our species, but only as an innate potential. He said we do not arrive in the world with our humanity realized, but it should be the goal of our striving, the sum of our efforts, our values. Hence the divine in our species is our formation for humanity. All great and good people, legislators, inventors, philosophers, poets, artists, have contributed to it by their example, work, schooling, and teaching—all noble persons in their life-circumstances by educating their children and observing their duties. Humanity is the treasure and bounty of all human endeavor; [creating it is,] as it were, the art of our race. The task of humanity is to gain knowledge of human nature, to develop its powers and abilities in a way befitting its nature, to gather all who are called human beings into the one city of God, governed by one law, the spirit of universal reason. Herder said: I would hope that I could encompass in the word "humanity" everything I have said about the noble formation of human beings for reason and freedom, for fulfillment and mastery of the earth, because they have no more noble word for their vocation than what they are themselves, i.e. "human."

If humanity is the highest achievement to be realized in human beings, the absolute human character, then we already find in it the viewpoint from which Herder understood Christianity. Christianity itself is the purest humanity; it requires, according to Herder, the purest humanity on the purest path. This idea of humanity and its relationship to Christianity only expressed what had already been the dominant tendency of the era. A transcendent Christianity with its antiquated dogmatism, in which the human could never be given its due vis-à-vis the divine, had long since been rejected. People sought to naturalize and rationalize the entire content of Christianity as much as possible, but in the process they gave all of it an overly subjective and individual character. Herder's idea of humanity was at least a more definite, more concrete, and more objective concept, from which a more important point of view arose for considering [Christianity] historically and the task of doing so. What we see in the entire course of development of Christianity is simply the realization of the idea of humanity. Protestantism has its great historical significance in the fact that, after so many aberrations of piety renouncing what is human (such as the asceticism of monks), it validated the purely human interest in religion and Christianity. For this reason, Herder pushed emphatically to humanize Christianity and the Bible: Christianity is human, and the Bible the most human of all books. His *Briefe über das Studium der Theologie* begins by saying that it remains true that the best way of studying the knowledge of God (theology) is the study of the Bible, and the best reading of this divine book is a human reading.[5] The Bible must be read humanly because it is a book written by humans for humans. The more humanely we read the Word of God, the closer we come to the purpose of its author, who created humans in his image, and who acts humanely in all works and good deeds, whereby he reveals himself to us as God.

Herder did not intend to diminish the divinity of the Bible and of Christianity in any way. His entire effort was apologetic. To those who despised the Son of Man because of his form as a servant, and who put the Bible aside as an archaic and incomprehensible book, Herder wanted to present Christianity in all its greatness and grandeur by showing how the human element was as such also the divine. The fundamental idea of Herder's view of Christianity is that the human is divine and the divine human. The purer the human is in its essence, all the more does it inherently bear the stamp of the divine; and the more immediately the divine reveals itself, the more it appears in the shape of the human. This view was quite well suited to reconcile with Christianity the religious consciousness that had been alienated by the old transcendent dogmatism. In a time that wanted everything to be human and natural, tangible and understandable, Christianity also had to become humanly accessible; and it was always better if instead of being rationalized it became at least humanized.

However, this left much that was unclear and vague: as much as Herder always tried to emphasize that both divinity and humanity must be shown to be present in Christ in an inner union, he never succeeded in formulating this unity clearly and specifically. Because for him the human aspect remained the more important and essential one, he could not, despite his intention, avoid making Christianity seem one-dimensional, especially in his later theological writings.

Just because he did not offer a theological system of his own, and because what he wrote about Christianity, the Bible, and theology was presented not by a learned theologian but by a great national author who spoke in a more popular vein to an educated public, his ideas were able to have a quite significant impact on the dominant views of the time. He did not bother with detailed exposition and scientific rationales but asserted what he wrote only in its general application and meaning. Herder provided the strongest support for the view in the general intellectual climate of the

---

5. First published in 1780–81. See "Letters Concerning the Study of Theology," in *Against Pure Reason* (n. 2), 218.

time for which he was a leading and emphatic spokesperson—the view that only the human is the substantial essence of Christianity, and that therefore Christianity cannot be something foreign to and different from human nature, or something utterly supernatural and beyond reason. He represented the general climate of his time by this specific form, one expressing his own individuality—the form of the idea of humanity.

Schiller and Goethe

With all the diversity of Herder's intellectual striving and work, he was also a theologian and a theological author. So he certainly warranted attention here. In moving on from him to examine Schiller and Goethe, we might ask what significance they have for the history of the Protestant church and theology. Though great poets, the products of their genius have so little of an authentic Christian character that they appear to fall wholly outside our field of view. People have often asked about their relationship to Christianity, with the particular point of emphasis being their judgments and statements about religion and Christianity, and what else about them might be Christian. Although the results of this effort were rather sparse, the important thing people hoped to find with them was not the personal aspect, something Christian as such. Rather the issue here can only be how their great importance to the spirit of the times influenced contemporary attitudes about Christianity. We cannot claim that the era became more Christian because of them in the usual sense of being Christian. But neither can we claim that it became as un-Christian as some believe, although the effect they initially had on the time can only be described as their further weakening the import of the positive and specific elements in Christianity.

The same is true of poetry as of philosophy. The more an era immerses itself in philosophy, tries to satisfy in it the highest intellectual interests and makes philosophical truths the absolute content of its consciousness, the more indifferent it becomes to the absolute content of religion, believing to find already in philosophy what only religion appears able to provide, namely everything that is salvific and produces happiness.[6] Poetry is also such an intellectual power, and there are times when everything else must subordinate itself to the aesthetic interest awakened and widely disseminated by it. When what is beautiful delights minds, when the ideals of art and the magnificent figures of poetic genius satisfy fantasy, the ideal world

---

6. This view of philosophy of religion is expressed already in Baur's *Die christliche Gnosis, oder die christliche Religions-Philosophie in ihrer geschichtlichen Entwiklung* (Tübingen, 1835).

created by poetry takes over the human attraction to the supersensible and appears to completely satisfy it. This produces indifference and coldness toward the religious aspect; the proper sense of the supersensible in religion is lost; the aesthetic cultivation becomes the highest measure by which we judge everything; poetic utterances with their lovely, appealing language are more valued than the sayings of sacred scripture in their simple truth; the theater is more interesting than the church, and we are led to believe that it is permissible to replace the one by the other.

Schiller[7] in fact wanted to elevate the stage to be a moral, even a religious institution, one above all to be exalted and strongly supported by the modern state. In his essay "The Theater Considered as a Moral Institution,"[8] he said in all earnestness that the purpose of the theater is a religious one, and that only when religion is allied with the theater is religion safe from subversion. To him the theater symbolizes, as it were, the Last Judgment, in which virtue finds its reward and vice its punishment. It is a living mirror of morals and, more than any other public institution, a school for practical wisdom, an unerring key to the most secret pathways of the human soul. Only in the theater do the mighty ones of the world hear the truth; only there do they see the human dimension. The theater is the shared channel in which the light of wisdom from the rational, better side of the people streams down and spreads in gentler rays throughout the entire state. It is the school for tolerance, and a wholesome effect on education can be expected from it. Indeed, Schiller expected from the theater what previously had been expected only from the church, that with its consolations the theater would lift people above the worries of life.

This is very characteristic of a period in which an aesthetic orientation began to gain such prominence, and it gives an indication of how aesthetic interests can clash with religious interests once they have gained such an important influence on the educated portion of the nation. If, at the same

---

7. Johann Christoph Friedrich von Schiller (1759–1805) was a poet, philosopher, physician, historian, and playwright. As a young man he had strong religious interests. Born in Württemberg, the son of a military doctor, he later moved to Weimar where he began a long association with Goethe. Although he wrote philosophical and aesthetic essays as well as many famous poems, his most important contribution was to the theater. His famous plays included *The Robbers, Intrigue and Love, Don Carlos, Wallenstein, Maria Stuart, The Bride of Messina*. Two lines from Schiller's poem "Friendship" are quoted at the end of Hegel's *Phenomenology of Spirit*: "The chalice of this realm of spirits / Foams forth to God his own infinitude." His "Ode to Joy" was incorporated into the final movement of Beethoven's Ninth Symphony and later became the anthem of the European Union.

8. "Die Schaubühne als eine moralische Anstalt betrachtet." See Schiller's *Sämmtliche Werke* (Stuttgart and Tübingen, 1812–15), vol. 2.

time, we consider that both poets in their most widely read works do not shy away from making comments about religion and Christianity that are occasionally injurious to sensitive feelings, then we are less inclined to have a very favorable notion of their positive influence on the Christian religious consciousness of the time. But if we were to base our judgment about them solely on that, it would be highly one-sided. If everything that gives people a more earnest and elevated awareness of greatness and nobility, of truth and goodness, of what lifts them above everyday reality to the ideal world and makes them enthusiastic about ideas—if all of this is also beneficial to religion and Christianity, then their works are to be highly esteemed in that regard. Schiller in particular had a tremendously inspiring and ennobling effect on his morally weakened age through the rigorously moral spirit of his poems, which reflected greatly the influence of Kant, whose philosophy he admired greatly and whose loftiest ideas he popularized in their noblest form. This he did by means of the great ardor with which he praised the majesty of the virtue that is independent of all earthly success, and directed our gaze from the dust of earthly existence upward to heaven by the fervent and genuinely Protestant antipathy, with which his noble soul was imbued, against all that denigrated humans and reason, all that denigrated the dignity of the human race.

When Goethe and Schiller also praised religion and Christianity primarily in their moral, noble, and beautiful manifestations, they did so free of any harsh one-sidedness; and even when they appeared to step too much to one side or the other, they did so only to restore the balance that in their opinion had been disturbed. Schiller, for example, in his much criticized poem "The Gods of Greece," looked back from the Christian world to the Greek land of fantasy. He brandished the flaming sword of his genius not against Christianity but rather against its soulless, abstract theology, which had banished the living God from the world and transformed everything into dead forces of nature.

Brilliant thinkers, such as these two poets, distinguish themselves especially by standing free, above contradictions and contentious parties. Their natural versatility, their intellectual vision penetrating the heart of the matter, their objective way of looking at things, do not permit them to take sides and become partisans of only one position. The characteristic greatness of Goethe's[9] nature was his completely free, calm, unbiased attitude

---

9. Johann Wolfgang von Goethe (1749–1832) was Germany's foremost poet, novelist, and playwright. He took up residence in Weimar in 1775 and become an important civil leader there. His works include *Faust, The Sorrows of Young Werther, Wilhelm Meister's Apprenticeship, Elective Affinities, Prometheus, Theory of Colors, Italian Journey, West-Eastern Divan*. Enormously influential, he was a free-thinking "non-Christian."

and ability to maintain a proper balance in all things, standing above the clash of opinions and views, secure in his self-knowledge. This applied to Goethe's view of the theological currents of his time. He loathed equally the view of Christianity that emphasized the supernatural in the interest of orthodox beliefs, and the rationalism of the Enlightenment, which he regarded as being too shallow, too soulless, too insipid. How cleverly and aptly he satirized the vacuous and fanciful neology of the likes of Bahrdt, Nicolai, and Basedow[10] in his *Faust* and elsewhere! With just a few words he dealt a far more painful and deadly blow to this superficial rational dilettantism than an expert apologetic theologian could have done with an extensive and thorough rebuttal.[11] He felt more sympathetic to philosophers of the Enlightenment, even to the views of Lavater and Stilling,[12] who were close friends from his youth. Whenever people got too pushy with their Christian views, wishing to convert him, he reacted curtly and said openly that he was not un-Christian, nor anti-Christian, but most decidedly non-Christian. It would be entirely against his nature to limit himself to Christianity, to have to find everything in it alone; it seemed to him confining to believe that everything of absolute importance to human beings was to be seen in Christ, a single individual. A letter to Lavater expressed his view so characteristically that it merits quoting here; it makes his entire view of Christianity evident.[13]

> It lifts up the soul and is the occasion for the pleasantest of reflections when one sees you grasp the exquisite crystal vessel with such fervor, fill it with your own foaming, deep red drink, and quaff again the overflowing foam with such relish. I do not begrudge you such bliss of finding all enjoyment in one single individual; and even though it is impossible that a single individual can be sufficient, it is marvelous that an image is left to us from olden times in which you can invest your all and see yourself reflected, even idolizing yourself in him. I am afraid I can only experience it as unjust and a theft that you pluck all the precious feathers of the thousands of birds under the heavens as though they had been usurped, in order to adorn your bird of paradise. This is what is bound to irritate and seem intolerable

---

10. Carl Friedrich Bahrdt (1741–92), Friedrich Nicolai (1733–1811), Johann Bernhard Basedow (1724–90).

11. [Baur] Goethe, "Prolog zu den neuesten Offenbarungen Gottes verdeutscht durch Bahrdt," *Werke* (Stuttgart, 1827–42), 13:109: "Da kam mir ein Einfall von ungefähr, / So redt' ich, wenn ich Christus wär" (Then a notion came to me by chance, / So I would say if I were Christ perchance).

12. Johann Kasper Lavater (1741–1801), Johann Heinrich Jung-Stilling (1740–1817).

13. See *Briefe von Goethe an Lavater: Aus den Jahren 1774 bis 1783* (Leipzig, 1833).

to those of us who, through people and the wisdom revealed to them, take on the role of pupils and as sons of God worship him in ourselves and in all his children.

Schiller expressed similar thoughts when he sang in his poem "The Gods of Greece": "To enrich one beyond all others was foreign to this lovely paradise"; and it is the same as Strauss said in his famous statement that it is not the nature of the idea to pour out its entire fullness into a single individual.[14] Another letter from Goethe to Lavater expressed the same basic conviction: "You take the gospel as it is for the most divine of truths. But a voice from heaven would not convince me that water burns and fire extinguishes, that a woman bears a child without a man, that a person rises from the dead—I take these to blaspheme God and God's revelation in nature. You find nothing more beautiful than the gospel; I find these thousands of pages written by ancient and more recent people whom God has blessed to be equally beautiful, and equally useful and indispensable to humankind." These are utterances that might easily cause offense; but examined more closely, are they not simply the same as what philosophy and speculative theology arrive at in different terms from their point of view?[15] It was clear to Goethe from his worldview that Christianity cannot be something utterly transcendent and supernatural; that it must also again be understood as something natural and rational, that Christ, if he is to be taken as a human individual, cannot be placed absolutely above all other human beings as something utterly different from what they are. This way of looking at things, found in the works of both authors and widely disseminated by them, also contributed to stripping away the particularistic, narrow, and one-sided aspects that still adhered to that view of Christianity;

---

14. David Friedrich Strauss, *Das Leben Jesu, kritisch bearbeitet*, 4th ed. (Tübingen, 1840), §151. ET: *The Life of Jesus Critically Examined*, trans. George Eliot, 2nd ed. (London, 1892), 779–80.

15. Baur's own position is spelled out most clearly in the following passage from *Die christliche Lehre von der Dreieinigkeit und Menschwerdung Gottes*, 3 vols. (Tübingen, 1841–43), 3:998–9: "Idea and reality can never be joined together in such absolute unity that the idea does not transcend every manifestation given in reality, indeed every single individual; therefore the idea can actualize itself only in an endless series of individuals. In every single individual the non-being of the idea must be posited, *be it only as a minimum*.... As certainly as the idea of humanity must actualize itself, and as certainly as it is established essentially in the unity of God and the human being, just as certainly can it be actualized only by virtue of the fact that it enters into the consciousness of humanity at a specific point in a specific individual. However, no matter how highly in other respects one may place this individual, in virtue of the idea of this unity that comes to consciousness in him, he must still stand in a subordinate relationship to the idea; and a God-man in the sense of the ecclesiastical doctrine embraces in itself an irresolvable contradiction."

to removing its transcendent, miraculous character that makes it an eternal puzzle to clear-headed reason. Their universal worldview became the natural basis that was henceforth gained for the more liberal comprehension of Christianity.

And why should everything that the consciousness of the time acquired through them in deeper intellectual content, richness of ideas, and grandeur of insights also not be seen as promoting the Christian religious life? We ask what raises such spirits so high above others, what gives them such a deep and broad reach, what it means to offer praise and tokens of universal, voluntary, and enthusiastic gratitude to Schiller at the centennial celebration of his birth,[16] such as have scarcely been shown another human being, let alone a poet. What else can one see in this celebration, if all aspects of it are not superficial but enclose an inner kernel of truth, than the obvious fact that so many thousands recognize in him a genius who not only brings joy by the beauty of his poetry but also awakens something in them, a spiritual good, an addition to their consciousness that lifts them above ordinary everyday life? It is a shared feature of their humanity that unites them with so many others. What Schleiermacher once said of himself as a teacher, and honored to such a high degree in his teaching activity, that his calling was simply to bring to awareness what was present already in any ordinary person, also holds good for the influence that such poetic geniuses [as Schiller] have on others. Their power over minds and spirits consists in bringing to expression what already inherently lies deep within the human being; it only needs to be expressed in order to find general resonance and to be recognized as something of truly human interest to every thinking and feeling person, a truth the awareness of which weaves a spiritual bond around all, thereby creating a single nation of brothers and sisters. The deeper such highly gifted minds reach into what is inward in human nature, and—like a few others who have this ability—the more they know how to take this content raised from the depths and express it in a clear and generally understandable way, and to set it before the soul in a vital vision that captures mind and spirit—the higher they then stand above their time as brightly shining stars, and all the more certain are they to be honored, in the eternal radiance of their names as geniuses, who also fulfill their duty, and it is not a small one, in bringing humanity along its earthly path toward the higher supersensible goal of its existence.

---

16. [*Zeller*] The final paragraph of this section is an addition provided by Baur in 1859 when he gave these lectures for the last time, on the occasion of the centennial celebration of Schiller's birth. In his earlier manuscript, only one sentence is found that concurs with the beginning of this addition.

The Romantics

The poetic uplift the German nation received from its two great poets was most closely related to the general tendency of the time to strive to surpass itself, to break free from the actual state of affairs and all that could so little satisfy the deeper yearning of the spirit—to break away as completely as possible in order to create a new ideal reality (*neue ideelle Wirklichkeit*) through the deepening of spirit within itself. The ideality with which these poets rose above the spiritless platitudes and triviality of their time, and became the leaders of a new epoch of the German spirit, is in principle the same as what philosophy calls "idealism," the general form of philosophical consciousness of the new age. Goethe and Schiller found the ideals of their poetic sensibility in the visual art forms of classical antiquity; and they looked back to antiquity. For them, genuine style and true ideality were to be found only in the art of antiquity. Art that did not achieve the purity of antiquity or at least approach it was in their eyes either not art at all or a highly inferior art.

The esteem the two poets had for antiquity contrasted with Romanticism, which assumed a particular aesthetic orientation especially through the two Schlegels, Tieck, and Novalis,[17] among others. If one understands Romanticism to mean the view that the ideals of beauty and nobility are not to be sought only in a world as distant from us as are the ancient Greeks and Romans, that instead the spiritual life of the Romance and Germanic peoples of the Christian Middle Ages and of later times is also of particular aesthetic interest, then Romanticism is entirely correct, and we should fully acknowledge that, in addition to Voss[18] (the classical translator of the Greeks and Romans), it was mainly the two Schlegels who, with their splendid translations, made the works of the great poets of England, Spain, and Italy accessible to a wider public and awakened the sensibility and interest for this new and important part of the *belles lettres*. They not only contributed much to the universal culture and education that sets Germans apart from

---

17. The brothers August Wilhelm Schlegel (1767–1845) and Karl Wilhelm Friedrich Schlegel (1772–1829) were poets, translators, philologists, leaders of German Romanticism, and co-founders of the *Athenaeum*. August Schlegel's translations turned Shakespeare's plays into German classics. He was a professor of Sanskrit and translator of the *Bhagavad-Gita*. Friedrich Schlegel collaborated with Novalis, Tieck, Fichte, and Caroline Schelling, whom he married, and in 1799 published *Lucinde*. Johann Ludwig Tieck (1777–1853) was a poet, translator, novelist, and member of the Romantic circle in Jena. Novalis was the pseudonym of Georg Philipp Friedrich von Hardenberg (1772–1801). His short life revealed his literary, philosophical, and scientific gifts.

18. Johann Heinrich Voss (1751–1826), a German classicist, was known for his translations of Homer's *Odyssey* (1781) and *Iliad* (1793).

other nations; they also expanded and enriched German national identity, and especially developed the German language, which—in the superb translations by which Voss and the Schlegels set the example—first fully developed its boundless potential for growth. They also laid the foundation for the new study of art and literature, which took as its goal to understand and grasp each [creative] spirit on its own terms, and to view all the works of the most diverse artists, whatever their aptitude for what is highest, as parts of a single imagination and a single art: they provided a new basis for appreciating the individuality and nationality of these artists.

This, however, by no means exhausts the concept of Romanticism; there is much more to it. While Goethe and Schiller sought refuge from their own reality, but not from reality as such, they returned to the ancient paragons and attempted to emulate them. But out of despair over the empirical mindset surrounding it, Romanticism abandoned the soil of nature and reality entirely. It fought against reality by means of the imagination (*Imagination*). Imagination's element is fantasy (*Phantasie*) left entirely to itself—a fantasy that, if it abandons itself entirely to its subjective moods and caprice and overleaps all of reality's laws and conditions, becomes fantastic or fantasizing (*phantastisch*).[19] Fantasy in Romantic idealism corresponds to the "I" in Fichtean idealism. A true and complete human being was supposed to be fantasy and only fantasy, and every limitation of fantasy by reality was said to be a limitation and devaluation of human nature, a loss of a person's inborn infinity. In order that nothing takes on the shape of solid reality, and everything remains sheer form, fantasy's sheer hocus-pocus, Romanticism ultimately always in turn negates its own structures by intentionally destroying the illusion it has introduced. It does so by means of wanton self-parody or Romantic irony, which is what this highest standpoint of completely free Romanticism is called.

From this purely idealistic antithesis to reality issued that audacious aristocratic hubris with which the Romantics not only attacked everything trivial and commonplace in ordinary life, but declared everything in ordinary life as such to be trivial and commonplace. The Schlegel brothers emerged as art critics with a theory of art that tossed out all previous principles and rules, and wished to have their authority alone considered as the

---

19. [Baur] Cf. Hermann Theodor Hettner (1821–82), *Die romantische Schule in ihrem inneren Zusammenhang mit Göthe und Schiller* (Braunschweig, 1850), 49: "The Romantic School is the doctrine and practice of subjectively self-oriented, objectless, fantasizing fantasy (*phantastischen Phantasie*). It calls itself 'Romantic' because, in the nature of the case, the subjectivity and inwardness, the mysterious, ominous glow of medieval romantic poetry, is infinitely preferable to the clearly sculpted and objectively oriented poetry of the ancients, with its measured dignity and cheerful harmony."

highest law. The Romantics spoke the same language even in the field of morals; they often enough derided morality and ethical life, not merely in their writings but also in the way they actually lived. Bourgeois morality was considered to be narrow-minded and Philistine. For example, we need only think of Friedrich Schlegel's *Lucinde*, which was meant to provide a Romantic reconfiguration of everyday life, but which went so beyond the trends of the time that even Schleiermacher could write his well-known *Letters on Lucinde* to that effect.[20] Even Schiller had to endure being referred to as "he of leaden morality" by the Schlegel brothers, who enjoyed making such derogatory references. They found his solemn, moral spirit distasteful, and they arrogantly felt themselves superior to conventional moral concepts.

However, this is not the place to characterize Romanticism according to its excesses; let us merely mention its relationship to Christianity and to Protestantism in particular. Goethe's and Schiller's classical orientation valued the genuinely humane spirit of Greek antiquity as the highest moral and religious norm. This orientation formed the basis for their indifference toward specifically Christian views. In any event, it does no harm to a Christianity sealed off in its church dogma if, time and again, it is compared to classical antiquity's free and universal idea of humanity. The relationship of Romanticism to Christianity is of quite a different nature. Just as Romanticism differs from classical antiquity by already revealing a Christian character, it also typically shows a preference for Catholicism. Because the forms and topics it held on to were medieval ones, Romanticism had a bent toward Catholicism. This can also be explained by the fact that such abstract interiority and subjectivity could, when exaggerated, suddenly change over into its opposite, an all the more concrete reality. This turning from reality, the flight from the present, from the clarity of the comprehensibly ordered, clear world of the new age, the freeing of fantasy from all the constraints of common sense—these traits led Romanticism into the chiaroscuro world of medieval Catholicism, where it could move about most freely. However, what first began simply as the play of poetic fantasy soon became entirely serious reality. It is well-known how this trend toward medieval Catholicism ultimately brought several renowned members of the Romantic school into the bosom of the Catholic Church. The author of *Lucinde* represented himself as a faithful son in the service of this church. For him and others, this step was also the consequence of the unbounded pursuit and craving for sensual pleasure on the part of the Romantics, which they regarded,

---

20. Schleiermacher was deeply influenced by Schlegel's Romanticism, which he embraced in his *Vertraute Briefe über die Lucinde*, ed. Karl Gutzkow (Hamburg, 1835), as well as by his seven-year relationship, from 1798 to 1805, with Eleanore Christiane Grunow, wife of a Berlin clergyman.

practically and theoretically, as the most sublime aspect of life's poetry, but which could only end with their own spiritual decadence.

Romanticism also played a role in politics, where it made itself quite unpopular. Some Romantics, such as Friedrich Schlegel, were willing tools of the Restoration. This caused the reputation of Romanticism to be damaged all the more, and things got to the point that Romantics were seen as reactionaries. Ruge[21] defined a Romantic as someone who used the education gained in our time to challenge the Enlightenment, and who rejected and fought against the principle of a humanity self-satisfied in the areas of the sciences, the arts, ethics, and even politics. This conception of Romanticism was even applied to the philosophy of Schelling during its last phase in Berlin.[22]

However, these reactionary ecclesiastical and political endeavors, and in particular the catholicizing efforts, can be attributed only to the aberrations of Romanticism. Romanticism originates from an essentially Protestant principle. For what else is it but the Protestant principle of freedom, the free being-for-self of the subject, when Romanticism claims the right to understand and judge in its own fashion, according to its own individual norms, everything that has taken a particular form in the spiritual life of peoples? In art and science as well, there should be no Catholic uniformity. Even the entire character of Romanticism as subjectivity—its so-called mania for immediacy, its poetry of the infinite, its breakthrough from the finite to the infinite to comprehend it sensually and emotionally—originated as a genuinely Protestant immersion of the subject within itself. It was the reversal of consciousness from flat Enlightenment prose to a poetry that fertilized the hard ground of rationalism (*Verstand*) with new currents of enthusiasm, breaking through the barriers separating the world of the finite from that of the infinite. In this sense all those persons in whom the first wing-beats of a new age were most powerfully felt at the beginning of the century were Romantics, not merely poets like Novalis, but also Schleiermacher, Fichte, and Schelling. Only Hegel with his principle of mediation and his disciplined thought was from the outset hostile to the Romantics. To appreciate Romanticism, one must ultimately take into consideration that its one-sidedly subjective orientation is simply the same path that Protestantism

---

21. Arnold Ruge (1802–1880), imprisoned during his youth for student agitations, became an exponent of German political and philosophical liberalism. He jointly authored a book called *Der Protestantismus und die Romantik* (Halle, 1839–40). Later he briefly collaborated with Karl Marx.

22. Schelling converted to Catholicism and during his last phase in Berlin developed a "positive" philosophy of revelation. See below, pp. 352–54.

too had previously followed. According to Hettner,[23] p. 38, subjectivism is the secret of the new Romantic poetry. Only the individual, the subject, is in the right. The world opposing the subject, namely, the object, is completely subordinated to the subject and its willful play. We see the same principle of subjectivity here: it announces itself in the most diverse manifestations in its power and strength, as well as in its eccentricity and exuberantly excessive behavior. At a time when French military power overwhelmed everything, the German mind fled to the inner world of Romanticism as well, where it found a substitute for the external world.

German Philosophy: Kant

The philosophers Kant, Fichte, Schelling, and Jacobi form a distinctive line. The actual process of spirit struggling for awareness of itself in its depths can be seen in the course of development philosophy took because of them. Thus they demonstrate most specifically how the consciousness of the time related to religion and Christianity. Hegel[24] opens the history of modern German philosophy with the words:

> *The philosophy of Kant, Fichte, and Schelling.* These philosophies reveal and express the revolution in the form of thought to which spirit has advanced most recently in Germany, and its impact can be seen in the course that thinking has taken. Only two nations, the Germans and the French (despite or perhaps because they are so antithetical), have participated in this great epoch of world history, the innermost essence of which is grasped by the philosophy of history.[25] Other nations have not participated; their governments and peoples have, but they have done so politically, not inwardly. In Germany, this principle has come to the fore in thought, spirit, and concept; in France, in reality. The reality that has come to the fore in Germany appears as the force of external circumstances and the reaction against it.

23. See n. 19.

24. Georg Wilhelm Friedrich Hegel, *Vorlesungen über die Geschichte der Philosophie*, ed. K. L. Michelet, 3 vols., 1st ed. (Berlin, 1833–36); 2nd ed. (Berlin, 1840–44), 3:534–35 (vol. 15 of Hegel's *Werke*); ET: *Lectures on the History of Philosophy*, trans. E. S. Haldane and F. H. Simson, 3 vols. (London, 1896), 3:409 (our translation).

25. Hegel's text reads "grasped by world history" instead of "grasped by the philosophy of history." In his *Lectures on the Philosophy of World History*, ed. and trans. R. F. Brown and P. C. Hodgson [Oxford, 2011]), 87–88, Hegel says that "world history is the progress of the consciousness of freedom," and he finds this consciousness coming to a culmination in his own time. The American Revolution could be considered an "inward" revolution, but Hegel makes no mention of it.

Thus Hegel sees in the course of German philosophy a revolutionary movement similar to what was found in France. This is not to be understood simply based on the general similarity that all revolutions have with each other, whatever their kind, but from the unity of this principle. The same principle that swept through this period and inspired a political revolution in France blazed a new path for itself in Germany in the world of thought. Is this not a clear analogy? The old monarchy with its absolutism was just as transcendent a system of abstract, traditional, and dogmatic concepts as was the dogmatism of the old metaphysics. Both structures collapsed as soon as people inquired into the foundations upon which they stood. In France this happened as the national consciousness grasped itself from within, and in Germany as thinking spirit reverted to a consciousness of its own. In both cases there is a return of spirit into itself, a deepening of spirit within itself, and the emergence of a general principle in which spirit knows itself as the sovereign power over all that is not itself.

Kantian philosophy called itself "critical" and began with a critique of reason, pure and practical, and of judgment.[26] This critique was meant to be only the basis of a new system; however, it already contained everything essential to this philosophy. Prior to any cognition, it wished to explore the cognitive faculty itself. Therefore it is an analysis of *thinking*, of the various elements and functions that can be distinguished in thinking and in which thinking expresses its activity. These activities lead to general concepts, determinations of thought or categories, and the result is that the cognitive faculty has real objective content only insofar as it focuses on objects given within the framework of space and time. Once it no longer remains within this sphere but goes beyond it, it becomes transcendent and devoid of content. Hence there is no theoretical cognition of the supersensible, and everything that the old metaphysics asserted about the supersensible is sheer dogmatism.

The novel and characteristic feature of Kantian philosophy is that its analysis of thinking and its critique of the cognitive faculty are done exclusively from the standpoint of consciousness, and it above all asks how things stand with consciousness—what in consciousness is subjective or objective. Kant's philosophy leads our knowledge into consciousness and self-consciousness, and hence becomes idealism because according to it everything emanates from consciousness, although this philosophy just

---

26. Immanuel Kant (1724–1804) was the pivotal figure of modern philosophy. His three great critiques were the *Critique of Pure Reason* (1781, 2nd ed. 1787), the *Critique of Practical Reason* (1788), and the *Critique of Judgment* (1790). These were followed by *Religion within the Limits of Reason Alone* (1793) and the *Metaphysics of Morals* (1797). His *Prolegomena to Any Future Metaphysics* was published in 1783.

remains at the level of subjective and finite cognition. For finite cognition, self-consciousness is what is substantial or existent in itself (*an sich Seiende*), but Kantianism cannot secure any reality for pure self-consciousness or exhibit being in it. There is still an inherent barrier that self-consciousness cannot overcome, namely, the things-in-themselves (*Dingen an sich*), which lie beyond consciousness and are for consciousness the inaccessible ground of phenomena. What is existent in itself lies outside consciousness, and thus consciousness still remains a single and limited consciousness. Even though for Kantian philosophy this boundary was still so fixed that it could not get beyond it, Kantianism nevertheless established the principle that had to result in a comprehensive shift in worldview. In this regard Kant is comparable to his compatriot Copernicus,[27] but we must not view what is epoch-making about their discovery in the usual manner. The usual view is that the discovery in the visible world that our earth is not the center of the universe, about which the sun and all the stars rotate—that the earth is only a tiny point in the universe, one that like all the other planets rotates around its sun—caused substantial humiliation for humankind; and that similar consequences from this discovery followed in the invisible world, in the realm of thought. So now was the time to fold the wings of speculation, which until now had spanned the entire heavens; the time to call back the troops deployed in all directions, to gather and assemble them and focus all the forces on the one brightly illumined point of what is actually thinkable. And who would deny that there was greater gain from this enhanced self-knowledge and self-limitation of reason, than from all the purported conquests in a field that humans nevertheless could not claim as their own as it was extended and defined heretofore? What is certain and withstands challenge is, after all, to be preferred over what is uncertain or built in thin air. To see things in this way would only be analogous to the humbling of humanity and the limitation of reason.

However, the parallel between Kant and Copernicus is found above all in the fact that that through them the focus of our entire view of the world shifted from one side to its opposite [from realism to idealism]. Just as after Copernicus the earth, having been central, was reduced to a diminutive point in the solar system, so too after Kant reason, confined to the finite and sensory domain, as opposed to things-in-themselves, simply became conscious of its own futility (*Nichtigkeit*). By contrast, according to the old

27. [*Zeller*] Cf. Kant, *Kritik der reinen Vernunft*, ed. G. Hartenstein (Leipzig, 1853), preface to the 2nd ed. (1787), 18. [*Ed.*] Kant himself makes the comparison. Nicolaus Copernicus (1473–1543), like Kant, was born and lived in Polish Prussia, but he was ethnically Polish (Mikolaj Kopernik) whereas Kant was German. See *Critique of Pure Reason*, trans. Norman Kemp Smith (London, 1929), 22, 25n.

metaphysics reason was the actual focal point of the whole, to the extent that, by its conceptions and inferences, reason stood in an equally real and substantial connection with the entire domain of the supersensible—just as the earth, according to the old worldview, was the major anchor of the entire universe. Kant and Copernicus severed this connection; but what for Copernicus is simply humiliation is for Kant the greatest exaltation. Although Copernicus considered the earth to be just a diminutive point in the whole, it is still the very point from which the entire cosmos is comprehended and construed by the human spirit; just as according to Kant the consciousness that distinguishes itself from the things-in-themselves, by making this distinction transcends it, and that serves to make it clear that this distinction is constitutive of all reality.

In this sense, the system of Copernicus, like that of Kant, exhibits the same shift from a worldview of realism to one of idealism—the spiritualization or intellectualization of the world as perceived (*die Vergeistigung der Weltansicht*), in that the thinking and differentiating spirit recognizes itself as the spiritual/intellectual power over what has been distinguished by it. What is revolutionary about Kantian philosophy is that transcendent realism was recognized as being null and void, was critically dissolved and taken back into spirit's consciousness by this process; and, through the connection of everything given to the consciousness of the all-determining focal point, it was posited in self-consciousness. Even though Kant let the unknown [and unknowable] thing stand as the limit for consciousness, it had already been subsumed (*aufgehoben*) in the "I" of self-consciousness by the principle of his philosophy.

Now, however, the main thing became the relationship between practical reason and theoretical reason. The more that theoretical reason must acknowledge its finitude, the more practical reason becomes aware of its unconditional and absolute nature. The unconditional moral ought (*Sollen*) is what is absolute. All morality of action rests on the conviction that one should act with a consciousness of the [moral] law and for the sake of the law, out of respect for the law and on account of the law itself. The human being is a moral creature and has the moral law within him- or herself, a law whose principle is the freedom and autonomy of the will, as opposed to the heteronomy in which the will takes determinations by something other than itself for its own purposes. The will is free self-determination; it is autonomous, absolute spontaneity, the principle of freedom. Hegel says[28] that a great and highly important tenet of Kantian philosophy is that Kant

---

28. Hegel, *Vorlesungen über die Geschichte der Philosophie* (n. 24), 3:551 ff.; ET 3:423ff.

has brought back into self-consciousness itself what is essential for it, what counts as law, as in-itself. When we are searching for how we should judge the world and history according to one purpose or another, what should we choose as the ultimate purpose? But for the will there is no other purpose than the one summoned up out of the will itself, the purpose of its own freedom. It is great progress that this principle has been established, that freedom is the ultimate axis about which the human being pivots—this ultimate pinnacle that lets nothing impose on it, so that one allows no authority or thing to override human freedom. Kantian philosophy was responsible on the one hand for the widespread appeal of the idea that human beings have within themselves something absolutely firm and unshakable, a solid core, so that they have no obligations that do not respect this freedom.

This is the principle, but there is more to it. Practical reason establishes law, but its law has no content. The law is said to be nothing other than just identity, agreement with itself, universality; the sole form the principle has is identity with itself; the universal, the non-self-contradictory, is something empty and remains devoid of reality. Thus the principle of practical reason is therefore free will, the simple moral ought. On this absolute ought Kant bases all the reality of the supersensible, and theoretical reason is inadequate for it. What the will is in itself must actualize itself in the particular will, in the will of the individual. The particular will should be in accord with the universal will. The human being ought to be moral, but there remains the sheer ought. The goal can be attained only through an infinite progression; the unity of the universal and the particular will is only postulated, hence the postulate of the immortality of the soul.

The second postulate concerns the harmony of nature with the rational will, with the good. The idea of the moral law is the good as the final purpose of the world; however, because the moral law stands over against an external and independent nature, the contradiction between morality and happiness must first be overcome. It is overcome in the idea of the highest good, in which nature accords with reason; in other words in virtue of the existence of God as the being or causality that brings about this harmony.[29]

These two postulates are supposed to provide the bridge from the sensible world to the supersensible world. However, morality would not be morality if the particular will accorded with the universal will in such a way that what is sensible would be determined by what is universal without a struggle. Nature would no longer be nature if it simply accorded with the concept of the good. Hence the contradiction between the two sides is

---

29. Baur is too condensed here. The existence of God is a third postulate in addition to freedom and immortality. God insures that ultimately one will have happiness as commensurate with one's moral worth.

ongoing; there is only an infinite ought that never arrives at the reality of being; there is no actual absolute, only an absolute ought.

In its relationship to Christianity, Kantian philosophy offers various aspects for our consideration. Above all it was entirely in the interest of Christianity for Kantianism to unmask, in its emptiness and nothingness, the eudaemonism, the familiar morality of happiness and utility still so widespread at the time, and to condemn it in no uncertain terms. Kantianism purified and corrected moral concepts, and the earnest strictness of its categorical imperative, the rigor of its moral teaching, forcefully and actively influenced the spirit of the time. This moral orientation is entirely in tune with the spirit of Christianity, which finds nothing more objectionable than moral laxness and indifference. Also, the humiliation of theoretical reason, by demonstrating its inability to cognize anything supersensible by its own means, appeared to be entirely in accord with the Christian belief in revelation; but it equally had to raise the concern that practical reason was said to provide a complete substitute for the unsatisfied theoretical need.

Nevertheless people conceded the possibility of a supernatural revelation and formulated it in Kantian principles. They said that because humanity at large or in part is found to be moral, and because people cannot realize the idea of what is morally good other than through a supernatural revelation, this situation sufficiently justifies not simply the possibility but the necessity of such a revelation. But it is hard to see how such a case could ever occur if practical reason, by virtue of its autonomy, must be capable on its own terms of bringing moral principles to the fore at all times. The question about the possibility and actuality of a supernatural revelation had a purely theoretical significance. The important thing was that a philosophy that elevated practical reason to an absolute principle turned the entire nature of religion into moral categories, and in any given religion it could only recognize as its substantial content what agreed with its own moral principles. This was the standard that also had to be applied to Christianity, and Kant himself views it from this vantage point in his work, *Religion within the Limits of Reason Alone*.[30] This work was revolutionary in that it was the first presentation of a philosophy of religion based on the principles of modern philosophy. In it, Kant described the relationship of the historically given religions both to one another and to the absolute religion, that is, to what he held to be the absolute of religion.

Philosophy of religion is a critique of the history of religion based on the moral principles of Kantian philosophy. Kant calls this endeavor a historical

---

30. *Die Religion innerhalb den Grenzen der blossen Vernunft* (Königsberg, 1793, 2nd ed. 1794). ET: *Religion within the Limits of Reason Alone*, trans. Theodore M. Green and Hoyt H. Hudson (Chicago and London, 1934).

representation of the gradual establishment of the rule of the principle of the good on earth. The perspective under which he places the history of religion is the progression from statutory institutional faith (*Kirchenglaube*) to pure rational faith (*Vernunftglaube*).[31] The further this progression advances in a specific religion, the more this religion approximates absolute religion. Therefore, Kant sees Christianity as contrasting markedly with earlier religions. According to him, if one seeks the institution (*Kirche*) that, from its earliest beginnings, contains the seed and principles for the objective unity of true and universal religious belief, which it gradually approaches, then Jewish faith (pagan beliefs falling outside the scope of this treatise) is related in no essential way at all with *this* institutional faith, that is, it stands in no conceptual unity with it. From its earliest formulation, Jewish faith merely embodied statutory laws as the basis of a political nation, and therefore actually was not a religion. Kant substantiates this opinion further.

The situation is quite different with Christianity; it completely forsakes Judaism and is based on an entirely different principle. The teacher of the gospel not only declared Judaism's servile faith to be inherently futile, opposed to the moral faith that alone saves human beings and, by changing life for the good, proves its authenticity as alone salvific. The teacher also gave in his person an example of the archetype of the humanity well-pleasing to God. Although Christianity contains these elements of a religion of pure reason, it does not present itself to us in its historical appearance as a religion of pure reason. Its early history is obscure, and we do not know what effect its teaching had on the morality of its adherents. After Christianity was introduced into the wider public, its history has little to recommend it in terms of the beneficial effect one rightly expects from a moral religion. Only in the present time, says Kant, has reason begun to disentangle things that, in their nature, ought to be morally and spiritually uplifting, from the burden of a faith constantly exposed to the whims of the interpreter. Reason adopts the principle of humble modesty in regard to all that is called revelation, but it also validates the principle that sacred history, which was merely a matter of institutional faith, can and should have no influence of its own on the adoption of moral maxims. Instead institutional faith is given only to vividly portray faith's true object, virtue striving for holiness, which must always be taught and explained as aiming for what is moral. It must repeatedly be emphasized in this regard that true religion does not deal with the knowledge or the confession of what God does or has done for our blessedness, but rather with what *we* must do to be worthy of it. So Christianity is

---

31. Baur, following Kant's usage, distinguishes between *Kirchenglaube* (translated here as "institutional faith") and *Vernunftglaube* several times in the following paragraphs.

indeed the absolute religion, but only insofar as it contains the principles of purely rational faith. That is precisely why we can view all that is in fact positive in its miracles and mysteries as only the form and vehicle of moral rational religion. For the means by which Christianity can be brought into harmony with itself as both a positive religion and an absolute religion is the moral interpretation. Because of the natural need of all human beings to always require something concretely sensible in relation to the highest rational concepts, moral faith can only start from an empirical faith, a historical institutional faith that is already at hand as something given. Such a revelatory faith must be interpreted in a way that accords throughout with the universal, practical rules of a purely rational religion.

The theoretical aspect of institutional faith cannot interest us morally if it does not contribute to the fulfillment of all human duties as divine commands. This may nevertheless be, or seem to be, a strained interpretation of the revealed text, but it must be preferred to the literal interpretation, which either has no moral import or even works against what motivates it. This moral interpretation by Kant is wholly analogous to the old allegorical scripture interpretation of the Alexandrines;[32] the one is as arbitrary and subjective as the other. If positive religion or revelation inherently already contains the ideas of the moral rational religion, and if they must first be elicited from the revelatory documents by an interpretation, allegorical or moral, then one must ask: Why do these ideas appear from the beginning in a form in which they are so disguised that they can only be recognized with great effort? Kant has no answer to this question, but says only that the pure rational religion finds statutory institutional faith already in existence. Thus the two stand alongside each other in completely unmediated fashion; they are indeed related as content and form, but one cannot tell how they fit and belong together. Viewed in this regard, despite Kantian philosophy's negative relationship to the positive aspect of Christianity, it is still inclined to recognize a deeper moral content in it. Kant accepts that there is radical evil, a natural inclination of humankind to evil; and for him the idea of a Son of God is also a practical postulate. The Son of God is the personified idea of the principle of the good. The principle gaining dominion over human beings, insofar as it is personified, is humanity in its full moral perfection, the archetype of moral behavior in all its purity—the human being alone well-pleasing to God from all eternity, and for whose sake everything has been created. If religion is the form and vehicle of moral rational faith, then it is this because religion personifies moral concepts. It is a matter of

---

32. Clement of Alexandria and Origen.

distinguishing form and content. The form is transitory, the moral content enduring.

Fichte

Fichtean idealism is the consequence and consummation of Kantian philosophy.[33] Fichte's doctrine of God made apparent how subjective everything would be here as sheerly a construct of the "I" or self (*das Ich*). Already in Kant the existence of God, as a mere postulate of practical reason, is a mere presupposition, although Kant did not speak against the objective reality of the idea of God. Fichte, however, substituted the idea of a moral world order for the idea of God, thereby eliciting a very serious protest on the part of the church. In his essay "On the Ground of Our Belief in a Divine World Governance," published in the *Philosophisches Journal*, which he edited with Niethammer, he expressed his doctrine of God thus (vol. 8, 1798, p. 11):[34]

> I must absolutely assume that the purpose of morality can be achieved, can be achieved by me; that is, each of the actions I complete, and my circumstances that condition these actions, are related as means to my assumed purpose. My entire existence, the existence of all moral beings, the sensible world as our common stage, now take on a relationship to morality, and an

---

33. Johann Gottlieb Fichte (1762–1814) arose from a peasant background to become one of Germany's great philosophers. He struggled to support himself during his youth and his studies were frequently interrupted. He was dismissed from a teaching position at the University of Jena on the charge of atheism, and finally ended up in Berlin where he joined the newly founded University in 1810. He died of typhus in 1814. His major work was a *Wissenschaftslehre*, published in various editions between 1794 and 1813. Baur cites several of Fichte's key writings on religion in the following pages. Recent translations of his works include *Science of Knowledge with the First and Second Introductions*, ed. and trans. Peter Heath and John Lachs (New York, 1970; Cambridge, 1978); *Attempt at a Critique of All Revelation*, trans. Garrett Green (New York, 1978); *The Vocation of Man*, ed. R. Chisholm (New York, 1986); *Early Philosophical Writings*, ed. and trans. Daniel Breazeale (Ithaca, NY, 1988); *Foundations of Natural Right*, ed. Fredrick Neuhouser, trans. Michael Baur (Cambridge, 2000); *The System of Ethics*, ed. and trans. Daniel Breazeale and Günter Zöller (Cambridge, 2005); *Addresses to the German Nation*, ed. and trans. Gregory Moore (Cambridge, 2008).

34. "Über den Grund unseres Glaubens an eine göttliche Weltregierung," *Philosophisches Journal einer Gesellschaft Teutscher Gelehrten*, ed. F. I. Niethammer and J. G. Fichte, 10 vols., 1795–1800; 8 (1798) 1–20. Baur's quotation consists of excerpted passages from pp. 11 ff. This was the article that led to the charge of atheism; see *J. G. Fichte and the Atheism Dispute*, trans. Curtis Bowman, commentary by Yolanda Estes (Farnham, UK, 2010), 17–29, esp. 24–26, although the translation is ours. On this and the next few pages, references are added in square brackets, most likely by Zeller, to Fichte's *Sämmtliche Werke*, ed. J. H. Fichte (8 vols., Berlin, 1845–46); in this case to 5:184.

entirely new order appears, of which the sensible world with all its immanent laws is only the passive foundation. The realization of rational purpose is only achievable through the action of a free being—but it most certainly is achieved in this way, according to a higher law. Doing right is possible, and every situation is evaluated based upon the higher law. As a consequence of that arrangement, without fail moral deeds succeed and immoral deeds miscarry. . . . Our world is the tangible material of our duty. This duty is what is genuinely real in things, the true raw material of all appearance. The force with which belief in the reality of this duty presses upon us is a moral force. . . . Viewed in this way as the result of a moral world order, one can indeed call the principle of this belief in the reality of the sensible world "revelation." Our duty is what reveals itself in it. This is the true faith; this moral order is the divine that we accept. This faith is constructed by doing right. This is the only possible confession of faith—to accomplish happily and unabashedly what duty commands on each occasion, without doubt and without sophistry about the consequences; doubt and sophistry are the true atheism, actual unbelief. The divine thereby becomes living and actual for us; each of our actions is accomplished with this assumption, and all of its consequences are contained only in it. . . . This living and operative moral order is itself God; we require no other God and cannot grasp any other. Reason provides no grounds for going over and above this moral world order, and, because of a conclusion from what is grounded to the ground, for positing a special being as its cause. Understanding in its original form does not require such a conclusion and does not know such a special being; only a philosophy that misunderstands itself does so.

Fichte's article containing these statements was directly followed by another article in the same journal on "The Development of the Concept of Religion," but this led to the well-known charge of "atheism," also directed against Rector Forberg, the author of the second article.[35] The journal that contained these articles was confiscated in Electoral Saxony and then also drew the attention of the Weimar court to the danger of Fichte's teachings. His teachings were deemed openly contradictory not only to the Christian religion but also to natural religion. The letter of 18 December 1798, requiring the confiscation, read: "Since experience sufficiently teaches what un-

---

35. "Entwicklung des Begriffs der Religion," *Philosophisches Journal* 8 (1798) 21–46. See *Fichte and the Atheism Dispute* (n. 34), 31–47. The author was Friedrich Karl Forberg (1770–1848), rector of a lyceum in Saalfeld.

happy consequences come from tolerating those deplorable efforts to spread even further the increasing tendency to unbelief, and to uproot the concepts of God and religion from the hearts of the people, then, for the general good and in particular also for the security of states, we too, with a view to our own lands, should not be indifferent if teachers in bordering lands publicly and openly confess such dangerous principles."

The government of Weimar was thus asked to punish in earnest the article's author as seems fitting, and to issue generally repressive orders so as to vigorously halt similar excesses at the University of Jena and at gymnasiums and schools. The additional threat was made that, in case of noncompliance, children of Electoral Saxony would be forbidden to study at the University of Jena. Similar demands to ban the accused writings reached other Protestant royal courts. Hanover agreed to comply, but Prussia, which had issued its well-known Edict on Religion ten years earlier, declined. Fichte released an "Appeal to the Public,"[36] which, however, only made the contradiction of his view with commonly held opinions clearer. He anticipated his official dismissal from his teaching position and resigned in advance. Then Fichte went to Berlin, where he was not unwelcome. King Friedrich Wilhelm III is even quoted as saying: "If it is true that Fichte is on hostile terms with the dear Lord, then let the dear Lord settle it with him—it does not concern me."

Fichte himself later backed away from these most extreme views of his idealism, which were considered to be atheistic. This is particularly evident in his essay "On the Way to the Blessed Life or the Doctrine of Religion" (Berlin, 1806).[37] In place of the absolute I (*Ich*) he substituted God, indeed God as the absolute unity of all being and life, apart from which there is no being and life, and the eternally unbroken circle, which it is the merit of the science of knowledge (*Wissenschaftslehre*) to have discovered. This is the eternal contradiction in regard to the absolute or *Ansich* (in-itself), that it should be something for the I and consequently in it, yet also not be in it but said to be outside it, because otherwise there would be no *Ansich* and it would no longer be said to exist (*bestehen*). There should no longer be any separation between the absolute or God, and knowledge in its deepest roots in life; rather they should completely coincide. Since Fichte posits as an immediate unity what first should be mediated by speculation, this new doctrine of God is given a mystical aspect. Fichte locates the essence of re-

---

36. *Appellation an das Publikum über die durch ein Kurf. Sächs. Confiscationsrescript ihm beigemessenen atheistischen Aüsserungen* (Jena and Tübingen, 1799).

37. *Die Anweisung zum seligen Leben oder auch die Religionslehre* (Berlin, 1806). See *Sämmtliche Werke* (n. 34), 5:399–580. ET: *The Way Towards the Blessed Life: or, The Doctrine of Religion*, trans. William Smith (London, 1849).

ligion in the flight from the finite into the infinite. As long as human beings still want to be something on their own (*für sich*), true being and life cannot develop in them. What we are in ourselves and have in the form of ourselves, the I, reflection in consciousness (*Reflexion im Bewusstsein*), must become one with being in itself (*Sein an sich*). Fichte says there is a bond higher than all reflection, which binds together pure being and reflection: God's love. In this love there is being (*Sein*) and there is existence (*Dasein*); God and humanity are one, completely fused and blended (*verschmolzen und verflossen*). Our love of God is God's own love of himself in the form of feeling, because we are not capable of loving him; rather God alone is capable of loving himself. This love is the source of all certainty, truth, reality, perfect blessedness. Accordingly the essence of religion is God's love of himself, or the unity of being and existence, of God and humanity, mediated by love.

Fichte himself did not leave unanswered the question that presents itself here as to how the divine-human unity of Christianity relates to this version of divine-human unity. However, since in his philosophy of religion the finite does not come into its own over against the infinite, his philosophy of religion can only stand in a purely negative relationship to the historical element. Without a doubt, as Fichte puts it, Jesus of Nazareth (taking into account his genuine reality) possessed the highest knowledge, serving as the basis of all other truths, of the absolute identity of humanity with divinity. Even though the philosopher indeed finds the same truths completely independently of Christianity, with a wholly different consistency and clarity, it remains forever true that we, together with our entire age, and with all our philosophical investigations, stand on the soil of Christianity, and that all those since Jesus who have come into union with God have done so only through and by means of him. However, it is a merely historical and by no means a metaphysical proposition that the eternal existence of God has assumed a human personality above all in Jesus and in no other human being. Only the metaphysical brings blessedness, not the historical. The metaphysical component of any phenomenon consists only of what does not stand on its own as a mere fact, but follows from a higher and universal law and can be derived from it. If someone is truly united with God and in communion with God, it is entirely a matter of indifference as to how he or she arrives there. It would be entirely senseless and wrong to repeatedly recall the path rather than to live in the reality of it. How the whole of humanity emanates from the divine being can be understood as a general metaphysical truth. But that the absolutely immediate existence of God, the eternal knowledge or word, pure and unadulterated as it is in itself, with no admixture of obscurity or darkness and with no individual limitation, has presented itself in Jesus of Nazareth in a personal existence both sensuous and human, is a historical proposition valid only for the time of Jesus and the founding of Christianity, and for the requisite standpoint of Jesus and the apostles. For us what could count as the original historical fact is only what is evident, that Jesus first knew and taught this universal truth. However, this fact gains metaphysical significance by an employment of the understanding that soars above this fact when we strive to grasp its foundation and perhaps to this end pose a hypothesis about how Jesus the individual, as an individual, proceeded from the divine being. This makes it quite clear that the God-man did not exist as a historical individual. But it is not so clear what significance Christianity as a historical phenomenon nevertheless has for religion, inasmuch as the essence of religion consists in the realization of the idea of the unity of God and human beings. Although the person of Jesus is denied a specific or metaphysical dignity, such must be accorded him from a historical perspective. We cannot deny that this universal metaphysical truth at least first came to consciousness in Jesus; and so that, although intrinsically every human being can rise up to this consciousness through his or her own nature, nonetheless only Jesus, in virtue of his historical position, became, and still always is, the mediator of this truth for the consciousness of humanity as a whole.

Therefore, can it be as pointless and off the mark as Fichte says it is to continuously remember the path by which this truth entered humanity's consciousness? What significance there accordingly is in the historical aspect being related to the metaphysical aspect! How clearly the necessity arises, from the Fichtean standpoint, of recognizing the truth—the truth that alone makes for blessedness—not merely in the one element on its own account but in both together! What would the metaphysical truth be without its historical mediation, if it did not actualize itself in the consciousness of humanity by appearing in history, and doing so not merely in scattered individuals but in the organic nexus of historical development, thus emerging out of the abstract region of philosophy into the concrete life of religion, and becoming part of the collective consciousness of a religious and ecclesial community? And what, on the other hand, would the historical aspect be—everything that has objectified itself in such a broad scope in the history of humanity and has been incorporated into human consciousness—how subjective and contingent would it be in all its external objectivity if it could not also be grasped in its true objectivity, and thus in the final analysis as a metaphysical truth grounded in the essence of God himself? Thus it is always a matter here of the vital conjunction of the two opposed aspects, the metaphysical and the historical; but for Fichte himself, the two sides still remain in an unmediated, abstract dichotomy.[38]

It was characteristic of Fichte's idiosyncratic view of Christianity that he preferred to base it on the Gospel of John. Fichte says: the philosopher can only work with John, because John alone respects reason. He bases this on the proof the philosopher alone deems valid, the internal proof. Anyone who wants to do the will of him who sent me will perceive that this teaching is from God.[39] The other evangelists of Christianity depend on external proof by means of miracle, which, for us at least, proves nothing. Moreover, John alone among the evangelists contains what we seek and desire, religious teaching (*eine Religionslehre*), whereas the best the others can offer, absent any additions and interpretations from John, is nothing more than morality, which for us is of inferior value.

This then is the extent to which Fiche went beyond the Kantian position. It was a very important shift in the perspective of that period that people now wanted to know only about religion and not morals, and also strove to understand Christianity in these terms. As much, however, as a philosopher such as Fichte recognized the absolute significance of religion and Christianity, he bestowed little of rational significance on the positive aspect of Christianity. Like Kant, Fichte reserved the right to select from Christianity only what he considered important and could best combine with his own philosophy. Worth noting in this regard is how Fichte understood Pauline Christianity. In his "Characteristics of the Present Age" (1806),[40] he said that

> Christianity is no method of atonement or expiation (*Aussöhnungs- oder Entsündigungsmittel*). The human being can never disengage himself from the Godhead—and insofar as he presumes to do so, he is a nonentity, which on that very account cannot sin. Instead the oppressive delusion of being sinful was

---

38. This paragraph is a clear exposition of Baur's own conviction about the interplay of metaphysical and historical truth. It recalls, at the end of his career, what he wrote at the beginning of it: "Without philosophy, history remains for me forever dead and mute" (*Symbolik und Mythologie oder die Naturreligion des Althertums* [Stuttgart, 1824], xi). To which could be added: Without history, philosophy remains forever abstract and ideal. The truth is the mediation of the ideal and the real.

39. "Doing the will of him who sent me" occurs many times in the Gospel of John. E.g., in John 4:34 ff., Jesus speaks of "the will of him who sent me" and subsequently is critical of those who require "signs and wonders" in order to believe.

40. *Grundzüge des gegenwärtigen Zeitalters* (Berlin, 1806), 420. See *Sämmtliche Werke* (n. 34), 7:190–91; Baur's quotation includes the bracketed insertion. The third sentence contains an allusion to Genesis 4:15. ET: *The Characteristics of the Present Age*, trans. William Smith (London, 1847), 200–201 (followed here with some revisions).

merely a mark on his forehead, that he may thereby be directed to the true God. In the hands of such ages [as that of the appearance of Christianity], however, Christianity was necessarily changed into a means of atonement and expiation, and assumed the form of a new covenant with God, because these ages had no need of a religion, and indeed no capacity for receiving one, except in this shape. And thus the Christian system that . . . I called a degenerate form of Christianity, and the authorship of which I ascribed to the Apostle Paul, was also a necessary product of the whole spirit of that age as concerns Christianity; and that this man and no other should have first given expression to that spirit was quite accidental; for had he not done so, someone else, who had not risen superior to his age by infusing his spirit intimately into true Christianity, would have done the same; as everyone does, even to the present day, who has filled his head with these images, and who dreams of a necessary mediation between God and human beings, and cannot even conceive of the contrary.

Around this same time Fichte wrote the following about the place of theology in the structure of the university sciences, in his "Plan for an Institution of Higher Learning in Berlin" (1807):[41]

> A school for the scientific application of reason (*Verstandesgebrauch*) assumes that any topic it takes up can be understood and penetrated in its most basic foundations. Accordingly, any subject that forbids the use of reason and presents itself from the outset as an insoluble mystery would, by its very nature, be excluded. Furthermore, if theology were to insist on a God who willed something without any reason, whose will no one could comprehend by their own means—for instead God himself had to intervene directly through a special envoy to communicate that such a message had been sent, the content of which was provided in certain holy books couched in enigmatic language, and on the proper understanding of which the blessedness of humanity depended—then a school based on the application of reason could not deal with it. Only if theology were to clearly renounce having exclusive knowledge of secrets and magical means, and to loudly proclaim that the will of God could be known without any special revelation, and to state that these books are certainly not a source of knowledge but only a vehicle

---

41. *Deducirter Plan einer zu Berlin zu errichtenden höhern Lehranstalt, geschrieben im Jahr 1807* (Stuttgart, 1817), 50–51. See *Sämmtliche Werke* (n. 34), 8:97–204, quotation from 130.

for teaching people—a vehicle entirely independent of what the authors are supposed to have really said, a vehicle by the actual use of which it therefore must be explained what the authors should have said (the latter, what they should have said, having to be known elsewhere, indeed prior to its explanation)—only under this condition can the material previously possessed by theology be taken up by our [scientific] institution and examined in accord with that assumption.

Moreover, in the same vein Fichte added[42] that the public teacher (*Volkslehrer*), in order to address his immediate task of educating people religiously (*religiöse Volksbildung*), should above all have to form his religious system in the school of the philosopher. It was certainly unnecessary to link his instruction to the biblical books in order to understand the biblical authors in the sense that they truly intended. This had doubtless not been the case up to then in exegesis, so it is a matter here not of innovation but only of acknowledging the true state of affairs, and all that is required is a prudent surrender of an unnecessary and vain effort. In its essentials, this is entirely the Kantian standpoint that Fichte does not transcend. Even though he does not, like Kant, reduce religion to pure morals, in his view the truly Christian position is only what is intrinsically rational. For Fichte too, just how Christianity is to be grasped as a historical phenomenon in its purely historical objectivity still lay outside his purview. A proper sense of the historical significance of Christianity is lacking in his case as in Kant's. As a philosopher, he remains curt and blunt in his treatment of Christianity.

Fichte was one of the most significant men who stimulated and invigorated this entire epoch to a remarkable degree. He was not simply an acute abstract thinker, like a few others, but also a person of great practical energy and moral force. His philosophical system, as abstract as it is in its idealism, already also has a thoroughly practical tendency: everything is the activity of the "I"—is deed, action, the free self-determination of the boundlessly self-activating I that supersedes its own self-posited limits. What especially distinguishes him is his popular impact and literary activity. Not only did he frequently seek to popularize his philosophical system, his idealistic worldview, as he did in his book "The Vocation of Man" (1800).[43] He was also driven to understand the present day and its challenges, which he addressed in his "Characteristics of the Present Age,"[44] lectures delivered in 1804–5

42. *Deducirter Plan* (n. 41), 60; *Sämmtliche Werke*, 8:137. Baur paraphrases.

43. *Die Bestimmung des Menschen* (Frankfurt, 1800). ET: *The Vocation of Man*, trans. William Smith (London, 1848).

44. *Grundzüge des gegenwärtigen Zeitalters* (n. 40). ET: *The Characteristics of the Present Age* (n. 40).

in Berlin and published in 1806 in the interest of awakening the national consciousness at a time when that was sorely needed. He accomplished the latter in his powerful "Addresses to the German Nation,"[45] which he delivered in the winter months of 1807–8 in the Academy Building of Berlin, although his voice was often drowned out by the drums of the French marching through the streets, and well-known informants were present in the auditorium. Several times the rumor circulated in the city that he had been detained and taken into custody by the enemy. In these lectures he developed chiefly the idea of a new national education of the German people. They were a powerful wake-up call that rang out effectively to the German nation. They appealed in the noblest language, with fiery enthusiasm for freedom, fatherland, and German nationality, at Germany's time of deepest ignominy and humiliation, for a rebirth of the nation through moral force, and held out hope for the onset of better times. "The sunrise has already occurred, and gilded the mountain peaks, and it prefigures the day to come." Fichte at least experienced the beginning of Germany's struggle for freedom in 1813, but he died in January 1814 as one of the noblest Germans ever to have worked, with the purest zeal and most powerful spirit, for the great cause of the German nation.

Schelling

When Fichte retraced his steps from the absolute "I" of his Kantian idealism to the idea of God, and found the absolute of philosophy in the unity of God and human beings, in other words the unity of being and existence, another philosophy had indeed influenced him, the philosophy of Schelling,[46] which

---

45. *Reden an die deutsche Nation* (Berlin, 1808). ET: *Addresses to the German Nation* (n. 33).

46. Friedrich Wilhelm Joseph Schelling (1775–1854) is the youngest of the four great German idealist philosophers (Kant, Fichte, Schelling, Hegel) but is generally listed third in terms of the evolution of ideas and on the basis of his early genius. He was born in Württemberg and at the age of 15 attended the theological *Stift* in Tübingen, where his roommates were Hegel and Hölderlin. At this time he also developed a fascination with natural science. In 1798 he was called to the University of Jena and in 1803 married Caroline Schlegel. While in Jena he collaborated with Hegel in editing a journal. He then moved on to Munich, where he remained from 1806 until 1841, when he was called to Berlin. As a member of the Berlin Academy, he gave lectures in which he developed a new system of "positive" philosophy in rivalry to the speculative philosophy of Hegel, with which he had been in disagreement for many years. His major published works all came within a twenty year period from 1795 to 1815. These include *Philosophische Briefe über Dogmatismus und Kritizismus* (1795), *Ideen zur eine Philosophie der Natur* (1797), *Von der Weltseele* (1798), *System des transcendentalen Idealismus* (1800), *Philosophie und Religion* (1804), *Philosophische Untersuchungen über*

opposed the one-sidedness of the previous philosophy. The idealism that secluded itself in its selfhood (*Ichheit*) had no sense for nature and the reality of things; it remained only at the standpoint of subjectivity, which evoked objectivity as its natural antithesis. Thus the philosophy of selfhood then opposed the philosophy of nature; however, the principle posited in selfhood should not be annulled but also be claimed for nature. The basic idea from which Schelling proceeded is that nature too is a system of the rational, and the absolute can only be the identity of the subjective and objective. Nature carries over into spirit, and spirit into nature. Each can be made the first, and that must happen to each: both the I and nature must be made the first principle.

This is not the place to enter into a closer exposition of Schelling's teaching; we should only indicate the new standpoint that it attained in the consciousness of the time. The main point is that with Schelling in a single stroke philosophy became once again the science of the divine. Early on Schelling himself depicted this revolution in the outlook of the time, and the enthusiasm it had to infuse in those who themselves embodied that consciousness. In his "Portrayal of the True Relationship of the Philosophy of Nature to an Improved Fichtean Teaching,"[47] he says the following:

> Antiquity has opened up once more, and the eternal springs of truth and life are again accessible. Spirit is once again allowed to play joyously, freely, and boldly in the eternal stream of life and beauty. In all seriousness, what now stirs is a completely new era in contrast to its predecessor, and the old era has no inkling as to how sharply and completely the two eras contrast. Largely blind to it and sensing its own impotence, its own lack of insight and aptitude, the old era wants to appropriate a part of what is better. Fichte is the philosophical blossoming of this earlier period and to that extent its limit; it is scientifically expressed in his own system, and that system will forever remain its lasting monument. If his era rejected him, it is because it lacked the ability to see its own image reflected in his teaching, an image he sketched out forcefully and freely, without doing so in a bad way.

---

das Wesen der menschlichen Freiheit (1809), and *Über die Gottheiten von Samothrake* (1815), which Schelling regarded as a "supplement" to the unpublished manuscript versions of *Die Weltalter*. Prior to his acquaintance with Hegel (beginning in 1832), Baur was deeply influenced by Schelling.

47. Schelling, *Darlegung des wahren Verhältnisse der Naturphilosophie zu der verbesserten Fichte'schen Lehre* (Tübingen, 1806), 46. Here and in the following paragraphs, Zeller inserts in square brackets references to Schelling's *Sämmtliche Werke*, 14 vols., ed. K. F. A. Schelling (Stuttgart, 1856–61); in this case to 7:50.

Thus the lively spirit awakened in Schelling's philosophy of nature forcefully disengaged itself from the barren lifelessness and abstraction of the Fichtean worldview. Yet the Kantian-Fichtean idealism that posits the I as infinite is so much the necessary presupposition of Schelling's standpoint and for directly transitioning to it, that we were simply able to open the new period with Kant and Fichte, and not with Schelling.

According to Schelling, God as the absolute is the identity of subject and object, of knowing and being, of ideal and real, of infinite and finite. However, this unity is not abstract unity but a concrete, internally alive unity, that is, the kind of unity in which God is posited as both difference and unity, not sheer being but also becoming, a necessary life-process. A being that would be sheerly itself, as something purely one, would necessarily be without a revelation within it, because it would have nothing in which it would reveal itself. It does not reveal itself when it is merely itself, when it does not have an other within it, and is itself the one in this other; thus when it is not as such the living bond of itself and an other. What is or exists as one must, in its being, necessarily be a bond between itself and an other. This other cannot be distinct from the one, for it can only be the one, but as an other. In the being itself, what is as one must therefore necessarily be a bond between itself as unity and itself as the contrary, or as multiplicity, and this bond is precisely the existence of this essential being itself. Thus what truly exists is neither the one as one, nor the many as many, but precisely just the living conjunction or copula of both. Indeed existence, taken by itself, is this very copula and none other than it. Multiplicity regarded in identity with unity is none other than the very existence of this unity itself; the multiplicity is in no way separate from it.

This living identity, in which there is both conflict or life, and the unity or moderating (*Sänftigung*) of life, Schelling calls the divine nature giving birth to itself. This being or essence (*Wesen*) gives birth to itself eternally in form, and in this birth just produces itself, i.e., unity. Eternally and without any beginning, it involves antithesis. However, by revealing the original harmony of its identity with itself within this antithesis, the [divine] being comes forth from this antithesis as the All, or absolute totality. This in turn also sheds light on the antithesis abated by being or essence, in other words by the form within it, and essentially in it—thus the fact that the One is the All and the All is one—and so existence completely brings forth all of existence. This eternal appearing-in-another of being and form, following from being, is the kingdom of nature, or the eternal birth of God in things, and the equally eternal return of all things into God. Viewed essentially, nature itself is merely the full divine existence, or God regarded in the actuality of his life and in his self-revelation. This eternal bond of the self-revelation of God, whereby the infinite is the finite and then again the latter is resolved into the former, is the wonder of all wonders, the wonder of the essential love that, through the opposition, alone presses toward unity with itself—in other words, the wonder of the vitality and actuality of God. The fact that God is living and actual, and not dead, is for this reason not something incomprehensible (although for most people this seems to be the most incomprehensible thing). It is self-evidently clear as the bright sunny day (although to them it had to seem the contrary, as the abyss of all incomprehensibility).[48]

If the being or nature (*Wesen*) of God is defined in such a way that it belongs to God's nature to reveal itself, and in this self-revelation to pass through the moments of a life process conditioned by the being of God, then of itself the idea is equivalent with history, and history is nothing other than the self-actualization of the idea. Under this general viewpoint, Christianity too can be regarded simply as a moment of the divine life-process. This is the perspective from which Schelling comprehends Christianity, as found in his *Lectures on the Method of Academic Study* (1803), where he speaks for the first time about his philosophical vision of Christianity. Schelling says:[49]

> What is true of history in general is especially true of the history of religion, namely, it is founded upon an eternal necessity, and consequently it is possible to construct it. By means of such a construction history becomes closely bound up with the science of religion. The historical construction of Christianity can have only one point of departure, namely, the view that the world as a whole, and hence also its history, necessarily shows two different aspects and that the opposition between them, which is that between the modern world and the ancient world, is sufficient to account for Christianity's nature and special characteristics. The ancient world represents the "nature" side of history in the sense that its dominant idea—what gives it unity—is that the infinite exists only in the finite. The end of the ancient world and the beginning of modern times, whose dominant principle is the infinite, could come about only when the true infinite was embodied in the finite—the purpose was not to deify the finite, but to offer it up as a sacrifice to God in his own person and thus to reconcile the two. Hence Christianity's leading idea is

---

48. In the text Baur cites *Darlegung der wahren Verhältnisse* (n. 47), 60 (*Sämmtliche Werke*, 7:59).

49. Schelling, *Vorlesungen über die Methode des academischen Studium* (Tübingen, 1803), Lecture 8, pp. 179–81, 184–85 (*Sämmtliche Werke* [n. 47], 1.5:292 ff.). ET: *On University Studies*, trans. E. S. Morgan, ed. Norbert Guterman (Athens, OH, 1966), 88–89, 91.

> God become incarnate, Christ as culmination, the closing out of the ancient world of gods. In him, as in the ancient gods, the divine principle becomes finite, but the humanity he assumes is not humanity in its highest estate but in its lowest. He stands as the boundary between the two worlds, decreed from all eternity yet a transitory phenomenon in time. He himself returns to this invisible realm and promises the coming of the Spirit—not the principle which becomes finite to stay finite but the ideal principle which leads the finite back to the infinite and, as such, is the light of the modern world. . . . The reconciliation of the finite which had seceded from God, a reconciliation effected by God's birth in the finite world, is the basic idea of Christianity; the idea of the Trinity, which expresses the whole Christian view of the world and of its history, is a necessary part of it. . . . The true relation [of this idea to the history of the world] is as follows: the eternal Son of God, born of the essence of the Father of all things, is the finite itself, as it exists in God's eternal intuition; this finite manifests itself as a suffering God, subject to the vicissitudes of time, who at the culmination of his career, in the person of Christ, closes the world of the finite and opens the world of the infinite, i.e., the reign of the Spirit.

Schelling distinguishes this comprehension of Christianity, as the speculative view, from the ordinary, purely empirical view.

Schelling's philosophy has the great merit of awakening a new interest both in the world-historical significance of Christianity in general, which can be recognized only from the standpoint of speculative interpretation, and in the content of its positive dogmas. Precisely those dogmas of Christianity that were most discredited by a shallow rationalism people now learned to grasp as not merely the deepest mysteries of faith but also as the supreme problems of philosophical speculation. Schelling's philosophy surely did not provide a support for orthodox faith. As Schelling specifically explained in his *Essay on Freedom*,[50] he is of the opinion that "clear rational insight into even the highest concepts must be possible, because only in this way can they become real to us, be accepted by us, and be eternally grounded." Indeed, he goes further and agrees with Lessing that "the development of revealed truths into truths of reason is absolutely necessary if the human race is to be assisted by them."[51] If Christianity is regarded in this

---

50. Schelling, *Philosophische Untersuchungen über das Wesen der menschlichen Freiheit* (1809); *Sämmtliche Werke* (n. 47) 1.7:412. ET: *Of Human Freedom*, trans. James Gutmann (Chicago, 1936), 94 (our translation).

51. Gotthold Ephraim Lessing, "The Education of the Human Race," no. 76 in *Lessing's Theological Writings*, ed. Henry Chadwick (Stanford, 1957), 95.

way, the result can only be that the divine-human significance that Christ has as this specific, single individual must be detached from the individual and be viewed, in his person, as the universal characteristic of humanity. Fichte already said: "The eternal word becomes flesh at all times in every individual without exception who sees his unity with God to be a vital one, and who really and in fact surrenders the whole of his individual life to the divine life in him, entirely in the same way that Jesus Christ did."[52] Thus Schelling too could only assert a universal incarnation of Christ. Ordinarily one cannot greatly object to such an understanding of Christianity as long as it is not a matter of the further, related question as to how it can be justified in relation to the gospel story. Schelling too did not address this issue. Hence a doctrine of God such as Schelling's must have been all the more objectionable to those who did not share his same philosophical standpoint. Just as the charge of atheism was brought against Fichte, so it was Schelling's pantheistic worldview that collided with theism. This brings us to the last major representative among our philosophers, Jacobi.[53]

Jacobi

Jacobi's philosophy[54] dates back to the time of Kant and in essence is very closely related to it. Like Kant, Jacobi asserts that cognition (*Erkennen*) can pertain exclusively to finite objects. God, the absolute, the unconditioned, cannot be demonstrated, because demonstrating and conceiving mean deriving something from conditions, but a derived absolute could not be

---

52. Baur gives no indication of the source of this citation.

53. [*Zeller*] In the above discussion of Schelling, the form of his views found in the essay on freedom is not expressly taken into account. In one of Baur's earlier manuscripts available to me, from which a significant portion of the presentation of Schelling in the present lectures is taken, the treatment of the freedom essay is thoroughgoing. I believe that what Baur provides in the present lectures should be more satisfying than it is, since he himself discussed Schelling, and specifically his essay on freedom, much more adequately (and in a form rather similar to the above-mentioned manuscript) in his *Dreieinigkeit und Menschwerdung Gottes* [Tübingen,1843], 3:806ff., and earlier in *Die christliche Gnosis* [Tübingen, 1835], 611ff.

54. Friedrich Heinrich Jacobi (1743–1819) was educated for a career in commerce and never held an academic position, but in 1807 he was appointed president of the Munich Academy of Sciences. He became involved in a controversy over Spinoza's alleged pantheism (*Über die Lehre des Spinoza*, 1785), in the atheism controversy focusing on Fichte (*Jacobi an Fichte*, 1799), and in a dispute with Schelling over pantheism (*Von der göttlichen Dinge und ihrer Offenbarung*, 1811), to which Schelling published an extensive rebuttal the following year. He developed a philosophy affirming that faith, not knowledge, is the means by which human beings apprehend supersensible realities; and he embraced the personal God of theism.

absolute and unconditioned. We have consciousness of God, and indeed the thought of God is immediately bound up with the fact that God exists. This knowledge is not demonstrated or mediated but is rather an immediate knowing. In their representation and thinking, human beings advance beyond what is natural and finite to something supernatural and supersensible, the existence of which is as certain as their own existence. The certainty that this supernatural something exists is identical with their own self-consciousness: as certainly as I exist, so certainty God exists. The supernatural can be spoken of simply as a fact.

Jacobi calls this immediate knowledge "faith." He also calls it "revelation," an inward revelation of God befalling human beings, in which they apprehend by reason what they cannot grasp by their understanding—in the way Jacobi was given to distinguish between reason (*Vernunft*) and understanding (*Verstand*). As highly, however, as Jacobi regarded this revelation and faith, he did not intend to speak of faith in a revelation in the ecclesiastical sense of the word. He was a warm defender of religion and Christianity, but could scarcely claim for himself the title of Christian philosopher. He said of himself[55] that he is a Christian at heart, a pagan in understanding, and "swims between two streams that will not unite in him."[56] Just as everything was offensive to him in philosophy that was demonstrative and mediating, and brought knowledge into the form of a system, so too in theology he fostered the same antipathy to a dogmatics whose positive statements were far too removed from immediate religious consciousness. But his philosophy was said to announce its Christian character all the more by maintaining faith in a personal God, as the foundation of all revelation, over against the pantheistic tendency of the time.

This brought him into a lively conflict with Schelling over the theistic and pantheistic concepts of God. In his work "On Divine Matters and Their Revelation" (1811),[57] Jacobi directly accused Schelling's doctrine of God

---

55. [*Zeller*] In his well-known letter to Reinhold, which is printed in the Schleiermacher work cited below [just prior to Schleiermacher's letter to Jacobi].

56. [*Baur*] Cf. Schleiermacher's letter to Jacobi from 1818 (*Aus Schleiermacher's Leben in Briefen*, 4 vols. [Berlin, 1858–63], 2:341ff.): "My philosophy and my dogmatics are tightly linked and do not contradict each other, but nonetheless neither of them wish to be finished, and as long as I can recall, the two have been brought into greater harmony and drew ever nearer to each other. . . . If understanding and the heart or feeling are different orientations, they are not antithetical, and must themselves be one in the unity of self-consciousness. One cannot be a Christian at heart and a pagan in understanding." But this was not the case with Jacobi. If he wanted to apply this distinction to himself, he had to say that he was also a pagan at heart because when it came to positive Christianity he was an enlightened rationalist.

57. "Von den göttlichen Dinge und ihrer Offenbarung," in *Friedrich Heinrich*

of being atheism. Twelve years earlier, he said, the worldly offspring of the critical philosophy, the *Wissenschaftslehre*, claimed that the moral world-order alone is God. This claim caused a sensation; but shortly thereafter, the second child of the critical philosophy—the doctrine of monism or identity, the philosophy of nature, which completely and intentionally erased the distinction that the first still allowed to stand, the distinction between natural and moral philosophy, necessity and freedom—no longer raised any eyebrows. Without further ado, this philosophy explained that over and above nature there is nothing, that nature alone exists, that nature is the one and all. This philosophy has surrendered the doctrines of God, immortality, and freedom, and all that remains is the doctrine of nature, the philosophy of nature. The system of absolute identity is in fact and in truth identical with Spinozism, which Jacobi declares to be atheism. The philosophy of nature asserts that all dualism, whatever its name, must be exterminated, and it in truth claims the identity of reason and unreason, of good and evil.

In his "monument" to Jacobi's essay and its accusation of an intentionally deceptive and false atheism,[58] Schelling responded with all the sharpness and bitterness of one who had been personally attacked. He emphatically opposed the view of someone who "accepts a God once and for all complete, and therefore a lifeless, dead God,"[59] or "the concept of a shallow theism, which allows no distinction in God, whose being (in which all fullness dwells) is described as absolutely simple, purely empty, insubstantial, but still discernible."[60] Schelling says that, if he is to be a living God, God must give birth to his own eternal being (*Wesen*) and have a life and therefore also a destiny. Thus God cannot be thought of merely under the abstract concept of being (*Sein*). God must also be thought of under the concrete concept of becoming (*Werden*); but every becoming presupposes distinctions and moments by which the original One must go forth from itself in order to mediate itself with itself.[61]

But this very point was the major issue about which all the opponents of Schelling's teaching raised the most serious objections. There is nothing

---

Jacobi's Werke, 6 vols. (Leipzig, 1812–25), 3:247–462.

58. Schelling, "Denkmal der Schrift von den göttlichen Dinge des Herrn Friedrich Heinrich Jacobi und der ihm in derselben gemachten Beschuldigung eines absichtlich täuschenden, Lüge redenden Atheismus" (1812), in *Sämmtliche Werke* (n. 47), 8:19–138.

59. "Denkmal," 95 (*Sämmtliche Werke*, 8:72).

60. *Sämmtliche Werke*, 8:62.

61. [Zeller] See Schelling's *Das Wesen der menschlichen Freiheit* (n. 50), in *Sämmtliche Werke* (n. 47), 1.7:403 et passim [ET 84ff.].

more offensive, as another writer maintained,[62] than the idea of a God who evolves to actual completeness from an initially dark, non-intelligent, and unethical principle, and who becomes personal only at the end of time. If the assumption that makes God into a God who first becomes God in time intrinsically destroys the concept of God, then we completely annul faith in an intelligent and moral world order and in providence. For if God is first revealed as wholly personal and actually complete at the end of time or the world, and if God first attains a higher stage of completeness through the creation of the world—but in creating the world is not yet in possession of his most supreme quality—then the world would not be the work of the most perfect wisdom, goodness, and holiness, and we would be in the sad situation of standing under a being about whom it is hardly certain whether, because of his limitations, he would have the power in every age to do what he knows and wills to be the best, or whether he actually would know and will what is best. It is hardly certain whether it is not through error, indeed through being seduced by moral defect in his world creation and world governance, that he is incapable of aiming for the best and realizing it in the whole and in each individual part. Put succinctly, the same doubt that every theory of a preexistent and independent matter, or of a chaos as the ground of all things, is subject to, applies also to Schelling. This is the doubt as to whether the chaos does not pose such obstacles to the world order as to make it even impossible to fully realize the intentions willed by a wisdom and love not yet wholly evolved. This is the principal objection that can be raised from the popular standpoint of deism [theism]. Here philosophy in its development since Kant arrived at a point at which it lingered for quite some time, in order to become clear about the antithesis in which it saw itself caught up. The entire consciousness of the age was divided into pantheistic and theistic worldviews, and both claimed the same interests. Pantheism,[63] however, obtained this significance not merely in philosophy

---

62. [*Baur, in the text*] Friedrich Gottlieb Süskind, in his essay, "Prüfung der Schellingschen Lehre von Gott, Weltschöpfung, Freiheit, moralischem Guten und Bösem," *Magazin für christliche Dogmatik* (1812) 17.

63. Where Baur speaks of "pantheism" in this book we today would use "panentheism" (a term apparently not common at the time). Pantheism does not mean literally that all things, or the world or the universe, *are* God. Hegel says that no philosophy or religion has ever maintained such a view (*Lectures on the Philosophy of Religion* [see p. 317, n. 1], 1:375–78). Rather, all things are *in* God; God is the power, substance, principle, or spirit of all things. God is not a "supreme being" apart from the world (traditional theism), but the essential being (*Wesen*) of the world. God dwells within the world, and the world within God, but they are not identical. One of the issues raised by panentheism is whether God can be regarded as "personal." God is not personal for Schleiermacher because his God is absolute undivided causality, but Hegelian panentheism defines God as "absolute spirit," which posits its own otherness and knows itself

but just as much or even more in religion, and thus we arrive at a further major phenomenon of our period.

Schleiermacher: *Soliloquies, Speeches on Religion, Christmas Eve*

We set Schleiermacher[64] apart from those men who represent the general culture of the time, and from the philosophers in whom the intellectual movement of the time takes its course in the specific form of philosophy. He had many points of contact with both groups, since he was one of the most versatile thinkers, but he cannot be assigned to either of these categories. We can only designate the distinctive sphere in which he was active—the field that he created for himself in this age so rich in new configurations of intellectual life—as the area of religion. This explains why he has such great significance for us here.

The beginning of Schleiermacher's literary activity coincides exactly with the beginning of the period with which we are concerned here. His *Speeches on Religion* appeared at the end of the previous century, in 1799, and his *Soliloquies* greeted the dawn of the new century. These two works, which are most intimately related, contain the foundation of Schleiermacher's individuality to such a degree that the essential elements of his thought are already found here, despite the wealth of content Schleiermacher subsequently produced, and despite the extent to which his philosophical and theological system in its developed form surpassed these first writings. In these two works, the spirit newly soaring out of the old century into the new hits us like a fresh morning breeze. The youthful enthusiasm with which they are composed makes itself felt by how the genius of the new century stirs in them with powerful wing beats. The whole movement of the age is spirit's going-within-self, its self-examining and self-comprehending, a self-mirroring and self-portraying. Spirit immerses itself in its innermost

---

through this other; and this is the very definition of "personhood."

64. Baur discusses the early work of Friedrich Schleiermacher (1768–1834) here, while his later work is analyzed in Part Two (pp. 172–98), specifically his *Glaubenslehre* (see n. 42 on p. 172). The works discussed here are: (1) *Monologen: Eine Neujahrsgabe* (Berlin, 1800). ET: *Soliloquies*, trans. H. L. Friess (Chicago, 1926). (2) *Über die Religion: Reden an die Gebildeten unter ihren Verächtern*, 1st ed. (Berlin, 1799); 3rd ed. (Berlin, 1821). ET: *On Religion: Speeches to Its Cultured Despisers*, trans. John Oman from the 3rd ed. of 1821 (London, 1893); trans. Richard Crouter from the 1st ed. of 1799 (Cambridge, 1996). (3) *Die Weihnachtsfeier: Ein Gespräch* (Halle, 1806). ET from the 2nd ed. of 1826 by W. Hastie as *Christmas Eve: Dialogue on the Celebration of Christmas* (Edinburgh, 1890); by Terrence Tice as *Christmas Eve: Dialogue on Incarnation* (Richmond, VA, 1967).

self-consciousness, in order to have itself solely within itself and to withdraw itself from everything that is not itself—and in this knowing of itself as the unity of all connections, to know itself as the free, self-determining, absolute subject.

Schleiermacher takes this stand in his *Soliloquies*. It represents Fichtean idealism in its most subjective form: the self in reflecting upon itself (*das Ich in der Reflexion auf sich selbst*) becomes aware of its infinite inwardness with all its subjective connections. Schleiermacher says that, for himself, freedom lies in this contemplation of the self by the self, in all that is original and, as what is first, is thus what is most inward.

> When I withdraw into myself to contemplate it [freedom], my eyes are lifted from the realm of time, and my vision is free from every restriction of necessity. Every oppressive feeling of bondage disappears, my spirit discovers its creative nature, the light of divinity begins to shine upon me, banishing far hence the mists in which it [enslaved humanity] sadly strays in error. The self revealed in my meditations is no longer a creature of fate or fortune; the hours of happiness I have deserved, the results achieved by my efforts, and whatever I have actually put into execution, all these are of the world; they are not myself.... We live not only as mortals in the realm of time, but also as immortals in the domain of eternity, that our lives be not only earthly but also divine. The stream of time bears with it in its course my mortal deeds; ideas and feelings change, I cannot hold fast a single one. The scene of life, as I picture it, hurries by; upon the next inevitable wave the stream will carry me on toward something new. But as often as I turn my gaze inward upon my inmost self, I am at once within the domain of eternity. I behold the spirit's life, which no world can change, and no time can destroy, but which itself creates both world and time.[65]

The language of the proudest self-feeling permeates these *Soliloquies*. The self apprehends itself as a world to itself: the inner determination of its nature by the All, in terms of which it is what it is, here becomes, in virtue of the original unity of the self and the universe, understood as a pretemporal intelligible act of free self-determination by the self; and as such it boldly opposes all external influences and refuses all dependencies. The physical world must serve the self. As a system of organs and, so to speak,

---

65. Schleiermacher, *Soliloquies* (n. 64), 18–19, 22 (translation slightly altered); see the whole of 16–22. The antecedent of *jene* in the second sentence is uncertain. It could be *Knechtschaft* (enslaved humanity), as Friess translates it, or it could be *Freiheit* (freedom), which consists in self-contemplation.

as an extended body, the physical dimension must help the self to execute its purposes. But the spirit finds itself benefiting infinitely more from the community of other spirits. Even when the resistance of nature or the adverse conflict of other human powers with one's own results in failure, the self is not dependent on the chance alignment of external circumstances. Inner action is not hindered by the impossibility of external deeds. What is denied to the individual in actuality by external consequences, contacts, and conditions, is formed inwardly but no less truly for oneself by imagination (*Phantasie*)—this divine force, which alone frees the spirit, carries it far above every power and limitation, and without which the human sphere would be fearfully circumscribed. Empowered from within by itself, the self submits to nothing.

How are Schleiermacher's *Speeches* related to the position he takes in the *Soliloquies*? We can say that it is the same relationship as that between Fichte's idealism and Schelling's philosophy of nature. The self of idealism works itself free from its vulnerability to the objectivity of nature, by perceiving nature as the absolute but without denying its own absoluteness, because the same intelligence, the same selfhood, is active in both places, on the one side in the form of subjectivity, on the other in the form of objectivity. Thus the free and self-determining self of the *Soliloquies* is replaced by the conditioned and dependent self of the *Speeches*, whose self-consciousness is determined by its connection to the universe; but it is the same with the self-identical self, since in the self's knowing about its dependence, it is, in this very knowing about itself, the self-conscious subject. The universe and the self mutually presuppose each other—the universe made subjective in the self, and the self having in the universe the objective ground of its consciousness, determined in one way or another. Idealism is only the other side of pantheism, which in its intellectual form has the ideal point of its unitary status in the self-consciousness of the self.

Schleiermacher was among the first who looked back to Spinoza with particular favor and sought to give the narrowly self-enclosed idealism an agreeable equilibrium in the universal worldview of pantheism. The following notable passage about Spinoza is found in his *Speeches on Religion* (p. 47):[66]

> What, then, shall become of the highest utterance of the speculation of our days, completely rounded off idealism, if it does not again sink into this unity [with the eternal, in which the human

---

66. Schleiermacher, *Über die Religion*, 3rd ed. (n. 64), 68–69. ET: *On Religion* (Oman translation of the 3rd ed.), 40. Baur's page citation is to the 4th ed. of 1831, and the words in square brackets are his. On Schleiermacher's "pantheism," see n. 63.

being becomes completely one with it in the immediate unity of intuition and feeling]; if the humility of religion does not suggest to its pride another realism than that which it so boldly and with such perfect right subordinates to itself? It annihilates the universe, while it seems to aim at constructing it. It would degrade it to a mere allegory, to a mere phantom of the one-sided limitation of its own empty consciousness. Offer with me reverently a tribute to the manes of the holy, rejected Spinoza! The high world spirit pervaded him; the infinite was his beginning and his end; the universe was his only and his everlasting love. In holy innocence and in deep humility he beheld himself mirrored in the eternal world, and perceived how he also was its most worthy mirror. He was full of religion, full of the Holy Spirit. Wherefore, he stands there alone and unequalled; master in his art, yet without disciples and without citizenship, sublimely above the profane tribe.

This apotheosis of Spinoza can demonstrate very well the influence he had already exerted on Schleiermacher when the latter still stood at the most abstract point of idealism. Pantheism and idealism most inwardly permeated him so as to create a new worldview in which the universe is reflected in the self, while the self itself regards itself, in the fullest awareness of its subjectivity, as the midpoint in which all the rays of the universe are gathered and united. Strauss rightly remarked[67]—about Schleiermacher's comment on Spinoza, that "he saw himself reflected in the eternal world and witnessed how he too was its most favorable reflection"—that such a self-reflecting is foreign to Spinoza. Spinoza does not regard the subject this highly; his God loves human beings only in so far as he loves himself, that is, not as free personalities but only as contained in the attributes and modes of substance.

This remark designates the standpoint of the *Speeches on Religion* all the more strikingly. The universe is the eternal process in which life in the totality of its forms is produced. In the same way, within the universe, humankind is the summation of all the interrelated components that are widespread in earthly space and temporally complementary, components that spirit and matter can enter into under the conditions of this planet. So each one, in his or her place, is a divinely willed part enhancing or completing this totality. Viewed in this way, the countless combinations of diverse talents that the individual perceives in the characters of others appear to him merely as assured elements of his own life. The human world as such appears simply as his own many-sided and more clearly excellent self. He

---

67. [*Baur, in the text*] David Friedrich Strauss, *Charakteristiken und Kritiken* (Stuttgart, 1839), 25.

himself appears as a compendium of humanity, embracing the whole of human nature. Schleiermacher's worldview affirms the conjunction of universal and particular life, the sacred marriage of the universe with incarnate reason, from which our entire life and consciousness solely emerge—a union that, because in it consciousness and object are one, does not occur in consciousness, but leaves its traces in consciousness only in fleeting, disparate moments. In the efforts of the self to reestablish that original unity in every moment of actual existence, it sometimes imagines the objects and sometimes forms them; it sometimes represents and knows, and sometime acts. It is itself determined, in other words determined by the objectivity; and on the other hand it is determined inwardly and thus directly in feeling, which, as the third to knowing and doing, forms one's own sequence of intellectual activity. This brings us to the point where Schleiermacher's worldview is essentially pious or religious.

Schleiermacher directed his *Speeches on Religion* to "the cultured among its despisers," and believed he must first justify to them why he still speaks of religion. His first speech, called "Justification," begins as follows:

> It may be an unexpected undertaking, and you might rightly be surprised that someone can demand from just those persons who have raised themselves above the herd, and are saturated by the wisdom of a century, a hearing for a subject so completely neglected by them. I confess that I do not know how to indicate anything that presages a fortunate outcome for me. . . . The life of cultivated persons is removed from everything that would in the least way resemble religion. . . . You have succeeded in making your earthly lives so rich and many-sided that you no longer need the eternal. . . . All this I know and am nevertheless convinced to speak by an inner and irresistible necessity that divinely rules me, and cannot retract my invitation that you especially should listen to me.[68]

Twenty-two years later, in the preface to the third edition of these *Speeches*,[69] Schleiermacher says that, when one now looks around among the cultured, "one might more likely find it necessary to write speeches to the pious and literal-minded, to those condemned by ignorance and lack of love, to the superstitious and super-faithful." Already by 1821 a reversal had occurred such that, instead of the disdain for religion among the cultured, the exact opposite appeared. Thus the times must have once again become

---

68. Schleiermacher, *Über die Religion*, 1st ed. (n. 64), 1–3. ET: *On Religion* (Crouter translation of the 1st ed.), 77–78. In the 1st ed. this speech is called "Apology."

69. Schleiermacher, *Über die Religion*, 3rd ed. (n. 64), xiv (no ET).

a religious era, in which these speeches, along with their repeated editions, had doubtless played a very important role. But how should we explain the overwhelming disdain for religion among the cultured at the time of these *Speeches'* first appearance? How should we understand it? We must transpose ourselves back into an age in which religion still belonged to the very substance of life and was the essentially determining principle in all human affairs, and everything obtained its form and color from religion—an age in which the church's faith was still fully respected and valued, and in which it was not yet thought possible at all that human beings could find their true well being in anything other than this faith and it alone. This age disappeared as the new enlightenment and culture, which dissolved and destroyed the substance of the old faith, became more widespread. The tighter and more immediate was the bond by which the whole essence of religion was connected with the faith of the church, was thus identical with it, such that they could not be separated or distinguished from each other as form and content, all the more necessary was it that, with the diminishing of faith in the doctrines and propositions of the church, religion itself lost its hold on the consciousness of the age. When the old form had become completely unworkable for the content of the religion, there was no new form the essential content could assume when it was divested of its contingent form.

Thus what Schleiermacher meant by the disdain of religion was not simply a passing half-heartedness and resentment toward it; rather it was the existing void and emptiness in the general consciousness at that time owing to all the sudden changes—a void and emptiness that had to be filled in turn by something that was not yet at hand. To the consciousness of the age, everything called religion had become something completely external, foreign, inessential. This consciousness must first become reacquainted and reconciled with religion, by religion proving itself to be an essential element of intellectual life, of human consciousness itself. This was not accomplished by philosophy since for it the connection with religion only consisted in the fact that the absolute, with whose concept it was concerned, was viewed from the objective standpoint of the idea of God. Schleiermacher first accomplished it, and the peculiar importance of his *Speeches on Religion* consists in the fact that it restored to religion the substantial center that had been removed from it, the very thing religion as knowing taught, what religion is in itself, in its essential and inseparable connection to the consciousness of humanity as such.

If we define the task that Schleiermacher set for himself in the *Speeches* as one of wanting to give to religion once again the substantial meaning it had lost in the consciousness of the age, this is by no means to be understood as his simply wanting to restore the old religious faith. He wants nothing whatsoever to do with "the orthodox and fearful lamentation whereby they seek to rear again the fallen walls and gothic pillars of their Jewish Zion."[70] Least of all is he concerned about dogmas and systems; he declares his contempt specifically for those who locate the essence of religion in such dogmas and systems, and acknowledges that the culture of the age is rightly opposed to such a religion.

> The perfect form of doctrines and systems is often all that matters, but it is not the consummation of religion. Indeed, not infrequently, the progress of the one has not the smallest connection with the other. I cannot speak of this without indignation. All who have a regard for what issues from within the mind, and who are in earnest that every side of the human being be trained and exhibited, must bewail how the high and glorious is often turned from its destination and robbed of its freedom in order to be held in despicable bondage by the scholastic and metaphysical spirit of a fearful and indifferent time. What are all these doctrinal edifices, considered in themselves, but the handiwork of the calculating understanding, wherein only by mutual limitation each part holds its place? What else can they be, these systems of theology, these theories of the origin and the end of the world, these analyses of the nature of an incomprehensible being, wherein everything runs to cold argumentation, and the highest can be treated in the tone of an ordinary academic controversy? And this is certainly—let me appeal to your own feeling—not the character of religion. If you have paid attention solely to these dogmas and opinions, therefore, you do not yet know religion itself, and what you despise is not it. Why have you not penetrated deeper to find the kernel of this shell?[71]

Schleiermacher wanted to direct the entire nature of religion back to what is inward, to show its living root in the deepest inwardness of human beings. In the second speech, on the nature of religion, he developed his now-famous proposition that religion belongs neither to the domain of science nor to that of ethical life, that it is essentially neither cognition nor action, that its distinctive domain is shown to be simply religious feeling (*Gefühl*). Our feeling, to the extent it expresses the being and life shared by ourselves and the All, and to the extent we have its individual elements as a working of God within us, mediated by the working of the world on us, is our piety (*Frömmigkeit*). The individual aspects of it are not our knowledge

---

70. *Über die Religion*, 3rd ed. (n. 64), 4. ET: *On Religion* (Oman translation, revised), 3.

71. Ibid., 24–25 (ET 15, revised).

or the objects of our knowledge, not our works and actions or the various arenas of our activity, but simply our sentiments or sensations (*Empfindungen*) and the influences on us, connected with them, of everything living and moving around us. These alone are the elements of religion, but they pertain to everything else too. Indeed, Schleiermacher maintains, there is no sentiment that would not have been pious, and the absence of piety signifies a diseased and corrupted condition of life, which must then be imparted to the other areas of life. Every individual feeling, whatever may have initially aroused it, is thus destined to become pious. Just as in cognition the idea of the absolute is the supreme and defining aspect, and in action the absolute as will, so the feeling side of human beings is completely formed for the first time when, in every excitation of feeling, the self finds itself determined not by this or that finite thing or relationship alone, but by the universe via it.

The spiritualization of religion, its liberation from everything that is not essentially religion itself, is attained, according to Schleiermacher, when religion has withdrawn from objectivity entirely into the subject. Whatever religion is, it is essentially only subjective, as feeling, sensation, immediate consciousness; everything else is more or less contingent.

In addition to the general definition of the nature of religion, what especially merits our attention in these *Speeches* is their comprehension of Christianity. If religion is as subjective as Schleiermacher takes it, an infinite multiplicity of religions is possible. Just as the universe in its infinitude is perceived in endlessly different ways, the relation of human beings to the universe can be grasped in endlessly different forms. So the nature of religion is modified in different subjects in the most diverse ways. However, the more the nature of religion is regarded subjectively, all the greater weight does Schleiermacher place on what is common in it: religion has the impulse within it to form a community. If a new intuition of the universe is once given to an individual, he speaks about the revelation he has received and thereby attracts to himself a circle of receptive people, which extends as far as the power of communication emanating from that individual reaches. If there are a number of such individuals, then there are also diverse, individually defined religions in which [what] religion [is], to the extent that its nature involves a common element, arrives at its concrete reality and existence. This concreteness of its existence is the positive aspect of religion. While people formerly made the positive religions a special object of their animosity, instead preferring a natural religion and even speaking of it with respect, Schleiermacher reverses this situation. The positive religions are precisely the specific shapes in which religion must present itself, and the so-called natural religion can make no claim at all to being something similar. "Natural religion" is only an indeterminate, meager, and impoverished idea, to which in reality nothing actually can correspond. A truly individual construction of religion is possible only in the positive religions; only in them is religion individualized in its more operative, forceful, and solid shapes. A specific intuition lies at the basis of every positive religion in this sense, an intuition providing the basis for grasping it as an entire phenomenon.

The basic intuition of Christianity, as Schleiermacher defines it, is none other than the general resistance of everything finite to the unity of the whole, and the way in which the divinity handles this resistance, how it mediates this enmity toward it, and how it sets bounds to the ever-increasing divergence by individual points dispersed across the whole, points that are at once finite and infinite, divine and human. Perdition and redemption, enmity and mediation, are the two inseparably connected reference points of this way of sensing things, and the shape of all religious content in Christianity and its entire form is determined by them.

The historical interest of these *Speeches* consists chiefly in the fact that, on the one hand they are indeed the foundation for Schleiermacher's entire theological construction, but on the other hand they disclose a not insignificant difference between his earlier and later standpoints. Schleiermacher himself felt and acknowledged this, and took pains to add numerous notations or explanations to later editions of his *Speeches*,[72] which harmonized as much as possible the earlier portrayal of his views with the later one, and to convert bold expressions into harmless ones, in order to sidestep the offense that could be taken at many of those earlier passages. But he did not succeed in eliminating the overall impression that the *Speeches* are essentially different from the later writings. What is the point in obscuring their youthful character? Their greatest interest for us is the very fact that we see reflected in them a true image of the time in which they first appeared. As much as Schleiermacher spiritualized and inwardized the nature of religion, he also made it sublime and removed its limitations. Every sound sentiment is indeed for him also in itself a pious one; religion as such is the intelligible contact of the self with the universe; and where Schleiermacher understands the nature of religion at its deepest source as every act of the life of a being taking shape on its own *and* as a being within the whole—as both together—he provides only a fleeting description in images and poetic intuitions.[73]

> It is fleeting and transparent as the vapor that the dew breathes on blossom and fruit, it is bashful and tender as a maiden's kiss,

---

72. Starting with the 3rd ed. of 1821.

73. *Über die Religion*, 3rd ed. (n. 64), 72–74. ET: *On Religion* (Oman translation of the 3rd ed., revised), 42–44. Baur paraphrases the first part of the quotation.

it is holy and fruitful as a bridal embrace. Nor is it merely like, it is all this. It is the first contact of the universal life with an individual. It fills no time and fashions nothing palpable. It is the holy wedlock of the universe—immediate, raised above all error and misunderstanding—with reason incarnate, in a creative, productive embrace. You lie directly on the bosom of the infinite world. In that moment, you are its soul. Though through only one part of your nature, you nevertheless feel, as your own, all its powers and its endless life. In that moment it is your body, its muscles and members pervade you as your own, and your musings and presentiments set its inmost nerves in motion. In this way every living, original moment in your life is first received. This is the domain to which it belongs, and from which every religious emotion is aroused.

How feeble and abstract, in comparison to all of this, is the feeling of utter dependence of the *Glaubenslehre*; but it is also an essentially different concept, since the "utterness" of this feeling is intended to exclude precisely the inward reciprocity of freedom and dependence that forms the essence of religion according to the *Speeches*. This essence has its basis in the fact that the pantheistic worldview thoroughly dominates the *Speeches*, where God and the world are not yet held apart when one always just talks about the universe, the world or, at most, about the world spirit. The issue is also the relation to Christianity, but with the specifics missing in this definition. The essential aspect of Christianity is not yet, as in the *Glaubenslehre*, faith in redemption through Jesus of Nazareth; rather the essence is found in whoever simply recognizes as such the mediating powers by which the divinity maintains a connection between itself and the world hastening away to its ruin. At this point, one or several human beings are seen as bearers of this mediation, Christ or oneself, this or that person within Christianity. Its principle remains genuinely Christian, despite all the shortcomings in form and material, as long as it is free. Likewise, what Christ can impart to his followers is not the blessedness that arises from his sinlessness but rather sadness or pensiveness (*Wehmuth*), which resonates as the basic mood of his soul in all his speeches, that is, the feeling of an unsatisfied longing, one directed to a great object and conscious of that object's infinitude. This longing is specifically directed to the fact that human piety is a persisting, uninterrupted condition, and there remains no fiber or stirring in human nature where it has not been present and pervasive.

In another brief writing from this period, the conversation *Christmas Eve* appearing in 1806, we encounter, a little later in Schleiermacher, a theological treatise that also belongs together with the *Soliloquies* and the

Speeches because of its literary form, that of dialogue. Its task, as Schleiermacher indicates in the preface to the second edition,[74] is to show "how the most varied ways of understanding Christianity may peacefully coexist in an ordinary living room, not by [the participants] ignoring each other but by amiably engaging each other in common reflection and sharing of views." In one of its conversation partners, named Ernst by Schleiermacher, we already find the characteristic grounding of faith in Christ as one who is from the outset completely sinless and perfect, the God-man, by arguing backwards from contemporary Christian experience, as the *Glaubenslehre* does. Since according to Kant the existence of God is not to be demonstrated from the concepts of pure reason, but is based rather, via practical reason, on faith in the sense that practical reason's essential demands cannot be satisfied without a God who will realize these demands in the future, Schleiermacher cannot demonstrate the divine humanity of Christ historically; but Christ's having existed in the past must necessarily be presupposed in order to account for the experience that inherently makes a Christian. Just as for Kant the existence of God is called a postulate of practical reason, so for Schleiermacher the dogma of Christ could be called a postulate of Christian experience. In similar fashion the other three conversation partners represent various aspects of Schleiermacher's characteristic theological position. The legal scholar Leonardt, "the unbelieving scoundrel," introduces the skeptical criticism that is so essentially a part of Schleiermacher's theology. Eduard's preference for the Gospel of John is likewise authentically Schleiermacherian; and his quest for a speculative foundation of christology is an all the more interesting inquiry, given how the later Schleiermacher carefully guarded himself against getting involved in this speculation. But here too, in the figure of Joseph, he allows the conversation to be called back from the inhospitable regions of objective thinking to the subjectivity of feeling, in which on his view everything religious has its proper home.

General Condition of Theology: Dogmatics

It is very indicative of our period that now, after we have become acquainted with its distinctive spirit and its productive power in various fields, we can briefly summarize what is properly theological. A period that had so little sense for the positive and traditional, and that far more felt imbued with the fresh impulse to try its hand at new creations and to open new avenues for

---

74. Schleiermacher, *Weihnachtsfeier: Ein Gespräch* (2nd ed., Berlin, 1826) (n. 64). Quotation from the Tice translation (n. 64), 25–26.

the universal striving of spirit, could not be very productive in the field of theology.

At first there was of course no shortage of works in dogmatic theology, ones taking distinctively different directions. But we do not recognize in them any more profound opposition. The influence of Kantian philosophy was widespread, and the only distinction that arose was whether one was more or less inclined to its principles. This was at most the case in the dogmatic writings of Stäudlin, Ammon, and Eckermann.[75] But even such theologians did not dare to challenge and reject the concept of a supernatural revelation. The general preference was to not articulate contrasting positions sharply but to be satisfied with general definitions that specifically allowed the truly major issues to remain undecided. They preferred to stick to a historical approach to biblical and dogmatic ideas. Even works that did not combine dogmatics and the history of dogma in their titles, as Stäudlin's did in 1801,[76] were far more a history of dogma than a dogmatics. Since these theologians did not desire either to maintain or to abandon the traditional concepts and doctrines, they believed they had done their duty when they had at least acknowledged them in their historical significance and defended them against objections, when countering these objections seemed to be a fair and nonpartisan thing to do.

At least the previously dominant indifference toward the positive and ecclesiastical elements no longer appeared to the same degree when people devoted more attention to the church's theological framework, and regarded the task of a textbook on dogma as presenting dogma's cohesion in more detail. This was the case not merely with Reinhard's *Dogmatik* but also with Augusti's *System der christlichen Dogmatik nach dem Lehrbegriff der lutherischen Kirche* (1809) and Bretschneider's *Handbuch der Dogmatik der evangelischen-lutherischen Kirche* 1814).[77] In general the dogmatic textbooks of this age, and I also include here Schott's[78] *Epitome Theologiae christianae dogmaticae* (1811), offer a scientifically very meager and unsatisfying picture in terms of content and form. They are almost entirely aggregates of materials and devoid of pointed criticism as well as systematic character and consistency.

When one describes the professors of our own University, including Süskind, the two Flatts, and Bengel, as forming their own theological

75. Karl Friedrich Stäudlin (1761–1826); Christoph Friedrich Ammon (1766–1850); Jakob Christoph Rudolf Eckermann (1754–1837).

76. *Lehrbuch der Dogmatik und Dogmengeschichte* (Göttingen, 1801).

77. Franz Volkmar Reinhard (1753–1812); Johann Christian Wilhelm Augusti (1771–1841); Karl Gottlieb Bretschneider (1776–1848).

78. Heinrich August Schott (1780–1835).

school because of their dependence on Storr's theology,[79] the reason for this is simply that they principally adopted an apologetic position and most decisively validated supernaturalism as the foundation of Christian theology. Furthermore, these theologians entirely shut themselves off from the influence of present-day philosophy. They were in part declared disciples of Kantian philosophy, at least of its moral principles, and made considerable use of it for their apologetic purpose of portraying biblical revelation as in accord with reason, and bringing it into agreement with the principles of a boiled-down philosophy aware of its limits.[80]

Daub, *Theologumena*

In the dogmatic field of that period, there is only one distinctive and especially first-rate work. This is Daub's *Theologumena, sive doctrinae de religione christiana, ex natura Dei perspecta repetendae, capita potiora* (1806),[81] written from the perspective of Schelling's philosophy of nature. This *Theologumena* sought to be a philosophical prolegomenon to dogmatics, a presentation of the philosophy of religion. The content of religion develops from the idea of God. God is treated first—God's nature, existence, and attributes—followed by religion with the subdivisions of reconciliation, piety, and public worship, the latter rubric itself containing the doctrines of the God-man, the divine education of the human race, and its public consecration for the kingdom of God through baptism and the eucharist. Only in the third part is the doctrine of religion addressed, including also the doctrines of the spiritual nature of God and of the Trinity. Closer inspection reveals that these three major parts in fact treat of God in himself (or the attributes of the Father), of God as the Son, and of God as the Spirit.

Thus it is the idea of the Trinity that lies at the basis of this *Theologumena*; but that God in his nature is a triune God is not based on the idea of God itself. It is always only human reason, or the reflective understanding,

---

79. Friedrich Gottlieb Süskind (1767–1829); Johann Friedrich Flatt (1759–1821); Karl Christian Flatt (1772–1843); Ernst Gottlieb Bengel (1769–1826). Based on the work of Gottlob Christian Storr (1746–1805), these theologians comprised the original Tübingen School.

80. [*Zeller*] On this older Tübingen School, see the author's history of the Tübingen theological faculty in K. Klüpfel, ed., *Geschichte und Beschreibung der Universität Tübingen* (Tübingen, 1849), 216ff., 389ff.

81. Karl (or Carl) Daub (1765–1836) was a professor in Heidelberg from 1795 until his death. Seeking a speculative reconstruction of traditional dogma, he was influenced successively by Kant, Schelling, and Hegel. The *Theologumena* was written during his Schelling phase. His *Dogmatische Theologie* (1833) was Hegelian in orientation.

that posits these moments of differentiation within God; it is not yet clear whether God is absolute spirit, positing these moments itself and becoming self-determining by means of them. The basis for this overlap of the subjective standpoint into the objective standpoint is that Daub indeed treats first of God, but then of religion and the doctrine of religion, thus starting out from the objective idea of God but only knowing how to make this progression by juxtaposing reflective reason to the objective idea. Overall this *Theologumena* still very much lacks the dialectical development of the idea. And the relationship of the biblical-historical and ecclesiastical-dogmatic materials to the speculative element in Christianity is not yet worked out with clarity and specificity, nor is it dialectically mediated. Daub sees the idea directly in the stories of the Bible and the dogmas of the church, but whether its relationship to them is simply affirmative or also includes a negative aspect is not yet the subject of reflection. Still the balance lies on the side of the idea, to which the facts and dogmas are at least not indispensably attached. From the standpoint of Daub's *Theologumena*, the historical facts of Christian revelation can only count as symbols; but Daub enters into no speculative investigation about the extent to which these symbols are necessary for conveying religious consciousness. With all its speculative intellectual content, the *Theologumena* remains far too bound up in an abstract schematism. It remains very much a misunderstood hieroglyph, which nonetheless had to be an indication of very serious thinking as opposed to the shallow and spiritless rationalism and supernaturalism of that time.

Rationalistic Exegesis: Venturini, Paulus

Dogmatics has to define and establish the concept of the supernatural in Christianity, but dogmatics is concerned only with the concept in general terms. The special task of the critical and exegetical treatment of the New Testament writings is to come to an understanding of, and engage itself with, the supernatural and miraculous in the narratives of the gospel story. Just as in the various periods of the history of the Christian Church one major difference was whether the supernatural in Christianity is more just a matter of faith, or is to be treated as a cognitive task, a matter for rational reflection, so too it is a no less important question as to how one can connect a more freely arrived-at and rational view, disassociated from belief in miracles, with the narratives of the gospel story. This question gains all the greater significance the more deeply and generally the rational view has permeated the consciousness of the age, and the less one can close one's eyes to its contradiction with the content of the New Testament accounts. Whether the response to this question is more or less satisfying depends, to a large extent, on showing whether the theological view of an age is, on the whole, based on principles and thoroughly elaborated. From the entire standpoint already assumed at the beginning of our period, nothing else could be expected than that people would try to work on the gospel story in this sense too.

The *Natürliche Geschichte des grossen Propheten von Nazareth*, which appeared already in 1800, was a work of this sort. The anonymous author was Venturini.[82] The gospel story could not have been treated more arbitrarily. It was transformed into a web of fanciful events, and we lose its ultimate threads in the enigmatic obscurity of a secret society. And yet this way of treating the gospel story essentially differs so little from that followed by Paulus,[83] in his *Kommentar über das Neue Testament*, that the later parts of the *Natürliche Geschichte* are utilized in detail in the *Kommentar*. This *Kommentar*, which first appeared in 1800 and the years following, extended only to the gospels. It is the true representative of this [rationalistic] mode of comprehension and is in fact the most remarkable theological product of this period. It makes very clear what was still the standpoint of this era and its two aspects, typically expressing both equally—the freedom of theological consciousness and the constraints on it. On the one hand, the author of the *Kommentar* is convinced that no actual miracles are found in the gospel story, that everything, however supernatural it appears, has happened in a wholly natural fashion. On the other hand, and equally the case, we have before us in the gospels exact and faithful reports, doubtless composed very soon after the narrated events by those who saw and heard what transpired. As much, therefore, as the author attests to the freedom of his theological consciousness by liberating himself completely from the traditional belief in miracle, equally great is the tenacity with which he adheres to the literal truth of the gospel stories. He can think of them in no other way than that everything actually happened the way it has been understood and stated, just as we read it in the text of our gospels.

The well-known skill of Paulus's exegesis consists in uniting these two assumptions. It knows how to remove everything supernatural and miraculous merely by interpretation, employing means none other than that provided by the text itself. Indeed, it does not remove it at all but shows that

82. Karl Heinrich Georg Venturini (1768–1849).

83. Heinrich Eberhard Gottlob Paulus (1761–1851), student of Storr in Tübingen, leader of theological rationalism, and professor at Heidelberg from 1811 to 1844. The 2nd ed. of his *Philologisch-kritischer und historischer Kommentar über das Neue Testament* appeared in Leipzig, 1804–8, in 4 parts.

the supernatural and miraculous were not there from the beginning, that we only need to open our eyes to see clearly enough before us a wholly natural origin of the material, to see that it is only error and misunderstanding if people earlier found something completely different in the gospels. To this end Paulus indulges in the greatest arbitrariness in grammatical and philological matters when it comes to the importance he gives to individual components of speech, to prepositions and conjunctions, etc.[84] In this regard he was simply a true student of his teacher Storr; for while Storr's own exegesis hardly suffered from aversion to miracles, he understood very well, in the interest of his biblical belief in revelation, how to find his preferred meaning in the words of the biblical text; and his arbitrary approach received its deserved punishment when it led to the extreme of Paulus's exegesis—as indeed Paulus also claimed about himself, by saying that his way of treating the New Testament was simply the consequence of Storr's method.

The main point, however, is the rule established by Paulus that every narrative must be tested historically-pragmatically, as a whole and in details. As a whole it is a question of whether a narrated event is impossible either generally or in the indicated circumstances; or else if it is actually conceivable, or capable of existing, in the real world as such, in that place and time, in keeping with circumstances of the participants and the operative natural conditions. In individual instances the impartial researcher must keep in mind all the plausible views about what is essential, and what is contingent or nonessential in a narrative, and then choose the most likely construal of the data. It must be mentioned in particular that a narrative never completely contains all the external, and especially all the internal, or psychological, circumstances of an event. After one has carefully assembled the information about the people and the locality involved, about the whole nexus of facts, one should never be deterred from placing oneself, so to speak, as a living observer, in the scene. Perhaps the writer, who seems to take much for granted, does not do that himself, although an observer, taking it all in, must have done so. Transposed into this standpoint, the interpreter can and must often fill out the narrative with circumstances that the narrator has not even mentioned, because either they were too familiar to him or were too far removed from his way of thinking and powers of observation.[85] It is

---

84. [Baur] For example, the miracle of Jesus' walking on the sea is simply explained by the fact that ἐπὶ does not mean "on" but "in" (ἐπὶ τὴν θαλάσσαν, Matt 14:25) The pious J. C. Lavater became so indignant at this that he spoke of Paulus in the strongest terms (see the life of Paulus by K. A. von Reichlin-Meldegg [Stuttgart, 1853], 1:266).

85. [Baur] Thus Paulus claims that the feeding of the five thousand was nothing less than a miracle, but it came about merely because the [wealthy] people brought out the stocks they had at hand [to feed the others]. To find this in the story, one only needs

just as necessary that the interpreter try to separate his own viewpoint and consequent findings about the narration and the author, from the factual circumstances, even though those findings were said to involve the facts by filling in a minor gap in the emphasis of the historical narrative. The desideratum that everything as it is narrated might have flowed smoothly from the most exacting historical examination will never make things so accommodating by simply taking the narration and the facts to be simply interchangeable.

The main point, therefore, is the distinction between fact and judgment. The two were originally intertwined, as seen especially from the inclination to derive every striking experience from an invisible and superhuman cause. The chief task of the pragmatic historian is therefore to separate these two components. But we do not see from this why this intertwining of the factual and ideal originally occurred, precisely among those who stood so close to the facts, and must have known best how things stood. Thus, in order to relinquish nothing of the literal truth of the narrative text, the judgments or findings, as distinguished from the facts themselves, must at least be judgments of persons who are situated in the theater of action and direct participants. Facts and the account should not be so widely separated that the account, even if incorrect, does not convey an immediate impression of the facts. It is well-known that Strauss's *Leben Jesu* shows how Paulus's pragmatically based natural explanation of the gospel story occupies a noteworthy position intermediate between the older and the most modern views.[86] Paulus's explanation shares with the older view a favorable opinion of the literal truth of the narrative, and with the modern view it shares the assumption of the narrative's natural origin. The one seems to stand in total contradiction to the other. It can only appear as a psychological mystery how these two assumptions on which Paulus's interpretative method rests could be found in one and the same consciousness in such an unnatural tension. But this standpoint is even more remarkable when it shows us what barriers first had to have been broken through, when the view already based on the consciousness of the time was that the substance of the gospel story is not absolute miracle, and that with the reports of the gospel story seeming to say quite the opposite, when what people formerly saw in them was said to be mediated in natural fashion.

In this regard Paulus's explanation is of course interesting for its own sake. But equally remarkable is the result following from it. Since there is

---

to complete what is necessary at the relevant place.

86. David Friedrich Strauss, *Das Leben Jesu, kritisch gearbeitet*, 4th ed. (Tübingen, 1840), §6. ET: *The Life of Jesus Critically Examined*, trans George Eliot, one-vol. ed. (London, 1892), 46–50. On Strauss and this work, see below, pp. 328–33.

inherently no recognition of anything as miraculous, what is reported as miracle in the gospel accounts can only be interpreted as based on misunderstandings, wrong conceptions, and erroneous judgments, which already occur in the theater of the action itself. We do indeed arrive at a very concrete picture of the original circumstances; but this concreteness (*Anschaulichkeit*) only serves to show us clearly that the entire gospel story rests on a series of the most ordinary and trivial events. We must of course wonder how everything here could have been so misunderstood, have been grasped and portrayed so wrongly and defectively; and we comprehend even less how the occasion for this could have been things of such an ordinary character. Jesus is none other than an itinerant country rabbi, in the best of cases a wise and virtuous man, and the works he did are kindly and humanitarian deeds, involving medical skill, chance, and good luck. The miracle at Cana was a wedding entertainment; awakenings from the dead happened only to those just apparently dead; the transfiguration of Jesus was based on the confused memory of half-awake disciples, who saw Jesus standing with two strangers in beautiful mountain lighting. Paulus's *Kommentar* very contentedly displayed the most superficial and arbitrary rationalism, together with the appearance of sound scholarship and the self-satisfied mien of a pragmatism that knows best about everything. It all proceeds here so prosaically and soberly that we cannot comprehend how primitive Christianity took hold of people's imagination, and how in their consciousness it could be filled with the divine content by which it entered into world history.

New Testament Criticism: Eichhorn, Schleiermacher

One could only move beyond this harshness and unnaturalness in understanding the gospel story by the route of criticism. Here it is especially worth mentioning the turn for the better that New Testament criticism at that time took with Eichhorn's *Einleitung in das Neue Testament*, which appeared in 1804.[87] With the well-known proto-gospel hypothesis,[88] it opened up a series of investigations that, hypothetical as they initially were, attained an ever-greater significance in the history of Protestant theology.

---

87. Johann Gottfried Eichhorn (1752–1827), an Orientalist and New Testament scholar at Göttingen. His *Einleitung* was published in Göttingen in 3 vols, 1804–14.

88. The hypothesis that an original, now-lost gospel served as a common basis for all three of the Synoptic Gospels. Baur regarded this as a purely literary invention with no credible external evidence. See *Kritische Untersuchungen über die kanonischen Evangelien* (Tübingen, 1847), 23–27.

We have already spoken about Hug's *Einleitung*,[89] which chiefly challenged this hypothesis. We can see from Schleiermacher's open letter of 1807 on First Timothy[90] what field criticism also had yet to cultivate, in the canonical epistles. In this letter Schleiermacher provided a brilliant display of his critical acuity, which was epoch-making despite its receiving only censure and rejection at the time, and it contained a premonition of more recent results attainable along this path.

Historical Theology: Planck, Marheineke

Of the remaining theological literature, two larger works merit special attention: Planck's[91] *Geschichte der christlich-kirchlichen Gesellschaftsverfassung*, which appeared in five volumes, 1803–9; and Marheineke's[92] *Christliche Symbolik oder historisch-kritische und dogmatisch-comparative Darstellung des katholischen, lutherischen, reformirten und socinianischen Lehrbegriffs*, of which, however, only the *System des Katholicismus* appeared, in three parts, 1810–13.

Planck sought to provide purely a history of the Christian Church as an external social institution, which would single out only what belongs to the proper history of this society. He did not conceal the fact that by this work he also wanted to contribute something to the philosophical mentality of this age, which, in one way or another, had indeed made the church an object of speculation, and to lead this mindset back to a purely historical viewpoint. Planck was no friend of philosophical speculation, but he was a great master of the so-called pragmatic approach to history. Despite the merits of his historical research, Planck's work also bore to a high degree the marks of the subjective mode of treatment generally characteristic of this age. What was called "pragmatism" was just this subjectivity of the entire standpoint. It was the same historical pragmatism in which Paulus's *Kommentar* found the innermost principle of its way of grasping the gospel story. Planck himself provided the clearest proof of this connection: not long after the completion of that work, he wrote in 1818 a *Geschichte des Christentums*

89. See above, p. 26.

90. Friedrich Schleiermacher, *Über den sogennanten ersten Brief des Paulos an den Timotheos: Ein kritisches Sendschreiben an J. G. Gass* (Berlin, 1807). Schleiermacher challenged Pauline authorship on philological grounds. Baur later confirmed this challenge on historical-critical grounds.

91. Gottlieb Christian Planck (1751–1833), professor of church history in Göttingen.

92. Philipp Konrad Marheineke (1780–1846), professor of theology in Berlin. On Marheineke, see p. 205, n. 70. Baur discusses him several times subsequently.

in der Periode seiner Einführung in die Welt durch Jesus und die Apostel, which distinguished itself from Paulus's procedure only in that Planck was not as wary of miracle; rather he used miracle itself as a means to explain the introduction of Christianity into the world, with the aid of clever little inferences based on the concurrence of various favorable circumstances. Nothing is more spiritless than this rationalism, or this mixing of rationalism and supernaturalism, in which finite subjective reason supposes it can puzzle out in the best possible way the most hidden thoughts and motives behind people's actions, while in its narrow-mindedness failing to surmise what an entirely different spirit is pervasive in the objective course of the movement of history.

It comes down to Planck saying that in a strange way a wise Jew has a plan to make the whole world blessed, and in an even stranger way it succeeds. Here everything is a plan, a cunningly applied and calculated plan. The apostles, as he sees it, have an especially clever method of converting all the teaching of Jesus into history. Paul, the keen thinker and speculative Jew, grasps Jesus' plan more readily than the other apostles. His reflection on it results in his describing the Messiah's kingdom as destined for pagans as well as Jews. He wants to bring unity into the plan, and it dawns on him that Jesus did not want to make Judaism into the universal human religion. From there it is only a further step to the great discovery that indeed Jesus' plan involved the abolition of Judaism and its entire suppression by a purer and more spiritual theory of religion, and perhaps this constituted the major vocation of the Messiah.[93]

After Planck said everything possible against accepting a miracle in the conversion of the Apostle Paul, he nevertheless felt himself tempted to see the strongest ground for assuming an actual miracle in what followed thereafter. We could at all events be easily persuaded that the higher wisdom, which foresaw this result, held it to be sufficiently important to account for the extravagance of the miracle, and that could then also have made it easier to believe in it. If Paul had not become an apostle, then either providence would have to have made other arrangements to secure the good it intended for humanity through Christianity, or else Christianity would never have spread within the world in this form. How fortunate it therefore is that Christianity met up with a man like Paul, for otherwise providence would have needed an even more extravagant miracle! It is truly narrow-minded to calculate everything in terms of total cost, as to whether providence brings something about at less cost this way or that. So here everything hinges on

---

93. [*Baur, in the text*] Cf. Uhlhorn, *Jahrbücher für deutsche Theologie* 2 (1857) 640 ff. [*Ed.*] The reference is to an article by Gerhard Uhlhorn, "Die älteste Kirchengeschichte in ihrer neuen Darstellungen," 603–78.

the most petty motives. There is no more striking example of pragmatic historiography than Planck's history of Christianity.

Marheineke's *Symbolik* sets itself apart by its more objective view of history, one in which Planck's idea of a symbolics replacing the old polemics has been carried out by what is, on the whole, a successful portrayal of the system of Catholicism. Since then symbolics[94] has assumed its own independent position among the theological sciences.

Theological Journals

Finally we will identify the various directions taken by representative theological journals. The Storr school, via Flatt and Süskind, published, up until 1812, its *Magazin für christliche Dogmatik und Moral, deren Geschichte und Anwendung im Vortrag der Religion*.[95] The organ for rationalism was the *Theologisches Journal*, edited by Gabler.[96] In the area of speculative theology, Daub joined with Creuzer in 1805 to edit *Studien*.[97] According to the latter's dedication, men filled with the idea of wisdom, and seeking only what is good and true in both old and new, endeavored here to win acceptance for this absolute idea in each of their disciplines and to revive them by doing so. Just as Creuzer in this journal above all provided an idea and demonstration of the old symbolics, so Daub made the first attempt at a speculative treatment of the Christian science of religion: instead of judging Christianity from the standpoint of subjective reason, his purpose was to recognize and grasp the absolute reason made objective in Christianity. Creuzer had the same idea in regard to the ancient pagan religions.[98]

---

94. A study of the confessions or symbols of different theological systems, Greek, Catholic, Lutheran, Reformed, sectarian, etc.

95. This journal was published in Tübingen, by Flatt, 1796–1802; by Süskind, 1803–12.

96. This was the *Neuestes theologisches Journal*, edited by Johann Philipp Gabler, 5 vols. (Nürnberg, 1796–1800).

97. Published by Karl Daub and Georg Friedrich Creuzer in 6 vols. (Frankfurt, 1805–11).

98. Baur was familiar with and influenced by Creuzer's *Symbolik und Mythologie der alten Völker, besonders der Griechen*, 4 parts (Leipzig and Darmstadt, 1810–12).

PART TWO

From 1815 to 1830

1

Introduction

Political Conditions

By 1815 the French Revolution's march of conquest through Europe had been ended. The powerful force that emerged as a result of the revolution had been pushed back within its natural boundaries. After this overwhelming opponent had been defeated, what now emerged, to replace a universal monarchy embracing nearly all the European states, was not just a political equilibrium. For instead people could also hope that everything so forcefully thrown out of joint by the great world events since the beginning of the revolution, all that had ensued as a consequence of it, would be restored, as much as possible, to the way things were beforehand. In France, what a great reversal suddenly followed, with the return of the Bourbon monarchs![1] After the revolution had taken place in the mother country, what then seemed to be clearly impossible was now, just a short time later, more than just a possibility. With the return of the Bourbons and the reestablishment of the old French royal throne, restoration became the watchword of these times.

In Germany it was inconceivable to reinstate the old German Empire [the Holy Roman Empire] that had collapsed from within long before the revolution, all the more so because the new German Confederation that the Congress of Vienna settled upon and established was supposed to take the place of the former empire.[2] Yet however much people at that time sought,

---

1. Members of the Bourbon family ruled France from 1589 until the execution of Louis XVI in 1793, during the French Revolution. Louis XVIII, followed by Charles X, returned the Bourbons to the throne for the period of the Restoration, 1814–30.

2. The Congress of Vienna (1814–15), with emissaries from major countries in attendance, reestablished the boundaries of European states following the Napoleonic wars. The Congress created the German Confederation of 39 German states, which replaced the old Holy Roman Empire and lasted until 1866, when the Austro-Prussian

as far as possible, to reinstate the old forms, to heal the damage done to [traditional political] legitimacy by the revolution and its consequences, the rulers and the defenders of the "monarchical principle" were hardly able to carry through with this effort to the extent they wished. The consciousness of this era had become entirely different. The ideas and tenets people had struggled so long and hard to hold on to were already so firmly rooted that they were unable to let go of them so easily, however much the political circumstances [after Napoleon] had changed. The rights and freedoms people now had they indeed regarded as the achievements they had won in the previous period, and everything must rely on maintaining them. The old ways had first of all to be accommodated to the new ones; people had first to understand the limits within which the old was supposed to exist legitimately alongside the new. Political states must first be constituted on this foundation. Hence the period of the restoration is also the period of constitutions.

When Louis XVIII became the successor to his father's throne, he could base his rule only on the constitution guaranteed in the Charter of 1814,[3] which had securely put in place all the institutions of the nation, ones to which it believed itself to be entitled as a result of the revolution. In Germany the circumstances were of course different, although the concerns were on the whole the same. Here the wars of independence first awakened the national self-consciousness. The great work of liberating Germany had been accomplished by the popular uprising, by the energy and self-sacrifice of the people. As soon as a favorable point in time for casting off the yoke of foreign rule seemed to be at hand, the princes themselves had appealed to the people. The Proclamation of Kalisch[4] had already promised a rebirth of Germany based on the nation's own innate spirit. In a famous proclamation [subsequently] issued by the king of Prussia, the king had addressed himself to his people.[5] After the struggle for freedom and the resulting peace, the claims of the people could not go unrecognized in the process of establishing Germany's internal state of affairs. Article 13 of the Vienna Act con-

---

War marked its end. Austria was the dominant party in the legislative body, or Diet, of this loose confederation, which had no executive body.

3. Louis XVIII issued the Charte Constitutionelle, the Charter of 1814, which set up a constitutional monarchy and parliament, while preserving freedoms resulting from the French Revolution.

4. Kalisz (German, Kalisch), a city in Poland, was at this time near the border of the Kingdom of Poland (as part of the Russian Empire) with German states to the west. The Proclamation of Kalisch (25 March 1813) was made to the Germans (who were facing Napoleon's expansionism) by the Russian field marshal, Prince Kutusow-Smolenskoi. It held out to the Germans the promise of restoring their empire.

5. See above, pp. 14–15.

cerning the Confederation stipulated that there will be a system of political representation in each state of the Confederation. One might have hoped not only that this stipulation would actually be carried out in practice, but also that the ideas and the aspirations the nation's best men had been working to realize for a number of years would, on the whole, increasingly come into play.

But what unhappy, dismal pages of the German nation's history lie before us when we look back to the era after 1815, this period of unfulfilled promises, of the most bitter delusions, of the most shameful betrayal of the people by the princes. In this period, the longer and more deeply each German just had to feel all the pain and all the justifiable anger, the more bitter then were the fruits from the seeds sown at that time.[6] In time of need the princes had appealed to the people to fight for the princes' cause as the people's cause. However, as soon as the princes saw themselves securely on their thrones once more, there was no longer a people that possessed rights, but only a people to heed the sovereign decrees. The 1815 acts establishing the Confederation spoke of political representation.[7] But only five years later the Austrian presidential envoy said, in a September 1820 address to the diet of the Confederation, that one must look upon the formulation of article 13 of the Acts of Confederation as one of the leading causes for the conditions in Germany, seeing as how this article contained the promise that there shall be a system of political representation in each of the states of the Confederation.

However, a time had not been firmly set for introducing political representation, nor the form it would take. Doing so had become impossible, given how very different the internal conditions of the individual states were. "Representation" was understood to mean none other than what it has always meant in Germany. So that meaning was far from envisaging the introduction of any kind of popular rule, of the sort people might demand in various places based on a foreign [i.e., French] model, despite that model being thoroughly incompatible with the existing monarchical states that still constituted almost all of the Confederation. This is why no firm decision might be reached as to [representation for] the existing occupational groups or social classes (*ständischen Arbeiten*) in the various states of the

---

6. [*Zeller*] It is perhaps not necessary to recall that this was written down in 1849 or 1850. In the transcript available to me [from later lectures], this passage has a milder tone.

7. The German term *landständisch* (here and below translated, together with *Verfassung*, as "political representation") refers back to a medieval political arrangement in which various classes or occupations had their own designated representatives to the government.

Confederation, prior to the Diet of the Confederation reaching agreement about an interpretation of article 13 that upheld the corresponding monarchical principle. The Prussian cabinet, no longer having the counsel of Stein, Humboldt, or Gneisenau,[8] declared that more recent legislation by the Confederation, with Prussia's participation, aims to thwart the combined political efforts of a few lands of the Confederation, efforts undertaken in such haste, and the democratic principles lying at their foundation. At that time the German people, and all matters in the interest of German freedom, were treated with disdain. In Prussia, in the state that owed its triumphant rise again solely to the impetus coming from the people, and where nothing more was envisaged than a participatory political system, thought was given only to building up the bureaucratic system of the police state as fully as possible. The South German states (such as Württemberg) had lost their old representative political systems in face of the sovereign power of kingdoms created by Napoleon, and only through protracted and difficult struggles could they succeed in gaining a place in their political documents for the essential rights of the people. As soon as they believed they had finally accomplished this political work, they only experienced anew how little inclination there also was to uphold the sworn constitutional rights.[9]

Thus the constitutional states simply became the arenas of a struggle in which, in its constant conflict with the monarchical principle, the popular principle repeatedly and ultimately had to meet with defeat. Given how individual states specifically stood in relation to the Diet of the German Confederation, which was completely dependent on the absolutist regimes of the large states, there could always be an ostensible pretext and a suitable mechanism for restricting and suppressing every justifiable attempt at developing constitutional freedom. In this context one need only call to mind the Carlsbad Decrees,[10] which played such a grievously infamous role in

---

8. Heinrich Friedrich Carl, Baron von Stein (1757–1831), a liberal Prussian statesmen, championed German nationalism in opposition to Napoleon's imperialism. Karl Wilhelm von Humboldt (1767–1835), Prussian first minister of education, founded the Friedrich Wilhelm University of Berlin (later named the Humboldt University). August Wilhelm Anton, Count Neithardt von Gneisenau (1760–1831), was a distinguished officer in the Prussian army and General Blücher's chief of staff in the defeat of Napoleon at Waterloo.

9. [Zeller] The transcript reads: "and then this once again made for a very unwelcome experience."

10. The Carlsbad Decrees were a set of reactionary restrictions introduced into the states of the German Confederation, adopted by a conference in Carlsbad, Bohemia in 1819. They banned nationalist fraternities (Burschenschaften), removed liberal university professors, and expanded censorship of the press. The conference was called by Austrian Minister of State Metternich after the liberal fraternity student Karl Ludwig Sand murdered the conservative writer August von Kotzebue. Only in 1848 were the

most recent history. They were a net artfully cast to ensnare irretrievably any efforts at freedom. How profoundly upsetting all this had to have been to the hearts of the German people! Also mainly to the university youths who, since the wars of independence in which they had themselves taken part, had had a very vital interest in German politics, and who had sought to realize their ideal of German freedom and unity, doing so with youthful enthusiasm and youthful energy. Anyone living through these times knows this. Despite the success in putting down any outbreak of the anger festering internally, there was only a deceptive calm, one that sooner or later had to see these antithetical positions, held together only with difficulty, now come apart.

The political aspect of this entire period is to be viewed from the perspective of such an antithesis. Two principles are constantly battling each other: the free popular principle, which comes on the scene with full awareness of its own internal and external justification, and the monarchical principle, which, by basing itself on its outdated entitlement and its positive power, disputes the basis for the existence of that popular principle, and regards any ground given to that principle as just a concession it was forced to make. Even where both sides came together on the common ground of a constitution, of legally based entitlements, this was no internal, conciliatory unity, but instead was simply a condition of hostile tension, of reciprocal mistrust, of an ongoing resistance. Ultimately it could only end by the two principles once again abandoning their collaboration, which had only been brought about under duress and artificially, and with one of them decidedly gaining dominance over the other.

Ecclesiastical Developments

We now turn from the domain of politics to that of the church. Here too we meet with analogous circumstances and antitheses, ones certainly expressing repeatedly, and in the same way, the general consciousness of that time in its various forms. Although they do not involve mutual confrontation with the same harshness, these circumstances and antithesis nevertheless are, on the whole, inherently of the same character. Here too the prevailing orientations are, in general, restoration, and reaction or resistance to it. The response in the Catholic Church was most emphatically to speak out for restoration. The response in the Protestant Church at all events took on the character of resistance. Just as the wars of liberation as such were earnestly

---

Decrees abrogated by the Bundestag. Many scholars, including Hegel, struggled with censorship restrictions.

attuned to the national spirit and internalized it, they also aroused a deeper religious concern that could not coexist with the previously prevailing indifference toward the positively historical (*das Positive*) and the ecclesiastical. People became not only more religious but also more ecclesiastically minded; they embraced a new confidence in the contents of the old church teaching, in the basic truths on which the Protestant faith rests; ecclesiastical awareness vigorously asserted itself again; ecclesiastical issues were of contemporary interest and significance, and that was very readily able to take a very one-sided direction.

It is in fact remarkable what a difference there is in this regard between the preceding period and this one. The earlier period was so productive in its philosophical ideas and systems—ones that also had a profoundly engaging significance for theology—and it was indifferent to the positive and ecclesiastical. In this second period things now apparently sought to go the other way; the times turned toward trust in Christianity's positive and ecclesiastical aspects. However, since the already-won, freer ideas and outlooks could not just cease to continue affecting the spirit of the time, and cease to exert their influence on theology, the opposite view then grew all the stronger, and a struggle among opposing principles and orientations had to arise in the church's domain similar to the struggle in the political domain. Here too in the church, as there in politics, the whole effort was aimed at drawing boundaries between opposing groups in such a way that the unifying of people was not internally conciliatory but instead stopped short with merely external arrangements. As we will come to see in what follows, there was a constitutional system on the soil of theology too, one inherently with the same ambiguous character as that of the system of constitutional monarchy, since it consisted of elements bound together simply by artificial ties. Hence sooner or later this system had to dissolve, owing to its own inner incompatibility.

2

History of the Catholic Church

The Papacy: The Restoration Politics of Pius VII

By starting with the head of the church, we clearly see, first of all, how the church favored the side of restoration in the period directly following the collapse of Napoleonic rule. Papal rule was reinstated in keeping with its essential foundation when Pius VII[1] not only took up his seat in the Vatican as an independent ruler but also, as a result of the Congress of Vienna, took back the former territory of the Papal States except for a small stretch of land on the far side of the Po River. So, happily, the pope recognized the fact that the Protestant princes too deserved well of the chair of Peter; and yet papal consistency bade him to protest not only against the partitioning of lands along the Po and the Austrian occupation of the region of Ferrara, but also against the French retention of Avignon, and the secularization and dissolution of the German Empire. As one can readily understand, the Vienna statesmen were unwilling to go so far as falling in line with the pope's wishes. He could not easily disregard this fact if he was simply to succeed in also restoring the chair of Peter by establishing the old hierarchical relationships. How much had changed since the beginning of the revolution in all the states that stood in some sort of relation to the papal seat! What a task the pope saw before him when, after the dissolving of so many old ties, he sought to undergird a new, secure order.

---

1. Pius VII, pope 1800–1823. The French Empire annexed the Papal States in 1809 and removed Pius to France. The Congress of Vienna restored the Papal States to the church in 1814. However, the church lost control of its properties in Avignon, where popes had resided in exile in the fourteenth century, and Austria retained possession of the church's former legation at Ferrara, on the north side of the Po River. On Pius VII, see also above, pp. 26–35.

The way Pius VII grasped his task, and the spirit with which he moved to carry it out, could not have been made known more clearly than he did so in the first major papal act upon his return: the reinstatement of the Jesuit order. Indeed, on 7 August 1814 the pope went, with great ceremony, to the Jesuit church, where he himself celebrated a mass at the altar of St. Ignatius.[2] In the adjoining oratory, before the aristocratic congregation, in the presence of cardinals, bishops, and about fifty Jesuits coming over from Sicily together with the provincial or father superior, the pope had the master of ceremonies read the bull *Sollicitudo omnium ecclesiarum*, which formally and ceremonially reinstated the Jesuit order throughout the entire Catholic world, with its former constitution unchanged and with all the privileges granted to it by former popes. In the bull the pope affirmed that he believed himself to be complicit in a grievous sin when, amidst the storm that raged around the little ship of Peter, he had neglected to restore to it the sturdy oarsmen who stood ready to bring it safely through the surging waves threatening it at every moment with unavoidable destruction. [He said that] the Catholic world, by common consent, demanded the reinstatement of the Society of Jesus; that almost daily the most urgent requests were directed to him on this matter, coming from archbishops and bishops, as well as from the most distinguished persons of every social class. In doing so he spoke quite openly about the plan to employ every means that he could always use in the interest of the hierarchy. Pius VII bestowed his complete favor on the order. On the very day of their reinstatement the Jesuits were given back the three palaces they had previously possessed in Rome. In the years that followed they received very generous support for founding their colleges [or religious communities] in Viterbo, Urbino, Orvieto, Ferrara, Terni, Tivoli, Fano, Ferentino, and Benevento.

Before we follow the Jesuits in the new theater of their activity, we wish to see how Pius VII sought to find his bearings with the relations of the various political states to the Holy See.

---

2. St. Ignatius of Loyola (1491–1556) founded the Jesuit order. The Jesuits (the Society of Jesus) were especially known as defenders of the papacy. Pope Clement XIV had suspended the order in 1773 to placate Spain and Portugal, which were angry about Jesuit actions in their colonies.

Success in Italy, Spain, and France

The times were quite favorable for the pope's designs. With new interest in the restoration, people gladly returned to the old established relationships. In Spain the Concordat of 1753, and the 1762 pragmatic sanction of Charles III, once more became the effective norms.[3] Ferdinand VII reintroduced the Inquisition, which had been abolished not merely with the rise of Napoleon but also by the Cortes, despite all the objections of the papal nuncio.[4] In 1815 the grand inquisitor issued edicts against the new and dangerous teachings by which the greater part of Europe had been brought to ruin in the most lamentable way, and now also endangered Spain.

The pope had every reason to be satisfied with [conditions in] Sardinia and Tuscany. This was less the case as to Naples. The king of Naples delayed in sending the riding horse for St. Peter, which attested to the old dependence of his kingdom on the Holy See. There was lively debate about whether or not this was purely a worldly obligation, and the pope threatened the king with future divine punishment. In contrast, Ferdinand[5] declined to admit the Jesuits to his land, and placed restrictions on its clerics corresponding with Rome. For his part the pope refused to install the Neapolitan bishops, and three-quarters of these dioceses were vacant. After lengthy negotiations, finally, in February 1818, the ministers representing the two courts, Consalvi and Medici,[6] concluded a concordat at Taormina [in Sicily]. Appointment even to those positions that had previously been filled by Rome was conceded to the king, whereas the pope retained significant influence on the filling of lesser positions. The pope's correspondence with the clergy was freed from all state oversight. The king's former jurisdiction over clergy became restricted or abolished, monasteries were set up once more, ecclesiastics were again qualified to own property, and they were promised the return of what had been taken from them.

In 1815 the leading voices in France were very much of a mind to undergird the restored state by the institutional church; so there was even

---

3. The Concordat of 1753 contained the pope's agreement to continue, in Spain, royal control of the selection of those who were appointed to ecclesiastical offices. We are unable to confirm information about the 1762 pragmatic sanction.

4. Ferdinand VII, king of Spain 1808 and 1813–33, reinstituted the Inquisition in 1814. It had been abolished by Joseph Bonaparte (ruled Spain 1808–14), and by the Cortes of Cádiz in 1813.

5. This is Ferdinand I, king of the Two Sicilies (which included Naples), not Ferdinand, king of Spain.

6. Cardinal Ercole Consalvi (1757–1824) was the secretary of state under Pius VII and played a key role in restoring legitimist principles. We are unable to identify the Medici who represented Naples.

talk of annulling the Napoleonic concordat and entering into a new one. Simultaneously, its structural articles ought to be repealed and the number of dioceses, suitably endowed, significantly increased (from sixty to ninety-two). This would have made the church more independent from the state, and the clerical endowments and establishing of new bishoprics would have imposed very significant costs on the state. The intent of the [proposed new] concordat was to sacrifice Gallican freedom wholly to papal power. But this was the very thing that incited the most decided opposition. It aroused a general outcry, and a great many pamphlets pictured the dangers that lay ahead. Guizot says that when the hand of monasticism reaches out for the property it lost, and when the Inquisition gains a foothold on French soil, it is as though Gregory VII has once again seized the crown.[7] Indeed that is why there was no concordat enacted. In the commission seated in 1816 to confer about the plan, there arose such a conflict that they did not risk bringing it to the Chamber of Deputies for its consideration. Yet later on, after lengthy deliberations, the number of bishoprics was increased. In 1822 their administrative areas were laid out so that they largely coincided with the areas of the political departments or divisions. Hence since that time there are eighty archiepiscopal and episcopal churches in France.[8]

Affairs in Germany

German affairs were especially important to the pope. To him, the condition of the German church seemed very distressing. In his address to the cardinals on 15 November 1817, he exclaimed: "So many churches blessed with titles and riches have lost their splendor and, at the same time, their estates. Almost all go without their statutory protections and their servants. The spiritual administration lies in chains, church discipline is no more, and the most thriving monasteries have become barren." These conditions called for new arrangements. This took place via concordats concluded with individual states. The first was Bavaria. This concordat already came into being in 1817, but it nevertheless encountered difficulties because of how the kingdom was organized politically. The Roman Curia believed that its rights were impaired by the way the concordat specified the civil circumstances of Catholic ecclesiastics, most especially because of the basic provision that

---

7. François Pierre Guillaume Guizot (1787–1874) was a prominent French historian and liberal public official after the fall of Napoleon. Cardinal Hildebrand (1020–85) became Pope Gregory VII in 1073 and fought successfully with the Holy Roman Emperor, Henry IV, over the powers of the church vis-à-vis the civil authorities.

8. [Zeller] Four more were added [in 1859] because of the annexation of Savoy.

the Protestants had fully equal rights.⁹ The prelates in the state assembly declined to swear allegiance to the state. However, since the king insisted on fulfilling the concordat, and in 1821 issued the interpretation that the oath to the government only concerned civic matters and bound one to nothing in conflict with divine law and the precepts of the church, the papal nuncio allowed the new appointees to be sworn in.

Negotiations with the smaller states—Württemberg, Baden, Hesse-Cassel, Hesse-Darmstadt, Nassau, Oldenburg, Mecklenburg, and so forth—were far more difficult. The plan of a commission meeting in Frankfurt in 1818 appeared to the Curia to tend too much toward democracy. The rural pastors too were supposed to participate in the election of someone to a diocese. When a vacancy occurred, the rural pastors of the diocese, collectively, were to select a panel with members at least equal in number to those from the cathedral chapter, and the body of electors was to consist of the two groups. No one could be chosen who had not held a pastoral or teaching office for eight years. The pope feared that the nobility, which those in Rome always viewed as the foremost supporters of the German church, might on this account be completely disqualified from holding episcopal office, and he declared that such treachery to the church would never be allowed. Together with this democratic element the Frankfurt plan also did include a very monarchical element. The electoral body should not name a bishop directly, but instead should only nominate three persons. Before they did so the sovereign was indeed to have the right to exclude *personas minus gratus* (those lacking his favor) from being nominated, and then after these proceedings to make the definitive choice from among the three nominees. But these arrangements must have just made the pope all the more displeased. The princes had what amounted to a direct right to appoint bishops; as Protestant princes they would have exercised the right of patronage over the Catholic churches. Only for as many as four months, or at most six months, was the pope entitled to express reservations regarding the selection of a bishop, at which point he could forestall the process longer should the archbishop have reason to allow that. If under these conditions no agreement could be reached, then they would just have to establish a new arrangement. Also, the negotiations with Hanover, under Pius or Consalvi, were unsuccessful. In Prussia, by contrast, there was effortless agreement on the basic procedures in 1821. The Roman Curia was amenable to these proposed reductions in the number of dioceses and to letting a few of the old episcopal seats be eliminated.

---

9. The Bavarian Religious Edict of 1818 gave equal civil rights to non-Catholics.

Other Matters in the Reign of Pius VII

Just as in his reinstatement of the Jesuit order, Pius VII also made the spirit of his reign known by condemning the Bible Societies[10] in 1817, declaring them to be a pestilence. He stated that they are *impiae novatorum machinationes* (impious new schemes), an *inventum quo ipsa religionis fundamenta labefactantur* (a device disruptive of the very foundations of religion). [He said that] translations of the Bible are more damaging than they are useful. On other matters, the soul of his government was his secretary of state, Cardinal Consalvi, who undoubtedly possessed diplomatic talent at a high level but was more flexible and versatile than he was energetic and creative. He endeavored to iron out as much as possible different mutually opposed interests, and to avoid an outbreak of hostilities. He knew how, with great ingenuity, to manage the requirements of each current situation, but he was in no position to bring about something tenable for the future. Since Consalvi was away for a long time at the Congress of Vienna, the pope relied mainly on the guidance of Cardinal Pacca,[11] who was especially concerned to restore the ecclesiastical chapters and the monasteries, for the Papal States had lost a significant part of their revenue from these sources and had to assume a new burden of debt. Also the ecclesiastics and the nobility regained their old entitlements, but the provinces and provincial cities lost their special political status. The Papal States were divided into seventeen delegations [administrative districts], each of which was presided over by an ecclesiastic as delegate, or a cardinal as legate. However, the more exclusively governance fell to the hands of ecclesiastics, the more public conditions took a turn for the worse, and the old disorder und uncertainty returned.

The revolutionary element had by then already established itself in the Papal States, and as a result had become quite dangerous to the papal regime. It emerged then under the name of the Carbonari.[12] When the 1820 revolution in Naples was supposed to lead to an outbreak in the Papal States too, the movement was suppressed by an army from Austria. The contemporary revolutionary movements in the old Catholic lands of Spain and Portugal also took an anti-Roman direction. It was especially noteworthy how the

10. Baur is referring to Protestant groups evangelizing by circulating copies of the scriptures, such as the British and Foreign Bible Society (founded in 1804), which spread to other countries and spawned other groups, as far away as Russia.

11. Cardinal Bartolomeo Pacca (1756–1844) served as pro-secretary of state during Consalvi's absence. Later he was a candidate for the papacy itself, but was passed over for a less inflammatory candidate.

12. The Carbonari was a secret society that arose in Naples to oppose the Bourbon restoration, and that spread to other regions such as the Papal States where, as a secular movement, it opposed theocratic rule.

old spirit of opposition in Jansenism[13] contributed to them. Jansenists held seats mainly in the Cortes in Spain. At one time the leader of the Cortes said directly to the papal nuncio that people join Jansenism without being apprehensive about a schism. In the Catholic Church itself people attached themselves to existing opposition factions.

Pius VII lived to see, once again, the establishment of a general peace and the consolidation of his supreme ecclesiastical vision. However, he became sufficiently convinced that a profound, intransigent hatred for the old order continually threatened, a hatred suddenly venting itself in powerful outbreaks. He died on 21 August 1823.

Leo XII and Pius VIII

The next pope was Leo XII (Annibale Sermatti della Genga). He belonged to the faction of the *Zelanti*,[14] the reactionary cardinals. Under Pius VII, Leo was an opponent of Consalvi's liberal administration. As cardinal he also displayed unfavorable attitudes toward the Jesuits, and he put every possible obstacle in their path. As pope, he generally behaved quite differently than he did before. He may have had good intentions in handling affairs, but he was quite inept and unlucky. Under Leo, what Consalvi had accomplished was in turn ruined. He made himself universally detested; from prince to beggar, no one was his friend. His papal acts that people disapproved of included the beatification of Julianus, a Spanish Franciscan, in 1825, and the proclamation of a Jubilee Year[15] for 1825, something not celebrated for the past fifty years. The beatification truly made Catholicism and Christianity a laughing-stock. The principal miracle documenting the worthiness of Julianus for beatification was said to have been that he once pulled a half-grilled bird from the cooking spit and released it to fly away alive. About the same time the pope summoned all believers to make a pilgrimage to Rome,

---

13. Jansenism, a reform movement in French Catholicism, followed the teaching of Cornelius Otto Jansen (1585–1638), who emphasized extreme versions of Augustinianism about original sin, grace, and predestination. The church opposed Jansenism and the pope banned Jansen's book in 1642, although the movement continued for centuries as a Jansenist church.

14. [*Baur*] In more recent times there are two factions in the Curia, a zealous, harsh faction that will give up none of the ancient claims, and a politically shrewd faction that at least takes into account the newer circumstances of the times, to the extent that it resolves on certain concessions. The *Zelanti* are the first faction, the liberals or *Politici* are the second.

15. Jubilee years were times of solemnity that popes typically proclaimed after twenty-five year intervals.

not only to pray for the eradication of heresies, but also to praise God for victory over the conspiracies of this century against human and divine right. Of course people were not especially drawn to the latter cause, owing to the ongoing activities of the Carbonari. More important factors are that Leo did not merely ally the apostolic throne with the Spanish republics in South America, but also completed the still-pending concordat with the smaller German states, which he did with his 1827 bull. He died on 20 February 1829.

Pius VIII (Francesco Saverio Castiglioni) had also belonged earlier on to the zealous faction, although subsequently he was no less opposed to the disciplinary actions of Leo XII. As pope, he sought to become more conciliatory. During his papacy, which lasted only until November 1830, he could not accomplish anything. He was at an advanced age, beset with ill health, and much troubled by philosophy, the Bible Societies, and the Carbonari.

The Fortunes of the Jesuit Order after Its Suspension

The reinstatement of the Jesuit order, and the activity beginning anew with it, are so very important for the history of the Catholic Church that we will take up this topic next.

The Jesuit order had not in fact ceased to exist following its suspension, and the order itself was confident about its speedy reinstatement. Pius VI had been so favorably disposed toward the order that the only thing lacking was a public declaration to that effect. Doubtless its reinstatement would even have occurred much sooner had the events of the French Revolution not posed an obstacle to it. The difficulty was that the revolution was also very conducive to the objectives of the Jesuits, since they sought to make quite clear, with regard to the revolution, the ruinous consequences of suspending their order. They contended that by tearing down the Society of Jesus the ancient bulwark of the throne and the altar had been torn down; that the natural result is simply that this century's audacious Jansenist philosophy now also raises its head against the rulers who are robbed of their most reliable support. [They said that] only if the order is speedily aroused from its grave—the order that has sufficiently proven that it understands how to keep the people in obedience to the ecclesiastical and secular shepherds set over them by God—may one hope to lead back those who have gone astray, and to protect from contagion by the revolutionary poison those who are still faithful. Such overblown statements made sentiments in the palaces so favorable to the Jesuits that, prior to 1814, steps were taken toward their reinstatement. The Fathers of the Faith, founded in 1792 by

Archduchess Maria Anna[16] and approved by Pius VI, were just Jesuits under another name. In Naples and Sicily, at the request of King Ferdinand IV, the order had already been reinstated by a papal brief or letter.

In Russia the Jesuits had unusual fortunes. When they were expelled from all the domains of orthodox Christianity [in the West] they found a very benevolent protector in the Russian empress, Catherine II.[17] She believed the Jesuits would become very useful to her, making it all the easier to render amenable to Russian rule her new subjects in provinces recently gained by the partitioning of Poland. Also, by making such a stand in opposition to the pope, she took pleasure in showing how little concern she had for his authority. The Jesuits set up a novitiate, and Pius VI silently assented to the election of a vicar-general of the order in Russia. Emperor Paul I was even more favorably disposed toward them owing to his hatred of the revolutionary ideas taking hold around him. In 1800 he granted the Catholic parish church in his capital city to the Jesuits, and authorized a teaching institution as its foundation, one that soon became a formal college. He also supported in the warmest way the efforts of its vicar-general, Franz Kareu,[18] to obtain from the new pope, Pius VII, at least to some extent a formal reinstatement of the order. A papal brief or letter in 1801 declared the establishment of the order for Russia, and named Kareu the general officer of the order for Russia. Tsar Alexander I was also very much a friend of the Jesuits, to the extent that the vicar-general of the order, Tadeusz Brzozowski, conceived and carried out the bold plan of placing all the educational affairs in Russia in the hands of his society.[19] To this end he elevated its college at Polotsk to university status and bestowed on it all the powers of the other Russian academic institutions. In this arrangement all the schools of the order in Russia had the privilege of not being under state jurisdiction and only being under the new university. This happened in 1812.

But when the Jesuits had hardly reached this goal they made such presumptuous use of this hard-won victory that matters soon took a turn for the worse. Contrary to the laws of the realm, which strictly forbade any enticement to defect from the dominant faith, they cast their nets among the adherents of the Greek [Orthodox] Church and drew a large part of the Greek Catholic followers entrusted to their educational institutions over to

16. The Fathers of the Faith was an independent group of ex-Jesuits. Maria Anna (1770–1809) was an archduchess of Austria.

17. Catherine II (the Great) was empress of Russia from 1762 until her death in 1796, when her son Paul became her successor and ruled until 1801.

18. Franciszek Kareu (1731–1802), vicar-general of the Society of Jesus in Russia.

19. Tsar Alexander I ruled Russia from 1801 to 1825. Tadeusz Brzozowski (1749–1820) was the nineteenth vicar-general of the Jesuit order.

the Roman Catholic faith. With their proselytizing activity they made inroads into prominent families in such a bold way that the emperor, however much he favored them, in January 1816 decreed the closing of their college at St. Petersburg and their banishment from this capital city as well as from Moscow. For them this was a very severe blow, and papal intercession was of no avail. Since they sought to gain revenge by subversive, conspiratorial activities, in March 1820 they were banished from all the domains of the Russian monarchy and banned from it for all time. These measures were motivated by their political duplicity, their proselytizing activity, their disruptive meddling in the family life of prominent households, and their crass way of taking advantage of the weakness of the female sex.

All the activities of the Jesuits have only one motive, their own advantage, and no other purpose than the endless expansion of their power. They are incomparably clever at putting a favorable light on the most reprehensible deeds by appealing to one or another rule of their society, and their conscience is just as elastic as it is malleable and supple.

The Generals of the Jesuit Order since Its Reinstatement

After the universal reinstatement of the order, the general of the order in Russia became the general of the order everywhere. But Brzozowski found himself in an unusual situation. The emperor may have had good reasons for not allowing him to leave Russia, despite how urgently he requested permission to obey the repeated summons of the Holy Father and take up residence in Rome. Up until his death in February 1820 he had to remain in Polotsk, in a situation amounting to captivity. When a new general was supposed to be chosen after his death, for reasons that remain unclear Cardinal-Vicar della Genga sought to prevent, by every means, the coming together of the general congregation that is alone entitled, by the rules of the order, to elect its general. Finally, in October 1820, at the first regular meeting of the chapter, Father Luigi Fortis of Verona, age 72, was chosen as general. He soon had the welcome experience of della Genga, so harshly disposed to them as cardinal, becoming, as Pope Leo XII, an all the greater patron of the order. He handed over to the Jesuits the Collegio Romano (the Jesuits' seminary, in which the Jesuits provide the education not only for all future priests of the Papal States but also for all the pupils of the different national colleges in turn established by the Jesuits), as well as several other institutions the Jesuits had previously sought in vain to have restored to them. After Fortis died in 1829, the new leader chosen was Father Johannes Roothaan, born in Amsterdam in 1785, who held this office until 1853. People praised him, saying that the order had not had such a prominent leader since Aquaviva,[20] one equipped to such a high degree with all the spiritual gifts requisite for his position. He was in fact the regent of the Papal States.

The Jesuits in Italy, Spain, and Portugal

As for the lands in which the Jesuits for the most part became established after the universal reinstatement of their order, they got their best reception in Naples. King Ferdinand I[21] had already been completely favorable toward them before their reinstatement. In June 1815, as soon as he had returned to Naples, he summoned the Jesuits from Sicily, restored to them the old college with all its estates, and placed the education of the people wholly in the Jesuits' hands. New favors were extended to them under the two following regimes, those of Franz I and Ferdinand II. They had an even more illustrious position in Sardinia, where King Victor Emmanuel I, who from longstanding unhappiness was full of bitter hatred toward all things new, was so very enthusiastic about the institutions of the good old days that, after his return [to Sardinia], he spared no time in recalling the followers of St. Ignatius, as the strongest pillars of the throne and the altar in his state. Already in 1815 the Jesuits opened their college in Turin, linking it with a novitiate in Genoa. The University of Genoa had to restore to the Jesuits the landed property appropriated from them by the government of the republic that had existed in 1773 when the Society of Jesus was dissolved. Of course the residents of Genoa were very much against this. Under Victor Emmanuel and his successor, Charles Felix, their reach continually expanded. Not only did they have the most important influence on the entire government, which they tempted to pass the most arbitrary measures; they also took under their control the entire educational establishment. A royal decree in 1822 combined the *riforma*, the highest educational authority over the whole educational establishment, with the Universities of Turin and Genoa, and the Jesuit order was in fact designated as the supreme educational authority for the Sardinian state.[22] The Jesuits enjoyed comparable favor in the Duchy of Modena, where at the same time they took over leadership of all

---

20. Claudius Aquaviva (1543–1615) of Naples was the fifth general of the order and laid the foundations for its educational system.

21. King of the Two Sicilies. Prior to 1816, he had been Ferdinand IV of the Kingdom of Naples and Ferdinand III of the Kingdom of Sicily. The joint kingdom included all of southern Italy and Sicily.

22. At this time the Piedmont region, including Genoa and Turin, was part of the Kingdom of Sardinia.

educational affairs and exercised such unlimited censorship that they were allowed to remove and burn all literary works in private libraries that they found offensive. In contrast, they did not succeed in establishing themselves in the same fashion in Parma and Tuscany, or in the Duchy of Lucca.

Beyond the boundaries of Italy, the reinstatement of the Jesuits was nowhere welcomed with greater pleasure than in Spain. King Ferdinand II declared the accusations people made against them to be fabrications devised by the enemies not just of this order but of the Christian religion, a religion that is still the first bastion of monarchy. Disregarding the objections of the Council of Castile, the king decreed the reinstatement of the Society of Jesus in all of Spain, and the restoration to it of estates not already sold. At that time Spain was so submissive that twenty-five of the foremost cities sent most urgent requests to the king to pardon the admirable sons of St. Ignatius. There was rejoicing when people were assured that the holy fathers would soon arrive. The Jesuits became the heart of a notorious cabal, which quickly made Ferdinand's government so detested that in 1820 a new revolution was the result. The reestablished Cortes abolished the Jesuit order and decreed the appropriation of its holdings by the state. As soon as French intervention enabled Ferdinand to regain his former power, the Jesuits were once again favored by him. In Spain too they got control of almost all public education.

Things were different in Portugal. The prince regent of Portugal and Brazil, John VI,[23] had indeed registered a most energetic protest against the reinstatement of the order, emphatically declaring that the Jesuits were never to be allowed in his territories, nor would he ever be involved in any transactions with the Holy See in Rome. Throughout the entire rule of King John VI, until he died in 1826, the Jesuits could not set foot in Portugal. However, Dom Miguel[24] believed "in promoting the well-being of his beloved subjects" and also not failing to include the Jesuits. Except that his decree contained the stipulation, objectionable to the Jesuits, that neither should their former estates and privileges be restored to them, nor should they be entitled to restitution for them. (Thus fate willed it that the descendent of the Marquis de Pombal[25]—the very man who drove the Jesuit

---

23. In 1807 the French army entered Portugal, and John, then the prince regent, fled with his family and government officials, to the colony of Brazil, which then became John's kingdom in 1815. In 1821, after revolution in Portugal, John returned to become king of Portugal (until 1826), and in 1822 his son Dom Pedro became king of Brazil, now declaring its independence from Portugal.

24. Miguel Maria Evaristo de Bragança (1802–66) was King Miguel I of Portugal, 1828–34.

25. Sebastião José de Carvalho e Mello, Marquês de Pombal (1699–1782), as prime

order out of Portugal and was the major contributor to its suspension—his granddaughter, the Countess of Oliveira, was the warmest admirer and most decided patron of the pious fathers.) Nevertheless in December 1830 they first got back their old establishment in Lisbon, and at the beginning of 1832 they recovered their old established, famous college in Coimbra. They had hardly begun to enjoy the use of these new acquisitions when all this ended when the rule of Don Miguel ended.

The Jesuits in Austria, Bavaria, and Elsewhere in Germany

In the states of the Austrian monarchy the Jesuits were permitted to appear under their true name only in Galicia, where the Dominican monastery at Tarnopol was granted to them for a college, and soon thereafter converted into a secondary school. At the time of the Congress of Vienna they already sought to be permitted in the Austrian states. Yet they were unsuccessful, since Metternich still harbored no special fondness for them. Their supporters therefore took a different path, and the fourth wife of Emperor Francis I of Austria, a Bavarian princess, is said to have had a hand in the affair. The Jesuits were introduced as Liguorians. In 1732, Alfonso Maria, from an old lineage of Neapolitan nobility, the Liguori, founded a new spiritual order with the vocation of following the example of Jesus Christ the savior and redeemer.[26] The order was supposed to work mainly among the lower social classes. However, in its efforts and precepts, in its requirement of unconditional obedience to the will of its leader and of the pope, and in its moral philosophy too, it was the true image of the Jesuit order. The Liguorians, or Redemptorists, were thus able to stand in for the Jesuits. What was disallowed for the one was allowed for the other. By imperial decree in 1820 the first house for the order was allocated to them in Vienna. Notwithstanding the declaration of the court that the Liguorians' calling was exclusively to promote the spiritual welfare of the lower classes, and that they were to confine their activities to the confessional and to the instruction of lower class youths, the appearance of the order caused a great sensation. However, in facing scorn and ridicule, they did not allow themselves to be disconcerted in the pursuit of their goal, and in a short time they knew how to insinuate themselves into the higher social classes. Even Foreign Minister

---

minister of Portugal, banished the Jesuits from the country in 1759.

26. St. Alfonso Maria de Liguori (1696–1787, canonized 1839), a priest from Naples, together with twelve companions, founded the religious order of the Liguorians, or Redemptorists, in 1732.

Metternich ultimately became their enthusiastic patron. He recognized them as being the most useful instrument for carrying out his plan to suppress all nationalistic efforts, especially in Italy, and to base the power of Austria on the antipathy the Italian princes manifested toward all reforms. In showing favor to the order, Metternich imposed conditions on it, limitations the Liguorians happily accepted, knowing full well how easily they could circumvent them. These concerned the acceptance of bequests and donations, the admission of foreigners, of novices, as well as seeking the approval of the state administration in adopting schoolbooks, giving notice of all changes in instructional personnel in their teaching institutions, and following the regulations of the local diocesan bishops in the discharge of all priestly functions.

In Bavaria, the Jesuits requested permission to set up a residence in Munich, in exchange for which they would undertake to work most effectively for the religious rebirth of the Bavarian people. In 1826, King Ludwig's decision in response to their request was that he had no need of them for his Bavaria. Despite all the efforts of the Jesuits, that is how things remained until the bishop of Eichstädt at that time, now the archbishop of Munich, Count von Reisach, who was himself a Jesuit, in 1837 in Rome promised the king[27] to introduce the Jesuits into Bavaria, as it were, under the name of Redemptorists, and to create for them a permanent settlement. However, they did not gain it in Munich as they hoped; instead it was in Altötting, in 1841.

From 1824 onward the Jesuits formed colonies one after another in the Rhine province of the Kingdom of Prussia, in Düsseldorf, Cologne, Coblenz, and in other cities. This happened with the silent assent of King Friedrich Wilhelm III, and yet it was overshadowed by the ban, issued in 1827, on attending foreign Jesuit schools, principally the German College in Rome that was restored by Pius VII and was designated to equip Germany with ecclesiastics who had an authentically Jesuit education.

In Saxony, where Kings Friedrich August and Anton had Jesuits for their father confessors, since 1827 the rumor was that the founding of a formal Jesuit college was already decided on and approved. Only after the uproar in 1830 did the government give assurance that there was never any thought of introducing the Jesuits. The consequence was that, as the estates of the realm demanded, the new constitutional document of 1831 had to include the stipulation that no new monasteries would be permitted, nor would Jesuits or any other ecclesiastical order ever be accepted in the land. In Saxony, people were always very alert to any Jesuitical inroads. When in

---

27. Ludwig I, King of Bavaria 1825–48, was the monarch who first rebuffed the Jesuits and then later allowed them into the state.

1844 the rumor spread that a Catholic church designed for the Jesuits had been built at Annaberg on the border with Bohemia, this caused such an uproar in all of Saxony that the plan for a colony, supposedly introduced via that church, had to be abandoned. Through the deviousness of Jesuitical proselytizing schemes, they brought Duke Friedrich Ferdinand of Anhalt-Köthen to Paris in 1825 to renounce his Protestant faith. The renunciation, at first kept secret, soon thereafter had to be acknowledged publicly. Köthen would have become the seat of a Jesuit mission, and only the duke's death in 1830 prevented the outbreak of the people's mounting bitterness. And yet the Jesuit mission in Köthen only ended in 1848.

The history of the Jesuits in the Netherlands is so closely connected with the history of the Dutch Catholic Church that it cannot be treated separately. So we are simply left with France, where the Jesuits played a more significant role than they did in any other land.

The Jesuits in France

The Jesuits did not first come to France because of the Bourbons; indeed they were already there. Under Napoleon, through the intercession of Cardinal Fesch, who was their patron, in 1800 they gained formal admission to Lyon, from which they spread more widely, going under the name of Fathers of the Faith, and they set up educational establishments at Amiens, Belley, and in other cities. When they gained too much ground, even drawing in pupils of the polytechnic school in Paris, in 1804 Napoleon commanded the closing of all the institutes of the Fathers of the Faith and of all other male congregations. Even so, the command was not strictly enforced. Toward the end of Napoleonic rule, with the protection of their patron they even had several residences in Paris. After the return of the Bourbons the Jesuits made every effort to resume their activities legally. For good reasons Louis XVIII could not consent to it, although, notwithstanding that fact, under his regime they already had all they needed for extending their influence ever more widely in France. In their interest Louis XVIII issued an order in October 1814, by which the so-called "minor seminary" was removed from the oversight it had previously been subject to under the university.[28]

---

28. [*Baur*] There are two kinds of seminaries, a higher seminary for actual theological instruction, and a lower seminary as preparation for it. The latter kind consists of the "minor seminaries," which are secondary schools, paralleling the gymnasiums. In fact they were under the oversight of the bishop, but, like all educational establishments under imperial rule, they were placed under the oversight of the university. The bishops always sought to exempt them from university oversight, and they succeeded in doing so right at the onset of the restoration.

Since the bishops could freely choose the teachers, but most of them of course sided with the Jesuits, the instruction in almost all these seminaries fell into the hands of the Fathers of the Faith. They were none other than Jesuit bodies, with the one at Acheul near Amiens especially standing out as the greatest educational institution of France during the restoration period. Also, the Jesuits' establishment at Montrouge, near Paris, where since 1818 they had their principal novitiate for France, was entirely aimed at attracting the aristocratic world and making connections with the most respected and wealthiest families.

The September 1816 order of Louis XVIII, which allowed the conducting of missionary preaching everywhere to mitigate the shortage of priests, was just as important for the Jesuits. They made the most extensive use of these so-called missions. They were the best means to exert political influence on the people, to set before them the horrors of revolution, the sacrileges committed against religion and its servants, and to stir them up against the Charter of 1814 and all the more liberal institutions and endeavors of recent times. In this way the Jesuits exerted a very great, but also highly deleterious, influence that poisoned family life, especially exercising it on the lower social stratum, an influence they knew best how to make use of in particular through the business dealings linked to their missions. In order to work on the people in as sensuous a way as possible, they linked festive ceremonies with their missions, some being of a quite theatrical sort. For instance, when the mission to a place ended, a gigantic cross decorated with lilies was carried in a procession to a specific site and consecrated with festive ceremonies. Each believer fastened to the cross a metal heart with his or her name inscribed on it. This heart was said to represent symbolically that the church draws to itself the hearts estranged from it, and heathen France becomes, so to speak, converted anew.

The *congrégation*, however, was the principal means by which the Jesuits spread their net over all of France. A distinctive feature of the order was that, alongside the members actually living wholly according to the rules of the order, it also had those who were more loosely connected with it, the seculars or laity who remained wholly in their former circumstances and yet were connected with the order in a way advantageous to both parties. They were the affiliates, the Jesuits in short robes (*à robe courte*). The ever more widespread influence of the order in France since the restoration relied on this system of affiliation, an association with extensive ramifications. After the Count of Artois, who was the king's brother,[29] and

---

29. Charles X (ruled 1824–30), the brother of Louis XVIII, is the king Baur mentions in our text below, who tried to restrict freedom of the press and dissolved the Chamber of Deputies. He was deposed by the July 1830 revolution.

the Duchess of Angoulême both became members of the congregation, it came to be the rallying point for all the enemies of the Charter and the constitutional monarchy, for all the ultra-royalist and Ultramontane[30] efforts to restore absolutism in church and state. Father Ronsin was head of the congregation in France, and it was divided up into multiple branches for the different social classes. There was a congregation of the nobility whose members were princes, dukes, counts, marquises, cardinals, deputies, and prefects. There was a congregation for the upper and middle classes of the bourgeoisie, another for the craftspeople and the military, and several for the social underclasses, the servants, children, thieves, and other criminals. These congregations went by various names. There were societies for the spreading of the faith, for the defense of the Catholic religion, for the sacred mysteries, for the holy sacraments, for the sacred heart of Jesus, for the sacred heart of Mary, for the holy rosary, for the sacred tomb, and so forth. The members pledged themselves to promote, with all the services they could offer, the noble causes of God and the Blessed Virgin, and to make monthly or weekly contributions that would provide major funding at the disposal of the Jesuits.

Organized in this way, the congregation formed a covert government alongside the constitutional government, one that in 1820 was already strong enough to put through the three notorious laws, those against the press and against individual freedom, and the law altering the rules for elections in the Chamber of Deputies. Minister Villèle[31] was appointed from the membership of the congregation, every post in the civil service was occupied by agents or creatures of the congregation, and it oversaw and controlled everything, even in private life. In the very last months of the rule of Louis XVIII, the Chamber of Deputies took up a resolution regarding the reestablishing of ecclesiastical corporations, namely, the reintroduction of the Jesuits. Nevertheless the cause failed at that time owing to opposition in the Chamber of Peers. But there could be no doubt that under the new king, Charles X, who was completely loyal to the Jesuits, the resolution would soon be taken up and enacted. Charles X ascended the throne firmly predisposed to overturn, wherever possible, the religious freedom sanctioned by the Charter. However, general animosity toward the Jesuit order then broke out ever more decidedly.

30. Ultramontanism was the movement seeking to maintain or restore the absolute authority of the papacy over other and distant nations and dioceses; from a term meaning "beyond the mountains," i.e., beyond the Alps.

31. Comte Joseph de Villèle, the minister of finance under Louis XVIII, became president of the Council of Ministers in 1822, and continued as a very influential figure in the government of Charles X.

It was already a serious omen for the Jesuits when the two newspapers that were the major organs of the opposition to the Jesuit order, the *Constitutionel* and the *Courier-Français*, had in 1825 spoken freely about the hope for appeal [of those repressive laws], when the Jesuits had been accused of attempting to topple the throne, and the wildest religious anarchy and contempt for the church and its servants was spreading. In France this information aroused the liveliest interest, and encouraged new attacks on the order. In particular, the report by the Comte de Montlosier[32] in 1826 was very influential. Although genuinely a royalist, he wrote that the essential nature and the impulses of the congregation show very persuasively, and demonstrate from uncontestable facts, the dangers the order poses for religion, society, and the throne. For that reason he presented a petition to the Chamber of Peers, and its spokesperson, Count Portalis the Younger,[33] recognized the necessity of intervention against the unlawful existence of the Jesuits in France, and so proposed and carried out the transmission of the petition to the president of the Council of Ministers. Their most resolute political opponents got involved in this matter of the Jesuits, in order to do battle jointly against this most dangerous enemy of civic and religious freedom in the land. This opposition to the Jesuits became so determined that, mainly because of it, Villèle was toppled from his ministerial post.

Martignac,[34] Villèle's successor, appeared as a resolute opponent of the Jesuits. The main blow they suffered occurred with the 1828 ordinances decreeing that the eight Jesuit colleges masquerading under the heading of "minor seminaries," those at Aix, Bordeaux, and elsewhere, should be eliminated or else placed under the oversight of the university. It was also stated that no one may function any longer as either director or teacher in such a minor seminary without it being assured in writing that this person did not belong to any religious congregation banned in France. The French bishops sought to see the ordinances as being the most flagrant interference with their rights. But they had to comply with them when Pope Leo XII himself declared that the French government was within its rights when it sought to disallow the intrusion of any ecclesiastical corporation expelled by the law

---

32. This aristocrat wrote a pamphlet opposing the Jesuits and the increasing influence of the clergy: *Mémoire à consulter sur un système religieux et politique tendant à renverser la religion, la sociéte et le trône* (Advisory memorandum about a religious and political system aiming at the overthrow of religion, society, and the throne).

33. His father, the elder Portalis, had been Napoleon's spokesperson on religious matters.

34. The Vicomte de Martignac, a lawyer, and minister of the interior, replaced Villèle as prime minister in 1828 and veered away from the previous policy that was favorable to the Jesuits.

of the land. Of course the Jesuits were pleased that Prince Polignac[35] soon became head of the ministry in place of Martignac, and that the cultus and instruction became entrusted to a disciple of the Jesuits, even though the July ordinances of 1830 had, as everyone knows, catastrophic consequences.

The Relations between Protestants and Catholics in France

One of the major points of general interest in the history of the Catholic Church is the mutual relations of Catholics and Protestants in Catholic states. France provides the most important phenomena belonging under this heading, and these phenomena are most closely connected with the matters we have just been discussing.

The return of the Bourbons brought French Protestants the Charter and a liberal constitution. Hence they too had reasons to join in the public jubilation with which the Bourbons were received in France. However, although the Protestants gave little reason to be mistreated, among Catholics in isolated regions in the south of France the old hatred of heretics cropped up right away. This happened most especially in Nîmes and the area surrounding it. Already in 1814 the Catholics made threatening statements about rescinding the Charter and about a new St. Bartholomew's Day massacre.[36] The Protestants were said to be blameworthy for all the harm that had befallen France since 1789. They alone supposedly had contrived the Revolution, the Terror, the military conscription. They alone preached atheism, regicide, and the pillaging of churches. There can be no doubt that the Jesuits had their hands in the game. In 1814, when no one had yet been killed, several thousand Catholics surged through the streets of Nîmes, shouting furiously: "Let us make sausages from Calvin's blood; let us wash our hands in Protestant blood."

In the next year too, after the second Bourbon restoration, there were bloody events and horrid acts of violence. Peaceful citizens were driven from house and home, were shot, stabbed, imprisoned, plundered, and their houses burned. Women were whipped on the public streets, and graves were desecrated. Protestants could not carry on their businesses, and their

---

35. Auguste Jules, Prince de Polignac, appointed as a prince by the pope, became the last Bourbon prime minister in 1829, succeeding Martignac. The July ordinances of 1830 were a strict version of those of 1820, which are described above in the text.

36. On 23 August 1572, the eve of St. Bartholomew's Day, Catholic mob violence was incited in Paris against the Huguenots (French Calvinists). Over several weeks the mob violence spread to other places in France, and thousands of Huguenots were killed.

churches stayed closed for several months. Notwithstanding the Charter, religious gatherings faced the greatest risks; they could only be held in secret. When the Duke of Angoulême came to Nîmes in November, 1815, he deplored the fact that the Protestant churches were still closed, and he directed them to be reopened. Even so, it was not possible, with armed power, to prevent disruption of Protestant worship services. The Protestants were met on the way into church with the cry: "Away with them; they should not have our churches; off with them to the wilderness!" The Catholic mob forced its way into the churches and there were tumultuous scenes. No one seriously intervened against this fanaticism; the authorities were too passive and weak, and when they did take action the blame always fell only on the Protestants, whereas people entirely excused the Catholics. The absolutist reaction sought to conceal and to play down these scenes as much as possible, although rumors of them still reached to places where one could not be silent about this mockery being made of Protestant religious liberty.

In November 1815 two societies held a meeting in London. One consisted of dissenting preachers from all the confessions, and the other consisted of the members of the Protestant Society for the Protection of Religious Freedom. The meeting was to confer about the situation of their Protestant brothers and sisters in France, and about the most expeditious way to improve their lot. The decision was to turn to the government of England and do their utmost to help. Also, the local councilor in London addressed the Prince Regent[37] with an urgent request that he take appropriate measures against the inhuman persecution of Protestants in the south of France. This step at least involved denying that the absolutist reaction was a force for good. After this the same fanaticism also repeatedly threatened to break out as it did in 1820, after the murder of the Duc de Berry,[38] although the government, no longer sure of itself, clandestinely sent to Nîmes an order to maintain the peace. Nevertheless, even in 1830, when the July Ordinances, and the opposition they met with in Paris, became known in Nîmes, Reformed Protestant citizens were injured and one was killed. However, the more well-disposed people of all religious and political parties joined together to maintain public order.

In the meantime the bloody events in Nîmes and its environs nevertheless remained isolated phenomena. Apart from them the absolutists found no favor elsewhere in France, and we must acknowledge that the government left each one to his or her own faith, paid the stipends of the

---

37. The Prince Regent was the son of King George III (who became deranged in 1811). He became King George IV in 1820.

38. Charles Ferdinand, Duc de Berry, the king's nephew and a Bourbon supporter, was assassinated in February 1820 by a Bonapartist fanatic.

Protestant pastors, increased their numbers, increased their revenues, built churches for them, and placed the control of Protestants' ecclesiastical matters in their own hands, something that had not been done even under Napoleon. Privy Councilor Cuvier,[39] the famous natural scientist, became the director of those matters and, as such, he was the head of Protestant teaching institutions via his agent, minister Martignac. Cuvier held the position of director of non-Catholic religion and of Protestant instructional affairs until his death in 1832, whereupon the theological faculties of Strasbourg and Montauban, along with the other Protestant teaching institutions, came once more under Catholic control. It is also deserving of mention that in 1817 the government did not stand in the way of public celebration of the jubilee (300th anniversary celebration) of the Reformation, nor did it interfere with the 1830 jubilee of the Augsburg Confession.

Although Louis XVIII had been approached from several quarters, and in fact by the pope, to restrict religious freedom where it is not to be banned, he was still steadfast in allowing the Protestants to enjoy all civic and political rights, and to protect and sustain their worship, just like he did for the Catholics. The Roman Catholic and apostolic religion was of course exalted as the state religion, but the king himself did not concede that this article, as the main statement, would, on the contrary, have relegated the other article that promised equal freedom and equal protection to all religions, to being merely a subordinate clause in the Charter of 1814. He remarked that it is not proper to treat this rule as an exception [to the main statement], and this remark was definitive regarding the wording of the article from the constitutional documents pertaining to religion. Upon his coronation at Rheims, Charles X too did not decide, like his forbear [Charles IX], to adjure the rooting out of heretics. On the contrary, article ten of the Concordat of 1817,[40] which people attributed mainly to the influence of his faction, was not suited to his winning the hearts of people.

Although one article of the systematic legal plan for reinforcing the concordat certainly set forth the rights of the Protestant Church, people still saw in that article the seed of a second revocation of the Edict of Nantes.

39. Georges Cuvier (1769–1832), a prominent zoologist, was a leading figure in developing the young sciences of comparative anatomy and paleontology. As minister of the interior, he was in charge of the national education system, and was an advocate for the Protestant Church in France.

40. The Concordat of 1817, between the papacy and Louis XVIII, while never in force in France, did include provision for the suppression of heretics. It repealed elements from the Concordat of Bologna (1516) that led to the religious persecution of Protestants and ultimately to the revocation of the Edict of Nantes in 1685. The original edict in 1598 gave religious freedom and civil rights to the Huguenots (French Protestants).

In that article, in order to furnish a new proof of his religious zeal, the king promised to use every means to remove the abuses and obstacles that stood in the way of religious interests and executing the laws of the church. Even though the Concordat of 1817 did not go into effect, still, because of the continuous infringements on the Charter, and because of so much that people could infer about the intentions of the government, these things constantly fed their distrust. The things included: the attempts to place in the hands of the Catholic clergy, along with popular education, the registry of births, marriages, and deaths; the designation of a bishop as the minister of public instruction; the opening of several Jesuit colleges; the education of the Duke of Bordeaux by Jesuits; the introduction of dogma into the Napoleonic Code or civil law, via the law concerning the desecration of sacred sites; the disparaging of Protestants by the missionary preaching of the Jesuits, and by the pastoral letters of bishops in royalist newspapers, with the permission of the censor; the permanent distinction between the state religion and authorized religion; the favoritism shown to the Catholics' means of proselytizing and the impediments to switching over from the Catholic Church to the Protestant Church; the reinstatement of the Feast of Corpus Christi procession, and the demand that the Protestants decorate their houses for the celebration; the unrelenting attempts to have the article of the penal code that prohibits gatherings of more than twenty persons, apply arbitrarily to the worship services of the dissidents.

In 1818 the requirement the Catholics imposed on Protestants with reference to the Feast of Corpus Christi came before the courts. Odilon Barrot, who litigated the matter for the Protestant complainants, said it was significant as an issue for the state, and its resolution was in the utmost interest not only of all Protestants, but of every citizen. He showed that in France the state could have no religion of its own and must remain neutral with respect to the different religions practiced; that the decoration of houses at the Feast of Corpus Christi is a religious act no Protestant, in fact no one, can be obliged to perform except by moral compulsion, so conviction in this case would be contrary to the constitution. The high court accepted his position unconditionally. The Jesuits mounted the main attack on freedom of conscience via the law put forward in 1825 by their patron, the Count of Peyronnet, who was the minister of justice. This law concerning the desecration of sacred sites and sacrilege was adopted in both Chambers despite such men as Count Molè, de Salvandy, and the Duke of Broglie, who had declared it to be an unconstitutional infringement on religious freedom. As the Duke of Broglie remarked in his speech in the Chamber of Peers, the law could only have as its purpose the solemn proclamation of the principal dogma of the state religion.

The majority of people worship the deity concealed in the host, and they wish to guard this conviction by penal law. But should legislation be allowed to invent crimes by infringing on conscience? There is a huge difference in that whoever desecrates the holy tabernacle or the host is, for a first degree offense, sentenced to death, for a second degree offense sentenced to the punishment for patricide, whereas in other cases—desecration of other objects used in the cultus, or creating a public disturbance—there are only the usual punishments. This distinction has its basis solely in the sacred character of the object that is profaned. But on what does this sacred character rest? It rests on belief. The belief alone makes it a crime. Without this belief the distinction between the different kinds of objects employed in the cultus vanishes. Since this belief cannot be forced upon the citizens, and many may be assumed not to hold it, how can one make it the basis of a criminal law? Barrot's address to the court quite correctly pointed out the consequences that this law involved for the Protestants. At present one may wish to embrace only the Catholic religion, but when one has once erected the scaffold, what then awaits the one who not only does not believe Catholic dogma, but openly teaches that it is idolatrous? According to the Charter, the civil law stays neutral toward the different creeds. The slightest privilege given to one confession leads irresistibly to intolerance and to the ecclesiastical authority holding sway over the secular authority. Whereas this law meant little in practice, since the government itself did not know what steps it should take with it, it was noteworthy for showing the influence that Jesuit principles exerted at that time, even on both chambers of the legislature.

On the topic of individual Catholic countries and the import of noteworthy changes in them for the history of the Catholic Church, we have nothing further to add with respect to France. So we come then to look at Belgium, a country we have not yet spoken about.

The Catholic Church in Belgium

The new system of government in the newly-created Kingdom of the Netherlands, as a result of the Congress of Vienna, established as a principle the unrestricted freedom of religious groups and the completely equal standing of all citizens of the state, without distinction as to religion. The Belgian bishops objected resoundingly to this principle. In 1815 they publicly expressed their view by repudiating the new system of state government because freedom of religious belief and giving equal rights to different religious confessions would only benefit the heretics that every true Catholic must condemn. Hence they even refused to swear allegiance to the new constitution that is "suppressing and demeaning the Catholic religion." They were unwilling to grant absolution to those responsible for it, and gave their blessing in advance to rebellion against it. The bishop of Ghent, Maurice de Broglie, was the leader of these rebellious prelates. He even declared that prayer for a Protestant prince is a sin. He was wholly influenced by the Jesuits. Provoked by this, the king commanded the Jesuits to close their novitiate in Distelberg and to remove themselves promptly from the country. Since Bishop Broglie was a defender of the Jesuits and proceeded to advocate for them against the government's statute, and to arouse the people, he was supposed to be taken in for judicial investigation, but he escaped it by fleeing to France.

Given the state of affairs, a Protestant government such as that of William I[41] could not be very well-disposed toward the Catholic clergy and the Jesuits. However, what still especially incensed them was not merely the religious confessions having equal rights, but the provision in the constitutional document that leadership and oversight of public instruction was entrusted to the king, as being a principal concern of the state government. This was entirely calculated to free the nation from the hands of centuries-long priestly control, and to enhance public instruction through cultivation of the intellect. Thus the bishops and the Jesuits saw themselves all the more called upon to oppose the government in the most persistent way. Still they would not have achieved their goal so easily had the government not aroused political opposition to itself by suspending trial by jury, restricting freedom of the press, and other missteps. The king had ordered the closing of the numerous boarding schools and private schools not compliant with existing laws, ones set up by clerics and mainly led by Jesuits. As opposed to them, a Philosophical College was to be set up in Louvain, one in which each person who wished to enroll in an episcopal seminary had to have completed a philosophical course of study. However, the archbishop of Malines declined to assume oversight of this Philosophical College, and the bishops did not want to accept into their seminary any student from this college.

Since the ecclesiastics of course saw that, if they claimed for themselves, as a priestly right, the leadership in public instruction, they could not successfully contest the government's exercising exclusive control of this supervision, owing to their having demanded a comparable monopoly for themselves. Thus unqualified freedom of instruction became the point at which Ultramontanists and liberals formed what was inherently a highly

---

41. Willem Frederik (1772–1843), king of the Netherlands 1815–40, ruled over a country combining the Dutch in the north and the reluctant Belgians (Flemish) in the south. A strong supporter of the Dutch Reformed Church, he was disliked and opposed by the Belgian Catholics.

unnatural alliance. The liberals based their position entirely on the government having taken away the right to direct and supervise instruction, and the Ultramontanists looked upon victory for the liberal opposition with the confident expectation that, if instruction were only to be at once unconditionally free, it would not become difficult for them to bring the great majority of people into their hands. The 1830 revolution separating Belgium from Holland was principally the work of this coalition of liberals and Ultramontanists that had materialized. The Ultramontanists now attained that for which they had striven. The complete separation of the church from the state, enunciated by the constitution, gave the clergy unhampered license to make the greatest inroads. The Belgian schools, high schools, and universities, and thus the education and training of the younger generation, were removed from the government's influence, and this played into the hands of the priests and monks, while the concomitant right removed all limitations on the construction of cloisters and cooperatives. Hence the number of such institutions in Belgium has since grown out of all proportion.

The Catholic Church in Italy, Spain, and Portugal

We come now to the traditional Catholic countries of Italy, Spain, and Portugal. The circumstances of the church in Naples were determined by the aforementioned concordat. Apart from the concordat, Sardinia reverted to conditions prior to 1799; the old laws were in force once again, and the pope exercised his previous rights. Insofar as they were still the property of the state, the estates confiscated by the French government were returned to the church, although the pope allowed the state to utilize part of them. Here too people reverted to their old ways, in that the Waldensian communities[42] had once again to suffer under the oppression of the hierarchical regime. Piedmont had previously belonged to France and had complete religious freedom. Like the Catholics, the [Waldensian] ecclesiastics were paid a stipend by the state. This stipend was taken from them once again, and they only got it back after England and Prussia had made representations to the court at Turin on account of how the Waldensians were treated. As a result their situation markedly improved.

My previous remarks have shed light on how in Spain, where such a huge breach in the hierarchical-political system had come about owing to Napoleonic rule, efforts were made to bring everything back to the way it

42. The Waldensian movement began in France in the twelfth century. It rejected some Catholic doctrines, and its members were persecuted in medieval and Reformation times, and in the latter period tended toward a more Protestant-like form of Christianity.

was, by reinstating the Inquisition and the Jesuits. From their hostility to the French, people agitated against every reform arising from the prior period and reminding them of it. The cloisters and orders were reestablished, and everything was then suddenly supposed to once again be just about as it had been under Philipp II.[43] Monks and ecclesiastics worked toward that goal, in particular also through the so-called "missions," just as they did in the instruction of youth. People paid homage to the pope, especially through the reestablishment of the Rota,[44] the papal nuncio's tribunal for decisions not directly adjudicated by the pope himself. The 1820 revolution and reestablishment of the constitutional Cortes also resulted in ecclesiastical reform. It was wholly in the interest of the Cortes that limits be set to the overly powerful clergy. In 1820 the ecclesiastical estates were nationalized, as a result of which all cloisters were abolished except for fourteen of them being put at the disposal of the king. In 1822 there ensued a reorganization of the ecclesiastics, in particular reducing by half the number of cathedral officials. This followed in the wake of the short-lived French intervention, and the reaction now beginning was a reestablishing of the former system. Yet a stop was put to the Inquisition. The struggle between the two factions, the papal party and the liberals, first took a new direction after the death of King Ferdinand VII.[45]

What we previously observed regarding the Jesuits explains why Portugal did not march in lockstep with Spain when it came to restoration of the hierarchy. A consequence of the Spanish revolution involved the convoking of the Cortes in Portugal too, and the adoption of the Spanish constitution, albeit with numerous significant modifications. Issues raised in the assembled Cortes included the abolition of cloisters, the capping of festival days or holidays at seven religious ones and six national ones, and the cessation of the patriarchate of Lisbon, since the patriarch was unwilling to go along with the new political system and stirred up the priests against the secular authority. There had been a patriarchate in Lisbon since 1717; the ambitious and splendor-loving King John V[46] had influenced Pope Clement XI to establish it. To magnify his splendor, the patriarch had been made both a papal legate with the highest authority and a cardinal. The cessation of the patriarchate was a show of force against the clergy, which was very

---

43. Philipp II (1527–98) was king of Spain from 1556 to 1598, when the Inquisition was still going strong.

44. The Rota is a tribunal of the Curia, the group via which the church is governed by the pope. The Rota has jurisdiction over matters appealed to it from the dioceses.

45. Ferdinand VII (1788–1833), the exiled heir apparent, became king in 1813. Waves of repression and revolution marked his rule, which lasted until 1833.

46. John V, "the Magnanimous," reigned as king of Portugal from 1706 to 1750.

much in danger of suffering a major loss of its wealth and privileges. Yet before meaningful measures could be carried out, Dom Miguel[47] usurped the throne. After he had broken his oath to Dom Pedro's new constitution, he favored the priestly faction and persecuted the liberals most ferociously.

The Catholics of Ireland

Catholic Ireland deserves mention on its own. In no land with a population consisting of Catholics and Protestants has there been more severe oppression of Catholics than in Ireland, where they are by far in the majority. Because of the Protestant conquest of the land the Catholic clergy lost its power and wealth. The one thing left to it, something it knew full well how to use, was its respect among the great majority of the people. With an awareness of the privileged status it lost owing to its suppression, and of its numerical superiority, Irish Catholicism always appeared openly opposed to its non-Catholic adversaries. It constantly endeavored to emancipate itself from Protestantism. One step in this direction was the abolition of the Test Act of 1673.[48] This act obligated anyone holding an office to affirm upon oath that he was not a Catholic, and in fact repudiated the doctrine of transubstantiation and the adoration of the saints. This act completely barred Catholics from taking a seat in Parliament and from appointment to national and local offices. On 2 May 1828 the House of Commons rescinded this act, as well as the Corporation Act that paralleled it. What then appeared in its place was the sworn declaration by each officeholder that he would never use the resources afforded by his office in a way detrimental to the state church or, in the exercise of his legal rights and privileges, to cause difficulties for it. In April 1829 it became legally enacted that the same civil rights were extended to members of the Roman Catholic religion along with extending them to the remaining Christian religious denominations.

We now still have to take a look at the circumstances of the German Catholic Church as it took shape in consequence of the concordat.

---

47. See n. 24. Pedro I, successor to King John V in 1826, subsequently resigned the throne. Miguel, brother of Pedro and regent for John's daughter Maria, got the Cortes to proclaim him king in 1828, and he ruled until 1834.

48. The Test Act, passed by the British Parliament in 1673, required all office holders to belong to the Church of England.

The Catholic Church in Bavaria

The point at issue was the various concordats concluded with the pope. Here in Germany there had just been concordats, so it would necessarily have been in the Germans' interest to make the structure of the German Catholic Church in relation to the papacy a matter of common concern. However, each individual state was left to make its own arrangements with the pope, as best it could. The motion put before the Congress of Vienna by Baron von Wessenberg, the vicar general of the Diocese of Constance, to establish a German national church under one primate, failed to be approved; also, the Congress did not enact the article that proposed to add Austria and Prussia to the German Confederation Act (1819), and which would have promised the Catholic Church a constitution that, as guaranteed by the Confederation, was supposed to secure the church's rights and the necessary means to defray its expenses. Since Bavaria was opposed to the motion, nothing to that effect was included in the Confederation Act; thus no common ground was found and the national church idea was abandoned.

Bavaria was then the first to negotiate with the pope on its own. The Concordat of 1817 divided the entire Catholic population of Bavaria into eight dioceses, headed by two archbishops and six bishops. The bishops of Augsburg, Regensburg, and Passau were under the archbishopric of Munich and Freising; the bishops of Würzburg, Eichstadt, and Speier were under the archbishopric of Bamberg. The ecclesiastical positions were richly endowed. One of the most notable articles of the concordat is the fifth one, which makes the leadership of episcopal seminaries and the appointment of their teachers the province of the bishop, without any involvement on the part of the state. According to article twelve, the king is bound, in light of these prerogatives, and to show that he is obliging to the Holy See, to make known what the churches and schools of the cloisters have possessed and what they can still have in the future, and to ensure that a few cloisters shall be reestablished with the necessary financial backing for both monks and nuns providing religious instruction and teaching the sciences, and then also for assistance to pastors. The concordat additionally specified that the church's possessions are forever indivisible and secure, that the king shall appoint the archbishops and bishops with the pope then installing them in office, and with jurisdiction over them residing in Rome. Article thirteen gave certain censorship rights to the archbishops and bishops. Printed materials offensive to them because these materials make statements contrary to sound morality, to the faith and discipline of the church, were said to be prohibited. According to the constitution, no decrees and statutes may be promulgated and enforced by church authorities without prior consultation with the king and with his assent. In contradiction with this, the concordat states that the archbishops and bishops can communicate with ecclesiastics and with their diocesan officials regarding their pastorates, and can freely announce their instructions and what they ordain in ecclesiastical matters. Communications of the bishops, ecclesiastics, and people with the Holy See in spiritual matters and church affairs shall accordingly be completely free.

It is clear from these stipulations how much the concordat conceded to the pope. Nevertheless, in Bavaria there were serious efforts to secure Protestant parity with the Catholics.[49] Alongside the two archbishops and one bishop in the upper house of Parliament,[50] another member was the president of the Protestant [i.e., Lutheran] church council. The elected representatives in the lower house included twelve representatives from Bavaria's Catholic ecclesiastics and six Protestant ecclesiastics. The government of Maximilian Joseph, under which Minister Montgelas[51] in particular sought to lead Bavaria by major reforms taking a progressive direction, and to make Bavaria an independent state, was by and large a very liberal government. It abolished nearly two hundred cloisters. Under the government of King Ludwig, who made Munich a "second Rome" for the arts,[52] Ultramontane aspirations could also very easily gain a foothold, and people thought nothing of shifting now to one side, now to the other. Yet in 1829 the Bavarian government decreed that indeed in keeping with the Peace of Westphalia,[53] and even more so with the principles of the Bavarian constitutional document, with the Religious Edict as part of it, the Protestant co-religionists are not to be regarded as *haeretici*, as heretics, and consequently also are not to be excluded from being godparents along with Catholics. However, in 1830 it was decreed that because baptism is a religious act, and the godparents assume the responsibility, when necessary, of taking the parents' place in seeing that the children receive religious education according to the tenets

---

49. The Bavarian Religious Edict of 1818 gave civil rights to Protestants, equivalent to those of Catholics.

50. According to the 1818 constitution, the upper house of Parliament consisted of government officials, large landowners, and the king's appointees. The lower house consisted of elected representatives of small landowners, peasants, and towns.

51. Maximilian Joseph, or Maximilian I (1756–1825), was Bavaria's first king (1806–25). Count Maximilian von Montgelas (1759–1838), foreign minister and exponent of French radical thought, set civil power above ecclesiastical power and brought Protestant scholars (Schelling, Hegel, et al.) to Bavaria.

52. Ludwig I (1786–1868) was king of Bavaria, 1825–48. Initially a liberal, he later gravitated toward a reactionary position. He collected the priceless art works that made Munich museums the center of the arts in Germany.

53. The Peace of Westphalia (1648) ended the Thirty Years War (1618–48) and protected the religious rights of Lutherans and Calvinists.

of the Catholic Church, Protestants could only be allowed to be baptismal godparents if a Catholic at the same time assumed the position of an actual godparent, with its attendant religious obligation. What happened with this relationship later on under King Ludwig's government belongs to the history of the next period.

The Catholic Church in Prussia

The July 1821 bull [from Pius VII], *De salute animarum*, divided the Catholic populace of the Prussian state into eight dioceses. Heading these dioceses were two archbishops, a prince bishop, and five bishops. The archbishop of Cologne is over the suffragans or diocesan bishoprics of Trier, Münster, and Paderborn. The archbishoprics of Posen und Gnesen are combined forever as one administrative unit. The bishop of Kulm is the suffragan under the archbishop. Directly under the papal see is the prince bishop of Breslau. Also, the bishopric of Ermeland is directly subordinate to the pope alone. Each archbishop and bishop has a suffragan alongside him. The cathedral chapters of Cologne, Trier, Münster, Paderborn, and Breslau have the right to choose their own archbishop or bishop, of course doing so from the collective ecclesiastics of the Prussian state. For the churches of Gnesen and Posen, or Ermeland and Kulm, the king retains his previous right to participate in the selection. Some honorary and prebendary positions are filled by the pope, some by the archbishop or bishop, provided that the reigning sovereign assents to the appointment. Filling the positions of provost and canon that become vacant during the six papal months is the prerogative of the pope, and the bishops shall appoint the chapter heads and canons for vacancies during the other months.[54]

What in the concordat seems to be conceding too much to the pope and the bishops, with these provisions, was supposed to be in turn compensated for by private covenants and instructions. The pope obliged himself to fill the positions reserved to him in accord with the government's wishes, and directed the chapters, in cases where they have to make the choice, to choose a bishop agreeable to the king. But since this was only specified by several articles, it was also a quite precarious arrangement. Catholic theological faculties at Bonn and Breslau, and an academy at Münster with a

---

54. According to the Concordat of Vienna (1448) between the papacy and the various governments of the Holy Roman Empire, the pope had the right of "collation" ("bestowal") if a bishop died in an even-numbered month, and the local authorities had this right if he died in an odd-numbered month.

theological faculty and a philosophical faculty, exist to educate Catholic ecclesiastics.

Similar to how it is in Prussia, matters involving Catholic ecclesiastics in Hanover came into line with the bull of March 1824. The Catholic populace of Hanover was under the two bishoprics of Hildesheim and Osnabrück. Since Osnabrück was in the process of endowing a bishop and lacked a chapter, it was supposed to be under the oversight of a vicar general whom the pope had to appoint as *episcopus in partibus* (in the role of bishop) so that he could carry out the episcopal functions. The chapter holds the election of the bishop; the naming of canons alternates between the bishop and the chapter; and the government has the right to strike off the ballot those candidates who are *personas minus gratas*, less acceptable.

The Ecclesiastical Provinces of the Upper Rhine

After first Bavaria, and then Prussia and Hanover, each made their own arrangements, the smaller states—with Württemberg, Baden, the Electorate of Hesse, and the Grand Duchy of Hesse among the leaders—did not give up on the plan to enter together into negotiations with the pope. In 1818 a commission met in Frankfurt in order to establish the principles for finalizing a joint concordat with the pope. They set out from a more radical standpoint and adhered completely to the liberal principles of the more recent Catholic canon law. But when a deputation went to Rome to negotiate with the pope on this basis, it encountered very great obstacles. After those sent had been kept waiting for a long time, they finally received a detailed presentation of the views of His Holiness concerning the 10 August 1819 Declaration of the United Protestant Princes, with forty-four of its points indicated as proposals made to him that he could not consent to. Both sides were still too far apart in their principles and demands for them to be able to reach an agreement. Hence they contented themselves with setting the boundaries of the bishoprics and prescribing the incomes of the bishops and the chapters.

The bull *Provida solersque* of August 1821, based on the consent given at that time by the sovereign princes, organized the Catholic Church's affairs in each of these lands by establishing an archbishopric and four bishoprics to serve Württemberg, Baden, the Grand Duchy of Hesse and the Electorate of Hesse, Nassau, Frankfurt, Mecklenburg, the Saxon Duchies, Oldenburg, Waldeck, Lübeck, and Bremen. Under the archbishoprics of Freiburg there were [the bishoprics of] Mainz, Fulda, Rottenburg, and Limburg. Further specifications were added in the bull *Ad dominici gregis custodiam* of April

1827. What then followed in the individual states was ratification by the sovereigns of these lands and the filling of the bishoprics. Early in 1830 the affected governments, in unison, decided on and added thirty-nine paragraphs that completed the groundwork on which rests the position of the Catholic Church in these lands vis-à-vis the Protestant Church and the government. However, only six of the states assented to those papal specifications, and they now formed the Ecclesiastical Province of the Upper Rhine—namely, Württemberg, Baden, the two states of Hesse, Nassau, and Frankfurt.

The second bull specified how the bishops and canons were to be chosen. When the seat of an archbishop or a bishop becomes vacant, the chapter of the cathedral church in question, within one month's time, makes known to the appropriate prince of that land the names of those candidates belonging to the clergy of the diocese who, in accord with canonical regulations, are deemed worthy of episcopal office. If one of these candidates is not acceptable to the prince of the land, the chapter shall strike his name from the list, while this still leaves a sufficient number of candidates. Then the chapter will proceed to the canonical election of the bishop or archbishop, and within a month's time the pope will be apprised of the choice. If that person meets the canonical requirements, the pope confirms the choice; if not, the pope allows the chapter to make another choice. When the position of canon is vacant, the bishop, or alternatively the chapter, within six weeks' time, presents the sovereign of the land with the names of four candidates, at which time the prince is entitled to cross off the list the less favored candidate(s).

The thirty-nine paragraphs show that the provincial governments are very conscious of their own national laws and are guarding against possible encroachments on them. Paragraph five, taken from Austrian canon law, contains the stipulation that, before they are published and put in force, all bulls, papal briefs, and other announcements from Rome must receive the approval of the reigning sovereigns; and even in the case of acceptable bulls, their binding force and validity last only so long as nothing differing from them is introduced in the state via new ordinances. Approval of the state is necessary not only for all newly-published papal bulls and constitutions but also for all earlier papal regulations, as soon as they become applicable. The provincial sovereigns' approval of both these bulls includes the explicit safeguard that in no way can one derive or infer from them something that could have been prejudicial to royal prerogatives or impaired them, or would be contrary to the law of the land and the government's ordinances, to the rights of archbishops and bishops, or to the rights of the Protestant Church and confessional groups. The guaranteeing of the rights of archbishops and bishops can be of significance only over against the papacy. From this safeguard, as well as also from several stipulations of the thirty-nine paragraphs, what clearly comes across is the intention to maintain the autonomy and independence of the Catholic provincial churches over against Rome.

Hence in a June 1830 document to the bishops of the Ecclesiastical Provinces of the Upper Rhine, Pope Pius VIII made known quite clearly his dissatisfaction with the thirty-nine paragraphs. In his papal brief he spoke of a scandal of innovation. For all that, the new provisions regarding Catholic ecclesiastics of the aforesaid states were willingly adopted, except that in Electoral Hesse they encountered opposition from the clerics of Fulda. Catholic ecclesiastics in Württemberg and Baden had already made provision in advance for the university education of Catholic ecclesiastics—in Baden through the entirely Catholic University of Freiburg, in Württemberg through a Catholic faculty that had distinguished itself very much by its scientific orientation since its 1817 merger with the provincial university (it had previously been in Ellwangen). Hesse-Darmstadt set up a Catholic theological faculty in Giessen in 1830, and Electoral Hesse did so in Marburg, in collaboration with Nassau, although it was in turn disbanded upon the protest of the bishop of Fulda, who wanted Catholic ecclesiastics to be educated exclusively in the episcopal seminary in Fulda.

It is worth noting here, with regard to the filling of ecclesiastical positions, how the Roman Curia behaved in opposing Baron Ignaz Heinrich von Wessenberg.[55] Dalberg wanted his vicar general, Wessenberg, to become his successor as bishop of Constance. The cathedral chapter and the grand duke of Baden concurred with this wish. However, after Dalberg's death, when the cathedral chapter designated Wessenberg to become the administrator of the bishopric, the Holy See refused to confirm him, supposedly for the most serious reasons (*ob gravissimas causas*). What these reasons were soon became apparent. Wessenberg was suspected of heterodox teachings. Rome detested his reforming tendencies that were manifest in the introduction of German hymns, in the structure of pastoral conferences, in a freer version of church teaching, church rites, and church governance—despite the fact that not one specific heresy could be proven. Wessenberg decided to respond to Rome in person. In July 1817 he went there himself. Although Cardinal Consalvi assured the Holy Father that this step on Wessenberg's part showed that his heart was in the right place, the outcome was none other than Rome persisting in its refusal.

55. Bishop Wessenberg (1774–1860) was a liberal reformer who, after the pope refused to accept his appointment as bishop of Constance, nevertheless still served (with the Baden government's approval) as administrator of the Diocese of Constance, in disobedience to the pope, until 1827. On Dalberg, see p. 18, n. 4.

Switzerland

In 1814, in Switzerland, this papal aversion to the person of Wessenberg led to the bishopric of Constance being cut off [from the Swiss cantons], since the papal faction was prompted to set up a Swiss national bishopric. The end of lengthy negotiations in 1828 saw the establishment of several smaller bishoprics that, in parallel fashion, were supposed to report solely to Rome. The papal nuncio at Lucerne seized the opportunity to exert full control over cloisters and bishops. Catholic Switzerland became divided into six dioceses, as follows: 1) the diocese of Basel, with its seat at Solothurn, to which belong Catholics of the cantons of Bern, Basel, Solothurn, Aargau, Lucerne, and Zug; 2) the diocese of Lausanne and Geneva, with its seat at Fribourg, and consisting of the Catholics of Fribourg, Vaud, Neuchatel, Geneva, and a few from Bern; 3) the diocese of Chur-St. Gallen, with its seat at Chur and consisting of the Catholics of Graubündten, St. Gallen, Schwyz, Uri, Unterwalden, Glarus, Schaffhausen, Appenzell, Thurgau, and Zürich; 4) the diocese of Sitten, with the Catholics of Valais; 5) the diocese of Como and 6) the archdiocese of Milan, the two to which the Catholics of Ticino belong. When the most prominent cantons reformed their political conditions in 1830, the new political movement also became a religious-ecclesiastical movement, and the liberal factions had not only the aristocrats for their opponents, but also the Ultramontanists.

The Trends of the Times: Advocates and Struggles

As we see from the foregoing, the general tendency at this time was in part directly toward restoration, toward the creation of ecclesiastical conditions that, as much as possible, were once again as they were before the revolution, and in part structuring the circumstances resulting from the political changes in a way at least appearing to be in the interest of the Holy See. Ever since the papacy had extricated itself once more from its profound humiliation and once again enhanced its position in the public mind—owing very much especially to the worthy stance exhibited by such a sorely tested pope as Pius VII, against the all-powerful sovereign in his unhappy time—Catholicism attained a new self-consciousness. It again became the faith of the people wielding power. People clung to the old institutions with renewed interest and once more acknowledged that Catholicism has the focal point of its unity solely in the papacy. In the scholarly domain too a decidedly Catholic outlook replaced the liberalism of the previous era, basing itself on the consistency of the Catholic principle; and the predominant tenor of

Catholic church writers increasingly came to express itself in the spirit of Ultramontanism.

Now people once again ventured to maintain that what alone makes for blessedness is the dogma of the Catholic Church in its full rigor, and to oppose the Protestants. One example of this sort was the book by Bishop Thomas Ziegler, *Das katholische Glaubensprincip* (Vienna, 1823), which declared it most necessary to state this truth specifically and firmly in our day, so that the terrible and poisonous monstrosity may not spread ever more widely, the indifferentism to which it would also assign Protestantism. Such outspoken contentions, repeated very energetically at that time, placed a Catholic at odds with his own church. F. W. Carové,[56] in his book, *Die allein seligmachende Kirche* (Frankfurt am Main, 1826), determined to portray that particular dogma inherently, and in its specific relation to the main dogmas of the faith setting the Roman Church apart from the remaining Christian confessions, as groundless and untenable, in order by his comprehensive elucidation of it to justify the Reformation according to its principle and its ongoing tendency. If the Catholic Church alone makes one blessed, then only as the Roman Church was it said to be all there is that makes for blessedness. Whereas the liberal theologians of the immediately preceding period had subordinated the pope to the church, so that the pope's authority blends into the authority of the church, now in contrast, the emphasis once again rests on the pope standing with absolute independence at the head of the church. Instead of saying, as people did formerly, that the pope is nothing apart from the church, now they said that the church is nothing apart from the pope. What therefore ought to follow as a direct consequence of the idea of the church is that the church also must have a pope. Without revelation, no religion; without the church, revelation has no specific meaning; without the pope, no church. Revelation with church and pope is the Catholic Church; the Catholic Church is the kingdom of God on earth, independent of worldly kingdoms. This, in short, is the concise line of argument in the book *Der Papst im Verhältniss zum Katholicismus* (Lucerne, 1817).[57]

With this strictly Catholic orientation, the polemic against Protestantism also had to become more strident. This was especially the case in France, where the newspapers of the restoration period—such as the *Journal des Débats*, the *Gazette de France*, the *Quotidienne*, the *Drapeau blanc*, the *Etoile*—did not fail to include calumnies and invectives directed at

---

56. Friedrich Wilhelm Carové (1789–1852), lawyer, philosopher, statesmen, wrote a number of books attacking the Roman Catholic Church, including *Ueber die allein seligmachende Kirche* in 2 vols.

57. Franz Geiger, Canon of Lucerne, is the author.

Protestantism. Also, such famous writers as Abbé Lamennais[58] went after Protestantism with the most hateful accusations. Lamennais contended that Luther and his followers persuaded a part of Europe that sovereignty resides in the people, and soon thereafter the blood of kings flowed on the scaffold. In a writing of 1826 Lamennais says that people cast their eyes on Europe and ask: Where do sound religious, moral, and political doctrines exist today apart from the Catholic Church? What other faith has taken the place of the Christian faith? What other bond than hatred toward Catholicism keeps the Protestants going? What have they in common but this very hatred? And what do those who, with further aims, reject the scriptures, revelation, and God himself, wish to do but destroy? And whence does general destruction lead us?

[According to these critics] the revolutionaries call for schism, that is, Protestantism, simply in order to hasten the dissolution of society. Schism would have made France the most isolated nation of Europe. Separated from its Catholic neighbors it would have been a perpetual stumbling-block for all peoples, those who could not escape the fact that this change, at once political and religious, threatened their peace more than war does, because it generously feeds the most restless minds of our day. As religion, Protestantism perpetually has that effect; without doctrine, it is just mere negation, and in this form of its own it lacks everything needed to be a substitute for the Catholic faith. It is not possible for a people to practice Protestantism without making it godless. From whichever side one looked at it, whether it be the political system or the religious system, one would always reach the same conclusion: without the pope, no Christianity; without Christianity, no religion; without religion, no society. Separating from Rome, causing a schism, founding a national church—that amounts to proclaiming atheism. That the Protestants' teaching would lead to indifferentism, to deism and atheism, was the most severe reproach that could be leveled against them. In addition, people especially charged them with lacking unity, with opposing every authority both secular and spiritual, and with showing very indiscreet fervor by disseminating the Holy Scriptures through the Bible societies.

The Protestants in France had no lack of men who knew how to salvage the reputation of the Protestant religion by writings vindicating it. Standing out in particular were Vincent and Stapfer.[59] Vincent was a pastor

---

58. Félicité Robert de Lamennais (1782–1854), a French priest, authored the *Essai sur l'indifférence en mattière de religion* (1818–24), which attacks the notions of religious tolerance and individual judgment in religious matters. The writing Baur refers to below in the text is likely *De la religion considérée dans ses rapports avec l'ordre civil et politique* (1825–26).

59. Jacques Louis Samuel Vincent (1787–1837) was a French Protestant theologian

in Nîmes, where he died in 1837. His writings of this kind are: *Observationes sur l'unité religieuse, en réponse au livre de M. de Lamennais* (Paris, 1820), and *Vues sur le protestantisme en France* (Paris, 1829). Stapfer had been a professor of theology in Bern, and he later lived in Paris, as fellow of the Paris Tractate Society and contributor to *Le Christianisme au XIXe siècle*, published in Paris beginning in 1818, which was the most important journal of Protestant literature.

In Germany a principal organ of the Ultramontane party was *Der Katholik*, which appeared first in Mainz in 1819, and was later published in Strasbourg.

As to the efforts from the side of the liberal faction, we can mention here only the attempts made to discontinue [clerical] celibacy. This issue, in which it was assumed that the state had the right, on its own, to abolish the rule of celibacy because it is simply a disciplinary rule having no effect on dogma, got brought up several times in the provincial Diets of southern Germany—first in Württemberg in 1824, then in Baden in 1828 where twenty-three Catholics in Freiburg addressed a written petition to the Baden chamber that interceded on behalf of abolishing celibacy. However, the Baden chamber declared that it lacked the authority to take up this matter. In 1830 the Darmstadt chamber resolved, in response to a similar proposal, to express to the government the wish that it use its influence, in every way possible, for the discontinuance of celibacy. In 1831 in Baden too a renewed proposal received a favorable reception, a proposal to which 156 Catholic ecclesiastics from Baden assented. In that same year an association of Catholic ecclesiastics formed for the purpose of influencing, in every legitimate way, the discontinuance of celibacy. There was also a similar association in the Diocese of Trier. The governments were not very inclined to agree to this. The Württemberg government expressed its disfavor concerning the association simply because Catholic congregations will find it disturbing.

---

and prolific author. Baur mentions *Bermerkungen über die Auctorität in Religionssachen* (Paris, 1821), for which we cannot find a French title; instead we list Vincent's *Vues*. Philipp Albert Stapfer (1776–1840), a Swiss politician and philosopher, was born in Bern and later settled in Paris. He was familiar with Kant and wrote *Considérations sur les rapports de la lecture universelle et intégrale des Saintes Écritures avec l'état moral des individues, le bonheur des peoples, et la cause du Christiansme* (1823).

3

History of the Protestant Church

Ecclesiastical Conditions Linked to Political Conditions

The era with which we begin this period marks an epoch for the Protestant Church too. It is not by chance that the sudden changes ensuing in the church coincide with the political revolution, for the one, like the other, has its deeper reasons in the general consciousness of the age. The political pressure to which the German nation was subjected, and the liberation from it, something only to be seen as accomplished with the aid of a higher [i.e., divine] power, put the nation in not just a more serious frame of mind but also a more religious one. People now came around again to having a favorable view of the positive and ecclesiastical elements of religion. The tranquility accompanying the generally peaceful conditions turned, of its own accord, into an attitude in which people could direct their attention to so many things that had previously been neglected under the pressure of political events, and they could give thought to rectifying the deficiencies also becoming perceptible in the life of the church. Since in the state, the launching point for the German people's great national movement or turn for the better, the rulers themselves, from their own personal interest, were very much devoted to the newly awakened religious and ecclesiastical sensibility, this gave people all the more reason to expect a favorable outcome from the reforms of the church that now became the order of the day. However, in people's experience church matters were much the same as in political affairs. Thus while the personal interest taken by sovereigns seemed to be beneficial for matters of the church, their getting involved too directly in these affairs had to be detrimental. The same mistrust that became such an impediment to political development also had to make its influence felt in ecclesiastical matters.

Negotiations Concerning Ecclesiastical Conditions in Prussia

If we first of all consider the ecclesiastical issues now up for discussion, then the close connection between the political and the ecclesiastical movements at that time is of course evident in the fact that the need for reforms in the church is nowhere expressed more outspokenly than it is in Prussia. The three issues becoming of general interest were indeed first raised in Prussia during the initial years of this time period. They concerned: the administration of the Protestant Church; the revision of liturgical forms; and the unification of the two Protestant confessions.

As for the first issue, following upon renewed interest in the church, major emphasis now fell on introducing into the Protestant Church an orderly presbyterial and synodal system. Already in December 1813 the committee of ecclesiastics and educators of the Kurmark[1] administration issued a request to the ecclesiastics of the Kurmark, to declare to them its ideas for not merely introducing individual synods into the Prussian state but also a synodal system of the Protestant Church. Thus in 1814 twenty-two superintendents, or senior Protestant ministers, gathered in Berlin to confer about what they, as supervisors of a major part of the ecclesiastics in the Kurmark, could and must collaborate on to bring about new life in the church, as well as to form a common front regarding possible proposals for a new arrangement for the church. They all accepted the principle of a completely free synodal system as the one starting-point for those wishing to reform the church. However, in order to introduce the matter most promptly, the attendees decided to turn directly to the king with the request to seat a commission of ecclesiastics who would submit proposals to him as the head of the state and the church. He consented to their wishes. The appointed commission issued the plan from the members of the aforementioned gathering. This was the occasion for the publication of the "Baselines for a Future Administration of the Protestant Church in the Prussian State. Three Proposals of Superintendents Küster, Neumann, and Triebel."

---

1. The Kurmark ("electoral march") was a state controlled from medieval times by the margraves of Brandenburg (and Brandenburg subsequently became part of Prussia). The Kurmark discussed by Baur was a general superintendency of the Evangelical Church in Prussia, geographically located within the March (or boundary) of Brandenburg.

Several years later, in 1817, a second plan, not from a designated authority but nevertheless official, was made public, a plan for a synodal organization for the Union of the two Protestant confessions [Lutheran and Reformed] in the Prussian state. Schleiermacher right at that time published his observations about the synodal administration set up for the Protestant Church of the Prussian state.[2] But in a postscript he added a criticism of the plan, from which we see clearly how little the plan met his cherished expectations. To him the plan looked far too much like a government, which could at that time do everything to pose obstacles to every freer political development, also taking no pleasure in a freer development in the life of the church. Albeit in the name of the synodal system, the plan was simply calculated to keep the church in the age-old state of immature dependence. Hence it was in line with what the government itself hoped for; it was no progress but instead a step backward. Schleiermacher said (*Werke*, 5:276) one can simply surmise that there is a very essential difference between the perspective of the earlier public announcement and that of the later plan. The plan interprets all the actual synodal advice in proposals to the authorities as being minor matters, whether that be the case because it takes the proposals as such to be unnecessary and the needs of the church to be insignificant, or else because it wishes instead to keep legislative control over church affairs fully and indivisibly in the hands of the state's ecclesiastical authorities, and only seems to leave the giving of advice up to the synods. One could almost say it is as though a fear of deliberative assemblies had gotten into their heads; that, based on a combination of very specific and entirely improbable stipulations, spurious complexities, and certainly calculated reservations, the plan has almost negated the [influence of] synods and consistories, and that the superintendents and general superintendents are the only real players. The plan looks to be a reinterpretation of the initial public announcement, one in turn almost entirely effacing its content. Matters organized according to this plan would make the synods completely superfluous.

The plan was nevertheless taken under consideration along with another one involving a new ecclesiastical organization of the Protestant congregations, considered first by the district synods of the provinces and thereafter by the provincial synods. In their judgment several of these synods spoke very decidedly in favor of introducing a presbyterial and synodal system. One of them was the Provincial Synod of Westphalia, which also

---

2. Friedrich Schleiermacher, "Ueber die für die protestantische Kirche des preussischen Staats einzurichtende Synodalverfassung" (1817), in *Sämmtliche Werke*, div. 1, vol. 5 (Berlin, 1846), 217–94. Baur's interest in and knowledge of church polity is related to his responsibility for teaching *Kirchenrecht* in Tübingen.

made its judgment known via a publication: "Transactions of the Provincial Synod of Westphalia Concerning the System and Organization of the Church, Lippstadt, 1 to 12 September 1819." Especially noteworthy is the declaration the delegates of the United Provincial Synod of the Margravate of Brandenburg (*Grafschaft Mark*) included in the proceedings of the synod. The declaration stated that the Protestant congregations united in the regional synod of the Margravate of Brandenburg, both the Lutheran and Reformed confessions, in association with the congregations of the lands of Jülich, Cleve, and Berg, have until now enjoyed a free, presbyterial system, according to which the church of these lands presents itself as an autonomous, free, and independent community, and governs, regulates, and administers itself through freely chosen representatives. Up until now the state only exercised the right to confirm the decisions, judgments, and choices proceeding from the assemblies of the presbyteries, and the district and provincial synods; or, if these decisions, etc., were at odds with the existing civil laws, to decline to confirm them. This system bases itself on the church regulations of these lands, which had been confirmed initially by the Great Elector, Friedrich Wilhelm, in 1662 and 1687, and thereafter by all the successive sovereigns of the land.

While this system in the Prussian state is only typical of the Protestant congregations in the provinces referred to, it served for the time being as a constant reminder of how improvements in the church were to be introduced. In these provinces it had its origins in the pure and pious sensibilities of the people themselves. Unlike in most of the other Protestant lands of Germany, it was to become effective independently of its being encouraged, ordered, or supported by the civil authority, indeed often in face of the strongest efforts to counteract it. They declared openly, in the name of the united congregations in the district synods of the Margravate of Brandenburg, that they will never, by freely consenting, accept any other system—not because of blind devotion to what is in place and customary, but instead with the conviction, confirmed by repeated experience, that this system is the only one appropriate for a Protestant Union of churches. Notwithstanding similar declarations of this kind passed by other synods as well, nothing further transpired as to this whole matter. After the official publication in March, 1817, first made by the consistory of the province of Brandenburg, and also issued subsequently by other consistories, with reference to the presbyteries and the union of Protestant ecclesiastics in district and provincial synods, a general synod of the lands was supposed to follow five years later. Yet no further mention was made of it, and for readily comprehensible reasons. At a time when the Carlsbad Decrees[3] had been issued, people soon had

3. See p. 104, n. 10.

sufficient reasons to bring a halt to the reform of the ecclesiastical system.[4] A general synod of the land would certainly have been, in an ecclesiastical setting, the same thing that [the rulers] did not want in a political setting, namely, a general representative body of the land. Long after these proceedings what finally appeared, without any basis for it, was, by a 5 March 1835 order of the cabinet, a church structure for the Protestant congregations of the Province of Westphalia and the Province of the Rhine, in which the presbyterial system was approved for these provinces.[5]

The Ecclesiastical System in Southern Germany

In the states that acquired new constitutional forms after 1815, the rights and circumstances of the Protestant Church were specified in the constitutional documents.[6] The reforms of the church system that people spoke about after 1821 still never came to pass. The consistorial control wholly dependent on the state government continued on its former course, and fairly often relied on the government's very arbitrary actions.

In Bavaria the system of governance for the Protestant Church was standardized along the lines of the 1818 constitutional document, in the May 1818 edict concerning internal church affairs of the Protestant congregations as a whole in the Kingdom of Bavaria. The supreme consistory, standing directly under the ministry of the interior in Munich, held the highest episcopacy and the leadership, deriving from it, over internal church affairs. Under this supreme consistory were the two consistories in Ansbach and Bayreuth, and a third consistory in Speier for the Palatinate. Every four years a general synod, meeting at the seat of the consistory and led by a member of the supreme consistory, provided counsel about internal church affairs, in the presence of a royal commissioner. A further step toward constituting the Protestant Church in Bavaria was supposed to be the creation of presbyteries. In 1821 the election of church elders was ordered in the Protestant congregations, but this order directly elicited a very vigorous opposition to it in the congregations. People feared compulsory belief and hierarchical authority. The provincial governments of Ansbach and Bayreuth formally protested against this directive, saying that one first

---

4. [*Baur, in the text*] Cf. Heinrich von Mühler, *Geschichte der evangelischen Kirchenfassung in der Mark Brandenburg* (Weimar, 1846), 332.

5. [*Baur, in the text*] See *Allgemeine Literatur-Zeitung* (Nov. 1835) no. 178.

6. [*Baur, in the text*] See, for instance, the *Württembergische Verfassungs-Urkunde*, §§71 ff. [*Ed.*] *Verfassungs-Urkunde für das Königreich Württemberg vom 23 September 1819* (Stuttgart, 1843).

of all had to know how things were supposed to be; that people could not choose a church governing body before it was determined what its sphere of activity ought to be. The mistrust was so great that the government had to give up its apparently well-intentioned plan. A few years later, after 1825, a synodal system was indeed introduced, but only with very restrictive specifications. There were two church dioceses, each one having its own general synod, with the deputies of the congregations chosen by the pastors. The supreme consistory had the right to exclude [from its membership] half of those elected to the general synod from the district assemblies. Also, the advice of the general synod could be effective solely within a narrow sphere, one determined from above.

Church Ritual in Prussia

The second issue under discussion in Prussia at the same time as the first one did not have the desired outcome. In 1814, at the impetus of the king, a special commission was seated to initiate improvements in the liturgy for the Protestant churches in all of the king's states. The congratulatory letter with which Schleiermacher greeted the members of the commission appointed by the king to establish new liturgical forms (*Werke*, 5:157)[7] was a bad omen for the completion of the commission's assigned task. Schleiermacher did of course profess his delight that now, with one grand gesture, the most important thing happened for reclaiming external freedom, and for establishing the foundation for people's new life and happiness by directing their courage and zeal within, so as to make secure what has been gained, to make the power awakened coalesce and grow stronger in new bonds of love, and to seek out the more deeply underlying reasons for previous troubles and clear them away. On the other hand, however, he also spoke out very openly about the difficulties and hesitations that confront the discharging of such a task. Not only for the well-being of the church but also because of the greatest dangers posed to the church, the commission could not accomplish its task on its own. If such improvements are supposed to come about, a new, vital system for the church would have to be created, one from which all else would proceed of its own accord, if and when that would be appropriate. If people must hand over future changes in the liturgy and the rites to the control of ecclesiastical representatives, why is not a system first

---

7. Schleiermacher, "Glückwünschenschreiben an die hochwürdigen Mitglieder der von der Sr. Majestät dem König von Preussen zur Aufstellung neuer liturgischer Formen ernannten Commission" (1814), *Sämmtliche Werke*, div. 1, vol. 5 (n. 2), 157–88.

created so as to see what is needed for the present as also proceeding from this system? The main difficulty Schleiermacher had about this matter was that it rested on an arbitrary directive on the part of the king. Moreover, he was doubtful that a commission with the task of establishing liturgical forms that not only fit with the clear theological framework of the Protestant Church but maintain that framework intact—forms proving to be effective in themselves—was in fact endowed with the full standing of an ecclesiastical assembly of the land. This arbitrary and purely personal factor came to the fore in an ever more striking way.

Even before anything of the general results of that commission's labors had become known, in 1816 a new liturgy was introduced in the garrison church in Berlin and in the court and garrison church in Potsdam, a liturgy not coming from that commission. Among the various objections Schleiermacher posed in his critique of the liturgy, which appeared right at the same time,[8] the most significant one is that the liturgical element, the established form, is given precedence and preaching is relegated to the background. Schleiermacher's main issue was now also the general issue for the church. He expected something essentially better and more suitable in this area. He thought that if the Protestant ecclesiastics of the land, united in a well-ordered synodal system, could collaborate in a set way, then neither could individual caprice go far astray in dealing with the sacred business of public worship, nor would there be a shortage of likeminded people who willingly come together on a fruitful and recognizable common ground. Otherwise people would reproach the ritual with being Catholicizing and be indifferent or passive toward it: Catholicizing because it adopted, as much as possible, many elements from the ancient church, the general tenor of which drew more on Catholic features; indifferent because, in the interest of the idea of union, it excluded everything reminiscent of confessional differences.

Nevertheless such views did not deter the king from formally introducing the liturgy, not only as the church ritual for the Prussian army in 1822, and in augmented and somewhat altered version in 1822 as the church ritual in the court and cathedral church; nor also from commanding its introduction to the superintendents and pastoral clergy. At first the majority of the clergy spoke out against it, but many of them adopted it. After that,[9] general adoption of the ritual became ever more decidedly urgent, but not without endangering freedom of conscience. So ritual became a live issue, and then also became the topic of discussions about church law. People

---

8. Schleiermacher, "Ueber die neue Liturgie für die Hof- und Garnison-Gemeinde zu Potsdam und für die Garnisonkirche in Berlin" (1816), *Sämmtliche Werke*, div. 1, vol. 5 (n. 2), 189–216.

9. Reading *Darauf* instead of *Da auf*.

were driven to ask whether, as a rule, princes of Protestant lands have the right to issue liturgical regulations of this kind. There were absolutists who ascribed a sovereign right to reigning princes as such in the context too, ones such as Augusti.[10]

Here too it was Schleiermacher who established the correct perspective, by an important statement expressed at the right time. His article, "Über das liturgische Recht evangelischer Landesfürsten, ein theologisches Bedenken von Pacificus Sincerus" (1824),[11] occupies a much respected place in more recent literature on Protestant church law. It is the most fundamental defense of the so-called collegial system, over against the territorial system on the basis of which people wished to justify the imposition of a liturgy by order of a government cabinet. The only other option, if there are to be churches conducting publish worship in the state, is the ruling prince being entitled, with regard to the regulation of divine worship, to solely a negative role, which essentially means that all new regulations of the church are subject to the sovereign's approval; that he is empowered to forbid anything he finds therein that is detrimental to the state. This in no way includes the ruler having other rights too that bear upon the internal operations of the church insofar as they do not concern the state itself. In these other respects the ruler would be someone in the church like any other member of it.

Thomasius,[12] the leader of the territorialists, set out from interests that are now no longer a factor. In fact he made souls anxious at the prospect of control by the clergy of the Protestant Church. The prospect of clerical rule coupled all that is inflexible and oppressive about the papacy with all the uncertainty and disquietude of control by many. His view was that the church must be ruled either by the clergy or by the prince, and of course purely by the prince as such and in virtue of the power conferred on him as ruler. However, Schleiermacher's opinion is that one should not fear the evangelical ecclesiastics in German lands arrogating to themselves control over people's conscience, and therefore no extraordinary constraint against their doing so is needed. But if it is a baseless contention that liturgical

---

10. [Baur in the text, augmented editorially] Johann Christian Wilhelm Augusti, *Kritik der neuen preussischen Kirchenagende* (Bonn, 1824), and *Nähere Erklärung über das Majestätsrecht in kirchlichen und liturgischen Dingen* (Bonn, 1825).

11. In Schleiermacher's *Sämmtliche Werke*, div. 1, vol. 5 (n. 2), 477–536.

12. Schleiermacher refers, in the article previously cited, to Thomasius, *Vom Verhältniss der Religion*, 30 ff. (Schleiermacher's *Sämmtliche Werke*, div. 1, vol. 5, 480). This must be Christian Thomasius, *Vollständiger Erläuterung der Kirchen-Rechts-Gelahrtheit, oder Gründliche Abhandlung vom Verhältniss der Religion gegen der Staat*, 2nd ed. (Frankfurt and Leipzig, 1740).

authority should derive directly from the royal prerogative of the prince, then one can only view such a prerogative as something transferred by the church to the prince. If this would make the prince into principal bishop of the church, then such an inherently inappropriate expression would only mean that the prince takes upon himself the concern for allowing this self-constituting society to have the form suitable to it, and for watching over its continuing existence. However, transferring the prerogative to the prince would therefore make him not the protector and patron of the church, its principal patron, but instead make him its principal bishop. In this fashion, together with concern for the church's union, there also falls on the prince the task of initiating regulations for the church as a whole. Thus the prince can exercise this prerogative only if doing so means the advancement of the community for its own sake, and if the way it is exercised actually corresponds to a need. A conscientious Protestant prince, once called upon for liturgical regulations, cannot be too careful about not letting them originate with his cabinet. Since a structure for this is established in the church, the proper and truly best way of serving the church, when it comes to exercising the liturgical prerogative, would be none other than by means of the existing authorities or corporate bodies for the administration of church rules in general.

If the question then is what the form for the administration of church power would be in Protestant lands, it would be called the consistorial system.[13] Schleiermacher raises this issue in order to link it directly with the further issue as to what progress the form of the church's governance would have to make in order to gain a fully substantiated and appropriate exercise of the liturgical prerogative. The answer to this question is that almost nothing would be gained by merely refining and improving the consistorial system; doing that still could not rid it of its similarity to the state administrative authorities and, as experience from the entire period since the Reformation sufficiently proves, it has the unfortunate feature that the entire power of the church could become forced into the forms of the state government, contrary to the nature of the church itself. The result would be that the members [of the consistory] seek their highest honor in being civil servants like the other councilors of the sovereign, and acknowledge nothing higher than his personal authority, which therefore means that his private opinions, views, and perhaps also personal predilections, influence

---

13. The term "consistory" (from the Latin, *consistorium*, place of assembly or council) has a long history in European (especially German) Protestantism. A consistory is basically a church governing body and/or court. The question at issue is whether consistories are self-governing or subject to state control (through the appointment of bishops, or by a secular authority acting as a bishop).

them. These things are entirely inadmissible in matters of the church and would always also divert the exercise of the liturgical prerogative from its true goal. The consistorial system is to be looked upon as only a transitional feature, one the Protestant Church has indeed held onto for much too long for its own good in most of the lands. If both the church governance as such, and also the liturgical prerogative in particular, are supposed to be administered in such a way in the Protestant Church as to be in line with their original, well-founded basis in the church itself, what is heretofore the consistorial system could only pass over into the presbyterial system.[14]

History shows that this presbyterial system is the most suitable one for the Evangelical (Protestant) Church, from the incontestable fact, as seen most definitely in France, of how the church has shaped itself in no other way than this. It is clearly evident that this system makes the life of the church prosper everywhere it extends to, and has proved victorious over all kinds of temptations and persecutions. Thus what more meritorious thing could Protestant princes have done than by putting the finishing touches to, and completing, the work carried over from the onset of the Reformation—that of shaping the organization and cohesion of the Protestant communities—by giving each of the churches of their lands this system that is capable of so many modifications suitable to remaining conditions? At that time Schleiermacher could only deplore the fact that the proposal set before the assemblies of ecclesiastics and introduced most enthusiastically by them, for setting up presbyteries and admitting lay members on the same footing in the synods, or district and provincial presbyteries, was undercut by those who brought a halt to this course of events right from the start. When dealing with the question of the liturgy, the time was all the more ripe to raise this issue anew. As such, this question at least had the benefit of bringing the principles of church law into the inquiry from a different angle.

This was also the occasion for Marheineke's book.[15] He insisted on the unity of church and state, that the two are in principle one, and only

---

14. A presbyterial system consists of a body of presbyters or elders (from Greek *presbyterion*), who govern a district of the church. The elders are both teaching elders (ministers ordained by the presbytery) and ruling elders (laypeople elected and ordained by individual churches). The advantage of a presbyterial system from Baur's perspective is that (for the most part) it cannot be controlled by the state and is not governed by a hierarchy of bishops. However, the Church of Scotland is a national church, and the Reformed Church of Hungary has bishops.

15. [*Baur, in the text*] Philip Marheineke, *Über die wahre Stellung des liturgische Recht im evangelischen Kirchenregiment* (Berlin, 1825). [*Ed.*] Marheineke's views on this topic reflect those of Hegel as worked out in his *Philosophy of Right* of 1821. The church is the realm of piety or religion, while the state is the realm of ethical life (*Sittlichkeit*), but ethical life and religion are present in each in different forms. This model is quite

that unity is to be denied which takes no account of the difference in their features. In the church, ethical life exists as piety; in the state, piety exists as ethical life. This oneness of church and state, the quest to conceive of the church being together with the state in a different sense than the old territorialists had entertained, was still a very unclear and underdeveloped concept at that time. It was of no practical significance for the question at hand, which is of course not so much a matter of the relationship of church and state as it is instead a matter of the relation of the person of the ruler to the church.

Meanwhile, [the authorities] knew how to derail the opposition to the ritual by various devices: awards and advancement rewarded those ready to oblige; threats and demotions frightened the recalcitrants; and there was the full import of a king's decrees. They especially sought to be sure about candidates for future ecclesiastical positions. Since 1829 the candidates had, by written declaration at the second examination, to commit themselves to accepting the ritual, just as, since 1822, they committed themselves to accepting the Union. Also, the authorities decided upon several changes. In 1828–29, particular versions of the ritual appeared for the different provinces, ones more or less taking account of liturgical differences of individual regions. In this arrangement they gave the ritual a fair amount of latitude in practice, and were satisfied with the declaration to accept it in its essentials. Except they did not allow the Union to be endangered by emphasizing any confessional differences retained in the liturgy. Thus opposition to the ritual gradually dissipated. Favorable reception of the idea of union also proved helpful for the ritual. In fact, the ritual was most closely associated with the Union from the outset, for it was said to be the liturgical expression of the Union. In 1829 and 1830, on the occasion of the three hundred year jubilee of the Augsburg Confession, general introduction of the ritual was successful almost everywhere in the old provinces, and those objecting to the ritual were at least in favor of the Union.

Celebration of the Jubilee of the Reformation; Harms, Ammon, and Schleiermacher

The most important and consequential issue at that time was the one concerning the Union [of the Protestant confessions]. It principally came into play via celebration of the jubilee of the Reformation in 1817, which was a significant occurrence for ecclesiastical developments at that time. Since it appeared only a few years after the political and religious exaltation of

---

different from that of a state (territorial) church.

the German nation, people welcomed it all the more so as the celebration of a glorious event for the German nation. In energetic exultation at the political freedom they regained, and with an eye to it, people fortified their Protestant consciousness. The memory of the three-hundred-year-old Reformation was widely celebrated with lively enthusiasm for the Protestant cause, and for the especially closely-related conception that, at that time too, Germany had become free from the yoke of foreign domination and, in the most important matters, had achieved its spiritual independence.

From this common starting point, however, interest in the Reformation could then take two very different directions. On the one hand, people could not be unaware that, owing to changes it had undergone particularly in recent times, the Protestant faith was no longer the same as it had been earlier on. Hence, in looking back to the origins of the Protestant Church, they saw themselves called upon to lament the falling-away from the old faith of their ancestors. On the other hand, people could only look upon it as progress that the general consciousness of their own time had gotten over so much that had previously just resulted in dissension and schism.

No one took up the former position with greater zeal than the archdeacon at the Church of St. Nicholas in Kiel, Claus Harms, in his pamphlet, "Das sind die 95 Theses oder Streitsätze Dr. Luthers, theuren Andenkens. Zum besondern Abdruck besorgt und mit andern 95 Sätzen, als mit einer Uebersetzung aus Ao. 1517 in 1817 begleitet."[16] He sought to come on the scene as a second Luther, and constructed his own pope and Antichrist based on reason and conscience. For instance, his ninth thesis reads: "The pope of our time, our Antichrist, we can call reason as related to faith, and conscience as related to conduct (in keeping with the position these two occupy over against Christianity—Gog and Magog[17]), with a threefold crown having been placed on these two, the crown of legalism, praise, and punishment." His thesis 15 reads: "Calixtus,[18] who separated the teaching of virtue from the teaching of faith, has placed conscience on the seat of majesty; and Kant, who taught the autonomy of conscience, has raised up the same thing." Thesis 47 states that, "in matters of religion, if reason wants to be more than a layman, then it will become a heretic. Furthermore, it appears as though all the heresies have been let loose once again—propo-

---

16. Claus Harms (1778–1855) was a fervent evangelical who attacked reason as "the pope of our time." See "Die Reformationthesen" in *Lutherischen Beiträge* 18.4 (2013) 238–54.

17. See Revelation 20:8.

18. Calixtus (George Callison, 1586–1656) was a Lutheran theologian who was accused of heresy for teachings leaning too far in the direction of Catholicism, or else of Calvinism.

nents of conscience and of naturalism, Socinians and Sabellians, Pelagians, synergists, crypto-Calvinists, Anabaptists, syncretists, millenarians (*Interimisten*), and so forth. Reason runs rampant in the Lutheran Church: tears Christ from the altar, tosses God's word out of the pulpit, casts filth into the baptismal water, adulterates the godparent position with all sorts of people, does away with the directive of the confessional, drives out the priests and all the people after them, and has already done so for a long time. Is one not still committed to these things? Is that commitment not being truly Lutheran, instead of being like Carlstadt[19]?"

This is how the zealous man, in his 95 theses—containing in part obvious falsehoods and half-truths, in part just commonplace truths, in part ones ineptly stated in form and content, ones invoking Luther's theses in just the most vainly arrogant way—blusters in opposition to reason and conscience, and to everything not befitting his own sensibility. Their impact was very slight. Schleiermacher said about them that—with their going back and forth between common and local shortcomings, between matters near and far, between well-known and obscure writers, with their oracular half-truths and their perplexities not worth resolving, with their straining for brilliance and wit—they made little impression on him; that it is a pity to see the writer in such haste and so mistaken. His theses are in no way like lightning flashes that, although they do not actually set on fire, still always have the power to strike and kindle. Instead they are for the most part like rockets that do not wish to climb, that explode too soon, that in a nice, orderly way complete only a small part of their trajectory and are then just a transitory, entertaining flash.

Nevertheless the theses were not entirely without an impact. It was a sign of the times that a theologian such as Chief Court Preacher Ammon[20] in Dresden greatly praised the theses and declared them as a group to be time-honored truths. He believed he had to enhance the impact of Harms's theses by his *Bittere Arznei für die Glaubensschwäche der Zeit* (Dresden, 1817). So this was a time when theologians who otherwise always put in a good word for reason now lamented the weakness of faith in their day, and who believed they must remedy the situation by their exhortations. However this did not go without a contemporary rejoinder. See Schleiermacher, "An Hrn. Oberhofprediger D. Ammon über seine Prüfung der Harmsischen Sätze, 1818" (*Werke*, 5: 327 ff.).[21] Schleiermacher demonstrated to Ammon

---

19. Carlstadt (Andreas Rudolf Bodenstein, d. 1541) joined Luther as a reformer, but broke off from him by becoming too iconoclastic.

20. Christoph Friedrich von Ammon (1776–1850), a theologian, was a defender of rational supernaturalism, a middle position between rationalism and supernaturalism.

21. In Schleiermacher's *Sämmtliche Werke*, div. 1, vol. 5 (n. 2), 327–407.

the inconsistency of giving unqualified consent to theses that stand in direct contradiction with Ammon's own dogmatic contentions. However, he thought he was able to discover the hidden motive for Ammon's doing so simply in the fact that now, when everyone manifests a strong inclination to revert to more stringent theories of revelation, someone in Ammon's position must be very desirous of positioning himself between the two factions, the rationalists and the supernaturalists, so as to seem to belong to both—belonging to the latter in virtue of the time-honored element that is not to be discarded, and to the former in virtue of what one skillfully introduces in other places. When Ammon deems it necessary to proceed with a more specific and more precisely stated confession, then it seems expedient to him to state freely and in a loud voice that the Augsburg Confession is his standard, one from which he would no more deviate than he would from the Bible. When experience establishes that the churches come to lack rational preachers, or when the people cannot be satisfied with the church's supreme commissars, who are content with the new creed or for some other reason, then Ammon could put this no more splendidly than by such an acquiescence to Harms's theses.

At the same time Schleiermacher also has something else to say to Ammon, about the bitter and vehement tone with which Ammon has spoken out about the Union of Protestant congregations of both confessions, a union already concurrently set in motion in Berlin. Ammon's main reason in opposing the Union of the two Protestant confessions, into one undivided church, was that the fellowship of the altar was not based on the fellowship of unbelief or half-belief, but instead based on full or complete belief; that by the Union people will be seduced into being indifferent to doctrine. Schleiermacher himself was very well-disposed toward the matter of the Union. [He held that] even though separation has proved beneficial thus far, the all-too-evident partiality of the authorities is gradually diminishing. We may hope that our day wants to get past the time when there could be such a universal authority; at least that the dividing line between the two churches is already much too flexible to be able to be effective; that the more the two churches come into contact peaceably, the more the causes of misinformation will disappear; that the more widespread the recognition of the reciprocal relation, in Protestantism, of individual freedom and the uniting power of the whole, then all the more so must there be change in how the endeavor of keeping to one's own path is related to the unifying endeavor. The unifying endeavor can now become dominant, with all Protestantism becoming one, and keeping to one's own path can only serve to firm up minor differences that may not further disrupt the unity of the whole. If people can be made to discern clearly that there are disagreements within each church, ones not detrimental to its unity and greater than those that separate the two churches, it thus follows that separation would no longer have any inner force, that it is just the result of old habits perpetuated automatically, and that the unifying force will be victorious. But this victory cannot come about from mere discernment, and the unifying force therefore can express itself only when a particular desire for unity is effective and operative, since where this desire is not felt, this force can always be repelled. Interest in the Union rested mainly on this desire. The Union had indeed long been a very important concern for Schleiermacher himself. Already in 1804 he had offered his own opinion, in these very terms, about the separation of the two Protestant churches, about its disadvantages and the suitable and feasible manner of uniting them.

The Union; Introducing It in Prussia

The 1817 celebration of the jubilee of the Reformation brought home, very much of its own accord, the conception of a unification of the two separate Protestant Churches.[22] If ever, the time for it now seemed ripe. The very prince who had already make known his zeal to improve the status of the Protestant Church, by introducing a new ritual, believed himself especially called upon in this instance to be the advocate for the Protestant Church. On 27 September 1817 the king of Prussia issued the well-known order of his cabinet that became the initial foundation for the Union. It was directed to all the consistories, synods, and superintendents, and expressed the lively wish for a union. The Reformed Church should not become Lutheran, or the Lutheran Church become Reformed. Instead, both of them should become a revived Evangelical-Christian Church in the spirit of its founder. The hope is for the success of this enterprise, heretofore frustrated by the ill-fated spirit of sectarianism, to be secured now under the influence of a better spirit, one setting aside the nonessentials, and for the main thing in Christianity to be that in which the two confessions are one. Such a truly religious union of the two Protestant Churches, separated only by external differences, would be suited to Christianity's grand purpose. This salutary union, indeed sought so long and so often in vain, and now once again so openly wished for, in the nature of the case no longer faces any obstacles.

22. The Prussian Union was established through a series of decrees by King Friedrich Wilhelm III in 1817. There was resistance to it for many years, and this resistance assumed different forms under changing political circumstances. The Prussian Union is now part of the Evangelical Church of Germany (EKD). For a summary of the details, see the article "Prussian Union of Churches" in Wikipedia. This article includes a bibliography in both English and German.

Friedrich Wilhelm III had a great personal interest in ecclesiastical arrangements of this kind, so it was not by chance that this very exhortation for union came from him. In it he followed up simply with the administrative principles for moving forward with it.

After Johann Sigismund[23] switched from the Lutheran confession to the Reformed Church, the Reformed royal house stood opposed to the strictly Lutheran established church. This kind of situation constantly made the princes concerned to alleviate, as much as possible, the resulting tension between them and their subjects, and in doing so also the opposition between the two confessions. The Protestant established church had for long been unable to adjust to the Reformed cathedral in Berlin being its royal mistress. The Great Elector Friedrich Wilhelm,[24] to whom the Reformed churches were indebted for receiving the same privileges and the same freedom of conscience as the Lutherans in the negotiations regarding Osnabrück,[25] had to complain very much about the fact that the zealots sustained the mutual distrust, bitterness, and hatred among the citizenry. The strong measures he took against them were mainly redirected away from accepting the sharp antitheses in Lutheran doctrine. In 1656 he decreed that one should not be bound to any ordinances from the Formula of Concord,[26] but instead be bound solely to the Holy Scriptures of the Old and New Testaments, and to the ancient creeds that are in accord with them, and to the Augsburg Confession. In a decree of 1662 he even specified that the consistories should summon and bind preachers to God's Word alone, and not to human precepts. In that same year he forbade attending Wittenberg University for philosophical and theological studies, since it was the main seat of the Lutheran zealots.

23. Johann Sigismund was the Elector of Brandenburg (1608–19). Together with his son Georg Wilhelm, Sigismund switched over to Calvinism in 1633.

24. Friedrich Wilhelm (1620–88) was the "Great" Elector of Brandenburg from 1640 on. He was a committed Calvinist, and yet his policy was one of religious toleration. Under him, the Collegiate Church of Berlin (the Supreme Parish Church of the Holy Trinity) became Calvinist in1632, and remained so until 1695.

25. At the Peace of Westphalia (1648), Osnabrück was officially recognized as biconfessional (Catholic and Lutheran). The prince-bishopric would be held alternately by a Catholic bishop and a Lutheran bishop.

26. The Formula of Concord (1577), signed by 8,000 pastors, solidified the Lutheran Church in its opposition to various controversial movements that had emerged within it. It was more detailed than the earlier Augsburg Confession (1530). Hajo Holborn, in *A History of Modern Germany, 1648-1840* (New York, 1967), writes (133) about the Great Elector that: "Since he himself did not espouse the more radical tenets of Calvinism, he felt it possible to find a common basis of peace in the Scripture and the Augsburg Confession, while declaring the special codifications of faith, including the Formula of Concord, matters for individual decision."

The fact that the Reformed element was greatly strengthened by the influx of so many Reformed refugees served very much to gradually lessen the tension between the prince and his subjects. The call of Spener to Berlin, and the establishing of the University of Halle, show that King Friedrich I knew how to utilize pietism, newly arisen at that time, in order to attenuate Lutheran zealotry.[27] A union of the two Protestant churches was already attempted at that time, but it only led to a harmonious relation in which, in 1722, both parties arranged to live in mutual love and freedom—so that the desired union would not be hindered but rather fostered. Friedrich Wilhelm I put his full mental energy into a plan of unification. In particular, he was concerned to make the public worship of the two churches more uniform and the Lutheran worship simpler. When the laity and the clergy complained about coercion of conscience, he issued a new decree, declaring that, instead of being zealous about subsidiary matters, pastors should instead teach their congregations how true Christianity does not consist of external, superfluous ceremonies, but rather of true conversion and transformation of the heart.

Friedrich II[28] had indeed not worked for a union of the churches, but he paved the way for it in the most fundamental way. He did so by allowing the differences to co-exist while certainly guarding against arousing them by precipitate action, and while protecting the free activities of science, research, and criticism. One exception in the series of these efforts at union was Friedrich Wilhelm II,[29] the successor to Friedrich II. He issued his notorious edict for the Prussian states in 1788. It stated that one should not have the audacity to revive any more the deplorable, long-refuted errors of the Socinians, deists, deniers of transcendence (*Naturalisten*) and other sects, and to disseminate such things among the people with much boldness and effrontery, under cover of the misused label of enlightenment. "We want to see an absolute stop now put to this mischief in our lands, all the more so since we regard it as the primary duty of a Christian ruler to pro-

---

27. Philipp Jakob Spener (1635–1705), "the Father of Lutheran Pietism," was appointed provost and consistorial adviser at the St. Nikolai Church in Berlin, in 1691. The University of Halle was founded in 1694 as the Friedrichs-Universität, and was a center of pietism and the German Enlightenment. Friedrich I (1657–1713) succeeded his father as elector of Brandenburg in 1688, and crowned himself as the first king of Prussia in 1701.

28. Friedrich II ("the Great") (1712–86) was king of Prussia, 1740–86.

29. Friedrich Wilhelm II (1747–97) was king of Prussia, 1786–97. He did away with freedom of the press and religious freedom in 1788. The edict on religion of 1788 was issued by Johann Christoph Wöllner, the king's chief adviser for domestic administration. The edict affirmed religious toleration, but said the Protestant ministers must adhere to the old or traditional tenets of their faith. See Holborn (n. 26), 374.

tect the Christian religion in his state from all adulteration and to uphold it—a religion whose preeminence and excellence has long been proven and established beyond any doubt—in all its supreme dignity and in its original purity, just as this is taught in the Bible, and has once been established according to the convictions of each confession of the Christian Church in its existing creedal documents." Thus the very thing that the Union was supposed to alleviate the edict sought to have emphasized most pointedly, the difference in the confessions. But in the repugnance it evoked the edict had precisely the opposite effect and, as soon as Friedrich Wilhelm III became the ruler, one of his first royal acts was to suspend the religious edict, with the declaration that reason and philosophy must be the inseparable companions of religion. Thus the work of union in 1817 was also no singular or unprecedented effort. It arose from the administrative policies of the Prussian rulers and from the stance taken by the Reformed confession over against the established Lutheran Church—the Reformed confession being the more flexible element when it found a place on the throne.

The Union in Baden, the Palatinate, and Nassau

Nevertheless matters had not yet come so far as people thought. A serious look at the situation shows that an internal process first had to take place. People usually supposed that everything was cleared up by declaring outwardly that previously existing differences are abolished and the same rights are secured for all parties—in setting aside all the dogmatic issues people thought should be laid to rest because they were in agreement on the main thing, uniting in the ecclesiastical fellowship by a common celebration of Holy Communion. After the events in Prussia, and as a result of interest in the Union resulting from the celebration of the Reformation, the Union was carried out in the aforementioned way in several lands, namely in Nassau, Rheinbaiern,[30] and Baden.

In 1821 there was a general synod of Lutheran and Reformed ecclesiastics in Baden. With the approval of the grand duke, as the supreme Protestant bishop of the land, it published a union document whose essential point was that the Augsburg Confession and Luther's Catechism, which heretofore had been the main confessional documents in Baden Lutheranism, and the Heidelberg Catechism, the main confessional document of the

---

30. Baur uses the term *Rheinbaiern* for what became the Palatinate in 1837. During the period he is discussing, this area along the Rhine was an administrative district of the Kingdom of Bavaria, from 1816 to 1837, when the name was changed from the *Rheinkreis* to the Palatinate (*Pfalz*).

Reformed Church in Baden, retain their normative standing in the united Protestant Church. These three documents appeared prior to the separation into two churches, which in fact first occurred because of the Formula of Concord. Prior to it, the two churches in Baden had differed solely with respect to their teachings about Holy Communion, for the doctrine of absolute predestination is not found in the Heidelberg Catechism. With regard to the teaching about Holy Communion, the general synod regarded it as the church's duty to link the presentations of the two catechisms with points included from Calvin's *Institutes*, to the extent that they could be reconciled. In celebrating Holy Communion, the broken bread and the cup should be placed in the hands of the communicants. Those who wished to celebrate it according to the old-established Lutheran or Reformed rites should be able to do so at a special Sunday worship service. With these arrangements it was decided that there should be a new ritual and a new book for religious instruction. From a dogmatic perspective, people accordingly wished to stick just to doctrines lying outside the scope of confessional differences.

The 1819 union in the Palatinate showed even less concern for denominational issues. According to it, regardless of the respect due to the confessional documents, scripture alone was to be recognized as the basis of faith and the norm for doctrine. From this we indeed see that the Union could be understood in very diverse senses. There could be no talk of a union as such unless people were determined to see beyond the divisive confessional differences. This concern for a union could move forward to the extent that, for the most part, people wished to hear no more about the dogmatically-based doctrinal differences and held just to the general points that were undisputed by both sides. On the other hand, however, the question always had to arise as to what extent the theological frameworks of the different confessions were entitled to maintain their validity, after the Union took place. The goal of the Union did not in itself require considering the creedal documents, those containing the doctrines making for differences, to be completely superseded, provided that, in acknowledging the differences, people also just held onto a common element in which they could all know themselves as one.

Further Deliberations and Disciplinary Measures for Promoting the Union in Prussia

It is undeniable that, when the matter of the Union was first talked about in Prussia, people started out with the assumption that, in contemporary consciousness, dogmatic conflicts had become less significant than was in fact the case. The more the prevailing rationalistic mode of thinking sought to capitalize on the Union for purposes of its own, so as to free itself from the positive element in the church's creeds as such, the more the confessional antitheses cropped up once more, precisely in virtue of the Union. In the beginning people still had an insufficiently clear awareness of the overall elements involved, and of the diverse interests that clashed with one another on this matter. In the fresh enthusiasm aroused by the celebration of the Reformation, the Union was also attractive to the ecclesiastically-minded from a genuinely evangelical standpoint, although even those people soon seemed to be put off by so much that followed from the Union. Since the Union, in which the two confessions came together, had to find itself expressed, first and foremost, in the shared features of the culture, that very thing was also the locus of the principal difficulty.

When a district synod of ecclesiastics from both confessions, convened in Berlin in 1817 with Schleiermacher as its chairman, declared its assent to the Union, the members also united in recognizing a fellowship of divine worship and the sacrament, including a uniform practice in the breaking of bread and the procedure for distributing the elements: Christ our Lord said, "Take it and eat" and so forth. Of course at that time Chief Court Preacher Ammon[31] in Dresden had objected to it. He held that, as the sum and substance of a church's confession of faith, the celebration of Holy Communion indeed presupposes the most complete unity in doctrine. Any church that is not trifling with sacred matters considers the unity of faith an essential criterion of its inner being and life. Whoever, under the pretense that each one may independently think whatever one wishes, and who wants to bring together, at one altar, rationalists, Schwenkfelders,[32] Unitarians, and Greeks can of course assemble at regular intervals a fellowship of God-worshipers, although surely they will never form the fellowship of a truly Christian church.

The new ritual then arrived with its liturgy. The liturgy is the church's most active profession of its faith. Thus, as the common liturgy for two previously separated churches, the ritual of course necessarily presupposes the inner union of these churches. However, since the introduction of the ritual was not preceded by a union in doctrine, the ritual had to avoid anything specifically expressing matters of controversy between the churches, ones involving one or the other's profession of faith with regard to the articles of faith. Adoption of the ritual included the declaration that adopting it on

---

31. See n. 20 and the work cited in the text.

32. Kaspar von Schwenkfeld (c. 1490–1561) created a Protestant sect, somewhat like the later Quakers, the followers of which were persecuted by both orthodox Protestants and Catholics.

behalf of one's confession did not involve accepting points that are not specifically and unambiguously presented by the ritual. The ritual was couched in these terms. The statements referring to articles of faith in which the two Protestant confessions differ were modified in such a way that their composition very carefully softens the distinctively Lutheran features and, in doing so, chooses a mode of expression compatible with a Reformed type of teaching. Devoted Lutherans could not accept these modifications without denying their faith. Indeed they had to say that the wording is intentional; that one could take it however one wished; that instead of being an expression of faith, it could only strengthen and foster doubt. Thus, however simple and straightforward the matter seemed to be at the outset, it became very complicated in its consequences.

The celebration of the jubilee of the Augsburg Confession in 1830 was supposed to mark a further step toward merging the Lutheran and Reformed Churches. On the day for celebrating the jubilee, when congregations introduced the rite of breaking the bread as the symbolic expression of assent to the Union, the general superintendent opened it up to wider participation and the king was most pleasantly aware of it. Therefore they had to make advance preparations so the bread-breaking rite would be introduced gradually, and the congregations would be guided so as to be in agreement with this rite. Only clinging in one-sided fashion to some distinction or private interest disruptive of this faith could place difficulties in its path. Avoiding them depended first of all on gentle instruction and then also on giving up those divisive terms "Reformed" and "Lutheran," and on the two formerly separate, but now united, confessions being united under the heading of "Evangelical" or "Protestant." At the same time it was decreed that, in the filling of Protestant pastoral positions, neither the Reformed nor the Lutheran confession would be taken into account. The Lutheran Church should only continue to the extent that adherence to the Lutheran rite of Holy Communion, albeit in keeping with the ritual, would, without the breaking of the bread, only be allowed for individual congregations and individual persons. These Lutheran congregations should not be entitled to clerics of the Lutheran confession except when, with evident dissatisfaction about the appointment of a Reformed teacher, people stay away. The assumption is that a non-unified congregation will be promptly dissolved, and this dissolution is then regarded as complete even though a majority of the current members had declared themselves in favor of the Union.

Dogmatic Alignments: Rationalism and Supernaturalism

The issue of the Union had to revert time and again to the dogmatic foundations of the confessions. In this respect the whole issue could only be resolved dogmatically. So a very natural follow-up to what we have already said here about the Union is further consideration of the dogmatic alignments and antitheses that can be distinguished in this period.

The issue of the Union provides us with two recognizably different kinds of alignment that are mutually opposed. On the one side people wanted to move on beyond the antitheses to a unity in which the differences balance out and annul themselves. On the other side, however, the antitheses go back within themselves and, with new energy, brace themselves in mutual opposition; and the more one wants to neutralize them, the more they hold fast to their own distinctiveness. Since an internal mediation of the antitheses is not possible, and the task of unifying them cannot be abandoned, what we have is just an outward unity brought about by concessions on each side. In this regard the course the theological development takes is very analogous to political developments.

Just as the period we are looking at now was, in political life, the time of constitutions—the establishment of the kind of governmental forms that were supposed to mediate the main political antithesis, that between democracy and monarchy, in the form of constitutional monarchy—there was also a similar mediation of dogmatic antitheses in theology. People had to be content to bring together the antitheses and reciprocal concerns to the extent that an overall unity came about. But since this unity could not be an internally mediated unity, sooner or later the whole threatened to come apart again, and the antithetical positions could only take a hostile stance toward each other.

If the task of historical examination is to bring the various antitheses, political and ecclesiastical, dogmatic and confessional, together as much as possible under one and the same perspective, then here we are certainly at a point where we see political and theological forms of consciousness at the same stage of development. However, we recognize that, because of the Protestant principle, in all these initiatives there are antithetical positions that are equally justified, ones mutually opposed here and grasped in an ongoing process of development, whereas in the Catholic domain, on the contrary, it is always just a matter of carrying on with the principle of absolutism in its pure form, a principle that, as such, tolerates no antitheses and excludes any free initiatives.

The first major phenomenon that presents itself to us in the theological domain is the stricter antithesis built up between the two mutually opposed systems of rationalism and supernaturalism. Each one sought to conceive of itself according to its own distinctive principle, in order to hold consciously to its ground. Rationalism found its main defenders in Röhr[33] and Wegscheider. The well-known *Briefe über den Rationalismus*, first published by Röhr in 1813 but without identifying himself as the author, constitutes the first methodically-developed presentation of the rationalist view of Christianity and way of grasping it. Christianity is nothing supernatural; it is purely natural in its origins. The miracles that cloak it have had their existence solely in the narrators' view and portrayal of such events, ones in which people sought to see a direct action of God. However lofty one's view of him, Jesus is a purely human phenomenon.

But however much rationalism divests Christianity of its supernatural status, it takes great pains, on the contrary, to ascribe to it all the good qualities it can have without presupposing its supernatural origin. There are, as the rationalist sees them, the great facts of world history, the unmistakable workings of divine providence, the purest and most universal rational religion and, as its founder, Jesus, the human being most excellent in wisdom and virtue. On the one hand, accordingly, in everything involving his origin, nature, and individuality, Jesus is reduced to membership in the series of ordinary human beings; while on the other hand, what has begun with him is, on the whole, the greatest and most important thing for humanity—something, so it seems, that depends on this specific, singular individual in such a fortuitous way that it becomes the main point for which rationalism cannot provide a satisfactory explanation.

If Christianity is something so infinitely great, as even the rationalist interprets it, then how does that square with the fortuitous character of its origin? If in its entire contents Christianity is the purest expression of reason, why should precisely just this one individual have been the instrument in which human reason came to this consciousness of itself? Rationalism wishes to trace Christianity back to what is rational as being what is necessary in itself although, to rationalism, what is rational always in turn appears as what is merely fortuitous, purely personal, subjectively arbitrary. It is with this essential shortcoming that the rationalist perspective presents itself in Röhr's *Briefe* too, which has also made that obvious by its skillful presentation. Röhr developed this perspective principally in connection with his historical grasp of Christianity.

---

33. Johann Friedrich Röhr (1777–1848), rationalist theologian, chief pastor at Weimar (1820). His *Briefe* was published in Aachen.

Wegscheider,[34] the second main proponent of this view, also elaborated it in the form of a dogmatic system. If rationalism wants to develop its principles and perspective dogmatically, it can only do so critically. Since rationalism subjects the existing system of church dogma to its criticism, and demonstrates that system's untenability on every important point, it sets up an opposed system in this critical and negative fashion, one that can maintain itself in its truth only inasmuch as it has refuted that other system. The main content of that rationalistic dogmatics consists of the critical analysis of the church's system by breaking it down into the various constituents from which it arose and, without having a deeper and firmer foothold in rational thinking, has nevertheless become the one authority for reason. Wegscheider's *Institutiones theologiae christianae dogmaticae* [Halle, 1815] was wholly concerned from the outset with rationalistic dogmatics in particular. In the long series of its editions (it was republished eight times between 1815 and 1844), it became the main textbook for rationalistic dogmatics, a truly classical authority for its many adherents. The more the orthodox, revealed faith continued to thrive, the more Wegscheider considered it his task to combat it by rational faith.

What Wegscheider wrote in the preface to the fifth edition (1826) is very characteristic of his standpoint. On page viii he says:[35]

> In this age of ours there have been those who gave too little notice to the superiority in reason and intelligence that God gave to human nature as opposed to other animals. Instead they wanted to force on us a religion wholly foreign to reason. There have also been those who rejected the first principles of reason, perhaps from questionable motives, or from some deeper motivation, or by claiming enlightenment and revelation of divine matters far exceeding human limits. They are those who demanded a return to religion. For my part I have striven to commend once again the right use of reason and the foundation of rational theology. As much as possible I have sought to emphasize and affirm, and again better shed light on, the truth of this view: that all doctrines of the faith must be judged by the highest ethical standards, and that these doctrines must be subjected to a refining process, with scripture itself being the sole guide. Moreover, be it far from me to think of imitating those who recently have begun to dress up their own mystical and scholastic philosophy

---

34. Julius August Ludwig Wegscheider (1771–1849), professor of theology at Halle from 1810.

35. Baur quotes this lengthy passage in Latin. We give only an English translation, thanks to Gerald Culley, retired University of Delaware professor (Greek and Latin).

fraudulently, in the rags of the ecclesiastical orthodoxy they brag about. Determined to follow no one but some among the older and more recent philosophers—those who have commended their teachings to the fairest judges, by subtlety in combination with the best evidence—I have labored to establish a system of reasonable Christianity. For the Christian religion indeed best displays its divine origin and authority when thus exposed, its temporal shrouds stripped away, and when called back to the truth and path within it that fits the principles of reason. After all, we owe reason itself to the grace of God; and its dignity and strength is approved by all posterity. So then, all those most memorable things based in fact, by whose help reason was first handed down and propagated, should be reclaimed from the providence of God.

This passage quite typically expresses all that is essential to Wegscheider's rationalism. As authentically intellectual rationalism (*Verstandes-Rationalismus*), it sets itself decisively over against all that is mystical, and likewise what is mystically speculative—as being revealed faith. Wegscheider considered the main task of Protestantism to be the further development of Christianity and Christian theology into the purely rational faith. When he first published his *Institutiones* in 1817,[36] the jubilee year celebration of the Reformation, he dedicated it to the manes of Luther. The rationalist therefore goes further along the path first opened up by the Reformers. When he refines the truth, so as to rid it of all that, considered in light of the scientific Enlightenment, must be viewed simply as outdated and lacking any rational foundation, he simply goes farther along the path first opened up by the Reformers.

Just as rationalism made itself into a consistently worked-out system in this fashion, so too supernaturalism sought to comprehend itself as in principle antithetical to rationalism. In the struggle between rationalism and supernaturalism at that time, what mainly carried weight for the defenders of supernaturalism was that excessive arrogance on the part of reason led it to suppose it could derive all that is unadulterated [truth] simply from itself. Hence the supernaturalists did not want merely to hold on to the given facts of revelation; instead it should be demonstrable, from the essential nature of reason itself, that there is need for a cognition going above and beyond reason. So supernaturalism too supported itself on reason in order to justify itself in principle over against rationalism, except that it grasped the essence of reason in quite a different way than rationalism did. Rationalism

---

36. This appears to be the 2nd ed., the 1st being published in 1815, as Baur suggests a little earlier.

took reason to be a self-sufficient capacity for cognition of truth. Thus for supernaturalism the essential nature of reason was, on the contrary, simply what it was not for rationalism, namely, that reason has in it a deficient and negative aspect. In any event one can only gravitate to the side of supernaturalism because, if reason is nothing more than what rationalism takes it to be, then it is only limited, finite, subjective reason that cannot rise above the antitheses in which it is situated, and is aware that it never occupies the standpoint of absolute reflection.

However, supernaturalism does not object to rationalism merely because of the limited and finite nature of its rational knowledge, or because of its self-deception when it wants to have within itself what can only be for it through a supernatural revelation, and when it closes itself off to the higher source of the knowledge of truth, a source indispensable to reason. For supernaturalism even raises the accusation of atheism against rationalism. We find this done in Tittmann's[37] work, *Über Supranaturalismus, Rationalismus und Atheismus* (Leipzig, 1816). In his interpretation, rationalism's line of argument is that it is contrary to reason accept a divine revelation, and so rationalism as such cannot hold the view that God works directly in nature. If reason disallows divine revelation because it cannot regard anything beyond comprehension to be true, then it also cannot believe in God's being, essence, and influence, because all this is utterly incomprehensible. Put succinctly: the rationalist cannot believe that God is the absolute cause of the world, which can only be thought of as working in a supernatural and incomprehensible way—but whoever denies such a being is an atheist.

Thus in order to justify and understand itself, each of the two views and orientations grasps its opponent in its most extreme form. Supernaturalism declares atheism to be the ultimate consequence of rationalism, and rationalism believes it can see in supernaturalism simply an abandoning of reason, a repudiation of all rational thinking, inasmuch as supernaturalism has so little confidence in reason, scarcely wants to stand up for an independent principle for the knowledge of truth, and is left with sticking in purely external fashion to what is given externally.

In the period we are speaking about, the general effort at that time proceeded not merely to keep the antitheses apart and to comprehend them in their differences, but also to unite them as much as possible. Yet since an inner mediation was impossible from this standpoint, only an external mediation was possible, a uniting of the antitheses by a bond of reciprocal, mutual limitation. So this very effort forms a further element in the history of these theological orientations. However much the two positions,

---

37. Johann August Heinrich Tittmann (1773–1831), professor of philosophy and theology in Leipzig, and cathedral canon in Meissen (1815).

rationalism and supernaturalism, had been conceived as in constant, mutual controversy and discord, the one could nevertheless hardly disengage from the other; each one always needed its opponent, albeit only as its partner in controversy, in order to maintain its own position. With all their differences, both stood on the same ground to such an extent that neither one could completely refute the other. What often enough happened was that, without expecting it, someone had gone over to the other standpoint as this in fact happened in the case of Bretschneider,[38] who, from the outset a supernaturalist theologian, ultimately counted as one of the main representatives of the rationalist view. So long as rationalism had its theistic foundation, it could not utterly rule out the principle of revelation; moreover, supernaturalism had so many rationalistic elements in it that it could not adhere to a more strictly antithetical stance. It was therefore natural that people made various attempts at mediation, given the conviction that there is no utterly exclusive antithesis here, that the one can exist alongside the other, that belief in revelation can be combined with rational faith.

The issue of the possibility of such a mediation was first raised by Reinhard.[39] In the *Briefe* that he published in his *Geständnisse seine Predigten und seine Bildung zum Prediger betreffend* (Sulzbach, 1810), he stated, with his keen intellect, that he knows no third option, that either reason must be unconditionally subordinate to revelation, or revelation to reason, and that he has decided in favor of the first of these. Tzschirner[40] did not think he could agree to such an absolute contradiction between reason and revelation, rationalism and supernaturalism. He was convinced that a consistent and tenable system could be constructed, one in accord with both the principle of the biblical system and the norm of a rationalism accepting revelation, and one avoiding an objectionable syncretism. He though that a decision for one or the other of these systems ultimately rested on subjective views and needs. However, he himself united rationalism and supernaturalism by accepting that the purpose of revelation would only be to undergird an ethical and religious institution by the prestige of one sent by God to confirm the truths of the religion of reason and to impress it on human hearts. On this view the right of reason to examine the origin and contents of revelation could not be called into question. Tzschirner elaborated on this insight in several writings, especially in his *Briefe veranlasst durch Reinhards*

38. Karl Gottlieb Bretschneider (1776-1848). He accepted the Bible as inspired, but allowed for complete, rational criticism of dogmas.

39. Franz Volkmar Reinhard (1753-1812), professor of theology and philosophy at Wittenberg from 1780.

40. Heinrich Gottlieb Tzschirner (1778-1828), professor of church history and the history of dogma in Leipzig.

Geständnisse (Leipzig, 1811), and in his *Memorabilien für das Studium und die Amtsführung des Predigers*, vol. 1 (Leipzig, 1810), in a presentation evaluating the dogmatic system found in the Protestant Church.

Following this precedent, the possibility and necessity of such a mediation became the leading issue at that time. Numerous writings appeared that bore this theme right on the title page. Supernaturalism wanted to be rational, and rationalism to be accepting of revelation. Even Schott's *Briefe über Religion und christlichen Offenbarungsglauben* of 1826[41] was wholly devoted to this issue. There should be no antithesis between rational religion and Christianity, for Christianity is itself the expression of the highest reason. Both of course stem from one and the same source, the divine reason. Of its own accord reason tends toward something positive and historical, and what is positive and historical has an unmistakable relation to the ideas of reason, ideas that satisfy the most important needs of the human heart and spirit. With regard to the purpose and goal of rational religion and of Christianity, a factual difference is of the least importance.

Now all of this sounded very enlightening. But if one asked about the manner of this mediation, people did not know how to provide a satisfactory answer. How did it help to maintain that Christianity and the religion of reason are in agreement, so long as one was not clear about how to take all those things portrayed in Christianity as God's direct and supernatural operations? If Christianity as an external phenomenon rests all of that on revelation and miracle, how can one declare what is rational and natural to be the substantial content of Christianity? Accordingly, how much had to be first excluded from consideration, and what right did one have to undertake this process of exclusion? The whole mediation of rational faith and revealed faith, as people attempted it at that time, was a highly capricious and one-sided affair. Either too much or too little was conceded to belief in revelation and miracles—too much by supposing that Christianity could be purely rational in its content but supernatural and miraculous with regard to its events; too little by taking the supernatural aspect of Christianity far too lightly and disavowing it, without being able to explain why Christianity appears to be so supernatural and miraculous, if all this nevertheless does not belong to its truly essential nature.

---

41. Heinrich August Schott (1770–1835), *Briefe über die Religion und christlichen Offenbarungsglauben: Worte des Friedens an streitende Parteyen* (Jena, 1826).

The Standpoint of Schleiermacher's *Glaubenslehre*

So at that time people still vacillated between opposed orientations and systems. Hence the essential merit of Schleiermacher's *Glaubenslehre*,[42] the first edition of which appeared in 1821, is above all to be seen in its putting an end to such an ill-defined controversy between rationalism and supernaturalism and, on the whole, occupying a standpoint depriving the previous antitheses of their significance. Schleiermacher disposed of the old controversy, as to whether Christianity is essentially supernatural or rationalistic, by taking Christianity entirely as being what it is according to the testimony of immediate Christian consciousness, inasmuch as everything in it is related to the redemption taking place through Jesus of Nazareth. For Schleiermacher, therefore, all that is apparently essential to Christianity in the view of supernaturalism, but on the other hand is nevertheless absolutely miraculous—this being the actual point of contention between rationalism and supernaturalism—is allotted no place in his system. In its content and form, Schleiermacher's *Glaubenslehre* excels by far all the preceding labors in Christian dogmatics, so we can rightly call it epoch-making. All that more recent philosophical and theological science has produced Schleiermacher applies as the foundation for a new and distinctive way of grasping Christianity and for a methodically elaborated theological system. Schleiermacher himself regarded his *Glaubenslehre* as his consummate work, as the ripest fruit of his many-sided scientific activity, as the center in which his intellectual directions, starting out from various points, came together as one, in a magnificent worldview.

Yet we can also regard Schleiermacher's *Glaubenslehre* as simply the product of the period we are speaking about—as the most complete expression of that striving to unite antitheses that by nature cannot be mediated internally, but which, all the more so, are said to be conjoined in an external bond of unity that, sooner or later, has to dissolve once more. In the theological domain of Schleiermacher's *Glaubenslehre* we have what, in a

---

42. Friedrich Schleiermacher, *Der christliche Glaube nach den Grundsätzen der evangelischen Kirche im Zusammenhange dargestellt*, 1st ed. (Berlin, 1821), 2nd ed. (Berlin, 1830). The work is often referred to as the *Glaubenslehre*. 2nd ed. cited by Baur (and in our notes below). ET of 2nd ed.: *The Christian Faith*, ed. H. R. Mackintosh and J. S. Stewart, (Edinburgh, 1928); *Christian Faith*, 2 vols., trans. Terrence N. Tice, Catherine L. Kelsey, and Edwina Lawler (Louisville, 2016). With his *Glaubenslehre* Schleiermacher (1768–1834) became the major theologian of German Protestantism in the nineteenth century. Baur discusses Schleiermacher's earlier works (by which he was especially influenced) in Part One (pp. 77–87). He developed his criticism of the *Glaubenslehre* as early as 1827–28. He continues his discussion of it in comparison with Hegel's *Philosophy of Religion* in Part Three, pp. 319–24.

constitutional state, is the governing document that unites the democratic and monarchical principles in the form of constitutional monarchy—that is until the never-resting opposition from the democratic principle breaks through the absolute right of monarchy and completely abolishes the limits this document sets up. The *Glaubenslehre* likewise wished to draw up, so to speak, a constitutional compact between the democratic principle of reason and the monarchical rights of Christianity, but this artfully concluded bond has no inner permanence in this case too. It is from this perspective that we wish to consider the *Glaubenslehre* here, as a phenomenon very characteristic of our period.

In the aforementioned attempts at mediating between rationalism and supernaturalism, supernaturalism always came off badly, for even the supernaturalists sought to rationalize the content of Christianity as much as possible. Things appear quite the reverse in Schleiermacher's *Glaubenslehre*; it certainly wants to have nothing to do with reason and philosophy, and protests against the supposition that it is already dealing with something other than the pure content of positive Christianity. The *Glaubenslehre* attaches itself so closely to the traditional doctrines of the ecclesiastical system that one scarcely believes there is nevertheless such a great difference between it and that system. Schleiermacher expressly declares his allegiance to a properly concrete supernaturalism, stating that, in his view too, Christianity has come on the scene in world history in a supernatural way; that its essential character is the redemption accomplished by Jesus of Nazareth. The whole of Christianity uniquely hinges solely on the absolute significance of the person of Christ, which is equally historical and archetypal. As Schleiermacher describes Christian consciousness, it takes its course in the antithesis of sin and grace in such a way that everything belonging to the work of redemption rests on the doctrine, adopted from the old Protestant dogmatics, of a human being's complete incapacity for the good. The redeemer alone is active and the redeemed one's stance is solely receptive and accepting. Redeemed persons accept into themselves the redeemer's pure sinlessness and highest perfection. In virtue of these qualities, the redeemer is distinguished from all others who, as opposed to him, are in need of redemption. He alone does not need redemption; instead he is the principle of redemption.

However supernaturalistic all this sounds, it nevertheless has an entirely different sense for Schleiermacher. It would be a very major error to want to believe that Schleiermacher's intention is for his *Glaubenslehre* to provide a new support for the church's system of doctrine. It is easy to show, for each main concept of Schleiermacher's *Glaubenslehre*, that it is based on a way of looking at things that is very different from the church's system.

The *Glaubenslehre*'s Position on Belief in Miracles

Of course Schleiermacher too maintains that Christianity has a supernatural character.[43] But when he links directly with this the contention that the supernatural is not utterly supernatural, that instead everything supernatural is also in turn natural, then we indeed see from this how matters stand with Schleiermacher's supernaturalism. He rules out the supernatural far more strictly and decisively than rationalism does. Rationalism of course denies miracles although, on its theistic foundation, rationalism was not in a position to cut away the roots of the concept of miracle. Miracles are the most direct result of ordinary theism. Once we think of God as extraworldly, absolute will, then we must also admit to this will's operation in the world. But this operation, as the intervention of a transcendent principle into the course of the world, can only be a supernatural operation, a miracle. Hence rationalism has no right, based on its supernaturalist assumption about the God-world relation, to contest this consequence.

At first Schleiermacher absolutely did away with the concept of miracle, by grasping God's relation to the world in a pantheistic, not a theistic, way. People of course have strongly challenged the view that Schleiermacher was a pantheist, and Schleiermacher himself most earnestly protested against the reproach of pantheism continually aimed at him. However, if one can justifiably call "pantheism" the view defining God's relation to the world as an immanent relation, then Schleiermacher's *Glaubenslehre* too must be allowed to fall under this heading. "God" and "world" of course always remain two essentially different concepts if, in the final analysis, God and world are simply so distinct that, as Schleiermacher says, God is the absolutely undivided unity, but the world, even though posited as unity, is still only the unity that is internally divided and fissured, a unity that is at the same time the divided state of all the antitheses and differences, and all that, on account of this characteristic, is multiplicity. However, God and world are still therefore only different in the way that Spinozism too can and must distinguish them: which is the relation between *natura naturans* and *natura naturata*.[44] Hence everything just falls within the sphere of nature; everything divine is still natural, and there can be no operation of God that,

---

43. On miracles and the supernatural, see *Der christliche Glaube* (n. 42), §14 Postscript and §47.

44. See Spinoza, *Ethics*, part 1, prop. 29. The distinction is between "nature viewed as active (*natura naturans*), and nature viewed as passive (*natura naturata*). . . . [The former is] that which is in itself and is conceived through itself. . . . [The latter is] that which follows from the necessity of the nature of God. . . ." *The Chief Works of Benedict de Spinoza*, trans. R. H. M. Elwes, 2 vols. (London, 1883), 2:68–69. On Baur's use of the term "pantheism," see p. 76, n. 63.

as in the concept of miracle, would act as transcendent to nature, in other words, would be supernatural. However much singular phenomena might nevertheless rise above the series of other phenomena, they still always belong to the same immanent network of nature. Since in the nature of the case it cannot be otherwise, it is just completely fictitious to speak of the supernatural and the miraculous.

Schleiermacher of course calls the redeemer's appearing within humanity a miracle, inasmuch as his own distinctive spiritual substance cannot be explained from the substance of the human sphere of life to which he belongs. Instead it can only be explained from the universal source of spiritual life and based on a creative divine act. However, the universal spiritual source, or the original power of spirit, is itself to be regarded as the power of nature, therefore not deriving from a creative act of God in a different way than does any other operation of natural powers. Schleiermacher does not avail himself of a philosophical challenge to the concept of miracle. He takes up this issue not as a mission of his own, but only from the standpoint of the *Glaubenslehre's* stance on religious consciousness. However, he does also dispense with the concept of miracle dogmatically, by establishing from this perspective the thesis that the concerns of piety can never give rise to a need to grasp an event in such a way that, in virtue of its dependence on God, its being conditioned by the network of nature would be utterly superseded. In other words, no religious need could be the reason for something necessarily being a miracle. Moreover, the concept of miracle is not a concern of philosophy, so it should also not be a concern of religion. Thus the question can only be whether or not the events of the gospel story force us to acknowledge miracles; whether or not our concept of the person of the redeemer, however highly he is placed, is formed in accord with scripture if we do not also recognize, as essential elements of his personality, his supernatural conception and birth, his resurrection and ascension, in the way church doctrine maintains all this. Schleiermacher was unable to avoid dealing with this question in his *Glaubenslehre*. But his way of answering it only shows how little miracle as such can have any sort of meaning for him.

Schleiermacher has this to say about Jesus' supernatural conception:

> Thus, the general concept of supernatural procreation remains essential and necessary if the distinctive superiority of the Redeemer is to remain undiminished; however, the further determination of the concept as procreation without male assistance in the process does not cohere at all with the essential features regarding the Redeemer's distinctive dignity. Thus, in and of itself the further determination of the concept is also definitely not a component of Christian doctrine. Accordingly, whoever

embraces further determination of the concept does so only on account of the narratives containing it in the New Testament Scriptures. Thus, belief in it belongs only to doctrine regarding Scripture, . . . [and all persons have] to decide on the matter for themselves in accordance with proper application of basic principles of criticism and of the art of interpretation that they have found trustworthy.[45]

Schleiermacher maintains that the matters of Christ's resurrection and ascension, as well as the prophecy of his returning to judge, cannot be set up as actual components of the doctrine of his person. Since Christ's redemptive activity rests upon God's being within him, a direct connection between these matters and that doctrine cannot be demonstrated. The disciples recognized him as the Son of God apart from any premonition of his resurrection and ascension, and we can say the same about ourselves.

Of course this makes evident the complete ambiguity and sophistical-dialectical ingenuity of Schleiermacher's *Glaubenslehre*. Schleiermacher can regard each element of Jesus' life as not actually miraculous, because in general for the *Glaubenslehre* there are, from his standpoint, no miracles. But why does he not say this straight out? Why does he make it appear as though he is not questioning the factual reality of these miraculous occurrences, as though it is not a matter of the facts but only of their meaning? And with what right can Schleiermacher maintain that all those miracles, which he too speaks of as facts, in no way have the meaning for the person of the redeemer that people routinely attribute to them? We can of course only form our concept of the redeemer from the gospel story. Why should it then be so inconsequential whether or not the extraordinary character said to have belonged to the life of the redeemer is considered to be an essential element of his personhood?

Nevertheless it is clearly self-evident that, when matters actually stand the way the gospel story tells it with regard to Jesus' birth, resurrection, and ascension, these miraculous events must count for us as a main proof that his entire appearing as such has a supernatural character, one belonging to the concept of the redeemer. However, if one indeed does not wish to cast doubt on the factual reality of those miracles, while assigning them no essential meaning for the person of the redeemer, then this is a halfway house that one cannot possibly continue to occupy. If they were supposedly just something incidental and nonessential for the redeemer, then he can be thought of just as well without those miracles as with them. The natural

---

45. Schleiermacher, *Der christliche Glaube* (n. 42), 2:74 (§97.2); ET (2016) 2:599 (the two volumes are numbered consecutively).

consequence we can draw from this is surely that there have in general been no such extraordinary events, and accordingly also no miracles.

This is also in fact what Schleiermacher thinks. Whoever generally accepts no miracles can only regard the birth, resurrection, and ascension of Jesus as not being miraculous. But why does Schleiermacher not tell us this openly and candidly? Why does he just speak about it as though for him it was of no importance at all to concede the factual reality of these miracles? On this whole question he dealt only with what the miracles mean for the person of the redeemer. Indeed how can he say about the birth of Jesus that whoever takes it to mean a supernatural procreation can hardly find a basis, in the supernatural element the New Testament narratives contain, for depriving it of historical character or departing from a literal interpretation of it? This is straight out false. For whoever accepts a supernatural procreation of Jesus only in Schleiermacher's sense is denying it in the sense in which the gospel story has Jesus being procreated supernaturally. How can he at the same time take the content of the gospel narrative to be historical truth?

According to the principles of Schleiermacher's *Glaubenslehre*, the story of Jesus can involve nothing miraculous and truly supernatural; the whole of Jesus' life can only have taken a natural course. But when Schleiermacher still never expresses clearly and openly how his *Glaubenslehre* differs from the church's doctrines, and always just wants the basis for such an essential difference in his standpoint to be regarded as of minor importance, the reason for this can only be that he wants to have his *Glaubenslehre* appear as more orthodox than it actually is. No other work of dogmatic theology has so methodically disintegrated and undermined the bedrock of the orthodox view of Christianity as Schleiermacher's has—in part by its general principles, in part by the critical analyses it makes of individual doctrines—and no other one is less willing to admit it, and the fact that it calls for an open break with the church's teaching. Whoever is not misled by these orthodox superficies and the skillful play with ecclesiastically-sounding expressions and formulations, albeit ones constantly taken in a different sense, sees clearly enough that here everything functions quite differently than it seems to. One must recognize this distinctive character of Schleiermacher's *Glaubenslehre*, this skillful effort to conceal the modern philosophical point of view under the cloak of the old orthodox faith, if one is to grasp it as the product of an era that makes it its highest task to unify, in this outwardly plausible way, the antitheses that existed at that time and could not be mediated in another way.

Its Teaching about Sin and Redemption

Redemption is another major concept of Schleiermacher's *Glaubenslehre*. Redemption mediates the antithesis of sin and grace into which religious consciousness is divided.[46] Here too Schleiermacher's *Glaubenslehre* gives the impression of holding firmly to the Christian Church's strict concept of redemption, in denying that human beings have any natural capacity for doing what is good, and saying that redemption alone transposes us from the sinful condition to the state of grace. Schleiermacher's *Glaubenslehre* makes this one of its principal points of departure.

Even before the *Glaubenslehre* appeared, Schleiermacher came forward, in opposition to the rationalists, as a defender of the strict Augustinian-Calvinist doctrine. He did so in his essay, "Über die Lehre von der Erwählung," published in the Berlin *Theologische Zeitschrift*, vol. 1 (1819), when he commented on Bretschneider's *Aphorismen* (1817).[47] Bretschneider had admitted that there is a thesis in the Lutheran Church's theological system contradicting the Lutheran theory of divine election, namely, the thesis that human beings are entirely incapable of change for the better and are naturally resistant to the divine grace that alone is said to bestow this capacity, whereas the Calvinist theory harmonizes most precisely with divine election. Schleiermacher declared that he too fully agrees that the two different theories of election relate, in these mutually opposed ways, to the teaching that divine grace is indispensable for a human being's conversion. Yet this point was not always suitably emphasized. Instead it was kept in the background, and many people presented the matter as though that doctrine of grace would be equally compatible with both theories about election. Hence the unreserved way in which the *Aphorismen* acknowledged this point is very commendable, and it is therefore a matter of choosing whether: to recognize the indispensability of divine grace for salvation (but also wishing to leave aside the strict Calvinist formula of election); or, to take the route of the Lutheran formula with its consequences (but in doing so also renouncing the indispensability of divine grace and wanting to stand on one's own feet). When it came to this choice before him, Bretschneider definitely decided that the Lutheran theologian must, without hesitation,

---

46. See the introduction to Part Two of *Der christliche Glaube* (n. 42), §§62–64.

47. Schleiermacher's essay (1–119 in the original) has recently appeared in English as *On the Doctrine of Election: with Special Reference to the Aphorisms of Dr. Bretschneider*, trans. I. G. Nicol and A. G. Jorgenson (Louisville, 2012). Karl Gottlieb Bretschneider (1776–1848) was general superintendent of the Evangelical Lutheran Church in Gotha. The work to which Schleiermacher refers is *Aphorismen über die Union der beiden evangelischen Kirchen in Deutschland* (Gotha, 1819 [the date given by online catalogues]).

abandon the former option because this teaching is not found in scripture and because the Calvinist theory follows from it strictly and necessarily.

In contrast, Schleiermacher adopted the opposite position and sought to portray the Calvinist theory as the only consistent one, except that he softened the frightful (*horribile*) aspect of the Calvinist decree by considering damnation as a necessary stage of development. Once the idea of the world involves the human race being first redeemed from the power of sin by the appearing of the divine Son—and with this appearing serving as an indispensable feature of that idea, a feature foreseen and foreordained by God—then it also follows that all of this has been foreordained; that therefore all the different ways in which human capacities concerning divine things became entangled directly in the most varied stages of degradation and impotence, must have emerged prior to Christ, in accord with the divine decision regarding persons in their own place and time. Through Christ the divine Spirit entered into this manifold fullness of degraded being, in conjunction with the preaching of the Word, and in this very way the Son became human in Christ. Thus spiritual life came about as a consequence of the divine decree, as did its impact on natural life. This impact happened accordingly as the Christian Church, the collective bearer of the divine Word as it affected the multitude capable of being enlivened, reached a moment, predetermined here or there by God as formative for the individual's life— a moment therefore also conditioned by all the preceding circumstances and all the concurrent events, right down to the most apparently contingent ones—in which the longing for redemption, a goodness that never completely disappears from human nature, opens one up to being fully receptive to the influence of the Spirit.

These statements indeed contain all the principal features of Schleiermacher's system. Even though Schleiermacher maintains, on the one hand, a human being's natural incapacity for the good, and on the other hand, that nothing conditions the divine decree for human blissfulness, in other words maintains the necessity of redemption, it turns out that this thesis is not so much in the interest of church teaching as it is instead presented in the sense of a system that, as pantheistic, can also be simply deterministic. If the God-world relation is defined as Schleiermacher does, then freedom too can be conceived only as the universal dependence of the finite on the absolute. This determinism of his system Schleiermacher already expresses in his definition of the concept of religion, when he defines religion as the feeling of utter or absolute dependence.[48] Yet knowing oneself as utterly

---

48. *Der christliche Glaube* (n. 42), §4. Schleiermacher uses *schlechthinnig* ("utter") here but says in a marginal note that it has the same meaning as *absolut* (see ET [2016] 1:18–19).

dependent still does not constitute the essence of religion, if the antithesis posited in self-consciousness—the antithesis between higher and lower, or God-consciousness and sensible consciousness—is not known to be cancelled out. Sensible consciousness and God-consciousness, or sin and redemption, are the antitheses in which consciousness is situated. Just as sensible consciousness is the predominant element on the one side, and determines the whole of human self-consciousness, so God-consciousness has this role on the other side. However, in redemption there lies the possibility of the sudden change from the one side to the other, a change in which sensible consciousness is suppressed and becomes subordinate, so that, in its uniting with God-consciousness, the God-consciousness becomes the predominant and utterly determinative factor. Redemption is the freeing of God-consciousness from the predominant power of sensible consciousness.

However, what is the ground of redemption itself? Obviously it is grounded in the same determinism that is the heart and soul of the whole system; in other words, in the fact that, if it once belongs to the essential nature of self-consciousness to separate itself into the antithesis of sensible consciousness and God-consciousness, then both the one and the other are predominantly grounded in the same way, in the nature of self-consciousness itself. It belongs to the immanent process in which self-consciousness is engaged with itself that the predominant element is in part sensible consciousness and in part God-consciousness. Since here we are entirely within the sphere of self-consciousness (for the feeling of dependence, the pious consciousness, the Christian consciousness, are of course just determinations of the self-consciousness), and the principle of self-consciousness is, however, the I or self (*das Ich*), so we see clearly the idealistic character of Schleiermacher's *Glaubenslehre*. Within self-consciousness there is no other antithesis but that of the empirical I and the absolute I. The antithesis within the sphere of the feeling of utter dependence is therefore posited as the antithesis, in turn canceled out, of the empirical I and the absolute I; and the two, sin and redemption, or the inability of sensible consciousness to become one with God-consciousness, and their becoming one in virtue of redemption, are facts of self-consciousness.

Insofar as all this would be purely idealistic, how then does Schleiermacher undertake to give this idealism a Christian stamp and to convert the facts of consciousness into the facts of the Christian account of revelation? He does this simply by replacing the abstract concept of redemption with the concrete person of a redeemer. If God-consciousness has in it the power to gain predominance over sensible consciousness and to become one with it, then there must also be an absolute point of this unification, one at which sensible consciousness is entirely determined and pervaded by God-consciousness, an absolutely full strength of God-consciousness. If we will substitute the person of the redeemer for the concept of redemption, then the distinctive feature of the redeemer can only reside in the fact that he presents within himself this absolutely full strength of the God-consciousness. And since any relative preponderance of God-consciousness over sensible consciousness is conditioned by the fact that there is also something absolute, this relative preponderance accordingly has what is absolute as its necessary presupposition; and thus each event by which the God-consciousness in the individual gains preponderance over the sensible consciousness simply proceeds from the redeemer. Accordingly, whereas the absolutely full strength of the God-consciousness is on the side of the redeemer, there is, on the side of all the other human beings juxtaposed to the redeemer, simply no strength of God-consciousness at all, an absolute inability to redeem themselves or to extricate themselves, by their own sensible consciousness, from the state of bondage of their God-consciousness, and to free themselves from this bondage. Accordingly, they are sheerly receptive to the redeemer, in whom they see all that makes possible the God-consciousness being one with sensible consciousness; and they feel themselves supported within this state as something imparted from the side of the redeemer, as something done by the redeemer, from whom alone all redemptive activity proceeds.

But who can fail to see the artifice in this entire procedure, the arbitrariness in this way of constructing the *Glaubenslehre*, when the concept of the redeemer, taken from Christian consciousness and given in the person of Jesus of Nazareth, is put in place of the concept of redemption as an essential element of self-consciousness when self-consciousness divides itself into the antithesis of God-consciousness and sensible consciousness? It is mere self-deception when another and very different subject is set over against the subject of self-consciousness, which is itself situated within the antithesis between God-consciousness and sinful consciousness; and the activity of this other subject is alone said to impart what nevertheless belongs to the nature of self-consciousness. If sin and redemption, in other words, sensible consciousness and God-consciousness, are the two mutually opposed elements of self-consciousness, then each one is equally the act of the subject. This deceptive feature in the *Glaubenslehre*'s presentation, what its teaching cannot conceal, is the fact that what is inherently the subject's own doing is said to be only something imparted to the subject. The ambiguity in making one's own act also in turn the act of the redeemer is, of its own accord, conspicuous when Schleiermacher himself, in describing Christ's redeeming activity as consisting in taking up the believer into the full strength of Christ's own God-consciousness, recognizes in this activity the essentially teleological character of Christian piety, in virtue of which not only the impeded condition of the higher life, but also the stimulation of the higher life in our own self-consciousness, appears as the particular act of our own individual life; and when, since in virtue of the distinctive character of Christianity, this very stimulation in that same self-consciousness is grasped as the act of the redeemer, Schleiermacher supposes he can unite the two [the self-consciousness and the redeemer's act] in no other way than by making this stimulation the act of the redeemer done as his own act, and the distinctive activity of the redeemer being the producing of this act in us. This vacillation between one pole and the other is explainable only from the fact that what is supposedly seen as the redeemer's act is still actually and inherently just the particular act of the subject itself. Only by presupposing this ambiguity can one hold fast to the teleological character of Christianity. What he calls "imparting" is only the immanent act of the subject itself, and that becomes ever clearer in how Schleiermacher develops this point.

As opposed to the powerlessness of the God-consciousness, the constraint on the feeling of utter dependence that constitutes the essence of sin, redemption is the liberation of God-consciousness, the facility with which we are capable of instilling God-consciousness into the various sensuous activations of self-consciousness. But why should this facility be considered something sheerly imparted to us, since God-consciousness is also present in each moment of sin and proves to be operative in human beings through the very fact of their being aware of God? Just as sensible consciousness is always posited at the same time as God-consciousness, so too God-consciousness is never something lacking in sensible consciousness. For, once God-consciousness is posited as an active force, then it is completely inconceivable that it should not demonstrably also be something forceful in the degree to which it pervades the other operative elements [of consciousness], and comes to prevail over the sensible element.

If, as Schleiermacher says (1:357),[49] that it belongs to the original perfection of human beings to reach "those states of self-consciousness in which God-consciousness can be realized," then the emergence of God-consciousness in its full strength is grounded in the human being's nature itself, and it is simply the consequence of human development that God-consciousness is initially suppressed and tethered by sensible consciousness and must first be freed from this constraint. However, this is the very reason one also cannot maintain—when the constrained feeling of utter dependence becomes free, in other words when we have this facility of being able to instill God-consciousness into the various sensuous activations of self-

---

49. *Der christliche Glaube* (n. 42), §60 (ET [2016] 1:355).

consciousness—that this is just something imparted to us or just has its basis in the acts of redemption, since the external acts of the redemption taking place through Jesus can impart nothing that was not originally grounded in human nature. Hence these external acts just awaken this feature of human nature and bring it to active expression.

Hence, as Schleiermacher states (1:384):[50] ". . . if both constraint on the impulse to God-consciousness and expedited development of it are to be equally the act of one and the same individual, and consequently opposites are to be explained on the same basis, then, in relation to the doer, the two must cease to be opposed." To be sure we do not find such an antithesis if sensible consciousness and God-consciousness are in the same way the elements of a human being's spiritual nature, or moments of one's spiritual development; if one and the same subject is indeed on the one hand someone in need of redemption, inasmuch as sensible consciousness is one's prevailing feature, but on the other hand is also someone capable of redemption in virtue of never being deprived of the power of God-consciousness.

For an even more precise understanding of how nonessential the distinctively Christian is in Schleiermacher's *Glaubenslehre*, compare it with Kant's *Religion Within the Limits of Reason Alone*. The two principles Schleiermacher sets apart can be traced back to Kantian ones.[51] It is easy to see how the mystical ambiguity enveloping Schleiermacher's *Glaubenslehre* gets cleared up in the bright light of Kant's rationalism.

The Christology of the *Glaubenslehre*

Nevertheless we still have to analyze the main part of Schleiermacher's *Glaubenslehre*, the christology consisting of the major thesis that, as redeemer, Christ is both archetypal (*urbildlich*) and historical.[52] With this thesis Schleiermacher's *Glaubenslehre* most decidedly renounces all that is rationalistic, in order, purely and unconditionally, to devote itself to the church's faith and to cast itself into the arms of the church. But, however fine the threads from which the ingenious web of this *Glaubenslehre* is spun, they nevertheless cannot conceal the deception at its foundation. The conception of a Christ equally archetypal and historical supposedly says: Christ is the redeemer in virtue of his totally abolishing the constraint on the feeling of utter dependence, a constraint making it impossible for all human

---

50. *Der christliche Glaube* (n. 42), §63.1 (ET [1928] 263, modified).

51. See above, pp. 57–59. The Kantian principles are those of good and evil; the Son of God is "the personified idea of the principle of the good."

52. *Der christliche Glaube* (n. 42), §§93–99.

beings to be satisfactorily aligned with God-consciousness. In other words, he is the redeemer in virtue of his archetypal status that essentially sets him apart from all other human beings, namely, the constancy of his God-consciousness manifest through his freedom from error and his sinlessness, the constancy that, as the absolutely full strength of the God-consciousness, was the being of God in him.

But how does Schleiermacher demonstrate this archetypal character? He cannot hold fast to the unity of the archetypal and the historical itself, posited in the concept of the redeemer, since where the archetypal character was supposedly evident in its historical actuality, he seeks to restrict the concept of it as much as possible. This amounts to saying that it is not something involving the thousands of circumstances of human life, such that the redeemer must be archetypal also for all knowing or for all the artistry and skill that develops in human society. Instead it only involves the strength of God-consciousness providing the impulse for, and determining, all the moments of life. So the archetypal character of the redeemer extends no further than this. Yet it is not only a matter of very strictly isolating this special sphere in which the redeemer is said to be, or to have absolutely been, the redeemer, whereas with regard to the rest of his personal being he was subject to the imperfection of all finite existence. Also, isolating it on the whole changes nothing, since God-consciousness too, in its development and its appearing, is necessarily subject to the conditions of finitude.

Of course here too there is once again a restriction, for the miraculous element of the archetypal character comes in only at the beginning of the redeemer's life and not in its continuation. Yet since we never in fact conceptualize the beginning of life, the requirement that this completely archetypal character has a complete historicality also gets fully satisfied if, from this point on, he developed in the same way as all others, so that from birth onward his powers gradually unfolded and, starting at zero when they first appeared, built up to proficiency in the sequence natural to the human species. This also applies to his God-consciousness, which has developed in him too, as all consciousness just gradually does in making its actual appearance in the human manner.

But how does this square with Schleiermacher's contention about Christ's sinlessness, with the utter inability to sin Christ is said to have had in virtue of his archetypal character? Such an attribute ruling out any internal struggle, any wavering of the spiritual life between good and evil, and so any development, is utterly incompatible with human nature. The possibility of sinning is essential to a human being in virtue of one's freedom as conditioned by various inducements, some sinful and some rational. Christ could in no way have had a human nature if he did not also have this possibility of sinning. Therefore if the God-consciousness in Christ, albeit conditioned through a natural development, is, in all the moments of his life, nevertheless said to have been only what is determinative but never what is determined, then this God-consciousness would be an absolute power doing away with the comparability of Christ's nature to the nature of other human beings—and it is not understandable how one can still speak of a natural development. However, if a natural development is completely unthinkable, then the entire appearing of Christ becomes something sheerly docetic or nonhistorical. Or else, if it is said to be historical, it is no sinless appearing and accordingly lacks the archetypal character. Thus time and again the link Schleiermacher wants to make between the archetypal and the historical in Christ is broken.

In order to concede the perfectibility of Christianity, the possibility of going beyond Christ in a certain sense, Schleiermacher distinguishes Christ's essential nature from his appearing. Schleiermacher maintains that Christ's conditioned and imperfect circumstances, the language in which he expressed himself, his national identity, are features that have also affected his thinking and acting, but just superficially so. Their inner core was still truly archetypal; and if the ongoing development of Christianity, in its teaching and life, increasingly overcomes those temporal and national limitations within which Jesus' acting and speaking operates, this would be no going beyond Christ but just a more complete portrayal of his inner essence.

But what now comes clearly into the picture, as Schmid justifiably remarks about Schleiermacher's *Glaubenslehre*,[53] is his separation of the historical Christ from the ideal Christ, in this distinction of Christ's appearing from his essential nature that does not appear. For the historical Christ can only be the one coming forward in the appearing; so the development of his essential being supposedly involves having gone beyond this historical Christ. Were this essential being the historical essence of Christ, it had to be able to be recognized in Christ's appearing, that is, in his teaching and actions. It had to be the enduring and determining feature in the phenomena or individual moments of Christ's life. Yet here the essential nature is said to be something not recognizable in the appearing, something more than his appearing. Consequently it cannot be the essence of the historical Christ, but instead is a concept or an ideal that is independent of his appearing, therefore beyond history, a construct of thinking or the imagination. Thus the believing Christian is said to rise up beyond the Christ of history to this ideal Christ.

53. Heinrich Friedrich Ferdinand Schmid (1811–85), *Über Schleiermacher's Glaubenslehre mit Beziehung auf die Reden über die Religion* (Leipzig, 1835), 265 (page number cited in the text).

Now it is self-evident that the pure idea of humanity dwelt in Christ as his innermost essence. This idea was unable to fully present itself in him, given the limitations of his day, an idea that consequently can be presented ever more fully in a period of higher spiritual growth. However, this is not the idea of the essence exclusive to Christ, or of the archetypal status exclusive to Christ. Instead this idea resides in each human life, making its appearance there as the basis of one's own essential nature. Therefore setting forth this essence more clearly does not mean setting forth more fully the distinctive essence of the historical Christ. Instead it consists of the idealizing of Christ, that is, relating the appearing of Christ to the pure idea of humanity, whereby the historical Christ, as nonessential, moves into the background. That is because another distinguished historical personality could, more or less happily, have served this purpose, and only the ideal Christ be made the actual basis of Christianity.

Just as the concept of Christ as equally archetypal and historical proves to be untenable in this way, so too we do not see what necessity there is, from the standpoint of Schleiermacher's *Glaubenslehre*, to presuppose such a Christ. In this case too Schleiermacher takes Christian consciousness as his point of departure, so that Schleiermacher's Christ too is the result of an analysis of Christian consciousness. As members of the Christian community, Christians are conscious of the efficacy of a principle restricting and annulling the power of sin in themselves. We cannot derive the efficacy of this principle from the Christian community itself, such that it would be produced by the reciprocal influence of one's fellow members. For, in the collective life of sin in which, first of all, they find themselves, each one both generates sin on one's own and is on the receiving end of it from others. This efficacy can only come from someone who, on the one hand, would be sinless and perfect (as the efficacy of the principle presupposes), but on the other hand, stands in the kind of relation to the Christian community such that his personal attributes can be imparted to it, that is, someone who is its founder. By concluding from the efficacy to its cause, Schleiermacher's *Glaubenslehre* arrives at its Christ.

What we find operative in our Christian consciousness can only be brought about by Christ; and just as we conclude from this effect to the efficacy of Christ, so the same conclusion also holds good for inference from Christ's efficacy to his person. What Christ brings about in us through the mediation of the Christian community is the empowering of God-consciousness in its relation to sensible or sensuous consciousness. That is, we find it easier for us to break the superior power of sensuousness in ourselves, to relate all the impressions we receive [from the world] to religious feeling and, in return, to allow all our activities to proceed from religious feeling. The very thing that Christ brings about is the consequence of what he was. We owe to him the ever-intensifying empowerment of our God-consciousness, and so this God-consciousness must have been present in him, in its absolutely full strength, in such a way that it—in other words God in the form of consciousness—was alone operative in him, and in Christ God became a human being. Furthermore, if Christ brings about in us the ever more complete overcoming of sensuousness, then this sensuousness must have been utterly overcome in him. In no moment of his life can the sensible consciousness have successfully contested the God-consciousness; never did he waver and struggle. The human nature in him was sinless, indeed such that it could not possibly sin, owing to the higher power in him being essentially superior to the lower one. This is how, by inferring from the one factor [his efficacy] to the other one [his sinlessness], Schleiermacher's *Glaubenslehre* arrives at its archetypal Christ.

However, one need only analyze this conclusion in order to see how unfounded is the main result it supposedly establishes. [The line of argument is that] if individuals feel themselves supported in their religious consciousness, then this support must also have a cause; and when individuals receive this support not from themselves but instead from the community to which they belong, they can only seek it in this community; and when this community has become what it is because of its founder, one must also resort to the founder. But what then is the justification for assuming that what exists in only a relative way, in all the individuals belonging to the Christian community, is in the founder of that community in an absolute way?

If God-consciousness is superior to sensible consciousness in varying degrees, then there must also be a highest degree, or an original strength, of God-consciousness. But where can the basis for this original strength of God-consciousness be except simply in God-consciousness itself? That is, as surely as God-consciousness belongs to human nature as such, so surely must it also have within itself the power to develop itself from itself as fully as befits its own essential nature. If God-consciousness presents itself as something especially strong in the founder of the Christian community, then the founder has this full strength of his God-consciousness from the same source from which individuals each have their own God-consciousness, from the original strength of the God-consciousness implanted in human nature as such. But what is the basis for assuming that this original strength of God-consciousness has produced itself in him, in this one [Christ], such that he is completely identical with it?

If God-consciousness can be thought of simply as a power and tendency implanted in human nature as such, then it is a feature of the nature of God-consciousness that it evolves in the most manifold forms and levels. However, each single individual, no matter how highly placed, stands as such just in a subordinate relation to the universal feature belonging to the distinctiveness of human nature as such. Hence there is simply no justification for identifying a specific individual with humanity as a whole, or with humanity's spiritual tendency, in saying that the strength of the God-consciousness that is something merely relative in all other human beings is something absolute in Christ, and that the support for the strength of the God-consciousness in each individual could only come from the absolute strength of Christ's God-consciousness.

What can therefore only be said about God-consciousness itself, inasmuch as it belongs to the perfection of human nature, Schleiermacher transfers directly to Christ; and he assumes as absolute reality in Christ what can be thought of in humanity as a whole only as an infinite capacity of development. Schleiermacher's entire christology rests on the presupposition that, in Christ, his absolute reality must possess what inherently belongs to the idea of humanity or is in it as its power and tendency. That is precisely what Schleiermacher is referring to when he says that Christ's appearing, and the establishing of a wholly new life, is to be regarded as the creation of human nature as now complete for the first time. In this way of putting it, the redeemer was already instilled in a nontemporal way in the initial creation of the human race, even though what appeared at that time was just the incomplete state of human nature. Consequently this position maintains the necessity of the redeemer's appearing within humankind, for all other human beings are related to the redeemer simply as lower levels are related to the highest, perfect level. Thus what is in all others in only a relative way must have become real absolutely in Christ. For, as Schleiermacher himself says (2:34),[54] "as soon as one concedes the possibility of a constant progression in the strength of God-consciousness but denies that the completion of that progression exists anywhere, then one also could no longer maintain that creation of the human being is or will become complete. This is so, because in the constant progression of God-consciousness completion always, of course, remains posited only as a possibility . . . [if it] is posited in the concept but exists in no individual."

But what basis can there be for maintaining that the creation of human nature is not completed unless the idea of humanity is realized in a specific, single individual in an absolute way? If the creation of human nature is completed when it is in actuality what human nature ought to be according to the idea, then it is possible that the essence of the idea involves explicating

---

54. *Der christliche Glaube* (n. 42), §93.3 (ET [2016] 2:567).

itself in an endless diversity of individuals; and what follows from the essential nature of the idea is simply that there cannot be any talk at all about a completed creation of human nature in this sense. If we consider human nature from the perspective of the self-realizing idea, then, in the very nature of things, idea and actuality cannot completely coincide at any single point, because the idea is what is infinite, and what is actual is only something finite, something temporally conditioned. At whatever point, or in whichever individual, one therefore wants to pinpoint the idea as captured within actuality, the idea inexorably and forever presses beyond it.

Schleiermacher also uses this same contention as the basis for speaking about the unity of the archetypal and historical elements in Christ. He says that, in virtue of the connection between the will and the understanding, sinful humanity has no ability at all to generate a spotless archetype, and therefore that what is archetypal could not at all have been present in the consciousness of humankind if indeed it were not already something historical; that the ideal Christ would accordingly have the historical Christ as its necessary presupposition. However, this contention could only be based on the fundamental principle of empiricism, that *nihil in intellectu esse potest, quod non est in re* (nothing can be in the intellect that is not in reality). But if there is also an ideal knowing, ideas independent of all experience, hence also an idealizing thinking, then we cannot escape the evident truth that Schleiermacher's Christ—since his unity of the archetypal and the historical is in no way sustainable—emerges only in an idealizing way. He is the ideal human being, or the idea of humanity, in a specific individual in whom the idealizing imagination finds its most natural point of contact, seen in its concrete appearing.

However, what also vanishes at this point is any semblance of orthodox christology and orthodox Christianity, which is what Schleiermacher's *Glaubenslehre* seeks to provide. If we further reflect on how the entire structure of Schleiermacher's *Glaubenslehre* rests on the doctrine of the person of Christ, with its particularly close connection of its doctrine about the work (*Geschäft*)[55] to the doctrine of the person of Christ, then, as soon as we have recognized the untenability of uniting the archetypal and the historical elements we see the entire edifice of this *Glaubenslehre* collapsing internally. It is the least stable precisely where it most intends to be conscious of its identity with the teaching of the church. So it is merely an illusion to suppose that here one is standing on the solid ground of ecclesiastical Christianity, and to suppose this is simply taking up the task of moderating the inflexible

---

55. On the work of Christ, see *Der christliche Glaube* (n. 42), §§100–105.

definitions of church doctrine as much as possible, of smoothing over the rough edges, and converting the old formulations into modern parlance.

The Pantheism of the *Glaubenslehre*

Indeed, Schleiermacher's *Glaubenslehre* is so minimally on the soil of ecclesiastical Christianity that not once does it occupy the standpoint of theism. The concern of theism is most specifically expressed in the idea of personhood. But this is the very point where the ambiguity belonging to the character of Schleiermacher's *Glaubenslehre* can be detected most clearly. Zeller's article on Schleiermacher's doctrine of the personhood of God[56] has treated this issue so exhaustively that here it is enough to indicate briefly its main results. The way Schleiermacher interprets the relation between God and the world completely excludes accepting God's personhood in his system. There is personhood only where spirit as subject distinguishes itself from objectivity, or from what is other to itself. If Schleiermacher has then abolished this distinction on God's part in relation to the world; if he has equated the divine causality with the totality of finite causality, considered under the form of eternity; if he has expressly stated that one can conceive neither of God's being without the world nor of God's being apart from the world; if he has limited the entire distinction between them by calling the totality of existing being, considered as unity, "God," and as a multiplicity, calling it "world"[57]—then he would in fact have misunderstood himself in the most incomprehensible way if, in addition, he still wanted to maintain that God has personhood. There is certainly no longer any distinctive locus for God's being and operation; the entirety of divine causality is said to proceed within the world. Where then can even just the simple activity of a personal self-consciousness, existent on its own, find a place in this system? However, Schleiermacher not merely does not maintain the personhood of God; he also states most explicitly that he does not know how to think of divinity as an isolated, individual object, and that any such portrayal of divinity in religious knowledge would just be empty mythology.

The impossibility of Schleiermacher's *Glaubenslehre* accepting the personhood of God stands out in particular in how it treats the doctrines of the divine attributes and the Trinity.[58] Taken as a whole, the concepts

---

56. Eduard Zeller, "Erinnerung an Schleiermacher's Lehre von der Persönlichkeit Gottes," *Theologische Jahrbücher* 1 (1842) 263–87.

57. See *Die christliche Glaube* (n. 42), §§46.2, 51, 57.1.

58. The *Glaubenslehre* treats of God's essential nature as undivided absolute causality. The so-called divine attributes do not denote distinct aspects of God's nature but

of the divine attributes in Schleiermacher's case express just the oneness of absolute causality, a causality in itself utterly single and undivided, and not subdividing into objectively different forms of the divine life and operations. The distinctive nature of the human eye is what makes us simply incapable of beholding the unitary ray of the divine light in its untinted purity. To us, its varicolored refractions within the finite appear as just so many originally different streams of light. A God whose essential nature is just the wholly simple nature of pure being, in which there are no internal distinctions, in which knowing and willing, decision and execution, the possible and the actual, may not be posited separately—a God of this kind is impossible to think of as personhood. For all personhood is a comprising of internal distinctions in the unity of consciousness. Where there is no distinction, consciousness is therefore impossible, as color is impossible where there is clear, unrefracted light. It logically follows that Schleiermacher also gives no objective significance to the doctrine of the Trinity, but instead demotes it to being a statement of formal connections.

The *Glaubenslehre*'s Relation to Church Teaching

Since there can be little doubt about Schleiermacher's real views, we must constantly ask why he did not speak clearly and candidly himself, but instead always in such a way that his actual views must first be drawn out from the total context of his system. We must ask why he even had the obvious concern to conceal his views under skillful turns of phrase and to give the impression that he did not want to deny the personhood of God forthwith. He repeatedly declares belief in the personhood of God to be a matter of dogmatic indifference, as opposed to belief in God's vitality. In particular, compare with this the explanation on pp. 137-38 of the third edition of the *Reden über Religion*,[59] where he seeks, in a quite sophisticated way, to inter-

---

only various modifications in how the feeling of utter dependence relates to God—whether it expresses the general relationship between God and the world (God as eternal and omnipotent, etc. §§50–56), or the consciousness of sin (God as holy and just, §§79–84), or the consciousness of redemption (God as love and wisdom, §§164–69). To predicate "mercy" of God is to use an "anthropopathic" term (§85). The doctrine of the Trinity is treated in a brief "conclusion" (§§170–72) because it is not an immediate utterance of Christian self-consciousness but expresses only a "Sabellian" (modalistic) distinction between the divine essence as such or God ("Father") and the union of this essence with an individual person ("Son") and with the common life of the church in the world ("Spirit"). This is not a distinction within the supreme being as such, and no mutability may be ascribed to this being.

59. Schleiermacher, *Über die Religion: Reden an die Gebildeten unter ihren Verächtern*, 3rd ed. (Berlin, 1821), 198–200 (explanation 19, attached to p. 164, with

pret it as a sheer misunderstanding if one supposes that he is approximating in some fashion to belief in the personhood of God.

The concern from our standpoint is exactly the opposite. While Schleiermacher made every effort to conceal and skillfully mask[60] his real views, by presenting as nonessential what nevertheless has the most essential significance for his system, we can only proceed by demolishing this pretense and bringing to light the underlying truth in its unvarnished character. However, Schleiermacher's concern to mask his real views is not merely a feature of his own *Glaubenslehre*. It is generally typical of that time, since the same tendency is also manifest in other instances. Although people could hardly be in agreement with a system supporting itself simply on the principle of authority and not giving the freedom of the subject its due, they nevertheless hardly wished to make an open break with it. So they were inclined to come to terms and bear with that system, both by making compromises with it and by setting boundaries around what one might call the "constitutional rights" of each part of it. In needing an organization based on a form that could bring together the antithetical elements at least externally, people proved to be far more in agreement superficially than they were inwardly; they were satisfied to have a formal structure (*Rechtsform*) to which they could adhere. The old principles retained their formal structure, since people left them superficially in place and were averse to contesting them openly. When it came to the subject matter of the new principles, people found it sufficient to make them felt too, within the overarching authority of this older structure.

Schleiermacher's *Glaubenslehre* is circumspect to a fault in seeking to circumvent and mitigate, as much as possible, its contradiction with church teaching; it is deliberately artful in interpreting ecclesiastical tenets and formulations in a sense that Schleiermacher could not possibly regard as their true and actual sense. Very often one cannot suppress the thought that this is an intentional deception.[61] In any event Schleiermacher remains a master

---

reference to *Der christliche Glaube* [n. 42], §8 Postscript 2). Baur's page citation (137–38) is actually to the 4th ed. of 1831, which is more compact than the 3rd (322 pp. vs. 461 pp.), but otherwise identical. ET: *On Religion: Speeches to Its Cultured Despisers*, trans. John Oman (London, 1893), 115–16. The *Reden* was first published in 1799. Schleiermacher added the explanations to the 3rd edition in light of his recently published *Glaubenslehre*. These were retained in subsequent editions.

60. Baur here uses *verschleiern*, which is a play on the meaning of Schleiermacher's name in German, "veil-maker."

61. [*Zeller*] I leave this passage as it is, although perhaps it will prove offensive to many of Schleiermacher's admirers. Even granted that the verdict above attributes too much to this theologian, it nevertheless ought not to be suppressed. That is because it is indicative of the standpoint of the one passing judgment. At one time Baur had

in the art of dealing with dogmatic formalism in a truly diplomatic way. Our only reproach of Schleiermacher in this regard redounds from him personally to the era characterized by this constitutive formalism.

Our analysis so far has shown how Schleiermacher's *Glaubenslehre* is wholly a matter of this ambiguous position in which it presupposes the subject matter of the church's system, but in truth continually contests it and annuls it in principle. Another convincing proof of this is Schleiermacher's treatment of eschatology. It is clear that all the doctrines people usually include in eschatology can find no place in a system taking such a negative stance toward everything transcendent. However, saying this straight out would have been far too discrepant with the diplomatic sagacity of this dogmatics. Hence a form must be found that will make it appear the *Glaubenslehre* is not inherently opposed to these doctrines; that it merely leaves them in place with the proviso that they are left to a future vindication better than they have found so far. This is the meaning of the section on prophetic doctrines,[62] which Schleiermacher puts toward the end of his dogmatic system. Our only task in this case, says Schleiermacher, is just to show how those doctrines have sustained themselves in the church from time immemorial and without also investigating them anew in our confessional writings, but only as an attempt to spell out an insufficiently supported future sense that goes under the name of prophetic doctrines, with the bases for them and their dubious character. As Schleiermacher said in his prefatory remarks, the imagination, to which people still fall prey, will take for its object a possible future state that is quite unlike our own range of experience at the time. So, in order to remain Christian, we must stick with the safeguard of the exegetical art and just work with the material it presents for us, without resorting to the play of arbitrariness or to putatively new revelations.

How can Schleiermacher speak, even only in this sense, about prophetic doctrines, if what they themselves nevertheless presuppose is belief in immortality, or the idea of one's personal continuation beyond death, when his basis for immortality is more than just shaky? Schleiermacher initially denies the religious element of belief in immortality, but at the same time, in order not to let it disappear, he maintains that belief in the continuation of personhood goes together with our faith in the redeemer. For, when the redeemer himself ascribes such a continuation to himself in all that he says

---

thought it not possible that such a rigorous thinker as Schleiermacher should have himself disguised the contradiction, so openly evident, between his own dogmatics and the church's dogmatics.

62. *Der christliche Glaube* (n. 42), §§157–63. These prophetic doctrines are the return of Christ, the resurrection of the flesh, the last judgment, and eternal blessedness.

about his return or his reunion with his own, then, since he could say this only about himself as a human person, it follows that the same thing must hold good for us too. Hence the redeemer is the mediator of immortality in this specific sense; for, if human nature's lot not be personal immortality, then also a uniting of the divine essence, conjoined with human nature, to such a personhood as that of the redeemer, would not have been possible. Vice versa, because God has decided to perfect and redeem human nature by such a union, this is also of course why the essence of the human individual who was conscious of the redeemer had to be forever a bearer of this immortality. This is the true Christian certainty of this belief.

But this certainty does not provide the slightest guarantee for the reality of what is believed. When Schleiermacher at the same time declares that one cannot maintain a connection between belief in the continuance of personhood and God-consciousness in itself, then there is no basis, even with reference to Christ's person, for why the constancy of the union, in his person, of the divine essence with the human nature, should be thought of as a personal continuation, inasmuch as the distinctive superiority of the redeemer resides only in his God-consciousness, and his God-consciousness in itself has no inner connection with the belief in personal continuance. Hence that belief in the constancy of the uniting of the divine essence with the human nature in Christ's person is none other than the belief that the consciousness which, through Christ, has become a being of God within his human nature, will forever remain the consciousness of the humanity, and it has utterly nothing to say about the personal continuance of the single individual.

The Internal Coherence and Historical Significance of the *Glaubenslehre*

This *Glaubenslehre* is so deceptive about each significant point that, where it seems to affirm that point, it instead denies it. If even Schleiermacher believed he could, simply in this ambiguous fashion, make a generally valid case for the freer, rational view that lies at the basis of his *Glaubenslehre*, we nevertheless can see in this ambiguity simply the transitory aspect of his *Glaubenslehre*. This form of presentation was brought about simply by a particular concern. We can locate what is essential or substantial in his *Glaubenslehre* only after stripping away this temporal form. This essential element stands out as what is enduring and ageless. But what does it consist in? What does Schleiermacher's *Glaubenslehre* have to offer for conceptualizing Christianity in its essential rationality?

This rationality's essential character consists in the fact that it makes Christian consciousness its principle, and develops the entire content of the Christian faith based on the testimony of Christian consciousness.[63] Since Schleiermacher relies on Christian consciousness for the content of the Christian faith and its essential determinations, and sets this consciousness above scripture, this says that, for the subject, faith is not merely something given externally; faith is nothing foreign to it from the outset; faith has an internal point of connection in the subject's consciousness. Thus the major historical significance of Schleiermacher's *Glaubenslehre* is that it is the first thorough attempt to set forth the content of the Christian faith as an original possession of the human spirit, as not a content entering into the spirit from outside it, but instead one arising from spirit's own innermost depth. As distinct from the principle of Schleiermacher's *Glaubenslehre*, rationalism is one-sided, in that it sets faith and thinking in such an antithesis from the outset that thinking can never know itself as being inwardly one with faith or belief. For rationalism, faith's content is something utterly given, a purely historical object, and thus thinking's task is simply to free itself from the specific elements of faith as something foreign to reason. In contrast, Schleiermacher grasps the specific elements of the Christian faith as being something immanent to the subject, so that for him Christian consciousness is just a modification and form of general religious consciousness. Hence what Christian consciousness also has, as such a special modification, cannot be superseded by the substantial element of religious consciousness as such. This of course says that Christianity can contain nothing that would not also be inherently rational. Inasmuch as it is Christian, the Christian consciousness cannot fail to recognize that this specificity it has is something mediated by what is historically given; but inasmuch as the immediacy of consciousness is the principle, this shows that, as principle, it may contain nothing that, as Christian, contradicts the immediate testimony of self-consciousness.

Consciousness as such is the power overarching everything. Hence in Schleiermacher's *Glaubenslehre* Christian consciousness takes a thoroughly critical stance toward what belongs to the content of the Christian faith. The entire *Glaubenslehre* is a continuous critique, in which rational thinking

---

63. Schleiermacher says that description of human states of consciousness is the "basic form" suitable to Christian theology, into which, because it is based on inner experience, nothing alien can infiltrate from dogmatics and metaphysics. Propositions about God and the world are theoretically reducible to the first basic form (self), but doing so "at the present time" would leave the *Glaubenslehre* without historical orientation or an ecclesial character, and would fail its purpose of explicating religious language with its rhetorical and poetic elements (§30.2–3; ET [2016] 1:183–85).

asserts its rights with regard to each tenet of the Christian faith, at any event to those in particular that Schleiermacher's *Glaubenslehre* emphasizes. On the one hand Christian consciousness has for its principle the principle of rational thinking, the I or self of self-consciousness; on the other hand it relies on the idea of community, which idea belongs to the essence of religion. So, from this starting point Schleiermacher's *Glaubenslehre* takes a direction acquiring an increasingly speculative character,[64] although it did not commence as speculation. Individuals become determined in their religious consciousness by the community of which they are members. Over against subjective consciousness, the community appears as the objective power, as the sphere in which alone the religious consciousness and the lives of individuals have their objective reality and truth. But the religious community on which the individual depends, as a member of it, has this objective significance only owing to the spirit holding sway in it. This is the Holy Spirit, as the shared spirit of the collective consciousness, shaping the believers. Had this religious truth not been given as a historical truth, not become objectively actual, through the power of this Spirit in the religious community of which it is the principle, then for the subject too it would only count as something subjective and not count as objective truth.

What then is this spirit itself, which is the principle so powerfully operative as the shared spirit of the common life? What brings it forth from the community in which it has objectified itself, and which is the distinctive sphere of its operation, to ever more intensify itself in the subjective consciousness of the individual? The answer, first and foremost, can only be that it is the spirit of Christ as redeemer. But we must then immediately ask how Schleiermacher's Christ relates to this spirit objectifying itself in history. This is the point at which there stands out most clearly the way in which Schleiermacher's *Glaubenslehre* relates the standpoint of subjectivity to that of objectivity; the way in which Schleiermacher, of course based on his originally subjective standpoint, presses on to an objectivity determining the subject—yet still does not push through to the point where this objectivity can simply be the absolutely self-determining principle. There always remains a limit here that Schleiermacher leaves in place. On the one hand he of course takes his standpoint within subjective consciousness, and always only wants to go as far beyond it as is necessary in order to

---

64. For Baur "speculative" entails an element of objectivity as well as subjectivity (a mirroring of the objective by the subjective, and of the subjective by the objective). Schleiermacher himself says that "speculative consciousness" is "the supreme objective function of the human spirit," while religious self-consciousness is "the supreme subjective function," and that the two functions cannot be in conflict (§28.3; ET [2016] 1:178). See also n. 72.

conceive of the experiences of the inner life as operations of a cause that lies beyond consciousness. On the other hand, however, the community from which alone this cause is derivable, the shared spirit determining the collective consciousness, comes to be regarded as the objective factor that just subjectivizes itself in the subject. But these two aspects, the objective and subjective ones, still stand side by side as wholly unmediated, and what is lacking is the unity in which they reciprocally permeate, and coalesce with, each other.

This unity is still not given by grasping the shared spirit as the spirit of Christ. Schleiermacher differentiates Christ from the Holy Spirit in such a way that Christ is God's being in a human individual, and the Holy Spirit is the uniting of the divine essence with human nature in the form of the shared spirit enlivening the collective life of the faithful. While this formulation, describing the Holy Spirit as the absolute principle implanted in humanity and operating within it in an ever-widening circle, is more suitable, what is especially striking is that it places Christ in a subordinate relation to the Holy Spirit. If the significance of Christ's personhood resides in the embedding of the new life-principle in humanity, and this principle is the Holy Spirit, then Christ's person is just the suddenly emerging point of light, the entry point for all that pertains to the essence of redemption, as the principle establishing in humanity's consciousness a new community, the point of departure for mediating the new consciousness of human beings' reconciliation with God, a reconciliation that is the imparting, and the presence, of the spirit itself. However, since Schleiermacher then eliminates any objective relation of the Son or the Spirit in an immanent trinitarian relationship, we see very clearly here the deficiency in his system. The objectivity to which he moves on from subjective consciousness is only historical objectivity, the spirit objectifying itself in the historically given religious community. But how and whence the spirit has entered into humanity's history, and what has determined it to objectify itself in history in this way, lies completely beyond the horizon of this standpoint.

The spirit as the shared spirit of the religious community of course presupposes the incarnation of God in Christ, or God's being in him. However, since Schleiermacher lacks any objective concept of God's essence, this being of God in Christ is, as Schleiermacher characterizes it, in part a merely abstract, contentless representation, and in part a bringing into view here of all that makes God's being in Christ, in other words the oneness of the archetypal Christ and the historical Christ, into a completely untenable representation. If the Holy Spirit is humanity's truly spiritual consciousness, and if Christ is not said to be either a mere individual or the absolute I of consciousness, then Christ can only be humanity in itself, the universal human being, or rather the eternal spirit becoming human within humanity and realizing itself in humanity as its concrete shape.

Earlier on Schleiermacher had taken up this [view of Christ] as being not merely ideal but actual, of Christ not merely existent in a single individual but present substantially in humanity itself. He did so in his *Weihnachtsfeier*,[65] where he has human beings finding redemption only in the human being in itself (*der Mensch an sich*), in which there is no defect or corruption and no need for redemption; and where he says, about this human being in itself, that a person will be redeemed only when human being in itself, the unity of eternal being and becoming, dawns on himself or herself. Humanity eternally becomes this human being in itself. But this human being in itself must enter into one as one's own thought. One must bear in oneself the consciousness and spirit of humanity, must envisage and build up humanity as a living community of individuals; and only in this way does one have within oneself the higher life and peace of God. This takes place in the church, where the human being in itself is and would be presented. Each person in whom that self-consciousness dawns comes to the church. The church is, so to speak, humanity's self-consciousness, as opposed to which all else is insensible to it.

As the universal human being, this Christ has a wholly different reality than does the artfully constructed Christ of the *Glaubenslehre*. On the contrary the *Glaubenslehre*, via its concept of the Holy Spirit as the spirit operating in the religious community, leads over, in speculative fashion, into the principle intensifying subjective consciousness. The question is just how the spirit, operating as the principle of humanity, has itself entered into humanity. This question is not answerable on the soil of the *Glaubenslehre*.

De Wette's Philosophy of Religion and Dogmatics

Schleiermacher's *Glaubenslehre* has such great historical importance that, unless one knows it in detail and has looked somewhat deeply into the internal coherence of its skillfully organized system, one cannot follow the course of development taken by the most recent theology. We may locate de Wette[66] here alongside Schleiermacher—not as though he in some way

---

65. Schleiermacher, *Weihnachtsfeier. Ein Gespräch* (2nd ed., Berlin, 1826); ET by W. Hastie as *Christmas Eve: Dialogue on the Celebration of Christmas* (Edinburgh, 1890); by Terrence Tice as *Christmas Eve: Dialogue on Incarnation* (Richmond, VA, 1967).

66. Wilhelm Martin Leberecht de Wette (1780–1849), was a theologian and biblical scholar who was influenced by Herder and other leaders of Romanticism and the Enlightenment. He taught first in Heidelberg and then Berlin, but after a controversy

is Schleiermacher's peer as a theologian, but only because, on the one hand, he too strives characteristically to disavow the rational justification for ecclesiastical dogma while, on the other hand, maintaining dogma intact under the deceptive appearance of an artfully devised theology. For this purpose de Wette distinguishes two essentially different elements in the concept and essence of religion, religion's truth and its beauty, in other words, belief and feeling, a dogmatic aspect and an aesthetic aspect. Religion can come alive only in feeling. The ideas of religious belief, grasped with one's speculative ability, are, so to speak, lifeless and rigid. They have no application to life if they are not grasped with feeling and introduced into life, since this speculative ability merely involves subordinating what is particular to the idea.

De Wette divides religious feelings into three kinds, or three aesthetic ideas. The idea of the *human vocation*, grasped by feeling, presents itself in the feeling of *inspiration*, that is, in the mindset with which we pursue a higher purpose in human life, or else sense it intuitively and look upon it as actual or nevertheless becoming actual. Inspiration is the cheerful, untroubled outlook on the world that gives us a presentiment, in the endless purposiveness of temporal phenomena, that we are in the kingdom of God on earth. The idea of *good and evil* is found in the feeling of *resignation*, an idea that, as irresolvable conflict, bears within itself its resolution. Conscious of our guilt, we bow down before the holy omnipotent one, and in this submission we recover the feeling of our higher worth and of inner peace. In this spirit, we rise above what is finite and become conscious of our everlasting worth; we confidently face the end and submit to outwardly inevitable necessity, because our spirit regards itself as higher than what it appears to be, and nothing can crush its inner freedom. The feeling of *devotion* is the presupposition for these other two feelings, those of inspiration and resignation. With inspiration, we cannot grasp the divine element in phenomena unless we have a presentiment of the spirit of God itself within the world. With resignation, we cannot rise above the phenomena unless we have confidence in the eternal goodness that guides everything for the best and resolves its perplexity. Therefore in the feeling of devotion, what is for

---

transferred to Basel, where he became a figure of great influence. He published widely, including *Biblische Dogmatik Alten und Neuen Testaments oder kritische Darstellung der Religionslehre des Hebraismus, des Judenthums und Urchristentums* (Berlin, 1813); *Über Religion und Theologie* (Berlin, 1815); *Lehrbuch der christlichen Dogmatik* (Berlin, 1813–16); *Lehrbuch der historisch-kritischen Einleitung in die Bibel* (Berlin, 1817); *Religion, ihr Wesen, ihre Erscheinungsformen, und ihr Einfluss auf das Leben* (Berlin, 1827), and *Das Wesen des christlichen Glaubens* (Basel, 1846). Baur discusses de Wette's contribution to the history of biblical criticism in the introduction to his *Vorlesungen über neutestamentliche Theologie*, ed. F. F. Baur (Leipzig, 1864), 12–14 (ET: *Lectures on New Testament Theology*, ed. P. C. Hodgson, trans. R. F. Brown [Oxford, 2016], 71–73).

our understanding just the empty form of absolute oneness, and so readily assumes the appearance of something merely thought and contrived, becomes faith in God, the firm foothold and point of support for our inner life, the fundamental source of all the other religious feelings.

Feeling acquires its more specific character from these three aesthetic ideas. The task of the philosophy of religion is then to keep feeling, so defined, apart from the understanding, as two particular spheres, so that what is kept out of the one can, on that account, still have its positive import in the other. What the understanding must recognize as something untrue can, for all that, have its truth in the form of feeling. The eternal ideas stand above and beyond the understanding and feeling. However, in this way of looking at things, just as the understanding ends up everywhere in mysteries, gets only so far as what is finite, and the ideas are the unattainable, the infinite, so feeling can only envisage the ideas in pictorial shapes, in symbolic outer garments.

The application of this general theory to Christianity is then made in the following way. Just as every history is, on the whole, symbolic, that is, the expression and likeness of the human spirit and its activity, so the appearing of Christ, his life and death inasmuch as it involves the complete unveiling of his divine-human status, is to be regarded as symbolic, that is, as the graphic portrayal of supersensible ideas. Christianity's character as revelation consists in this very portrayal, because in fact the eternal ideas of reason make their appearance in Christianity in their greatest purity and fullness. Rationalism is no more than the philosophical perspective on the revealed faith, or the consciousness of the relationship between idea and symbol in Christianity. As a result of this symbolic perspective, the miracle narratives in the gospel must be considered, from the standpoint of those who report them, first and foremost as symbols of the ideas that they found in the history of early Christianity. The temporal element in these ideas must then be separated out from the eternally religious element and, with the help of the religious element, these symbols have a more or less fruitful meaning for us too.

Jesus' miraculous conception and birth belong in this sphere of time-dependent mythical symbolism. Christ is conceived in the womb of a pure virgin, and that portrays symbolically the ideas of religion's divine origin and Jesus' divine stature. We can indeed concur with the gospel writers in this ideal view of Christianity's origin, although our understanding resists the miracle. The miracles that Jesus performs portray the divine spirit in him as lord of nature, and give evidence of his spirit's superiority, by which he captures people's admiration and fills them with awe. The factual events in themselves, and their relation to nature and to nature's laws, are not significant for us, although they do involve the idea, very meaningful for us, of the independent power of the human spirit, and they embody the sublime teaching about spiritual self-confidence. His resurrection and ascension are to be considered from the same symbolic or aesthetic perspective. Indeed one can say that the life of Jesus is, on the whole, the embodiment of religious ideas. The basic religious ideas are so clearly expressed in his teaching, and the ideas of inspiration, of resignation, of devotion, are just as clearly expressed in his life story.

What holds good for grasping the gospel story also holds good for treating the church's dogmas. One must of course leave their form intact, but simply give them symbolic meaning. De Wette, who in fact takes up the dogma of Christ's divinity in this sense, is far from wanting to overturn it, although he holds that thinking of divinity united with humanity in one individual is a self-contradictory concept, because it involves thinking of the divinity as degraded to being something finite and actually no longer divinity as such. However, this doctrine should not be a concept, but instead be an aesthetic idea. The pious Christian, convinced of the divine truth of Jesus' teaching, convinced that God's wisdom and grace have obviously been infused into his teaching, and being deeply affected by the purity and sublimity of Jesus' character, believes Jesus is the embodied deity and beholds it in him, but without reflecting on this or asking how it is possible, since believing it shows one's vital feeling is genuine. Therefore, away with all those barren dogmatic formulations! Moreover, the Bible and the people's faith know nothing of them. For us Christ counts as the one sent by God, as God incarnate, as the image of God. One should not be too sparing in glorifying him or be too apprehensive about these expressions. However, one ought never forget that one is speaking not about intellectual truths, but solely about religious beauty; and whoever speaks of them to people should never do so except with the impetus and warmth of pious inspiration.

De Wette states that this is the advantage of distinguishing the intellectual and the aesthetic points of view. Whoever gives credence only to the intellectual viewpoint in religion must repudiate these doctrines; and that is what all the rationalists have consequently done. We, however, can and must let these doctrines stand, as belonging to the aesthetic perspective, as a beautiful, meaningful picture; not perhaps as a poetic creation of pious fantasy, of extravagant inspiration, but as the result of a historical, religious experience. But in doing so we excise the metaphysics from it and take up an ethical standpoint. This perspective speaks not so much about Christ's essential nature as it does about his character. The extant dogmatic specifications are otherwise readily derivable from the circumstances of the natural and ideal perspectives from which one can view Jesus. Considered in natural terms, he is a human being; considered in ideal, aesthetic terms, he is God; and just as both viewpoints are in principle one, there is then just one person, the God incarnate, and not two persons but instead two natures.

De Wette and Schleiermacher

This is the essential content of de Wette's theory as he elaborated it in his *Über Religion und Theologie* (1815, 1821), and in his *Lehrbuch der christlichen Dogmatik* (1816, 1821). Kant had already understood the church's dogmas as symbols of rational ideas, but had not gone so far as setting aesthetic beauty alongside what is true in itself, as its equal. Treating dogmas as symbolic posited in religious consciousness a dualism that lacked a mediating unity. Of course de Wette did set the ideas, as something absolute, above belief and feeling. Yet what objective significance do the ideas have here if they are unreachable by the understanding, and if what presents itself in feeling is only a pictorial way of intuiting them? And if understanding and feeling are juxtaposed as equals, what value then can aesthetic feelings and intuitions have if, as soon as the understanding reflects about them, it must say that they only rest on untrue representations. One should simply ponder how things stand with the divinity of Christ, when it is maintained, from the side of the understanding, that Christ is just a human being, while on the other side one without reservation, and even necessarily so, assigns to him the predicates "God" and "God incarnate." [De Wette asks:] If Jesus' early followers simply elevated him to divine stature, based on their own misguided, subjective standpoint, would not their fellow Christians, who saw that subjective view taking hold, have faced extraordinary pressure to join in that same religious enthusiasm?

Not only can we show the untenability of such a theory; we can also point out, for our purposes here, that the dogmatic ambiguity typical of the period we are discussing is also recognizable very distinctly in this instance. The rationalists who, like de Wette, have inwardly parted ways entirely with dogma, are still averse to admitting this break openly, and so constantly create the illusion that they are fully orthodox believers in Christianity as it really was. If they did not also believe in the supernatural and miraculous aspect of Christianity, they still always sought to give the appearance of believing in it. With their view of Christianity they stood on clearly human ground, although the human side of Christ was still at least said to be always cloaked with the semblance of this supernaturalistic belief. To be sure they no longer believed in the divinity of Christ, although, even if Christ was merely a human being, what harm could it do to speak of him as "God"? The only purpose of this deception is to artfully link up the rational point of view with the church's dogma. We see it in its unvarnished form with no other theologian in such a pronounced way as with de Wette. How can it be surprising that the result was a very prompt and serious protest at such intentional self-deception? What it all amounts to in this case is a completely unresolved dualism, one also underlying Schleiermacher's *Glaubenslehre*, with the only difference being that Schleiermacher knows how to conceal this duality far more skillfully.

It is truly dualistic when, on the one hand, Schleiermacher proceeds from a basic outlook utterly incompatible with everything supernatural and miraculous, and on the other hand constructs his position in such a way that all the elements of the church's belief system seem to be fully warranted in his *Glaubenslehre*. In order to clarify this discrepancy or bifurcation between Schleiermacher's philosophy and his dogmatics, a recent article (*Jahrbücher für deutsche Theologie*, 2:831)[67] stated that this bifurcation is undeniable; but the very thing personally distinctive about Schleiermacher is that his religious concerns are much broader and much more demanding than his philosophical system can allow for and satisfy. He has not found a scientific form corresponding to the rich contents of religion; however profound and original he may have been as a man of feeling, he still did not have scientific accomplishments sufficient for configuring this religious content freely on its own terms. He experienced the tension between believing and knowing; and where his dogmatics seems to be formulated too artfully, that is not a matter of hidden intentions, but instead of leaving natural necessity to seek out what is, according to him, the mediation of his own bifurcation.

However, it is just typical of Schleiermacher himself that in no way does he make such a bifurcation evident. Put succinctly, he never even admits that his philosophical presuppositions are insufficient for the contents of his religious feeling. To the contrary, his entire dogmatics is organized so as to have his philosophical presuppositions appear as the completely adequate foundation for the testimonies of religious consciousness. When he wants to dispense with miracle in his dogmatics, he states that religious concerns have no need to grasp an event in a way that its dependence on God cancels out its being conditioned by its natural connections.[68] Had Schleiermacher

---

67. Repentent Dr. Sigwart in Tübingen, "Schleiermachers psychologische Voraussetzungen, insbesondere die Begriff des Gefühls und der Individualität," *Jahrbücher für deutsche Theologie* 2 (1857) 829–64. Christoph Sigwart (1830–1904) later became a professor of philosophy in Tübingen. He was the author of several books, including a *Logik* (Tübingen, 1873–38) and works on Spinoza and Zwingli.

68. *Der christliche Glaube* (n. 42), §47.

actually been aware of such a bifurcation, he would have had to admit this dualism just as openly and honestly as de Wette did. Instead we find Schleiermacher neither making such an acknowledgement nor deciding for one side or the other. Instead, his own way is and remains always presenting the matter as if the two sides would be in complete harmony. It is not even remotely thinkable that religious consciousness would contain something contradictory to rational thinking and not at once be fully satisfying [rationally], if not today at least in the future. Schleiermacher hardly wants to admit to such a clear contradiction; instead he seeks in every clever way to conceal it. Hence one must always ask in turn why he has done this. Should something that must, of its own accord, strike every thoughtful reader of his *Glaubenslehre* have simply escaped his own keen understanding?

Hence if we put Schleiermacher and de Wette side by side, the interesting thing in this juxtaposition is precisely that the one [de Wette] openly and honestly admits what the other seeks to conceal with every artifice and effort—the dualism of reason and belief, of philosophical and religious concerns.

The Nature of Dogmatics at That Time

From the foregoing, we see how dogmatics, as one of the theological disciplines, works out its concerns and the direction it predominantly takes. On the one hand what counts is giving validity to the autonomy of reason; on the other hand people considered it an essential requirement to show genuine regard for the theological framework of the church, to recognize the historical justification for it, and to engage with it in dogmatic terms—whether that be by merely criticizing it as the rationalists did, or by acknowledging in it an inherently rational content that is only adequately expressed in thinking consciousness in the way we find this done by Schleiermacher and also by de Wette. The positive feature of Christianity, in the form of the church's theological framework, was such a significant element of the contemporary consciousness that no dogmatician would have been permitted to deny his ecclesiastical consciousness and to ignore the theological framework of the church. Friends of uniting the churches, such as Schleiermacher, could only treat dogmatics in keeping with the same basic tenets that underlay the Union. In the preface to the first edition of his *Glaubenslehre*, Schleiermacher emphasized, as its particularly distinctive feature, that it is written, first and foremost, with a view to the uniting of the two communions of the Evangelical (Protestant) Church.[69] Nevertheless, this distinctive feature

---

69. Schleiermacher, *Der christliche Glaube* (n. 42), 1st ed., viii–ix. The two

consists only in the fact that it was able to take examples from the symbols of both confessions. So one of course inherently would have had a larger selection and could counter-pose milder passages to the harsher ones, on the whole neutralizing one theological framework by the other. If Christian consciousness was the highest principle, of course the two confessions could only have equal standing relative to it.

Marheineke

We still have to mention Marheineke's *Grundlehren der christlichen Dogmatik*,[70] which merits special attention in the history of dogmatic literature. The first edition (1819), worked out according to the principles of Schelling's philosophy, was received with marked disfavor, at a time when Schleiermacher's *Glaubenslehre* too still had to contend so much with prejudice directed at its pantheistic character. In the second, completely revised edition (1827) this work forged its own path in virtue of its strictly scientific stance. Marheineke made the strictest scientific demands on dogmatics, in quite a different way than Schleiermacher, who only sought to facilitate the expression of pious consciousness. Only then, after it transpired that this discipline finally lost confidence in itself and became the subject of irony, could a more honest, scientific spirit begin to stir and give rise to the need to see dogmatics too finally set for once in its element, that of science (*Wissenschaft*).[71]

Marheineke saw spurious forms of science in both ways of thinking, rationalism and supernaturalism, into which theology at that time had bifurcated itself and fallen into decline. This antithesis would not be overcome

---

communions are the Lutheran and the Reformed.

70. Philipp Konrad Marheineke, *Die Grundlehren der christlichen Dogmatik* (Berlin, 1819); 2nd ed., *Die Grundlehren der christlichen Dogmatik als Wissenschaft* (Berlin, 1827). After teaching in Erlangen and Heidelberg, Marheineke (1780–1846) was appointed to a professorship at the newly established University of Berlin in 1811. Influenced earlier by Schelling, Marheineke became a disciple of Hegel after the philosopher's arrival in Berlin. He offered a right-Hegelian theological interpretation of Hegel's *Lectures on the Philosophy of Religion*, which he edited for publication, after Hegel's death, in 1832. His own lectures on Christian morals, dogmatics, and history of dogma were published posthumously.

71. *Wissenschaft* means the creation or production of *Wissen* (knowledge) in a disciplined, critical fashion, and in this context refers to humanistic, theological, and philosophical knowledge production. Hegel's speculative philosophy claimed to be "the science of the experience of consciousness"; and the goal of Marheineke, Baur, and others was that of a scientific theology, which would inwardly unify reason and revelation, knowledge and faith.

by subordinating one of these two antitheses to the other, and by seeking to bring about their outward unification. Instead it would be overcome only by the keenest grasp of the two antitheses and pointing out their inner contradiction. Rationalism falsely teaches a reason that knows nothing of divine revelation. As self-negating, it necessarily goes to an extreme; if this contradiction was not resolvable, then theology had to be abandoned. The science no longer burdened with this antithesis would involve the truth of supernaturalism and of rationalism. Correctly defining this concept of revelation and reason gives the two positions the possibility of attaining inner unity and thus attaining scientific knowledge.

Marheineke considered science in this sense to be the fruit of the Reformation, the essence of Protestantism. Reforming the faith awakened the spirit of the boundless activity that, in true religion, knows what is past as also present and eternal. Hence it can also bring the past forth from itself, fresh and new in ever-changing forms, without becoming unfaithful to itself and to the Christian religion with which it is one. Owing to that great spiritual movement, we have gained this freedom, this sacred right, of a free and independent knowledge; and henceforth the identical desire of all ages [for freedom] is to be defended against all blind faith in authorities. Now, finally, it is time to recognize, specifically and plainly, what all dogmatics has disregarded, and to see that dogmatics cannot carry out its task without taking more than just external notice of philosophy. Philosophy, especially philosophy from Descartes to Hegel, shows forth the truth-investigating spirit in its movement through all its essential moments. Hegel's greatest merit is to be seen in this very fact, that he has speculatively assimilated and concentrated the entire history of philosophy. Hence there is nothing more unworthy of a dogmatics in our day than ignoring this movement of spirit and, after such advances in its most kindred science, still being content with empty abstractions and constructs, or with that crude empiricism to which people still today seemingly want to confine all theology.

Here we encounter the influence of a new philosophy on theology, a philosophy that then was not yet generally known and was still only quietly establishing its power, yet soon thereafter became a very important phenomenon of the time. Indeed we are also speaking most decidedly here about the antithesis in which the standpoint newly established by philosophy stood in relation to Schleiermacher's position.[72] Schleiermacher was happy about

---

72. In another work Baur suggests that Schleiermacher's "feeling of absolute dependence," just because it lacks "an absolute with an objective content," "involves on its own the inner compulsion to pass over to Hegel's standpoint of objectivity." *Die christliche Gnosis oder die christliche Religionsphilosophie in ihrer geschichtlichen Entwicklung* (Tübingen, 1835), 668–69. This is how Baur interprets the progression from

his contention, which, to be sure, sounded somewhat paradoxical, that his *Glaubenslehre* had nothing to do with philosophy.⁷³ The contrary contention [i.e., Marheineke's] was that theology (*Glaubenslehre*) was now said to be science just because of its philosophy. Yet the standpoint adopted [by Marheineke] is like [Schleiermacher's] standpoint in the same circumstance in relation to rationalism and supernaturalism, as two antithetical, mutually annulling ways of thinking, two equally subordinated standpoints, beyond which one must ascend to an absolute standpoint. The difference is just that, whereas Schleiermacher makes Christian consciousness his principle, and so occupies the standpoint of subjectivity, Marheineke in contrast sets out from the objective idea of God. Where Schleiermacher simply develops the content of the Christian faith from Christian consciousness, Marheineke sets up a system of speculative theology. We can only go further into it in connection with Hegelian philosophy. Here we may simply remark, first of all, that, if the untenability of Schleiermacher's *Glaubenslehre* is evident in its Christ being likewise archetypal and historical, for Marheineke too the doctrine of the incarnation is the point at which his scientific dogmatics has not yet become sufficiently engaged critically (*auseinandergesetzt*) with the church's dogma.⁷⁴

New Testament Criticism: Gieseler and Bretschneider

However, in order to reach an understanding as to what the church's dogma was, one first had to take a further decisive step in New Testament criticism and exegesis. The main critical issue occupying people's attention still involved the genesis of the gospels. The most significant writings on this topic are Gieseler's 1818 book,⁷⁵ and Bretschneider's *Probabilien über das johanneische Evangelium* (1820).⁷⁶ Over against Eichhorn's hypothesis about

Schleiermacher to Hegel in the present volume as well.

73. *Die christliche Glaube* (n. 42), §28.3

74. As a right-Hegelian, Marheineke argued that the traditional doctrine of Christ as the God-man can be affirmed by scientific theology (see *Grundlehren* [n. 70], 2nd ed., 175 ff.), whereas Baur's view was that the divine idea cannot be exhaustively identified with any single individual but only with humanity as a whole (see below, pp. 327-28). Christ has an exemplary but not exclusive role.

75. Johann Carl Ludwig Gieseler, *Historisch-kritischer Versuch über die Entstehung und die frühesten Schicksale der schriftlichen Evangelien* (Leipzig, 1818). Gieseler (1792–1854) became professor of theology at Bonn in 1819 and at Göttingen in 1831. His main work was a multi-volume *Lehrbuch der Kirchengeschichte*, the last part of which was published posthumously (Darmstadt, 1824–57).

76. Karl Gottlieb Bretschneider, *Probabilia de evangelii et epistolarum Joannis, apostoli, indole et origine eruditorum judiciis modeste subjecit* (Leipzig, 1820).

the original gospel (*Urevangelium*), Gieseler set the traditional hypothesis that Schleiermacher presented in his 1817 work on the Gospel of Luke.[77] Bretschneider's book brought out a very important issue, although Schleiermacher himself thought that people at that time did not think it amounted to much and it could not in fact be taken seriously. Of course whoever believed that, in the archetypal Christ of Schleiermacher's *Glaubenslehre*, one has the most firm center of one's own Christian consciousness also cannot be mistaken in one's confidence about the authenticity of John's Gospel. The dismissive way Schleiermacher speaks at every opportunity about critical issues regarding the Gospel of John can be explained simply based on the dogmatic bias of his christology. See, for example, his [posthumously edited] lectures on *Einleitung ins Neue Testament*,[78] and his *Reden über die Religion* in the 1821 edition, where he states (p. 305):[79]

> Nothing surely betrays less feeling for the essence of Christianity and the person of Christ, as well as less general feeling for, and understanding of, what brought about these great events and what must be the conditions for them that were actually their foundation, as the view that formerly appeared somewhat cautious by contending that John mixed much other material of his own into the speeches of Jesus, but that today, after furtively becoming stronger and equipping itself with critical weapons, ventures a blunter contention, namely, that John is not at all the author of this Gospel, for instead someone else later invented this mystical Christ. For how could a Jewish rabbi have such an effect—someone with a kindly disposition, a somewhat Socratic morality, a few miracles, and a gift for uttering pleasing maxims and parables, yet having nothing more to him (indeed one will always also have to excuse him for a few foolish acts, according to the other gospel writers)? How, I say, could someone like that have produced such a result as a new religion and church? It

---

Bretschneider (1776–1848) served as general superintendent in Gotha from 1816 until his death. He was a representative of rational supernaturalism.

77. Friedrich Schleiermacher, "Über die Schriften des Lukas, ein kritischer Versuch" (1817), in *Sämmtliche Werke*, div. 1, vol. 2 (Berlin, 1836), 1–220. Johann Gottfried Eichhorn (1752–1827) proposed that an original, now lost Aramaic gospel lay at the basis of the canonical Gospels, each revising the *Urevangelium* with its own interests in mind. Schleiermacher contended for the historical authenticity of the Gospel of John.

78. Schleiermacher, *Sämmtliche Werke*, div. 1, vol. 8 (Berlin, 1845).

79. Schleiermacher, *Über die Religion*, 3rd ed. (n. 59), 442–43 (explanation 14 to p. 416). *On Religion*, trans. Oman (n. 128), 262. Baur cites the pagination of the 4th ed. (see n. 59), but the quotation corresponds exactly to the text of the 1821 ed. The translation is ours since Oman gives an abbreviated version.

leaves us with the conception of a man who, like that, is inferior to Moses and Muhammad.

The question would therefore be whether or not the origins of Christianity are understandable without presupposing the authenticity of the Gospel of John. It will be evident in what follows how people answered this question. In any event it is clearly not a critical standpoint when one answers critical questions, which can only be resolved in purely historical terms, by investigating individual instances, when one wants to reach a decision in this fashion, via general assumptions. The customary and long-standing preference for the Gospel of John, because of which people at that time gave far too little thought to how much of the truth of the gospel story taken from the Synoptic Gospels had to be sacrificed because of it, had its main basis of support in Schleiermacher's theology.

Church History: Neander

It is striking how little of significance was accomplished in exegesis right up to the end of this period. In contrast, greater activity began to make itself felt in the domain of historical research. Of course Neander came on the scene in 1812 as a writer of church history, with a monograph on the Roman emperor Julian.[80] In it Neander expressed his distinctive approach at that time, most especially in his interest in prominent individual personalities who represent the general character of their era, and in the kind of epochs and turning points of history in which great antitheses emerge. Christianity in particular comes into contact with phenomena to which it contrasts and thereby discloses itself all the more in its own distinctive light. Julian's era was such a time, one in which paganism, with all its splendid symbolism and all its impressive speculation, faced off against Christianity. Soon thereafter Neander drew a similar picture based on materials drawn from medieval history, in his book *Der heilige Bernhard und sein Zeitalter* (Gotha, 1813). Just as Neander's orientation in his choice of topics focused on what is individual, so these monographs inherently also bear the stamp of Neander's individuality by the features they especially emphasize, by the way they are arranged and, overall by the rather genial way they are treated. Other works by Neander of the same kind include: *Genetische Entwicklung der vornehmsten gnostischen Systeme* (Berlin, 1818), in which Neander seeks to demonstrate, in a way similar to his book on Julian, how the true charac-

---

80. August Neander, *Über den Kayser Julianus und sein Zeitalter: Ein historisches Gemälde* (Leipzig, 1812). Neander (1789–1850), a convert from Judaism, was a Protestant theologian and professor of church history in Berlin from 1813 until his death.

ter of Christianity directly revealed itself all the more vividly in its contact and struggle with oriental Gnosticism; *Der Heilige Johannes Chrysostomus und die Kirche besonders des Orients in dessen Zeitalter* (Berlin, 1821); *Antignosticus, Geist des Tertullianus und Einleitung in dessen Schriften* (Berlin, 1825).

Neander's procedure awakened interest in historical research on special topics that were the necessary preparation for larger works encompassing church history as a whole. Several more monographs of this kind appeared, such as Ullmann's *Gregor von Nazianz, der Theologe* (1825).[81] Neander himself soon undertook the writing of an *Allgemeine Geschichte der christlichen Religion und Kirche,* with the initial volumes [of what became six] appearing in rapid succession (Hamburg, 1826–1830). About the same time Gieseler began his *Lehrbuch der Kirchengeschichte*. We need elaborate no further on the subsequent preeminence of these two very famous works on church history.

Neander's works express their author's subjectivity. We see this from how Neander himself lacks any more definite philosophical and theological outlook. Instead he occupies a comfortable position of faith in which there are only fluid distinctions between the most general antitheses, those of divine and human, natural and supernatural. In particular, the kinds of phenomena that must fall under the heading of those general issues get dealt with rather vaguely and indecisively. Just as Neander supports his subjective outlook in the interest of his individuality, he on the whole therefore leaves individuals fully entitled to their freedom, although in doing so his history becomes an aggregation of individualities; and where individuals should have become subordinate to the universal, to the historical progression conditioned by spirit's general course of development, what prevails is just the free play of individuals. Neander rightly does not want to look through the lens of a philosophical or dogmatic school, but he also lacks the vision made keener by the specificity of the concept.

Where the historian concentrates attention, deciding on a specific outlook, this was said to emphasize the more general perspectives conveyed by the unity of the idea. Yet Neander's presentation becomes broad and nonspecific. Neander's most general perspective is simply the religious perspective. In the foreword to his *Kirchengeschichte* Neander articulates his task as one of portraying the history of the church of Christ as an eloquent demonstration of Christianity's divine power, as a school of Christian experience,

---

81. Carl Ullmann, *Gregorius von Nazianz, der Theologe. Ein Beitrag zur Kirchen- und Dogmengeschichte des vierten Jahrhunderts* (Darmstadt, 1825). Ullmann (1796–1865) taught at Halle for most of his career and was co-editor of *Theologische Studien und Kritiken*. He was a mediating theologian oriented to Schleiermacher.

an edifying voice heard throughout the centuries, a school teaching and admonishing all who are willing to hear. So the character of Neander's *Kirchengeschichte* is predominantly religious, edifying, and practically oriented. It dwells especially on the history of missions and on all that vividly calls attention to Christianity's religious and ethical influence. Its predilection for individual factors is linked to a special fondness for providing plentiful extracts from the biographies of missionaries and other persons who, on account of their effectiveness and personal experiences as Christians, have special significance for Neander and form for him, so to speak, a Christian hagiology. In Neander we frequently come upon apocryphal anecdotes that have no significance for a general church history.

Gieseler's *Lehrbuch der Kirchengeschichte* has no inclination for such things; its presentation is all the more sober, dry, and unimaginative. The whole is thus clear and orderly, and its greater superiority just consists in providing materials for church history, assembled diligently, accurately, and with critical understanding.

Theological Orientations and Their Publications; the *Evangelische Kirchenzeitung*

To sum up briefly what else is characteristic of our period, we distinguish three different principal orientations, each of which made an impact and also sought to gain wider influence through its own publications: the rationalistic orientation, the strictly ecclesiastical orientation, and the mediating one.

The mediating orientation includes the large group of those theologians who increasingly found Schleiermacher's theology to be expressing their own religious convictions, or else thought they might at least accept this theology as they interpreted it. Given the heightened concern for ecclesiastical orthodoxy, and the harsh way the other two factions opposed each other, it was all the more desirable to have, in Schleiermacher's theology, a firm foothold over against two equally extreme orientations. The followers of Schleiermacher's theology therefore also included those who believed, on the whole, that in it they had found the correct, middle path; that it distanced itself both from the one-sidedness of a rationalism making faith superficial, and from an exaggerated orthodoxy that wanted to concede no legitimacy at all to rational thinking in conjunction with faith. They paid the least attention to the very thing that is the most distinctive characteristic of Schleiermacher's theology—that its view of God's relation to the world did away in principle with the supernatural, and could no longer find any place at all for miracle in the proper sense. They simply clung to the fact that it sought to unite both concerns, that of faith and that of understanding matters of faith. Even those theologians who were supernaturalists in a different sense stood up for Schleiermacher when the distinctive principles of his theology allowed that. These groups created their journal, *Theologische Studien und Kritiken*, since 1828 edited by Ullmann and Umbreit, in collaboration with Gieseler, Lücke, and Nitzsch.[82] It quickly became the most widely-read theological journal.

Since 1815 *Bengels Archiv für die Theologie und ihre neueste Literatur* had replaced *Suskinds Magazin* as the publication representing Tübingen supernaturalism. In 1828 the *Tübinger Zeitschrift für Theologie*, edited by Steudel, became associated with *Bengels Archiv*.[83]

The rationalist faction was not just represented by such theologians as Wegscheider and Röhr. At the beginning of this period it also had men heading it up such as Paulus, Voss, and Krug,[84] those who knew how to gain more general recognition for the principles of rationalism by their activities, partly on behalf of the general interests of Protestantism, partly on behalf of the liberal ideas and endeavors at that time.

Krug took part in all the political, religious, and theological issues of the time. Voss applied his Protestant zeal in his 1819 attack, made in his well-known blunt fashion, against the friend of his youth, Count Friedrich Leopold Stolberg,[85] shortly before Stolberg's death, because of his conversion to the Catholic Church in 1800. He thought he could show that the conversion took place under disreputable circumstances, owing to the proximity of Münster Catholicism and the fact that the well-known Catho-

---

82. On Gieseler and Ullmann, see nn. 75 and 81. F. W. C. Umbreit (1795-1860) taught theology and Old Testament in Heidelberg. Friedrich Lücke (1791-1855) was a theologian in Göttingen and later became a church official. Karl Immanuel Nitzsch (1787-1868) held various church positions.

83. Ernst Gottlieb Bengel (1769-1826) was a professor in Tübingen when Baur was a student. Johann Christian Friedrich Steudel (1779-1837) taught biblical theology there from 1815 until his death. He and Baur were on friendly terms until the Strauss controversy, and Baur's articles were published in the *Tübinger Zeitschrift für Theologie* during the 1830s.

84. On Röhr and Wegscheider, see nn. 33 and 34. Heinrich Eberhard Gottlob Paulus (1761-1851), rationalist theologian, professor in Heidelberg (discussed above, pp. 91-94); Johann Heinrich Voss (1751-1826), poet and translator, anti-Catholic polemicist; Wilhelm Traugott Krug (1770-1842), philosopher, successor to Kant in Königsberg, then professor in Leipzig.

85. Johann Heinrich Voss, *Bestätigung der stolbergischen Umtriebe: nebst einem Anhang über persönlichen Verhältnisse* (Stuttgart, 1820). Cf. C. F. A. Schott, *Voss und Stolberg, oder der Kampf des Zeitalters zwischen Licht und Verdunklung* (Stuttgart, 1820). Stolberg (1750-1819) was also a poet and translator.

lic deviousness in proselytizing had played a role in it. People generally thought the angry old man would have been far better off staying out of a situation where surely one can never truly see the reasons behind someone's decision. Because of the peculiar bitterness of Voss's unbending Protestant nature and his antipathy—demonstrated in his *Antisymbolik* [Stuttgart, 1824-6] directed against Creuzer—toward everything he suspected of being a furtive veiling of the truth or indeed a very cunning priestly deception, he was driven, in his elder years, to wield his well-polished sword against the proselytes of Catholicism. The publication in which this attack occurred was also wholly suited to providing such information uncovering the intrigues of Catholicism, just as Voss supposed he was able to provide it in his article, "Wie Fritz Stolberg ein Unfreier ward."

The *Sophronizon* of Paulus (begun in 1819)[86] also had mainly an anti-Catholic tendency in the way it made its general mission the presentation of the case for rationalism, which, as simple reflection shows, is in line with its motto: "Just as surely as there can be nothing better in all things than thinking and acting rationally, so too surely everyone can only stand behind the principles of rationalism." In another journal, one entitled *Der Denkglaubige*,[87] Paulus also sought to gain for rationalism the popular appeal he thought it could not fail to have once people let themselves be persuaded what a fine thing faith in reason would be. Based on this effort by the rationalists to popularize their views and principles, there arose the idea of issuing a church periodical intended for the wider public, one in addition to the existing scholarly, theological journals. The *Allgemeine Kirchenzeitung* founded in Darmstadt in 1822 by [Ernst] Zimmermann, the court chaplain, soon became a principal organ of the rationalistic faction. With its symbol, the three interlaced hands on its vignette, and with its motto, "We all believe in one God," it alluded to a community of all three Christian confessions.

The more the antitheses sharpened and the opposed positions rode into battle against one another (which happened in several places, for instance in Leipzig, where Hahn,[88] in an academic disputation in 1827, demanded that, as deniers of transcendence and non-Christians, the rationalists should be

---

86. *Sophronizon oder unparteiische, freimütige Beiträge zur neuern Geschichte, Gesetzgebung and Statistik der Staaten und Kirchen* was a journal edited by Paulus. The name is based on Romans 12:3, "I say to everyone among you not to think of yourself more highly than you ought to think, but to think with sober judgment (σωφρονεῖν)." Its 13 volumes were published between 1819 and 1831. The third number of volume 1 contains the article by Voss, "Wie ward Friz Stolberg ein Unfreier?"

87. Published in Heidelberg, 1825-29.

88. August Hahn (1792-1863).

dismissed from the church, and in Denmark, where Clausen[89] was attacked most vehemently in 1826 on account of his independent interpretation of Protestantism), the more natural it was for there to be a church periodical that was not just general in nature but also evangelical.[90] It deserves mention here since it soon enough gained renown of its own, and it is still today a main organ of its faction. This periodical was established in 1828 in Berlin, by Professor Hengstenberg. It brought together under its banner all those who took it to be their special task to contest the wrong-headed orientation of the spirit of the day by the strictest maintenance of the church's teaching. In the prospectus of 21 June 1827 it named as its associates: Neander and Strauss[91] in Berlin, Tholuck in Halle, Heubner in Wittenberg, Hahn, Lindner, and Heinroth in Leipzig, von Meyer in Frankfurt, Scheibel in Breslau, Steudel in Tübingen, Krummacher in Bremen, Olshausen in Königsberg, and Rudelbach in Copenhagen. Yet several of these men soon saw themselves obliged to withdraw from participation in a publication whose principles they could less approve of the more overtly they came to the fore.

The *Evangelische Kirchenzeitung* soon established itself as a bureau of clandestine reports that the editor had submitted to him from all parts of the world and published recklessly; as an organ of the most malicious and hateful allegations that made it its special business to single out and accuse, before the wider public, the most respected men as being unbelievers because they were not believers of the *Evangelische Kirchenzeitung* kind. Charges in 1830 against two very respected Halle teachers, Gesenius and Wegscheider,[92] aroused the greatest indignation. Based on information from their lectures, they were denounced for ridiculing Christianity and leading the youth astray. This should have led to intervention by the state government. The ministry then did indeed take the usual course of investigating the accusation made against Professors Wegscheider and Gesenius in the *Evangelische Kirchenzeitung* (1830, nos. 5, 6, and 15). However, its official statement with reference to the faculty of evangelical theology expressly acknowledged that nothing had been discovered pertinent to the lectures

89. Henrik Nicolai Clausen (1793–1877).

90. The *Evangelische Kirchenzeitung*, established by Ernst Wilhelm Theodor Hengstenberg (1802–1869), who was professor of Old Testament in Berlin from 1826 until his death. Baur tangled with Hengstenberg and his journal during the Strauss controversy. The *EKZ* was published from 1827 to 1920.

91. Not David Friedrich Strauss but Friedrich Strauss (1786–1863), professor of theology in Berlin.

92. On Wegscheider, see n. 34. Wilhelm Gesenius (1786–1842) was a colleague in Halle.

of the professors cited that would be a reason for intervention by the state. The statement remarked in addition that, without wishing to influence decisively the different dogmatic systems in theology, His Majesty expected from all theology teachers a dignified treatment of sacred topics and also that, with their varying points of view, they should constantly keep in mind that their lectures educate young theologians for the Evangelical Church. So the denunciation did not in fact accomplish its purpose.

Neander took this occasion to renounce his association with the *Evangelische Kirchenzeitung*.[93] Making special reference to the deleterious article directed against Schleiermacher, Wegscheider, and Gesenius, he declared that his stance toward the *EKZ* had now changed because, in several instances, its procedures involve principles completely in conflict with his own and, he is convinced, continuing with them could only be ruinous to the church. He thoroughly disapproved of the fact that existing differences among learned theologians, whether presented in lectures or in writings, are brought before the tribunal of the laity who lack a scientific theological education, by the sort of periodicals that are first and foremost designed for practical Christian concerns. Neander also declared, very emphatically in his conclusion, his opposition to using student notebooks or verbal remarks about them in accusations against their academic teachers. Such a procedure could only open the door and the gate to all sorts of capricious slander arising from misunderstandings or misrepresentations, to restricting the openness of academic lectures, to upsetting the reciprocal trust that should exist here between teachers and learners, and introducing an extremely destructive system of second-guessing into one's way of thinking. Hengstenberg's audaciously confident rebuttal was that of course the laity have the ability, as well as the duty and the right, to distinguish between teachers of theology and heretical teachers.

In the matter of Halle the special goal was to make the public aware of the terrible wrong that had been committed against the Evangelical Church by installing rationalist professors in the evangelical theological faculty, and to demand that the sovereign who had both the right and the duty to intervene would fulfill this obligation. This was the language the *Evangelische Kirchenzeitung* took the liberty of using and made its hallmark. However shameful for it the success of such a step as that taken against the two teachers in Halle should have been, the *EKZ* did not let that deter it from continuing with obstinate consistency on this path once taken. It knew too well what support and sympathies it could count on. To such men as

---

93. August Neander, *Dr. Neanders Erklärung über seine Theilnahme in der Evangelische Kirchenzeitung* (Berlin, 1830).

this Neander's declaration, however estimable and appropriate, nevertheless lacked decisiveness and soundness. Even though people wanted nothing to do with the offensiveness and scandalous character manifested by the *EKZ*, they nevertheless were increasingly too much in step with it as regards certain views and principles for them to be able to break openly with. How else would an inquisitorial authority such as the editorship of the *EKZ* at that time have been able to maintain itself for so long? But however much Neander, in a case like this one, was horrified by the principles of the *EKZ*, its editor still remained his dear friend, someone whose serious convictions, tied to these principles, only deserved respect. On the same occasion, and in the same sense, other theologians also spoke up, ones such as Bretschneider, Ulmann, Schott, and Baumgarten-Crusius.

Since from the outset the *Evangelische Kirchenzeitung* followed the same principles and the same procedures, we can now say something more specific here about its nature. In his *Beleuchtung des Wesens und Treibens der Berliner Evangelischen Kirchenzeitung* (Breslau, 1839), Schulz[94] has described the main features of the congregations united under the banner of the *EKZ* as follows. First, it does its best to restore, to their original condition, the old traditions that have lost their earlier significance, or passed into oblivion, in the Evangelical Church—on the one hand through progressive spiritual development, on the other hand because of new modes of life as such—and to secure for them a new, insofar as possible everlasting, stability. Second, those associated with the *EKZ* want to be regarded as alone the true church, and without further ado they describe themselves as the faithful, as the Evangelical Church, and their newspaper as the organ of the Evangelical Church. Third, they have a shared and ever constant hostility toward the friends and promoters of light and freedom in the affairs of religion and church; a blind, at times truly ridiculous, self-generated rage against what, in the most indiscriminate way, they find it useful to paint, with the broadest brush, as rationalism and rationalist, with the disreputable intent to instigate malicious suspicions among the uninformed by this misleading name-calling. [To them] rationalism is the actual enemy, and from the outset the *EKZ* has made this struggle its main task. Using the term "rationalism," it disparages and persecutes everything that lacks the hues of its faith, calling it absolutely reprehensible, soul-destroying, a monstrous creation of hell. The rationalists are the born and sworn enemies of Christ; and they cannot depict too often, in the darkest colors, the dread and horror creating the critical state of the church, the devastation and upheaval in the church

---

94. David Schulz (1779–1854), professor of theology in Breslau, defender of a historical, rational orientation against orthodox Lutheranism.

because of the rationalists, their denial of transcendence, their atheism and its irreligious wickedness.

It is very characteristic of the spirit of the time that it is this party, as a result of being so very presumptuous and knowing how to utilize the circumstances at that time so effectively in the interests of its own hierarchical despotism, that still crops up so prominently at the conclusion of our period. In 1829, in his second open letter concerning his *Glaubenslehre*, published in the *Theologische Studien und Kritiken*,[95] Schleiermacher made the following statement (without expressly mentioning the *Evangelische Kirchenzeitung* but unmistakably referring to it): "The soil lifts up right under our feet where this ominous larva wants to crawl out from the self-enclosed religious circles that declare all research outside the entrenchments of an age-old literalism to be satanic." From such a beginning this soon came to pass in the fullest sense. Just in order to oppose, in the most dogged way, all that the progress of that time involved of its own accord, what is age-old, in the way it appeared to this party, was supposedly validated anew in its unconditional authority. But the greater the energy with which the one side pursed this direction, all the sharper its antithesis had to become.

---

95. "Dr. Schleiermacher über seine Glaubenslehre, an Dr. Lücke, Zweites Sendschreiben," *Theologische Studien und Kritiken* 2.3 (1829) 481–532, quotation from 490–91. ET: *On the Glaubenslehre: Two Letters to Dr. Lücke*, trans. James Duke and Francis Fiorenza (Chico, CA, 1980), 55–89, quotation from 61 (our translation).

PART THREE

From 1830 to Most Recent Times

1

Introduction: Political Conditions

Eighteen-thirty is an epochal year in more recent history because, in France, the old dynasty fell and a "bourgeois monarchy" or "citizen monarchy" took its place.[1] France was then still the political center of gravity. The struggle between the two mutually opposed principles, a struggle begun in France with the first revolution, now entered a new phase of its development. Since the revolution intensely involved general interests by no means just related to France, people saw very clearly that, even though the initial impetus for it was forever in France, the revolution was just the beginning of a movement also taking hold in neighboring lands.

The restoration period consistently pursued the mission indicated by its name. Under the pretense of constitutional forms it sought to regain absolute power for the old monarchy. It succeeded to the point that people saw it as ultimately encroaching on the constitutional forms, and that made the inwardly rebellious national consciousness once again an energetic reaction. The well-known ordinances of Charles X, while outwardly preserving the semblance of legality, abrogated the state's constitution and destroyed the old dynasty in one fell swoop.[2] The great catastrophe ensuing within the brief span of three days showed the weakness of the foundation on which the constitutional throne stood; it showed how little the constitution, with its current system of governance, had been able to unite inwardly the two powers it was supposed to unify.

If ever there was a revolutionary movement indubitably expressing the general will of the people, this July Revolution[3] in France was it. Whatever

---

1. Louis-Philippe (1773–1850), who earlier had renounced his titles as son of the duke of Orleans, became king of the sovereign people following the 1830 revolution, hence was called the "citizen king."

2. These actions of Charles X (king of France, 1824–30) led directly to the July Revolution of 1830. See also p. 122, n. 29.

3. The demonstrations and the three days' fighting (27–29 July 1830) forced the

multiple divisions may have existed in France, the nation was completely at one in its antipathy to the old dynasty and to its reinstatement, and could only see in it a shameful concession made to the enemies of revolutionary France. Hence the causes of the July Revolution lay far deeper; they were not just the events at that time, and sooner or later things had to come to a head. It had become impossible for Charles X to rule in tandem with the representative constitutional form as it had become elaborated during the fifteen years of the restoration period. Every concession he was able to make to the liberal party always just resulted in new and greater demands, until finally there were no more concessions left to make. But it was equally impossible to do away with the representative government and rule without it, as Charles X ultimately sought to do. That is because, in the battle that his doing so had to provoke, the government stood opposed not only to a political party but also to the entire nation. Thus the old throne went under without struggling or resisting, and foreign powers did not even dare to intervene with force, despite seeing how perilous was the attack on the monarchical principle.

But it also became evident, soon enough, that the new revolution in no way brought about the great change that people should have expected from it. Instead of the old Bourbon lineage, the younger Bourbons ruled. Now the important thing was the fact that the new citizen monarchy had to be a throne fenced in by republican institutions; that the Charter would now, for the first time, have to be a reality. Yet based on the natural antithesis of the two principles, monarchical and democratic, a new struggle developed in which the democratic principle lost more and more of the ground it originally held. Although Louis-Philippe did not indulge in any constitutional violations as striking as those of his predecessor, he did have a much better understanding of how to take advantage of human concerns and passions in order to advance his own goals; and, by seeming to offer the guarantee of tranquility and peace, of how to win over the part of the nation that had rested everything first and foremost on the security of its possessions and the promotion of material prosperity.

However, a condition similar to that under the restoration soon set in. Dissatisfaction increased in proportion to people's growing belief in their entitlement to complain about deception and breach of faith on the part of the citizen monarchy. A major part of the bourgeoisie who had joyfully greeted Louis-Philippe's assumption of the throne became very uneasy, since not one out of all the expectations people tied to the new monarchy had been fulfilled. They saw forced aside almost all the figures who had

---

abdication of Charles X, gained power for the bourgeoisie, and led to the kingship of Louis-Philippe.

come forward in the glorious revolution, as leaders of the people's faction. People heard from all quarters that the government was about to revert to all the misguided ways of the restoration. However indignantly the friends of the government might have dismissed it, no one could possibly conceal the fact that the most unambiguous events only seemed to strongly justify this complaint. So time and again the government even believed that its adroit and crafty political strategy had thwarted the attacks of an energetic opposition. The conflict repeatedly calmed down, its twists and turns just giving rise to the conviction that the opposition between the two principles mutually at odds here is an irreconcilable antithesis. So now too the end result could be none other than the kind of catastrophe that had occurred previously.

However fortuitous may have been the circumstances that toppled the throne of the July regime,[4] even more abruptly and ignominiously than those toppling the restoration, they made manifest unambiguously where the real power lies when it comes to the decisive confrontation. Here we see a nation for the most part desiring nothing less than a revolution—a nation up to that point governed by using the term "revolution" to scare people, and with every reason to see its government's continued stability as the surest guarantee of its material interests—suddenly and completely breaking with this government and able to plunge anew into all the hazards of a revolution. How else explain this, except by recourse to the unrelenting disgust aroused by all the corruption of the July regime? Long before it toppled, this regime had lost any basis in public opinion for its continued existence. People had finally become weary of seeing themselves constantly taken in by new deceptions. They felt compelled to destroy the pretentiousness of a power that sought to have, based on itself and its own absolute power, what it received solely and exclusively from the hand of the nation, and thus could only become a despotism.

The great contradiction inherent in a bourgeois or citizen monarchy sooner or later must annul itself internally. Where the principle of the people's sovereignty has become so deeply impressed on the entire consciousness of the nation, it must in turn make itself felt, in its overarching power, wherever conditions are suitable for it. It may even be caught up for a long time in a struggle, one in which it is so entangled with the principle standing opposed to it that, in its subjection, it seems defenseless. But this is only the necessary dialectical process every principle, albeit having already

---

4. Baur is now apparently referring to the February Revolution of 1848 in France, a popular uprising that led Louis-Philippe to abdicate in order to avert outright civil war, and resulted in the formation of the Second Republic. See p. 234, n. 6.

entered into humanity's consciousness, must first undergo in its external development.

However, what gives this latest French revolution its great historical significance is the broad context in which its effects extended to neighboring lands. Whereas the July Revolution itself had already elicited revolutionary movements in most of the German states, now it was as though the spirit of the people awakened from its slumber and became self-aware. The same principle of the people's autonomous will, which had now for the third time toppled the throne in France, had in the meantime also struck deeper roots in the German people's consciousness. For long enough people not only believed, from practical experience, that the constitutional forms of individual states are, for the most part, just an illusion; they also became fully aware that the German Confederation's governmental system is far beneath the dignity of the German nation—that it degrades the German nation far below other nations to which it is comparable in power and culture, and, in the interest of the monarchical principle, makes a mockery of this nation's proper standing. No governmental form was as unanimously judged to be as objectionable, and with greater indignation and more profound contempt, as the Diet of the German Confederation was. In contrast to the Diet, the German nation apprehended itself in its national consciousness. The freedom and unity of Germany became the mighty battle cry of the time, and the first national German assembly[5] constituted itself under the principle of the people's sovereignty. In its initial enthusiastic fervor its power was sufficient to give it a position commanding respect, over against the princes.

We can think of the changes that had made their way into all the public affairs of the German nation as not being great enough to enable building further on the foundation of the German nation's constitutional rights that had already been deliberated about and set forth. The same thing was true for spiritual life and for the independent development of those disciplines that had most to suffer from disfavor at this time, as was in fact the case with theology in its dependence on the church, and this had the most important consequences. When everything people at that time believed was already securely theirs got turned into the exact opposite, and what ensued, instead of the hoped-for results of the striving for freedom, was just a stronger reaction, we can, based on the political course of events, draw the same conclusion as to the general character of the most recent period. Whichever side may be in the ascendancy, the effort at this time is always the move

---

5. The Frankfurt National Assembly consisted of 809 members freely elected from throughout Germany. It met from 18 May 1848 until 31 May 1849. It drafted an imperial constitution, providing for a parliament and the office of emperor (offered to Friedrich Wilhelm IV, but he declined it). Political confusion ensued and the Assembly was disbanded on 18 June.

to escape from unsteady vacillation between mutually opposed principles and to dispense with all forms that lead to a merely apparent and external mediation. The more frequent such reversals, the better one learns how to think of oneself as being beyond the real antithesis of principles, and it becomes ever clearer that one can choose to position oneself decisively on one side or the other.

Hence it is characteristic of most recent times that the antitheses stand out more clearly, and all the phenomena pertinent to them, in people's political and social lives, take on a sharper and more pronounced character. The more quickly such a reversal often occurs—as we saw in 1852 in France, where the [Second] Republic had been suddenly replaced by the absolutism of a strictly unitary authority and the plan of 2 December[6]—people just see all the more clearly how little this has to do with a mediation, and how only one side or the other can stand its ground and exert its influence. Whether it be the principle of autonomy, of free self-determination, of aspiration toward further progress, or the principle of authority, of unconditional subjection, of sticking conservatively to traditional ways, people are increasingly less reticent about the consequences that result from one or the other of the two principles. People are aware that it is a matter of principles, and of deciding between them. This is the perspective from which we also mainly have to grasp and evaluate the most recent phenomena in the realm of the church and theology.[7]

---

6. In 1851 Louis-Napoléon (Napoleon III, 1808–73), who had been elected president of the Second Republic, staged a coup, making himself dictator. In 1852 he became emperor, which marked the beginning of the Second Empire (1852–70), an authoritarian regime.

7. [*Zeller*] The last two paragraphs, starting from "We can think of the changes ...," have the following form in Baur's 1850 manuscript, and I pass it on as an expression of his political sentiments at that time: "As disheartening, for every German soul, as the complete fruitlessness of all these unifying efforts may be, they have at least had the result that contemporary consciousness has grappled with the antitheses of the two principles, in such a way that there has been a complete break with the authority of the monarchical principle, inwardly if not outwardly. The more clearly people have become aware of the consequences of the two principles, the less possible it is to perpetuate the previous deceptions and to make attempts at mediation that just rest on false presuppositions. Whatever the further course of events may be, the antitheses stand out clearly, and the autonomous national will is conscious of its spreading power. However, what results, first and foremost, in the political domain is generally the characteristic feature of this latest period. Overall, where spiritual development can only proceed via more deeply engaged antitheses, and where the antitheses face off against each other in a sharper and more pronounced way, people dispense with all forms that only offer a one-sided, apparent mediation. Nothing should count that is not in a position to conceive of the spirit as free, released from every merely external authority and based on the principle of its own self-consciousness."

2

The History of the Catholic Church

A. The Papacy

If we start out from political history as the way to orient ourselves regarding the character of this period as such, then the connection between the political and ecclesiastical domains is most directly evident in the Papal States. The revolutionary movements emanating from France in fact also impacted the Papal States as they did Italy as a whole. Even though they first of all just involved the pope's secular authority, the Papal States at the same time also had to be a concern of his spiritual authority, since both were inseparably one in the person of the pope.

Gregory XVI; Unrest in the Papal States; Reaction

The contention is that the disastrous ordinances of Charles X had also been brought about principally at the suggestion of Rome. The greater the hopes they had built up, the more the news of the July Revolution caught people by surprise. Yet papal politics soon knew how to accommodate itself to the new circumstances. Louis-Philippe hastened to give the pope assurance that he himself would also be a firm support for the church in facing the storm of unbelief; that if he is just given time, then everything will be restored to order. Shortly before his death Pius VIII[1] therefore imposed on the French clergy the obligation to submit without reservation to the new order of things, to also include the new ruler in their prayers, and to follow him truly and obediently.

---

1. Pius VIII was pope only from 31 March 1829 to his death on 30 November 1830.

However, it was far more difficult to deal with the tempest at hand in the immediate vicinity. The people of Italy had long looked impatiently toward the moment that allowed them to break their hated chains. The July Revolution in France was greeted with unmixed joyfulness. Above all, the banner of the freedom and unity of the Italian people ought to have been raised in the Papal States and in the neighboring small principalities, because here one had expected the least resistance, given the weakness of their regimes. When Gregory XVI was elected pope on 2 February 1831, Bologna was already in an uproar. The papal legate departed, and the commission he had put in place to maintain the public peace and safety called itself the provisional government of the city and province of Bologna. The movement quickly developed throughout all the provinces of the Papal States, from the Po River, along the coast of the Adriatic Sea, right up to the border with Naples. It even crossed over to the west of the Apennine Mountains, for the two delegations of Perugia and Spoleto in central Italy joined in. At one time the newly-elected Holy Father in Rome felt himself so seriously threatened that arrangements were made for him to embark from the harbor at Civitavecchia. But in Rome itself the revolutionary movement encountered resistance. Not only did the Romans not participate; they even spontaneously took up weapons in defense of the city.

Meanwhile even more important steps were taken in Bologna. The current regime proceeded to make drastic improvements in all branches of the government. It convened official representatives from all the provinces of the Papal States that had renounced the secular rule of the pope, and they convened in a legislative assembly that began its work on 26 February in Bologna. Right away the assembly reached a unanimous decision that the pope's secular authority was ended in the regions represented at the congress. They united in one state and adopted the name "The United Italian Provinces." It was led by one collective government, while retaining the previously existing provincial divisions with their independent provincial administrations. A commission outlined the basic features of a new constitutional form. The seat of the government was to be Bologna, with a president heading up the executive authority.

However, this arrangement only lasted briefly. Austrian troops marched into the Papal States and put an end to the revolution. A special commission was seated to pass judgment on those participating in the revolution. Yet the strict measures planned could not be carried out. The official representatives of the other royal courts joined with the French ambassador to get the pope's consent to improvements in governance and to doing away with abuses that, to the shame of the papal administration, had become public knowledge because of the uprising in Romagna [the region around

Bologna]. So on 5 July 1831 a papal edict announced the reorganization of the entire system of governance in the Papal States. The official representatives of the royal courts, with the concurrence of the French emissary, were so satisfied with it that the Austrian troops left the papal territory directly following the edict.

But in the provinces themselves the edict in no way had the pacifying effect that people promised it would. Directly after the Austrians departed, the emissaries of the five powers sent a communiqué to Bologna that discussed and demonstrated the great crimes of the Papal State's governance, stating that even an honestly-intended community and provincial governance system would be an insufficient remedy, so long as the secular authority was not completely separate from the spiritual authority. Although a few improvements were put in place to eliminate what were essentially abuses, the uprising in the legations continued. Owing to the introduction of papal troops and the brutality permitted them, bitterness reached such a high level that the Austrians had to be called in once again.

Now, however, under pressure from the Chamber of Deputies, the French government too could not look on passively. A French naval squadron with marines suddenly appeared in the Adriatic Sea and took control of the city of Ancona in February 1832. This aroused the most widespread hopes in the Papal States and in all of Italy. The inhabitants of Ancona treated this with such high spirits and exuberance that, on account of the sacrilege their rebellion committed against the heritage of St. Peter, the pope issued an anathema and excommunicated them from the Catholic Church. Yet together with the French expedition to Ancona, this move was only intended as a ruse. In order to reassure the French nation, the ministry had made a show of acting energetically, whereas the whole matter was arranged with the Viennese cabinet. French occupation restored papal control in Ancona, and there was no more talk about the improvements announced by the previous year's edict. So long as French troops occupied Ancona, and the Austrians occupied Bologna and the most prominent cities of Romagna, the Papal States remained outwardly calm. However, the fire of revolutionary excitement continued to glow beneath the ashes. Not until 1838 did the French leave Ancona, and the Austrians leave Bologna.

The uprisings that broke out in various places in following years, such as the one in Rimini in 1845, were indeed put down by the Swiss Guards and the brutal bands of papal volunteers, but on the whole the state did not gain anything by doing so. While the political consequence was the imprisonment of a major part of the educated Roman youth, or else the need for them to leave their home country, the state administration carried on in its old capricious and disorderly way. Its finances in particular fell into the greatest disarray. The indebtedness of the Papal States under Gregory XVI well-nigh doubled, from 20 million scudi to 40 million.²

When Gregory XVI died, on 1 June 1846, people were completely indifferent when it came to their verdict on his reign. He had no sense for what the times demanded, but instead knew how to lead the ecclesiastical regime in the rigidly uncompromising way of former popes. He was most energetic where what counted was sticking to old principles and prerogatives, maintaining Catholic dogma with the strictest consistency, and leading the opposition to the forces seeking changes. From the pope's standpoint, the ultimate reasons for all the lamentable phenomena of that time lay simply in the fact that people no longer troubled themselves about the authority of the church's dogma, and constantly made that dogma the object of attacks due to the mania for change.

Gregory XVI had already expressed his profound sorrow about this in his pastoral letter or *Epistola encyclica* of 26 May 1832. He located the cause of such widespread unbelief in science. He had scientific knowledge in mind when he said, right in the beginning of his epistle:

> The schools and gymnasia are echoing, in an awful way, with strange distortions of ideas, ones attacking the Catholic faith no longer secretly but by undermining it; for a horrific and wicked war is now waged against it, openly and publicly. Since the spirits of the youth have been subverted by the instruction and example of their teachers, a great injury to religion and a most dreadful perversity of character has now become widespread.³

As the text continued, it did not place the blame for all these calamities simply on indifference, or on the false opinion that one can become blessed via just any creed if one simply lives a moral life. Instead, it also singles out the direct source from which all the revolutionary movements emerge as "the nonsense that freedom of conscience must be claimed and defended for all," and Protestantism.

> Indeed to this extent (namely, so that they may corrupt and overthrow all the laws of the authorities, introducing slavery in the guise of freedom) they bring together the most wicked, nonsensical positions and plots of the Waldenses, the Beghards, the Wycliffites, and other sons of Belial of this kind. And those old hands surely do not focus all their might for any other reason

---

2. The scudo, a silver coin that served as the currency of Italy, was worth about one dollar.

3. Gerald Culley (see p. 167, n. 35) assisted with the translation of this and the following passages in Latin.

except, in celebrating Luther, to be able to exalt themselves, being free from all [authorities]; and to gain that goal more easily and quickly, they very rashly undertake things more shameful than one can imagine.

The pope also expressed his abhorrence of freedom of the press, since it provides the easiest way to spread the most harmful and shameful teaching and errors. The Index is a very salutary device for countering it. Yet the Holy Father ultimately put his trust in the fact that the Holy Virgin Mary, "who alone has put an end to all heresies," will guide his efforts to the most felicitous outcome. If one understands the striving for freedom, of former times and of the present, from this perspective, then papal absolutism is fully justified from the fact that it catches sight of an utterly reprehensible principle inherent in the striving for freedom. However, this poses the great issue of the day in an extreme way, such that if suppression of all efforts at freedom proves unsuccessful, then the result must be a decisive break with the papacy. Each concession made to the striving for freedom carries with it the consequence of threatening to do away with the papacy. The next pope was destined to find this out.

The First Years in the Reign of Pius IX

Gregory XVI died on 1 June 1846. In the conclave the choice of a pope wavered between Cardinal Lambruschini who, as secretary to Gregory XVI, had ruled in his stead, and Cardinal Mastai Ferretti, the archbishop of Imola. After just two days, Cardinal Ferretti emerged from the conclave as the newly-elected pope. This choice apparently was in line with the principle that had, for the past hundred years, been the rule: that a pope from the zealous faction has to be followed by a political or diplomatic pope, one chiefly occupied with ecclesiastical affairs, the kind of pope who makes the church's internal governance the main focus of his activity. All aspects of Cardinal Mastai's personality very much commended him as a man with a good-natured, conciliatory disposition and firm character. He was trusted as someone not insensitive to contemporary, progressive developments.

It is no small matter for a papal election to have been greeted with such approbation and loud jubilation as was the case of Pius IX.[4] Owing both to his outward and very imposing figure, and to his vigorous age (for a pope) of 54 years, he apparently combined in himself all the qualities to make him a favorite of the people. The expectations people had for him were in no way

---

4. Pius IX reigned as pope until his death on 7 February 1878, long after the time period covered in these lectures.

disappointed. Day after day his popularity grew, because of his affable and kindly demeanor—respectably plain and folksy, far from any vain display and extravagance. The more people could see from his actions how very convinced he was himself about the necessity of thoroughgoing reforms, the more their confidence in him grew.

People anxiously awaited the granting of a general amnesty for those imprisoned and excommunicated for political offenses. They counted on it from the outset, yet the process dragged out. When the decree of amnesty was finally announced on 16 July, a stupendous celebration occurred not just in the Papal States alone but in all of Italy. With new enthusiasm the cry of *Evviva Pio nono* ("Long Live Pius IX") rang out everywhere. Like an electric shock, the amnesty had an inspirational impact on the entire populace, but made quite the opposite impression on the government. In Rome itself the traditionalist church faction found grounds for opposing it, because it appeared to be something far too questionable for the beginning of his papacy. In addition to the amnesty, the appointment of Cardinal Gizzi, as the Vatican's general secretary for internal and external affairs, met with great approval. He was a trusted friend of Pius IX, who had to count on Cardinal Gizzi's active support for his reform plans.

At first Pius hoped to be able to bring about the necessary reforms via the advisory council consisting of six cardinals he appointed to it. But he was soon disappointed, for he met with obstinate opposition from several of the cardinals. However, Pius did not let this deter him, for he instead formed a new advisory council made up of younger prelates. He did not just wish to be independent of the cardinals; instead he even transferred several important state positions, formerly held only by clergy, to laymen. All the pope's actions expressed his decided conviction regarding the necessity of thoroughgoing reforms, and the firm decision to continue forward on the path once taken, without allowing himself to be scared off by the impediments that the efforts at reform had to confront as a matter of course.

But if we ask whether the political broad-mindedness that Pius IX exhibited to such a high degree, and that made him such a distinctive phenomenon on the papal throne, also rested on the deeper foundation of an enlightened and more liberal, ecclesiastically religious outlook, then we find a very explicit answer to this question in his pastoral letter of 9 November 1846, which he sent to the Catholic bishops. He too could not sufficiently lament an era in which the most vehement and fearsome war is waged against the entire Catholic cause by those who, joined in an impious company estranged from sound doctrine and turning its ears away from the truth, have taken great pains to dig up from their obscurity all sorts of monstrous opinions, to exaggerate their power, and to spread and disseminate them among the people. They include not just the deniers of revelation and the blasphemers, but also those who are subject to the great error of misusing reason and declaring the Word of God to be a human product. They impudently make bold to expound and interpret God's Word according to their own discretion. Yet God himself has established a living authority, the one supposed, by its unerring judgment, to teach and reaffirm the true and correct sense of God's heavenly revelation, and to settle all controversies in matters of faith and morality.

His additional words about the malicious Bible societies then belong in the same context. By reviving the device of the ancient heretics, they translate the books of Holy Scriptures into all the common languages, contrary to the most sacred rules of the church. Often they do so accompanied by wholly perverse commentaries, and they circulate these books, in huge numbers and at great expense, to all the people of every race, even to the uneducated, free of charge; and with no thought given to making people aware that, by rejecting the divine tradition and the authority of the Catholic Church, anybody can interpret the Word of the Lord according to his own private opinions and twist its meaning. Furthermore, the pope spoke about: the perverted instruction in philosophical courses of study; the appalling doctrine of indifference toward religion; the hateful attacks on the holy celibacy of the priestly class, attacks causing great distress even among a number of clerics who, in lamentable fashion and forgetful of their office, succumb to, and are stained by, the attractions and enticements of sinful pleasures; the communist doctrine, of course entirely contrary to natural law and which, if once put into practice, would do away with human society at its foundations; and so forth.

In short, this is entirely the same tenor as that of the pastoral letter of Gregory XVI. How then could Pius IX, as pope, put things any differently? The question is how political liberalism is compatible with this religious and ecclesiastical absolutism, which concedes no validity at all to what is not Roman Catholic, and thus sees in Protestant freedom only a damnable defection from the Roman Catholic faith. Is there not a contradiction here that necessarily develops internally and also makes the striving for political freedom just a deceptive pretense?

Meanwhile, despite signs that those favoring reactionary means were at work, the popularity of Pius continued, and the reforms and new directions he settled on were met with well-deserved approbation. The most important of these were the municipal government system of Rome, and the state advisory council. The Roman municipal system consisted of a hundred-member council with a senator as its head and eight conservators. The state advisory council consisted of deputies from the provinces who were supposed to participate as social class representatives conferring about the governance of the Papal States. Both these bodies were constituted in a way that seemed to promise that their decisions would hold up, that would let them utilize to the fullest extent the rights granted to them, and would put into practice the principle expressed in creating them, namely, that governance of the Papal States should no longer be exclusively in the hands of the clergy. Also, the creation of a citizen militia (*guardia civica*) was a political measure only a pope such as Pius IX could have countenanced.

The Austrian occupation of the city of Ferrara, the uprising resulting from it, and the energetic protest Pius registered against it, seemed that it must, of its own accord, push him to the further step of positioning himself at the head of the Italian nationalist movement. Yet the discord with Austria, owing to dissension in Ferrara, was finally settled peaceably, and Pius did not neglect to curb at every opportunity the excessive expectations of him that people entertained. He particularly seized the occasion to counter the opinion that his political position conflicts with his ecclesiastical position. In his formal speech of 17 December 1847, he very emphatically denied that he could ever have intended to compromise the repute of the Holy See and the tenets handed down, or to cherish other traditions as being in complete agreement with those handed down by the ancient church, but most especially those of the Roman Church. It makes him painfully sad that so many enemies of Catholic truth set out to place the most fanciful opinions on the same footing as Christ's teaching, or to confuse it with them, and to disseminate the godless system of religious indifference—indeed that some of them level the most detestable insult at Christ, making him out to be, so to speak, a partner in their foolishness. They in fact wish, from a few regulations certainly containing nothing contrary to religion, and enhancing the well-being of the citizens of the Papal States, as well as from the amnesty granted at the beginning of this papacy, to conclude that the pope is so benevolently disposed toward the entire human race that he believes one can also obtain blessedness apart from the Catholic Church. Accordingly people have caused a new and more severe vexation to the pope, and he cannot find the words to express his horror about it.

This was in fact a reply to a document addressed to the pope in September 1847 by Giuseppe Mazzini, formerly a Genoese lawyer and now the main leader of the Young Italy party. In it Mazzini reminded the pope of the huge obligations of someone in his exalted position. He wrote:[5]

5. Giuseppe Mazzini (1805–72) was an Italian nationalist and republican who worked tirelessly for the unification of Italy, fully achieved shortly before his death. His open letter to the pope in 1847 was written from exile in London. Baur provides a German version.

> Europe is in a terrible crisis of doubt and longing. In virtue of current forces, which have been expedited by the popes and the hierarchy, the faith is dead. The Catholic faith has succumbed to despotism, and Protestantism is submerged in anarchy. There are only the superstitious or the hypocrites, and no believers. The kings, the governments, the privileged classes battle to seize power by force, and because of them the people suffer. We no longer have any heaven, and that is why we also no longer have any social community. But humankind cannot live without heaven. We will therefore more or less quickly have a religion and a heaven—not kings and the privileged classes, but instead the people. The pope can hasten this moment. He should take the leadership of a new humanitarian religion, declaring that humankind is holy and God's servant; that all who infringe upon humanity's entitlement to progress and free association are taking an erroneous path; that God is the source of every government; that those who are the best in reason and spirit, in genius and virtue, are entitled to be the leaders of the people. But the main duty of the head of the church is, above all, establishing the unity of Italy.

The youth of Italy rested such hopes on Pius IX. Enthusiasm for him had not yet grown cold.

The Year 1848; Retreat of the Papists; The Roman Republic

The public newspapers from early 1848[6] went overboard reporting the joyful testimonies and touching scenes involving the pope and the people. They happily praised a prince whose main efforts had only to be directed at restraining his subjects' public declarations of love for him, and setting bounds for it. At the same time there was no lack of signs of unrest. The people's clubs evidently wanted to see how far they could go before the

---

6. The year 1848 brought revolutions throughout Europe, which led to the abdication of Louis-Philippe, the resignation of Metternich, freedom for Hungary, the adoption of a declaration of rights and a representative assembly by the German states in Frankfurt (see p. 224, n. 5), and the arrival of Mazzini in Milan, who pressured Pope Pius IX to join the war against Austria. In 1849 the Habsburg monarchy regained control: with the help of Russian troops it suppressed Hungary and blocked further steps toward German unification for another twenty years. Counter-revolutionary forces prevailed elsewhere too, in France and Italy. "A dialectic of radicalization on the left and military reactions on the right had emerged in many parts of Europe by the later stages of the revolution" (Richard J. Evans, *The Pursuit of Power: Europe 1815–1914* [London and New York, 2016], 212–13).

pope would decide to resist them; what took place in Naples was even more upsetting.

The pope could not disregard the demands for a constitution. After repeated assurances as to how seriously people were working on it, but also how difficult a matter it was in a state consisting of a twofold regime, what finally emerged was not only a reform ministry with just two of its members clerics, but also the long-awaited constitution. On 14 March the basic constitutional law of the state was announced; the day before it had been accepted in the consistory of cardinals. In Rome at least, it was received with great jubilation. Alongside the College of Cardinals, which remained the senate wholly inseparable from the person of the pope, the new governmental system put in place two advisory assemblies or chambers, an upper chamber of members appointed for life, and an elected chamber of deputies.[7]

Impressed by reports from Paris, but chiefly from Vienna and Milan, and the resulting feelings in Rome (the Austrian ambassador was in fact insulted), Pius faced a great predicament. He could not remain uninvolved; he supported the volunteer militias, and resolved to dismiss the Jesuits. Although urgently warned to exercise restraint, in a public address to the Italian people on 31 March, he recognized the voice of God in the occurrences of recent months. In this case we see more than a human work. He said that, for one to whom this voice is given, it is a joy to interpret the silent eloquence of God's works. The heart is moved by many a religious and noble phenomenon.

However, when people put further pressure on the pope, and after the commander of his troops had already crossed over the Po River, and people demanded that he sign a declaration of war against Austria, he steadfastly opposed doing so.[8] Ongoing tumult in Rome could not move him to sign a declaration of war. On 29 April he held a consistory at which he declared in his formal statement that, as the successor of Peter, he would have to lovingly embrace all peoples; that every war is a terrible thing; and that he is quite horrified at the thought that people want to install him as the leader of an Italian republic. He was in no position to stifle the ardent zeal of those of his subjects who wished to take part in the events occurring in northern Italy. So he was simply faced with what many mightier princes than he have had to deal with. He just sent his soldiers out to protect the borders of the Papal States. He repeatedly made the same declaration that, when it came to

---

7. [*Baur, in the text*] See the *Allgemeine Zeitung*, 23 March 1848.

8. The territory of Venetia, just north of the Po River, was controlled by Austria. Well after the revolt of 1848–49, Austrian ceded it to Italy (1866).

the peace of the entire world and specifically that of Italy, as the Father of all the faithful he could not become a participant in political factions and did not wish to do so. Despite the preparations for war and the ongoing conflict with the people's clubs, he at least succeeded in sticking to his position. The pope was continually in a tense relationship with the chamber of deputies and with Minister Mamiani,[9] for both were in favor of war and demanded that the pope declare war against Austria.

The enthusiasm for Pius IX had already substantially abated, and confusion in Rome increased until finally there was a public outbreak on 15 November with the murder of Count Rossi.[10] Prior to the February Revolution in Paris, Rossi had been the French ambassador in Rome. After Mamiani was dismissed from his dual offices, an effort was made to form a new and durable ministry. Rossi, as head of the cabinet, became minister of the interior and minister of finance. He endeavored, via stronger regulations, to establish peace and order and to counteract the anarchy of the various factions. That is why he was stabbed by an assassin on 15 November, on the steps of the chamber of deputies. From how strikingly people accepted this act one could see how public opinion was opposed to the pope. It was the beginning of a series of very consequential events.

The People's Club (*Circolo popolare*), in conjunction with the Club of Leghorn (*Circolo Livorno*), and together with Tuscan anarchists and demagogues, sought to force on the pope a democratic ministry. On 16 November this led to a belligerent demonstration. The program of the people's petition called for: a democratic ministry, recognizing Italian nationalism, pursuing war against Austria, and calling a constitutional assembly. When the crowd reached Montecavallo, the Quirinal Palace, a deputation was sent in to the pope. Initially he remained firm and protested against the violence. But when the tumultuous scene in front of his palace became ever more threatening, with projectiles even penetrating his antechamber, he signed the document submitted to him.

After this the pope was like a prisoner subject to the caprice of demagogues. The movement he himself had set in motion now took such a turn that he was enchained by the very powers he had unleashed. It is no wonder

---

9. Terenzo Mamiani della Rovere (1799–1885), an intellectual, a diplomat, a man of many parts, was a strong supporter of the *Risorgimento*. Named minister of the interior and minister president of the Papal States on 4 May 1848, he was dismissed from those offices on 2 August, only to return as foreign minister on 23 December.

10. Count Pellegrino Rossi (1787–1848), an Italian who was a professor at the Collège de France, went to Rome as the French ambassador in 1845. He opposed efforts to unify Italy with the pope as its president, and was assassinated in Rome on 15 November 1848.

that the pope sought to extricate himself from this painful situation. After most of the cardinals had already fled from Rome, the pope too fled during the night of 24-25 November. Under the protection of the Bavarian ambassador (Spaur), the pope escaped to Gaëta. From Gaëta he issued a manifesto in which he declared that, to his great regret, he had been forced to leave Rome owing to the latest unfortunate uprising; that the protest already made before the diplomatic corps, against the forcible installation of the ministry, he now repeats before all the world; that all the enactments issued in the meantime are declared to be lacking all legal sanction, are null and void. At the same time he seated a governing commission.

Meanwhile the People's Club in Rome took the lead of an anarchist regime. A provisional junta was proclaimed. The triumvirate of Corsini-Camerata-Galetti declared the intent to take over leadership of the state until a constituent assembly of the Papal States would be summoned, and that it would make provisions for what transpires thereafter. These plans made no mention of the pope at all.

For his own part the pope protested not only against the summoning of a so-called national assembly of the Roman state in order to introduce new political forms; he also, on 1 January 1849, condemned it as an atrocious, ecclesiastically scandalous crime against his own independence, one deserving of the punishment threatened by divine as well as human law. He recalled the decrees of the Council of Trent,

> in which the church again and again imposed its punishment, and declared its greatest anathema above all on anyone who should venture to be guilty of any sort of crime against the secular sovereignty of the Roman pope. Hence, although his conscientious duty compels him to protect and defend the sacred pledge of the patrimony of the bride of Christ, which is entrusted to his care, he can, on the other hand, still never forget that he is the representative of the one who, in exercising justice, also leaves room for mercy. Day and night he prays for the return and rescue of those who have gone astray, and hopes it will not be long before the day he sees, coming back once again into the fold of the Lord, those of his children who today cause him so many troubles and such grief.

The Romans still had no great desire to return to this fold. Reports from various quarters are in agreement that the papal anathema itself made not the slightest impression on the people; that in Rome people laughed about it and made light of this harmless reminiscence of a distant era. Indeed it even produced the opposite effect. Since it reminded people of earlier sins by the popes, a long suppressed resentment of the priestly regime came to a head. Only now, after the papal message of excommunication, was the convening of the constituent assembly not in doubt. All the social classes resolutely demanded that the spiritual authority be divested of the worldly scepter. As for heavenly matters, people were heard to say that priests and cardinals may continue to carry on with them, but that they have ruled this visible world unscrupulously, indeed being the true and ultimate reason for all sorts of corruption and depravity.

The constituent assembly had scarcely convened on 5 February when it decided, in one of its first sessions, to set up a Roman republic. The ceremonial removal of the pope's secular power and the installation of the new government were announced from the Capitoline Hill on 9 February. Triumvirs were named, with executive authority. According to one of the laws promulgated by the national assembly on 18 February, all the moveable possessions and real property of mortmain, that is, of pious foundations and religious corporations and so forth, were considered to be, and appropriated as, the property of the state. The full committee of the Roman ministry expressly declared that its program included extirpating anything that remains from the clerical system. How this program greatly furthers religion is, more than anything else, proof for the holiness and integrity of what the republic did.

While the Romans, with the greatest enthusiasm, were constituting the republic, news came about the Battle of Novara.[11] It had a disturbing impact, but only served to increase the boldest resistance. Now a dictatorial triumvirate was named, with Mazzini, the well-known agitator, as its head. The pope protested against both the setting up of a Roman republic and the expropriation of church property. More significant, however, was his now calling for intervention by the Catholic powers, namely, Austria, France, Spain, and Naples. In April the French government announced its intention to intervene in Rome. But this made a very unfavorable impression on the public, for people generally disapproved of restoring papal rule, and they found the principles of the French government unsuitable, forming an obstacle to the creation of a different republic. Soon afterward French troops landed in Civitavecchia and from there approached Rome, but encountered unexpected resistance. Under Garibaldi's[12] leadership the Romans gave laudable proof of courage and bravery, the French suffered severe losses,

---

11. On 23 March 1849 Austrian troops defeated an Italian army under the king of Sardinia-Piedmont, at Novara, a town near Milan. This incident showed a lack of support from small states in the Italians' war of independence.

12. Giuseppe de Garibaldi (1807–82), Italian patriot who led numerous campaigns in the struggles for Italian independence.

and only after a siege drawn out to the end of June could they take possession of the city.

The French occupation now proved to be adequate protection against all the democratic movements, yet the pope still remained away from his home base. The pope's relationship with the Romans could be no different than that of all his predecessors; it was as poor as it could possibly be. He finally gave in to Austrian advice, and on his own initiative he promised several reforms in finance and governance. However, even the most modest hopes and wishes tied to them remained unfulfilled. Everything was just organized in hierarchical fashion and no thought was given to a secular administration. The same applied to the amnesty declaration of 18 September. The amnesty involved so many exclusionary provisions that political persecution went on as it had before.

Pius IX and the Papacy after 1849

The pope did not venture to return to Rome until April 1850. His reception was cool and ambivalent, his relationship with the Romans remained tense, and one can see most clearly from the way things are now that the papal rule can maintain itself only because of the French troops that still occupy Rome. A strong argument against the divine character of the papacy is that the very regime supposedly the wisest and most beneficent in principle is the most hated and notorious regime, for by the most flagrant abuses and imperfections it undercut the authority of the state, not merely politically and financially but also morally. On the other hand, however, all it had to undergo in more recent times has made the papacy even more tenacious. However things stood in the Papal States, the pope could always count on foreign help, and the world has retained such faith in the papacy and its infallibility that the pope may always be confident when the strength of this faith is put to the test. In this connection one need only call to mind the official endorsement of the dogma of the Immaculate Conception of the Virgin Mary.[13]

Still more significant is the observation as to the value that Catholic and Protestant regimes, even in most recent times, have placed on being on the best possible footing with the Roman Curia. This is shown by the most recent concordats, with Austria in 1854 and Württemberg in 1857. The pope stated publicly that he was especially happy to conclude the concordat

---

13. The teaching of the Immaculate Conception, stating that Mary herself was immaculate when conceived in the womb of her mother, was made an official dogma by Pius IX in 1854.

with Württemberg. Now too the concordat with Baden[14] puts the finishing touches on concordat politics. In the summer of 1857, when the pope visited many of the provinces of the Papal States, returning via Florence to Rome, we saw the powerful influence the papacy was still in a position to exert in the region, by the direct impact its presence has on hearts and minds. The pope was received everywhere with great jubilation and all sorts of demonstrations of the most devoted adoration and subservience. Catholicism so far seems to be inseparable from the integrity of the papacy.

More recently, however, a most serious crisis has emerged. After the Italians' struggles for freedom, long since proclaimed to Emperor Napoleon III by Sardinia, had received such powerful support, it was necessary, when war broke out in the spring of 1859, for the Austrians to withdraw from the provinces of the Papal States they had heretofore occupied, with the result that these provinces turned to open rebellion against their papal sovereign.[15] The Peace of Villafranca did not preclude restoring sovereigns to their renegade Italian states. However, the French emperor had played a major role, indirectly and directly in the Italians' revolutionary striving for freedom. So as not to get caught up in too great a self-contradiction, together with the nationality principle the emperor had put in place, he had to link to the restoration a stipulation as to what would surely never happen, namely, that restoration would not take place via military intervention. At least for the inhabitants of the Romagna region the expectation is that they will freely return to obedience to their papal ruler.

Along with regulating other Italian affairs, the congress convened in Paris mainly had the task of deciding issues regarding the Papal States. Yet prior to the start of the congress Emperor Napoleon III revealed his intentions quite clearly: first, in the brochure undoubtedly inspired by the emperor and composed by his own publicist, Laguéronnière, and entitled "The Pope and the Congress"; then in the 31 December 1859 document the emperor directed to the pope. It stated that, with all due respect that the emperor has for the pope, and with all the concern the emperor has expressed for him and also for the preservation of the Papal States, the emperor's aim is nothing less than carrying out the plans that Napoleon I had for the pope,

14. [Zeller] 1859.

15. The Kingdom of Sardinia included extensive territory in the Piedmont region of northwest Italy. On 24 June 1859, at the Battle of Solferino in the province of Lombardy, controlled by Austria, allied French and Piedmontese armies defeated the Austrians at great cost to each side. The Peace of Villafranca, made between France and Austria in 1859, ceded Lombardy to France and then to Piedmont, and restored various deposed Italian dukes to their positions. However, by strengthening Piedmont and weakening the hold of Austria on Italy, it began the process of unifying Italy.

namely, divesting him of his secular power, limiting him to the city of Rome and, as a substitute for his previous revenues, making him a pensioner of Catholic states. It directly demanded that, from his love of peace, of his subjects' well-being, of the common good, of European tranquility, the pope should give up his papal provinces.

The pope of course declared that, for his own part, he was resolved to oppose this most emphatically, and would never assent to such a crime against the heritage of Peter. Shortly after receiving Louis Napoleon's document, in his New Year's address, which gives a résumé of that document, the pope declared it to be a monumental hypocrisy and a web of contradictions. In his encyclical of 19 January, and in the foregoing address, he rejected most decidedly the demand to relinquish provinces to the insurgents, and elaborated on the reasons why he could not do this.[16]

The most important leaders of the Catholic clergy, including the French clergy whose bishop of Orleans stood out by speaking candidly about it, had already protested the outrageous act of seizing these most ancient entitlements and calling into question all the legal concepts and factual considerations. Similar sounding declarations came from all quarters, signaling the most heartfelt sympathy for the pope on the part of all of Catholic Christianity. One cannot predict what will come of this. Given the French emperor's position vis-à-vis the other European powers, he will not find it difficult to follow up on his plans. Even the Catholic clergy's opposition is not much of a deterrent.

Whatever the immediate outcome may be, for us Protestants the most important factor is simply that, within the Catholic Church itself, there is a growing recognition that the Christian church can also endure without there being a secular regime, without a representative of God and Christ presiding over a papal political state. If the pope is no longer a secular ruler, then, even as spiritual head of the Catholic Church, he will no longer be so very significant; he will no longer be treated as a sovereign equal in rank to other rulers; Protestant princes will no longer be very interested in concluding concordats with him. His demotion in this regard can in general be viewed as just the beginning of a series of changes gradually offsetting the imbalance between Catholicism and Protestantism.[17]

---

16. [Zeller] He could not surrender what is not his own but belongs to all Catholics. By such a surrender he would be violating his solemn oath, the dignity and rights of the Holy See, and encouraging the rebellion in other provinces, as well as offending against the rights of all Christian princes.

17. [Zeller] I let this passage stand as presented in the 1860 manuscript. Baur wrote it around the end of January or the beginning of February in that year. Since then we have had the opportunity to learn more about the future course of events deleterious

B. The Most Recent History of the Jesuits

The Jesuits in France under Louis Philippe

Here too our attention is drawn above all to France. If the entire character of the government of Charles X is what embittered the French nation to it, the Jesuits were the principal cause of the new revolution. Fear of the Jesuits drove them straight away to the borders of the land. People unleashed their fury at several of the Jesuit establishments, those at Montrouge and St. Acheul. The new government found it necessary to show, through new regulations, what a serious matter it was to oppose Jesuit influence in the future. In 1831 Louis-Philippe issued an ordinance cancelling the decree of 25 September 1816 that had allowed Jesuit missions in France, and consequently forbidding these missions. In the same year the minister for worship issued a circular letter to the governing bodies of all the higher schools that called upon the archbishops and bishops to comply more strictly with the ordinance of 16 June 1828, with regard to the minor seminaries. In fact the main provision directed that no one may be a principal or a teacher for an institution dependent on the university, or in the religious seminary, if he has not declared in writing beforehand that he does not belong to any forbidden religious association.

But the Jesuits soon knew how to take advantage of the new circumstances. However much the new government made it a fundamental principle to neutralize, and strictly oversee, the pretensions of the priests, it was very much in its own interest, by respecting religion and carefully cooperating with the priesthood, to establish public trust and consolidate the social bonds of the new order. The more this succeeded, and the more the public opinion of religion improved, the more the Jesuits saw their opportunity to gradually emerge once more from the quiescence into which they had retreated. They very skillfully set about drawing public attention to themselves. Even before their influence had otherwise become noticeable, a member of the their society, Xavier de Ravignan,[18] became famous in Paris

---

to the pope's secular rule. . . . [Ed.] Zeller continues with a lengthy note describing events in 1860 and 1861, including a papal bull of excommunication, the defeat of papal forces by the Piedmontese in September 1860, and the rejection in 1861 of papal claims to secular power by the German theologian Johann Joseph Ignaz von Döllinger (who later refused to accept the 1870 dogma of papal infallibility and became a leader in the movement resulting in the formation of the Old Catholic Church).

18. Gustave François Xavier Delacroix de Ravignan (1795–1858), a Jesuit who preached at Notre Dame in Paris, throughout France, and also in Belgium and London. Author of *De l'existence et de l'institut des Jésuits* (7th ed., Paris, 1855), which is mentioned below in the text.

and all of France for his splendid addresses from the pulpit. This was just the opening round of the sensation the Jesuits soon created by their involvement in a very important issue.

About this same time, after the tragic death of the duke of Orleans, when Louis-Philippe was very much concerned to gain the approval of the senior priesthood for his dynasty, the French clergy unanimously raised a clamor for freedom of instruction. In France since 1808, public instruction was under the exclusive oversight and direction of the university. An imperial decree of 1808 ordered that no school, no teaching institution of whatever kind, may be established without the permission of the University of France; that no one may open such a school, or teach publicly as such, who is not a fellow of the university and a graduate of one of its faculties. Only the major seminaries, the episcopal seminaries dedicated to educating the priesthood, were exempt from this rule. The Charter of 1830 had included freedom of instruction among the freedoms it guaranteed. Yet from experience in Belgium people had learned in the meantime how to sidetrack the Charter's promise to carry out this law. But now, in 1842, the senior clergy pressed for unconditional freedom of instruction and, in doing so, battled against the university.

People saw why the Jesuits were interested in this matter from the manifesto the aforementioned Ravignan included in his 1844 book, *De l'existence et de l'institut des Jésuites*. It was the impassioned apologetic for the Society of Jesus to which he publicly declared his allegiance. He boldly derided the law of the land by candidly admitting that more than two hundred Jesuits resided on French soil, and he demanded a revision of the major anti-Jesuit proceedings, and a moral and material rehabilitation of the order. Whereas the government ignored this presumptiveness and the university left unanswered the attacks made on it, two professors at the Collège de France, Michelet and Edgar Quinet,[19] in particular responded with their powerful polemic against the Jesuits. In a series of lectures they sought to show how the essence of Jesuitism and the purpose of Jesuit instruction is the stifling of individualism by rote learning. To this end they looked at the order in all aspects of its internal organization and its historical operations, and demonstrated, from Loyola's *Spiritual Exercises*, his profound hostility to the freedom of the spiritual life; and from the *Constitutions* demonstrated his striving for moral servitude and the negation of the individual, the stifling of every nobler social impulse, and his hostility to political freedom.[20]

19. Jules Michelet (1798–1874), French historian, professor at the Collège de France (1838–51). Edgar Quinet (1803–75), French historian and man of letters, and anti-clericalist.

20. Saint Ignatius of Loyola (1491–1556) founded the order of the Society of Jesus

After these lectures, public attention turned increasingly to the Jesuit issue, which had become one with the issue of the freedom of instruction. The government now saw an occasion to introduce a new draft ordinance regarding the freedom of secondary school instruction (of classical or grammar school instruction). This ordinance was especially aimed at the Jesuits, and its main provision was that every principal and all teachers in private institutions should be required to provide assurance that they did not belong to any forbidden congregation or association. The commission of the chamber of peers adopted the provision, and this became the occasion for very lively and extensive discussions, between the opponents and defenders of the Jesuits, regarding the Jesuits and their stance toward the state. The Jesuits themselves took advantage of the leniency the government still showed them, in order to set up more institutes, and in a short time the number rose to more than twenty Jesuit houses dispersed throughout all of France. The Jesuit house in the *rue de Postes* in Paris was the center of their widespread activity.

But the more secure the Jesuits believed their situation to be, the more that misled them into opening the public's eyes regarding them. One legal proceeding implicating them involved Affenaer, one of their treasurers, in April 1845. It established judicially the generally known fact of the order's illegally organized existence in France, and also gave people an even further look into the non-priestly, commercial dealings of the pious fathers. The government could no longer be indifferent to such an obvious offense against the laws of the state. The outcome was that the friends of the society themselves quickly gave their opponents an opportunity to call the proven facts to the attention of legislative authorities, and this resulted in further and more serious steps taken to suspend the institutes.

An association of zealous Catholic residents of Marseille had appealed to the chamber of peers with a petition asking that Professors Michelet and Quinet be prohibited from lecturing. In the lively discussion about this, with almost everybody recognizing both the inappropriateness of the lectures and the impossibility of forcibly stopping them, Cousin[21] ended a lengthy discourse by a very direct attack on the Jesuit order, and by rebuking the government for previously and demonstrably being unlawfully tolerant of it.

(1539) and became its first superior general (1541–56). His *Spiritual Exercises*, deriving from his devotional practices in 1522, received the approval of Pope Paul III in 1540. He also composed the *Constitutions* of the Jesuit order.

21. Victor Cousin (1792–1867), a French philosopher, peer, and holder of various public offices, became the minister of public instruction in 1840.

This is how things stood when, in 1845, Thiers[22] felt moved, in the chamber of deputies, to interrogate the ministry [of public instruction] about enforcing the laws pertaining to religious congregations. He introduced the fact that in a few years' time the Jesuit congregations have become very widespread. He believed himself well-informed in contending that today the society has become large enough to divide itself into two provinces, those of Lyon and Paris; that it has twenty-seven houses, and at least three or four times as many professors as are reported in public documents; what is more, that this number is increasing. Instead of a half-hidden existence able to be denied, a congregation prohibited by the law of the land is now proven to exist and its existence is acknowledged in the law court. Not taking action in the face of such facts is no longer tantamount to tolerating the failure to enforce the laws of the state; it is tantamount to revoking these laws. He said that if the law now remains silent, then in 1845 we are talking about summoning the Jesuits back to France. This brilliant speech was greeted with loud applause from all sides.

The main topic of the discussion linked to this speech was the rights of the state and the validity of the law. The discussion dealt with the past edicts of parliament and the extent to which they still apply; also the laws of 1790 and 1792 from the era of the revolution, and the Napoleonic Code.[23] The issues discussed included: the law of Messidor XII[24] that is now still the main legislative act governing [religious] orders; the concordat and laws governing organizations; the specifics of the penal code; finally, the charter and freedom of worship. The deliberations on all these points removed all doubt regarding the rights of the state vis-à-vis the Jesuits, and the chamber of deputies accepted both the legal rationale for the state's rights as well as the appropriateness of pursuing them. The only issue then was how this matter should be resolved. Two ways presented themselves: the legal route or the administrative route. Either the Jesuits could be hauled before the court based on the laws governing associations, because of their unauthorized opening of the community houses, and because of their participation in illegitimate associations; or, by applying the decree of Messidor XII,

---

22. Louis Adolphe Thiers (1797–1877), a historian and French statesman, held numerous public offices.

23. The Napoleonic Code, or "Code Civil," introduced by Napoleon in 1804, modeled itself on Roman law and made the civil laws (involving persons, things, and ownership) uniform.

24. The First French Republic established a new calendar. Messidor (equivalent to 19 June to 18 July) was the tenth month. This calendar, adopted in 1793, sought to remove Christian elements, and began the year with the autumnal equinox and the first month, Vendèmiaire.

the police and authorities could shut down their houses without further ado. The government was unwilling to settle on either course of action. It believed it must find a more lenient procedure, and promised diplomatic negotiations with the spiritual authorities, with Rome. So the chamber concluded its deliberations with the declaration that it is universally agreed that the laws of the state are applicable here; that their application has become necessary; and that whatever the outcome of the negotiations may be, the law must be enforced.

Despite the defiant protestations made by several bishops, the government had no choice but to comply with the decision of the chamber. Count Rossi, the French ambassador to the papal seat, was instructed to demand in Rome the voluntary withdrawal of the Jesuit order from France. The general of the Jesuits, Father Roothaan,[25] initially wanted to refuse consent to such an unwarranted expectation. The college of cardinals, charged with this matter by Gregory XVI, also stated unanimously that its reply to the proposal of the French court was simply to reject it. Yet soon thereafter a ministerial publication broke the news that the Jesuit issue has been settled according to the wishes of Louis-Philippe. After the matter itself had miscarried, Count Rossi or the pope prevailed upon the Jesuit general to at least make a face-saving concession. Father Roothaan agreed to the pretense of recalling his underlings from France, and the French government promised, in return, to temporarily close just the main Jesuit establishment on the *rue de Poste* in Paris, and a few others that had drawn the most public attention to themselves—such as those in Lyon, Avignon, and St. Acheul—but to tolerate the remaining Jesuit institutes as before, and in general to carry on with the greatest forbearance.

The Jesuits could certainly make such a compromise. A voluntary renunciation without the civil authorities commanding it, and without a formal legal expulsion, made it easier for them to return later on. Also, only a few of them left the country; the rest just carried on more circumspectly. The government press proclaimed this result to be a splendid victory of diplomacy; but everyone saw the disgraceful game that had been played with the nation. When Louis-Philippe soon thereafter approved of the Jesuit order even in foreign lands, and championed the interests of Ultramontanism and Jesuitism in the Swiss civil war stirred up by the Jesuits, the provocation was so extreme one could justifiably contend that the royal court's conduct in the matter of the Jesuits also essentially contributed to the downfall of the Orleans dynasty in the February 1848 revolution.

25. Jan Roothaan (1785–1853), born to a once-Calvinist family that emigrated from Frankfurt to Amsterdam, became a Jesuit in Russia and rose to the top ranks, being elected superior general in 1829.

The Jesuits in Switzerland; the *Sonderbund* War

Switzerland is the land that came closest to France in the severity of its experience with the Jesuits' pernicious influence, in fact even in political affairs.[26] After its reinstatement, the Jesuit order sought to establish itself in various places, in Graubünden, Valais, and Fribourg. In 1818 the Jesuits were formally introduced into Fribourg, and the canton's educational institutions were assigned to them. They also set up a first-rate boarding school in a magnificent building. When the papal nuncio suddenly moved, in 1835, from Lucerne to Schwyz, right away the local community of Schwyz expressed the desire for a Jesuit college to be situated in the principal town of the canton. In a short time they collected the necessary funds both for this purpose and for setting up a boarding school on the model of the one in Fribourg. But even this was not enough. The government also handed over to the Jesuits the secondary school in Schwyz, together with all its endowed property. Schwyz than became the principal center of the Jesuitical, Ultramontane intrigues in Switzerland. The liberal governments of neighboring cantons, specifically those of Aargau, Lucerne, and Solothurn, soon had to feel the effects of all this. Even the Zürich riot of September 1839, upon the appointment of Strauss,[27] was closely connected with the Jesuitical and Ultramontane efforts in opposition to liberalism. Just as the Jesuits had their best friends in the aristocrats, so too they aroused the fanaticism of the people in accomplishing their purposes.

The canton of Lucerne in particular had to face the rise of the Jesuits. Already in November 1839 Josef Leu von Ebersole,[28] for years the leader of the Ultramontane faction in Lucerne's grand council, had proposed handing Lucerne's higher educational institution, endowed by their forefathers, over to the Society of Jesus. The grand council did not do so, but people rested their hopes in 1841 on the pending changes in the government and complete turnover of the grand council's membership. When the people were given the impression that religion is in peril, they brought down the

---

26. The *Sonderbund* War (discussed later in this section) was brief in duration, 3–29 November 1847. Eight cantons principally consisting of a conservative Catholic population resisted liberalizing forces from the other (Protestant majority) cantons that sought to replace the traditional sovereignty of individual cantons with a more centralized government. The separatist alliance (*Sonderbund*) capitulated and the Swiss Confederation was formed.

27. The highly controversial scholar, David Friedrich Strauss, was appointed professor of dogmatics and church history, but the public outcry in Zürich was so great that the offer was rescinded.

28. Josef Leu, a conservative Swiss politician (born 1800 in Weiler Unter-Ebersol, murdered in his bed in 1845), later added "von Ebersole" to his name.

liberal government and introduced a system of governance putting the state entirely in the hands of the clergy. The newly elected governing council even presented the governmental system to the pope for his approval. Now only Roman Catholic Christians were said to have political and civil rights. In that same year, Leu von Ebersole, together with eight other members of the grand council, reintroduced the proposal to invite the Jesuits to Lucerne and hand the higher educational establishment over to them. Now the proposal also included the decision to make inquiries regarding the life and activities of the Society of Jesus, as well as the terms under which they would be inclined to take over the higher educational establishment, wholly or in part. However, the Jesuit issue had now already become the theme not merely of Lucerne politics, but also of Swiss politics as a whole.

Yet before matters were resolved, as a result of the Jesuit intrigues the three original cantons, together with the cantons of Fribourg, Zug, and Lucerne, formed a Catholic *Sonderbund* that in fact introduced a split in the confederation. A seventh canton, Valais, was added to the *Sonderbund*[29] after the liberal government had collapsed in 1840, not only because of the intrigues of the Jesuits but also because the liberal faction had suffered total defeat in the battle of Trent in 1844. We can see the fanatical religious hatred, practiced by the victorious Ultramontane party, from what Bishop de Preux, a follower of the German College in Rome, stated in the grand council of Valais. He said the maxim of reciprocal tolerance goes directly counter to the fundamental canon law of the Catholic Church. Because it alone is the true church, the Catholic Church cannot be tolerant of Protestants, whereas the Protestants are duty-bound to be tolerant of Catholics, because the Protestants cannot say that their church is the only true church.

In Switzerland people were now generally convinced that a religious and civil war was inevitable if the Jesuits were not dismissed from the confederation. The need to ban them was expressed in many of the people's associations and assemblies. However, a resolution presented to that effect in the Swiss Diet in 1844 failed to pass, and Lucerne, the current headquarters of the Jesuits, defiantly embraced the Jesuit colony in this canton. Yet in September of that same year an agreement was reached with the Jesuits, the force of which was that the theological education establishment there would be handed over to the Jesuits as a training school in Lucerne for priests and the associated pastors of the town. Making the Jesuits subordinate to the educational council was of course one of the conditions; but this was merely a ruse, since they were at the same time allowed to live and operate in the

29. The members of the *Sonderbund* were the cantons of Lucerne, Uri, Schwyz, Zug, Fribourg, and Valais, with the other two (Obwalden and Nidwalden) treated as one (Unterwalden) by Baur to get his number of seven.

canton in accord with the church-sanctioned rules of their order. Of course in Lucerne's system of governance the people's veto could still pose an obstacle to a Jesuit colony. But the foray by irregular troops in December 1844, and the insurrection of Lucerne's liberals against the Jesuit brigade, led to the complete triumph of the Jesuits. What now began in Lucerne, under Sigwart-Müller[30] and his associates, was a reign of terror, against which even the Swiss Diet, called into extraordinary session at its new seat in Zürich in February 1845, dared raise no objection. In March of that year the weakness of the Diet resulted in a second foray by irregular troops, which ended just as deplorably as the first one did. Directly thereafter came the ceremonial installation of the Jesuits in Lucerne.

Nevertheless their triumph did not last long. Public opinion turned ever more decidedly against them. In April 1846 the Swiss Diet met and deliberated about expelling the Jesuits and dissolving the *Sonderbund*. However, since the reactionary party still held the governing power within most of the cantons, no firm decision could be reached. Only after the more decidedly liberal faction had succeeded in taking the helm of government in the majority of the cantons, would the twelve other cantons reach the decision, in July 1847, that designated the *Sonderbund* as an illegal entity and directed that it be dissolved. Since people saw in the *Sonderbund* simply the work of the Jesuits, the declaration by the seven *Sonderbund* cantons, that they do not go along with this decision but are instead opposed to implementing it, resulted in the further decision by the Swiss Diet in September 1847, that the Jesuits are to be expelled from the confederation.

As inadequate as the *Sonderbund's* means of resistance seemed to be, it was very daring in relying on the European diplomatic corps caught up in the nets of the Jesuits. Metternich and Louis-Philippe not only encouraged and supported the *Sonderbund* by advice and other means; they also restrained Pope Pius IX from interfering and, by threats and intrigues, sought to impede the Swiss Diet from carrying out its decision. The Diet was not deterred by this. After every effort at an amicable settlement was exhausted, in November 1847 the Diet confirmed its earlier decision and summoned the army of the confederation to implement it under its banner. In a brief campaign the army destroyed the entire edifice of the *Sonderbund* and crushed the Jesuit regiment. Switzerland cleansed itself of the Jesuits, and the revised governmental system of the canton of Lucerne expressly

---

30. Constantin Sigwart-Müller (1801–69) took over leadership of the Ultramontane party from Josef Leu in the 1830s. He held various offices in Lucerne and in the confederation, was active in escalating hostilities in the canton, and went into exile in Austria when the *Sonderbund* collapsed in 1847, only later returning to Switzerland.

stipulated that the Jesuits, and their affiliated orders, may no longer be introduced into the canton in any form.

The Fate of the Jesuit Order since 1848

Yet what happened in Switzerland in 1847 was just the prelude to the great catastrophe that would befall the Jesuit order in the following year. Lively interest in the happy outcome of the *Sonderbund* war, and people's outspoken pleasure in particular at the well-deserved punishment of the Jesuits, made it clearly evident how public opinion was very much opposed to the Jesuits. The February revolution in France, in which too, as we already noted, the Jesuits just reaped the bitter harvest from the poison they themselves planted, gave the signal for a general popular uprising against the Jesuits. In all the Catholic lands where a national uprising occurred, the people were aroused to take vengeance on the Jesuits. They promptly agreed that the Jesuits, as the declared enemies of all spiritual and political freedom and of any national progress, were no longer to be tolerated in the midst of civilized society.

In those very lands where the Jesuits were most firmly implanted—the motherlands of Catholicism—the will of the people spoke out most decidedly in opposition to the Jesuits. As soon as the Lombards were caught up in overt resistance to Austrian domination, and Sardinia had changed its political system, the existence of the Jesuits in northern Italy was no longer assured. In February 1848 the popular movement against them was still so threatening that the government directed them to vacate their establishments without calling attention to it. In Turin and Genoa, public fury against the hated order broke out openly. Important discoveries supposedly were made when the people stormed the Jesuit college in Genoa. In July 1848 the Sardinian cabinet reached the decision, which became a matter of law in August, forever banishing the Society of Jesus and its affiliated orders from the monarchy. Those who were natives received a small pension from the state if they left religious orders; the foreign Jesuits had to leave the country. Their property reverted to the state.

Things went no better for them in southern Italy, in Naples and Sicily. King Ferdinand II, who was very devoted to the Jesuits, even advised Father Roothaan to recall his underlings from Naples, because their presence was incompatible with the new governmental system of the kingdom. They finally left the capital city when threatened by the populace. In July the parliament in Sicily banned the order. The foreign fathers were deported, the local ones received a modest pension, and the state took the order's property. Even in the Papal States, in Rome, the people forcefully demanded the departure of the Jesuits, and the pope himself requested it. Yet before the pope's advice was followed, the preaching of a Jesuit hostile to reform, and the heightened bitterness of the people, led to a papal decree in March 1848 that ordered that the Jesuits be completely banned from the Papal States, and that their property be confiscated by the treasury. During the night they left the city. The natives who were secularized remained in the land and received a pension. The Jesuit college in Rome was returned to the secular clergy, and the other establishments under the care of the Jesuits simultaneously fell into other hands. Roothaan, the Jesuit general, boarded a ship for England with a considerable number of his underlings. Many of the refugees from Rome and Italy took themselves to America.

In other lands affected by the revolutions in February and March, the Jesuits also met a similar fate. In Austria, in Vienna and Linz, ominous popular movements arose in opposition to the Ligurians. They were driven out of many places and, to forestall further outbreaks of popular hatred, the emperor therefore ordered the suspension of the Society of Jesus and the Ligurians throughout the realm. Nevertheless they soon wormed their way in once more, even into Vienna, under the protection of their patrons in the higher aristocracy and in the imperial family itself. Galicia too expelled the Jesuits. Sentiments differed only in the Tyrol, where they had with difficulty first inserted themselves just ten years before. A deputation from the community declared to Archduke Johann that the Tyroleans would never allow the decree banning the Jesuits and the Ligurians to be carried out in their land. This was in part because the Tyroleans wanted nothing at all to do with the political upheaval in Austria that resulted in the expulsion of the Jesuits. Before the February revolution, a government decree in Bavaria had already suspended the Redemptorist mission at Altötting. Those who were to continue their missionary activity in America were provided with a small pension from the state.

In opposing the long-detested Jesuit order, the people therefore spoke out in such a widespread and resolute way. The stronger the national and political turn for the better in 1848, the more directly it took aim at the Jesuits as the primary obstacle to the new aspirations. Everywhere that the new movement forged a path, the Jesuits had to quit the field ahead of it. Yet as quickly as the storms of the February and March revolutions swept the Jesuits away, they by no means cleansed the soil of them forever. As soon as the political reversal came about, the Jesuits emerged once more from the hiding places to which they had resorted in face of the danger threatening them, and they sought anew to regain the dominance that had been stripped from them. People heard the same thing from all sides: that the Jesuits are coming back and regaining possession of what they relinquished. They regained their college in Rome, their Father Roothaan reappeared, and, following the pope's return, everything resumed its former course.

As the contest of the old ways with the new ones, of reaction with revolution, became more a battle of principles, the reactionary party in Catholic states, in order to be victorious, increasingly had to overcome its disdain for the Jesuits. People now also recognized once again that the Jesuits were the time-tested support for absolute monarchy. As one might have expected, they also made greater inroads with the populace. The supposition had been that 1848 provided very strong evidence against the Jesuits. Once the people had delivered such a verdict on the order and it had become so unpopular with the public, whose general conviction had been so loudly expressed, the important point seemed to be that the Jesuits are the sworn enemies of all humanity and all civilization, of all spiritual and political freedom; that they are always traitors to the people's cause. But all too soon the people and the Jesuits once again became on friendly terms. By their publicly manifested zeal for the religion, the missions the Jesuits organized in so many places were wholly calculated not merely to commend themselves to the higher echelon of society, but also to gain popularity and get people to witness contrary to the revolutions of 1848. The large crowds for their missionary preaching showed how very successful they were. Today they once again seek to become influential mainly in terms of morality. Hence, wherever they can, they are especially involved in setting up educational and teaching establishments, and in taking control of the instruction. Thus in Austria, for instance, they have gained possession of various professorships and academic institutions. Just as Catholicism cannot exist without its pope, so too it cannot exist without its Jesuits. Furthermore, it also remains the case that Jesuitism is the natural consequence of Catholicism.[31]

C. The Conflicts between Rome and Germany Prior to 1848

I place together under this heading phenomena having a shared feature. They evidence a distinctively German interest standing opposed to Roman Catholicism, to the extent that they involve either basic principles the governments of the German states had to uphold over against Rome, or a

---

31. [Zeller] More recently the Jesuit order has suffered a significant loss in Italy, owing to its expulsion from Naples and Sicily, and from other lands annexed by [Sardinia's Principality of] Piedmont. To the contrary in Germany, even where it is legally prohibited, as a rule no serious obstacles are placed in its path.

form of Catholicism as it was able to take shape only in Germany, under the varied circumstances in which Catholicism and Protestantism were mutually related. The first and most important topic under this heading is the controversy about *mixed marriages*. In order to understand this issue correctly, we must go back somewhat in time.

The Controversy about Mixed Marriages: The State of Affairs up until 1837

According to the principles of the Roman church, mixed marriages could not be allowed. However, it was naturally the case that, in a land where the two confessional groups were in such close contact, no church prohibition could prevent them. As time passed they became more frequent, and the church found it necessary to issue certain stipulations about what it had to let happen, so as to not let things get entirely out of hand. Especially noteworthy in this regard are regulations announced by Benedict XIV,[32] the first more specific ones on this topic. His 1741 declaration pertaining to the Netherlands led off with the main theme that mixed marriages are abominable, reprehensible, damnable, and cannot be condoned by the See of Rome; and yet, in order to avoid even greater evils, there is no obstacle to the See of Rome granting a dispensation for them. Hence he declared the ecclesiastical validity of mixed marriages. However, to make the church a party to them as little as possible—for it would be party to them in a formal marriage ceremony—he held that the sacrament of marriage is to be performed not by a priest but instead by those entering into the marriage. Hence the validity of the marriage satisfies the form prescribed by the Council of Trent, if the priest, acting just as a qualified witness, is present when the engaged couple utter the wedding vows. This is termed "passive assistance without performing the marriage."

In 1748, in response to a query from Poland, Benedict issued the constitutional edict that a mixed marriage could be approved only under three conditions: a Catholic education for all its children; assurance that the Catholic partner will participate in his or her faith; and in the expectation that the non-Catholic partner will return to the bosom of the Catholic Church. Yet the pope wished to overlook what Friedrich the Great decreed for Silesia in 1750, that children of mixed marriages are to be brought up in the religion of the parent of the same gender until the age of fourteen.

In Germany up until 1825, some mixed marriages took place without promising the children would be educated as Catholics, and some only

32. Prospero Lorenzo Lambertini (1675–1758) was Pope Benedict XIV (1740–58).

with this promise. However, in 1825, by order of the Prussian cabinet, the clergy was not allowed to require such a promise. Since the Catholic clergy then of course required no promise, but in protest refused, without further explanation, to perform the marriage, this led to negotiations with the See of Rome, which resulted in the March 1830 brief of Pius VIII. According to it a dispensation for a mixed marriage would be expressly made, but only conditional upon the promise that the children be raised as Catholics. Since this decision was not in line with that of the government, in June 1834 an understanding was reached with Count Spiegel, the Archbishop of Cologne, about putting the papal brief into practice. The archbishop agreed, in his pastoral letter sending the brief to pastors, and in an instruction to the general curacy, to present an interpretation entirely opposite to that of the brief's contents and purpose. According to this agreement, and contrary to the brief, things were supposed to remain in accord with the cabinet's 1825 order.

Whereas that papal brief allowed for just "passive assistance" in cases where no suitable guarantee was given as to the Catholic upbringing of all children, and so forth, according to the understanding with the archbishop the wedding will only be refused if the bride is certain that all children will be raised as non-Catholics, and in this certainty clearly evidences culpable irresponsibility and indifference toward her religious faith and her future parental duties. In fact a case like this surely cannot arise, since it is unthinkable that the Catholic partner, when informed about Catholic marriage, would be of such a mind as this provision assumes. Therefore the government, acting through the bishop, gains the very thing that the pope, in his brief, affirms is never to be conceded. Yet at the same time the very brief with which the episcopal understanding hardly concurred was published to the bishops with the approbation of the king.

When news of this reached Rome at the beginning of 1836, the cardinal secretary of state had a discussion about the matter with the Prussian ambassador. The ambassador explained that certainly the papal brief had indeed been approved by the king, but only after Archbishop Spiegel had given assurance that it did not contradict the laws of the state. However, it is out of the question that the bishops received secret instructions from the archbishop. In order to mollify the pope, the archbishop and three bishops (those of Münster, Paderborn, and Trier) were induced to send documents to the pope in which they reported on this matter in line with the government's sense of it. Yet even before these documents took their roundabout way to Rome via Berlin, the bishop of Trier had sent a different document to Rome in which he gave a discrepant report about the course of events. He said that, pressed by his conscience in facing his death, he most earnestly repented of the fact that he too had been a party to that arrangement.

Droste-Vischering and Dunin

In the meantime Baron Droste-Vischering,[33] the suffragan bishop of Münster, became the successor to Count Spiegel, who died in 1835. He was made the archbishop as a result of his declaration that he would indeed take care to uphold the agreement adopted in compliance with the brief of Pope Pius VIII about mixed marriages and in force in the four dioceses—in other words, to in no way weaken or overturn it were it expedient to do so; and that he would apply the agreement in the spirit of love and conciliation. As archbishop, he had sent to the pope a document consonant with those of the three aforementioned bishops. However, after the bishop of Trier's second document had become public knowledge, the archbishop believed that he was bound by the original understanding only to the extent that he found it in agreement with the papal brief—for only subsequently had he been apprised of the understanding's contents. Now he declared he found that, given these instructions, permission for a Catholic marriage without the betrothed promising, in advance, a Catholic upbringing for the children, obviously contradicts the brief. Hence when such cases arise he always instructs the pastors involved to never allow the marriage if such a promise has not been made.

Negotiations between the Prussian government and the archbishop about this matter were inconclusive. At this point the government demanded that the archbishop resign from his office, because he was not fulfilling the conditions under which he was selected. Since the archbishop did not agree to do what was expected of him, on 20 November 1837 he was, as we know, removed from Cologne to Minden. In issuing this order, the government justified it based on the accusations made against the archbishop, that he acted contrary to his word and his duty, contrary to existing laws and regulations, and that he attempted to undermine and subvert these laws, not only keeping the government in the dark about this, but rather having made it believe quite the opposite. [The order also said] it should not go unnoticed that the archbishop's whole way of doing so bears unmistakable marks of links with the hostile influence of two revolutionary factions that

---

33. Clemens August zu Droste-Vischerung (1773–1845). Elected archbishop of Cologne in 1835, formally installed 29 May 1836. On 20 November 1837 he was taken to Minden and placed under house arrest. He was released in 1839 and lived thereafter in Münster.

seek to incite people and confuse their consciences in order to carry out their destructive and wide-ranging plans.

When this interference with the seat of the archbishop took place, the cathedral chapter was instructed, when it follows the canonical rules suitable and adapted to the case of a *sedes impedita* (impeded seat), that it should forthwith maintain intact the internal management system of the diocese as well as initiate the restoration of an orderly ecclesiastical government in canonical fashion, and also report to the papacy about the whole incident. People must have been very anxious about the steps the pope would take. On 10 December he had already summoned a consistory of cardinals to a formal address in which he could not express with more sadness his deep distress about this injustice done to the church. This address was entirely calculated to win over public opinion to favor his cause. It set the tone for the energetic opposition that emerged on the part of Catholicism regarding this matter from that time onward. Bunsen,[34] the Prussian emissary who came to Rome directly after the pope's address, and had not been apprised about this already-accomplished act on the part of the Holy See, found himself in a very awkward position. When he inquired about the meaning of the address, he was just told it is to be viewed as a public protest against a public circumstance; as a solemn objection to a public and scandalous encroachment on the sacred rights of the church.

It is quite understandable that the archbishop's arrest on 20 November was very upsetting for the Catholic population in the Rhine Province and in Westphalia. In many places it led to disturbances, but they were readily suppressed. More important for the government was the fact that it could rely on the cathedral chapter in Cologne, which was itself dissatisfied with the archbishop. The only issue in this regard was whether or not the pope would confirm the election of its dean, Hüsgen,[35] whom the chapter chose to be its administrator, and who had already been for many years its vicar-general in spiritual affairs. The confirmation was long in coming, but finally, in May 1838, the pope approved of Dean Hüsgen in his capacity as the archbishop's vicar-general, heading up the archdiocese's governing system until the archbishop should return.

The government steadfastly maintained the legal force of its controversial instructions to the bishops of the western provinces, and to their successors in office, with regard to mixed marriages, while proving to be lenient and conciliatory on other matters. After the affair had run its course to this point, the literary controversy began with the publication of official

---

34. Christian Karl Josias von Bunsen (1791–1860), a Prussian diplomat.
35. Johann Hüsgen (1769–1841).

documents from both sides on the issue. These were appeals to public opinion, and presented the actual course of events with carefully selected documents. Among those who defended the interests of one side or the other, Görres[36] stood out. His *Athanasius* tackled the issue of the archbishop martyr with the full fervor of his grandiose presentation, and gave a new and powerful impetus to the enthusiasm [for Ultramontanism]. His book came out at the beginning of 1838, and was already in its fourth printing by Easter. He titled it *Athanasius* in order to establish a parallel between the famous archbishop of Alexandria and the new fighter against princely power. However much was written in opposition to Görres's *Athanasius*, it was all of far less significance than such a powerful polemic.

The controversy had begun in the western provinces of the Prussian kingdom, but also spread to the east. Although the archbishop of Gnesen and Posen, Martin von Dunin,[37] had stated in writing in 1830 that it was not customary in these dioceses to require this promise that all children of a Catholic mixed marriage ceremony be brought up as Catholics, at the beginning of 1837 he demanded that either the Prussian ministry officially publish the papal brief of 1830 in his archdiocese too, or else he be permitted to take the matter, in its present form, to the Apostolic See for a decision. Since the government rejected this demand, the archbishop, prompted by the pope's allocution, announced in a pastoral letter of February 1838 that he will immediately suspend any priest of his archdiocese who is so presumptive as to perform in a Catholic rite, or in some other way consent to, the marriage of a mixed couple, if the non-Catholic party has not pledged in advance, and most assuredly, that all the children of such a marriage shall be raised in the Catholic faith.

The government demanded that this pastoral letter be withdrawn. When the archbishop refused to do so, the government declared his illegal decree to be null and void, and forbade all holders of clerical offices to obey the decree, under threat of punishment. However, this then also aroused a Catholic self-consciousness in the Polish priesthood. It gave rise to protests from all the dioceses, declaring in one voice that they cannot do otherwise than obey the pastoral letter of their archbishop. The government then took

36. Johann Joseph von Görres (1776–1848) was a very prolific journalist and writer of books on philosophy, theology, and politics, who became a staunch defender of the Ultramontane position. His *Athanasius* (1837) defended the Catholic Church in opposition to the authority of the Prussian state.

37. Martin von Dunin—Marcin Dunin Sulgustowski—(1774–1842), archbishop of Gnesen (Gniezno) and Posen (Poznan) and primate of Poland, wrote a pastoral letter (27 February 1838) to his clergy, threatening their removal from office if they performed mixed marriages without getting the requisite promises from the couple. The Prussian government ministry held that he had overstepped his authority.

preliminary steps toward a criminal proceeding against the archbishop. The archbishop appealed to the ecclesiastical *privilegium fori* (special privileges) and steadfastly rejected all attempts to interrogate him judicially. In the pope's new formal address to the consistory of cardinals in September 1838, he presented the matter as though, based on the proceedings in Posen, the Prussian government was making unmistakable efforts to fundamentally destroy the system of church governance ordained by God, to separate each territory from the center of Catholic unity, and to make the church into a human creation. What followed in the Prussian state newspaper was a detailed statement that, in a very indecorous tone, accused the archbishop of falsely portraying the affair.

All the Prussian bishops became participants in the controversy and made it into a public issue. People hoped in vain for a more lenient attitude toward the archbishop after he was summoned to Berlin. In April 1839 the verdict of the higher regional court in Posen was made public. The court indeed acquitted him of the charge of treasonable actions and inciting the people against the government. However, because of his disobedience, and his unauthorized measures in his diocese and his failure to revoke them, it sentenced him to the loss of his office, to six months' imprisonment, and to paying all the court costs. At the same time he was declared unfit to ever again hold an office in the Prussian state. The strict verdict was not carried out in this way. The king accepted a letter from the archbishop as an appeal for leniency, and as a result suspended his removal from office and revoked his imprisonment, except that for the present he was to be confined to his residence in Berlin. However, he fled from Berlin and so was arrested in Posen and brought to the prison in Kolberg.

The Controversy Resolved in Prussia

This is how matters stood in 1840, when Friedrich Wilhelm III died and Friedrich Wilhelm IV succeeded him as head of state. The expectation was that a prince so favorably disposed to the church, and especially one so accommodating to the Catholic Church as Friedrich Wilhelm IV was, would have demonstrated what was then a different way of doing things, by taking a number of conciliatory steps. The change in government provided the best opportunity for him to set the matter aside and extricate himself from its many difficulties. First and foremost, the king allowed the imprisoned archbishop of Gnesen to return to his diocese. In a pastoral letter of 27 August 1840, the archbishop indeed urged people to be peace-loving in relations with non-Catholics, but also ordered his subordinates to refrain from any consensual act in concluding mixed marriages, because the law forbids requiring the guarantee that the children be raised as Catholics, and without that guarantee the church cannot allow such marriages. The situation of the other archbishop was handled via negotiations with the See of Rome. The outcome was that Archbishop Droste-Vischerung agreed, in view of his ill health, and via a brief of 24 September, that Johann von Geissel, the bishop of Speyer, be appointed his coadjutor with the right to be his successor. The king made public a document releasing the archbishop from his confinement, and honorably acquitted him of any blame for revolutionary intrigues. The archbishop then declared that he just wanted to pray for his church. However, he not only journeyed to Rome, where he was received very fondly by the pope, as a martyr for the church, but also believed that he must, in writing, advocate peace between the church and the state.

With regard to mixed marriages, people now adhered to the stipulations made by the Roman church in the brief of Pius VIII. Of the Prussian bishops, only the prince bishop of Breslau had heretofore let stand in his diocese the more moderate discipline of consecrating mixed marriages without the assurance that the children will be raised as Catholics. But he also believed he could no longer maintain this position in face of what was now the prevailing sentiment and practice. In order to escape the conflict into which his twofold position—vis-à-vis the government and the pope—had taken him, he carried out the resolution spoken of earlier, and gave up his bishop's crosier. As further reconciliation of the Catholic Church with the state, not only was a Catholic department set up in the ministry for spiritual affairs; also, in January 1841, by omitting the *placet* (consent) in the case of the teaching [on mixed marriages], communication was restored with the See of Rome.

Assessment of the Issues in the Controversy

We see here very clearly what we established as the general perspective from which to grasp the phenomena of the most recent period in the life of the church, namely, the tension and sharpening of antitheses. The lenient practice with respect to mixed marriages, a practice not only having taken shape of its own accord but also one that had even been introduced and approved by the bishops of the German Catholic Church, had to give way to the strict practice established by the stipulations of the Roman Church. The lenient practice was the consequence of the rapprochement of the two confessions, as this naturally occurs in a Protestant state, in a land with Catholic and Protestant populations. The strict practice can only maintain itself in the interest of the Roman hierarchy and Catholic absolutism. Hence in the controversy about mixed marriages we see how the laxer Catholicism that had become prevalent in German Catholic lands withdrew into itself, in order to embrace itself at the center point of its Catholic self-consciousness, and to place itself in an abruptly dismissive antithesis to Protestantism.

From the position of the absolute standpoint of Catholicism, or of the only salvific church, the Catholic view on mixed marriages is therefore completely justified. According to the principles of his church, it is utterly impossible for a Catholic priest to bestow his church's blessing on a mixed marriage. If he cannot wholly avoid participation in such a marriage, he can take part in it solely under the condition that at least the children of such a marriage in the Catholic Church will be saved. On the other hand, however, the state also has a claim with regard to marriage; it is also a matter for the state. Hence a Protestant state would completely fail to appreciate its interests if it wished to concede that all children born to a mixed marriage belong to the Catholic Church. However, we must go even further and ask: if both confessions once exist side-by-side with equal entitlements, then by what right as such are mixed marriages just addressed utterly in the interest of the Catholic Church? From its absolute standpoint, Catholicism of course believes the matter cannot be considered in any other way. However, the Peace of Westphalia[38] certainly ended Catholic absolutism in Germany. It recognized the full equal rights of the two co-existing confessions. However, it is then Catholicism's typical feature that, again and again, it thinks it should disregard its actually existing relationship with Protestantism; and so, despite that co-existence, Catholicism has assumed its own absolutism. Catholicism thinks it should constantly ignore the fact that it must co-exist with Protestantism, by acting as though there is no such co-existence at all.

The lenient practice regarding mixed marriages is therefore none other than the arrangement corresponding to the factually existing relationship of the two confessions; whereas the strict practice wishes to establish the absolute idea of Catholicism by completely failing to recognize the actual state of affairs, and doing so in a way for which there is no historical justification, at least in Germany. As for the state's relation to this absolute claim made by Catholicism, the Catholic priest's conscience is of course under no constraint when he refuses to consecrate a mixed marriage, although he has justice on his side all the more if he disobeys the call for all children of a mixed marriage to be raised as Catholics.

38. The Peace of Westphalia (1648) ended the Thirty Years' War. It confirmed the Peace of Augsburg (1555), which provided for the legal existence of both Lutheranism and Catholicism in the Holy Roman Empire. The Peace of Westphalia added the Reformed Church to this agreement.

In this controversy we have not just the antithesis between laxity and strictness, or between German nationalism and Roman Catholicism; we also have the antithesis of church and state. In the matter of mixed marriages, the interests of Protestantism can simply stand in for the interests of the state. The question is then whether the state must utterly subordinate itself to the church, or assert its free rights even over against the church. The second document of the Roman state, that of September 1839 written from the perspective of this question of principles, poses the controversial issue in beginning directly by blaming all the contentions of the Prussian government, regarding the affair of the archbishop of Posen, for starting out from the erroneous thesis that, in matters of religion, the church is subject to the authority of the state. The document declares that it is no surprise to the Holy See to hear, coming from the mouth of the Protestant government, the proscribed maxim that the church is subject to the state. The Holy See feels that a rebuttal is completely useless. However, it says the tendency is clear: to make the king's government the focal point of ecclesiastical unity for all Catholicism of the Prussian state; to cut the Catholic population of Prussia loose from the true and only center of unity, which is the pope in Rome; to introduce into the church a new governance system, opposed to the one given to the church by its divine founder; in short, to construct from the Catholic sector of the monarchy a new church, which would be something entirely different from a Catholic Church, since the nature and form of a church instituted by God does not turn upon the power and plans of human beings, and the Catholic Church can no longer endure where one alters and excludes the prerogatives and rights with which it has been invested by its founder.

From the Catholic standpoint all this is quite true and correct. However, when we bear in mind that there is not merely a Catholic confession but also a Protestant confession with the same entitlement, then the statement is no longer true. The Protestant counterpart to Catholicism's church, with its absolute entitlement, is the state, which can never let itself be controlled by the church. Hence it is correct to regard the controversy about mixed marriages as a contest of principles, inasmuch as, in the last analysis, it is dealing with the absolute relationship of Catholicism and Protestantism, in other words, of church and state. Accordingly, the emphasis falls on its characteristic feature, that an issue relating to practical life has developed into a controversy in which the two contesting parties face off in full awareness of their antithesis in principle.

The Controversy about Mixed Marriages in Württemberg

We may also note, in this same context, that the controversy arising in Prussia and spreading more widely found echoes in other lands where there was a mixed population of Catholics and Protestants. This also in fact occurred in Württemberg. Not long after the outbreak of the Cologne controversy, the Catholic clergy refused to consecrate mixed marriages in accord with the 1806 law that gave the two confessions equal standing. They were transferred as punishment for this. Mack,[39] professor of Catholic theology at Tübingen, received this punishment when, in an essay in the Catholic *Theologische Quartalschrift*, he spoke out very indecorously in opposition to the Württemberg government and the Protestants, about mixed marriages.

Finally, the elderly and infirm Bishop Keller of Rottenburg was moved, in the meeting of the Diet in 1841, to present the proposal that, to keep intact the autonomy of the church guaranteed by the governing system, measures suited to preserve peace in the church be enacted. In a series of articles he called for restoring to the church or the bishop the free exercise of the rights that the Catholic Church Consistory, as a state agency, had until then exercised in place of the bishops and in contradiction to the essential specifications of the Catholic Church's system of governance. One of these points concerned mixed marriages, for which the bishop proposed that the Catholic clergy play only a passive role, as arranged for in Austria via a papal brief. The entire motion made little impression on the chamber, since they certainly knew that the bishop, who was otherwise a faithful servant of the government, was in this case just the agent of an Ultramontane party. The chamber concluded that when substantial proposals from the bishop's camp are brought to the state government, it will give them due consideration individually, but that the motion as presented cannot be acted on. This decision did not lead to further discord, although the Ultramontane party vented its anger, to some extent in a very undignified fashion, about how its intentions miscarried, and it continued to be very active in its opposition to the government and to the liberal Catholics.

Hermesianism and Its Condemnation

Closely related to the controversy about mixed marriages, which originated in Prussia's Rhine Province, is the contemporaneous controversy about

---

39. Martin Joseph Mack (1805–85) was removed from his position as dean of the Catholic Theological Faculty and rector of the University of Tübingen, and reduced to being a country priest.

Hermesianism, which belongs to the same region. Here too we see once again the characteristic phenomenon of a form of Catholicism with affinities to Protestantism being suppressed with stubborn consistency by Roman Catholicism. G. Hermes,[40] a teacher of theology initially in Münster and since 1820 in Bonn, founded a school of theology that became the predominant one in the faculties at Bonn and Breslau. This school gained very significant influence owing to the reputation of its founder and his close personal relationship with the bishop of Cologne and other bishops in the region. Catholic theology, which under French rule had become ensconced in that region, first regained scientific import because of Hermes.

The work that, in addition to his very valuable academic lectures, made a name for him is his *Einleitung in die Christkatholische Theologie*, which appeared in two volumes (1819 and 1831). What is distinctive about Hermesianism is the method Hermes applied to the foundation of Catholic dogmatic theology. He set out from doubt and held that it is possible to transcend doubt, not by appealing to external authority but solely through insight into the truth and inner necessity of reason. As a theory of knowledge, which is what Hermesianism above all wants to be, it positions itself, broadly speaking, in relation to Catholic dogma in a way similar to how Kantian philosophy, as a critique of cognition, relates to philosophical dogmatism. Hermes says, in agreement with Kant, that arriving at the "that" (*Dass*) of existence or being [i.e., what actually exists] depends above all on "how" (*Wie*) it is known. One must distinguish the *principium cognoscendi* and *credenda* (the principle of knowing and believing) from the *principium essendi et creandi* (the principle of what is and is created).

According to Hermes there is a necessary rational belief, as a natural gift of God. It not only interconnects all scientifically valid certainty about the truth and reality of a natural revelation of God within us and outside us, and God's direct self-revelation within that reality; it also is the assured criterion for all that which is otherwise presented historically, as God's supernatural revelation and as an infallible authority, in particular in Christianity and in Catholicism. This necessary rational belief and its applicability to the evidence for Christianity is what constitutes the contents of Hermes's *Einleitung*. This position is in no way said to endanger the authority of the church, for it only substantiates that authority by showing that, in virtue of this God-given rational nature, every rational human being finds it necessary to faithfully acknowledge it as a higher divine authority standing above reason, and to trust its guidance in matters of salvation.

40. Georg Hermes (1775–1831) combined Catholic teaching with Kant's philosophy, in his *Philosophische Einleitung in die Christkatholische Theologie* (1819) and other writings. A papal brief condemned his teaching as heresy in 1835.

The two basic principles on which this faith rests are the two functions of theoretical reason and practical reason. These are human beings' only natural principles of reality and truth. In addition to them there are also supernatural, divine principles of reality and truth, ones met with in the supernatural revelation imparted by God. However, human beings who do not possess the principles of reality and truth naturally provided by reason cannot locate those supernatural divine principles either within themselves or externally. Hence rational belief is the necessary presupposition for belief in revelation.

This is the essential element in Hermesian theory. The entire theory sets out to demonstrate, in reason, the presuppositions necessary for accepting a supernatural revelation, and to analyze the various operations that play a part in doing so. Revelation through reason is in no way said to exclude, or detract from, divine grace through nature. However, the fact that it so manifestly places such great importance on the natural basis for revelation being given in reason, and that it leaves reason to develop, in the entire extent of its activity, on its own soil, independently of revelation, has cast suspicion on the teaching of Hermes. People surmise it involves a kind of rationalism that, although to a certain extent justifiable, could easily gain the upper hand over revelation. Hermes scarcely put forward any thesis deviating from Catholic dogmatics, and yet his entire way of understanding dogmatics was aligned with a rigorously understood dialectical procedure, with proof and [philosophical] thinking, such that it could have commended itself to the Catholic who implicitly dispenses with external authority.

Soon after Hermes died in 1831, the *Aschaffenburger Kirchenzeitung* raised the issue of Hermesianism's relation to Catholicism. Since the followers of Hermes responded, with the self-confidence of thinkers and independent scholars, to the suspicion as to their Catholic orthodoxy, and conducted themselves as the superior party, certain of being victorious, a definite bitterness then found its way into the controversy and soon bore its fruit. It seemed that people simply waited for the death of the Hermesians' patron, Archbishop Spiegel,[41] before striking a decisive blown against them. A papal brief, issued promptly in September 1835, condemned the teaching of the deceased Hermes and forbade publication of his writings. The brief stated that the nearly universal rumor from Germany judges Hermes to be a teacher of errors. Since the pope heard of this rumor via the denunciations and remonstrances from many of Germany's theologians and venerable ecclesiastics, he took it as his apostolic duty to have the writings of Hermes carefully investigated by theologians well-versed in the German language.

---

41. Archbishop Ferdinand August von Spiegel (b. 1764) died on 2 August 1835.

The judgment of these theologians was found to agree entirely with the general rumor. The cardinals too, the general inquisitors who were assigned to investigate the entire matter, issued a unanimous verdict of condemnation.

Prior to 1835 people in Germany knew nothing about the rumor referred to by the papal brief. The very bishops who, as friends of Hermes and his school, could have provided the most specific information about the orthodoxy of the Hermesians, had not been asked about it. People saw all too clearly on what a shaky foundation the pope rested his verdict. One of the Roman theologians assigned to scrutinize the writings of Hermes, Professor Perrone, a Jesuit, thought that he had disproven a statement by Hermes in his own work on dogmatics, but he subsequently had to concede that it was only a misunderstanding arising from his unfamiliarity with the German language. If one went on to ask what then in the teaching of Hermes was found to be subject to condemnation, the brief had nothing more specific to offer about that.

Hermes supposedly belonged to those who, from a desire for novelty, are forever just learning and never come to know the truth. By audaciously departing from the Holy Father's main road, he has taken a sinister path in his explanation and defense of the truths of the faith—namely, by taking doubt to be the basis of all theological inquiry, and reason as the initial norm and sole instrument for gaining knowledge of supernatural truths. The theologians convened for this scrutiny found teachings unbefitting the principles of Catholic truth; they found much that is poorly presented, is ambiguous, is grasped in an obscure and clever way so as to confuse and muddy the insight into Catholic dogmas, as well as much that is assembled from the errors and counsels of non-Catholics.

After the brief became public knowledge, the Hermesians, professors at Bonn and Breslau, declared that the Holy Father was simply deceived by the intrigues of their personal opponents; and that they firmly believed that, after looking more closely into the matter, the pope will restore the honor of one of the Catholic Church's most worthy clergy and one of the most profound and most upright searchers for truth, the purity of whose faith is still never in doubt. But as the *Aschaffenburger Kirchenzeitung* directly and very bluntly pointed out to them, the Hermesians were laboring under an entirely false hope.

As soon as Archbishop Droste-Vischerung had taken up residence in Cologne, he went to work everywhere against the Hermesians, for their founder had been personally distasteful to him. The Hermesians became increasingly less effective. A circular letter to the father confessors of the city of Bonn, from the archbishop, forbade them to read Hermes's writings and to attend the lectures of the professors known to have been his students.

This also led to conflicts and negotiations between the government and the archbishop, but with no result, since the issue of mixed marriages got in the way. All the steps the Hermesians took on behalf of their cause were completely in vain.

As a teaching condemned by the pope, Hermesianism now lost its standing. Many Hermesians resigned themselves to this, in keeping with the adage: *Roma locuta est, res finita est* (Rome has spoken, that settles it). In 1844, when Professors Braun and Achterfeldt in Bonn, who, together with Elvenich in Breslau, were the nominal leaders of Hermesianism, at least challenged the factual statement that Hermes had actually taught what, according to the papal brief, he supposedly taught, and they refused to approve the papal brief's contention that Hermes had, in his own character, been a reprehensible human being, they were removed from their academic positions upon the petition of the coadjutor in Cologne. Of course the Prussian government had not approved the papal brief of condemnation, since the brief had not been presented to the government for publication. But after the matter had taken such a turn, what opportunity could the government have had to retain those professors who were appealing to its conscience? While keeping their stipends, the professors were relieved of their official functions and relocated.

This also shows us that the case of Hermesianism involves the same antithetical orientations and interests as those in the issue of mixed marriages. However slight the scientific significance of Hermesianism is when considered from a Protestant standpoint, it unmistakably manifests the spirit of the German science that proceeds from Protestantism. Hermes offers a critical stance toward the dogma of his church. His method of treating dogmatic theology is said to be strictly scientific. The Hermesians validated the concerns of thinking reason even though, with these concerns, they wished at the same time simply to stay within the confines of the authoritative belief system. Hermesianism had within it the seed for developing a German national Catholicism, and soon enough it had to collide with Roman Catholicism. However, this is the very thing that brought Hermesianism down. Its opponents quite correctly had a foreboding of this tendency it embodied.

People have indeed said[42] the danger lying in the fundamental conception of Hermesian theology, that of introducing proofs for the beliefs of the Catholic Church via the justification of reason, is no greater than the danger residing in all of scholasticism. But we should also bear in mind the differ-

---

42. [*Baur, in the text, augmented editorially*] Karl Hase (1800–90), *Die beiden Erzbischöfe. Ein Fragment aus der neuesten Kirchengeschichte* (Leipzig, 1839), 78.

ence between the two times. In an era where Protestantism is such a clear and outspoken factor, it is also far less possible to conceal the magnitude of the dangerous consequences from the kind of path on which Hermes has set out. Where Hermesianism is headed makes it all the clearer how each of its growing, and seriously scientific, concerns is completely incompatible with Catholicism in its present condition. Catholicism, with its necessarily underlying principle of authority, unavoidably and directly clashes with it. However clear and incontestable the justification for Hermesianism may be, and however shoddy the motivation behind the papal verdict of condemnation, the utterly decisive factor is that of authority. The ease with which Hermesianism has been suppressed shows how powerful this principle of authority still is, even in German Catholicism.

If we bear in mind the import of the Hermesian school, the friends and patrons it numbered among the bishops, and what a spectacle—as the Hermesians accused it of being—was made of the enemies of the Catholic Church by such a measure so in conflict with the spirit of the time, then the outcome has to be surprising. On the other hand, however, it is also in the spirit of the time for people to directly grasp such an issue's importance in principle. If they have not yet reached the point where they are not to shrink, even in the most painful case, from a break with the principle, then every freer movement will always be suppressed by the power of the principle and its consequences.

Yet the question as to how a Protestant government is to conduct itself in such a case affecting its universities is of interest for its own sake. Did the Prussian government not have the right and the duty to deal with teachers who have a harmful academic stance and effect. Would it not have been in its own interest to stand up to Catholicism via Catholicism itself, and to promote the development of a German national Catholicism? A consideration of the other side is whether a Protestant government has the right to object when the highest authority of the Catholic Church has once made a decision regarding dogma. We have here the conflict between the state and the church. On the one hand, the state cannot allow anything else to have unconditional rights over it or its own affairs; on the other hand, the Catholic Church cannot subordinate itself to the state.

Under the statutes of the University of Bonn, insofar as the church is of course an interested party regarding the effectiveness of the Catholic theological faculty, that faculty is under the spiritual oversight of the archbishop. However, the statutes also contain the stipulation that, should a teacher belonging to the Catholic theological faculty give offense, or in some other manner, in a moral-religious context, conspicuously cause a scandal to Catholic faith and morals in his lectures or writings, then the archbishop is authorized to file a declaration to that effect. Based on that declaration, the government ministry will take serious and vigorous steps, and will provide a remedy. In this situation the ministry therefore also makes decisions about issues that bear upon what is taught.

But how will the ministry decide whether a teacher accused of giving offense to Catholic teaching has overstepped the bounds within which he is permitted to operate as to the scientific foundation of that teaching? Here scientific scholarship again and again collides with authority. If the government decides in favor of science, then authority takes the other side. And how can the government implement its decision if it is impermissible to engage in religious persecution? What would it have availed the Prussian government to defend the academic operations of the Hermesians if their lecture halls nevertheless remained empty? So this episode hardly provides a clear and definitive concept of state-church relations. The state will dictate to the church too, and yet the autonomy of the church stands opposed to the state. The Catholic Church in a Protestant state is under the state's authority, and yet the state acknowledges that the church is subject to the absolute authority of the pope. This is a contradiction that is still unresolved. As soon as the church relies on its principle of absolute authority, as it did in these two cases [i.e., mixed marriages and Hermesianism], and thus consciously sets itself over against the state, then the state sees itself being in no position to enforce its directives and laws.

Bautain

The subject matter in the controversy about Hermes involves the relation of reason and revelation. Now we have to mention another and similar controversy. Hermes became suspect to the church because he seems to rate reason too highly as opposed to belief or faith. Abbé Bautain,[43] professor of philosophy at Strasbourg and esteemed canon there, gained the disapproval of his spiritual superior because people thought he assigned too lowly a position to reason. This seems contradictory, but the contradiction is only an apparent one.

After repeatedly changing his philosophical outlook, Bautain finally stuck with the contention that reason can do nothing with reference to faith;

---

43. Louis Eugene Marie Bautain (1796–1867), a student of Victor Cousin, after a sudden conversion became a priest. He held that all genuine reason is based on the eternal divine reason as revealed in scripture, and one should stick to that reason alone. His *Philosophie du christianisme* (Paris, 1833) based his dismissal of other forms of reason in part on Kant's antinomies. Pope Gregory XVI condemned his fideism, and Bautain subsequently recanted his former views.

that reason first arrives at knowledge via faith, and in no way arrives at faith via knowing. He held that conclusive reasoning alone, apart from faith, cannot provide certainty about the existence of God. If reason or syllogisms alone sufficed to gain certainty about the infinite, then human beings would also have been able to obtain the knowledge of God on their own. If they had been able to grasp the idea of the infinite by their own powers, or if, assuming this idea of the nature of the infinite is innate, they had been able to have the awareness and certain knowledge of it on their own, then they would have had no need of a supernatural illumination, nor of grace, nor of preaching. They would then need neither God nor the church.

In opposition to this view, the bishop defended the position that God's existence and God's attributes can be demonstrated by reason alone. He contended that belief based on reason is the necessary presupposition for belief in the revealed religion because, apart from believing in God and God's attributes, one cannot even believe in the self-revealing God. The bishop in fact took offense at Bautain's contention because it seemed to him that it endangered the Catholic faith; for if one does not accept the results of the scholastic method, the faith is open to disproof by externally compelling arguments. Bautain's teaching contains nothing inherently non-Catholic, as Möhler too acknowledged in his open letter of March 1835 concerning Bautain.[44] But at the same time Möhler advised him to acquiesce to the bishop, given the existing misconceptions about it.

A papal brief of December 1834 had already also demanded a retraction from Bautain and his followers. The pope followed up in November 1835 by subscribing to the following six propositions set forth by the bishop. 1) The use of reason precedes faith or belief, and leads human beings on to faith via revelation and grace. 2) Conclusive reasoning can prove God's existence with certainty. Faith as gift of God follows upon revelation, so that, in order to prove God's existence to the atheist in a rational way, one cannot appeal to faith. 3) Certain proof of the Mosaic revelation is through the oral and written tradition of the synagogue and the church. 4) Proof of Christian revelation drawn from the miracles of Jesus has lost none of its power. In the oral and written tradition it is as compelling for all Christians as it was for the eyewitnesses. We must prove it through this twofold tradition to those who reject it or who wish to accept it. 5) One has no right to expect an unbeliever to accept Jesus' resurrection if one has not beforehand supplied convincing proofs of it. These proofs are in fact provided by the tradition, by conclusive reasoning. 6) Reason can with certainty demonstrate the

---

44. [*Baur, in the text, augmented editorially*] See J. A. Möhler, "Sendschreiben an Herrn Bautain," *Theologische Quartalschrift* 17.3 (1835) 421–53.

authenticity of the revelation that has been given to the Jews through Moses, and to the Christians through Christ.

We may doubt the sincerity of Bautain's acquiescence. From the six propositions we see quite clearly how the pontifical theology is obsessed with external proofs. Hence in this case too the freer, more spiritual orientation, the scientific weight, was on the side offering resistance to the church.

The Philosophy of Günther and Its Condemnation

More recently, the philosophy of Günther met the same fate as that of Hermesianism. Anton Günther,[45] a private ecclesiastic in Vienna, is the originator of a new system of philosophy dualistically juxtaposing God and the creation—and within creation juxtaposing nature and spirit. This system contends that positive Christianity so very much corresponds to rational thinking that human beings cannot disavow positive Christianity without relinquishing their own essential nature. In 1854 various writings by Günther were placed on the church's Index of prohibited books. Initially this was of course reputed to be the result of Jesuit intrigues. However, the pope had spoken very favorably about Günther, and gave assurance that he had nothing to fear from this accusation.[46]

However, a decree of the *Congregatio indicis* (the Congregation of the Index) on 8 January 1857 placed all of Günther's writings on the Index. Since this decree only condemned Günther's writings in general terms, those containing so much that is contrary to the teaching of the Catholic Church, the pope believed the decree must address specific themes, and he did so in a letter to the archbishop of Cologne on 15 June 1857. According to it, one may not suppose oneself guiltless of disobeying the decree just because it does not specifically enumerate Günther's objectionable teachings. The pope sorrowfully observed that in Günther's writings the pernicious system of rationalism, already so often condemned, fully (*ampliter*) prevails, although there is also no less that deviates from the genuinely Catholic doctrine of the Trinity. The situation is no better as to Günther's teaching about the incarnation, about the person of Christ, and as to his teaching about the human being, *qui corpore et anima ita absolvatur, ut anima eaque rationalis*

---

45. Anton Günther (1783–1863), an Austrian, was ordained a priest, then joined the Jesuits but subsequently left the order to reside in Vienna as a private ecclesiastic, that is, without specific appointment or office. The philosophical position he worked out in publications gained him numerous followers, some in high church positions. After his views were condemned, many of his followers joined the Old Catholic movement.

46. [*Baur, in the text*] *Allgemeine Zeitschrift*, July 1854.

sit vera per se atque immediata corporis forma (which is thus complete in body and soul, and how the soul is rational truly through itself and is directly the form of the body).[47] He teaches much more that conflicts with the Catholic teaching of God's absolute freedom *in rebus procreandis* (in creating things). Also to be condemned is his ascribing *jus magisterii temere* (heedlessly, the supreme right) to human reason and philosophy—which in religious matters *non dominari sed ancillari omnino debent* (ought to be entirely subservient, not dominant)—and he confuses all that counts as acknowledged truth in matters of believing and knowing. Finally, he also proves to be lacking in the respect one owes to the church fathers.

At the same time the brief states how very pleased the pope is that, in a letter of 10 February, Günther has most humbly submitted to the decree concerning his writings and submitted to the apostolic authority, and that most of his followers have followed his outstanding example.[48] From this we see that Catholic theologians almost wholly submit to the papal decrees. While the condemnation of Hermesianism elicited protests, Güntherianism silently submitted to the pope. Another difference is that the author of the Hermesian system did not disavow it himself in such a pitiable way as Günther disavowed his system. What should we think of a philosopher who, as soon as the pope demands it, right away declares that he now regards his teaching itself as false and erroneous? Who can believe that such a disavowal is sincere? If it were sincere, how irresponsible it would be to disseminate, in a series of writings, a teaching about which one could subsequently deliver such a verdict oneself! Of course there are always ones who, in such cases as those of Hermes and Günther, hardly have any other option than joining the chorus of the *pater peccavi* (father, I have sinned). For this is only a more recent example of what a corrupting principle resides in the papacy, when one cannot be a faithful son of the apostolic see without exhibiting before all the world the most contemptible lack of character in the most important matter of the spiritual life. In viewing such proceedings, all thinking Christians may count themselves fortunate in not being subject to such a regime.[49]

47. This Latin states the typical scholastic, Aristotelian view of the soul as the form of the body; hence, as embodied, gaining knowledge via sense perception. Günther's teaching involves a duality in human thinking by separating two functions: the "soul" (*Seele*), which belongs to the nature-principle; the "spirit" (*Geist*), which engages in ideal thinking (and can grasp revealed truths as necessary truths of reason, hence treating revealed dogmas as a kind of philosophy).

48. [Baur, in the text] See the *Theologische Quartalschrift* (1858) no. 1.

49. [Zeller] In the context of the ban on the Güntherian philosophy, in April 1860 the prince bishop of Breslau revoked the authorization to teach of Dr. Baltzer, professor of theology in Breslau, and also simultaneously that of his rival, Dr. Bittner.

What prevented the controversial issues we have been speaking about to this point from splitting the church was the fear of a break with the principle of the church [as the only saving church]. However, Catholics themselves also challenged this principle and contended that the system of Roman Catholicism would necessarily disintegrate from within because of its own consequences. Carové[50] presents this view in the most basic and most ingenious way, in his book *Über die allein seligmachende Kirche* (Frankfurt, 1826). He presents this dogma, in and for itself and specifically as related to the chief dogmatic statements that set the Roman Church apart from the other Christian confessions, as being unfounded and untenable. Thus via a series of de facto arguments the system is forced to acknowledge its own contradiction, in which it comes undone. Catholics such as Carové, who are quarreling with their own church, cannot find the Protestant Church's belief system congenial. So from such an attack, which in Carové's case was primarily elucidated just in scientific terms, one could see on what foundation such opponents of Roman Catholicism will stand if, within the Catholic Church, it once comes to a serious break with the principle of the church. This leads us to *German-Catholicism (Deutschkatholicismus)*,[51] which is especially pertinent here because it became an issue very closely connected with the 1837 incident in Cologne and its consequences.

German-Catholicism: The Sacred Tunic

The initial impetus for the German-Catholic movement was provided by the display of the sacred tunic [of Christ] in Trier in 1844. The movement is related to this tunic in the following way. According to church tradition in Trier, a tradition passed down from the Middle Ages, the Holy Virgin wove a tunic for her divine child, one that grew in size as he did. This is the seamless tunic for which the soldiers cast lots,[52] and the ancient church regarded it as the symbol of the indivisible church. Saint Helena, the mother of Constantine, found this tunic in Palestine and sent it to Trier via Saint Agricius, who preserved it there in the cathedral in 328. According to the

---

50. Friedrich Wilhelm Carové (1789–1852), German lawyer, philosopher, and publicist.

51. This term refers to a specific movement, as described by Baur below, not to German Catholics (or the Catholic Church in Germany) in general. To distinguish it from the latter, we hyphenate the term. *Deutschkatholicismus* also referred to itself as *Christkatholicismus*.

52. John 19:23–24 has the most detail. See also Matthew 27:33, Mark 15:24, Luke 23:34.

most ancient historical evidence, in 1196 Archbishop Johann, when consecrating the altar of Peter as the high altar of the cathedral, placed beneath it the sacred tunic, which he had found in the crypt of the Nicholas altar. The sending of the tunic by Saint Helena is already mentioned in the part of the *Gesta Trevirorum* written between 1106 and 1124. Apparently the tunic lay unnoticed, or at least uncelebrated, at the altar of Peter until Emperor Maximilian, who had read about it in the [Trier] chronicles, took the occasion of an assembly of princes in Trier in 1512 to locate and open the locked chest containing it.

The treasured tunic was then so readily venerated that, when money was needed for embellishments of the cathedral, they followed the custom of obtaining a bull from Leo X in 1514, which decreed that the sacred tunic be put on display at seven year intervals, with full indulgences granted to every pilgrim who is contrite and makes an offering. Nevertheless we know of only three ceremonial displays in which the public at large participated. All three occurred at significant points in time: 1585, after the restoration of the Catholic Church in that region; 1655, after the Thirty Years' War; 1810, after Napoleon decided that the sacred tunic, which had been given refuge in the interior of Germany prior to the French Revolution, was to be returned from Augsburg to Trier.

The decision of Bishop Arnoldi of Trier to display the sacred tunic in 1844 was based on the emotions that had been aroused in the populace of the Rhineland because of the dispute the archbishop of Cologne had with the Prussian government; [it was] based on confidence in them, and [intended] to strengthen them. The elderly Görres, the protagonist in every controversy, also understood these emotions as a demonstration of this kind, in his book *Die Wallfahrt nach Trier* (1845). [He wrote that] achieving this goal [making the pilgrimage to Trier] would be as splendid as anything one could ever have done. While the sacred tunic, framed under glass, hung in the chancel behind the high altar from 18 August until 6 October, more than one million pilgrims from all parts of the world marched past it in daily processions. Prayerful throngs stretched through the valleys of the Mosel and the Rhine, waving banners before them. They were greeted in every village with pealing bells, while at intervals there came boatfuls of pilgrims joining in pious singing. The reporters for Catholic newspapers described this as a great religious fair, a Catholic mass migration, a mighty current of old-fashioned faith taking hold of the populace along the Rhine—a sign of the times.

There were no promises made in advance about miracles from the sacred tunic, although miracles soon appeared of their own accord. The most sensational one was the healing of the grandniece of the archbishop of Cologne, a young Countess von Droste-Vischerung. On the morning of 30 August she stood on her crutches, facing the sacred relic in ardent prayer, when she suddenly cried out: "I can stand on my own feet," and let loose of her crutches. The facts of this miracle are like those of so many other miracles of the Catholic faith. Her spiritual excitement seemed to have so affected the maiden bodily that, with an effort, she could make her way on the arm of a guide and without her crutches; but her lameness was not healed, and in place of the crutches hung up next to the sacred tunic she soon thereafter had need of new ones.

Since all sorts of stories about the sacred tunic came into circulation for the use of the pilgrims, Protestant critics could hardly remain silent about such an ostentatious display of Catholicism. The main writing in this respect is that by J. Gildemeister and H. v. Sybel, *Der heilige Rock zu Trier und die zwanzig andern heiligen ungenähten Röcke: Eine historische Untersuchung* (3rd ed., 1845). It completely demonstrates that there is no historical trace at all for a discovery of the tunic by Saint Helena, and of its existence in Trier prior to the end of the first millennium. Given the unconscionable counterfeiting of relics at that time, Archbishop Bruno probably christened the garment, coming from who knows where, as the seamless tunic, and deposited it well-preserved in the Nicholas altar dedicated in 1121, where Archbishop Johann discovered it in 1196.

Ronge and Czerski

This tunic pilgrimage also became a literary phenomenon because it gave rise to a great many pieces written about it. One of them is especially significant, owing to the effect that it had. "Das Urtheil eines katholischen Priesters über den h. Rock in Trier. Von Joh. Ronge," bearing the date of 1 October, first appeared in the *Sächsischen Vaterlands-Blätter* of 16 October 1844.[53] The article did not challenge the authenticity of the sacred tunic; instead it attacked the idolatrous celebration in Trier. [It said] the founder of the Christian religion did not leave his tunic to his disciples; instead he bequeathed his spirit to them, for the tunic belonged to his executioners. The article lamented the hordes of people who have saved up, or gone begging, for the money for the journey and the offering, and have been led

---

53. Johannes Ronge (1813–87), Catholic priest and chaplain in Grottkau (1840–43), who was removed from this office because of a writing critical of the church. The newspaper article Baur cites was an open letter to Bishop Arnoldi of Trier. The article was widely circulated, and led to Ronge's excommunication. In 1845, in Laurahütte in Upper Silesia, Ronge founded a "Rome-free" church, which in March began to call itself "German-Catholic."

astray, leaving behind their occupations, their household affairs, the tilling of their fields; as well as lamenting the women and maidens who lost their purity of heart and their virginity while on the pilgrimage. The man who has displayed that garment to be revered, who misdirects the religious feelings of gullible human beings, who takes the offering money from the undernourished ones of the people, who exposes the German nation to the scorn of the other nations, is a bishop. However, this nineteenth-century Tetzel[54] should not deceive himself. While hundreds of thousands run to him, millions, like the author, are filled with horror and indignation at the despicable spectacle.

The author spoke out in this rhetorical pathos directed against relics and pilgrimages. But the greatest attention he excited was focused on the very fact that a Catholic priest uttered these words, and Protestants and Catholics applauded him enthusiastically. Johannes Ronge, the writer of this letter to Arnoldi (as people usually referred to it) was a priest already on bad terms with Roman Catholicism. Not much before this, the offense he had given by an article on the episcopal administrator of Breslau[55] led to his relinquishing his religious functions. After doing so he took over the instruction of the children of Protestant mining officials in Laurahütte, near the Russian border. He sent this letter to Bishop Arnoldi from Laurahütte. The episcopal authorities requested clarification as to whether he acknowledged himself to be the author of the article bearing his name and his title as a Catholic priest. When he said he was its author and refused to disavow it, he was punished by demotion and excommunication. The result of Ronge's letter was a new torrent of writings and rejoinders, speaking for and against the new "religious reformer," as people called him.

While Ronge's letter called for establishing a free Catholic Church, a number of pamphlets appearing directly after the letter did so in a more pronounced way. But that actually came to fruition in a different location, via another likeminded colleague in the Catholic Church. Czerski,[56] a Pole who was the vicar of the cathedral in Posen, was transferred to the small town of Schneidemühl because he was living with a Polish woman in a clandestine marriage, and after that he was suspended [from the priesthood] in March 1844 for breaking the rule of celibacy. When he had been sentenced to four weeks of penitential confinement because he had not appeared before the

54. Johan Tetzel (c. 1465–1519), a German Dominican preacher, sold indulgences granted for contributions to the building of St. Peter's in Rome. It was partly in response to this that Martin Luther posted his 95 Theses in 1517.

55. "Rom und das Breslauer Domkapitel" (1843).

56. Johannes Czerski (1813–93), leader of a schismatic sect of Catholicism formed in Schneidemühl (now Pila) in December 1844. Czerski, more conservative than Ronge, called his sect "Christian-Catholics."

investigating body, he declared in August 1844 that he resigned from being a Roman Catholic priest. In his document of self-justification he wrote:

> The correct understanding is that I am leaving behind the erroneous teachings of the Roman hierarchy, but I will not become a Lutheran or a Calvinist, for I remain a Catholic Christian, a Catholic priest, but one in keeping with the words of scripture, with the commands of Christ and his apostles.

Some twenty-four members of the congregation sided with Czerski and decided to establish a Christian-apostolic-catholic community on the foundation of the Holy Scriptures. After the provost of Schneidemühl, speaking from the pulpit, excluded the adherents of the new diabolical teaching from the sacrament, they united in a confession of their faith on 19 October. It was prefaced by a biblically-supported refutation of the Roman Church's new human ordinances and erroneous teachings: withholding the chalice, canonization and veneration of saints, effecting absolution by auricular confession and indulgences, mandatory fasting, rituals in foreign languages, celibacy, rejection of mixed marriages, governance by the pope. The confession of faith itself begins with the Nicene-Constantinopolitan understanding of the apostolic affirmation of Christ's divinity. The confession acknowledges: the Holy Scriptures as the only certain source of faith (of course understood in the sense current among every enlightened Christian); the seven sacraments as the medium of salvation instituted by Christ; the mass as the memorial of the sacrifice on the cross, beneficial for the living and the dead; also, Christ's body and blood being actually present in the sacrament of the altar. It even conceded a purgatory, although not one the Roman hierarchy teaches. The confession speaks in most personal terms by the statement: We acknowledge that not only can priests receive the sacrament of marriage; for, in order to be worthy examples for the people, in accord with Holy Scripture, they even ought to marry.

The leaders of the new community submitted this confession of faith to the closest state authority, the provincial government in Bromberg, on 27 October, together with the request that they be recognized as a separate Christian Catholic community, and given protection from persecution by the clerical vassals of Rome. The government did not reply. But it did tolerate the establishment of a private chapel in which Czerski, in gold-trimmed mass vestment, celebrated mass together with acolytes and hand bells, but doing so in the German language, and distributed the elements in both forms. In January 1845 the community consisted of eighty-five members, almost all belonging to the middle classes. Without Ronge, this merely local congregation in Schneidemühl would have faded away. However,

Schneidemühl provided a specific model for realizing Ronge's general appeal [to others].

The Further History of German-Catholicism Prior to 1848

Ronge made his way to Breslau in November 1844. There his faction gained a respected and learned adviser in Regenbrecht.[57] As canon, and professor of canon law at the university, Regenbrecht sent to the cathedral chapter on 15 December a letter of withdrawal, in which he harshly found fault with the age-old self-seeking and obfuscating efforts of the higher clergy, and he parted ways with a church whose efforts he could not reconcile with the spirit of Jesus.

After a call to Silesian Catholics to pledge loyalty to the new Catholic Church of Germany and to choose Ronge as its spiritual leader, the first assembly met on 22 January 1845 and Ronge set forth specific articles of faith. They repeated the usual protests against the Roman priestly religion, limited the sacraments to baptism and the Lord's Supper, and acknowledged the Holy Scriptures to be the sole foundation of faith, with the proviso that no external authority may be permitted to restrict free investigation and interpretation of them. In the deliberations on 2 February, about the confession of faith, they agreed upon the apostolic creed as the most ancient symbol still common to almost all Christian groups. However, at the same time they decided to give the symbol a form corresponding to the consciousness of today, one that would be accepted as the conditions for a universal Christian ecclesiastical community without any coercion of faith and conscience. Thus the Breslau confession replaced the old sacred formulas with more modern ways of speaking. The first article contained an addendum about the divine governance of the world, and the second one, with its purely practical Christian framework, omitted everything referring to what is divine and wondrous in the life of Jesus, even the resurrection. Then they elected a church governing body, and on 9 March they held the first worship service, in the prayer hall of the almshouse that the magistrate had assigned to them. The community, soon to number in the thousands, unanimously summoned Ronge as its pastor.

Similar to what happened in Breslau, smaller congregations popped up prior to Easter in about twenty towns in northern Germany, almost all of them among Catholics who lived scattered among a Protestant population. All these people came from the middle classes, most being community

---

57. Eduard Regenbrecht (1791–1849), Breslau professor of canon law, who wrote an *Erklärung* about departing from the church.

leaders who lived in mixed marriages. Where there was no cleric, laypeople led the gatherings. Before they joined the Breslau confession, those in Offenbach who were inclined toward German-Catholicism turned, in their own fashion, to Bishop Kaiser in Mainz, with the request that, to salvage Catholic Christianity, he would, as its supporter and leader, help to effect the remedy for the abuses they enumerated to him. With sadness the bishop is said to have advised them that if they did not wish to remain true Catholics they should instead become Protestants.

When this congregation in Offenbach sought to hold its first worship service, and Darmstadt issued a prohibition against German-Catholics opening an evangelical church, they improvised by making a large warehouse into a permanent church in which Chaplain Kerber, who had joined the movement in Breslau, preached about the uniting of all the confessions through love, together with abolishing all religious intolerance—the main theme of German-Catholicism. Because of its rationalist orientation, the Breslau confession differed from that of Schneidemühl, which held firmly to the basic ideas of the old ecclesiastical orthodoxy. Most of these communities concurred with the Breslau model. The Dresden community even declared its allegiance not merely to Holy Scripture as the one and exclusive foundation of Christian faith, but also explicitly to the reason made pervasive, and set in motion, by the Christian idea.

The first convocation of German-Catholicism, as proposed by Robert Blum,[58] met hastily in Leipzig, at the Hotel zur Stadt Rom, on the first day of the Easter holiday, 23 March 1845. Its purpose was in part to smooth over the differences that already now in fact existed, before they led to dissension, and in part to unify the scattered local congregations. The assembly met over four days, in five sessions. There were thirteen congregations represented by thirty delegates, with Kerber in Breslau at first the only clerical member, and Czerski and Ronge first arriving near the end. The main issue was the statement of faith. Czerski demanded in vain that they acknowledge the divinity of Christ. The Breslau–Dresden model completely predominated and, according to the official report, when the vote was taken, even the Schneidemühl group did not oppose it.

Thus the basic tenet they decided on was "that for us the Holy Scriptures alone shall be the sole foundation of Christian faith, and that understanding and interpreting them sets free the reason made pervasive, and set in motion, by the Christian idea." Their creed was: "I believe in God the Father, who created the world by his almighty Word and rules it in wisdom, justice, and love. I believe in Jesus Christ our Savior; I believe in the Holy

---

58. Robert Blum (1807–48) was a liberal agitator.

Spirit, a holy universal Christian church, the forgiveness of sins, and an eternal life." Specific points added to this are that the task of the church and of the individual is to make the contents of the religious teachings known in a vital way, commensurate with contemporary consciousness, and that, in complete freedom of conscience, the different ways of understanding these religious teachings provide no basis for separation or condemnation, because the Christian's primary duty is to make one's faith active by works of Christian love. All these were said to be features distinctive of the Protestant Church. They readily agreed on the remaining articles. In continuing Christian practices, the individual congregations are not supposed to be limited to recognizing just two sacraments. In this way a definite foundation for the new church was established, and the work of unification was apparently successful. The new church spread through all the regions of Germany in which a self-contained Catholic population or a resolute Catholic government did not stand in the way.

However, the Leipzig Council had not given careful attention to the original differences as to beliefs. Soon after it, in a letter to councilor Romberg of the evangelical consistory, and in an open letter to all apostolic-Catholic communities, Czerski declared in May 1845 his disapproval of the Leipzig confession of faith for denying the divinity of Christ, a confessional statement to which he did not subscribe. The first controversy conducted in print soon intruded into the life of the community, namely in Bromberg, because of the influence Romberg, the evangelical superintendent, had there. He declared Schneidemühl Catholicism alone to be fully authorized and recognized by the state.

The two factions soon divided the community into two separate communities. Ronge, who was traveling in southern Germany in the fall of 1845, wrote a document directed just as much against Czerski as it was against the Protestant hierarchy, which, like Rome, took up the task of fostering dissension and negating the great world-redeeming achievement of the Reformation. Czerski no longer looked upon the Reformation as its champions did. A Reformation in Germany going no further than Luther did three hundred years ago is historically unnecessary, for it has already happened here. What is needed, first and foremost, as the foundation of a universal church, is the moral courage to express full belief in it. "We have shown that courage, by breaking through a fifteen-century-old symbol of faith because it did not correspond to our religious consciousness today." Ronge located today's religious consciousness above all in the fact that, in the freedom of faith we have gained, Christ is no longer said to be an otherworldly God, but is recognized joyfully as our brother. This is the main point of the new Reformation, which he [Ronge] will defend to the limit. In the first Reformation

Germany lost its dominant place in the world; in the second Reformation Germany will regain it.

These statements expressed very openly the tendency of Ronge's German-Catholicism. Later Ronge and Czerski were indeed on friendly terms at the gathering in Rawicz on 3 February 1846. However, the split that had developed was too fundamental; setting aside the issue of personalities, it was in principle the same split as that between Luther and Zwingli over the presence of Christ in the Eucharist.

Anton Theiner, professor of Catholic theology in Breslau, had long been very active on behalf of peaceful reform of the Catholic Church, and he joined forces with Ronge in the work of reconciliation at Rawicz, for in June 1845 he had crossed over to the German-Catholic Church. German-Catholicism rejoiced that his membership gave it the endorsement of [theological] science. But already on 19 February 1846 he relinquished his clerical role in the Breslau community, although with the assurance that his further conscientious efforts would be to support the concerns of the Christian-Catholic community. Disagreements with Ronge were said to have been the cause of his resignation. In July 1846 Ronge informed the synod in Breslau anew about the spirit in which he continued to operate. He presented the task of Christian-Catholicism (*Christkatholicismus*), and principally of the synod, as functioning no longer as bishops and prelates but instead as citizens, farmers, preachers, and scholars, so as to refine Christianity into humanity.

The internal arrangements of the German-Catholic community involve the system of governance and the cultus. The system of governance rests on a common foundation of checks and balances among the parts sharing the leadership of the community. These are the governing body, the council of elders, and the community assembly. The formal statute of 1845 expressly gives women complete voting rights. Election of a cleric takes place by the community, on the recommendation of the governing body and the elders. Ordination is done by the governing body, which can also authorize non-clerics to conduct afternoon worship services. A committee of elders has to watch that the contents of the religious proceedings are compatible with the principles and specifications of the German-Catholic Church. Worship services shall consist essentially of instruction and edification, with the liturgy structured in particular in keeping with what the apostles and the early Christians instituted, and suited to the needs of the present day. Celebration of the mass is regarded as the actual focus of New Testament worship, for the Lord's Supper presents Christ's overall work of salvation and is no commonplace nourishment. In the Ordinary drawn up by Theiner, the norm adopted is the celebration of the Lord's Supper after the sermon, and it also still consists of the elevation of the Eucharistic elements. Directly before their distribution, there shall be an appropriate statement addressed to the communicants, a kind of general acknowledgement of sin, but no actual confession and absolution is required. If no communicants are present, the priest shall receive communion himself as representative of the community, as someone united in spirit with it. In any event worship predominantly assumes a simpler and briefer form.

An additional point to consider here is German-Catholicism's legal position in the eyes of the state. The more widespread German-Catholicism became, the governments of states in which such communities took shape had to face more directly the issue of whether they were to receive legal recognition. This issue could not arise at all for Catholic states such as Bavaria and Austria. In 1845 the royal authorities in Bavaria declared that the new sect is not a religion but instead radicalism and communism, and so membership in it is to be treated as high treason. The German-Catholics at Neustadt an der Hardt requested, in 1846, that they at least be granted what is granted to Jews. The answer they received was that, unless they return from their erroneous ways, they forfeit the rights enjoyed by adherents of religions warranted by the state. Austria forbade even the term "German-Catholicism" and any public mention of Ronge's sect.

In Prussia, since the issue of tolerance for dissidents had not yet come to a head, on 30 April 1845 an order of the cabinet directed the public authorities neither to support the course of such eventualities, nor to obstruct them. It in fact said: Stay out of such affairs. However, resentment and ill-will soon arose, quite naturally explainable based on the religious orientation coming to light in the Breslau and Leipzig confession. The ministry for religious cults, or the orthodox party that influenced the ministry, saw in this confession a defection from Christianity. Since almost everywhere the evangelical congregations had given the German-Catholics the use of their churches, a decree of the ministry, effective in May 1845, stated that the congregations did not have proprietary rights over their churches such that they could lend them to a foreign cultus without the approval of the designated church authorities; and that this approval could not be given at present, so long as the Catholic dissidents are not recognized as constituting a religious association of its own. The provisional, shared use of the Evangelical churches was nevertheless later allowed as an exception, and the government once again confined itself to leaving things as they are.

In several German states, for instance Saxony and Baden, the cause of the German-Catholics was very actively supported in the Chamber of Deputies, although even in these states the government had little inclination to grant full civil rights to German-Catholics. Each of the three possible standpoints the state could take vis-à-vis the German-Catholics had its particular advocate. Herr von Linde supported their unconditional exclusion; Herr von Hecker their unconditional acceptance; Herr von Richter their toleration with conditions imposed. In any events, practical considerations simply dictated the intermediate position.

German-Catholicism since 1848

Political movements of 1848 and legislation involving basic rights in the German nation proved to be very advantageous for the German-Catholics. Because of this legislation their existence was legally recognized; however, the ensuing reaction to this was very much to their disadvantage. The police monitored their gatherings as political associations and enforced such strict measures against them that German-Catholicism continually declined, and many of its congregations disbanded.[59] At its peak, German-Catholicism had about 60,000 adherents, about half of them in Silesia where the Breslau community was its most important one and best embodied its spiritual energy. Even thereafter, when so many communities of this kind disbanded, the Breslau community for the most part remained cohesive. In a gathering in June 1857, it discussed and approved a rule of life for the German-Catholic religious community.

The point at which German-Catholicism stood in its development in 1849, and its tendency at that time, are best seen from the manifesto issued in May 1849 by the provincial governing body of the Christian-Catholic community of Silesia, in the name of the fourth Silesian synod, especially in order to clarify the relation of German-Catholicism to the socio-political order. The manifesto stated that a great many people long for a change in social circumstances. History teaches that all progress in the social structure of a people has been achieved via changes introduced into their religious outlook. German-Catholicism too seeks to reshape the whole of human life by a revolution in the religious perspective of today's generation. German-Catholicism wants to make scientific research be shared by all of society. The fundamental ideas in the domain of thinking must also be recognized in their relation to the outward phenomena of life. The first duty of the Christian is to put knowledge into practice by works of Christian love. Love of one human being for another, unhampered by social customs, is what is holy. Christian-Catholicism wants to make the kingdom of God appear on earth, whereas in olden times it was made out to be an otherworldly affair. It

---

59. Zeller adds a footnote providing additional information about the German-Catholics beyond the date of Baur's composition.

redirects one's view from "up there" to "down here." It does not just embellish heaven with pleasures people renounced on earth, but instead seeks for earthly life the heavenly joys people are promised.

This statement answers the main objections people might pose to German-Catholicism, especially inasmuch as it gets lumped together with the concurrent movements in political and social life. German-Catholicism is not unaware of how it harmonizes with these movements. But we also ought not overlook the differences. The adherents of what is ancient, traditional and enduring, accuse German-Catholicism of atheism, of destroying Christianity, of doing away with religion. The reply to this is that, on the contrary, religion is everything for it; that it bases and maintains religion in the pure, authentic fullness of human life, the fostering of which is its sole and supreme goal. Furthermore, people mistake German-Catholics for socialists and communists. They of course are such, but only in a different sense. German-Catholics sanctify the aspirations of the socialists by elevating socialism to a cultus, to religion; and they likewise sanctify the principles of democracy, because human self-determination or freedom of the will cannot, in their view, be separated from human dignity. They see themselves as being the authentic and true bearers and promoters of all the nobler aspirations to which the activities of humanists, socialists, and democrats devote themselves. All these aspirations of the times first find their animating principle in German-Catholicism. For, only when the new vision of a people has become a sacred vision for them does it have enough force to also restructure the external conditions of humankind's life, to reshape society. From this we see clearly how German-Catholicism unites within itself different kinds of elements, and how deeply it has taken hold in contemporary movements. It sympathizes with all the radical tendencies of our day. The pinnacle of this movement is its idea of a religion of humanity, which, as immanent religion, was supposed to be the antithesis to the transcendence of ecclesiastical Christianity.

Initially German-Catholicism sought to have nothing to do with Protestantism. However, the Protestantism of the free Protestant congregations[60] was too similar to it for the two communities to be able to maintain a distance from each other. Their closer union was the main goal of the 1850 Leipzig meeting (which the police forced to move to Köthen). The manifesto to the German people, issued at Köthen on 25 May by the united leadership of the German-Catholic councils and the assembly of the union of free congregations, showed that the delegates from both sides were aware that

---

60. Congregations or sects not affiliated with the Lutheran and Reformed state churches.

there can be no more proximate and more important task than concluding a mutual association. This association came about under the name of the Religious Society of Free Communities. The association was not supposed to do away with previously existing differences, for they certainly made it clear that there are major, heartfelt principles on each side, and on this basis they extended the hand of brotherhood.[61]

We cannot pursue the history of German-Catholicism further here. It of course has gained its own historian in Pastor Kampe's extensive work.[62]

The Assessment of German-Catholicism

The whole question about the external and internal validity of German-Catholicism, about its present and future significance, has in the meantime been answered of its own accord by German-Catholicism's history up to now. It has in no way demonstrated as much vitality as one might have expected from its initial emergence. Nowhere has it taken on a firmer shape, one gaining a more profound hold on people's lives. This is not because of external impediments that, to the extent they existed, should rather have fostered its internal development instead of impeding it. The reason instead is that obviously German-Catholicism lacked inner vitality. Indeed, early on it came to a standstill. Just as every standstill of this kind is also always a step backward, that was the case here too. German-Catholicism is now already something no longer in fashion.

We can indeed locate the cause for this in the personalities of the men who started it. Ronge, for instance, had neither the fundamental makeup of a truly effective reformer, nor the sterling character that can command a high degree of moral respect. There is too much vanity and self-importance in his overall nature. The way in which, as a new reformer, he even set himself above Luther creates a very offensive impression. With catchwords and rants, in touring and triumphal processions, with festivals and ceremonial banquets, he and his associates supposed, in the most superficial fashion in which they expressed themselves, that they could constitute a new segment of world history. Although of course providence often makes use even of very insignificant instruments, the personality of such men is still always a measuring stick for also evaluating their works. Here, however, for all those

---

61. [*Zeller*] In some places the free [Protestant] congregations fully united with the German-Catholics, for instance in Königsberg in January 1860.

62. [*Baur, in the text*] Friedrich Ferdinand Kampe, *Geschichte der religiösen Bewegung der neuern Zeit*, in 4 vols. (1852–60). *Das Wesen des Deutschkatholicmus mit besonderer Rücksicht auf sein Verhältnis zur Politik* (1850) is by the same author.

who know how to judge such phenomena by their deeper foundations, this is the very factor that does not inspire much confidence.

One of those books with the most reassuring statements about the future of German-Catholicism, a book that merits special attention, is *Die Mission der Deutschkatholiken* (1845) by Gervinus.[63] He commences with the fact that the benefits of the Enlightenment period, the undeniable achievements of the great spirits of that era, are firmly established for us. But the shape of things at that time, in terms of the older orthodox forms of theology, both Protestant and Catholic, and the sole dominance of religious concerns then, are things we have now long put behind us. What a change is said to take place today in the church, in the religious circumstances of our people. Only when the church stood in the closest relation to the final achievement of a [German] national life, to the ordinary conditions shaping contemporary society and to society's religious needs today, has it been able to have an inner fullness of life and become more long-lasting. Hence Gervinus regards German-Catholicism as not merely one of the different versions of Christianity, one that could and should be tolerant of the state and also tolerant of the previously constituted other churches that exist alongside it. Instead he also regards this church as the only one still tenable and possible in our time, and he accordingly hopes that, with a normal progression of our culture on the route previously marked out by the great spirits of the German nation, all the other ecclesiastical communities will cross over into German-Catholicism, giving their own distinctive religious substance to it. He asks whether our clerics have given thought as such to what it means to have a church edifice and a religious edifice to which the entire educated sector of the people are indifferent, or from which they even turn away with contempt. What does it mean when the best part of the nation turns its back?

One can well imagine how the Protestant orthodox clergy took these words in favor of German-Catholicism. They saw in them a program of deism and atheism.[64] An impartial judge, however, must certainly give Gervinus his due, for the forms and rules still prescriptive for religious and church life, within Protestantism too, cannot be normative for all future time. What would Christian piety be if it could not have become broader than is customarily allowed—if it could not have detached and liberated itself from the orthodox dogma in which people perpetually locate the substantial nature of Christianity? It is an undeniable fact that, when educated

---

63. Georg Gottfried Gervinus (1805–71), historian and liberal politician.

64. [*Baur, in the text*] Cf. Gervinus, *Die protestantische Geistlichkeit und die Deutschkatholiken* (1846).

people are candid enough about their own religious consciousness, they admit that it is becoming less and less compatible with the old orthodoxy. Saying as much is not a declaration that this new outlook is to be deplored as just the disbelief of the time. There is also a justifiable disbelief. Unbiased historical research shows increasingly that so many things modern culture sees as a stumbling block can also be viewed as not genuine components of original Christianity.

The other side of the coin, nevertheless, is that Gervinus is quite mistaken if he supposes that the mission of German-Catholicism is to actualize the freer and more universal form of religion it still looks forward to. German-Catholicism is still caught up in the great misconception already embodied in its name. Why does it call itself "German-Catholicism"? Obviously because it sets itself in opposition not merely to Roman Catholicism but also to German Protestantism; and it wants to set over against the Reformation, from which Protestantism emerged, what it supposes to be another reformation, one going beyond the Protestant principle. But how is this possible? Whoever correctly understands the relation of Protestantism to Catholicism must also discern that there is nothing intermediate between Catholicism and Protestantism; that anyone who wishes to come forward as a reformer can only do his reforming based on the same principle that gave rise to Protestantism, and his further developments must go forward on that basis. Everything that seems to put Protestantism on a par with Catholicism, as if both were equally inferior forms of the Christian religious life, can only be viewed as in contradiction with the Protestant principle.

Since the German-Catholics never made clear their relation to Protestantism (something they ought to have done first and foremost), and since they did not wish to be Protestants (while still standing on the same soil as the Protestants), the outcome could only be their precarious position between Catholicism and Protestantism, one in which they had to languish. They must have lacked any historical foothold and connection, since they sought to begin anew, in contradiction with history, with what long existed and should only be carried forward as tempered by principle. So people say, "What more complete form of the Christian religious life is there that could not just as well have arisen from Protestantism rather than from German-Catholicism?" All that German-Catholicism preeminently assigns to itself—rationality, freedom, humaneness, removal of the barriers that separate the confessions from each other—is also found to be a consequence of the Protestant principle, and has indeed often enough been claimed by it and established there, as far as that could be done. Why then a new form, set up as neither Catholic nor Protestant and completely up in the air, whereas

Protestantism rests on a rich historical past, on the soil of which alone a new development can flourish?

People found it remarkable that the Roman Curia said nothing about the new movement; that Gregory XVI departed without excommunicating the apostates.[65] The supposition was that this happened either because of the pope's inattention to German-Catholicism, or because he thought it of little importance. Instead it was simply due to his wariness, and fear of the threat, of a new reformation in Germany. The pope found it all the more reassuring that the Protestant governments too cooperated so conscientiously with Catholicism in protecting and maintaining intact its time-honored stability. One would think that such an anti-Roman movement could be in the interest of Protestantism. But conservative principles may never be discounted, not merely in politics but also in matters of religion and the church. If we ponder the current situation of the Protestant Church and its governing principles, then it is certainly not wrong to fear that an attack essentially on the Catholic Church could all too soon become a danger to the Protestant Church too.

D. Möhler's *Symbolik* and the Protestant Response

Möhler's *Symbolik*

What we see, again and again, standing in the background of all the phenomena we have been discussing, is Roman Catholicism with its power and dominion, with its consistent claims, with the full energy of its self-consciousness. Whatever may be the reason for it, all the movements that arose in opposition to Roman Catholicism forever foundered on the eternal Rock of Peter, and that could only serve to strengthen and heighten Catholicism's self-confidence. It was manifestly aware of its power at that time, and we see clearly how its self-consciousness has grown from one period to the next. What a great different there is in this regard when we compare the period beginning in 1830 with the one that came before. We need only consider what voice makes itself heard in all the main Catholic publications, the number of which has greatly increased since 1830. This Catholic upswing, this boost in Catholicism's self-consciousness, is a feature of the most recent times, and its tendency is to sharpen as much as possible the antitheses in matters of principle.

---

65. Pope Gregory XVI died on 1 June 1846.

Möhler's *Symbolik*[66] is one of the foremost of the phenomena in which this sudden change in the consciousness at that time makes itself known in a characteristic way, and can first be more definitely pinpointed. The way in which the *Symbolik* itself emerged from the new boost in Catholic self-consciousness also made it the most powerful leverage for that self-consciousness. Since first appearing in 1832, it has been disseminated throughout the Catholic audience in a series of editions it underwent in a few years' time; and everywhere it met with unanimous approval. In the *Symbolik*, Catholicism gained a new scientific impetus, during an era in which it became important to show, in a first-rate way, that not only does Catholicism as such not fall short of the demands that more recent scholarship places on it; Catholicism also does not shrink from pitting itself against its opponents by using the weapons of science in the very arena where the battle of principles is fought. While the close proximity Catholicism in Germany had to Protestantism was often to its own detriment, owing to the issues that proximity stirred up and the conflicts that arose with its own principles, this situation also in turn should have become very advantageous for it.

No Catholic theologian was as conversant with the literature of Protestantism as Möhler was. He knew very well how to utilize, for his own standpoint, most especially the elements of modern culture and science emergent from the theology of Schleiermacher. A work like his *Symbolik* could only have been produced in Germany, under the stimulating influence of German Protestant scholarship. As Möhler himself admitted, he had taken the idea of such a *Symbolik* from Protestant theology. His intention in doing so was to make the reader clearly aware of the full scope of the confessional divide separating Catholics from Protestants. So he made it

---

66. Johann Adam Möhler, *Symbolik oder Darstellung der dogmatischen Gegensätze der Katholiken und Protestanten nach ihren öffentlichen Bekenntnisschriften* (Mainz, 1832); critical edition by Rupert Geiselmann (2 vols., Cologne and Olten, 1958). ET: *Symbolism: Exposition of the Doctrinal Differences between Catholics and Protestants as Evidenced by the Symbolical Writings*, trans. J. B. Robertson (London, 1843; 2nd ed. 1847; reprint with an introduction by M. J. Himes, New York, 1997). His earlier major work is *Die Einheit in der Kirche oder das Prinzip des Katholizismus dargestellt im Geiste der Kirchenväter der drei ersten Jahrhunderte* (Tübingen, 1825, 2nd ed., 1843). ET: *Unity in the Church or The Principle of Catholicism Presented in the Spirit of the Church Fathers of the First Three Centuries*, ed. and trans. Peter C. Erb (Washington, DC, 1996). Möhler (1796–1838) was professor of theology in the Catholic Theological Faculty of the University of Tübingen from 1826 until his departure in 1835 for the University of Munich, apparently because of his controversy with Baur. On this controversy, see Notger Slenczka, "Ethical Judgment and Ecclesiastical Self-Understanding: Ferdinand Christian Baur's Interpretation of the Protestant Principle in the Controversy with Johann Adam Möhler," chap. 2 in *Ferdinand Christian Baur and the History of Early Christianity*, ed. Martin Bauspiess, Christof Landmesser, and David Lincicum; trans. Robert F. Brown and Peter C. Hodgson (Oxford, 2017).

his task to indicate the antitheses very precisely; and never, or at any point, did he endeavor to disguise or conceal them. The view that there are no substantial differences, none vitally affecting Christianity, could only meet with contempt from the other side. For any opponent who is inwardly aware of having no sufficient basis [for his opposition] is self-contradictory; and yet in pursuing [his opposition], he must be contemptible.

Möhler emphasized the most recent change to occur, the revival of the older Protestant orthodoxy, as his particular motivation for publishing his *Symbolik*. The more this faction spread rapidly and began to become a force once again—in part by linking up with the long-standing pietist movements, in part at the encouragement of one of the most influential government cabinets in Germany—the more apparent became the need for Catholics to take their bearings in exact opposition to Protestant orthodoxy, and to once again become clearly aware of their own position over against it. From this perspective we see how the *Symbolik* is wholly organized so as to interpret the antitheses of Catholicism and Protestantism as an issue of principles in the strictest sense. Hence the author must also be very much intent on answering this challenge.

The result of Möhler's investigation is that, on all the points where he juxtaposes Catholicism to Protestantism, including in their scientific respects, Catholicism is so decidedly superior to Protestantism that one can only be astonished at how a religious system so very lacking in any internal justification can have maintained itself for so long, side by side with Catholicism. In Möhler's view and presentation of the two systems, they stand mutually opposed as do truth and error. In Protestantism everything is purely subjective; its universal feature is just something individual that gets elevated to universality, something that, as such, also has no objective focus. In Catholicism, on the contrary, everything is objective. Luther, Zwingli, and Calvin are the originators of the views they adopt, whereas no Catholic dogma can be traced back to some individual theologian as its creator. Catholic theologians find the dogma, on which they expatiate, as already a given for them. Their particular and distinctive contributions are to be most meticulously distinguished from the common elements articulated by the church, those handed down by Christ and the Apostles, just as these elements existed prior to those theologians. Thus the dogmas can also endure after those theologians and for that reason also endure apart from them—in general, quite independently of them.

This distinction between what is individual and what is universal is possible only in the Catholic Church, but there it is also necessary. As in life and so in science, the individual's free action is therefore just given greater scope when it is always compatible with the permanence of the universal element, that is, so far as it does not contradict the universal element and threaten to displace and undo it. In its relation to Catholicism, Protestantism presents such a contradiction to the universal element, such a danger of displacing and undoing it. That is why Protestantism was only able to emerge outside Catholicism, not within the Catholic Church. But that is the very reason why Protestantism is also the absolute contradiction to what is universal; it lacks anything universal and objective, and is therefore sheer subjectivity. In Protestantism, what is subjective and individual, in its contradiction to the objective and the universal, is also something untrue and empty, is absolute error, absolute caprice.

The Protestant Response; the Significance of the Dispute

We of course ought not expect any different verdict about Protestantism from a Catholic creedalist (*Symboliker*) if he did not wish to disavow the standpoint of his church. The disconcerting feature in this was only how a scientifically educated writer could have allowed himself to give such a thoroughly false and wrongheaded portrayal of all the main teachings of the Protestant system as we have here—in any event an extremely one-sided presentation. There is nothing so senseless and unreasonable that Möhler does not think it may be attributed to Protestantism. The more the Protestant theological framework was distorted in this way, the easier it was to cast the Catholic system in a favorable light. Indeed quite often what is truly the Protestant teaching (instead of the contentions foisted upon Protestantism) gets claimed for Catholicism. Such a procedure was of course necessary if the two theological frameworks were said to be related as truth and error. However, if Möhler himself could only achieve his purpose in this fashion, it makes it all the clearer that a *Symbolik* in the scientific sense that the Protestant associates with this concept, is not possible from the Catholic standpoint as such.

This is not the place to go further into individual points of Möhler's *Symbolik*. I believe that I have provided enough evidence for my contentions in my critique of it: *Gegensatz des Katholicismus und Protestantismus* (1833).[67] An attack of this kind on the Protestant belief system could not go unanswered from the Protestant side. Responses in addition to my book came from Nitzsch and Marheineke.

---

67. *Der Gegensatz des Katholicismus und Protestantismus nach den Principien und Hauptdogmen der beiden Lehrbegriffe: Mit besonderer Rücksicht auf Herrn Dr. Möhler's Symbolik* (Tübingen, 1834; 2nd ed. 1836).

When Möhler answered my book with a rebuttal,[68] other Catholic theologians also joined in the fray. This resulted in a theological controversy lasting several years, one important not only for justifying the Protestant theological framework but also for looking more deeply into the distinguishing characteristics of the two systems. If the issue was to be treated scientifically, then what mattered was not merely countering the opponents' individual points and establishing the truth of the Protestant dogma, for one also had to go back to the principles of each system and to understand them in their most general, antithetical character. In my own investigation I made doing so the main task.

If we do not take this standpoint, then the distinction between the two systems always remains just a relative one, and we cannot rebut what Strauss says in the preface to his *Christliche Glaubenslehre*:

> Viewed from a scientific basis, Protestant orthodox theology today stands incomparably closer to orthodox Catholic theology than it does to rationalism or to the speculative theologians of its own confession. Where the controversy concerns the autonomy or the heteronomy of the spirit as such, the related question—whether the principle of this heteronomy is said to be the church or the scriptures—can only be a minor concern. That is why it must appear to be a wasted effort to bicker about individual fine points concerning the doctrines of original sin, justification, the sacraments, and so forth, when the totality of those doctrines, together with the worldview forming their foundation, is placed in question.[69]

Strauss contends that, however strongly rooted the Catholicism-Protestantism antithesis also may have been in the disparities of national character and form of governance, this antithesis lost all significance in the domain of science. In fact there would not be much to say to the contrary if it were correct that Catholicism and Protestantism both belong under the heading of heteronomy.

In any event, since the essential nature of Catholicism must be located in the principle of heteronomy, then: either the antithesis of Catholicism and Protestantism has no absolute significance; or else it has this significance

---

68. *Neue Untersuchungen der Lehrengegensätze zwischen den Katholiken und Protestanten: Eine Vertheidigung meiner Symbolik gegen die Kritik des Herrn Professors Dr. Baur in Tübingen* (1834). Baur wrote another rejoinder: *Erwiderung auf Herrn Dr. Möhlers neueste Polemik gegen die protestantische Lehre und Kirche* (Tübingen, 1834).

69. David Friedrich Strauss, *Die christliche Glaubenslehre in ihrer geschichtlichen Entwicklung und im Kampfe mit der modernen Wissenschaft*, 2 vols. (Tübingen and Stuttgart, 1841), 1:vi–vii.

in the very fact that Protestantism and Catholicism stand to each other as autonomy and heteronomy. But we must then go on to ask: Is this autonomy not that very subjectivity and individual caprice the Catholic considers to be the actual essence of Protestantism? This is truly the Catholic view of Protestantism—the accusation made over and over against Protestantism from the Catholic side. Protestantism's entire historical development is invoked as evidence that it is none other than the self-aggrandizing operation of subjective free will.

This is the sense in which Drey too expressed the essence of Protestantism (p. ix of the preface to vol. 2 of his *Apologetik*).[70] He said that the subjectivity, caprice, and frivolity of all of Christianity's opponents supposedly finds its support in a principle false in itself and none other than something put in place by the Reformation with reference to the Bible. This subjectivity detached the Bible from the church, and it had to do so after it had cut itself off from the church; while at the same time it still felt the necessity to have a divinely attested authority and norm for the new faith, which could only be the Bible. Hence the Reformation set up the Bible all by itself as the sole norm of the new faith. However, this expedient, driven by the need [for an authority], had effects and consequences the Reformers, without weighing the matter and thinking clearly, had of course for the most part not suspected, but consequences that nonetheless had to come about in the natural course of things.

The first and most salient consequence was the unlimited freedom in scriptural interpretation given to individuals, to their own spiritual and moral capacities. The early Reformers embraced this consequence and so they joined individual freedom of interpretation, as a second principle, to the first principle, the exclusive authority of scripture. Soon, however, the overall error became evident. The divisions and controversies that second principle led to became manifest, and people resorted to colloquies and formulas of concord said to limit and constrain individual freedom. But this was none other than a return to the human authority recently repudiated so solemnly. It was of course an authority that could not, in any respect, avoid comparison with the authority of the church. People had once again gotten this authority off their backs, and the Bible, now cut off from the church, got the same treatment as the secular writings of the Greeks and the Romans. Indeed by mythologizing criticism and exegesis they introduced paganism

---

70. Johann Sebastian von Drey (1777–1853), professor in the Catholic Theological Faculty at Tübingen from 1813 on. Möhler was his student. *Die Apologetik als wissenschaftliche Nachweisung der Göttlichkeit des Christentums in seiner Erscheinung*, 3 vols. (Mainz, 1838–47); vol. 2: *Die Religion in ihrer Vollendung durch die Offenbarung in Christus* (Mainz, 1843).

into their heart and soul, into the Protestant doctrines and history, and the more recent speculative theology carried through with what this exegesis was unable to fully accomplish, leading to a new pantheism. In this way a development of the basic principle brought the other factors in its wake. From this standpoint, the latest school of thought can justifiably maintain that, through it, the Protestant principle has attained its full force; that its own [theological] standpoint represents the ultimate goal of the development of Christian consciousness. Over against what has blossomed into such a destructive principle, one can only hold fast to the Catholic standpoint by regarding the Bible as the church's book; and this fundamental principle is the basis for the preservation of Christianity.

This is the issue, what it is all about, grasped with the greatest precision. But is Protestantism then utterly dispatched because of the capriciousness it is charged with, thus the deplorable consequences following in its wake? The simple reply to all of this is as follows. The subjectivity that is the Protestant principle is not subjective caprice (*Willkür*) but subjective freedom (*Freiheit*). This subjective freedom, by which Protestantism itself first came into being, is the necessary progression grounded in the essence of spirit itself: the advance from objectivity to subjectivity, to the freedom and autonomy of the subject. With the same justification we have for saying that spirit would not be spirit, be this living, immanent process of mediation with itself, if spirit were only objective spirit and not also subjective spirit, we must also say that subjective spirit would not be what it ought to be as such, the free self-conscious spirit, if spirit's development had not progressed from Catholicism to Protestantism. The essential nature and the necessity of Protestantism can be conceived only based on spirit's essential nature. In its endless subjectivity, in the absoluteness of self-consciousness, Protestantism is itself spirit determining itself through itself. What is the supreme principle of spirit—that everything only is for self-consciousness, and through self-consciousness it has its true reality only in self-consciousness; that self-consciousness can know itself as one with spirit—is also the Protestant principle.[71]

71. Spirit's advance from objectivity to subjectivity leads to a mediation of subjectivity and objectivity and a consummation of absolute spirit. This means that freedom is not locked into sheer subjectivism (caprice); it also involves a relationship to the absolute, and it might be characterized as "theonomous autonomy." Baur does not use this expression, but he describes faith in similar terms in a passage from *Der Gegensatz des Katholicismus und Protestantismus* (n. 67), 157 (cited by Slenczka [n. 66], 57): "Faith is for the Protestant . . . the orientation of one's soul, encompassing the whole person and directing one to the highest goal of one's blessedness; the principle of one's religious life is what enlivens the innermost person. While people have their depth and inwardness in their proceeding from faith as the midpoint in which the whole of human spiritual

Putting it this way is, in the main, none other than the usual popular expression of this point, namely, that in Protestantism one leaves behind the state of childhood and dependence, of tutelage, in which the individual stands in Catholicism, and enters into the state of maturity and independence. If it is then in general necessary, and can scarcely be denied, that when people do not hold a far too abject conception of a human being's essential nature and spiritual freedom, there is then also a state of maturity and independence in which one is not merely guided and treated condescendingly by another's authority, but instead, in all things involving the most direct, subjective relation to another, one stands on one's own, is responsible for oneself, thinks for oneself. This condition is not only the justification for Protestantism's existence, but is also the recognition of its necessity. This maturity and independence, this spiritual freedom that Protestantism, as freedom of belief and freedom of conscience, appeals to above all as its most essential right, is its principle of subjectivity. How then can it be regarded as mere capriciousness?

Considered in this way, Catholicism and Protestantism present themselves as two forms and stages of spiritual development, ones that can only be comprehended, in their essential relation to each other, as based on the essence of spirit itself. Catholicism is naturally authoritative so long as the individual spirit's self-consciousness is not yet strong enough to have the inner impulse to break loose from the whole with which it is immediately one, and to grasp itself within itself. However, once this inherently necessary break has occurred, then along with it Catholicism is demoted from the absolute standpoint it previously occupied as the sole form of consciousness, and it is relegated to a subordinate stage at which it stands opposed to Protestantism simply as a moment that has been overcome. If even now Catholicism nevertheless wishes to assert itself as being absolutely significant, this gives rise to that self-contradiction on the part of Catholicism when it acts toward Protestantism—which now still exists and Catholicism cannot utterly deny that—as though Protestantism were not there at all, or else had no right to exist at all.

To say that Catholicism alone is truth, and Protestantism is merely error, is to speak quite ridiculously and absurdly, because everybody knows that in reality there is no such dualism. It is sheer arrogance to say there is.

---

activity is concentrated, and in which individual personal life has its innermost seat and hearth, faith is at the same time a renunciation of all that is personal, of one's own self; faith is simply being directed to what God offers, a pure surrender to it that arises from the deepest feeling of one's own indigence; it is an act that, however intensive and substantial, wants only to be receptive to what is given and not to fixate on itself in its own independent significance."

As long as a contention wanting to assert as truth something that is in itself false, can make that assertion deceptively, as pretence, then doing so gives rise to that equivocation and dishonesty, to that sophistical and Jesuitical character also found in Möhler's *Symbolik*, for that equivocation belongs to the nature of the Catholic polemic.

Since Protestantism can have no interest in taking matters otherwise than they actually are, Protestantism for its own part just has the purely scientific interest that in Catholicism, in the final analysis, always gets subordinated to hierarchically supported authority. [Catholicism] does not want Protestantism to be allowed its due place in history because it has a particular reason for not wanting this; or else, if this unwillingness is said to be an inability to do so, then Catholicism is subjectively incapable of following through with the general course of spirit, proceeding from the lower stage to the higher one. Catholicism walls itself off in a past that counts for it as absolute truth, whereas Protestantism is the endless progression in which all that is subjective and arbitrary is always just a self-annulling moment of the universal process of development.

This is the way to understand how the two systems stand vis-à-vis each other, an understanding based on the most recent discussions occasioned by Möhler's *Symbolik*, and provided for those capable of grasping this matter in its greater depth and its context. However, the negligible scientific contents and value of Möhler's *Symbolik*, as measured by the Protestant critique of it and by the empty show into which its arguments dissolve, were no obstacle to the reputation it gained. It has set the tone especially for the Ultramontane orientation that has since become increasingly dominant, both among Möhler's closer associates and also in wider circles.

The State of Catholic Theology Today

This would be the place to take an even wider look at the latest Catholic theology. But what more could we say about its character that the foregoing account has not already conveyed? The Ultramontane orientation is completely dominant, and whatever wishes to diverge from it and operate more freely always in turn founders on the Rock of Peter, the unavoidable obstacle. Papal authority presents an impediment to every attempt at an independent, scientific treatment of dogma. For all who in good faith have ventured on such an endeavor regarding the dogma of their church, their only recourse, sooner or later, is silent submission. In the issues we have been discussing we see clearly how vigilant the Roman Curia has been concerning all efforts of this kind, precisely in most recent times. Although we readily acknowledge the scientific accomplishments of Catholic theologians—and there is no shortage of these theologians lately, at least when it comes to the domain of dogma—in the Catholic Church the course of science is blocked from making any new, meaningful progress.

The Dogma of the Immaculate Conception

But there is another source from which Catholic dogma enriches itself with new content. The absolute power of the papacy is also sufficient for creating new dogma, as most recently in the dogma of the immaculate conception of the Virgin Mary. People were surprised by it, and yet the dogma simply accomplished the objective toward which Catholic dogmatics had indeed long aspired.

We can simply go back to the Council of Trent. The decree of this Council on 17 June 1546, concerning original sin, declared that its intent was for this decree to not also apply to the blessed and immaculate Virgin Mary, the Mother of God. Instead, by referring to the decrees of Sixtus IV, the Council observed that (in 1483) Sixtus IV proscribed any other opinions about her status as heretical.[72] Since then the popes, in partnership with the Jesuits, headed with increasing decisiveness toward making this a dogma of the faith. Indeed, in 1622 Gregory XV forbade everyone from expressing an opposed view, even in private conversations. In 1798, Clement XI enjoined the general celebration, throughout the entire world, of the Feast of the Immaculate Conception of the Virgin Mary.

The last step to be taken was reserved for Pius IX. Perhaps he held it to be particularly significant that he succeeded to the apostolic seat [in 1846] exactly three hundred years after the Tridentine decree. Soon thereafter he issued a sacred invitation to promote devotion to the Holy Virgin. Almost all his remaining decrees exude the greatest devotion to the Holy Virgin, whom he thanks for deliverance from all perils. He states that she is our most sweet mother, intercessor and advocate; our most dependable hope and greatest confidence; the all-powerful and most directly effective representative before God; the great patroness of the city of Rome to whom God has entrusted its direct protection; the one who, because of her fully influential advocacy with God, will ask for nothing in vain because she receives all that she asks for.

---

72. Pope Sixtus IV issued such a decree concerning the immaculate conception of Mary (namely, that she did not inherit original sin via her own birth) on 4 September 1483.

In 1847 Perrone, a Jesuit, submitted to the pope a treatise on the question of whether the immaculate conception of the Holy Virgin Mary could be established by decree as a dogma. That set things in motion. In 1849, Pius IX issued a circular letter to all the bishops, with the following points stated in the introduction. He said that, since his elevation to the seat of the prince of the apostles, it has been an exceedingly great comfort to him to know how, under Gregory XVI, in the entire Catholic world, the ardent desire had been aroused for the apostolic seat to finally establish, by a solemn declaration, that the holy God-bearer, our most beloved mother, was conceived without the blemish of original sin. From his youth onward, nothing has been so dear to, and valued by, the pope, as revering the most blessed Virgin Mary with one's whole heart, and promoting all that redounds to her glory. From the beginning of his pontificate he has prayed to God for enlightenment about what to do. For he drew support above all from the hope that the most Blessed Virgin would extend her motherly care to him—she who, because of the magnitude of her merits was exalted, above all the choirs of angels, to the throne of God; she who stomped on the head of the ancient serpent with the foot of her virtue and, standing between Christ and the church, has, at all times, rescued Christian folk from menacing perils. [He continues, to the bishops:] You know full well, esteemed brothers, that all our trust is placed in the Holy Virgin Mary; for God has set forth the abundance of all good things in Mary, such that when hope, grace, and salvation is prepared for us, we might know that it is mediated to us through Mary, because such is the will of he who wills that we receive all things through Mary. Thus for the pope the Blessed Virgin is an abundance.

At the conclusion of his circular letter the pope indicates its aim: that as soon as possible the bishops shall give an account of what devotion their clerics and faithful flocks have for the immaculate conception of the Blessed Virgin, and of how it was made known that this was a matter decided on by the Holy See. Naturally the bishops' reports were entirely favorable; they said it had long been forbidden to say anything against this practice. In the meantime the pope ordered a medal to be struck upon proclaiming a new dogma, and launched a jubilee, in order, by accessing the church's wealth, to be in an even better position for the imminent official act. For that purpose he assembled a number of selected bishops to seek their advice, not on whether the dogma is true, but instead on whether it was the opportune time for it and what outward form the announcement of it should take. The Jesuits certified that, toward the conclusion of the assembly, the Holy Spirit came down upon the bishops almost visibly, so that they urgently requested the pope to "teach us, instruct us, Peter; strengthen your brothers." Whereupon the new dogma was imparted to them from the infallible mouth [of the pope], and they extolled it together with praising the everlasting fidelity of the beneficent Holy See.

This is how the *dogmatica definitio de immaculata conceptione Deiparae* (Dogmatic Definition of the Immaculate Conception of the Mother of God) came about, as proclaimed by the pope on 8 December 1854, in the presence of 53 cardinals, 43 archbishops, and 100 bishops. People even found it especially noteworthy that the pope in fact convened no council, but only assembled bishops he himself selected, so that the new dogmatic decree was consequently seen to be entirely just a product of papal authority.

As expected, the Catholic Church greeted the decree with the greatest jubilation. The time was past when one could raise an objection to it. People heard only of feasts that were celebrated, of medals that were struck, of pillars erected to the honor of the Virgin Mary. It was especially interesting to compare the judgments expressing opinions about this in Protestant journals with various orientations. Most of them believed they had to see in it simply an event of most recent history that is equally deplorable and significant. In itself it is certainly a matter of the greatest indifference whether or not the immaculate conception of the Virgin Mary, which people have for a long time celebrated as a feast in its own right, is now also believed to be an issue of dogma.[73]

E. The Most Recent Conflicts of the Catholic Church with the Government of States[74]

A series of efforts in the Catholic Church dates from the movements in 1848. These efforts all aimed at the same goal, achieving as much independence and autonomy as possible for the church in relation to the authority of the state. In an era when the general order of things threatened to come apart, those steps took place not so much for consolidation, for maintaining the status quo in a stable central point, as they did instead simply with the intention of interrupting the general trend at that time, the trend toward the state as absolute monarchy, and utilizing this interruption in the interests of

---

73. [*Baur*] See the following. *Deutsches Museum* (1855) no. 3, 89: "Das jüngste Dogma der kath. Kirche." Kliefoth and Mejer, *Kirchliche Zeitschrift* (1855) no. 2, 287. "Der neue römische Glaubensartikel von der unbefleckten Empfängniss der Jungfrau Maria, ein Zeichen der Zeit." *Deutsche Zeitschrift für christliche Wissenschaft* (1855) [nos. 1–2, article by Julius Müller].

74. [*Zeller*] In the 1859–60 transcript, this section stands at the very end of the whole. I locate it here instead, where it naturally fits and where it occurs in the 1857–58 transcript. Perhaps Baur put it at the end in 1860 because he sought to anticipate further developments on the matter of concordats in southern Germany.

the Catholic Church. The same steps would also be pursued subsequently, after the political currents of the time had taken a quite different direction.

The German Episcopacy in 1848

In October 1848 a majority of the German bishops and archbishops met in Würzburg. A few Austrians also took part, one being the cardinal archbishop and prince of Schwarzenberg.[75]

This was in fact a German national council, but it did not adopt that label for the simple reason that it did not include very many of the Austrian bishops. Its proceedings were secret, although at the conclusion it sent out a general pastoral letter to all the faithful and issued a report. In this report the bishops declared that, in circumstances where concordats or similar agreements assure that public order in the state permits a free life and expression on the church's part, these compacts will be regarded as sacred; but that where restrictions on the life of the church and on the free operations of bishops are evident, they will be a matter of negotiations with the Holy See. In general the bishops felt obliged to uphold the freedom of the church and thus to demand unlimited freedom as to doctrine and instruction, as well as the establishing and guidance of its own instructional institutions taken in the broadest sense, including the right to be the sole inspector and watchdog of the clergy, the cultus, and the congregations.

Very indicative of these bishops' intentions is the solemn protest they made against their alliance with the [Holy] Father of Christianity being looked upon as a sin against their nationality, as un-German and dangerous. Hence they declared every kind of agreement restricting the free promulgation of spiritual regulations as essentially an infringement on the inalienable rights of the church. It is no surprise that, in the pope's response to the resolutions sent to him, his *Conventus Herbipolensis* of 17 May 1849 (sent from Gaëta), he manifested his great joy at how the bishops handled the matter.

The Catholic Church in Austria; the Concordat; the Position of the Protestants

In the meantime the basic rights of the German national council were acknowledged. They included every publicly recognized church and religious community as having independent rules and governance for its organization, and the possession and use of its religious institutes, endowments and

---

75. Schwarzenberg is in Baden, a part of which was under Austrian rule at this time.

foundations, specified for the purposes of instruction and charity. It was also determined that religious instruction in the public schools should be under the care of the pertinent church or religious community. These regulations were also adopted in the imperial government charter for Austria of 4 March 1849 (§2).

Directly thereafter, in April 1849, the Austrian bishops assembled at a conference in Vienna. Its outcome, in agreement with the decisions reached at Würzburg, was an arrangement with the government for an independent system of ecclesiastical property, for a different way of filling the position of bishop, for the filling of lesser positions by the bishops, for the influence of bishops on the appointment of professors of theology, and so forth. Without posing any obstacles, the government now consented to the desired plan by its decrees of 18 and 23 April 1850. There was to be free interaction with the pope, without prior approval from the secular authorities; consent to what the bishops promulgated to clergy and congregations was eliminated; the bishops were permitted to impose ecclesiastical punishments so long as those had no repercussions for civil rights; the bishops could suspend or dismiss clergy, declare their official income forfeited, and claim the cooperation of the state's executive power in carrying out their verdicts. In addition, in filling bishoprics the emperor promised to heed the advisory body of the bishops. There were to be no obstacles to the bishops fully implementing their decisions concerning the investigation of insolvent parishes and the establishment of diocesan and cloistral institutions for teaching theology. No one was to be allowed to serve as a teacher of the Catholic religion or as a professor of Catholic theology, in lower or higher public educational institutions, without the authorization of the diocesan bishop, and so forth.

These concessions retained their legal force despite the charter of 4 March 1849 having been in turn annulled by the imperial decree of 31 December 1851. The concessions are truly the opposite of the earlier Josephine legislation,[76] and so they also caused a great sensation when they were announced publicly in Austria. What then followed was the concordat of 18 August 1855, which made such great concessions to the church, and gave it such independent standing vis-à-vis the state, that everything still remaining from the Josephine canon law was completely annulled. Here everything pertaining to the Catholic religion and church was placed totally in the hands of the clergy. Inasmuch as the educational system has any relation at all to religion, it stands entirely under the clergy. In particular,

---

76. Joseph II (1741–90), emperor of Germany from 1765 until his death. As head of the Austrian government, he broke off relations with the pope, suppressed convents, imposed other restrictions on Roman Catholicism, and in 1781 decreed full toleration for Protestants and Greek Catholics.

the clergy can even exercise such unlimited censorship of books that it is fundamentally up to the clergy which books may circulate in the monarchy; for a book of any kind can be banned under the pretense that it is harmful to religion and the church. Appointment to ecclesiastical posts and to teaching positions affecting religion is totally vested in the clergy and the pope. What remains the emperor's prerogative is so limited by the church that all the rights reserved to him are just illusory. What does it mean that he can appoint bishops, when he cannot appoint anyone other than one of the three persons nominated by the church?

Notwithstanding all this, it does not appear to be the state's intention to let the church exercise its authority across the full range of the powers the concordat grants to it. Recently the bishops of Lombardy began to make full use of their rights to censor books, rights to which they believe themselves entitled according to the concordat. The government saw itself obliged to intervene, since for its own part it claimed the right to oversee the measures in which it is supposed to collaborate in the interest of the church. Such a right of oversight can become very extensive, but it gives rise to the following contradiction. On the one hand the concordat establishes that the Catholic religion shall retain intact all the prerogatives and powers belonging to it according to God's instruction and the church's decisions; while on the other hand, the government shall have this right of oversight of the church. So if the concordat's goal was to avert clashes between the state and the church, by the state granting the church its free standing, this goal will be difficult to achieve.

The Ultramontane clergy has indeed presented very broad claims that have decidedly intruded on the most important circumstances of life—on marriage, on the instructional system, on the burial of the dead. These clerics have also most obstinately resisted measures of the greatest importance for the national economy, and in individual instances have offered most remarkable defiance to the well-meaning intentions of the government and the laws of the land. The experience of a few years has already shown in what difficulties people have become embroiled owing to the concordat.[77]

77. [*Baur, in the margin*]. According to the publication, *Kirchliche Zustände in Oesterreich unter der Herrschaft des Concordats* (Leipzig, 1859), nothing has in any event come of all the concerns people had about the concordat. On the whole it views the concordat from a different perspective than the usual one. The state has simply acknowledged the inalienable rights of the Catholic Church, and it has surrendered none of its own rights over against the church. In appointing bishops, the emperor has to follow the recommendation of the bishops, especially those of the same ecclesiastical province. The government appoints the theology professors, and the bishop assigns their mission. Since the concordat, there has not yet been an episcopal ban on books. The comment as to marriage is simply that all of the laws concerning marriage enacted

Nonetheless, there are two kinds of issues to be considered with regard to the Austrian concordat. The first is that Austria is not a Protestant state but a Catholic state, one that has concluded the concordat with the pope. The second issue is that the government has given the assurance that, after the freedom of the Catholic Church is made secure, the same shall happen for the Protestant Church—although it is questionable whether the government is serious about that. The Austrian government has made an encouraging beginning by the charter of 1 September 1859, provided for the Evangelical [Calvinist] churches in Hungary, and by the following order of 2 September from the ministry of cults. The latter order, in elaboration of §55 of the charter, provisionally establishes a complete ecclesiastical system of governance for the Evangelicals in Hungary, that is, to the point at which the Evangelical Church will have to make further decisions about these specifics of the system. The governance system is so liberal that, when it goes into operation, no Evangelical church in a European land, other than those of the Scots and the Dutch, will enjoy such a system. However, it is dubious whether this may come to fruition, such that in the German lands under the Austrian crown the Evangelicals will be granted a truly comparable system of church governance. That is because the Protestants in these German provinces lack the basis and the concerns that led to the concession made to Hungary (cf. *Protestantische Kirchenzeitung* [1859] no. 40).[78]

Following the decisions of the Würzburg synod, the bishops in Prussia also came together with new demands to the government, in a statement in July 1849. In it, and based on the specifics of the document on governance from 5 December 1848, they derived further consequences in particular from article 12 that were consonant with constitutional rights, and to which the government readily consented. The revised governance document of 31 January 1850 confirmed article 12 of the 1848 document, and further established that: there are no impediments to religious organizations communicating with their superiors; the promulgation of ecclesiastical regulations is subject only to the restrictions to which all other public announcements are subject; there is an end to the appointment, nomination, election, and confirmation of the occupants of ecclesiastical positions so far as these acts

---

by state authorities since Joseph II, so far as they do not merely concern its civil consequences, no longer have any validity in Austria, and marital matters as such belong before the church courts. The secular authority provides only limited assistance in the implementation of episcopal verdicts concerning clerics. For violations of the state's laws, clerics must be arraigned before the secular courts. In Austria since the concordat, the clergy no longer has a privileged standing before the courts. The state administers the funding for religion and for schools.

78. At this point Zeller adds a lengthy footnote describing events in Hungary after late 1859, where the imperial charter for Evangelicals was not well-received.

are vested in the state and do not rest on the patronage or titular rights [of the church]. In conformity with these general specifications regarding governance, several particular ordinances established the Catholic Church's independence from the government. Rights previously exercised by the government and by state officials now came almost completely under the control of the archbishops. We see how very happy these concessions made the pope, from his not only appointing the archbishop of Cologne and the archbishop of Breslau as cardinals, but also awarding to Presiding Minister von Manteuffel the Grand Cross of the Order of Pius.

In Bavaria, where in 1847 a reaction already ensued against the strict Catholic faction that had previously been so dominant, and where this party did not wholly relax its efforts even after the abdication of King Ludwig in March 1848, the bishops likewise took steps in the same direction. At a conference in Freising, in October 1850, the bishops composed a statement to the king. In it they complained about the harm the Catholic Church in Bavaria still constantly suffered despite the concordat of 1817. They declared very emphatically that it belonged to the episcopacy alone to decide on what is essential or nonessential in the cultus. Since this issue involves matters of governmental controls that cannot be changed without the cooperation of the chamber, the government made it clear that it was not much inclined to concur. There has still been no decisive reply to the bishops' statement.

We see clearly how all these efforts were part and parcel of the overall trend in 1848. While the Catholic bishops too had hardly wished to give the appearance of revolutionary tendencies and political agitation, they just as little wished to lag behind in the assertion of demands that now seemed to be quite timely. We see this connection expressed with sufficient clarity in the statement of the bishops assembled at Würzburg, when they themselves declared that: as decidedly and strictly as the church too abhors and repudiates anarchical efforts of every sort, it also still has a vital interest in securing all that the general call for freedom from administrative patronizing and control truly involves. Furthermore, the church may not neglect to claim its rightful share in the promises the princes make to their people. After such important concessions had been made in the larger states, people thought they might move forward in the same fashion in the smaller ones. But one could already see in Bavaria what opposition the bishops' demands faced in states where—as was the case in southern Germany—there was already a long-standing system of governance. Hence what had taken place in the larger states rather quietly, gave rise in the smaller ones to a more intense conflict of church and state. This point leads us to the most recently arising conflicts in the ecclesiastical province of the Upper Rhine, those between the bishops and the governments of the states that belong to this province.

The Church Controversy in Baden

In January 1849 the archbishop of Freiburg issued a pastoral letter, which, in consideration of the decisions of the Würzburg council, held out the prospect of summoning his suffragens to a provincial synod for the coming spring. Since the uprising in Baden intervened, the five bishops of the ecclesiastical province of the Upper Rhine were only able to come together on a joint statement to their governments in March 1851.

In this statement the bishops demanded: eliminating all the so-called "March achievements" affecting the church, such as those involving civil marriages. Their demands included: free conferring of religious offices and benefices within their own dioceses by the bishops; the authority of bishops to freely control their subordinates and impose canonical punishments; no state control of boarding schools; no princely approval for filling vacant pastorates; no appeals to the state government in their exercise of punitive power over the clergy; relinquishing princely claims to official church titles (*Tischtitel*); doing away with the consent for publication of papal bulls and letters, and episcopal announcements to the clergy; free interaction for the bishops with Rome; no intervention by secular authorities in the filling of vacant cathedral chapter positions; independent administration of the property of Catholic churches and foundations; episcopal approval of appointments of teachers of religion in higher schools and universities; complete freedom to engage in popular missions and spiritual exercises; and so forth. All these demands stood more or less in opposition to previous practices and to the sovereigns' regulations, ones that the bishops had sworn to obey upon accession to their offices. In their conciliatory replies, which were as accommodating as possible, the affected states simply pointed out, first of all, that changes in the basic principles legally binding on the ecclesiastical province of the Upper Rhine could only be undertaken after mutual consultation and their adoption.

The government of Baden indeed issued the invitation to a conference scheduled for December 1851. Even before this conference convened, one could see the direction the bishops had decided to take. Professor Schmid in Giessen had been the canonical choice for the vacant episcopal seat in Mainz, but by a letter of December 1849 the pope had declared him unworthy of episcopal office and told the chapter to make a new choice. From the three candidates nominated, the pope singled out Ketteler in Breslau. Ketteler had shown himself to be the right man for this position, not only because, in his pastoral letter of April 1851, he opposed existing laws lacking [papal] consent, but also because he made arrangements to reinstate the discontinued seminary for priests in Mainz. Seven professors were appointed, and attending the seminary was given such priority that all those studying Catholic theology at the provincial university in Giessen left, so that the teachers at Giessen were completely unable to carry out their official duties.

In February 1852 the anticipated conference took place. Commissioners from the affected governments arrived in Karlsruhe to confer about the bishops' demands. At the same time the five bishops gathered in Freiburg [im Breisgau] and, after a brief consultation on 10 and 11 February, they issued the following declaration. First, they persisted unwaveringly with the points they specifically made in their statement of March 1851. Second, they said if their justifiable demands are not satisfied, they are resolved to proceed on their own, and thus to act as though each point would actually have been granted, and letting the chips fall where they may. This statement was obviously none other than a formal repudiation of their sworn obedience to the princes and the sovereigns' ordinances. The bishops' demands were not only so inherently extreme that no government, and least of all the government of a Protestant state, could consent to them if it did not wish to forsake the exercise of its sovereign rights; for their demands also could not find any support that would make them seem actually justifiable. Their argument was simply the absolute right of the church, and that seemed to make any further proof superfluous. This situation just expressed the absolute antithesis of church and state.

The governments of the affected states had promised nothing of the sort that was now demanded of them; they were not bound by any earlier commitments of this kind. In a case that could not be treated as comparable to the different matters at issue here, Pius VII himself had expressly pointed out that, after completing the external arrangements for the dioceses in the ecclesiastical province of the Upper Rhine, one "wants, going forward, to have a workable agreement regarding the churches." The bull of Leo XII, *Ad domini gregis custodiam*, on which the bishops principally rested their demands, had been issued without any attempt to provide for such an agreement. There was not even any existing private understanding between the princes and the bishops. Likewise with the creation and endowing of dioceses, the commonly agreed upon principles came about as publicly announced conditions; and people only assented to papal bulls in such a way that complete adherence to princely ordinances regarding the church was never in question. In a letter to the bishops, Pius VII made known his disapproval of restrictions on church practices by the [state's] ordinances governing the church. Even so, he wrote that bishops still must be fully obligated to carefully obey these ordinances. Whatever the pope thought of them, as always he gave them his blessing. So in this case the decision was that right is on the side of the government.

The government's response to the archbishop's protest of 12 April 1853 not only did not deter him from expressing, in the most blunt fashion, the principle of the church's autonomy vis-à-vis the state, in a new declaration by the episcopacy of the Upper Rhine ecclesiastical province on 18 June 1853, together with a special petition on 16 July; it also did not deter him from taking real steps. Without consulting a royal commissioner, the archbishop established a theological test when he sought to fill a pastoral position unilaterally, by drawing up an announcement of the appointment, and when he informed the members of the council with oversight of the Catholic Church that if, in two weeks' time, they did not declare their unconditional obedience to the archbishop's directives, in particular their firm resolve to support forcefully all the demands spelled out in the declaration of 18 June, then the punishment of excommunication would be imposed on them. The government sought in vain to get the archbishop to reverse his steps. On 4 November he simply retorted that he had not wanted to encroach on the government's sovereign rights; that his actions simply exercised his episcopal rights and duties, ones God and his church had bade him to exercise. [He said that] when it comes to one's terrible responsibility before God's judgment seat, no human authority is in a position to dissuade the bishops from their way of proceeding. One must obey God rather than human beings. The Almighty God manages all things for the well-being of his church. Martyrdom is the flowering of the church.

On 7 November the government appointed its own special commissioner whose approval was needed for any directive from the archbishop to be valid, and it threatened legal punishment for the promulgation, implementation, or overt recognition of any unauthorized directive, because such a thing would disrupt public confidence and order. On 11 November the archbishop nevertheless issued a pastoral letter to all the priests and faithful of his archbishopric, justifying his own way of proceeding, and on 14 November he pronounced the excommunication of the special commissioner as well as the council with oversight of the Catholic Church. In a circular letter on 14 November the government elaborated further on the state's right of oversight as applicable to the Catholic Church. It henceforth proceeded, by imprisonment and monetary penalties, secular prohibitions and the like, to take steps against those who respect the archbishop's commands more highly than they do the royal legislation. In response the archbishop imposed suspension and other ecclesiastical punishments on clerics who complied with the secular directive as opposed to his own commands. In the end the government decided to bring charges against the archbishop for resisting the authority of the state. Yet this also had no further consequences. The archbishop persisted in his stance and the government entered into negotiations with the pope. From this entire controversy people saw clearly that a Protestant government, after conceding so much in the meantime to the Catholic Church, and constantly dodging as much as possible the issue of principle, or else just making capricious decisions, now lacked any firm ground for forcefully and decisively, according to definite principles, taking steps against the effrontery of the Catholic clergy.[79]

The Württemberg Concordat and the Baden Concordat

Before this controversy could be resolved, the government of Württemberg concluded a concordat with Rome. The occasion for this concordat was the same conflict that in Baden put the state and the church in such an agitated condition. The Württemberg government had participated in the Karlsruhe conference, but from the outset was more inclined to be flexible. It entered into negotiations with the Roman See, aiming at more specific provisions for the Catholic Church's relation to the authority of the state. The result was an agreement made on 8 April 1857, which was then also officially published in no. 16 of the 1857 government newspaper, as the papal bull *Cum in sublimi Principis Apostolorum cathedra*. Incidentally, the official term for it is "convention," not "concordat," because the Roman Curia does not in fact conclude a "concordat" with a Protestant government, for it deems such a government to be heretical.

The contents of this so-called concordat principally, and almost exclusively, concern the position of the realm's bishops. Heretofore the official activities of a bishop were not only inherently limited in scope, but were also

---

79. [*Baur*] Noteworthy publications about this controversy include: J. B. Hirscher, *Zur Orientierung über den derzeitigen Kirchenzeit* (Freiburg, 1854); H. Ewald, *An die deutschen Bischöfe und Erzbischöfe päpstlichen Glaubens* (Göttingen, 1854); L. A. Warnkönig, *Der Conflict des Episcopats der oberrheinischen Kirchenprovinz mit Regierungen* (Erlangen, 1853). Each of the three represents a standpoint of its own. Hirscher's thesis is that the church is absolutely free and autonomous, and the state has nothing to dictate to it; that conflicts between church and state are to be resolved simply according to the saying, "One must obey God rather than human beings." Since the bishop represents the cause of God, and counts much the same as God, the plain meaning of that saying is that "one must obey the church, i.e. the bishop, rather than the state." With its thesis, the second publication cries out to the bishop: "You are absolutely in the wrong; you are a false Christian; you simply set out to negate Protestantism and the whole of Christianity. Away with you; you surely cannot compete any longer with the Protestants in scientific matters." The thesis of the third publication deals partly with the church, partly with the state. It grants that the state also has to dictate to the church in some things, because otherwise it could not be a state with police powers, something it must be. The important thing is therefore to set apart and spell out what the state can concede to the church without detriment to its police powers.

bound by conditions set by the state, ones that assured the government's significant influence [on them]. Now things were to be essentially different. The government relinquished the prince's consent to all purely ecclesiastical arrangements. [Church] authorities and the people can communicate freely with the bishop and with the Roman See. All church edicts can be published without prior scrutiny and approval by the government. In place of the previous formal oath for the bishop there is a new one, in which the person chosen of course swears obedience and loyalty to the prince "as befits a bishop," but which makes no mention at all of obedience to the laws of the land. Stipulations as to the election of the bishop and a member of the cathedral chapter remain in essence as they were; yet in these cases the government relinquishes the right to confirm cathedral chapter membership and other positions. The powers of clerical ordinaries increase in proportion to their decreasing dependence on the state. The bishop has the right to grant all the clergy's livings that are not subject to a legally acquired patronage; that is, of the 521 livings previously granted by the crown, the bishop confers 184, more than one third. In addition, the bishop has the right to regulate and to administer the examinations for acceptance into the theological seminary, and for admission to pastoral care positions, without any government participation; to ordain clergymen as well as bestowing the official titles he himself assigns to them; to regulate the canonical orders in accord with all that involves worship and religious practices; to summon and hold diocesan synods, and to attend provincial councils, without the need for the prince's approval for or supervision of them; to introduce into his diocese religious orders and congregations approved by the pope, although in each instance he shall make arrangements for this with the government.

Also especially important are the stipulations about the legal authority, or punitive power, given to the bishops over the clergy and the laity. The scope of this legal authority is surely inconsistent with the proper concept of the state. Legal or punitive authority is inherently important for the state, but it can only be exercised on behalf of the state, and for that reason it can only be exercised according to the state's laws and under the state's control. Also, according to the concordat, the subjects of the church are at the same time subjects of the state; so it is therefore in the state's interest to see that they are not subjected to courts and laws over which the state itself has no say. The same also holds good regarding censorship affecting the laity. The state cannot be indifferent if a bishop ostensibly issues church directives that infringe on the rights of citizens, and if he seeks to compel obedience to such directives by church-administered punishments.

In fact the concordat even goes very extensively into educational affairs, also with reference to the university. In their teaching office, the members of the Catholic theological faculty are under the control of the bishop. He can grant them permission to teach theology and can rescind that permission at his own discretion; he can receive [their] professions of faith, examine their publications and textbooks, and so forth. We see clearly, from these and other stipulations, what a significant portion of its essential rights and interests the state has forfeited so as not to step on the toes, not so much of the Catholic Church as a whole, but rather just those of the bishop and the Roman Curia.

The concordat will nevertheless become the topic of public deliberations, since, owing to its conflicting with the charter of the constitution, it cannot become legally valid without the approval of the estates of the realm. In the meantime several persons have publicly expressed their views about it, ones who, to the extent they come from the Protestant side, could only express their regret and consternation about it.[80]

Especially noteworthy is the treatise by Dr. Otto Mejer, the consistory councilor and professor of law at Rostock.[81] He says about the new concordat that, in its overall character, it is undoubtedly a document of surrender by the Württemberg government, a victory of the Roman Catholic Church over the Protestant state. For, despite its professed parity of the confessions, Württemberg is actually a Protestant state. This character of a surrender is already outwardly apparent from the fact that the entire concordat consists of one-sided promises by the government, only here and there interrupted by a concession on the part of the church. If one did not see this, it would nevertheless become clear by looking back to the deliberations in 1807. For, of all the negotiating points between church and state remaining at issue back then, there are now none that are not conceded to the Roman view and, where possible, to the formulas secured by the church. On more than one of the points the nuncio was willing to yield back then, whereas today it is the state that has yielded. Back then the church had not held itself aloof, and the consequences of its position, if there were any, now no longer hold good. It is very regrettable that in recent times public officials are so little aware of ecclesiastical matters, and from the outset allow themselves to be captive to the Roman Church.

---

80. [*Baur, in the text*] The treatise, *Das württembergische Concordat und seine Folgen* (Jena, 1857), special reprint from the newspaper *Minerva* (1857) vols. 1 and 2.2, very clearly and fundamentally illumines the different perspectives about it to be considered. See also: A. L. Reyscher, *Das österreichische und das württembergische Concordat nebst den separaten Zugeständnisse vergleichen und beleuchtet*, 2nd ed. (1858); Hofacker, *Das Württembergische Concordat* (Stuttgart, 1860).

81. [*Baur, in the text*] *Die Concordatsverhandlungen Württemberg's vom J. 1807* (Stuttgart, 1859), 79.

Mejer shows in particular how the concordat stands with respect to Protestantism.[82] The Roman Church, by not recognizing the Protestant Church at all, simply reckons Protestants to be baptized persons and declares them to be subject to its own episcopal jurisdiction, as belonging to the Catholic parishes in which they live and as those it must work to convert from heresy. In 1807, in its negotiations with Rome, the government stuck to the position that such notions will not hold good in Württemberg; that people have insisted on a formulation acknowledging that the newly instituted church order pertains merely to the king's Catholic subjects. The negotiations in 1819 involved this same intention on the part of the government. When the pope, in his bull of 1821, included not merely Catholics but all Christian inhabitants of Württemberg as diocesans of the bishopric of Rottenburg, the government did not ignore that; and when, in the bull of 1827, total authority was expressly assigned to the bishop, the government, upon the bull's publication, not merely invalidated this measure but also preserved the appropriate rights of the Protestant confession and church. What in the bull was contrary to this was also said to be invalid. This proviso would put an end to the concordat. For it would contradict article 4 of the concordat, according to which the bishop, in administering his diocese, has the freedom to exercise all the rights belonging to him by dint of his ecclesiastical pastorate, and to direct, according to canonical precepts, all that pertains to worship and those religious practices that have for their purpose the awakening and strengthening of the pious sensibilities of the faithful. These rights touch on the duties it is still necessary to carry out in accord with Catholic conceptions in relation to Protestants, but duties that [only] involve Catholics.

After the Württemberg proceedings, Baden too then thought it ought hesitate no longer about concluding a concordat. The date of the Baden concordat is 28 June 1859. As is well-known, it has provided even greater dissatisfaction and opposition than the Württemberg concordat did and, like it, will become the object of parliamentary deliberations. In comparing the too concordats, at the conclusion of his book Hofacker [n. 80] states that, if we ask which of the two concordats better preserves the rights of the crown and its sovereignty, the comparable position of the other branches of religion, and confessional tranquility, we can only say that, whichever one chooses, they both set aside these rights and do so almost to the same degree. On most points they are in verbal agreement, and they differ only owing to local circumstances.

---

82. [*Baur, in the text*] Ibid., 91.

The Baden concordat is drawn up with greater attention to the rights of the church, and it displays even greater subservience to the church's authority. It almost entirely obscures the bishop's status as a subject [of the state], makes even greater concessions regarding the educational system, and subjects all teachers at the University of Freiburg to a kind of censorship by church authorities. Two declarations by instructors at the University of Freiburg are pertinent to this last point. First, the memorandum of 1 December 1859, signed by eighteen university professors and two teaching associates, and concerning freedom of instruction at the University of Freiburg; and second, the memorandum by Protestant professors of Baden's Provincial University of Freiburg. In a codicil to the concordat, the government has given assurance to the archbishop that, in the future, any eventual complaints he may lodge against teachers at the university, against those said to clash in their instruction with Catholic teaching on faith and morals, shall be given every possible consideration on the part of the government. Because of this, the authors of the two aforementioned memoranda complain that, if control over lectures at the university is given to the archbishop, that will in fact put an end to freedom of instruction. The Protestant professors especially emphasize that, in their own instruction, they will be subject to the supervisory judgments of a church authority foreign to them, one fundamentally at odds with their own religious confession.[83]

F. Concluding Remarks

Up to this point we have followed the course of the major phenomena that determine the character of this period. It is not possible to go more specifically into individual instances, and for our purposes it is not necessary to do so. Nevertheless we might append a few matters from the particular histories of individual countries.

Spain, Portugal, and Italy

In the authentically Catholic countries of Spain and Portugal, the clergy was fully involved in the conflict of the political factions battling one another there.

---

83. At this point there follows a very long footnote composed by Zeller, to which he gives the heading "Further History of the Concordats in Southern Germany." In it he sets forth developments in Baden and Württemberg, going forward from 1860, as well as providing substantial discussion of events in Hesse-Darmstadt, Electoral Hesse, and Nassau.

After the death of King Ferdinand VII [of Spain], Queen Christina and their daughter succeeded him as heads of the government.[84] Christina only secured the throne with the help of the liberals, and by suspending the Salic Law. She did so in opposition to Don Carlos,[85] the legitimate heir to the throne, who was supported by the clergy acting under the name of the apostolic party. In the course of the civil war the state found it necessary to close cloisters in ever greater numbers. In 1837 it also abolished the tithe [tax] and declared all church landed estates to be the property of the state, by decision of the Cortes. After the nuncio of Gregory XVI had been expelled from the land by the regent, Espartero,[86] on account of his protests, the pope in a formal statement in March 1841 proclaimed his verdict that all the church-robbing decisions of the Spanish government were invalidated. This threatened a complete break with Rome. But before matters got to that point, and after Espartero's downfall, the government thought reconciliation with the pope would be a good thing. It reinstated the banished priests and recognized papal entitlements with regard to Spain. The ecclesiastical estates that were still recoverable it restored to the church. Since then reconciliation with the pope has been even more complete. The pope consented to all this in the concordat of 1851.[87]

In Portugal, Dom Miguel, the usurper under whom the clergy had total authority, was deposed by Dom Pedro just because Dom Pedro advocated the cause of freedom.[88] A decree of 28 May 1834 disbanded all the religious orders, confiscated all monastic properties, and abolished the tithe. In Dom Pedro's 1834 address on the opening day of the Cortes, he expressed his views about these matters as follows. He said when we consider the relation of these institutions to religion, we see that the religious orders have taken them completely away from the original spirit in which

---

84. Ferdinand VII, king of Spain, 1819–33; Maria Christina, queen (1833–43) and regent (1833–40) for Isabella II, who was queen 1843–70.

85. Don Carlos was the second son of King Charles IV, and brother of Ferdinand. The Salic Law that Maria Christina suspended had mandated an exclusively male succession to the throne.

86. Baldomero Espartero (1792–1879) was appointed the regent for Isabella in 1840, after Maria Christina had been driven into exile in France. In 1843 an insurrection resulted in Espartero losing power.

87. Zeller adds a brief note at this point, calling attention to the Spanish government's support for the papacy since 1859.

88. See p. 118, n. 24, and p. 133, n. 47. Dom Pedro, Emperor of Brazil, briefly ruled Portugal in 1826 as "the Liberator" before abdicating in favor of his 7-year-old daughter Donna Maria in order to return to Brazil. Two years later, Maria's throne was usurped by Dom Miguel, Pedro's younger brother. In 1832, Pedro came back to Portugal and in 1834 overthrew the usurper. He died a few months later of tuberculosis.

they were founded. They have been managed almost exclusively in line with the propensity for temporal and worldly interests that they profess to disdain. Viewed in political terms, they are corporate bodies estranged from the nation, indifferent to the well-being and woes of their fellow citizens, and zealous servants of any despotic and tyrannical regime, if only they can expect its favor and respect. Portugal in large measure owes the troubles it has so recently undergone to the impact of these bodies on individuals and families, an influence that in many cases has been all the more dangerous when it was exerted covertly. In return, the usurper driven from Portugal was received in Rome as a king. Yet even in this case people on both sides shied away from a complete break. In 1842, via promises on each side, the relationship was already so extensively established that Queen Donna Maria gained the pope as her godfather and, in doing so, received from him the gift of the golden rose. Three bishops nominated by the government were then canonically installed in April 1843.

In Italy, already before the recent events there described above, tension existed between the Sardinian government and the pope because of the Siccardian legislation that had abolished the clerical *privilegium fori* (special political law). Justice Minister Siccardi had this law enacted in the chamber in 1850 in order, in the explicit legal framework of the state, to bring about the equality of citizens under the law. Other privileges were also taken from the clergy, and cloisters were closed.[89] Because of his recalcitrance the archbishop of Turin was expelled from the country. The pope protested and threatened excommunication. Yet on this occasion the pope did not act on the threat.

France

In France, as a result of the July Revolution and the revision of the charter undertaken then, the article referring to the Catholic Church as the state religion was altered, so that now, in a word, the charter statement stood as merely a statistical notice: that the majority of the French people profess the Catholic religion. The wish in doing so was to make a concession placating the Protestants. So the Catholic religion supposedly lost any claim to dominance, and the freedom of the cultus was supposedly sanctioned to the greatest extent to which that could be done in relation to Catholicism.

The church knew how to manage quite well in conjunction with the Republic of 1848. The Republic's constitution assured the protection of each

---

89. [*Zeller*] In the way this has now also happened in Naples, after its unification with Sardinia.

cultus, and the priests had no intention of giving their blessing to the growth of freedom, and of praying for the sovereign people. In the battle with the socialists in June 1848, the archbishop of Paris had taken to the barricades. Also, the clergy was certainly satisfied with the May 1850 law governing instruction. It knew it was in good standing with Louis Napoleon, for it had contributed so much to his rise to power. He found this so commendable that he restored the Pantheon to the cultus as the Church of St. Genovese, and he returned the pope to Rome.[90] The concordat of 1801 also carries even more weight now.

Switzerland

In Switzerland, several smaller bishoprics standing directly under Rome had been established. This was done in the interest of the Roman hierarchy. However, after the 1830 revolution, public sensibilities about this now tended in the opposite direction. The articles of the Baden conference were especially important in this regard.

In January 1834, because of these articles, the diets of Lucerne, Bern, Aargau, Thurgau, St. Gallen, the Basel district, and Zürich came together to set up a national metropolitan confederation, for the purpose of better preserving the rights of the state authorities in matters of the church and the rights of the episcopates, over against encroachments by Rome. Although the decisions at issue deviated in no essentials from the rights of the established church holding good in most other Catholic countries, Gregory condemned them in May 1835, in a circular letter sent to the Swiss clergy, as being false, audacious, and wrong, as diminishing the rights of the Holy See, as destructive to the governance of the church and its divine institution, as subjecting the ecclesiastical function to secular power, as of course deriving from repudiated teachings, as headed toward all sorts of heresies and as schismatic.

The entire Ultramontane army of the faithful in the Confederation was activated in order to give suitable emphasis to this statement by the pope. Even in Aargau the Ultramontanes, in concert with the Jesuits in Switzerland, continually incited the Catholic population against the government, specifically to bring about a separation of the Catholic part of the canton from the Protestant part. After there had been a constitutional revision along the lines of the Baden conference articles, the Ultramontane faction

---

90. Zeller adds at this point a lengthy footnote about more recent tension besetting this era of good understanding between the state and the pope, arising from the French emperor's involvement in the Italian political situation.

dared to rebel openly, but the rebels were put down. Since the Aargau cloisters had in fact fostered and concocted the uprising, the government right away decided to do away with the eight cloisters, including the wealthy Muri cloister, founded by the house of the Habsburgs, and to convert its properties to the general functions of instruction and public charity. Action to reestablish the cloisters guaranteed by the compact of the confederation was then a continual issue for the federation diet, until the majority of the twelve cantons declared itself satisfied with the Aargau compromise, that three nunneries should be reestablished. The rest of the most recent church history of Switzerland is wholly connected with the history of the Jesuits.[91]

---

91. Zeller adds here a footnote about a new constitutional system for the canton of St. Gallen, a conciliatory arrangement leaving church affairs to the church and public education in the hands of the state, with a Catholic and Protestant advisory council.

3

The History of the Protestant Church

Catholicism always takes us to foreign lands in which it is more or less the sole religion. As the most recent history of Protestantism shows, it has the soil of its many-faceted and momentous development solely in Germany. We set the theological dimension apart from the ecclesiastical aspect and treat it first, because the distinctive principle at work in Protestantism resides in the theological dimension.

A. The History of Theology

Hegel: The General Character of His System

What we have emphasized as the distinctive character of the most recent period—the sharpening of antitheses, the orientation to principle, the striving for systematic completion, in order to pursue what hitherto remained undeveloped and indeterminate to its highest level and to bring it insofar as possible to a clear and specific conception—appears before our eyes in its first major manifestation, that of the Hegelian philosophy, for which reason we accord the latter the universal importance it has for this most recent epoch. Hegel[1] had worked most diligently for a long time in developing

---

1. Georg Wilhelm Friedrich Hegel (1770–1831) culminated the series of great German idealist philosophers beginning with Kant and continuing on through Fichte and Schelling. Hegel's system (logic, nature, spirit) was the most brilliant and comprehensive of all that were produced in the nineteenth century, and it continues to resonate today. During his lifetime he published only four books (*Phenomenology of Spirit* [1807], *Science of Logic* [1812–16], *Encyclopedia of the Philosophical Sciences* [1817, 1827, 1830], and *Philosophy of Right* [1821]), but the lectures he gave on a variety of topics in Berlin during the 1820s (logic and metaphysics, world history, ethics, art, religion, history of philosophy) became available when his collected works began to be published shortly after his death in 1831. Of decisive importance for Baur was the *Vorlesungen über die*

his system. For a number of years indeed people understood him to be the most important philosopher, as compared to Schelling who had had almost nothing to say, at least so far as major publications were concerned.[2] The overwhelming impact of Hegel's philosophy first began to be felt in the latter years of his activity in Berlin, indeed fundamentally so right after his death in 1831, and especially following the publication of his collected works,[3] which drew such general attention to his philosophy that it could come to be considered the dominant philosophy at that time.

The distinctiveness and the greatness of Hegel's philosophy is that in it the development of German philosophy—which took its point of departure from Kant, advanced further because of Fichte and Schelling, and had an orientation arising from how they reciprocally influenced each other—reached its culmination and arrived at that very unity prevailing as a matter of course. Hegel's system is the necessary consequence of the systems preceding it, which serve as its necessary presupposition. Hence, simply based on this entire context, this period came to be conceived as such an important period for the history of philosophy.

This period is idealistic, given how, since Kant, each philosophy self-aware of its task can only take up the standpoint of idealism, from which standpoint all existing being has its truth and actuality solely for consciousness; solely in the self-consciousness of the I, or self, knowing itself as the absolute subject. However, this philosophy is also pantheistic,[4] in the sense in which we can call it the reversal, grounded in Schelling, from the subjectivity of idealism to the objectivity of nature,[5] which is identical with God.

Philosophie der Religion, edited by Philipp Marheineke (Berlin, 1832); a second edition appeared in 1840 edited by Bruno Bauer, but Baur favored the first edition. The critical edition is edited by Walter Jaeschke, 3 vols. (Hamburg, 1983–85); ET: *Lectures on the Philosophy of Religion*, ed. Peter C. Hodgson; trans. R. F. Brown, P. C. Hodgson, and J. M. Stewart, 3 vols. (Berkeley and Los Angeles, 1984–87, reprint Oxford, 2007). The philosophy of religion is the only Hegel text with which Baur seems to have been thoroughly familiar.

2. Schelling continued to teach in Munich until he was called to Berlin in 1841, but he published virtually nothing after 1815. His Berlin lectures on the philosophy of mythology and revelation, discussed by Baur later in this section, appeared posthumously, beginning in 1856. See p. 68, n. 46.

3. *Werke. Vollständige Ausgabe durch einen Verein von Freunden des Verewigten* (Berlin, 1832ff.). The first critical edition of Hegel's works is being published during our lifetime: *Gesammelte Werke*, ed. by the Academy of Sciences of North Rhine-Westphalia in association with the Deutsche Forschungsgemeinschaft, 40 vols. projected (Hamburg, 1968ff.).

4. On Baur's use of the terms "pantheistic" and "pantheism," see p. 76, n. 63.

5. In Schelling's philosophy of nature, nature is the absolute's worldly (non-subjective) self-expression.

For we now have the two together, both idealism and pantheism. The actual character of this position consists in these two forms of philosophy posited together as the two sides of the same unity—the objective and subjective dimensions, the universe and the I, God and world, understood as a living process of self-mediation.

The basic idea of Hegel's philosophy is that of the immanent process, moving forward from moment to moment via the concept of the matter itself. Hence this idea posits its distinctive character in the method by which speculative thinking just applies itself to the objective course given by the nature of the matter itself. As the phenomenology of consciousness, Hegel's philosophy sets out from sensible consciousness, but of course seeks to demonstrate the inner drive and immanent necessity within sensible consciousness by which consciousness is driven on from one moment or stage to another so that, by proceeding through all the shapes of consciousness, until by grasping itself in its own presupposition, it finds its absolute resting point in the absolute. However, this is only one side of spirit's process, of the sphere in which Hegel's philosophy operates. The other side has its point of departure in the absolute itself.[6]

The absolute would not have been what is truly absolute if it had not, as the absolute spirit, been its own immanent movement; if it did not determine itself as being the finite and being finite consciousness, so that, as unity of the finite and the infinite it has the finite not outside itself but instead within itself, as the necessary element of its own mediation with itself. God, or the absolute, determines itself as absolute spirit because the principle of movement can only become known in the essential nature (*Wesen*) of thinking, inasmuch as God, or the absolute spirit, is also the thinking spirit. Without the principle of movement, God would not have been the living process of self-mediation. Thinking is essentially distinguishing. Thus God is the thinking spirit, and so God distinguishes himself from himself,[7] objectifies himself, sets an other over against himself, one that is not him-

---

6. Hegel's *Phenomenology of Spirit* sets out from sensible consciousness and moves through all the shapes of consciousness (consciousness, self-consciousness, reason, spirit), until it reaches absolute knowing. Hegel's *Science of Logic* constitutes the point of departure in the absolute itself (being, essence, concept, culminating in the absolute idea, which goes forth of its own accord into nature and finite spirit, and returns to itself as absolute spirit). Hegel's absolute entails an intensive relationality.

7. Baur and Hegel use the masculine personal pronoun (*er*), but both of them know that God is not a masculine person. God transcends gender and is not *a* person; as absolute spirit God is the intrinsic essence of personhood. Our languages do not allow us to express this easily. God is neither "he," "she," nor "it." The German reflexive pronoun *sich selbst* is not gendered, and it could be translated as "godself," but using this term frequently seems awkward.

self but an other he knows himself to be one with and with which he must come together in unity, because the absolute is the absolute only as the unity embracing everything and comprehending everything within itself. In this view we have of course the most universal categories and moments that determine the overall articulation of Hegel's system.

Hegel's *Philosophy of Religion*

We are just going to look specifically at the impact of Hegel's philosophy on theology. The prevailing direction theology had taken was that of Schleiermacher. Hence theology for the time being had resisted Hegel's philosophy, indeed took a form directly antithetical to it. Schleiermacher's *Glaubenslehre*[8] and Hegel's *Philosophy of Religion* occupied two essentially different standpoints. Whereas for Schleiermacher the entire content of religion is the immediate expression of consciousness, for Hegel it is all the explication of the idea of God. Thus the major difference between these reciprocal standpoints becomes prominent, first and foremost, with regard to the idea of God.

For Schleiermacher, the idea of God is the most general and emptiest of abstractions; for Hegel, it has the most concrete content. According to Hegel, God is not abstract, utter unity, but is the concrete unity that also has difference within itself; God is the self-movement of the idea, the immanent process of self-mediation. Hence for Hegel, God is essentially the threefold one (*der Dreieinige*), according to the three moments in which spirit's essential being explicates itself.[9] For Schleiermacher, on the contrary, the idea of the Trinity just has a merely external, purely formal significance. The concept of religion provides further specificity to this difference in their respective standpoints.

Schleiermacher takes the concept of religion in a wholly subjective way when he defines religion as the feeling of utter dependence. Hegel says straight out that religion is not a matter of the human being [as such], for it is essentially the highest determination of the absolute idea itself.[10] In other words, religion is the self-consciousness of God or absolute spirit; it is di-

---

8. See Baur's extensive discussion of this work in Part Two.

9. The three moments are identity, difference, and mediation; or in theological terms, the kingdoms of the Father, the Son, and the Spirit. The Trinity constitutes the basic structure of Hegel's *Philosophy of Religion*, whereas it is treated in an appendix in Schleiermacher's *Glaubenslehre*.

10. *Lectures on the Philosophy of Religion* (n. 1) [subsequently *LPR*], 1:318 (1824 lectures). See the whole of Hegel's discussion of "the speculative concept of religion" in the 1824 lectures, 1:314–64.

vine spirit's knowing itself through the mediation of finite spirit.[11] As Hegel defines it, religion is spirit self-aware of its own essential nature. Spirit is conscious, and what it is conscious of is the truly essential spirit, which is its own essential nature and not the essence of something other than it. This rests on the fact that God as spirit is simply *for* spirit, reveals himself in finite spirit, and is spirit's consciousness of itself, of its own essential nature, is itself God's self-consciousness. What God is as spirit—distinguishing himself from himself, being object to himself, but in this distinguishing being utterly identical with himself—also constitutes the content of religion. Religion is thus the way spirit relates to itself, as both finite spirit's knowing its oneness with the absolute—in short the elevation[12] of finite consciousness to its absolute content, in which it is superseded as finite—and also absolute spirit's own knowing of itself as being one with itself in finite consciousness.

Schleiermacher locates the essence of religion in feeling, and does so in order to designate religion as something actually belonging directly to a human being's own nature. Hegel's antithetical position essentially appears in his contesting this principal thesis of Schleiermacher's *Glaubenslehre*. Hegel says that what is rooted simply in my feeling is only something *for me* and *not* something that is *in itself*. God's roots are not merely in feeling; God is not merely *my* God.[13] People speak of a religious feeling, and say that belief in God is given to us in feeling; that feeling is the innermost ground for our absolute certainty that God exists. However, feeling can have the most diverse contents. The most contradictory and the most degrading things find a place in feeling, as well as what is highest and most noble. If God is in feeling he takes no precedence there over what is most disreputable, for the most regal flower sprouts from the same soil alongside the rankest weed. That something is a content in feeling does not make it something excellent. For our feeling involves not just what exists, is sheerly real and existent, but also what is imaginary and fictitious—all the good and all the bad things, all that is real and unreal.

Feeling is therefore the form in which the content is posited as completely contingent. So if God's existence or being is demonstrated in our feeling, that makes it just as contingent as anything else to which this kind of existence can be applicable. We call this subjectivity, but subjectivity in the worst sense of the term.

11. *LPR*, 1:318.

12. On the theme of "elevation" (*Erhebung*), see the 1827 lectures in *LPR*, 1:414–41. (Marheineke's edition of 1832 blended together passages from transcriptions of the lectures of 1824, 1827, and 1831.)

13. Hegel discusses "feeling" (*Gefühl*) in both the 1824 and the 1827 lectures, *LPR*, 1:268–76, 390–96.

Furthermore, feeling is something human beings have in common with animals; it is the animal, sensuous form [of consciousness]. Therefore when what justice is, or morality, or God, gets exhibited in feeling, this is the worst way in which such a content can be demonstrated. God *is* essentially in thinking. We must of course get beyond the suspicion that because God exists in thinking God exists *only* in thinking. This suspicion arises because human beings alone have religion, and animals do not.[14]

Nevertheless, Hegel even states in turn that God is also said to be in my feeling, in my heart.[15] People express the point that God is said to be not merely something I picture to myself, but rather something inseparably one with me. I should be characterized as I actually am, and so it is essential that all true content be in feeling, in the heart. Accordingly, what is in fact the difference between Schleiermacher and Hegel? It can only be the following. For Schleiermacher, religion as feeling is so very much the substantial essence of religion, that the nature of religion is something completely insignificant if it is deprived of this immediacy and made into the specificity of the concept. For him, the main thing is always just the purely subjective element in religion. According to Hegel, religion of course must also be subjective, but that is the least important thing that can be said about it. In saying that, one does not yet know what religion essentially is. What it is objectively can only be the topic of its thoughtful examination. Hence religion has its essential element not in feeling but in thinking, in the thinking consciousness in which the meaning of the idea of God is made clear in Hegel's sense.[16]

Does anyone want to deny the fact that all feelings without something objectively true as their basis are lacking in value? Whatever the weight one might place on the fact that *I* have this feeling, that *I* am the subject experiencing the feeling in this specific way, this assertion can only hold good where the I is the one and all. However, this subjective element also certainly has something objective outside and beyond it. Thus Hegel says this calls for a standpoint where the I in its singularity (because the I as such is surely the I just for itself, something singular just for itself) relinquishes itself in fact and actuality. I must be the particular subjectivity that has in fact been superseded. Thus I must recognize something objective that in fact counts as true for me, something recognized as affirmative that is posited for me;

---

14. Hegel writes (*LPR*, 1:273): "God *is* essentially in thought. The suspicion that God is only for thought, through thought, and in thought must at once arise because only human beings, not animals, have religion, and humanity distinguishes itself from animals by thought."

15. *LPR*, 1:274.

16. On religion and thought, see the 1827 lectures in *LPR*, 1:403–41.

something objective in which I am negated as this [aforementioned] I but which at the same time involves my freedom. If in fact something objective is said to be recognized [in the I], then that involves the I being determined as universal, simply counting as something universal in me.

This is the standpoint of thinking reason, and religion is itself this act or activity of thinking reason and rational thinking, taking itself as singular and positing itself as universal—superseding itself as singular so as to find its true self as what is universal. The I knows itself as universal, and this universal factor is God as absolute spirit. But it belongs to the essential nature of absolute spirit that it determines itself as being finite, subjective spirit, and in finite spirit it knows itself as identical with itself, has in it consciousness of itself, which consciousness is also in turn finite spirit's own consciousness of itself and of its oneness with God. Accordingly, religion is not feeling, but instead is thinking, and that difference obviously accounts for distinct positions that Schleiermacher and Hegel respectively assign to the philosophy of religion.

For Schleiermacher, philosophy has nothing at all to do with religion. Religion is what it is purely on its own, a distinctive sphere existing for its own sake. Although reflection plays a role in it by taking up into thinking consciousness the testimonies of religious consciousness, religion in its immediacy always retains an absolute standing of its own. In facing all of philosophy's claims to validity, Schleiermacher's theology of feeling can, in the final analysis, always appeal once again to one's own immediate self-consciousness. This is the true sense of the thesis that religion is neither knowing nor doing, but is instead simply a determination of feeling.

Now Hegel also of course grants religion its place in feeling. But what religion is as feeling loses it absolute significance as soon as thinking divests it of its immediacy. The main thing is then no longer what religion is subjectively, but instead what it is objectively, from the standpoint of thinking reason, at which point God is known as absolute spirit and is explicated in the idea of his essential nature. As Hegel expressly maintains, philosophy and religion have the same content, with their difference being only a matter of their form.[17] Philosophy, which operates in the element of thinking, of

---

17. In the 1824 lectures, *LPR*, 1:333: "It is the distinctive task of philosophy to transmute the *content* that is in the representation of religion into the *form* of thought; the content [itself] cannot be distinguished. Religion is the self-consciousness of absolute spirit: there are not two kinds of self-consciousness—not both a conceptualizing self-consciousness and a representing self-consciousness, which could be distinguished according to their content. There can only be a diversity in form, or a distinction between *representation* and *thought*." Because the content of religion (theology) and philosophy is the same—namely God, or absolute spirit—Hegel is able to say in his 1821 lecture manuscript that "philosophy *is* theology, and [one's] occupation with philosophy—or

pure thought, must separate out, and exclude, from its content all that just belongs to the sensible mode of representation (*Vorstellung*). Philosophy's form can only be that of the concept (*Begriff*) adequate to the matter itself. In contrast, religion operates in the sphere of sheer representation. Thus everything distinguishing representation from concept[18] also constitutes the difference of religion from philosophy.

However, as distinct from the concept, representation is the concept still bound up with sensible elements. In order to rise up to the concept, representation still must become cleansed of, and freed from, these sensible elements. Representation is linked to intuition (*Anschauung*), to the given in its empirical reality. What these elements involve, representation can only express in pictorial form, and much of it is fantasy and feeling. What the concept is in the unity and totality of its moments is something representation portrays only in one aspect or another, in a specific connection, only relatively and subjectively. Representation is only the reflection in which the pure light that is the concept's element appears in the most manifold hues. The most general distinction we must draw, in defining the relation between religion and philosophy, given all the identity of their content, is thus: the form of philosophy is the abstract concept, purified of all sensible elements; the form of religion is the concrete representation.

However, if this is religion's relation to philosophy, then proceeding from representation to the concept thus necessarily requires stripping away from representation all it has that is in itself sensuous and inadequate, and lifting out from it its pure thought-content (*Gedankeninhalt*). Schleiermacher's *Glaubenslehre* itself shows how impossible it is to stick, as a rule, with the immediacy of feeling, with sheer representation. Whatever superiority the *Glaubenslehre* may assume vis-à-vis philosophy, and however much it protests against any interference on philosophy's part, philosophy is nevertheless everywhere evident in it, and indeed in a very specific form, as a specific view of the relation of God to the world.[19] This entire relationship cannot be viewed merely as the expression of feeling and of immediate self-consciousness. Also, when one regards many doctrines and theses as of no concern to religion, and may banish them from religion into philosophy, in the final analysis one still always returns to issues on which speculative thinking alone can render a decision, and on which it is insufficient merely to appeal to feeling as the essence of religion.

---

rather *in* philosophy—is of itself the service of God" (*LPR*, 1:84).

18. On this distinction see *LPR*, 1:328–36 (1824 lectures), 396–406 (1827 lectures).

19. Friedrich Schleiermacher, *Der christliche Glaube*, 2nd ed. (Berlin, 1830), §§50–51; ET: *Christian Faith*, 2 vols., trans. T. N. Tice, C. L. Kelsey, and E. Lawler (Louisville, 2016), 1:279–92.

Accordingly, Hegel has just expressed clearly and consistently what Schleiermacher too must indeed have presupposed. Hegel's philosophy of religion is the necessary progression if, with thoughtful consideration, one has also simply gone on to where Schleiermacher himself had been unwilling to go.[20] This very consistency of the concept is then, however, also what springs from a standpoint essentially different from Schleiermacher's standpoint. According to this other standpoint, religion stands in a subordinate relationship with philosophy, and everything that belongs to religion's content receives its truth only in the philosophy of religion and speculative theology.[21] There is no "double truth,"[22] for there can be nothing true in religion and theology that philosophy must not also recognize as truth.

Since Hegel considers the world's entire development from the perspective of a process developing itself from moment to moment, Christianity too can be grasped simply as a specific moment of this process. Hence in his philosophy of religion Hegel assigned Christianity its specific place in the history of religion. In doing so, Hegel also established in speculative terms the fact that Christianity is nothing utterly suprarational or supernatural—a point rationalism had already expressed as its own principle, and one Schleiermacher's *Glaubenslehre* had made its basic presupposition and grounded dialectically in its own fashion.[23] For how, in the context of a process in which everything is conditioned by the necessity of the self-moving concept, could absolute miracle have found a place? The apparatus for a speculative theology, which is already unmistakable in Schleiermacher's *Glaubenslehre*, Hegel built up into a self-enclosed system.

The Hegelian School and "Positive Philosophy"

As soon as Hegel's philosophy became well-known, it not only found many opponents, but also aroused misgivings among those who, impressed by it themselves, could not at all events harmonize its consequences with their Christian religious interests. So the demand posed from this quarter was to go beyond Hegelian philosophy and from its pantheism to develop it further in terms of Christian theism. Schelling indeed seemed at that time to offer a

20. On the "progression" from Schleiermacher to Hegel, see p. 206, n. 72.

21. On the term "speculative," see p. 196, n. 64. Baur's "speculative theology," insofar as it can be discerned, is based on the Hegelian philosophy of religion. Baur does not appear to subordinate religion to philosophy in the way that Hegel's philosophy does. Rather, he regards religion as an independent and irreducible domain of human experience. In this respect Baur stands between Schleiermacher and Hegel.

22. On Hegel's critique of double truth, see *LPR*, 1:130–32.

23. See above, pp. 174–79.

way for doing so; at least that much was reported about his philosophy, the fact that people regarded it as suited for deliverance from the tyranny of the absolute concept and for reinstating a lasting peace between philosophy and religion.[24] Fichte, Weisse, Fischer,[25] and others were representatives of this orientation, which can be called "positive philosophy."

It is correct to locate the point of contention as wholly concerning the issue of personhood and comprising both the personal being of God and individual human beings as persons, with regard to their personal immortality. The issue of personal immortality got raised mainly by Richter's *Die Lehre von den letzten Dingen* (pt. 1, 1833; pt. 2, 1834),[26] and by an anonymous writing already having appeared in 1830, *Gedanken über Tod und Unsterblichkeit*, with Feuerbach later disclosed as being its author.[27] With reference to the latter work, Göschel[28] in particular made fruitless efforts to deflect the reproach directed at Hegel's philosophy, by his vain attempt, via several writings, to bring Hegelianism into agreement with Christian orthodoxy, an attempt gaining him dubious renown.

The main issue was the personhood of God. Since Hegel grasped the absolute simply as the idea maintaining itself in the process of what is finite,

---

24. During the 1840s Schelling gave lectures in Berlin on a new "positive" philosophy. Only after his death in 1854 were these lectures, on the philosophy of mythology and the philosophy of revelation, published in four volumes (1856–58).

25. Immanuel Hermann Fichte (1796–1879), son of J. G. Fichte, was a philosophical theist who defended the personality of God and was strongly opposed to the Hegelian school. From 1842 he taught in Tübingen, where he gave lectures on all philosophical topics. Christian Hermann Weisse (1801–66), initially a Hegelian, developed ideas closer to those of Schelling in his later years, and advanced (along with I. H. Fichte) a new speculative theism. He was the first theologian to propose (in 1838) the two-source hypothesis, which accorded priority to the Gospel of Mark along with a hypothetical sayings-source. Kuno Fischer (1824–1907) was a philosopher who taught in Jena and later in Heidelberg as successor to Zeller. The first volume of his major work, *Geschichte der neuern Philosophie*, appeared in 1852.

26. Friedrich Richter, *Die Lehre von den letzten Dingen*, 2 vols. (Breslau, 1833–34).

27. Ludwig Feuerbach (1804–72) was a post-Hegelian who advocated atheism and materialism. He is best known for his *Das Wesen des Christentums* (1841), translated into English by George Eliot as *The Essence of Christianity* (1854). His first book, *Gedanken über Tod und Unsterblichkeit*, published anonymously in 1830, was an attack on personal immortality; ET: *Thoughts on Death and Immortality*, trans. James A. Massey (Berkeley, 1980).

28. Karl Friedrich Göschel (1784–1861) was a Prussian jurist with an interest in theology. He wrote *Aphorismen über Nichtwissen und absolutes Wissen im Verhältnisse zur christlichen Glaubenserkenntniss* (Berlin, 1829), which Hegel reviewed in 1829 and quoted in the 1830 edition of his *Encyclopedia of the Philosophical Sciences*, §564. After Hegel died Göschel published *Der Monismus des Gedankens: Zur Apologie der gegenwärtigen Philosophie am Grabe ihres Stifters* (Naumburg, 1832).

Fichte objected that the oneness and identity with itself is nevertheless lacking in this process; yet to be instilled in this endlessly extending process is the simple, imperturbable eye (*Auge*), the steadfast self.[29] Strauss retorted to this that the absolute one and self *is* right in the endless other-becoming (*Anderswerden*); its movement within itself is likewise absolute rest; it of course possesses natural eyes and needs no implants [of its own], which could indeed have only been glass eyes.[30]

The decisive point, that the absolute must be personally individual, is something the positive philosophers of course always presupposed. But could one prove that by argument, for instance that there could have been nothing coherent in the world if God were not the original consciousness? That would just be the teleological argument for God's existence. However, absolute purposiveness is just the necessity of things themselves, and so one cannot, from the purposiveness of the world, infer an extra-worldly cause.

If the issue was how the personhood of the absolute is possible, then the thesis of Hegel's philosophy became generally understood as the affirmation that the absolute is actual only in its self-mediation, but that this mediation is not said to coincide with the bringing forth of the world. People then usually fell back on the Christian doctrine of the Trinity, although they did not know how to explain either the thorny points of this doctrine or the existence of the world. It is not worth the effort to linger any longer with this type of philosopher. After philosophy has defined the absolute as the unity of the finite and the infinite, if one wishes, in the interest of Christian theism, to set up yet another absolute above this absolute, then at least one ought not have passed this off as being philosophy.[31]

In any event the relation of Hegel's philosophy to Christianity and to Christian theology brings to mind still other, more profoundly engaging issues. For, based on this philosophy's speculative standpoint, from which

---

29. Immanuel Hermann Fichte, *Die Idee der Persönlichkeit und der individuellen Fortdauer* (Elberfeld, 1834), 36.

30. David Friedrich Strauss, *Die christliche Glaubenslehre in ihrer geschichtlichen Entwicklung und im Kampfe mit der modernen Wissenschaft*, 2 vols. (Tübingen and Stuttgart, 1841), 1:522–23.

31. Hegel's Trinity is best described as an "inclusive" or "holistic" Trinity rather than as an "immanent" Trinity distinguished from an "economic" Trinity (and certainly not as two absolutes). The inclusive Trinity encompasses both the inner, preworldly dialectic of the divine life, the immanent divine self-relations symbolized by the figure "Father," and the outward mediations by which the world is created and redeemed ("Son"), and God becomes absolute spirit, the unity of finite and infinite ("Holy Spirit"). See Peter C. Hodgson, *Hegel and Christian Theology: A Reading of the Lectures on the Philosophy of Religion* (Oxford, 2005), 129–31; also Hegel, *LPR* (n. 10), 3:185ff. (1824 lectures), 3:271ff. (1827 lectures).

it wished to give its full due to each moment of the concept, it left religious representations in their ecclesiastical form to have free rein in the sphere of representation, but at the same time, while keeping representation and concept distinguished, still had to accept that there is a certain internal connection between them. This then had to raise the issue as to what meaning the dogmas of positive Christianity have for Hegel's philosophy, dogmas whose articulation and terminology it had been so happy to appropriate. There has indeed existed a Christian-ecclesiastical dogma, which, inasmuch as it expressed the basic idea of Hegel's philosophy, seemed to be elucidated for the first time by this philosophy, and which the church for long held to be a profound, unfathomable mystery. But once this philosophy had its Trinity (*Dreieinigkeit*), why should it not also, and in the same sense, have had its God incarnate or God-man (*Gottmensch*), its reconciliation, and other matters of this kind. The Hegelian school and Hegel himself were happy with the supposition that, between their philosophy and Christianity, there is a relationship and harmony unlike what any other philosophy can enjoy. In one respect, they actually held this view themselves; in another respect, they were at least pleased to have others think it so.

Since the whole of positive Christianity hinges on the person of its founder, the entire significance of the question now before us is concentrated in the person of Christ, the God-man. For the Hegelian school, speaking of a God-man sounds just as speculatively profound as it does edifyingly Christian. Whereas people were previously accustomed to hearing from Schleiermacher just about a redeemer, Hegel's philosophy, as though conscious of a certain priestly status, now located its deepest significance in the God-man.

We see best with Marheineke[32] how one nevertheless has such a slight sense of the great gulf between the God-man for speculation and for the church respectively. After Marheineke has spoken in properly speculative terms about the unity of the divine nature with the human nature, about the divine nature as the truth of the human nature, and the human nature as the actuality of the divine nature, he then quite unselfconsciously makes the transition to the historical person of Jesus. He says that this oneness of God with the human domain is manifest and actual in the person of Jesus, as something come to pass, as historical; that in him the divine revelation has become consummately human. The idea of the God-man, of God incarnate, is inherently grounded in Hegel's system, for when the absolute is defined as the oneness of the finite and the infinite, that of itself involves conceiving the more concrete conception of the oneness of the divine with the human.

---

32. On Marheineke, see p. 205, n. 70, p. 207, n. 74.

Yet what a great leap it is to go directly from the divine-human oneness to the person of Jesus, even though, in doing so, one posits the more concrete expression of the God incarnate! How shall one think of these two, so far-separated moments, the speculative idea and the historical individual, as mediated with each other?[33] This was therefore the locus of a very pressing issue, one that first called for an even deeper investigation.

Proponents of Hegel's philosophy—such as Marheineke, Daub,[34] Göschel, Conradi,[35] and others—who were especially concerned to leave no doubts as to the orthodoxy of Hegel's teaching, believed the concept of the God-man or God incarnate, directly referring to Jesus, may indeed be regarded as fully justified because of the fact that the church's teaching and Hegel's philosophy joined hands in agreement about it. However, what then justifies giving precedence to the church's teaching as a teaching in existence prior to the philosophical critique? Surely also with reference to the church's teaching itself, the issue was precisely whether the kind of divine-human oneness the theory established can even exist in actuality, in a specific individual. Of course after Hegel's philosophy had given the concept of the God-man or God incarnate such significance in its system, people therefore had to address this issue more specifically, in the interest of philosophy.

Strauss's *Life of Jesus*

But there was also a pressing need to address this issue from the other side, that of New Testament criticism. This was because all the investigations bearing upon the authenticity, origins, and condition of the canonical scriptures had reached a point at which the reliability and historical truth of the gospel account as such had seriously been questioned. Since the gospel account is essentially the life story of Jesus, the significance of the person of Jesus is also in turn placed in question.

We will not go further into these details here. However, it was impossible to go forward on the already beaten path. Strauss's *Life of Jesus*,[36] which

---

33. For Baur's response to this question, see the quotation from his *Dreieinigkeit und Menschwerdung Gottes*, 3:998-9, on p. 46, n. 15.

34. On Daub, see above, pp. 89-90, incl. n. 81.

35. Casimir Conradi (1784-1849), author of *Christus in der Gegenwart, Vergangenheit und Zukunft* (1839) and *Kritik der christlichen Dogmen* (1841).

36. David Friedrich Strauss, *Das Leben Jesu, kritisch gearbeitet*, 1st ed., 2 vols. (Tübingen, 1835-36), 4th ed., 2 vols. (Tübingen, 1840). ET: *The Life of Jesus Critically Examined*, trans. from the 4th ed. by George Eliot (London, 1846, 2nd ed., 1892); reprint of 2nd ed., ed. P. C. Hodgson (Philadelphia and London, 1972). Strauss (1808-74) was one of Baur's students first in the lower theological school at Blaubeuren, then at

first appeared in 1835 and was viewed in light of this issue, came about because of the necessity of addressing the matter itself. His book is usually looked upon as a product of Hegelian philosophy. In any event Strauss himself had of course acknowledged, in the preface to the first edition,[37] that early in his philosophical studies he had come to share in the inner freedom of heart and mind from certain religious and dogmatic presuppositions; that unless this basic requirement is met, all critical erudition accomplishes nothing. Yet Strauss did not get the critical mindset, from which his work emerged, on the basis of the Hegelian school, since Hegelianism had already existed for some time without itself giving rise to a critical element of this kind [i.e., addressed to the biblical texts].

The contents and tendency of Strauss's work are of course well-known. Nevertheless, we might briefly analyze his methods here. As Strauss himself says, he sought to replace the time-worn, supernatural and naturalistic, ways of treating the story of Jesus with a new and mythical approach. The topic is the story of Jesus or, since the dogmatic understanding of Jesus' person is not to be separated from it, the historical Christ as such. This twofold topic involves: (1) the historical investigation concerning the gospel portrayal of Jesus' life; (2) the dogmatic investigation concerning the conceivability of the general circumstances under which Jesus' person is represented, and to which the concluding dissertation refers.[38]

The historical investigation deals with the difficulties in the gospel reports. These difficulties arise in part from the supernatural character of many of the narratives and speeches, and in part from the contradictions

---

the University of Tübingen (in the *Stift* or Protestant theological seminary). Shortly after becoming a *Repetent* or tutor in the *Stift*, he published his most famous book, which led to his dismissal. The end of his career in theology was sealed by the publication of his second book, *Die christliche Glaubenslehre* (n. 30). For a detailed discussion, see Ulrich Köpf, "Ferdinand Christian Baur and David Friedrich Strauss," in *Ferdinand Christian Baur and the History of Early Christianity*, ed. Martin Bauspiess, Christof Landmesser, and David Lincicum; trans. Robert F. Brown and Peter C. Hodgson (Oxford, 2017), chap. 1.

37. *The Life of Jesus Critically Examined*, 1972 repr. (n. 36), lii (preface to vol. 1 of the 1st Ger. ed.).

38. Following the introduction in which Strauss describes the development of the mythical interpretation (§§1–16), by far the greater portion of the book is given over to the historical investigation, (§§17–143), while the dogmatic investigation is limited to a brief concluding dissertation (§§144–52). On Strauss's original plan for the work, which envisioned a positive traditional part, a negative critical part, and a dogmatic part that would re-establish what had been destroyed critically, see Köpf in *Baur and the History of Early Christianity* (n. 36), 11. Later on in this section, pp. 363–68, Baur compares the "overwhelmingly negative" results of Strauss's work with his own "historical comprehension" of the New Testament writings.

internal to them, with one another, and with the contemporaneous history. In the first instance, the supernaturalist explanation stands opposed to a rationalist explanation. The other instances are alike in the harmonizing efforts that refuse to acknowledge any contradictions, and at most concede just apparent contradictions in minor matters or involving features about which even eyewitnesses could be mistaken. Strauss shows that both kinds are biased by unproven assumptions. When traditional church exegesis proceeds based on the twofold assumption that the Gospels contain historical accounts, and indeed supernatural ones, and when rationalism subsequently rejects the second of these assumptions while still just holding all the more firmly to the first one, then [biblical] scholarship cannot stop with rationalism's halfway measures. Instead it must also abandon the other assumption and first investigate whether, and to what extent, in the Gospels we stand, as a rule, on a historical foundation and soil. This is Strauss's presuppositionless approach, namely the treatment of the gospel writings according to the same norms of historical criticism that we apply to all other historical accounts. The result of this criticism is then the mythical interpretation of the life of Jesus, a procedure that has two aspects.

According to the first one, very many matters of fact in the gospel accounts are unhistorical. These include not only the stories about Jesus' birth and childhood, but also all the miracle narratives, most of Jesus' speeches in John, almost all the specific features in Christ's passion that seek to portray it as a special fulfillment of prophecies, and finally and most importantly, also Jesus' resurrection. That these accounts are unhistorical is substantiated in part by the impossibility or difficulty of understanding them in historical terms, either rationalistically or supernaturalistically, but also in part from the ease with which they could have taken shape even without a historical foundation, in other words on a far simpler and more natural basis.

This first line of argument brings up all the particular ways in which apologetics seeks to evade Strauss's point. Here is where Strauss—by wide-ranging erudition and undergirded by his mastery of classical languages—provides the most elegant proof of the dialectical virtuosity with which he knows how to single out the essential point in each view, to point out its difficulties in the most striking and most succinct way, to reduce nonspecific representations to their concrete content, to eradicate apologetic fallacies, and to marshal his very opponents against one another in matters where they are correct. Strauss accomplished this aspect of gospel criticism in its essentials.

The other component of his line of argument leads from the negative verdict that certain matters of fact are not history, to the positive task of explaining the origins of this nonhistorical material. The answer lies in the contention that such reports are mythical; that is, they are fabrications, although not made by individuals intentionally and consciously falsifying actual history. Instead they are not the product of traditions composed by design, but are gradual creations of the community. Strauss's explanation is that the tradition has been reworked by individuals to fit dogmatic assumptions, but without their being conscious of doing so.

For the first of these assumptions Strauss points to the faith of the community itself. The community was impelled toward a distinctive religious life through the impression made by Jesus' personality. It viewed its founder as ever more splendid the further away from him it came to be in time; hence it also found itself impelled to glorify his story in mythical terms. The second assumption involves the way the Jews at that time represented the messiah; how they elaborated on the Old Testament models and prophecies. Strauss says that, since people of course had a ready-made picture of the messiah, by acknowledging Jesus as being the messiah, they also transferred to the person of Jesus all the features that picture involved.

Nevertheless historical criticism only accomplishes one part of the task. Just like the historical reports about Christ, so too the testimonies of Christian consciousness about him must be put to the test by the critique of dogma. This takes place with reference to supernaturalism, to rationalism, and with regard to Schleiermacher especially as this touches on him. As opposed to Schleiermacher, Strauss seems to want to be conciliatory once more to orthodoxy, based on a speculative standpoint. In the preface to the first edition, he states that he knows the inner core of Christian faith to be completely independent of his critical investigations.

> The supernatural birth of Christ, his miracles, his resurrection and ascension, remain eternal truths, whatever doubts may be cast on their reality as historical facts. The certainty of this can alone give calmness and dignity to our criticism, and distinguish it from the naturalistic criticism of the last century, the design of which was, with the historical fact, to subvert also the religious truth, and which thus necessarily became frivolous. A dissertation at the close of the work will show that the dogmatic significance of the life of Jesus remains inviolate: in the meantime let the calmness and sang-froid (*Kaltblütigkeit*) with which, in the course of it, criticism undertakes apparently dangerous operations, be explained solely by the security of the author's conviction that no injury is threatened to the Christian faith.[39]

---

39. *The Life of Jesus Critically Examined*, 1972 repr. (n. 36), lii (preface to vol. 1 of the 1st German ed. of 1835). The translation softened *Kaltblütigkeit* into "insensibility," although George Eliot herself preferred "sang-froid." Baur paraphrases the last sentence

The critic is aware that the content of the highest religion, the Christian religion, is identical with the highest philosophical truth (2:687).[40]

Yet Strauss subsequently finds that the appearing of a person, in which the oneness of the divine nature and human nature would have been exclusively and individually present, would not be conceivable based either on Hegel's principles or on the deductions of Marheineke, Rosenkranz,[41] and Conradi. Such a thing would surely be inherently unthinkable, because it would not be the way of the idea "to pour out all its fullness into one single exemplar and be stingy with all the others." Instead the idea prefers "to distribute its riches in a multiplicity of exemplars that reciprocally supplement one another," positing itself in rotation and in individuals rising up in turn.

> The key to the whole of christology is that the subject of the predicates the church assigns to Christ is not posited as an individual but is posited as an idea, albeit a real idea, not as a non-existent Kantian idea. . . . Humankind or humanity (*die Menschheit*) is the uniting of both natures, the God become human who endlessly gives himself over to finitude, and the finite spirit recalling its own infinitude. Humankind is the child of the visible mother and the invisible father, of spirit and nature. Humankind is the miracle-worker, inasmuch as, in the course of human history, the spirit itself perpetually takes complete hold of nature and subjects nature to itself, as the powerless material basis of spirit's own activity. Humankind is sinless inasmuch as the course of its development is a blameless one. Impurity just always attaches to the individual, but it is removed from the species and its history. Humankind is what dies, rises again, and goes to heaven, inasmuch as higher, spiritual life for it always springs from the negation of its naturalness. By believing in this Christ, namely, believing in his death and resurrection, a human being becomes just in God's sight; that is, by enlivening the idea of humankind in oneself, in keeping with the feature that the negation of naturalness is a human being's only way to the truly spiritual life, the individual also comes to share in the divine-human life of the species.[42]

---

rather than quoting it directly.

40. This is Baur's reference to vol. 2 of the 1st ed. of *Das Leben Jesu, kritisch bearbeitet* (n. 36). In the ET, the reference is found on 757–58.

41. Karl Rosenkranz (1805–79) was a philosopher of the Hegelian "center" who taught for most of his career at the University of Königsberg. He wrote several books about the Hegelian system and the first important book about Hegel's life, *Hegels Leben* (Berlin, 1844).

42. *The Life of Jesus Critically Examined* (n. 36), 780 (our translation).

One must have lived through the period of Strauss's book itself to be able to form a notion of the emotions it had to have evoked. Seldom has a literary phenomenon readily created such a great sensation, so quickly and in such a widespread fashion, and summoned, with such lively interest, all the forces to a battlefield on which the various parties confronted one another. It has heightened the zeal of the conflict itself, to the point of the most vehement passions. Strauss's *Life of Jesus* was the incendiary spark that set off the already long-accumulated fuel as a blazing fire.

The Opponents of Strauss: Steudel, Hengstenberg, Tholuck, and Others

This was a very heartfelt matter above all for the older supernaturalism. Even before volume 2 of Strauss's work had appeared, people were made aware of the impact it had on the supernaturalist side through an essay by Steudel.[43] Steudel believed he had an especially pertinent reason for being in a direct position to extinguish the blaze that had arisen, since at that time Strauss was still a tutor in the Protestant seminary, and had tossed this firebrand "out from his closet" into the edifice of the old Tübingen theology. Steudel's intentions were very good, but he was completely unsuccessful. In this case the supernaturalist just made known the wholly inflexible tenacity of his nature, his inability to put himself in his opponent's place, as well as, for just one example, his inability to heed the distinction between mythic-artistic imagination (*mythenbildener Phantasie*) and deliberately fabricated reflection. In addition to the vaguely nonspecific and conventional character of Steudel's reasons, he frequently took the tone of a father confessor, unsuitably so, in [trying] to make a favorable impression. His main argument was that the facts of Christianity are not explainable without accepting a historical Christ. But in part of this apologetic he also turned the critic's view into the contention that there never was a Jesus, and in part of it he concluded too hastily, from the universal acknowledgment of this person's [existence], to the accuracy of the details in the Evangelists' accounts.

---

43. [*Baur, in the text*] "Vorläufig zu Beherzigendes bei Würdigung der Frage über die historische oder mythische Grundlage des Lebens Jesu, wie die kanonischen Evangelien dieses darstellen, vorgehalten aus dem Bewusstsein eines Glaubigen, der den Supernaturalisten beigezählt wird, zur Beruhigung der Gemüther." [*Ed.*] Published in the *Tübinger Zeitschrift für Theologie* (1835) no. 3 (July) 117–99, then separately as a book (Tübingen, 1835). Johann Christian Friedrich Steudel (1779–1837) was a professor of dogmatics and Old Testament in Tübingen, where he was the last prominent member of the old Tübingen School and founder of the *Tübinger Zeitschrift*. Baur was on friendly terms with him even through the Strauss episode.

Steudel's essay was in fact the forerunner of a whole deluge of rebuttals and rejoinders of various kinds. Here we can only look briefly at the most typical examples.

We start out with the most extreme example. No one can contest the fame of the *Evangelische Kirchenzeitung*'s editor for having led the way in this battle with the banner of orthodox faith. Just as Hengstenberg[44] repeatedly declared that the old supernaturalism of deism could not refute Strauss, so he made it his special calling to oppose Strauss, in an all-the-more glorious fashion in the well-known foreword to the beginning of the 1836 series—a foreword Strauss dubbed "the silly New Year's sermon"—and in later articles in June and July of that year. One ought not have expected it to be an actual refutation. Hengstenberg declares that Christian theology is of course said to equip well-intentioned people with weapons against doubt, but on the other hand it never claims to impose its explanations on those who hate the light because their works are evil. The evildoers include all those who engage in biblical criticism. Hengstenberg states that we must turn our backs on a person who invokes his own reason in opposition to the Word of God. There are also irredeemable, spiritual monstrosities, people without hearts. Strauss is such a person, or rather, as Hengstenberg says, Strauss just has the heart of a Leviathan, as hard as a stone, and as immobile as the lower millstone.

Nevertheless we must credit Hengstenberg with discerning Strauss's position at that time more accurately than many others did. He is very explicit that Strauss's critique is not solely the due consequence partly of Hegel's philosophy, partly of the rationalistic critique; and that one cannot concede that there is myth in the Old Testament and deny it in the New Testament. For Hengstenberg also recognizes that Hegel's philosophy is simply the consummation of more recent philosophy as such, and that Strauss's critique is essentially and necessarily a product of the time; that it is therefore not a matter of something singular and individual, but instead is wholly general in nature, involving the decisive struggle between Christianity on the one hand, and the philosophy and spirit of the time on the other. Indeed it is the struggle of faith and reason, for faith is necessarily counter to the corrupted reason of human beings. If not every irrationality is Christian dogma, every Christian dogma is nevertheless irrational.

After posing the issue in such a pointed way, Hengstenberg believes that he must raise his voice all the more forcefully, so as, in prophetic tones,

---

44. Ernst Wilhelm Hengstenberg (1802–60), professor of Old Testament at the University of Berlin and founder of the *Evangelische Kirchenzeitung*, a strictly orthodox Protestant journal (see Baur's description of it above, pp. 214–17. The "foreword" to which Baur refers extended over six issues from 2 to 20 January 1836.

to broadcast his lament about godless science and to urge vigilance in opposition to it. Our time is the time of Jeremiah. Like Jeremiah, Hengstenberg cries out: "O that my head were a spring of water, and my eyes were a fountain of tears, so that I might weep day and night for the slain of my poor people! . . . For they are all adulterers, a band of traitors" [Jeremiah 9:1–2]. The entire spirit of our time is corrupt at its foundations—theologians and non-theologians, thinkers and poets, Schiller, Goethe, and so on—one and all are from the seeds of the adulterer and the harlot, and they labor in service to the kingdom of darkness. But it is essentially the monster of pantheism that smothers all religion in its Moloch[45] arms, and which is the fulfillment of the prophecy about the human being of sin who sets himself up in the temple as God. In pantheism we have the end of all religion. There is even more religious content in fetish worship than there is in this system. [He says] it is a teaching of the devil, and Eschenmayer[46] has rightly called it "Iscariotism." Hengstenberg too goes after it with passionate, implacable animosity. And yet we also find in Hengstenberg passages that sound authentically pantheistic. Thus everything here, taken together, is nonsensical, and the main thing is always just the fanatical energy with which Hengstenberg speaks pompously in opposition to the Straussian Antichrist, in prophetic and apocalyptic phrases.

Strauss has aptly called the aforementioned book by Eschenmayer, *Der Ischariothismus unserer Tage*, the "monstrous product of the legitimate marriage of theological ignorance and religious intolerance, consecrated by a somnambulant philosophy."[47] It belongs in the same category as the articles of the *Evangelische Kirchenzeitung*, except Eschenmayer's fanaticism was seriously meant, whereas the fanaticism of the *Evangelische Kirchenzeitung* only serves as backdrop for its own hierarchical lust for power. A publication having as its most distinctive feature a mania for denunciation and, in general, whatever can cause an uproar, and that has feebly contended with rationalism, had simply to have been gratified to obtain new polemical subject matter in the form of Strauss's *Life of Jesus*. It made full use of it.

Works coming closest to Hengstenberg's standpoint include: Harless, *Die kritische Bearbeitung des Lebens Jesu von Strauss* (1836); Hoffmann, *Das*

---

45. Moloch was a Canaanite god associated with child sacrifice. See Lev 18:2; 20:2–5; Jer 32:35; etc.

46. Carl August von Eschenmayer (1768–1862) was a professor of philosophy and medicine in Tübingen during this period. He wrote *Der Ischariothismus unserer Tage. Eine Zugabe zu dem jüngst erschienenen Werke: Das Leben Jesu von Strauss, I. Theil* (Tübingen, 1835).

47. Strauss, *The Life of Jesus Critically Examined*, 1972 repr. (n. 36), liv (preface to vol. 2 of the 1st German ed. of 1836).

Leben Jesu von Strauss geprüft (1836); Tholuck, *Die Glaubwürdigkeit der evangelischen Geschichte* (1837).⁴⁸

Harless, one of the most hidebound defenders of the old Lutheran orthodoxy, supposed that he could do the most damage to Strauss's work by being completely unwilling to acknowledge its scientific significance. But Harless's book just provided evidence of his superficiality and his vain, snobbish presumptuousnss. He opines that the greater part of what is plainly untenable in Strauss's view is emphatically obvious to any reasonably educated person. Why then, if all this is so very self-evident, is there this great theological clamor?

Hoffmann takes a more scientific approach. But he too comes forward with the pretentious contention that the slightest concession ought not be made to the critique, as though he were the man to completely beat back Strauss's entire attack, and to do so at every point, conceding not even one foot of ground to the opponent. Whereas he gives the appearance of also bringing up to date what he takes to be the inadequate older supernaturalism, at the same time he simply has recourse to the age-old apologetic; in other words, he indulges in the most obviously circular reasoning (*petitiones principii*).⁴⁹

However, no one surpasses Master Tholuck in toying this way with modern culture and science. In the aforementioned writing he confronts the opponent in the most grandiose fashion, with all the tools of his extensive literary knowledge and all the polish of the most clever modern cultivation. No one also makes such an effort to seem to give his opponent the most fitting recognition, and yet setting himself apart from Hengstenberg's mania for denunciation solely by knowing how to dress up the most vindictive moral insinuations in fine-sounding phrases. One example is the following passage, which also is typical of the entire document's tone:

> That exalted genius who first fitted the sail to the mast, and who transferred the steam engine into the belly of the ship, like an

---

48. Gottlieb Christian Adolf von Harless (1806–79), at that time a professor of New Testament at Halle and a follower of Tholuck. Ludwig Friedrich Wilhelm Hoffmann (1806–73), a church official and theologian from Württemberg who ended his career in Berlin. Friedrich August Gotttreu Tholuck (1799–1877), a leading exponent of German pietism and Lutheran orthodoxy, who taught most of his career at the University of Halle.

49. [*Zeller*] In place of this verdict about Hoffmann, the transcript of the 1857–58 lectures just says: "Hoffmann's treatise is far more significant, except that its tendency is too strongly apologetic." In later years the author in fact seems to have expressed his judgments from the lectern in a milder way than he did in the manuscript prepared principally for his own use. Nevertheless I do not believe that this circumstance justifies my altering what this manuscript presents.

inner storm, is [for Dr. Strauss] the Son of God before whom he bends the knee; it is the ideal of humankind established as the image of God. And these tidings are welcomed at a time when the customs association is a more gratifying subject for debate than the divine and human natures in Christ, and the railroad to Augsburg is a more serious topic to examine than that ὁδὸς τεθλιμμένη (hard road) of Matthew 7:14.⁵⁰

The whole character of the book is this tasteless pathos of the most shallow tirades and rants. We can simply call it a masterpiece of charlatanism and pettifoggery. It all just relies throughout on deceptive make-believe, on being dazzling and impressive.

With the misunderstandings and misconceptions so often found in it alongside its declared focus, of course this text inherently has the obvious marks of something written hastily and heedlessly. Thus it possesses, as such, only very marginal scientific value for the main issue with which it is dealing. What is Tholuck wanting to say when, for example, he contends that, if the evangelists' story were not true, then Jesus had to be have been declared a fanatic? Or that, if one objects to the feasibility of the mythical structure, then what is left of Strauss's Jesus would not have been able to have this significance? Or that, if the necessity for miracles is said to throw light on the fact that the absolute spirit, who has put in place the universal natural law, could also have brought about such miraculous phenomena via the instrument of the human personal being the spirit assumed, phenomena no single one of those laws was capable of producing? In any event he even traces miracle back to what is merely extraordinary (*mirabile*) (pp. 92, 103).

Tholuck exhibits his exegetical capriciousness in dispelling the difficulties and contradictions of the gospel story, by how he interprets the census of Quirinius in Luke, chapter two. His proofs for the Evangelist's authoritative status are examples of his major cunning devices. Tholuck supposes that the Book of Acts already shows the authenticity of Luke's Gospel (p. 376). Indeed Tholuck even knows almost certainly (pp. 141, 152; cf. 66) that Luke wrote his Gospel in Caesarea, and that he probably heard the story of Jesus' childhood from Mary herself. With incredible boldness he assures us that the concluding verses of the Gospel of John contain a formal attestation of its authenticity, from an eyewitness. From such proofs one can conclude to [the accuracy of] all the rest. The whole of Tholuck's book is

---

50. August Tholuck, *Die Glaubwürdigkeit der evangelischen Geschichte, zugleich eine Kritik des Lebens Jesu von Strauss, für theologische und nicht theologische Leser dargestellt*, 2nd ed. (Hamburg, 1838), 92–93. The bracketed insertion is Baur's. The pages numbers cited in the text below are to this book.

an unmethodical, overwrought procedure, all of which is calculated for its immediate effect; it is the frivolous display of a witty presentation.

The Moderate Faction: Ullmann, Neander, and Others

Those who to some degree make use of Schleiermacher's theology are not to be numbered among these harsh opponents, but form a middle or moderate faction (*die Mittelpartei, die mittlere Partei*).[51] They include Ullmann, J. Müller, Lücke, Neander, Kern, and others.[52] These moderate opponents [of Strauss] do not wish to support all of Schleiermacher's positions indiscriminately and with equal rigor. They make concessions and express no opinion on many points, but in doing so they just get caught up in inconsistencies and half-hearted positions, in virtue of which their standpoint becomes completely uncertain.

Ullmann, in *Historisch oder Mythisch?* (1838),[53] dogmatizes wholly in the manner of Schleiermacher's christology, in order to demonstrate the historicality of an archetypal Christ. However, the main thing for him involves the historical proof. So he appeals to the external testimonies that are in fact so numerous in the four Evangelists, as, in fairness, one could always be expected to do. From this we see on what firm grounds these historical proofs rest. One of his most unusual arguments is that it is unthinkable for the Apostle Paul to have become a Christian if he had not also convinced himself of the historical truth of Christianity. Certainly the Apostle Paul could not have become a Christian without believing in the historical truth of Christianity. But what follows from this for the historical truth of the

---

51. Also known as the "mediating theology" (*Vermittlungstheologie*). See below, n. 125.

52. Carl Christian Ullmann (1796–1865) was professor of theology in Halle and Heidelberg, co-editor of *Theologische Studien und Kritiken*, and later head of the Evangelical Church in Baden. Julius Müller (1801–78) was a professor in Marburg and Halle, a close associate of Tholuck, and co-founder of the *Deutsche Zeitschrift fur christliche Wissenschaft und christliches Leben*, an organ of the mediating theology. Friedrich Lücke (1791–1855) was a professor of exegesis, dogmatics, and ethics in Göttingen, and a friend of Schleiermacher, to whom the latter wrote his "open letters" concerning the *Glaubenslehre*. August Neander (1789–1850), a convert from Judaism, studied under Schleiermacher in Halle and later became professor of theology at the University of Berlin; a prolific and popular author, his works on church history are discussed by Baur above, pp. 209–11, and his *Leben Jesu* just below. Friedrich Heinrich Kern (1790–1842) was Baur's colleague in Blaubeuren and Tübingen, where he taught ethics and other subjects.

53. *Historisch oder Mythisch? Beiträge zur Beantwortung der gegenwärtigen Lebensfrage der Theologie* (Hamburg, 1838).

gospel story as a whole and in its details? Vague arguments of this kind are the stock-in-trade of this group of apologists. That is especially the case with their vacillating indecision as to how they conceive of miracles, since they neither accept miracles in the absolute sense, nor do they relinquish them in such a way that, for them, time and again, the miracles of the gospel story, are not actual miracles.

Neander's *Leben Jesu* (1837)[54] is of course not directly aimed at Strauss, although it does wholly emerge from what Strauss set in motion. Since Neander is the chief representative of the moderate group, at this point we mainly have to address his position. In his foreword he describes his stance as intermediate between what he views as two extreme factions. [Neander says that] his view will not please those who wish, in an overbearing way, to change everything, the hypercritical ones who subject the Holy Scriptures to the subjective caprice of a hyper-rational, hair-splitting, frivolous discernment. Nor will it please those who suppose that, in this case, all criticism, or at least all criticism based on internal grounds, is malicious. On the one hand, he praised the Zürich faction[55] that has proven to be so dignified in its resistance to those capriciously seeking to overturn everything, and in its enthusiastic support for the sacredness of the faith of its great forefathers. On the other hand, however, he did not wish to concur in the one-sided position that regards it as wrong to give their due to the exponents—competent in their own way—of a standpoint [that this position] finds inherently objectionable; nor to express approval for the conceit that believes itself justified in haughtily disparaging the scientific competency of overmatched opponents; nor at all—by cleverly and humorously professed substance, in keeping with the unwholesome tastes of current literature—to concur in its concealing the weakness of its reasoning. Whoever dresses up his standpoint in this way can readily make it appear that he alone has the correct view.

But one can simply ask whether what Neander calls "hypercriticism" is not precisely the genuine and needful criticism. In any event, here he makes certain concessions to criticism. Often Neander is not simply satisfied with a mere "perhaps," a "not evidently so" (a *non liquet*), in place of a categorical assertion; for he even concedes that in the gospel narratives there are

54. *Das Leben Jesu Christi in seinem geschichtlichen Zusammenhang und seiner geschichtlichen Entwicklung* (Hamburg, 1837). ET: *The Life of Jesus Christ in Its Historical Connexion and Historical Development*, trans. from the 4th Ger. ed. by J. McClintock and C. E. Blumenthal (London, 1853). In this paragraph Baur draws on material found in the prefaces to the German editions.

55. Strauss's call to Zürich as a professor of church history and dogmatics was rescinded in 1839 when citizens took to the streets in protest.

possibly, and in individual cases actually, statements that are imprecise and in fact erroneous. He regards the accounts of Jesus' childhood as just fragments of the gospel tradition we may hardly assume are literally precise in their form and content, since they do not actually belong to the preaching of the apostles. He concedes that Luke could have been mistaken about the reason Joseph and Mary were present in Bethlehem, and that Matthew [could have] presented an erroneous supposition about the way in which the Magi, in Jerusalem, became informed about the birth of Jesus. Neander does not find it inconceivable that, in the gospel accounts of John the Baptist's utterances about Jesus, the views John expresses are inflated based on the narrator's subsequent standpoint. Neander also accepts that, since the Synoptic Gospels originated from a range of separate traditions, and incorrectly assigned, to a single set of circumstances, events occurring separately on various festival journeys, they combined them just as Matthew did in his concluding eschatological address, when he combined multiple elements from speeches made on various occasions.

Neander believes he is justified in all this, despite the [divine] inspiration of the New Testament writers, because, for one thing, this view does not do away with the natural distinctiveness and personal growth of the inspired writers, and for another, only the religious content of their accounts is inspired, not the historical content. Yet Neander knows how, from the latter of these claims, to also justify Jesus' accommodating himself to the popular conceptions held by the zealots (*Bessenen*); for Neander follows Schleiermacher in maintaining that these popular conceptions are in any event erroneous, and that it is not part of Jesus' teaching role to contest them, since they do not bear upon religious concerns. Compromises such as these are very dubious, and the information on which they are based is presented in a misleading and sophistical way. However, the curious thing is that Neander himself cannot avoid making them. Criticism is then said to confine itself to these secondary issues. But how is it possible to hold fast to criticism on these secondary issues and segregate it from any further use? On the one hand, only the time-worn arguments of the old apologetics are used in reply to the most fundamental critical doubts. On the other hand, these very arguments lose their cogency when one comes up with logically-contrived special cases in order to get the very outcomes one wants to avoid [i.e., conclusions based on criticism].

Let us highlight a few examples of this procedure. Neander takes up, as an issue of particular concern, the prior question about the authenticity of the Gospel of John. In its defense he remarks that such a portrayal could only have arisen from the soul of the most intimate disciple, not from the second century, strife-ridden by antitheses; that the writer of such a scripture could not be someone unknown (as if this were not also the case elsewhere, even for the canonical scriptures, for instance, with the Epistle to the Hebrews!); that a man like the Evangelist would, on moral grounds, of course have countenanced no such forgery, any more than he would, with good sense, have allowed such significant departures from the synoptic tradition, and the church would not have accepted them.

Neander provides several examples in his treatment of the infancy narratives. In order to deal more easily with the appearance of the angels, Neander assumes that a few of the shepherds ardently expected the Messiah to appear, and by a heavenly vision, in that night so significant for the salvation of humankind, they had been led to the place where the object of this longing was born. This changes the appearing of the angels into a vision. But how does that harmonize with the narrative text? In the extraordinary circumstances of Christ's birth it is striking that in Luke's account the customary purification offering and sin offering are said to have been made for it too; but a mythical tradition would have removed these features, which could not have been appropriate for Jesus' glorification—as though the very fulfilling of the law, which would have been the first requirement people set for being the Messiah, did not apply in the circle where the infancy narrative originated!

In order to provide justification for Jesus' speeches in the Gospel of John, Neander remarks that it is inherently unlikely that Jesus should have utilized only one kind of delivery. However, the Johannine manner of delivery is of course not just different from that in the Synoptics. Instead it presupposes an essentially different kind, one with a wholly different way of thinking and of looking at things.

Whereas Strauss is scandalized by Jesus tolerating Judas in his fellowship, while having long known that he is a betrayer, Neander appeals to the assumption that, from the outset, Jesus of course recognized the root of evil alongside the good seed in Judas, but hoped to overcome it. In John 6:70 Jesus already says to his disciples, "Yet one of you is a devil (διάβολος)." Neander also remarks that we ought not to assume Jesus had been informed about Judas betraying him, which he mentioned at the Last Supper, from a supernatural communication. Instead he probably learned it from his friends among the members of the Sanhedrin. But how is this authentically rationalist-pragmatic view compatible with the supernatural knowledge ascribed to Jesus in John 1:49 and 2:25?

Neander's stance on the miracles in the gospel story is especially significant. Naturally it cannot occur to him to deny them, but we surely do see that the supernatural in the strict sense is a troublesome issue for him. In part he turns to a general point, with the observation that miracle in connection with the divine's entry into history in Christ would be something in accord with nature; in part he seeks, in particular cases, the aid of an explanation of miracles we can certainly mark down as tainted by rationalism. Thus in cases of rising from the dead, he wants to leave it undecided whether the risen person was indeed really dead, or was just in a state resembling death. Neander hardly does this on any other basis than in order to take the sting out of miracles and make them to some extent more natural in character. With demonic possession, he will of course accept a higher and hidden cause for this condition, and trace it back to the collective realm of evil. However, the actions resulting from this condition are not magical or supernatural, but rather are ones connected with its psychological development.

Even with the feeding of the five thousand, he notes that there is at least no clear creating out of nothing, but only a multiplication of goods already at hand; in other words, a magnification of their same indwelling powers. This explanation once again manifests very clearly his naturalistic propensity, although it also does not make apparent what it supposedly achieves with regard to the narrative text. The account of the feeding of the four thousand is supposedly just an erroneous repetition of the other episode. When he takes up the changing of the water into wine at Cana in Galilee, he draws our attention to the fact that nothing actually had to have become wine from water; that there was only the energy of the water in its being given the potency of wine, as we find in the analogous phenomenon of mineral water.

Neander's *Leben Jesu* clears up the most important and most difficult points with very little effort, by half-measures, arbitrariness, and ineptitude. In this way the whole of it bears a clearly subjective stamp. Throughout it one just learns how Neander himself represents matters, not how they must be thought of in themselves. For what it lacks throughout is an internally coherent way of looking at history, one built upon methodical thinking. In his article "Zehn Jahre in der Theologie," published in the *Monatsblätter zur Ergänzung der Allgemeinen Zeitung* (1845) 471ff., Fock[56] properly characterizes the book as follows. He says it is the weakest thing Neander has produced; that in it the historical and critical Neander is in constant conflict with the believing and edifying Neander, and although Neander the believer for the most part tempers the historical and critical Neander, the result is an uncontrolled vacillation, a half-heartedness resulting in inconsistencies.

---

56. Otto Fock (1819–72).

After Neander had written his *Leben Jesu* as a result of Strauss's precedent, each of the various principal factions likewise believed it had to provide one too. Ammon championed rationalism in his *Geschichte des Lebens Jesu* (1842), and Pastor Lange did so for the more blatant supernaturalism, in his *Leben Jesu* (1844).[57] Both of them took up a time-worn standpoint that could not make any specific impact. Unlike them, Christian Hermann Weisse merits our attention here.

Weisse and the Hegelians

In his *Die evangelische Geschichte, kritisch und philosophisch bearbeitet* (1838), Weisse[58] did not just intend to provide a counterpart to Strauss's *Leben Jesu*; he also sought to surpass it positively.

Weisse declares himself in essential agreement with the negative, critical aspect of Strauss's work. On his own view too there are many unhistorical and mythical elements in the gospel accounts. He renounces the stories of Jesus' birth and childhood as historically untenable. He declares that the twofold miraculous account of feeding the multitudes is a misunderstood parable, and that Jesus' walking on the sea and his transfiguration are intuitive visions. He did not wish to count the resurrection itself as external, historical fact.

On the other hand, however, Weisse supposes that he can salvage a majority of the gospel's miracle narratives in their essential features, by assuming a miraculous energy indwelling Jesus as a spiritual, earthly ability, in virtue of spirit's universal power over nature. The phenomena of animal magnetism [hypnotism] supposedly provide the natural analogy to it. Weisse even wants to interpret belief in the resurrection as resulting from this magnetic energy. The historical fact is precisely just Jesus' followers' belief in the resurrected one's presence in the apparitions and phenomena they themselves experienced. Inasmuch as we actually feel ourselves compelled to think of the departed spirit of the crucified one as present personally in these phenomena, Weisse stipulates that the basis for this is the ability contained in the magnetic, miraculous endowment extended to the redeemer, in virtue of his world-historical priority over all other mortals, as one of his essential elements. Even after his death it still worked influentially and magically on his disciples and a few others, because they were predisposed, in body and spirit, to be influenced in this way.

57. Christoph Friedrich Ammon (1766–1850); Johann Peter Lange (1802–84). On Lange, see n. 129.

58. On Weisse, see n. 25.

The scientific value of Weisse's work is very much in question, owing to this peculiar hypothesis and others of a comparably subjective sort, such as, for instance, his philosophical theory about the person of Christ. But it more than holds its own, in part by its pertinent critical and exegetical observations that shed more specific light on the status of the gospel accounts (as Weisse, for example, correctly saw in regard to Christ's resurrection in the Gospel of John), and in part by its having raised more vigorously the issue of how the Gospels are related to one another. He correctly emphasizes how the concept of Christ in John differs from the depiction of Christ in the Synoptics, and stresses the reflective character of the Fourth Gospel. However, Weisse has rearranged the way of looking at the Synoptics by his superficially supported contention of the authenticity and priority of Mark, then followed by Luke, then Matthew, with each independent of the others but making common use of the collection of sayings attributed to Matthew the Apostle, and each pretty much said to have freely constructed his gospel.[59] He likewise has an unfortunate idea as to the Gospel of John, that a follower of the apostle composed it from fragments, didactic materials from the apostle that a later person enlarged upon by adding the narrative parts.

In speaking of Weisse, with his largely very free, critical standpoint, we have of course gone beyond where the moderate faction stands. We have then to ask who, in addition to Strauss, represents the faction Neander calls "hypercritical." Supposedly we should seek the representatives of this faction in the Hegelian school, from which, as people believed, Strauss's *Leben Jesu* itself had surely arisen. But we look in vain for overt acknowledgment of Strauss's criticism from this quarter. The Hegelians who delivered their verdict about Strauss's work adopted a very unphilosophical stance toward it. They wanted to have nothing to do with Strauss's reputed connection with Hegel's philosophy. Hence the issue now, of upholding the interests of free philosophical criticism, is then a matter of examining just the opinions of those who believed they had to maintain intact the traditional orthodoxy by using their philosophical categories.

One of the first of the Hegelian school to speak out about Strauss was Bruno Bauer, in a review of Strauss's *Leben Jesu*, published in the *Jahrbücher für wissenschaftliche Kritik*.[60] Bauer granted that the critique is fully justi-

---

59. On Baur's interpretation of the Synoptic problem, including his defense of the priority of Matthew, see Martin Bauspiess, "The Essence of Early Christianity: On Ferdinand Christian Baur's View of the Synoptic Gospels," in *Ferdinand Christian Baur and the History of Early Christianity* (n. 36), chap. 8.

60. Bruno Bauer (1809–82) was, at the time he wrote this review (Dec. 1835, May 1836), a right-Hegelian, which probably accounts for Marheineke's selection of him to edit the 2nd ed. of Hegel's *Vorlesungen über die Philosophie der Religion* (1840).

fied, but he absurdly demanded that it would have to reinstate what it destroyed a priori. The critique is only a half-measure, and does not lead to the actual comprehension of the object if it declares comprehending it to be impossible on account of the difficulty of doing so. Strauss retorted that this is saying one ought to pick peas, but with the proviso that they are all thought to be good ones.[61] Bauer in fact did as much. Based on the necessary realization of the idea, [Strauss says,] Bauer demonstrated not only the divinity of Christ itself in the usual way, but also the individual facts of his life. Thus the resurrection is based on his spirit's absolute power over his body, from which it would rather follow that in no way could he die. Miracle is based on the necessity for spirit to manifest itself not only in particular laws of nature, but also in its own totality as the absolute law of nature, so that, as Strauss says, in addition to apples, pears, and cherries, then fruit as such would also exist—as though each revelation would not be special on its own, and "miracle" would instead be lawlessness in place of lawfulness or regularity.

However, the pinnacle of Bauer's achievements is his deduction of Christ's supernatural procreation. Since an origin brought about by the private sexual act of individual persons would always just yield an individual as its product, and human nature as such would certainly have lacked at the time the power [needed] to produce [Christ], Bauer therefore supposes that this human being, said to present the essence of human nature purely within himself, would have to have been posited directly by the concept itself, and the human nature would not have been able to serve positively for that purpose, only just receptively. And since this receptivity would be present in the woman, more specifically the Virgin, in a direct way Christ has as his mother the Virgin and as his father the Spirit, which is the absolute necessity of the oneness of the divine and human natures.

Strauss rightly says that the craziness of this deduction always causes one to imagine being in Faust's witch's kitchen, and hearing an entire chorus of a hundred thousand fools speaking.[62] He parodies it with the following analogous line of reasoning. He says that since no individual poet absolutely realizes the idea of poetry, necessarily poetry as such must at one time have written the absolute poem on the absolutely receptive sheet of paper, without the mediating role of a human hand.

Shortly thereafter, Bauer switched to a left-Hegelian, anti-Christian position, which is described by Baur later in this section.

61. David Friedrich Strauss, *Streitschriften zur Vertheidigung meiner Schrift über das Leben Jesu und zur Charakteristik der gegenwärtigen Theologie*, no. 3 (Tübingen, 1837), 102; cf. 101–20 on Strauss's response to Bauer. See further, n. 67.

62. Ibid., 109.

The deductions of Göschel and Conradi,[63] among others, are not much more rational than this. Even Rosenkranz[64] only sets himself apart from them by conceding more in individual instances; by acknowledging the contradictions in the external history of Christ, and by abandoning narratives such as those of Christ's ascension and his supernatural procreation. But Rosenkranz also sticks with the thesis that substance, in order to be at the same time subject, must be an individual subject; therefore the idea of humanity united with God must also be realized in one individual, absolute appearance or phenomenon.

Schaller attempted a fuller grounding of this thesis in *Der historische Christus* (1838).[65] Schaller concedes that the species realizes itself not in a single individual but in the totality of individuals. Yet he believes that the concepts "species" and "individual" are only suited to nature, whereas the spiritual individual, as singular, is at the same time what is universal. This is merely playing with words. Schaller sees, however, that he is forced to resort in part to the general contention that the species will become personal only in the singular personality, and in part to one of Schleiermacher's analogous deductions, since he assumes that realizing reconciliation necessitates that reconciliation have an absolute beginning, an absolute reconciler, and that is beside the point he is making. The point of contention here was wholly the relation between idea and appearance, between what is universal and what is singular. Whereas Strauss advanced his well-known thesis that the idea would only realize itself in the multiplicity and diversity of individuals, these Hegelians maintain that the idea would not be real without its being realized in one single individual.[66] Strauss demonstrated very clearly that in this way the Hegelians came to contradict the principle of their own phi-

---

63. See nn. 28, 35.

64. See n. 41. Baur must be referring to Rosenkranz's *Kritische Erläuterungen des Hegelschen Systems* (Königsberg, 1840), part 3, chaps. 4–5, where he discusses Hegel's philosophy of religion and various responses to it, including Conradi's *Selbstbewusstsein und Offenbarung* (1832), Göschel's *Entwickelung des Hegelschen Unsterblichkeitslehre* (1835), and works by Marheineke, Eschenmayer, and others.

65. Julius Schaller (1810–68), a center-Hegelian, taught philosophy in Halle. The full title of his work is *Der historische Christus und die Philosophie* (Leipzig, 1838).

66. Strauss, *The Life of Jesus Critically Examined* (n. 36), §151 (779–81). The Hegelians have grounds for their claim in Hegel's *Lectures on the Philosophy of Religion*, where Hegel seems to argue for the actuality of reconciliation occurring in and through a single human being. For the relevant texts in *LPR* 3, as well as problems with the argument, see *Hegel and Christian Theology* (n. 31), 160–63. In any event, Baur's view is closer to Strauss's in that he does not believe that idea and actuality can *absolutely* cohere in any single individual (see the quotation from *Dreieinigkeit und Menschwerdung Gottes* cited on p. 46, n. 15), although he accords greater positive significance to Jesus as a bearer of the idea than Strauss does.

losophy. Only in representation are idea and appearance immediately one. But of course in the concept this immediacy is said to be sublated. What is the point of distinguishing representation from concept, if in the end the two of them are nevertheless one?

Strauss's *Streitschrifen* and "Vergängliches und Bleibendes"

This of course brings us to the circumstances in which Strauss addressed himself to his opponents. He could not remain silent for long in face of the attacks coming from all sides. He speaks out in his three-part *Streitschriften zur Vertheidigung meiner Schrift über das Leben Jesu und zur Charakteristik der gegenwärtigen Theologie.*[67] In the first part he analyzes, with regard to Dr. Steudel, "the self-deceptions of the rational supernaturalism of our day." In the second part he exposed the wholly uncalled-for verdicts of Eschenmayer and Menzel,[68] for their many ignorant shortcomings and their vehement insinuations. In the third, Strauss threw the spotlight on the *Evangelische Kirchenzeitung*, the *Jahrbücher für wissenschaftliche Kritik*, and the *Theologische Studien und Kritiken*, regarding their stance [in critical reviews[69]] toward his *Leben Jesu*.

In these various contests Strauss engaged in with his opponents, his position was so decidedly superior that even those he thought unworthy of a special reply, and only came under consideration in later editions of his *Leben Jesu*, could not expect their cause to be more successful. After so much negativity, Strauss believed that he must counteract the general reproach that his results are negative, with something positive and conciliatory. He sought to do this in the form of a soliloquy reminiscent of Schleiermacher's *Monologen*, in the brief journal article of 1838, "Vergängliches und Bleibendes im Christentum," which he also separately published in his *Zwei friedliche Blätter* in 1839.[70] This article was in part a precursor to his

---

67. See n. 61. "Polemical Writings in Defense of My *Life of Jesus* and as a Characterization of Present-Day Theology." Strauss intended to continue the series but finished only the first three numbers. Partial ET of the third number: *In Defense of My Life of Jesus against the Hegelians*, trans. Marilyn Chapin Massey (Hamden, CT, 1983). The "Hegelians" are B. Bauer, Ullmann, and Müller.

68. Wolfgang Menzel (1798–1873).

69. The reviews are by Hengstenberg, Lange, B. Bauer, Ullmann, and Müller.

70. Strauss, *Zwei friedliche Blätter. Vermehrter und Verbesserter Abdruck der beiden Aufsätze: Ueber Justinus Kerner, und: Ueber Vergängliches und Bleibendes im Christentum* (Altona, 1839). The latter article ("Transitory and Enduring Elements in Christianity") first appeared in *Freihafen* 1.3 (1838) 1–48.

dogmatics,⁷¹ to the extent that it identified the difference between criticism and supernaturalism as the difference between modern and traditional forms of Christian consciousness as such; and from christology it went on to another issue, namely, the belief in immortality, which Strauss had not yet explicitly contested. The other part was a peace proposal, to the extent that he said Jesus gained a position of the relatively highest rank, instead of an absolute status.⁷²

Proceeding from the point that we actually know the absolute only in the totality of the finite, albeit here in varying degrees, Strauss came to the significance of genius, and the thesis that the only cult for the cultured that remains from the decay of the time is the cult of genius.⁷³ As a religious genius, Christ joins the category of those highly gifted individuals we are accustomed to designate as geniuses in fields other than religion, for instance in the arts and sciences. Of course if Christ were therefore to stand alongside not only an Orpheus, a Homer, a Moses, but also Muhammad, he would not disdain the society of Alexander and Caesar, of Raphael and Mozart. Nevertheless a twofold consideration would, at least in part, supersede this unsettling juxtaposition. The first is that, in the various domains in which the divinely-related, creative power of a person of genius could show itself, the religious domain would not just stand, without further specification, as the foremost domain; for it stands to the rest as the center of the circle, inasmuch as the divine spirit draws near to human and immediate self-consciousness solely in religion. The second consideration is that, even within the religious domain, Christ, as the creator of the supreme religion, towers over the other founders of religions. However, since in Christ the oneness of the divine and the human could not appear in an adequate way, this did not utterly rule out the possibility that the minimal gap between Christ and the archetype, small as it is, might be even smaller in one or

71. *Die christliche Glaubenslehre* (n. 30). See below, pp. 371–74.

72. In this respect the essay is a further development of the revised christology that Strauss presents in the 3rd ed. of his *Leben Jesu* (1838), where he applies the category of "religious genius" to Jesus. Baur does not mention that some of his own ideas and criticisms are reflected in this version, but that in the 4th ed. of 1840 Strauss restores most of the original text, which paints a negative picture of the relation of the historical Jesus to the Christ of faith. See the Editor's Introduction to the 1972 reprint of *The Life of Jesus* (n. 36), xl–xlii.

73. This is not Baur's position. He does not employ the loaded category of "genius" but rather speaks of Jesus' proclaiming the righteousness of God and morality of conscience in such a simple but profound way that people began to think of him as the Messiah; thus his teaching became the foundation of the "Christian principle" of reconciliation. See his *Lectures on New Testament Theology* (n. 106), Part One. Strauss's reference to "the cultured" (*den Gebildeten*) recalls Schleiermacher's *On Religion: Speeches to Its Cultured Despisers*.

several later [religious] figures. So one also cannot maintain that it would be impossible for Christ to ever be surpassed in the future.

A Look Backward at the Straussian Movement

In looking back now to the beginning of the Straussian movement, and the course it took, we certainly cannot fail to recognize the importance of its consequences. There is no writing from the literature of more recent theology that has been so very epochal as that by Strauss. So we must now ask, first and foremost, why it made such a stir right from when it first appeared, and why it gained such great significance.

There is certainly nothing essentially new in what it brought to light. Its essential character is just that it compiled already existing materials, provided an overview of them, and from the given data drew out the obvious consequences contained therein. Even its mythical point of view is nothing new.[74] Already long before Strauss people accepted the presence of myths not only in the Old Testament but also in the New Testament. What reason therefore did they have for looking upon the New Testament as such an extraordinary phenomenon? The widespread astonishment this view aroused among theologians in fact bears witness to a certain lack of insight as to the true state of affairs. However, we can declare incontestably that Strauss's view first clearly and comprehensively brought together, and concentrated at a single point, what had previously been scattered in quite different places.

Since people now saw it all before them, all at once, as a unified whole, for the first time now they could be convinced to what extent, and on what basis, it all cast doubt on the traditional view of the truth of the gospel story. They saw how shifting and uncertain was the ground on which people heretofore believed they had a firm footing. One felt oneself taken unawares, and stricken. All at once something had come to light about which people up to now had no proper conception, although it had indeed long been at hand. The main strength of Strauss's presentation is the very fact that everywhere he is duty-bound not to conceal or cover up anything; to set forth the results in their unadorned contours; to express what is indefinite and undeveloped in the most specific way; to cut away, in the most rigorous fashion, everything that could obscure our clear understanding of the facts.

---

74. The mythical interpretation goes back to the rationalist theologians of the eighteenth and early nineteenth centuries, as evidenced by the literature Strauss cites in his Introduction. The body of the work draws out the conflicts between rationalist and supernaturalist interpretations of individual pericopes.

On the whole, his duty is simply to follow up on the interests of criticism itself as opposed to religious interests, doing so with all the dispassionateness (*Kälte*) of scientific research, so that he could hardly fail to make a very sharp impression.

The great significance of Strauss's book is, on the whole, the fact that it for the first time awakened religious and theological consciousness about the standpoint at which it found itself: how this consciousness itself proceeded wholly based on the consciousness of that time, was simply the distillation of it, and so was just something in which the consciousness of that time provided guidance with regard to the [religious] topics it was dealing with here. In a word, Strauss let the era behold its own likeness in a mirror he held before it. But in the consternation and astonishment seizing it upon looking at its own likeness, the public turned against the one who held up the mirror. Both the theological audience, and the educated public in general, very eagerly devoured Strauss's book, as we see from how quickly and repeatedly it was reprinted. Just as loudly and decisively, the voices of disapproval and indignation spoke out from almost all quarters. People felt offended; they believed the most sacred interests were imperiled, and just looked upon this book as a great public scandal. In Klüpfel's history of this Tübingen theological faculty (pp. 410ff.),[75] I have recounted the consequences this had for the author Strauss himself.

The Ecclesiastical Reaction

Upon its first printing, the impression the book made even aroused talk in Berlin about banning it. Neander nevertheless countered this talk by his own authoritative opinion, drawn up at the behest of the government ministry.[76] He declared his opposition to banning it because Strauss's book, as a link in the historical development of science, could not be ignored. The vocation of a teacher of theology is to bring his influence to bear, so that this book, proceeding from a mindset resistant to the spirit of the Christian church, would contribute to the advancement of science and thereby to the interest of the church. Although Neander acknowledged the book's scientific significance,

---

75. Baur, "Die evangelisch-theologische Fakultät vom Jahr 1812 bis 1848," in K. Klüpfel, ed., *Geschichte und Beschreibung der Universität Tübingen* (Tübingen, 1849), 389–426.

76. August Neander, *Erklärung in Beziehung auf einen ihn betreffenden Artikel der Allgemeinen Zeitung nebst dem auf höhere Veranlassung von ihm verfassten Gutachten über das Buch Strauss: Leben Jesu* (Berlin, 1836).

he had no choice but to impute it to the author's mindset, and to declare the author's standpoint to be completely reprehensible.

The more people stuck to this view of Strauss's book, the less they were able to accomplish scientifically in opposition to it. Thus even Lücke[77] thought as much, when he stated, in all seriousness, that the recognition of religious truth is precisely a matter of the heart and the will.

Thus it transpired that, since people treated a scientific issue as an issue of religious interests, and made this perspective more and more the prevailing and exclusive one, the result of Strauss's movement was the mutually opposed theological antitheses becoming increasingly sharper. The more Strauss took hold of his topic as a matter of principle, the more everything related to it also gained significance as a matter of principle. Liberal views people heretofore could have expressed in a wholly disinterested and harmless manner were now taken in a wholly different way. People saw them as simply the consequences of the Straussian criticism, and disputed them on the same terms. The supreme principle was that theology ought not be critical and skeptical, but just ecclesiastically orthodox. Now these theologians found it very advisable not merely to come to the aid of theology's weak scientific defense by appealing to people's Christian-religious consciousness, but also to draw the populace itself into the concerns at issue, a populace that anyhow could not remain oblivious to the Straussian movement. Thus it became increasingly hazardous to take the side of the Straussian critique, or even just to be inclined in that direction.

The Zürich uprising in September 1839[78] showed to what an extent popular religious fanaticism could be worked up by the bogeyman of Straussian anti-Christianity. It made it completely impossible for Strauss, a talented teacher, to work in the professional academic sector. But this was not just Strauss's own fate; since then it has more or less been the fate of everything viewed as suspect because of its critical orientation. As soon as there was rumor of such an appointment, right away the *Evangelische Kirchenzeitung* sounded the trumpets of Zion in order to alert the church to the impending sacrilege, and the highest authorities of the state were weak enough to let themselves be controlled by this influence. In filling a theological teaching position it no longer became the practice to ask mainly about a person's scientific or scholarly competence. Instead the issue above all was just whether the person is sufficiently devout so as, in the interest of the church, to make no concessions to science.

---

77. On Lücke, see n. 52. In the text, Baur refers to an article in the *Gött[liche] Anz[eige]* of May 1837.

78. See n. 55.

No further explanation is needed about how this allowed spurious interests to poke their noses into science; how, especially on account of its non-ecclesiastical orientation, the freedom and purity of the scientific studies of university young people had to have been disturbed by colliding with this apprehensiveness, and incurred the disfavor of the higher authorities. The very kind of men who considered it wholly in keeping with the times to speak, at opportune moments, in favor of free science, became ever more harsh and resistant to what they saw as not being along the lines of positive Christianity. The very same Neander, who believed that scientific interests would be harmed by banning Strauss's book, had no reservations about commending the Zürich uprising as a noble deed of the Swiss people's religious spirit. This orientation toward traditional orthodox belief, as it became dominant in opposition to the influence of Strauss's book, got a new impetus beginning in 1840, when the government of King Friedrich Wilhelm IV of Prussia, with its political and religious perspective, endorsed for the most part the view represented by the *Evangelische Kirchenzeitung*. It then declared open war against Hegelian philosophy, which had previously enjoyed the great favor of Minister Altenstein,[79] and it made serious preparations to purge all teaching institutions of Hegelianism's pernicious elements. However, since it seemed that the negativity of Hegelian philosophy could only be completely overcome by a comparable positive philosophy, attention turned to the philosopher who, simply by his long-standing silence, had retained his former philosophical renown.

Schelling in Berlin; Neander

In 1841, Schelling was appointed to the chair of philosophy in Berlin, vacant since Hegel's time, in order to raise a new banner in the main center of German science. People expected great things from this philosopher's mission. Schelling himself announced that he would not only establish "a mighty fortress" for philosophy, but would also for the first time procure for religion a genuine foundation and self-knowledge, in a new "philosophy of revelation."[80]

---

79. Karl vom Stein zum Altenstein (1770–1840) was, from 1817 until 1838, head of the Prussian Ministry of Culture, charged with reorganizing the Evangelical Church of Prussia and reforming the educational system; he supported Hegel's appointment to a professorship in philosophy at the University of Berlin.

80. F. W. J. Schelling, *Philosophie der Offenbarung*, ed. K. F. A. Schelling, *Sämmtliche Werke*, div. 2, vols. 3–4 (Stuttgart and Augsburg, 1858).

But what constituted this new "Berlin wisdom"? After the elderly Paulus in Heidelberg, bitterly hostile to any "mystery-mongering," obtained a transcript of Schelling's lectures and maliciously published it—which resulted in his being sued in the law courts—the great mystery was laid bare before the public.[81] Schelling's lectures consisted of a "negative philosophy" and a "positive philosophy." The negative philosophy is presented in the metaphysical doctrine of the three potencies. The first potency is called the infinite ability to be (*Seinkönnen*); in other words, the distinctionless unity of the ability to be and the ability to not be (*Nichtseinkönnen*). The second potency he calls the ability to be; and the third, the potency freely suspended between the ability to be and the ability to not be.[82] The positive philosophy tells how what is necessarily or blindly existent being (*Seiende*), the being from time immemorial (*das unvordenkliche Sein*), through an antithesis to what is contingent, is set in tension to this contingency and apprehends itself as free or as spirit. So then, with the freedom based on the renewed process of the potencies, it brings forth the world itself and the stages of revelation within it. The world, disrupted by the primal human being's fall from its original condition in paradise, ultimately returns once more to unity with itself.

This process of returning is the history of religion, which has two arenas or components, the mythological process,[83] and that of revelation. Via the mythological process the Son becomes the free Lord of all being. Since, by means of supernatural procreation, he also now enters into history himself, and through his death submits to the cosmic principle, he can bring this principle itself back to God and, through the spirit entering into humanity in the church, he can, in stages, bring humanity to its consummation.[84] Indeed this insignificant work (*dieses Wenige*), but most especially

81. On Paulus, see above, pp. 91–94. On the incident with Schelling, see Albert Schweitzer, *The Quest of the Historical Jesus*, trans. W. Montgomery (London and New York, 1910), 50.

82. [*Baur, in the margin*] One can indeed see from these potencies that we are dealing here with a truly negative philosophy. If we seek to make the matter somewhat clearer, we will see that these potencies are essentially none other than Hegel's categories. For this new philosophy of Schelling's is, on the whole, just a reproduction of Hegel's philosophy using new terminology that is supposed to conceal this secondary relation, but a terminology that just makes the whole thing all the more enigmatic.

83. Schelling, *Philosophie der Mythologie*, ed. K. F. A. Schelling, *Sämmtliche Werke*, div. 2, vol. 2 (Stuttgart and Augsburg, 1857).

84. [*Baur*] In the first volumes of the posthumous publication of Schelling's *Werke* we now have the authentic editions of his philosophy of mythology [n. 83] and philosophy of revelation [n. 80]. The latter is none other than a philosophy of religion, in the way it could just as well have been written by someone else who is not such a famous philosopher. It contains philosophical reflections, speculative examinations of

the particular way it is constructed, is such a gobbledygook that one can only wonder how there are people who could build so much upon it. The whole of Schelling's appearing in Berlin was a truly comical spectacle, performed with great fanfare. Neander played a major role in it.

Neander could not allow any volume of his own numerous publications to be released without the preface attacking Hegel's philosophy, and without venting there his anger about its miserable formulaic nature, philosophical popery, arrogant deification of the concept, and other similar ways of speaking. And yet Neander was Schelling's most enthusiastic admirer and devotee. Hence he even dedicated a particular volume of his church history to Schelling—for Neander, equivalent to admitting Schelling to a royal order—so as to bear witness to his gratitude for all that Schelling had accomplished in the service of their shared "holy cause" in the course of his being in Berlin; and to salute Schelling as the one who prepared the way for the new Christian period of history, the dawning light of which already approaches us from afar, to the extent that it shines in science.[85]

We now know what an idle fantasy this dawning was, and what the outcome of that shared holy cause was. In Neander's case, his passionate, partisan spirit intensified to the point of that notorious, derogatory performance in which, when theology students greeted him at his birthday celebration, he belittled two ways of thinking whose well-known advocates were two of his own colleagues, Hengstenberg and Marheineke. And what kind of talk is it for a theologian when Neander erupts, in one of his most recent prefaces, with the following words: "In defiance of all the emaciated and satiated Philistines, all the fools who cloak themselves in the semblance of an empty, vainglorious, scientific method, or let themselves be hoodwinked by it, I thus enunciate anew this motto: *pectus est, quod theologiam facit* (theology is accomplished by the heart)."[86] In keeping with this slogan, people called Neander's theology "the heart theology" (*die Pectoraltheologie*). This name appropriately designates its purely subjective character. Whoever thinks he comprehends the standpoint of another as Neander does, in hardly a scientific way, can of course just oppose it with the ardent, subjective conviction of his or her own heart. All is sympathy and antipathy, love and hate. One

---

the gospel story and Christian dogmas, but it leaves us completely in doubt as to what, above all, we might know about how we have to think about the supernatural aspect of revelation, if we do not wish to be left with an indefinite representation of it or with sheer contradictions.

85. Neander, August, *Allgemeine Geschichte der christlichen Religion und Kirche*, 2nd ed., vol. 1 (Hamburg, 1842). See the dedicatory statement.

86. We have read several of Neander's prefaces but cannot find this one. However, we have gained a clear impression of his piety and partisanship.

hates the opponent, taking him to be a person devoid of heart and soul, of spirit and life, of God and religion, simply because one cannot rediscover one's own self in him.

No theologian of high standing, in taking a partisan position, has shown himself to be so impassioned and intolerant, so insubstantial and limited, and at the same time so inconsistent, as Neander has. Given my former respect for Neander, it pains me to have to say this about him. But this is also typical of the time. When such men allow themselves to be dominated so much by the partisan spirit of the time, and allow the interest of their faction to so greatly influence them—something they have ample opportunity to do in their position—then we cannot be surprised at the fact that the antitheses become ever sharper, and church and science grow ever farther apart. By what right does Neander bemoan the inner strife of the time, in the way he makes this his constant complaint in all of his prefaces, when he himself does everything to sever the ties that are supposed to hold the antitheses together?[87]

It is characteristic of the most recent era to elaborate the significance of the antitheses in principle. This is the clearly expressed tendency of the time especially since Strauss. The false mediations just relying on pretense and deception ought finally to cease. People want to know, clearly and decisively, what is true and justifiable in each orientation. Hence what can no longer remain together must be separated. If the church can no longer put up with scientific criticism, then it must expel criticism from the church. If criticism can see in the church's faith just unhistorical assumptions, then there is nothing left for criticism to do but break with the church. However, it is undeniable that overstatement and capriciousness have also contributed very much to this sharpening of the antitheses, and to the hostile reaction the most recent criticism has elicited from the side of the church. Thus many believed the critical principle must lead to an extreme in which it had to annul itself if it were to be truly consistent.

Bruno Bauer

This is where Bruno Bauer, above all, is to be assigned his unenviable place in the history of the most recent theology. Not long after his review of Strauss's *Leben Jesu*, he broke with the orthodoxy he had previously wanted to elevate directly into the sphere of the concept by employing categories from Hegel's philosophy. This quickly brought matters to the most extreme point.

---

87. [Zeller] It is not irrelevant to point out that the above was written already in 1849. [Ed.] Neander died in 1850.

Bauer's basic idea was that criticism had reached a standpoint with him where it could declare the gospels to be just based on the self-consciousness of the gospel writers. In order to stick to his standpoint in its utterly pure form, he operated in abstraction from all the historical assumptions that form the basis for interpreting the gospels. The contents of the gospels are not to be interpreted based on the gospel tradition. That is because the accounts are created by the self-consciousness of individuals, not by the community (as though Strauss had ruled out this possibility). The mythical interpretation and the orthodox interpretation both occupy the same standpoint—taking the accounts as inexplicably substantial. There is no essential difference between saying "the gospels are verbally inspired" and saying "their contents have taken form in the tradition." Both versions are equally transcendent, and they undermine the freedom and unlimited character of self-consciousness. Furthermore, this self-consciousness is wholly abstract; it does not involve the specific, historically demonstrable and understandable representations and tendencies of earliest Christianity; it is, on the whole, just unlimited self-consciousness. So we have a similarly formulaic interpretation (*Formelmann*) as before. Just as inferences previously were made based on abstract categories, without the requisite role naturally played by objective facts, so now we have just the phenomena of consciousness without any historical mediation of them. The new critical standpoint rests solely on this syllogism: all being is first of all substance, and then self-consciousness; consequently, that must likewise be how things stand in criticism; [therefore] criticism in the wake of Strauss can only demonstrate that the gospel story is purely a work of self-consciousness.

Bruno Bauer employed this basic principle in his critique of the Gospel of John (1840),[88] albeit in a somewhat moderated way. Since this Gospel is actually for the most part a work of reflection, this is Bauer's best writing. In the form of a logical analysis he calls attention, often suitably so, to the inherent improbabilities of John's portrayals, specifically of the speeches, and justifiably points to the motives behind them and their artificiality. To be sure, even here he recognizes no guiding idea. His criticism of the Synoptic Gospels[89] is much less circumspect. This criticism is so unsystematic, and carried out so hurriedly, that at the outset the author obviously had no idea at all as to what the end result would be.

---

88. Bruno Bauer, *Kritik der evangelischen Geschichte des Johannes* (Bremen, 1840).

89. Bruno Bauer, *Kritik der evangelischen Geschichte der Synoptiker*, 3 vols. (Leipzig, 1841–42).

Bruno Bauer derived the basis for his view from Wilke's *Urevangelist* (1838).[90] At the same time as Weisse,[91] Wilke sought to argue for the priority of Mark over Luke and Matthew, by a laborious and detailed analysis that in other respects presupposed the traditional hypothesis. According to him, the self-consciousness of Mark, the writer of the initial gospel, would have been the ultimate source of the gospel account. Wilke's conclusion at the end of his work shows what the negative result of this critique amounted to. He states that if a man named Jesus existed, and if this Jesus provided the impetus for the revolution that, in the name of Christ, shook the world and gave the world a new form, then it is virtually certain that Jesus' own self-consciousness was not yet distorted by the dogmatic pronouncements of the Christ of the Gospels, and not yet torn from its moorings; then the character of Jesus' own personality gets salvaged. Conceived of as an actual historical phenomenon, the Christ of the Gospels would be someone humanity would have to have dreaded, a figure who could have inspired only fear and horror. The end result of this interpretation could only be that the very existence of such a man named Jesus is nothing but a spontaneous creation of self-consciousness.

Since Bruno Bauer had nevertheless been appointed a teacher of theology in Bonn, under the Altenstein ministry, the question soon had to arise as to whether the author of the critique of the Synoptic Gospels—and, what is more, the one who, in all his writings of that period, had gone to battle in truly fanatical fashion against the apologists and theologians, against their ignorance and hypocrisy—could still remain a teacher of theology.

In August 1841 the Eichhorn ministry[92] called upon the collective theological faculties of the Prussian universities to render a decision on the following issues. First, in light of that book [on the Synoptic Gospels], what would be its author's standpoint with reference to Christianity? Second, given the intended purpose of the universities, and especially of the theological faculties, could the freedom to teach (*licentia docendi*) be granted to him? [To the second question,] the Bonn faculty answered with an unqualified "no," as did the Berlin faculty with the exception of Marheineke, who, in a separate response proposed that Bauer be left to his academic activities, but

---

90. Christian Gottlob Wilke, *Der Urevangelist, oder exegetisch kritischen Untersuchung über das Verwandtschaftsverhältniss der drei ersten Evangelien* (Dresden and Leipzig, 1838). Wilke (1788–1854), after studies in Leipzig and a pastorate in the Erzgebirge, moved to Dresden where he wrote his book.

91. C. H. Weisse, *Die evangelische Geschichte kritisch und philosophisch bearbeitet*, 2 vols. (Leipzig, 1838). On Weisse, see n. 25. Wilke and Weisse worked independently.

92. Bauer was sent to Bonn by Minister Altenstein (n. 79) in 1839. But following his death in 1840, Altenstein was replaced by the anti-Hegelian Friedrich Eichhorn.

that, since he had in any event freely disavowed their theological character, he be granted a philosophical position with a commensurate salary. The majority of the Breslau faculty voted for revoking his teaching license. The Greifswald faculty divided evenly on the issue. The Halle faculty was very undecided, yet finally indicated that it was more advisable not to revoke Bauer's license, but instead, for the present, to just point out to him most emphatically the contradiction in which he found himself with his position as an academic teacher, as the result of his book. The Königsberg faculty declared itself most decidedly opposed to withdrawing the license.

Nothing might take place that would contribute to respect for theological science or for the church, when the church itself had no internal antidote or remedy, and when it therefore had to seek to make up for, and conceal, its own powerlessness by relying on the external authority of the state. Nevertheless everyone expressed their disapproval of criticism of this kind, including those who could not find anything directly anti-Christian in Bauer's standpoint. Bauer himself did all he could to destroy his opponents' illusion that his hostility was not aimed at Christianity as such, namely by an essay in the November [1841] issue of the *Deutsche Jahrbücher*, with the title "Theologische Schaamlosigkeiten."[93] In it he called the fruits of modern, self-contained faith "hypocrisy, dirty tricks, deliberate lies," and called the ultimate fruit of this faith "shamelessness." Thus in March 1842 the ministry decreed that his license to teach was revoked.

The *Deutsche Jahrbücher*

The very same journal, the *Deutsche Jahrbücher*,[94] in which Bruno Bauer found an outlet for his own orientation, had an alignment similar to his. Beginning in July 1838, it was greeted with such great fanfare, as one of the finest manifestations of the present-day German spirit. Thus it had itself to blame for quickly bringing on its downfall.

At the end of 1841 its editor, Arnold Ruge, already had said it was necessary to do away with Christianity. The essential form of the Christian view of the world is dualism. For someone who wishes to understand the unhealthy spasms of contemporary religious movements, the initial

---

93. In the same year Bauer published *Die Posaune des jüngsten Gerichts über Hegel, den Atheisten und Antichristen* (Leipzig, 1841). ET: *The Trumpet of the Last Judgment against Hegel, the Atheist and Antichrist*, trans. L. Stepelevich (Lewiston, NY, 1989).

94. It is more commonly known as the *Hallische Jahrbücher*, published by Arnold Ruge between 1838 and 1843. When the January 1843 issue was seized by the police, Ruge moved to Paris and, with Karl Marx, founded the *Deutsch-Französische Jahrbücher*, only one issue of which appeared in 1844.

"heresy" would be the necessary and inevitable abolition of Christianity and of the ancient dualistic religion. The second one would be the new religion set over against the old one, the religion of morality or ethics (*Sittlichkeit*), this-worldly religion (*die Religion des Diesseits*). The God of our future is not God above the world but a this-worldly God; it is spirit and its depth. The foreword to the 1842 series then contained the public declaration that, for the philosophically-oriented observer, theology and the Christian worldview could now only be of historical interest; that all attempts at an actual reconciliation of immanence with transcendence, of philosophy with Christianity, of freedom with the Christian worldview, must necessarily prove unavailing. Today science conceives of the entire standpoint of belief as uneducated and historically obsolete. Thus there is no longer any place for belief in the sphere of theological cultivation of the mind.

However, since belief, theology, and Christianity still occupy their position in practice and still seek to maintain it, the goal of an ongoing polemic against these factors could only be to attack them on the battlefield and gain the victory in practice as well. Hence the Christian worldview was to be contested with every available weapon. The names of Vatke, Schaller, Rosenkranz, Strauss, and others gradually disappeared from the *Jahrbücher*, and in their place Bruno Bauer and Ludwig Feuerbach now led the anti-Christian round dance, reacting negatively not only to theology and Christianity but to all their supposedly persisting features as such. Thus when the state authorities put an end to the *Jahrbücher*, it had long since come apart internally and condemned itself.

Feuerbach

This same Feuerbach,[95] taken together with Bruno Bauer and, in the last phase of the *Deutsche Jahrbücher*, pretty much keeping in step with him, is nevertheless to be set above him as a more high-minded, substantial personality. Just as Bauer, as a critic, sought to go beyond Strauss, Feuerbach, as a philosopher, believed he could not remain with Hegel. Because of this, the tendency of each of them was anti-Christian in a comparable way.

---

95. See n. 27. With his mention of the *Jahrbücher*, Baur may have in mind, in the first paragraphs, Feuerbach's *Ueber Philosophie und Christenthum, in Beziehung auf den der Hegel'schen Philosophie gemachten Vorwurf von Unchristlichkeit* (Mannheim, 1839), which is a separate publication of an article begun in the March 1839 issue of the *Hallische Jahrbücher*. Feuerbach's major work is *Das Wesen des Christentums*, published two years later, to which Baur refers below (n. 96). His *Grundsätze der Philosophie der Zukunft* (Zürich, 1843) is a valuable summary of his views; ET: *Principles of the Philosophy of the Future*, trans. Manfred H. Vogel (Indianapolis and New York, 1966).

It is incorrect to count Feuerbach as a member of the Hegelian school, for he protested most definitely against that and was clearly outspoken about his relation to Hegel. Feuerbach says Hegel belongs to the "Old Testament" of recent philosophy, and he himself therefore wants to be its "New Testament," its actual "gospel." In Hegel's philosophy God is given back to us as our own proper, essential being. God is thought by us, known by us, and this thinking and knowing is God's own knowing and thinking; our subjective activity is objective activity, our essential being is therefore God's essential being. However, at the same time this position holds fast to God in the religious sense, to God posited as an objective being distinct from us. Hegel fails to simply speak the truth. His position is based on the duplicity of religious consciousness, expressing not the self-identity of the human being but the identity of divine and human being. In truth, however, this latter identity is simply the displaced expression for the human being's identity with self. For Hegel, the divine-human oneness is always still a dualistic, bifurcated, equivocal oneness, not a true oneness, as also, in general, is the oneness of finite and infinite, of the natural and the spiritual, the sensible and the supersensible. It is because, for Hegel, the old hostility toward the natural and the sensible is fundamental. That is indeed clearly expressed by the fact that, according to him, nature is a falling away from the idea; it is the disjointed, cadaver-like concept, the concept gone astray, the "lost son" of the New Testament.

Feuerbach considered the necessary turning point of history to be the public acknowledgment and admission that God-consciousness is none other than species-consciousness; that human beings can and should simply rise above the limits of their individuality, but not rise above the laws or positive, essential determinations of their species; that human beings cannot think about, have some idea of, conceive of, feel, believe in, wish for, love, and revere, any being as absolute being other than the essential being of human nature. The principal thesis to which Feuerbach always returns, in its various applications, is that human beings can think of nothing higher than their own essential being; that "God" is just a human being's manifested inwardness, one's expressed self. Hence from this standpoint the absolute is not spirit in its distinction from nature; instead it is nature, is human nature in its oneness with nature as such (*Natur überhaupt*).

From this general definition of his standpoint we of course see how to capture the essence of religion in Feuerbach's case. If the divine essence is none other than the essence of the human being, then religion can only be a person's relation to himself or herself. Religion is the relation to one's own essential being, albeit not to one's own being as such but instead to an other essence, one set apart, distinct, indeed a confronted being.

The secret of religion is that human beings objectify their own essential being, and then in turn objectify themselves as objects for this being as it is transformed into a subject. They think of themselves, they are objects to themselves, but as objects of an object, of another essential being. This way human beings approach religion is rooted in the fact that religion is essentially practical, albeit only in an exclusively, and one-sidedly, egotistical sense. Feuerbach even says as much: that religion is a matter of the heart, of the subjectivity that sets itself in isolation and just refers to itself. The heart's desires want to be satisfied, it fancifully forms the representation of a subject that accomplishes this, and this subject is God. Since in religion one's consciousness falls back exclusively on one's subjective needs, in religion the universal aspect of human nature can appear only as a consciousness distinct from it, but a consciousness that, for this very reason, is itself necessarily in turn a subjective being.

The secret of theology is therefore anthropology. Feuerbach sought to gain general recognition for this thesis. Failure to recognize it is said to be the fundamental error of our time. In relation to self-conscious reason, the issue as to religion involves destroying an illusion, indeed the kind of illusion that is by no means inconsequential but instead affects humanity in a fundamentally destructive way; the way in which religion does away with the cogency of human beings' actual life, and so destroys their sense of truth and virtue. For where morality is based on theology, and what is right is based on what is divinely instituted, one can justify and argue for the most immoral, unjust, disgraceful things. Religion is envious of morality, sucks morality's best energies dry; and even love, in itself the truest and most inward sentiment, becomes, through religion's piety, just apparent, illusory love, since human beings' religious love just for God's sake is therefore only apparently love of people but in truth is just love of God. Faith sacrifices love of people for love of God.

Here then Feuerbach's difference from Hegel also emerges more pointedly. Feuerbach himself describes his philosophy of religion as in opposition to that of Hegel. What for Hegel has secondary, subjective and formal significance is for Feuerbach what is primitive or primary, is objective, essential. For Hegel, feeling is the form of religion; for Feuerbach, feeling is religion's essence. Hegel's image or likeness (*Bild*) is for Feuerbach the thing itself (*Sache*). Hegel identifies religion with philosophy, while *he* [Feuerbach] emphasizes the specific difference between them. Hegel separates the contents, the religious object, from its form or instrument, while *he* [Feuerbach] identifies form with content, instrument with object.

According to Feuerbach (in *Das Wesen des Christentums*, 1841),[96] what Christianity especially involves is the essence of religion, magnified and incarnated. It is, in its better part, something invented by the human heart, although also having all the heart's imperfect features. As the religion of the heart, Christianity is the human being's estrangement from the species and the world, its egoistic retreat to subjectivity, its withdrawal to its own desires and needs. In Christianity, human concentration was only on oneself, grasping oneself as the only being warranting attention, the only substantial being; detaching oneself from connection with the whole world, making oneself into a self-sufficient whole, in an absolute extra-worldly and supraworldly being. In Christianity we see, unambiguously, what religion as such is. If the clearest, most incontrovertible proof that, in religion, a human being is just related to himself or herself—that since, when we love God because God loves us, we are just loving ourselves—then, because the incarnation, as the supreme act of love, makes it completely obvious that God is a thoroughly human being, and when this incarnate God is said to have suffered for us, this therefore states very plainly that our love of God is just our own self-love.

If there is any theory we can justifiably object to as one-sided, Feuerbach's is it. Everything that has a twofold aspect for Hegel, an objective side and a subjective side, has for Feuerbach just the one aspect, the subjective side, which is now for him the whole. Hence everything in religion is just subjective; in religion there is nothing objective. Feuerbach wholly occupies the standpoint of Hegel's philosophy by seeking to conceptualize the essential nature of religion as a process of self-consciousness. However, for Hegel this process is just the subjective side of absolute spirit's determining itself as infinite consciousness. In contrast, Feuerbach declares that everything objective is transcendent. To be sure he shares Hegel's tendency, in that for Feuerbach everything transcendent must become something immanent, everything "up there" must become something "down here." However, for Hegel the universal as such has its own objective reality, whereas for

---

96. *Das Wesen des Christentums* (Leipzig, 1841). ET: *The Essence of Christianity*, trans. George Eliot (London, 1854). See the foreword by H. Richard Niebuhr and the introductory essay by Karl Barth to the Harper Torchbook reprint of the translation in 1957. Barth argues, and Niebuhr seems to agree, that Feuerbach carries to its logical extreme the nineteenth-century liberal theological tendency to focus on human subjectivity rather than the objective divine revelation in Christ; the only antidote is to make theology irreversible in principle, and that requires a new orthodoxy. Neither takes notice of Baur's critique of this work precisely from the standpoint of a liberal, Hegelian theology: Feuerbach fails to appreciate Hegel's dialectical *holism* and reduces it instead to an egoistic monism. This is a different critique than the one based on Kierkegaard's "infinite qualitative difference" between God and humanity.

Feuerbach all truth resides solely in what is sensible and actual, only in what the human being immediately is. If one can say that, according to Hegel, God is all and the human being is nothing, inasmuch as, for Hegel, the human being's essential nature has its truth only in God, then according to Feuerbach, on the contrary, human being is everything and God is nothing.

Theology dissolves into anthropology, but also everything universal and objective dissolves into the subjectivity of what is individual. The egoism for which Feuerbach blames religion becomes, as such, the principle of this standpoint. If it is true that human beings simply are self-relation, that one cannot conceive of anything higher than one's own essential nature, then it is just the further consequence of this standpoint when people take their species-consciousness to be something transcendent. With the same justification one can say that each individual I or self can conceive of nothing higher than itself.

What holds good is, on the whole, therefore just the principle of egoism. In adhering consistently to the proposition that human being itself cannot rise above itself, that all truth and reality reside only in that of which a person is immediately self-conscious, Feuerbach's teaching, itself arising from Hegel's philosophy, crosses over from that philosophy to communistic and other practical tendencies whose principle is the most subjectivistic egoism, denying everything universal and objective. This is therefore the point at which everything belonging to the most extreme aberrations of the day, in theory and practice, also appears in turn in its connection with science, with the highest spiritual aspirations of the age. The principle of this time is human self-consciousness as the absolute power over all, as the most immediate thing to which a person has to cling. But when one does not locate the truth of self-consciousness in what is universal (and doing so is for Hegel the main thing), the necessary presupposition for this omission is that one thinks and wills everything subjectively; and then everything giving unity and coherence to one's life resolves itself into one being brutally dominated by egoism.

Baur and the Tübingen School

Strauss's *Leben Jesu*, our main point of departure here, posed for itself the task of investigating critically and grasping historically the early history of Christianity from the life of Jesus. But the results were so overwhelmingly negative that the entire early history of Christianity seems to dissolve into a series of myths and traditions. The response from the critics was as unable to contradict Strauss's views as it was to further secure the old views.

So both sides faced a dilemma. If one chose to disregard the fact that through Strauss's criticism an irreparable rift had opened up in the previous representation of the gospel history, still the negativity of its results, and the unclear and indeterminate picture that it gave of the early history of Christianity, were so unsatisfying that one could not come to a halt at that point. As a consequence, one could see that the task that had become central to the time, that of grasping early Christianity historically, had not yet been solved. In the nature of the case things had to move on. And since the consequences that critics such as Bruno Bauer drew from Strauss's results only led to a self-annulling extreme, one could only hope to approximate a solution to the problem along another path. So the question had to be raised whether the negativity of Strauss's results did not reside in a deficiency of the investigation, of its critical method; and whether one could not from a different point of view penetrate more securely into the inner aspects of the early history of Christianity and bring light to bear on its obscurity.

This is where I may mention my own efforts at research into early Christianity.[97] I started my investigations long before Strauss, and thus began from an entirely different point. My engagement with the two Corinthian epistles first provided the occasion to bring more sharply into focus the relationship of the Apostle Paul to the older apostles. I became convinced that in the letters of the Apostle himself sufficient evidence is available to see that this relationship was something entirely different from what previously had been assumed—that, where people supposed a thorough harmony of all the apostles is to be found, rather an opposition exists, an opposition that, from the Jewish-Christian side, went so far as to call into question the authority of the Apostle Paul. A closer investigation of the Pseudo-Clementine Homilies, a writing whose importance for the history of the earliest period I had especially noted along with Neander, allowed me to see more deeply into the significance of this opposition in the post-apostolic period. It became increasingly clear to me that the opposition of the two parties, which in the apostolic and post-apostolic periods are to be distinguished much more sharply than hitherto has been the case, the Pauline party and the Petrine or Judaizing party, had a decisive influence not simply on the configuration of the sayings of Peter but also on the composition of the Book of Acts.

97. Baur does not address here his own stance in relation to the Hegelian school, or the effects of that stance on his works in church history and history of dogma. He could be described as a center-left Hegelian, who on the one hand rejects the absolute identity of the idea of divine-human unity with an individual human being, but who on the other hand affirms the positive historical significance of Jesus for Christianity, and who treats the history of the church and its faith with idealist categories influenced by Hegel. He is, in Martin Wendte's terms, "a historically informed idealist of a distinctive kind" (*Baur and the History of Early Christianity* [n. 36], chap. 3).

I published the first results of my investigation in the fourth issue of the *Tübinger Zeitschrift für Theologie* of 1831, [pp. 61–206], in the essay, "Die Christuspartei in der korinthischen Gemeinde, der Gegensatz des paulinischen und petrinischen Christenthums in der ältesten Kirche, der Apostel Petrus in Rom."[98] My investigations into Gnosticism[99] led me to the Pastoral Epistles, and the results of the latter study published in 1835[100] led to the conclusion that these letters could not have been composed by the Apostle Paul. Rather their appearance is to be explained from the same partisan tendencies that were the moving principle of the church as it took shape in the second century. Continuing engagement with the Pauline epistles, and deeper penetration into the spirit of the Apostle and of Pauline Christianity, solidified in me the view that a very essential distinction exists between the four major letters of the Apostle and the lesser ones, and the authenticity of most if not all of the latter must become very doubtful. What I subsequently gathered together and further expounded in my book on the Apostle Paul[101] is the result of investigations that placed me in this position totally independently of Strauss's critique.

If a period becomes more clearly known the more deeply one sees into its circumstances and its endeavors, into the antitheses operative in it, I believe I have attained a historical comprehension of a period of the most ancient history of Christianity, which hitherto has remained in principle immune from historical examination because, on the basis of a dogmatic assumption, people held that what happened [in the events recorded in the New Testament] was not at all possible in the ordinary course of events. I have shown how deeply antithesis itself penetrated into the heart of apostolic Christianity, and how the differences of a later period have their beginnings already in this first sphere. On this basis one can for the first time form a clearer and more concrete picture of the formation of the ancient church, its oppositions and conflicts and the way they were harmonized

---

98. "The Christ Party [or Faction] in the Corinthian Community, the Opposition between Pauline and Petrine Christianity in the Earliest Church, the Apostle Peter in Rome." Reprint in *Ausgewählte Werke in Einzelausgaben*, ed. Klaus Scholder, vol. 1: *Historisch-kritische Untersuchungen zum Neuen Testament*, with an introduction by Ernst Käsemann (Stuttgart-Bad Cannstatt, 1963).

99. *Die christliche Gnosis, oder die christliche Religions-Philosophie in ihrer geschichtliche Entwicklung* (Tübingen, 1835).

100. *Die sogennanten Pastoralbriefe des Apostel Paulus aufs neue kritisch untersucht* (Stuttgart and Tübingen, 1835).

101. *Paulus, der Apostel Jesu Christi* (Stuttgart, 1845); 2nd ed., 2 vols., ed. Eduard Zeller (Leipzig, 1866–67). ET of 2nd ed.: *Paul the Apostle of Jesus Christ*, trans. Allan Menzies, 2 vols. (London and Edinburgh, 1875–76).

into the unity of the Catholic Church.¹⁰² Ebionitism and Paulinism were the factors of the historical movement of that time. These results had to be of particular importance for the history of the canon. Despite the resistance they encountered, I believe I am right to assert that by means of these results the old, baseless concept of the canon as a self-contained unity has been destroyed forever.

My first series of critical works referred to the Pauline epistles and the Book of Acts accompanying them. When Strauss's *Leben Jesu* appeared and evoked its notorious emotional response, I remained a passive observer. The matter represented nothing new for me since I had witnessed the emergence of the work close at hand and had frequently discussed it with the author. However, I could come forward neither for nor against it because at the time I still lacked the fuller studies requisite for doing so.

Only after I had made the Gospel of John the subject of lectures did I find myself in a position to adopt a new and independent position in regard to the Synoptic Gospels. The fundamental difference of John from the Synoptics became so compelling for me that I at once formed the view of the character and origin of this Gospel that I set forth in the *Theologische Jahrbücher* of 1844.¹⁰³ In this way I attained a new ground for criticism of the gospel history. If the Gospel of John is not a historical gospel like the others, if it itself does not intend to be genuinely historical, and if it undeniably has an idealizing tendency (*ideelle Tendenz*), then it can no longer be taken together with the Synoptics and be juxtaposed to them. Thus it is no longer possible, using the Straussian tactic and *modus operandi*, for the Synoptics to win out over John, or vice versa. Thus the result is that no one any longer knows to which of them one should adhere in the gospel story. To the extent that the historical value of John sinks, that of the Synoptics correspondingly rises. We can no longer have any basis for doubting the credibility of the Synoptics for the sake of John. The disagreement between the two sides is entirely due to John. This is surely not to say that we have in the Synoptics a purely historical portrayal, but with them we nevertheless have a wholly different historical basis; and the question can only be whether, since now one of the canonical Gospels has been shown to be written with a tendency of a specific type, one or another of the Synoptic Gospels should not also be placed in the same category.

---

102. See *Das Christentum und die christliche Kirche der drei ersten Jahrhunderte* (Tübingen, 1853; 2nd ed. 1860). ET of 3rd Ger. ed., identical with 2nd: *The Church History of the First Three Centuries*, 2 vols., ed. Allan Menzies (London and Edinburgh, 1878–79).

103. "Ueber die Composition und den Charakter des johanneïschen Evangeliums," *Theologische Jahrbücher* 3 (1844) 1–191, 397–475, 615–700.

This occasioned my further investigation into the Gospel of Luke in the *Theologische Jahrbücher* of 1846,[104] following which I pulled the whole together and completed it in my second major work on New Testament criticism, the *Kritische Untersuchungen über die kanonischen Evangelien* (1847).[105] The more narrowly in this fashion the circle is drawn within which the original gospel tradition is to be sought, the more the task of criticism is simplified and illumined. The whole question is concentrated on the Gospel of Matthew. Also, because of this, the mythical approach Strauss applies with such a broad brush faces very essential constraints. If it is established that most of our canonical Gospels are to be seen as tendency writings, this raises the question as to whether, where previously it was believed necessary to take the gospel traditions as a myth, this tradition has not been modified in the interest of the author's literary tendency, or even that it is an outright fiction.

Since the tendency recognizable as the specific character of several of the Gospels can have its basis only in the distinctive circumstances of the time in which their authors have written, in the partisan stances they embody, then our stance as to gospel criticism can only be taken within the entire sphere in which such phenomena are evident to us, in the way they have to be presupposed in this case. We should not draw our historical horizons too narrowly. From this it is self-evident how important it is, not merely in the apostolic age but also in the post-apostolic age, to survey everything that can serve for more precise information about the different orientations that can be distinguished in this period. My investigations into the Gospels quite naturally are therefore linked with my earlier research into the Pauline epistles. They have their foundation and firm support in that Pauline research. On the other hand these investigations also contribute essentially to allowing the post-apostolic age to appear more clearly and vividly in its concrete shape. Our canonical Gospels are products of the post-apostolic age, with the antitheses and interests that are its moving forces.[106]

In doing this I have also permitted myself to give a brief sketch of my own activity in this area. Talented students, of whom I have been fortunate to have many, have further elaborated my views and principles, and have collaborated in their dissemination and reception. This has provided

---

104. "Der Ursprung und Charakter des Lukas-Evangeliums mit Rücksicht auf die neuesten Untersuchungen," *Theologische Jahrbücher* 5 (1846) 453–615.

105. *Kritische Untersuchungen über die kanonischen Evangelien, ihr Verhältniss zu einander, ihren Charakter und Ursprung* (Tübingen, 1847).

106. See *Vorlesungen über neutestamentliche Theologie*, ed. F. F. Baur (Leipzig, 1864; repr. Darmstadt, 1973). ET: *Lectures on New Testament Theology*, ed. P. C. Hodgson, trans. R. F. Brown (Oxford, 2016).

an occasion to regard me as the founder of a school. The "New Tübingen School" has become the customary label for the most recent critical direction. I make no claims of this kind, and I am content to have contributed what I can, to the best of my ability, to the research into the most important issues that occupy the present age. My critical standpoint is the only one from which Strauss's criticism can be both revised and carried further. My criticism is more methodical than Strauss's because it goes back to the question that Strauss, above all, is said to have posed so clearly. One cannot make the life of Jesus the object of criticism as long as one is not in a position to form a definitive, critical view of the writings that are the source of our knowledge of this life, and of their relations to each other. My criticism is for this reason also more conservative than Strauss's inasmuch as it knows how, from a specific point of view, to distinguish the historical elements from the non-historical. Whatever may be the future results of investigations undertaken with such great interest, in any event I believe I may with certainty hold that no view will succeed in obtaining more general recognition vis-à-vis mine before mine can be contradicted in its entire extent and on wholly other grounds and proofs than those that have been advanced against it thus far.

Dogmatic Theology: Nitzsch, Twesten, Marheineke, and Others

After following thus far the main direction theology has taken in its most recent course of development, we can now summarize succinctly the remaining points to be emphasized, ones arising from individual branches of the discipline.

An initial glance at the field of dogmatics shows us that the first half of our period [1830–1845] was very productive. Each of the major orientations had its representatives, who were confident about their cause. Nitzsch and Twesten adhere for the most part to Schleiermacherian theology.[107] Like Lücke, Ullmann, and others, they are Schleiermacher's students. However, one cannot say that, as dogmaticians, they are preeminently supporters of Schleiermacher's spirit. The very thing Schleiermacher as dogmatician most of all epitomizes, his independent stance vis-à-vis the teachings of scripture and the church, which enables him to continually resolve dogma's positive elements into the fluid forms of the general religious consciousness, is a

---

107. Karl Immanuel Nitzsch (1787–1868); August Detlev Christian Twesten (1789–1876). After teaching in Bonn, Nitzsch succeeded Marheineke in Berlin in 1847. Twesten succeeded Schleiermacher in Berlin in 1835, but he tried to reconcile the latter's views with orthodox Lutheranism.

feature they especially lack. In them, Schleiermacherian dogmatics has incorporated too much the rigid forms of orthodoxy.

In company with Schleiermacher, Nitzsch understands religion as a fact of mental or spiritual life, one originally rooted in feeling. However, he indeed parts ways with Schleiermacher by directly recognizing in this origin the necessity of objectifying feeling in knowing and doing, at least in a far more definite way than Schleiermacher did. The perspective guiding his understanding of Christianity emphasizes its enlivening effect, what Nitzsch calls its "salvific power." On this basis he has taken ethics up into dogmatics. The greatest merit of this treatment is a more vital and unitary presentation of the Christian religion as a *System der christlichen Lehre*, which is the title of his dogmatics (1829, with later editions).[108]

But appropriating this teaching inwardly is only possible in a speculative or intellectual way, as Nitzsch himself occasionally has to acknowledge (for instance, in the case of the Trinitarian doctrine, which seems to embody its essentially speculative origins). However, Nitzsch's principle excludes actual speculative treatment of the teaching. So there remain just in part echoes of an intelligible treatment, but ones stuck, as a rule, with mere approaches to it, with forceful language or original-sounding terms that lack any distinctive conceptual content; and in part a vagueness in his presentation and thinking, in which the most significant critical difficulties are dismissed with a few superficial remarks, and the self-contradictory representations as well as contradictions with the church's theological framework, are concealed by very general expressions. Thus in apologetics the difficulty the supernaturalist view has with prophecies and miracles gets hardly enough emphasis, when in each case the historical, rationalist interpretation gets conjoined with the orthodox, dogmatic interpretation, by accepting that the Old Testament speeches and history have typological [i.e., non-literal] meaning, and thus that scripture has a twofold sense—so that these things are supposedly made plausible by various rational artifices. Where there is no capacity for dialectical development, one far too readily adopts a peremptory, judgmental tone.

Twesten (*Vorlesungen über die evangelisch lutherischen Dogmatik*, pt 1, 1826)[109] is decidedly superior to Nitzsch in his reasonable reflections and clarity of presentation. However, the absence of an overall standpoint,

---

108. K. I. Nitzsch, *System der christlichen Lehre* (Bonn, 1829, 6th ed. 1851). ET: *System of Christian Doctrine*, trans. from the 5th Ger. ed. by Robert Montgomery and John Hennen (Edinburgh, 1849).

109. August Twesten, *Vorlesungen über die Dogmatik der Evangelisch-Lutherischen Kirche, nach dem Compendium des Herrn Dr. W. M. L. de Wette*, 2 vols. (Hamburg, 1826–37). The projected second part of vol. 2 was never published.

mysteriously covered over in Nitzsch's case, now also emerges all the clearer. These features are ultimately grounded in the forced combination of Schleiermacher's theology of feeling with the supernaturalist dogmatics of the old orthodoxy. On the one hand, religion derives from feeling, and the meaning of religious representations is measured with reference to feeling; on the other hand, these representations are said to have their own independent value and significance. On the one hand, Christian consciousness is the source and norm of faith; on the other hand, absolute authority is attributed to scripture, and this calls for scripture's harmony with the creeds, at least in essentials. Hence we have the contradiction that can hardly appear anywhere more clearly than it does with Twesten. He wants to interpret everything based on the nature of spirit, and to that extent in accord with reason, and at the same time to interpret it in supernatural terms; to posit religion as both immanent and transcendent for human beings. This is a contradictory position Twesten extricates himself from only by constantly vacillating between incompatible stipulations.

For Twesten, revelation is supposedly in part natural, in part supernatural, except that in one place he gives one of these aspects prominence while deemphasizing the other, and in another place he does the opposite. Miracles are said to also belong to the natural order of things, but to a higher order and therefore not the order of nature. He interprets inspiration in one place as psychological, à la Schleiermacher, and in another place as supernatural, based on its being miraculously imparted by the Spirit; first as confined to the essentially religious contents of scripture, and then described as providing both the contents and the wording (*suggestio rerum et verborum*). He puts aside the conflict of faith and reason by employing the pointless distinction that revelation does not contradict enlightened reason, but only contradicts unenlightened reason; that reason does not need to comprehend faith's content, but only needs to understand what it is, and so forth. Twesten departs so far from Schleiermacher that even the Athanasian doctrine of the Trinity, with all the aridity of the old Protestant scholasticism, found a place in his *Dogmatik*. After an interval, he continued this work in 1838, but then broke off with the doctrine of the angels and left the rest unfinished. In doing so it seemed that he wanted to say it was no longer suited to the times.

Here we pass over other, and less important, presentations of this kind. In Steudel's dogmatics, *Die Glaubenslehre der evangelisch protestantischen Kirche nach ihrer guten Begründung mit Rücksicht auf das Bedürfniss der Zeit* ([Tübingen], 1834),[110] supernaturalism summoned its remaining forces in

---

110. On J. C. F. Steudel, see n. 43.

the most unremitting struggle against Schleiermacher, Hegel, and Marheineke. See my own history of the Tübingen Protestant theology faculty, pp. 420ff. in Klüpfel's *Geschichte und Beschreibung der Universität Tübingen*.[111] We can also include here Hase's otherwise wholly eclectic dogmatics,[112] for it shares with the rationalistic textbooks of dogmatics the specific feature of being far more a history of dogma than being a dogmatics. In the published versions of Daub's and Marheineke's respective lectures on dogma,[113] speculative dogmatics has been reworked very substantially. From this same perspective, Vatke's book, *Die menschliche Freiheit in ihrem Verhältniss zur Sünde und zur göttlichen Gnade* ([Berlin], 1841),[114] merits special mention, as a scientific counterpart to J. Müller's *Die Lehre von der Sünde*,[115] which is in many points not a very scientific book.

Strauss's *Glaubenslehre*

By far the most important event in the area of dogmatics was the second major work by Strauss, *Die christliche Glaubenslehre in ihrer geschichtlichen Entwicklung und im Kampfe mit der modernen Wissenschaft* (1840).[116] It was supposed to do for dogmatics what his first book had done for the life of Jesus or the gospel story. Strauss himself declared, about the idea and tendency of this work, that all the previous antitheses, even that of Catholicism and Protestantism, have resolved themselves into the "main antithesis," that "between the standpoint of the Christian faith as such, and the standpoint

---

111. "Die evangelisch-theologische Fakultät vom Jahr 1812 bis 1848," in K. Klüpfel, ed., *Geschichte und Beschreibung der Universität Tübingen* (Tübingen, 1849), 389–426.

112. Karl August von Hase, *Lehrbuch der evangelischen Dogmatik* (Stuttgart, 1826; 2nd ed., Leipzig, 1838). Hase (1800–90) was a professor of theology in Jena and great-grandfather of Dietrich Bonhoeffer. In 1855 he wrote an open letter to Baur on the Tübingen School, to which Baur replied. These documents are reprinted in *Ausgewählte Werke in Einzelausgaben* (n. 98), vol. 5: *Für und wider die Tübinger Schule* (Stuttgart–Bad Cannstatt, 1975).

113. Karl Daub, *Die dogmatische Theologie jetziger Zeit* (Heidelberg, 1833); on Daub, see p. 89, n. 81. Philipp Marheineke, *Theologische Vorlesungen*, ed. S. Matthies and W. Vatke, 4 vols. (Berlin, 1847–48), vol. 2: *System der christlichen Dogmatik*. On Marheineke, see p. 205, n. 70.

114. Wilhelm Vatke (1806–82) was a professor of Old Testament in Berlin.

115. Julius Müller, *Die christliche Lehre von der Sünde*, 2 vols. (Breslau, 1844). ET: *The Christian Doctrine of Sin*, trans. from the 5th Ger. ed. by W. Urwick, 2 vols. (Edinburgh, 1868). Müller (1801–78) taught at Göttingen, Marburg, and Halle. As a disciple of Neander and friend of Richard Rothe, he was strongly opposed to Hegel's philosophy and Baur's historical criticism.

116. See n. 30.

of modern science." If heretofore "people have either, without further ado, rationalized the faith and the Bible, or Christianized speculative reason, or have neutralized both faith and reason in vague feelings or a careless mixture of both of them, by consequently concealing the harm done instead of remedying it, by suppressing the conflict instead of settling it, then things have to change if we want to move forward."[117]

Strauss said he prepared his *Glaubenslehre* to move in this direction.

> With this aim he traced, step-by-step, the origin and elaboration of each dogma, sought to transpose himself into the mindset of that time and the conscious steps from which the dogma organically arose, and he shed appropriate light on the truth, the magnitude and excellence, that he found in this way. But when he arrived at the high point of a dogma's elaboration by the church, he then immediately followed up with the further task of revealing, in the dogma's full maturity, the seeds of its downfall, by directly tracing this downfall through the stages of the dogma's downward course right up to the present day. However, what counted in the end was to be alert so as not to mistake a new coat of paint on the old structure for its actual restoration.[118]

Therefore the history of dogma was also said to be its critique.[119] Strauss says that "the subjective critique of the individual instances is like the outlet of a spring that any lad can stop up for a while, whereas criticism over the course of centuries, and carried out objectively, crashes down like a roaring river, and all the floodgates and dams are of no avail against it."[120] The writings of dogmatic science are said, in this way, to perform the same function as "the balance sheets in a business office."

> If those balance sheets do not make the business uniformly richer, at least it learns from them precisely how things stand with its resources, and that information is often worth just as much as an increase in those resources. Such an overview of how dogmatic theology's holdings stand in our own day is all the more a pressing need, when the majority of theologians harbor the greatest illusions about those resources. People vastly underestimate the impact that the criticism and polemic of the past two centuries has had on the overall foundation of the old

---

117. Strauss, *Die christliche Glaubenslehre* (n. 30), 1:vii–viii (partly paraphrased).
118. Ibid., 1:viii–ix (paraphrased quotation, with "he" substituted for "I").
119. Ibid., 1:71. "Die wahre Kritik des Dogma ist seine Geschichte."
120. Ibid., 1:x.

theology and, on the other hand, they vastly overestimate the dubious resources they believe they have found in the theology of feeling and in mystical philosophy. They suppose that these procedures, which place those results under a cloud, have for the most part already won out, and are certain to be the most substantial gain from this newly-opened well. However, it could be the case that these procedures as a whole are summarily misguided; and if these new excavations nevertheless dash their hopes, then failure would be unavoidable.[121]

The fact that such a failure or bankruptcy, such a disparity between credits and debits, is indeed the case, is the result of Strauss's work, which concludes with a very negative tone, as does his first book.

The issue could only be whether Strauss's negative conclusion regarding each dogma is in fact to be viewed as the objective verdict of the very history on the basis of which Strauss wants to embrace it as simply a given; whether that verdict does not depend on individual authorities whose worth can only be determined subjectively, and who can always be countered by others. However, when looked at in this way, the force of the line of argument in the individual instance, and the value of the result, might, in the larger picture, be conditional upon discovering the mindset behind, and essential tendency of, a historical act, from its surface, nonessential features; and that sets clearly before the eyes of any unbiased person the irreconcilable conflict modern science is conceived as having with traditional belief.

Strauss sees the distinctive task to which he has devoted all his energy as making people aware of this breach in the whole sphere of faith; of confronting each one with the agonizing matter of conscience, by treating it in a completely unsympathetic, scientific way; by asking how people can endure this conflict in their consciousness, and can go on thinking they can decide in favor of one side or the other. Here all the cardinal issues come to a head: the personhood of God, the immortality of the soul, the person of Christ. Here it seems no longer possible to yield to any further illusions and to escape acknowledging the transparently obvious negativity of the result. So it can only be left to each person to find the way to get over it and, subjectively and internally, come to terms with the conflict forcing its way into the general consciousness of the time. In any event this much is certain: that all those antitheses having their apex in dogmatics have still never entered

---

121. Ibid., 1:xi. Strauss's fondness for the analogy with business operations is also found in his correspondence. See U. Köpf on Baur and Strauss in *Baur and the History of Early Christianity* (n. 36), 27–28 n. 198.

into such a reciprocal tension that they seem only able to culminate with a complete break between science and the church.[122]

Mediating Theology; A More Modern Supernaturalism

We are now to treat the dogmatic standpoint where the antitheses, at their peak, are no longer understood to involve the conflict between theological systems and orientations, but rather the conflict between science and the church. Instead of disputing Christianity's positive elements with scientific reasoning, it is simpler by far to stick directly to actual features of the church, and to consider the church's consciousness as the barrier that all the nay-saying of science has to break through. This is most closely connected with what was taking place in the church itself.

The issue of the Protestant Union intensified people's ecclesiastical awareness, and the concerns of the Lutheran system in particular were strongly promoted. Thus major opposition now formed to any more liberal view of the ecclesiastical system. The confessionalism so very significant in all issues involving the church can, it goes without saying, also simply maintain the strictest orthodoxy in dogmatics. However, between the antithetical extremes posed by the mutual opposition of science and the church, an intermediate faction is nevertheless at work, seeking as much as possible to forestall such a breach between the two sides. This is the same faction we spoke of earlier as the Schleiermacher group.[123] It has comparable interests in both defending the project of the Union, and seeking to mediate and mitigate the dogmatic antitheses.

---

122. Baur speaks much more directly in his *Lehrbuch der christlichen Dogmengeschichte* (Tübingen, 1847, 2nd rev. ed. 1858), where he discusses Strauss's *Glaubenslehre* in the context of rationalist approaches: "Rationalism inherently has, in the nature of the case, no historical sensibility. . . . Although [Strauss's dogmatics] rests, in a quite different sense than do the usual textbooks, on the elaboration of the view that the history of dogma is also its critique, one nevertheless can also see quite clearly that, simply considered from a dogmatic point of view, the history always comes off badly. The [dogmatic] history as such is not the major concern, but instead the critique; and, since the critique itself is connected not with the positive aspect but with the negative, dogma only serves to build up its structure so that the structure is seen to collapse. To show that there is nothing in it that can be sustained, dogma appears in the final analysis to exist only to be criticized and critically negated." *History of Christian Dogma*, ed. Peter C. Hodgson, trans. R. F. Brown and P. C. Hodgson (Oxford, 2014), 78–79. These remarks led to Strauss's "renunciation" of his relationship with Baur (see Köpf in *Baur and the History of Early Christianity* [n. 36], 28–30), and Baur must have desired not to further alienate his former student.

123. See above, n. 51.

At this point we connect Ullmann[124] above all with Nitzsch and Twesten. Ullmann is a major advocate of this mediating theology,[125] particularly in his opposition to the Straussian orientation. We learn this best from his 1845 book *Das Wesen des Christentums*,[126] which appeared in several editions. Ullmann sees Christianity in properly Schleiermacherian fashion, grasping it not as doctrine but as life and the creative life-principle. He considers the person of Christ, as the God-man, to be the central point of Christianity as a whole. He defines Christianity as the religion that neither divinizes the natural domain in itself, in its bare form, nor denies and destroys what is in itself natural; instead Christianity transforms, sanctifies, and transfigures it. Christianity is divine in essence, human in form; divine in its origin, human in its actualization and development. For supernaturalism, Christianity is exclusively divine, superhuman, miraculous, extra-historical; for it Christianity would not be spirit and life, not present-day, self-certain, human truth. For naturalism and rationalism, Christianity would be turned around into something sheerly human, natural, and historical, without new divine, creative power or real connection with a higher world.

No one knows better than Ullmann how to traffic in such trite phrases. However, they are merely clichés, and as soon as one examines what they are supposedly saying, they leave all the important points completely undefined and unanswered. Such statements are in principle worthless. They hurt rather than help, since they only serve to create the pretense that something is really being said by this vacuous way of speaking. They continue to use Schleiermacher's expressions and characterizations, but they will have none of the general perspective or worldview on which these expressions have their basis in Schleiermacher and without which they have no meaning.

---

124. See above, n. 52.

125. Claude Welch, drawing on Baur, provides a summary of the mediating theologies, which in general sought to reconcile faith and science, historical Christianity and modern culture. He writes, in *Protestant Thought in the Nineteenth Century: Volume 1, 1799–1870* (New Haven and London, 1972), 142: "According to this schematism, one must then distinguish among the many varieties of 'mediation.' Thus F. C. Baur proposed to differentiate between the 'speculative theists' (e.g., I. H. Fichte, C. H. Weisse, and Richard Rothe) and the 'right of center' mediating theologians of either the Schleiermacherian type (e.g., Nitzsch, Twesten, Ullmann, Lücke, Umbreit) or the 'right-wing Hegelian' type (e.g., Liebner, Lange, Marheineke, Martensen, Dorner). Baur judged both of these latter groups to be moving toward a new supernaturalism."

126. Carl Christian Ullmann, *Das Wesen des Christenthums: mit Beziehungen auf neuerer Auffasungsweise desselben von Freunden und Gegnern: Eine Erörterung auch für gebildete Nicht-Theologen* (Hamburg, 1845).

The dogmatic works of Liebner, Lange, and Martensen belong in the same category, only with the difference that they include even more heterogeneous elements, and combine them into a speculative eclecticism.

In the first division of the first volume of his dogmatics, appearing in 1849, Liebner[127] sought to provide a speculative deduction of the Trinity and of the person of Christ, one as little ecclesiastically orthodox as it is philosophically tenable. It employs the strange conception of a universal personhood (*Allpersönlichkeit*) supposedly belonging to Christ as the primordial human being, a conception first proposed by Göschel and Dorner.[128]

Lange sets out from a christological perspective in his dogmatics, published in 1849.[129] The concept of the God-man is the center of the entire dogmatics for him too. In order to grasp the deepest foundation for the oneness of the divine and the human, he regards creation as the basis of all revelation, the goal of which is then attained in a sequence ever more perfectly developing the divine aspect in Christ as the God-man. Lange proceeds in very grand style in opposition to the supernaturalist school's representations, and speaks about revelation, miracles, and inspiration as if one should have supposed he wholly occupies the standpoint of the modern way of looking at things. But in Lange's case too this is all just empty words. He lacks any coherent thinking and engages in sheerly fantastic speculation. In also wanting to be witty and clever, he often instead just makes a comical impression. We see from his writings on church history how insignificant he is. Entirely lacking any concept of the need for historical criticism, the tenor of these writings is all the more hostile to the more recent research.

The Danish theologian Martensen[130] is far more worthy of our attention. His 1850 dogmatics gained deserved recognition in various respects in Germany too. At least it is methodical and circumspect in its formal aspects.

127. *Die christliche Dogmatik aus den christologischen Princip* (Göttingen, 1849), by Karl Theodor Albert Liebner (1806–71), a professor in Göttingen, Kiel, and Leipzig.

128. Isaac August Dorner (1809–74) studied theology in Tübingen, where in 1835 he published the first part of his *Entwicklungsgeschichte der Lehre von der Person Christi*. He served as a professor at several universities before arriving in Berlin in 1862. In this volume Baur discusses him only in relation to church issues, but in his *History of Christian Dogma* (n. 122), 346, 359–60, he evaluates Dorner's views on the immutability of God and christology.

129. Johann Peter Lange (1802–84), following a pastorate in Duisburg, was called to Strauss's intended position in Zürich, and later to Bonn. His *Christliche Dogmatik* was published in 3 vols. (Heidelberg, 1847–9).

130. Hans Lassen Martensen (1808–84), professor in Copenhagen and later bishop of Zealand, influenced by Schleiermacher, Hegel, and Franz von Baader, and also the object of Kierkegaard's attack on Christendom. *Die christliche Dogmatik*, translated from Danish (Kiel, 1850). ET: *Christian Dogmatics: A Compendium of the Doctrines of Christianity*, trans. W. Urwick (Edinburgh, 1886).

He wants to be a faithful adherent of the church's dogma, although in his own system the dogma is oft times also very quixotically interspersed with modern speculative conceptions.

Rothe, Fichte, and Weisse

Richard Rothe[131] without question is deservedly superior to the aforementioned dogmaticians. His *Theologische Ethik* (1845) is among the most important publications in the domain of systematic theology. Although Rothe calls his main work an "ethics," we quite properly introduce it here among the works in dogmatics. It is not ethics in the usual sense, for it is far more a dogmatics than an ethics. As such, it is a theological system arranged according to a first-rate plan and carried out methodically.

In his previous book, *Die Anfänge der christlichen Kirche* (1837), where he set out from the oneness of the religious and ethical domains, instead of keeping them apart as abstractly separate, he situated them as mutually and inherently related by understanding the ethical domain as the concrete realization of the religious domain. Thus in his *Ethik* too, the ethical is the principal concept that comprises within itself the whole of speculative theology. Rothe is very much aware of the task of science, of its stature and independence. However, if one wanted to set him alongside Schleiermacher, as someone of completely equal rank, in the way Schwarz does in his *Zur Geschichte der neuesten Theologie* (p. 280),[132] that would credit Rothe with too much importance.

Rothe himself describes his own standpoint as one of Christian realism, and as theosophy in Oetinger's sense, for Rothe acknowledged his own intellectual kinship with Oetinger.[133] Just as Oetinger's theosophy, in its antipathy to spiritualism, sought to have everything fittingly concrete and tangibly corporeal, Rothe too insisted on the real and corporeal, although for him theosophical realism ultimately amounted to a very contentless play of fantasy.

Rothe sets out from the absolute personality and trinitarian being of God. He puts the world, as the not-I or not-self, in contraposition to God,

---

131. Richard Rothe (1799–1867) studied theology in Heidelberg and Berlin and was a professor in Heidelberg and Bonn. His *Theologische Ethik* was published in 3 vols. (Wittenberg, 1845–8). Earlier he wrote *Die Anfänge der christlichen Kirche und ihre Verfassung* (Wittenberg, 1837).

132. Carl Schwarz (1812–85), *Zur Geschichte der neuesten Theologie* (Leipzig, 1856).

133. Friedrich Christoph Oetinger (1702–82) was a Württemberg theologian and theosophist who was influenced by Boehme and translated Swedenborg.

and defines the God-world relation as their absolute correlation: without a world there is no God. God posits himself in the world, although in the many stages of development, where each stage is conditioned by its predecessor stages, the developmental process of the creature presents itself as its own process. In human persons this process becomes an ethical task in which the creation's process carries on as an ethical process, which in turn also passes through a series of stages in which sin necessarily forms an unavoidable way station.

So far everything proceeds with the strict coherence of an immanent development. But as soon as Rothe's system arrives at the soil of Christianity, all continuity in the development ceases. He then speaks, all at once, of absolute unexplainable miracles and of creative acts without any mediating role on the creature's part. The historical development even comes to a final end with the physical second coming of the Lord, and the thousand-year consummation of God's kingdom on earth.

In the speculative element Rothe's dogmatics contains, it has more affinity with the philosophical orientation we mentioned earlier that, as speculative theology, shares the concern to undergird theism and opposes the pantheistic worldview arising from Schleiermacher and Hegel. This theism, with the idea of God's absolute personhood, sought to mediate God's self-understanding with his pervasiveness in the world, God's being-for-self with his omnipotent operations—in other words, to mediate transcendence with immanence. The most significant works belonging in this category are I. H. Fichte's *Spekulative Theologie* (1846) and Weisse's *Philosophische Dogmatik* (vol. 1, 1855).[134]

Weisse also calls his dogmatics a "philosophy of Christianity." In the earliest period of Christianity there was not yet any philosophy of Christianity. In the process of its development, Christianity then had not yet reached the point of tolerating, alongside it and unconditionally, an independent philosophy with the full range of epistemological endeavors such a concept would involve. With its abundant contents, grasped on their own in faith and not, strictly speaking, directly in knowledge, Christianity did not stand for being made into an object of these epistemological endeavors by philosophy. Christianity must first reach a point at which it does not merely tolerate, completely unconditionally, a philosophy alongside it, a philosophy that would just be guided by the idea of the truth as such and not by the idea of a specific religious truth; instead Christianity must actively create this philosophy, based on Christianity's own sphere of life, before it may

---

134. On I. H. Fichte and C. H. Weisse, see n. 25. Fichte's work is *Die speculative Theologie oder allgemeine Religionslehre* (Heidelberg, 1846). Weisse's work is *Philosophische Dogmatik, oder Philosophie des Christenthums*, vol. 1 (Leipzig, 1855).

hope to position itself as having a truly objective knowledge of itself. Doing so should therefore take place through philosophical dogmatics, which will for the first time procure for Christianity an authentic awareness and true knowledge of itself (p. 9).[135]

This is the age-old problem vis-à-vis Christianity that has occupied thinking spirit in every era. Weisse's work too wholly deals with this same issue: how we are to regard all the previous attempts of this kind—whether the philosophy that wants to thoroughly understand Christianity conceptually is completely free of assumptions of its own; and, if this is the case, whether by that very procedure Christianity does not lose some of the contents of its faith, contents essentially belonging to it. Like all the rest of Weisse's writings, this latest work is also marked above all by lack of clarity in dealing with the main issues, and by dogmatic pretexts. However, today we are in general so little attuned to philosophy that not very much attention even gets paid to this philosophical dogmatics. So far it has not gotten beyond volume one, which contains just the topic of the divine attributes and the introduction to the topic of the world.[136]

The Union Theology

Today the church has a far more decided impact on the domain of dogmatics than philosophy does. The consequence for dogmatics, from controversies arising from the issue of the Union, is that one cannot be a defender of church teaching unless one declares one's allegiance either to consensus dogmatics or to strict confessionalism. Since the principal opponents of the Union are the Lutheran theologians who categorically assert their confessional interests, Lutheran dogmatics constitutes the major opposition to consensus dogmatics. Those backing consensus dogmatics are chiefly the theologians belonging to the Schleiermacher school: Nitzsch, Lücke, J. Müller, Dorner, and others.

If the Union is not to be castigated for failure to affirm anything, it too must subscribe to a specific, dogmatic, theological framework. However, since the concept of union involves its distancing itself from confessional particularism, from divisive doctrines, the theological framework of the Union theologians can consist only of common elements on which the two

---

135. Baur here summarizes and partly quotes material from the introductory sections of the *Philosophische Dogmatik*.

136. [*Zeller*] The second volume, *Die Welt- und Menschenschöpfung*, containing the doctrines of creation, the original condition, and sin, appeared in 1860. [*Ed.*] The third volume, *Die Heilslehre des Christenthums*, appeared in 1862.

theological frameworks [Lutheran and Reformed] are in agreement. Nitzsch and J. Müller sought to formulate the confessional consensus in specific articles along these lines: Nitzsch in the charter document of the Protestant Union (1853); J. Müller in *Die evangelische Union, ihr Wesen und göttliches Recht* (1854).[137] But these efforts only reached the point of reducing those two theological frameworks to a happy medium by limiting them and toning them down; by a compromise in which their antithetical character lost its edge. This method of unification may be applied to a number of doctrines without any difficulty and without further import for the system. In the end, however, it necessarily founders on the divisive teachings that neither of the two theological frameworks can consent to modifying without surrendering their essential character.

Schleiermacher had first proposed the thesis on which this consensus theology rests: that only those features in Protestantism on which the two confessions actually agree could be essential ones. But Schleiermacher wanted to neutralize and disempower both theological frameworks by this thesis, in order to get beyond them, as outdated systems, and to take up a new standpoint suited to modern culture. However much Schleiermacher also sought to create the appearance that he was in complete agreement with the old system, we see clearly in his case how the new form of consciousness breaks through the old one. We also see that he retains the old form only so as to introduce the new consciousness and pave the way for it.[138]

However, the consensus dogmatics of every doctrinaire unionist is simply a self-deception, just on the basis of its own lack of intellectual freedom. It has been too confined to the particularism of the confessional system, while having the internal impulse to adopt a freer relation to that system, and not failing to recognize that it already occupies a standpoint above and beyond that system. But this dogmatics does not wish to acknowledge this confinement openly, instead looking forward to where its efforts are actually directed, and only looking backward, time and again, to the point at which the confessional differences had their original foundation. These doctrinaire unionists want what they hold, as the true contents of the Protestant faith, to be established based on the church's confessional statements. Yet they themselves must concede that they are unable to agree completely with either the Lutheran or the Reformed theological framework. For that very reason these dogmaticians want to have what they cannot find in either confession

---

137. K. I. Nitzsch, *Urkundenbuch der Evangelischen Union mit Erläuterungen* (Bonn, 1853). Julius Müller, *Die evangelische Union, ihr Wesen und göttliches Recht* (Berlin, 1854).

138. See the discussion of Schleiermacher in Part Two, Sec. 3.

be all the more certain in both, taken together. Yet the more detailed the comparison of these confessions, the more they stand as mutually exclusive.

This is the contradiction from which there is no way out; the circle in which one constantly rotates between the Union and confessional ties. People no longer have a proper sense of the old system, and yet lack the strength and courage to rise up to a new one. They know inwardly that they are no longer one with the church, and yet they dare not break with it openly. They hold fast to the Union with all its advantages, and yet they also cannot part with denominational ties. Can it be surprising that all the dogmatic products from this group of theologians are so very feeble, superficial, and platitudinous? Only the opponents of these union theologians, namely the Lutheran theologians, have a proper dogmatic standpoint. With all the repellent features of its particularism, the Lutheran system at least has the advantage of its standing, its decisiveness, and its consistency.

The Orthodox Theologians: Hofmann and the Erlangen Group; and Baumgarten

In addition to Kahnis in Leipzig, Philippi and O. Mejer in Rostock, and Kliefoth in Schwerin,[139] it is mainly the Erlangen theologians—Hofmann, Thomasius, Delitzsch, Harnack, Schmid[140]—who represent this orientation in Protestant dogmatics.

To the extent that the works of these theologians do not merely contain a secondhand presentation of the old Lutheran system—which is in fact what the writings of Philippi and Schmid do—the one standing out the most from the rest is *Die Schriftbeweis* by Hofmann.[141] However, with this very work we unfortunately encounter the way in which, even with orthodox Lutheran theologians, the clearest stream can be diverted into being a murky, shadowy one. Hofmann calls his work "scriptural proof," as a way of saying we ought not be satisfied merely with writings said to provide evidence by proving one or another individual point instead of the whole of a system, of proving this or that element in scripture instead of providing proof for all

---

139. Karl Friedrich August Kahnis (1814–88); Friedrich Adolph Philippi (1809–82); Otto Mejer (1818–93); Theodor Friedrich Dethlof Kliefoth (1810–95).

140. Johann Christian Konrad Hofmann (1810–77); Gottfried Thomasius (1802–75); Franz Julius Delitzsch (1813–90); Theodosius Harnack (1817–89), father of Adolf Harnack; Heinrich Schmid (1811–85). Hofmann and Thomasius are the major figures. On the Erlangen theology, see Welch, *Protestant Thought in the Nineteenth Century* (n. 125), 218–27.

141. J. C. K. Hofmann, *Die Schriftbeweis, ein theologischer Versuch*, 3 vols. (Nördlingen, 1852–55).

of it. Therefore, with respect to all the things one wants to prove from scripture, one should always have in view the whole of scripture. Scriptural proof in this sense was said to be a new theological principle, of a kind similar to Christian consciousness according to Schleiermacher, for Hofmann apparently took Schleiermacher's *Glaubenslehre* as his general model. "Scriptural proof" was supposedly neither the usual Protestant scriptural principle nor Christian consciousness.

Hofmann then incurred the reproach that he deviated in a major way from the authentic teaching found in the cardinal doctrines of the Lutheran system. Philippi charged him with doing that, in *Herr Dr. von Hofmann gegenüber der lutherischen Versöhnungs- und Rechtfertigungslehre* ([Frankfurt], 1856). [Philippi said that] in the church's doctrine of reconciliation Hofmann clearly and unequivocally cancels out the doctrine of vicarious satisfaction and, in the church's doctrine of justification he does away with the correlative doctrine concerning the imputation of Jesus Christ's righteousness. That is, Hofmann cancels out precisely what the church itself teaches about reconciliation and justification, because this very teaching is none other than these two doctrines as integrally connected and as correlatively requisite elements. Hofmann denies that the blood of the Son of God has been paid as ransom to God's wrath, that Our Lord and Savior has taken upon himself the guilt and punishment for our sins and paid the penalty for them by his death, and that accordingly we share in the forgiveness of sin, in other words, in justification, solely by acquiring the merit of Christ in faith. Hofmann expressly denies what the church unanimously and explicitly affirms throughout all its confessional statements.

In fact Hofmann's teaching is none other than a reiteration of the Socinian theory of reconciliation. [It is that] in Christ, God's holy love has inaugurated a new humanity. God's righteousness, as the Son's righteousness, has made humankind the object of the divine pleasure. Now the individual just needs to depart from fellowship with the First Adam and cross over to fellowship with the Second Adam, to the community of righteousness, in order to share individually in the divine pleasure. The sending and perfection of Christ is accordingly just an actualization of God's holy love, the commencement of a new history of humankind. Christ's death is no divinely ordained necessity, for one can instead consider it to be just a contingent and avoidable incident in human affairs.

In opposition to Hofmann, Philippi avows that it is precisely because of the Lutheran doctrines of reconciliation and justification, in their confessional form and formulation, that he is a Lutheran theologian, a Lutheran Christian, indeed a Christian as such. For whoever accepts the expiatory blood of God's Son as the ransom paid to God's wrath, as the satisfaction of God's righteous vengeance carried out vicariously, and so accepts this justification, or forgiveness of sin, and does this solely by faith, is one who accepts Christianity as such. Then he would likewise gladly remain with the religion of his forefathers, the religion of the seed of Abraham, according to the flesh.

Philippi had reproached Hofmann in the preface to the second edition of his *Commentar über den Brief Pauli an die Römer* ([Frankfurt], 1856). Hofmann's rejoinder, "Begründete Abweisung eines nicht begründeten Vorwurfs," was in the *Erlanger Zeitschrift* of February/March 1856. He made a further statement about this in his *Schutzschriften für eine neue Weise, alte Wahrheit zu lehren*, in two parts ([Nördlingen], 1857-58), which was also directed against his two colleagues, Thomasius and Harnack, who had likewise attacked him in *Das Bekenntniss der lutherischen Kirche von der Versöhnung und die Versöhnungslehre Hofmann's*, written by Thomasius with a postscript by Harnack ([Erlangen], 1857).

Hofmann's opponents share the view that what Hofmann teaches is not the teaching of the creedal documents, and that he just seeks in the most artful way to establish the fact that he agrees with them. Hofmann can appeal on far better grounds to similar sounding passages in Luther's writings, but Luther is not consistent in how he presents this teaching. The opponents are correct that the concept of satisfaction at issue here is always presupposed both in the ancient creeds and by Luther. It is a remarkable occurrence for such a departure from the church's teaching to have come to light in such an orthodox faculty as Erlangen's. Apart from this dispute, there cannot be any significant objection to Hofmann's teaching. It can be justified exegetically, and it not only has the support of ancient authorities, but also corresponds far more to a developed dogmatic consciousness than the church's consciousness does. But why then, if it is now not the church's consciousness, should that also not be openly admitted? Even with an inherently more liberal orientation, this captivity to church teaching ever remains the characteristic feature of our time.

A similar case occurred at the University of Rostock in Mecklenburg, where the strictly orthodox theological faculty likewise had a colleague in their midst, Dr. Baumgarten,[142] who caused the others to have very serious reservations about his orthodoxy. In addition to other factors at which they took offense, Dr. Baumgarten was accused of repeated departures from the church's theological framework regarded as binding in Mecklenburg. In April 1857 the government saw this as the occasion for demanding that the consistory consider the issue as to whether, and to what extent, Professor

---

142. Michael Baumgarten (1812-89).

Dr. Baumgarten's teaching, presented in five enclosed writings by him, agreed, despite all its innovations, with the contents of the creedal documents and the Mecklenburg ecclesiastical system. The judgment, composed in September 1857 by Dr. Kraabe,[143] Rostock professor of theology, resulted in Baumgarten being removed from his teaching position, while for the present retaining his current salary.

This event created quite a stir. People saw it as an unwarranted power play and a most striking infringement of academic freedom of instruction. The issue was the subject of much debate. Several notable publications about it were *Beleuchtung des über Dr. Baumgarten's Lehrabweichungen abgegebenen Consistorial-Erachtens* (1858), by Hofmann at Erlangen, and *Die Sache des Prof. Dr. Baumgarten in Rostock, theologisch and juristisch beleuchtet*, by Dr. Delitzsch and Dr. Scheuerl, professors at Erlangen. Both these writings express serious misgivings about the consistorial judgment, based on an injustice perpetrated against Dr. Baumgarten.

Baumgarten himself protested against such proceedings, and turned to theological faculties elsewhere, specifically those of Göttingen and Greifswald. Each of these faculties expressed its opinion in print: *Gutachten der theologischen Facultät zu Griefswald über das Rostocker Consistorial-Erachten* (Leipzig, 1859); *Gutachten der theologischen Facultät zu Göttingen über die in dem Erachten des Consistoriums zu Rostock gegen die Theologie des Dr. Baumgarten erhobene Beschuldigung fundamentaler Abweichung von der kirchlichen Lehre* (Gotha, 1859).[144] Each declared itself in Baumgarten's favor. Only Dr. Gass[145] of Greifswald cast a publicly-announced vote of his own, in which he found the consistorial judgment justified in designating as heretical anything it might find in Baumgarten's works to be departures from a standpoint materially and thoroughly binding for doctrine, based on Luther's writing on creedal matters. But this standpoint is untenable and lacks any internal rationale as to whether, and in what area, the contents of confessional writings can even be imposed as still binding on theology today. The Göttingen faculty stated as one its conviction that, despite his many contested and unfruitful theological themes, Dr. Baumgarten is not caught up in any fundamental departure from the Protestant confession; that, to the contrary, he is rooted, and abides, in the basic outlooks and truths of the Evangelical-Lutheran Reformation. Its statement was so detailed and specific that, as a result, there could be no suitable and justifiable complaint

---

143. Otto Carsten Krabbe (1805–73).

144. We cannot find online listings of these debates about Baumgarten. A *Gutachtung* is an expert opinion, a scholarly judgment.

145. Wilhelm Gass (1813–89).

lodged against him based on deviant teachings, much less any condemnation of him.[146]

Historical Theology

In turning from dogmatics to historical theology, the first thing to mention here is of course Strauss's *Glaubenslehre*, which is wholly designed to facilitate the critique of dogma, carried out in the context of the history of dogma. This work was largely the fruit of the historical research that preceded it, and it also essentially contributed to the furtherance of that research.

The time frame we are speaking about here has, as a whole, produced many works on church history and the history of dogma. Because of them and, in addition, such great enrichment of historical materials, our perspective on this history in its entirety has also become essentially different than it was before. An objective understanding and portrayal has replaced the subjective pragmatism that was the distinctive characteristic of the earlier period. We have not just endeavored to investigate, in a deeper and more multifaceted way, the inner connections between events, for we also learned how to grasp historical phenomena as appearances of the idea objectifying itself within them, and how to comprehend them as moments of the idea's immanent working within history. In my own writings on this topic of historical theology, I have made it my principal task to treat the earliest history of the Christian religion, and the history of dogma, from this perspective.[147] Since by discussing this here I would just be repeating things I have said previously,[148] I will tarry no longer with this branch of the most recent theological literature.

---

146. [Zeller] The controversy has been carried on since then in publications and official actions, including lawsuits for damages and condemnations, but without anything of consequence coming from it.

147. Baur contributed massively to this task through his foundational monographs on the history of the doctrines of reconciliation, Trinity, and incarnation, his multi-volume history of the Christian Church (Zeller notes that it should be included too), and his lectures and textbook on the history of Christian dogma. For an overview, see our translation of the latter, *History of Christian Dogma* (n. 122), especially Baur's introduction on the object, method, and history of the history of dogma (§§3–4, 6). That he was also a major contributor to New Testament studies reflects a range of expertise no longer imaginable today.

148. [Zeller] Cf. especially now *Die Epochen der kirchlichen Geschichtsschreibung*. [Ed.] Published in Tübingen, 1852. ET: *The Epochs of Church Historiography* in *Ferdinand Christian Baur: On the Writing of Church History*, ed. and trans. P. C. Hodgson (New York, 1968). The *Epochen* was intended as a general introduction to the five-volume *Kirchengeschichte*.

Biblical Exegesis

Exegesis also took a turn for the better in just the most recent period. Only a short time ago relatively little was done in the domain of exegetical literature; but now, all at once, it has come alive with activity. Instead of the arid, niggling, insipid exegesis of both supernaturalists and rationalists, people felt the need to grasp scripture in a fresher and more vital spirit, and to delve more deeply in their understanding of it. They sought to form for themselves a more concrete and vivid picture of the individuality of each writer and his distinguishing features. They not only worked at the fundamentals of individual scriptures; they also began commentaries intended to cover the entire New Testament canon. Indeed the exegetical works of Tholuck[149] and Olshausen[150] have the merit of spurring exegetical interest on at a time when it had to be given new life once more.

Olshausen's *Commentar über das ganze Neue Testament* (1830-),[151] which remains unfinished, sets itself apart by a certain freshness and independence. But linked with its efforts at a deeper investigation into the meaning of the text are very unusual and venturesome conceptions that become increasingly more forced the more Olshausen wants to put its supernaturalism into natural terms.

Tholuck too lacks a firm stance in exegesis. At least in his earlier writings he made numerous compromises that his rationalist opponents, Fritsche and Schulz, mercilessly exposed. His *Commentar über den Römerbrief*, in five editions, the first in 1824,[152] has, by comparing the older commentaries, gone back to the more profound and truly Pauline spirit in his interpretation of Romans. In the first edition he indeed gave a running account of the exegetical writings of the Church Fathers and the Reformers.

Among the most recent exegetes, Lücke[153] and de Wette[154] have a place of honor alongside Bleek, whose three-volume *Commentar über den Hebräerbrief* (1828-40) counts as a model of fundamental exegesis.[155] It is in

---

149. See n. 48.

150. Hermann Olshausen (1796-1839).

151. *Biblische Commentar über sämtliche Schriften des Neuen Testaments*, 6 vols. (Königsberg, 1830ff.); vols. 5-6 completed after the author's death by J. A. H. Ebrard and A. Weisinger. ET: *Biblical Commentary on the New Testament*, trans. A. C. Kendrick, 6 vols. (New York, 1856-58).

152. *Kommentar zu Briefe Pauli an die Römer* (Halle, 1824ff.).

153. Friedrich Lücke (see n. 52).

154. W. M. L. de Wette (see p. 198, n. 66).

155. Friedrich Bleek (1793-1859), *Der Brief an die Hebräer* (Berlin, 1828-40).

exegesis that these two theologians, whose names are so intertwined with the history of the most recent theology, are in fact primarily at home.

One of the most esteemed exegetical works is Lücke's *Commentar über das Evangelium des Johannes*, in its third edition ([Bonn], 1840). Here John is treated with the partiality the school of Schleiermacher reserves for him, and with all the sentimentality of a theologian of feeling such as Lücke. In its third edition, which had to take account of the Straussian critique, it collided head-on with that criticism. Lücke is not unreceptive to the toughest critical questions, although they cut too deeply into his heart, and he does not have the fortitude to make some concession to them and continue on regardless. In the end his theology of feeling must nevertheless always carry the day. Inasmuch as Lücke cannot avoid reaching a decision, he therefore avails himself of partial and vacillating explanations and artful hypotheses, like those on the issue of who wrote the Book of Revelation. De Wette occupies the same standpoint, for the two of them acknowledge their intellectual kinship, although de Wette has a more dispassionate nature, as he is more critical and skeptical than Lücke.

Shortly before his death de Wette finished his *Kurzgefasstes exegetisches Handbuch zum Neuen Testament* in 1848 [Leipzig, 3 vols]. Working on it was his daily task, as laudably one of the most faithful toilers in the theological field. Not only one of the most useful theological books, it is also very commendable in scientific terms. Here in particular he very propitiously put to use his own special talent, which is to author textbooks that are brief and compact, with appropriate selections and illuminating summaries. On the whole, de Wette was no systematician or historian but just an eclectic, someone who digested already given material, although he was wholly on his own distinctive terrain in such labors. His name will long endure in the history of theology, because in addition to his *Exegetisches Handbuch* there is his *Lehrbuch einer historisch-kritischen Einleitung in das Alte und Neue Testament*,[156] which is very valuable because it provides an overview of all the critical materials. One can readily use it for orientation everywhere in the New Testament. It provides a compilation of all the important exegeses, together with judgments that, from a strictly exegetical angle, evidence a fundamental proficiency in languages and unbiased scriptural research.

---

156. Two separate works in later editions: *Lehrbuch einer historisch-kritischen Einleitung in die kanonischen und apokryphischen Bücher des Alten Testaments*, 7th rev. ed. (Berlin, 1852); *Lehrbuch einer historisch-kritischen Einleitung in die kanonischen Bücher des Neuen Testaments*, 5th rev. ed. (Berlin, 1848). ET of the former: *A Critical and Historical Introduction to the Canonical Scriptures of the Old Testament*, trans. Theodore Parker, 2 vols., 3rd ed. (Boston, 1859). ET of the latter: *An Historico-Critical Introduction to the Books of the New Testament*, trans. Frederick Frothingham (Boston, 1858).

From the outset of his theological career de Wette was one of the most broad-minded critics, as well as someone who initially made far greater concessions to Straussian criticism than any of the older theologians did. On this point see in particular the foreword to his 1836 treatment of the Gospel of Matthew,[157] where he speaks specifically about this: "The return of many younger theologians to the old orthodoxy, under the protective shield of worldly power, is nothing but the result of a reaction and only serves to guard against acting hastily; the more philosophical way (*der Weg der Weltbildung*) is a higher road, of course clear only to the few, but it will be discovered and become the path despite all the precautions it calls for." The ensuing years shed even stronger light on the truth of these words.

Yet however candidly de Wette spoke about the results of his own critical research—how they also ensued in particular from his exegetical labors on the New Testament (for instance on the Pastoral Epistles whose authenticity he denied unconditionally, and Ephesians, whose Pauline origin he at first doubted)—he nevertheless lacked a firm standpoint and a consistent point of view. Submitting impartially to the force of arguments and counter arguments, he also constantly switched from one side to the other. On major issues like those involving the Gospel of John his judgment wavers far too much and is self-contradictory. So he could end up giving predominance to the view that his critical nature found unacceptable. The cause of this was partly reluctance to be so extreme, and partly a certain superficiality and shallowness in his general way of looking at things. The latest edition of his New Testament introduction is, above all, evidence of this; see *Theologische Jahrbücher* 1849 (339ff.) and 1851 (80ff.).[158]

Deserving favorable mention alongside de Wette, as a commentator on the entire New Testament, is Meyer, whose *Kritisch exegetisches Handbuch*[159] has the special advantage of grammatical and philological rigor. While there has been almost an excessive number of commentaries, especially on Romans, Rückert[160] in particular has accomplished a great deal in his exposition of the Pauline epistles, seen in the successful efforts

157. W. M. L. de Wette, *Kurze Erklärung des Evangeliums Matthäi* (Leipzig, 1836), viii.

158. These are references to articles by Baur: "Zur neutestamentlichen Kritik. Uebersicht über die neuesten Erscheinungen auf ihrem Gebiet," *Theologische Jahrbücher* 8 (1849) 299–370, 455–534; "Die Einleitung in das Neue Testament als theologische Wissenschaft. Ihr Begriff und ihre Aufgabe, ihr Entwicklungsgang und ihr innerer Organismus," *Theologische Jahrbücher* 9 (1850) 463–566; 10 (1851) 70–94, 222–53, 291–329.

159. Heinrich Wilhelm August Meyer (1800–73), *Kritische exegetische Kommentar über das Neue Testament*, 3rd ed. (Göttingen, 1855).

160. Leopold Immanuel Rückert (1797–1871) wrote commentaries on several of the Pauline epistles.

of an interpreter not so much theological as philological, who puts himself into the concrete situations of the epistles and understands the Apostle in human terms, and for that reason also more truly.

The fundamental principle, without which the idea and the aim of a biblical theology is unthinkable, is that there is nothing one has to be more on guard against than one's own conceptions and beliefs when one interprets the writings of the biblical authors; that therefore one has to take up a purely objective stance toward the New Testament writers as well, without bringing in a subjective interest, even be it the interest of faith. This principle cannot be acknowledged if one has not, by the general advances made today, risen to the stage of personal freedom requisite for doing so.[161]

Old Testament Theology: Hengstenberg

As for Old Testament theology in particular, we now have to mention Hengstenberg[162] first of all. He set for himself the general task of reestablishing the old orthodoxy and elucidating it with every means at his command. First he had to try to immerse himself in the area of scientific activity he had most affinity for [the Old Testament]. Nowhere has criticism ever caused such devastation.

Hengstenberg had the audacity to attempt a thoroughgoing restoration in this area too. In a series of publications (*Christologie* [*des alten Testaments*], 3 vols, [Berlin,] 1829–35; *Beiträge zur Einleitung ins Alte Testament*, 3 vols, [Berlin,] 1831–39), he busied himself with justification of the authenticity of the entire Old Testament canon, the orthodox interpretation of individual passages, namely those pointing toward the messiah, and also the historical credibility of the Old Testament narratives, based on examining them in detail. With all his might he threw himself into contested issues: the genuineness of the Pentateuch, of the Book of Daniel, and of the second part of Isaiah.

Hengstenberg knew as well as anyone how to reprimand the unscientific character and superficiality of the rationalists, and he sought to proceed in a strictly scientific way. But one could of course perceive what kind of scientific methodology this was from its irritable, vehement tone, and even more from the moral suspicions and accusations it relied on throughout. Thus in his *Beiträge*, vol. 2, p. xxxv, he provides an investigation into the reasons for opposition to the Pentateuch, the result of which is that the

---

161. The way in which Baur himself carries out this principle is seen in his *Lectures on New Testament Theology* (n. 106).

162. On Hengstenberg, see n. 44.

opposition bases itself: 1) on the contemporary inclination to naturalism, to alienation from God finding its consummate form in pantheism; 2) on the critics' aversions to the ethical mentality of these scriptures; 3) on the critics' inability to place themselves within the mindset of the Old Testament. Compare what he says in vol. 3, p. 467: that the Pentateuch "has such a thoroughly moral spirit that for this very reason it is utterly contrary to all the pantheists."

The a priori basis from which Hengstenberg derives his exegetical results is in part his spiritual affinity with the Old Testament, and in part genuine insight into the consequences of his standpoint. Whoever, like Hengstenberg, therefore knows how to accommodate himself to the representation of God's jealousy, anger, and vengeance (*Beiträge*, vol. 3, p. 458)—whoever has such great personal need for anthropomorphism, even of the crudest sort (vol. 3, p. 448),[163] so as to have something of his God in the bloody battles where even the bare idea [of God] is abandoned; whoever deems everything so perfect as he does with the system that every injustice and crime is forgiven more readily than is opposition to the people of the covenant (*Christologie*, vol. 3, pp. 145, 198); whoever is so little rooted in the enlightenment of our times and instead is so deeply saturated with the Old Testament spirit of exclusiveness, of fanaticism and hierarchy—must naturally be scandalized about someone who has accepted rationalism in dealing with the content of the Old Testament revelation.

However, even where Hengstenberg would perhaps have been personally inclined to make allowances for the spirit of today, insight into the connection of the individual passage with the whole forbade him from doing so. His conception is that, with each concession, one is acknowledging the critical principle; that then the critical axioms must also be applicable to the New Testament. Then at various points he perhaps would have set aside a miracle, although he perceives that miracles are the indispensable consequence of theism (*Beiträge*, vol. 2, p. xxv). Then perhaps he would have conceded a historical development in the case of prophecy, an advance from what is more indefinite and obscure to greater clarity and specificity. But a more proper instinct tells him (*Christologie*, vol. 1, pp. 103, 257; *Beiträge*, vol. 1, p. 187) that doing so would risk scripture's revealed character; that a direct revelation in the individual passage can just as well communicate the distant future as it can the near future, the most definite matters as well as the most indefinite ones; that when prophecy is not foretelling individual events quite specifically, it could just as readily have been derived from the

---

163. In this passage, Hengstenberg says that anthropomorphism is unconditionally necessary, and that its alternative is nihilism, as illustrated by deism.

universal needs and longings of the human heart; that one cannot possibly assume a constant development of Old Testament revelation, and so scriptures like the Pentateuch, Daniel, and the second part of Isaiah keep their ostensible authors; that therefore when even credulous theologians such as Nitzsch do away with the specificity of revelation, by symbolic interpretation of the prophetic numbers and other things of this kind, Hengstenberg simply ascribes that to the covert influence of a view arising from sheer unbelief. Thus it is precisely the consequences of criticism that form the mainstay of this reaction.

Hengstenberg was also able to carry through with his own standpoint in an unreserved way. Thus he contends (*Beitrage*, vol. 3, p. 507) that the vessels the Israelites took with them when they departed from Egypt had been given to them by the Egyptians, otherwise they would not have possessed them legally; that Jephthah [Judges 11:30–40] did not sacrifice his daughter but only consecrated her to God as a nun, because a human sacrifice would have been contrary to the spirit of the religion of Jehovah (on which see pp. 127, 143, and elsewhere). Based on the obviously rationalistic argument that a talking ass seems to violate the eternal boundary that chapter one of Genesis has drawn between the human world and the animal world, the talking ass in the story of Balaam [Numbers 22:28–30] gets interpreted away, declared to be merely a vision the prophet had. Even more striking is the hypothesis about John, chapter 4, where Hengstenberg cannot comprehend Jesus' conduct when, for him, it has to do with the woman's salvation and in general with success among the Samaritans; when the woman and her circumstances were at the same time symbolic of the Samaritan people (vol. 2, pp. 21ff.).

Hengstenberg pits himself against the ancient church's view of prophecy as such, when he contends (*Christologie*, vol. 1, pp. 299ff.) that the Old Testament prophets received their revelations in a state of ecstasy. From this he concludes that, in the case of the prophets, and without detriment to their higher status, what we find is not only that they delineate the future in an incomplete and fragmentary way, but also that they completely stand back from current conditions, by transferring the distant future into the present. We find the prophet transposed into the circumstances of a later time. An example is Isaiah, in the second part of his book, transposed into the circumstances of the Exile. With the prophets we find a synoptic vision of events far separated in time; a pictorial presentation in which what is to come is depicted according to present-day prototypes (for instance, Christ as a militant conqueror); an obscurity in presentation often illuminated only by its fulfillment. It is clear how useful this hypothesis is for apologetics, in order to derive messianic prophecies from a connection far and way devoid of any coherence; in order to justify an unfulfilled prophecy; in order to wriggle out of the unmistakable indications that a text is not authentic.

Later, after Hengstenberg had learned a few Hegelian phrases from Göschel[164] and others, he availed himself, in an even more elementary way, of the contention that prophecy rests on the idea. On this basis he referred to all the events in which this idea might present itself, for instance, by relating Joel's prophecy of the locust plague [Joel 1:4] to all the [divine] punishment for the degenerate Jewish or Christian theocracies; by relating the prophecy of Matthew 24 not solely to the destruction of Jerusalem and the Last Judgment but also to everything that occurs in the interim (*Christologie*, vol. 3, pp. 141ff., 374). On another occasion (with respect to the prophet Micah, ibid., 235), Hengstenberg hypothesized that a prophet's portrayal would consolidate in one overall picture the quintessence of all his different prophecies, divested of all their local and temporal features, with their individual contents said to be at the same time non-contemporaneous and contemporaneous. Hengstenberg himself boasted about this hypothesis, because with it one could leave all the historical references in place, since according to it the prophet ties together what belongs to these different circumstances and different times. Yet in truth its advantage is just that it leaves the door open for any capriciousness on the part of the exegete.

However, just as all these particular points are products of [exegetical] predicaments, so too they clearly originate under the influence of rationalism. Hengstenberg cannot escape partly accepting the rationalistic interpretation, may not surrender the orthodox interpretation, and so takes up a twofold and multiple relation to prophecy. I have characterized this orientation somewhat extensively in order to show what an internal contradiction it involves, what self-deception and untruth; indeed dishonesty and dissembling is wedded to such an eccentric position. One must maintain a great deal in opposition to one's own better convictions, once one follows a tendency such as Hengstenberg's.

In his *Theologie des Alten Testaments*, Vatke,[165] with all the rigor of dogged criticism, has taken the opposite standpoint, one accepting historical development. Only the initial volume has appeared. His basic idea is that Old Testament theology is to be understood as a history of religious development. Its beginnings are to be seen in a sensuous, barbarous cult of Jehovah that emerged from Sabeanism[166] by focusing on one of the heavenly bodies,

---

164. On Göschel, see n. 28.

165. On Wilhelm Vatke, see n. 114. The title of his book is *Die Religion des Alten Testaments nach den kanonischen Büchern entwickelt*, vol. 1 (Berlin, 1835). No further volumes were published.

166. The Sabeans were an ancient South Arabian people who are mentioned in

namely, Saturn. This cult was elaborated and refined by the prophets. The Mosaic legislation was only completed after the Exile, and for the most part was never put into practice. Ewald is the most recent authority in this field owing both to his history of the people of Israel, and to his treatment of the prophetic and poetic writings of the Old Testament.[167]

Ecclesiastical and Theological Journals: *Theologische Studien und Kritiken, Evangelische Kirchenzeitung*, and Others

An overview of the periodical literature of today will conclude this part, for it too is especially informative about how various orientations and factions are related. It is noteworthy that the number of theological periodicals has certainly increased right up to today, including especially those that have both an ecclesiastical and a practical orientation. Many of the numerous theological periodicals published today are quite insignificant. The ones that stand out are for the most part periodicals that began publication toward the end of the previous period.

From 1828 right up to most recent times, *Theologische Studien und Kritiken*, edited by Ullmann and Umbreit,[168] has championed the Schleiermacherian orientation. After it had once made inroads with the public at large it became the most generally accepted theological journal, one that now also apparently has the widest readership. At an opportune time, at the beginning of its third decade, Ullmann proceeded, in a preamble, to speak very grandly about the prominence and the wide circulation of his publication. It was established at a very auspicious time for a new theological journal to appear. Right from its inception it also contained contributions from such theologians as Schleiermacher, including his famous *Sendschreiben* concerning his *Glaubenslehre*,[169] a feature that had to be quite beneficial for boosting its reputation. In the long run, however, it has not

---

several Old Testament books and the Quran, and who reportedly had seven temples dedicated to the seven planets.

167. Heinrich Ewald (1803–75) taught in Göttingen, where in 1837 he lost his position because of his protest against the king's abrogation of the liberal constitution, then at Tübingen (where he feuded with Baur over the latter's interpretation of the canonical gospels), and later again at Göttingen starting in 1848. Included among his works are: *Geschichte des Volkes Israel bis Christus*, 3 vols. (Göttingen, 1843–52); *Die Propheten des Alten Bundes*, 3 vols. (Göttingen, 1840–41); *Die Dichter des Alten Bundes*, 4 vols. (Göttingen, 1835–57).

168. On Carl Ullmann, see n. 52. He and F. W. C. Umbreit (1795–1860) were colleagues in Heidelberg.

169. See p. 217, n. 95.

produced anything epoch-making, for indeed very much of it, particularly in the exegetical and apologetical line, is of very little consequence.

Since this journal has a very broad and undefined character, it makes it its business to keep its distance both from nonscientific devoutness (*Kirchlichkeit*) and from non-devout science. On the whole it sets out to please all factions as much as possible, at least by not only avoiding letting anything extreme come up, but also avoiding anything decisive and drastic. Everywhere it seeks to take the sting out of the antitheses and to neutralize them by a middle-of-the-road way of looking at things. By doing so it therefore had to emphatically commend itself to a public fond of this broad, moderate avenue. Ullmann also never failed to seize any opportunity for renewing public interest in his *Studien und Kritiken*, by speeches referring in particular to its importance. So just recently he celebrated its twenty-five year jubilee, or silver anniversary, at which, in a very unctuous sermon, he newly blessed the reader's bond with *Studien und Kritiken* as a marriage with the church and with science, therefore as a double marriage.[170]

Especially indicative of its theological character are several of Ullmann's essays that also appeared there, such as those on the sinlessness of Jesus, the essence of Christianity, and Strauss's *Leben Jesu*.[171] Likewise indicative is the approval they met with, simply thanks to their effort to modernize, as much as possible, the church's supernaturalism that it everywhere adheres to, and the way in which this supernaturalism is presented, by having it appear in an accommodating, inoffensive form, one Ullmann always takes great care to utilize. Overall, *Studien und Kritiken* has grown in keeping with the personality of Ullmann, its chief editor, in such a way that its theological character has shaped itself wholly in relation to him. As chief editor of a periodical designed for the wider public, Ullmann has to take into account all the trends of the time; so he has become not merely the managing director of his own faction, but also its theological diplomat and publicist. He is involved where it is a matter of mediating, of bringing people together, of ecclesiastical organization. He has a verdict and a voice in all important ecclesiastical issues of a scientific or practical kind, and the tenor of this voice is always one of mediation and guidance from the standpoint of modern devoutness, of tempered broadmindedness, but a broadmindedness sometimes taking very definitive steps against destructive liberalism. If such a voice makes itself known, then an article usually also appears in the

---

170. See *Theologische Studien und Kritiken* 25:1 (1852) 5ff.

171. See *Theologische Studien und Kritiken* 1:1 (1828), 3ff.; 9:3 (1836) 770ff.; 22:4 (1849) 961ff.

Allgemeine Zeitung[172] so as to call particular attention to the momentous nature of the opinion delivered on a most important issue by the renowned theologian, who is broadminded, as well as tempered and fair in his thinking. Ullmann's name has become even more famous because of this path carved out by *Studien und Kritiken* than it did from his otherwise respectable works in the field of historical theology.

The new Berlin periodical, *Deutsche Zeitschrift für christliche Wissenschaft und christliches Leben*, edited by Neander, Nitzsch, and Müller, has, since 1850, been published concurrently with *Studien und Kritiken*. These two journals compete with each other by trading in the same stale and superficial theology, which uses Schleiermacher's name simply as a cover for its scientific weakness.

Since 1856 another publication, the *Jahrbücher für deutsche Theologie*, edited by Liebner, Dorner, and others, has presented the orthodoxy reliant on Schleiermacher.

The principal organ for the older supernaturalism is the *Tübinger Zeitschrift für Theologie*, edited by Steudel. From its inception this journal contained elements that could not bode well for its successful existence.[173] When it was discontinued in 1840, the Tübingen publication that replaced it was the *Theologische Jahrbücher*, edited by Zeller beginning in 1842, which had a quite different tendency and allegiance.

The preamble of the *Jahrbücher* stated that so far all the forms of contemporary Protestant consciousness have had ample opportunity to speak for themselves and have their own organs—creedal, ecclesiastical orthodoxy; the theology of feeling; rationalism; eclecticism; even sectarian Lutheranism and the "new church." Only the theological science independent of all heteronomy, and basing itself solely on the power of thinking, has thus far had to be content with the meager space allotted to it in general literary periodicals or in theological journals of wavering allegiance. The *Theologische Jahrbücher* was therefore said to inaugurate a venue for those who, without reservations or ulterior motives of any kind, aspire to the advancement of science, purely and for its own sake. It sets out from the idea of free science. The first requisite for this journal is the necessary and justifiable recognition of free and consistent thinking in the theological domain too.

The *Jahrbücher* continued in this spirit until the sixteenth volume, with which it ended its run in 1857. I have been a contributor to it from the outset, and from 1847 onward I was also an associate editor. Those who

---

172. A leading daily newspaper in nineteenth-century Germany.

173. [*Baur, in the text*] See, for instance, Klüpfel's *Geschichte der Universität Tübingen* (n. 75), 418ff.

worked in this field were few, and the number of readers could not equal the thousands that Ullmann boasted of for his *Studien*. All the same, the *Jahrbücher* could have the consolation of not being a superfluous link in the theological literature.[174]

Periodicals such as those I named represent a specific theological orientation, but consider themselves to be simply a scientific instrument of that orientation. None of those with an ecclesiastical tendency, but that wish with this tendency at the same time to exercise control over science, can challenge the leading position the *Evangelische Kirchenzeitung*[175] occupies. Until today it has remained faithful to its appointed character. It continues, very decisively and persistently, to polemicize against everything that is not what it takes to be orthodox; and, despite constant assurances to the contrary, it relentlessly attacks not only views but also persons. In his publication Hengstenberg displayed a very hierarchical, political aptitude that wholly fitted him to be the leader of his faction. Since he clearly and definitively understood and expressed his own convictions and their consequences, as well as those of the opposition, he persecuted his determined opponents with all the fervor of fanaticism and all the tools of theological politics. He knew how to seize upon the half-heartedness of lukewarm and undecided people and, from the consequences of a freer standpoint, pressure them to adopt the opposite position. No sooner did he incite the adherents of his own faction when they wished to become lenient, than he called them back when they overstepped moderate orthodoxy by their excessive assertions. Of course he did not achieve the impossible, reestablishing a lost cause scientifically. But he did achieve what he actually wanted: under the shield of orthodoxy he acquired a power that made him and his publication names to be greatly feared by many. But as consistently rigid as he was in his truly hierarchical modus operandi, he was also savvy enough to contradict himself when it was in his interest to do so. This was evident most conspicuously in his conduct toward the traditional Lutherans.

Since Hengstenberg was very actively involved in gaining the assistance of the state authorities in pursuing his hierarchical goals, it was self-evident that he would have political absolutism go hand-in-hand with his ecclesiastical absolutism. Ever since its preamble of 1832, the *Evangelische Kirchenzeitung* has adopted a distinctively political character, in which it defended the doctrine of the divine right of the authorities, and of

174. Baur does not mention the *Zeitschrift für wissenschaftliche Theologie*, which started publishing in 1858, edited by Adolf Hilgenfeld, and to which Baur contributed for three years prior to his death.

175. Baur also discusses the *Evangelische Kirchenzeitung* (*EKG*) in Part Two (see p. 214, n. 90).

unconditional obedience in the most servile way, when it comes to what are in fact political matters. It depicted kings as the reflection of God's majesty, and with the same zeal it accused the unbelievers of being most closely connected with revolution, that is, with libertinism (although it was of course a different matter when this journal could not heap enough praise on the Zürich revolution of 1839, as the most glorious work of God).

When it came to church law, the *EKZ* upheld the regents' sovereign authority over the church, and with equal decisiveness it protested against the separation of the church from the state, as it did against all attempts at a synodal constitution. It gave very naïve reasons for its opposition to the latter, on page 11 of the 1832 series [vol. 10], as follows: "As things stand now, the Spirit of the Lord need only play its part in one person, and from that one person blessing goes out directly over his entire land." With a system of representation, on the contrary, "the leaven of God's Spirit must either pervade the entire corrupt multitude of electors ahead of time, or else the majority of electors subsequently." The Holy Spirit would sooner enlighten one person, the prince of the land as the supreme ruler of the church, rather than many as the electors. Why should the Spirit of the Lord not be able to come down upon the crowned heads of the church, and the church officials they have put in place, just as well as upon a disparate body of elected people?

Anyone has to read between the lines here. This statement means that, just as the Holy Spirit is said to have an easier time in its operations if it just needs to come down upon one person, so too with a leader of a hierarchical faction, someone like Hengstenberg, the Spirit operates much more surely with this one individual than with a majority, which, as Hengstenberg fears most of all, will also always surely include rationalists. By the way, all such servile utterances cannot deter the defender of absolutism from also, on occasion, in turn pitting defiant ones against the official disciplinary measures put in place by the king, and, among the same traditional Lutherans he abandoned to the executive authority of the state, sermonizing about the principles of the freedom of the church.[176]

It is quite understandable that, after 1848, the main theme of the *Evangelische Kirchenzeitung* was the February Revolution together with the events of March, the German National Assembly in Frankfurt, and demagogy in general. Right from the outset it summoned all the forces of the apocalypse against the new demonic powers that had broken out in France. [It said that] it is now beyond doubt that we are already in the time of Gog

---

176. [*Zeller*] See what the *Protestantische Kirchenzeitung* says on this matter, (1860) 619.

and Magog, and we now just have to anticipate that, before long, fire will come down from heaven. Demagogy is surely already inherently identical with Gog and Magog. We may simply assume that the very sounds of the three terms "Gog," "Magog," and "demagogue" make things as clear as they can be—that our demagogues are, as Gog and Magog, the latest offshoots of the Beast of Revelation [20:8]. Hengstenberg first enunciated this view in an essay in the *EKZ* soon after the March events in Berlin. After that he made it fundamental to his commentary on Revelation. So the *EKZ* is forever making a different contemporary theme the focus of its polemical harangues. Most recently it got very agitated about the Protestant Alliance.[177] Even in the most recent preamble, to the 1860 series, it begins right away by saying that Satan is once again loose in Italy because of princes being driven from their duchies; in Germany in the Schiller hundredth anniversary celebration, which is a demonstration of the unbelieving world against the growing power of the church; and so on.

The influence of this faction is to be attributed to the fact that, for so many people, the study of theology has become discredited, and it has suffered such a severe decline. People become averse to a theology that knows nothing higher than literalism and hierarchical subservience. That the theologians belonging to Hengstenberg's school operate at such a low level of scientific education and intellectual culture is common knowledge. It seems that most recently, even in Prussia, people have come to see how little such an exclusive orientation has to offer for the Prussian universities as such. On this very point, see also the *Protestantische Kirchenzeitung*, 1859, p. 377: "Revolutionary Orthodoxy."

In addition to the *Evangelische Kirchenzeitung*, we should also mention the *Erlanger Protestantische Zeitschrift*, edited by the professors of theology, and the *Kirchliche Zeitschrift*, edited by Kliefoth of Schwerin and Mejer of Rostock (since 1854).[178]

B. Ecclesiastical Affairs

The Union and the Traditional Lutherans in Prussia

We have left the issue of the Union [of churches] at the point where it was about to lead to further complications.[179] On this matter the two sides

177. See below, pp. 455–57.

178. [Zeller] The latter was replaced in 1860 by the *Theologische Zeitschrift*, edited by Dieckhoff and Kliefoth. Vilmar's *Pastoraltheologische Blätter* was added in 1861.

179. See above, p. 381.

became increasingly contentious. One side held that, because of the Union, the specific differences in their confessional documents should be eliminated, whereas the other side could not, and would not, do without a specific confession.

When it came to posing this issue in an extreme version, no one spoke out more openly for the former of these two orientations than Bruno Bauer did, in *Die evangelische Landeskirche Preussens und die Wissenschaft* ([Leipzig,] 1840). He declared the Union a tremendous inversion that has toppled the visible church. The Union is the Enlightenment become actual and statutory in the church; it is the revolution as consummated in the church. That is why it is feared and dreaded by the Protestant hierarchy; why it has to involve an even more heated battle. Should the state all at once renounce it, the Union will not be defeated, for those who have recognized it in its world-historical magnitude, as the last judgment on the willfulness of the church, will proclaim it before the world. Science will contend on its behalf with an even more cheerful spirit since, in the Union, science defends the law, the state itself, and the most precious legacy of its founders. The church as such cannot acknowledge a distinction between essential and nonessential elements in the system of its doctrinal articles. Therefore [from this perspective] when one community admits, declares, and actually demonstrates that it can no longer consider differences in the individual doctrinal points of the other confession as a basis for outwardly refusing church fellowship with it, then that community has in principle abandoned its own essential nature. Therefore it is established: the unavoidable condition for the Union is that the mutually exclusive doctrinal specifications have to be surrendered; that so long as they remain valid they are just mutually exclusive, and so long as they are just mutually exclusive, they remain valid. The Union puts an end to exclusiveness as such, and without ending it the visible church cannot continue carrying through with the Enlightenment.

Although this way of putting it, in its extreme form, captured the tendency essentially underlying the Union, it had to be the obvious concern of all church-minded people, from the outset, that the Union involved this risk; so one cannot be surprised by the resistance the Union in fact increasingly encountered. Lutheranism in particular still always had its adherents who opposed nothing more than they did a Union with Reformed Protestants. The strict Lutherans saw in the Union a defection from the faith of their forefathers, a poorly-concealed crossover to the Reformed confession.[180] Some leaders of this faction in Breslau were: Scheibel, who seems to

---

180. [*Baur*] For the following see H. T. Wangemann, *Sieben Bücher Preussischer Kirchengeschichte: Eine actenmässige Darstellung des Kampfes um die lutherischen Kirche im 19ten Jahrhundert*, 2 vols. (Berlin, 1859).

have been determined from the outset to be a martyr in the battle against the Union;[181] Huschke, a learned jurist, who led his faction in matters of canon law; and Steffens, the prominent philosopher of nature, who likewise professed his belief in the Lutheran confession with all the ardor of his religious feeling.[182]

Scheibel in fact just saw the Union as an undertaking of religious indifference and obvious anti-Christianity, whereas Steffens in contrast was unable to reconcile himself to the Union mainly because he clung to the Lutheranism in which he grew up, because it made a powerful impression on his youth, and he held to it most sympathetically in his congenial, individual way. Such leaders of this faction objected loudly not only to the liturgy but also to the Union as such, and to the state's provisions for accomplishing it. However, after the Union plan had been in the works for such a long time, the firm decision was to put the Union in place and in full force. After extensive proceedings, which Scheibel fully recounts in the aforementioned book, he was at first suspended, and when he pressed for a decision on his status, he was dismissed in 1832. Steffens's Breslau connection ended when he was called to Berlin.

People sought, with all the means at their disposal, to make the Lutheran community that had rallied around Scheibel receptive to the Union. Since even now, particularly in Silesia, there were some who persistently refused to accept the liturgy, as well as the Union, the year 1834 saw an order issued by the cabinet in which union and liturgy were treated separately. Joining the Union was even left up to the free decision of each [congregation], whereas acceptance of the liturgy was ordered as obedience to the ruler's command. Consequently the wishes of those who, from antipathy to the Union, were also resistant to the liturgy, were strictly and forcefully rejected as inadmissible. Even in churches not joining the Union, the official state liturgy had to be followed, with particular modifications allowed in each province. However, if it were not a matter of a non-Christian group, those who were not friends of the Union, but hostile to it, were at least allowed to constitute themselves as a separate religious fellowship. Of course this made very clear the contradictions that complicated all these arrangements. The liturgy was constructed with the specific aim of serving as the

---

181. [*Baur, in the text*] See Scheibel, *Actenmässige Geschichte der neuesten Unternehmung einer Union zwischen der reformirten und lutheranische Kirche, vorzüglich durch gemeinschaftliche Agende, in Deutschland und besonders im preussischen Staat* (Leipzig, 1834). [*Ed.*] Johann Christian Scheibel (1783–1843).

182. [*Baur, in the text*] See Steffens, *Wie ich wieder Lutheraner wurde und was mir Lutherthum ist* (Breslau, 1831). [*Ed.*] Philipp Eduard Huschke (1801–86); Henrich Steffens (1773–1845).

liturgical expression of the Union. Yet people now said that the adherents of Lutheranism are indeed not forced to accept the Union, but are forced to accept the liturgy as something the ruler commanded; furthermore, that they ought not be allowed to exist as a separate religious community. Yet there were said to be congregations both within the Union and outside it.

Since non-acceptance of the liturgy now counted as rebellion, in Silesia people created scenes that permanently stained the history of the Union. Rival pastors who declared their opposition to the liturgy and the Union, and who, in a unified consistory, wished to disobey, were suspended. When Pastor Kellner in Hönigen was suspended in September 1834, the congregation, while singing and praying, relentlessly and passively resisted the opening of their church, so that they would not be to blame for the desecration of the altar. Hence the army forcibly opened the church and, at Christmas, the first public worship service occurred according to the [official] liturgy. Kellner was arrested and investigated on account of the uproar. Recalcitrant members of the congregation were made compliant by quartering soldiers in the town.

Nevertheless the suspended clergy did not become disheartened. In February 1835 they held a synod in Breslau, at which they resolved to rescue the Lutheran Church by every legal means. Many widely scattered congregations introduced the old Wittenberg liturgy on their own and split off from the state church. Scheibel held them together mainly by his passionate faith, and also moved them to adopt an apostolic system of governance with strict church discipline.

Guericke,[183] professor of theology in Halle, now also came to the forefront in addition to Scheibel. In 1833, Guericke had announced his return to Lutheranism, which he had unknowingly and unwillingly forsaken. Afterwards, as a secretly ordained Lutheran clergyman, he had multiple run-ins with the authorities, and in 1835 he was dismissed from his professorship on account of how he ruthlessly attacked the royal ordinances. The government proceeded with unrelenting harshness against the Lutheran congregations and their clergy, with the result that some of them, weary of the pressure exerted against them by compulsory regulations of every kind, emigrated to America.

What also had to be especially vexing for the traditional Lutherans was that even theologians who formerly agreed wholly with them, as to their ecclesiastical views and principles, now went over to the other side after the government had taken this stance toward them. These theologians included Hahn, professor of theology in Breslau, Olshausen, professor of theology

---

183. Ferdinand Guericke (1803–78).

in Erlangen,[184] and above all the editor of the *Evangelische Kirchenzeitung*. As soon as the government intervened against the traditional Lutherans, Hengstenberg, who had previously been with them in heart and soul, as well as with Scheibel, Rudelbach, and others, now resolutely sided against them. Before this Hengstenberg only spoke of the sacred cause of the true faith and the church's confessions that his publication solely dealt with, irrespective of time and circumstance. Now he spoke about the *Evangelische Kirchenzeitung*'s stance toward the present time, how it could not fail to understand how bad things were. He spoke about the signs of the times, and said he is a sound judge of them; about the conditions that, in the wake of the July Revolution and the opposition arising against the authority of Protestant princes in church affairs, have provided the occasion for him to break his silence, because the reason for that silence has now been swept aside by other, more important considerations. He spoke out decisively against regarding the authority of princes in the church as something alien, obtrusive, and necessarily to be eliminated. People should turn to Schulz's exposure of this glaring contradiction[185] in order to get an idea of how completely vile this hierarchical servility is.

But the Lutheran separatists themselves remain disunited, since Guericke did not accept Scheibel's apostolic system of governance. They acknowledge that a Lutheran conscience could even accept the official Prussian church, and be reconciled with the government, if only Christ be preached in the church.

However, when the government then succeeded in implementing the Union in this way and silencing its opponents, it still could not avoid the contradiction that this arrangement naturally involved. All the government's pronouncements about the meaning and purpose of the Union contained self-annulling stipulations. The aforementioned 28 February 1834 order of the Cabinet could be interpreted in very different ways. It stated that the Union does not intend or mean any renunciation of previous creedal statements, nor does it entail nullifying the authority previously vested in the confessional documents of the two Protestant confessions. Entry into the Union just expresses the spirit of moderation and leniency that no longer allows the difference of the other confession's individual points of doctrine to count as the reason for refusing outward church fellowship with it.

---

184. On Hahn, see p. 213, n. 88; on Olshausen, n. 150.

185. [*Baur, in the text*] *Wesen und Treiben der Evangelische Kirchenzeitung*, 2:45–6. [*Ed.*] See p. 216, n. 94.

People interpreted this order of the cabinet in the following way.[186] They said it has reinstated the legally binding status of the creeds of both confessions, which seemed to be endangered; that the two confessions have been designated as one outwardly-united church fellowship; and that as a result, it likewise authorized that the united church no longer be regarded as the state church, inasmuch as according to it the members of the Lutheran and Reformed churches who find themselves within the state church are still not members of the united church if they belong directly to a church congregation outside of the state church. But in this case, then, one could simply deplore the contradiction contained in the order of the cabinet, with its conclusion that, in contrast to the friends of the Union, the cabinet may not permit those hostile to the Union to constitute a separate religious society.

Others maintain the contrary.[187] They say there is no such contradiction in the order; that it was certainly not the king's intention to grant such authority to the confessional documents, one by which they could still be foundational for separate confessional communities within the outward church fellowship of the state church. Surely the order of the cabinet itself expressly spoke about this authority of the confessional documents only as being the kind of authority that the Union does not invalidate, and therefore as consistent with the Union. Thus it describes the true sense of the Union as its no longer letting the different confessions' difference on individual doctrinal points count as the basis for excluding them from the external fellowship of the church. In taking this position, it states clearly enough that the continuing authority of the two churches' confessional documents should extend just to a certain point, where they are not in conflict, and no farther.

With this restriction on their authority, the Lutheran confessional documents are then no longer creedal statements of the Lutheran Church. They, and the comparably weakened Reformed confessional documents, are now just factors in the confessional documents of the Protestant state church, the ones that lump all the others together. If this is doubtless the correct interpretation of the situation, then we can in no way excuse the cabinet's order of blame for being indecisive and confusing. Lutherans who rested easy about the permanence of the creedal statements because of this order were deluded.

186. [*Baur, in the text*] See, for instance, Krabbe, *Die evangelische Landeskirche Preussens* (1849), 52. [*Ed.*] On Krabbe, see n. 143.

187. [*Baur, in the text*] For instance, Scheurl, in the *Erlanger Zeitschrift für Protestantismus und Kirche* (May 1854) 304. [*Ed.*] Adolf von Scheurl (1811–93), a professor in Erlangen.

Yet another difficulty had to crop up as soon as it came to practical matters: how things were to stand in the Union concerning those being ordained, or assuming religious vocations, in their sworn obligations to the creedal books. Should the creeds not be mentioned at all, so that this omission gives the appearance of approving the indifference imputed to the Union, even while continuing the obligation to the other symbols, just as they stand? How does the constant reminder of this discrepancy tally with the Union? In the new liturgy, the ritual of ordination combined specific citation of the Apostolic, Nicene, and Athanasian creeds, with making general reference to the familiar creedal books widely accepted in the Protestant Church, in the way they are correspondingly accepted in Prussia as the norms of faith. But what texts could have fit this description? Not even the Augsburg Confession. The February 1834 order of the cabinet stipulated that the clergy should be duty-bound to the Augsburg Confession too, but just upon special request, that is, only in special cases. So even in the revised liturgy this matter is left quite vague and undefined. Yet the church authority of the Union had to have a specific position in dealing with the antagonism between the respective factions that were for and against creeds, an antagonism that had by no means disappeared.

Following the commencement of the government of Friedrich Wilhelm IV in 1840, the matter of the Union entered upon a new phase with other pending issues. What most concerned the traditional Lutherans were coercive measures that had been relaxed under the previous government but were now reinstated by the new one. There had not only been the release of clergy still under arrest, upon their promising not to spread separatism by proselytizing; but also, alongside the unified Protestant state church, the government had tolerated a Lutheran Church with its own independent system of governance, one constituted in 1841 at a general synod held in Breslau. In 1845 the government made a general concession to the Lutherans that authorized their freedom in religious practices, and acknowledged the independence of their system of governance. At that time there were some thirteen to fourteen thousand of them, and they could only carry on a sectarian existence since, despite the freedom granted them, the era of exclusive Lutheranism was over.

The Bishopric in Jerusalem

From this tolerance shown to the traditional Lutherans, by only excluding a recalcitrant element from the domain of the Union, one should by no means conclude that the issues in question were to be treated as being of less concern. The king was equally enthusiastic about religion, the church, and orthodoxy, so his whole personal orientation guaranteed that everything related to religion would receive a new impetus. Except that the first idea coming forward as the king's very own creation just showed that his practical, common sense was quite limited.

In order to exhibit the romantic king in all his splendor—romantic because his ideal seemed to especially involve a uniting of different confessions—we may just mention that in 1841 he joined with the archbishop of Canterbury, the primate of the Church of England, in founding the Anglo-Prussian bishopric at the St. James Church in Jerusalem. The public announcement about the Prussian deed of foundation identified the purpose of the undertaking as simply acquiring the same advantages for Protestants that Catholics had in the Turkish realm, and in gaining the right of assembly for those professing the faith, as well as the right to freely proclaim Protestant truth according to the confession and liturgy of Protestantism, in the very place where Christianity originated.

Soon, however, deeper underlying purposes surfaced. People praised the king as the representative of genuine Protestant efforts at a union of all Protestant churches. So it was said that all the communities and peoples sympathetic to the Reformation should now also actually take the form they had when the teaching was given at the time of the Lord's messenger and his first followers, and when a power of rebirth and sanctification was at work. Indeed, not only was the bishopric in Jerusalem said to solidify the bond of union between the Christians of England and Germany; for they said members of the Protestant-Prussian church will also be consecrated by the hands of the new bishop, and both national churches will establish one communion above the sepulcher of the redeemer, a communion that will quickly become universal.

These expectations were officially endorsed by a document in which the archbishop of Canterbury publicly announced the discussions about the bishopric of Jerusalem. It contained the regulations set forth for the relation of the German congregations and clergy to the Anglican bishop. They were stated as follows. First, German clergy to be installed in German congregations will be ordained by the bishop according to the rites of the Church of England and will subscribe to the Thirty-Nine Articles. Second, the confirmation rites for catechumens of the German congregations will likewise be finalized by the bishop, according to the forms of the Church of England. A further result was that the articles of association contained the agreement that the crowned heads of England and Prussia would alternate in appointing the bishop of Jerusalem, but so as to give the archbishop of Canterbury the right of absolute veto over the Prussian appointment. Any doubts about the purely Anglican understanding as to instituting the bishopric were completely dispelled by the statement that the ultimate outcome of its founding could not of course be predicted with certainty, but one may nevertheless indulge in the well-grounded hope that, with God's blessing, it will pave the way for an essential unity, in discipline and doctrine, between the Church of England and the less-well-organized Protestant churches of Europe.

From these provisions people saw not only that the guarded suspicions they had from the very outset were quite well-founded, but also how much the German church had to play second fiddle to the Church of England. After they saw the light, public opinion spoke out so decidedly in opposition to the whole project that it could only be regarded as a complete disaster. With all the indignation of the German national consciousness, the 1842 article by Schneckenburger and Hundeshagen,[188] entitled "Das anglo-preussische Bisthum zu St. Jacob in Jerusalem und was daran hängt," lodged a very energetic protest against any and all Anglicanizing of the German Protestant Church, by recalling the saying in Job 15:2, "Should the wise . . . fill themselves with the east wind?"[189] This article sets forth in very trenchant fashion what in fact lies hidden in this masterpiece of diplomatic Romanticism: Anglicanizing the less-well-organized Protestant churches; establishing an advance post for Anglican rites and the Anglican system of governance; introducing Anglo-Catholic concepts of episcopacy into the free Protestant church; and so many other elements, from the stone arches of the ancient Cologne cathedral, the addition of which the same king so piously celebrated, right up to the new, Schellingian Johanneskirche. Yet how little cause Protestant Germany has to yearn for the dominance of a church that is ashamed of its own Protestant name, and whose founding was indeed a betrayal of the principle of the Reformation, is displayed here very clearly. Bunsen[190] is an especially sympathetic champion of the king in this predilection for the Anglican idea of episcopacy, and in the longing for hierarchy from which it springs. He has even written and published a complete plan for the organization of a German episcopal church. Whether the pious foundation, which even Hase has called a mustard seed of Protestantism on Mount Zion, might have been all it was rumored to be, is very much in doubt.

188. Matthias Schneckenburger (1804–48), professor in Bern. Karl Bernhard Hundeshagen (1810–72), professor in Bern and Bonn.

189. A fuller quotation of Job 15:2–3 makes the point clearer: "Should the wise answer with windy knowledge, and fill themselves with the east wind? Should they argue in unprofitable talk, or in words with which they can do no good?"

190. Christian Karl Josias von Bunsen (1791–1860), a Prussian diplomat and am-bassador to London. In 1845 he published *Die Verfassung der Kirche der Zukunft*.

Arrangements for a System of Governance in Prussia; the Protestant Conference; the 1846 General Synod

With exuberant planning of this kind taking place, nothing was accomplished in meeting the needs of the present. Yet each control by the church governmental body faced increasing difficulties. As people more and more had to realize, the harsh stance taken by the various factions meant that things could not continue as they had previously. Instruments had to be created that could make the church's voice heard. So they resolved to revive the synods once more, beginning in 1843 with the district synods, followed in the next year by the provincial synods. What the district and provincial synods had begun was then supposed to be completed by the general synod.

In any event, before this could happen yet another drama played out, the German Protestant Conference. It was the work of two court preachers, Grüneisen in Stuttgart and Snethlage in Berlin.[191] Their sovereigns knew how to get very much behind this enterprise in the interest of the Protestant Church. Even before public preparations had been made for the conference, Ullmann, who had been drawn in so as to attach a famous theologian's name to the cause, in 1845 published *Für die Zukunft der evangelischen Kirche Deutschlands, ein Wort an ihre Schirmherrn und Freunde*.[192] This was the prospectus for the proposed conference. People perceived this agitated, confused time as ever more urgently demanding a drastic remedy. Now, if ever, was the moment to implement a major and truly constructive measure for the life of the church. The goal was supposedly to enhance the inner strength, the independence and dignity, of the Protestant Church, by setting up a representative, presbyterial system of governance within each individual church, and by establishing an orderly relationship among the individual German-Protestant state churches.

Since the Protestant Church in Germany was not set up to facilitate embarking on a new course independently of its illustrious patrons and guardians, the first announcement about this course had to come from the German princes via their deputies; and when these princes had decided to pursue this course, the foundations for the arrangement had to be put in place. From the empty words of the prospectus it was Ullmann's function to first work up, one could of course see from his presentation, with all its polish and being composed for his royal audience, how relatively lifeless the whole affair was. Thus, at the beginning of 1846 deputies sent by their respective royal courts, and representing all the Protestant states except for

---

191. Carl Grüneisen (1802–78); Karl Wilhelm Moritz Snethlage (1792–1871).
192. On Carl Ullmann, see n. 52. The book was published in Stuttgart.

the free city of Berlin, did indeed assemble and held a conference lasting a month and a half, but we never heard anything of importance about the result of their deliberations. Nothing was officially announced about it, and what was reported elsewhere about it cast it in an almost completely unfavorable light. People thought it all to the good that nothing came to fruition from the proposals, many of which just aimed at limiting previously existing freedoms. The occasion for the whole conference was simply that the deputies wanted to find a new way to satisfy their personal ambitions via the role they could play as law-givers for the church, on behalf of their royal courts.

In that same year, at Pentecost, the general synod convened in Berlin. There were seventy-five participants, thirty-seven of them clerics and thirty-eight laypersons, but even the lay participants were not freely chosen by their congregations. The state's minister for clerical affairs was the chairman. The main issues were the confessional statement, the Union, and the system of governance.

Nitzsch[193] was the expert advisor in the committee charged with matters concerning doctrine; like all committees, its members were half clergy and half laymen. The committee set out from the assumption that, on issues of the confession and religious commitments, the status quo could not be maintained; that the Union should not be merely a union as to the cultus and the governance system, but should also be a union as to doctrine and the confession. A truly Protestant Union could only have its unifying principle in unity of belief, and this unity of belief must also be made explicit. But doing so is just a matter of setting forth the fundamentals of the Christian faith and setting them apart from what is not fundamental. Based on this, the Union would then not be the founding of a third church alongside the Reformed and Lutheran churches. Instead it would confirm the unity of the two previously separate churches. Likewise, it would also not have a new confessional basis, independent from the contents of the preexisting confessions. Instead it would return to the shared Protestant roots of the Lutheran and Reformed confessions. Their previous separation would be acknowledged as a departure from which the Union would return. Since, in the committee's view, ordination of clergy is where the foundation of the faith is manifestly expressed, the committee also proposed a form for ordination. As for the rest, although the state church is essentially the united church, it will nevertheless also allow for a confessional separation within it to some degree, insofar as that does not impact the church's fellowship. Hence when expressly desired, there could also be a religious vocation

---

193. On Karl Immanuel Nitzsch, see n. 107.

based on a separate Lutheran or Reformed creed. These were the essential proposals of the committee.

When it came to debating these proposals, the faction representing creedal orthodoxy very strongly opposed them. Its principal spokesmen were Stahl, Twesten, and Strauss.[194] [They said that] the committee's proposals aimed at founding a new church, but its religious symbols would be its legal basis as well as the Union. The Union would be no change in the confession of faith, but only the recognition that no separation of the church's fellowship would be necessary for the sake of doctrinal differences. Even rationalism could be happy with the kind of confessional statement that the committee recommended. It leaves everything too vague and indefinite; it would take us back into a period of doctrinal development, something we have been over and done with for more than a thousand years. [These spokesmen said] our time is a sick era that has no competency for formulating creeds.

The conservatives (*die Rechte*) wanted to keep everything at the status quo, whereas the liberals (*die Linke*) believed they must refuse any commitment to a specific doctrinal content. [The liberals] believed that Christianity is essentially a living power, not a doctrine; that the doctrine is always secondary, is what is changeable as opposed to the eternal aspect of faith; that one can of course be obliged to preach the faith, but not to preach a specific doctrinal content. The main spokesman for this position, alongside Count Schwerin, was Court Preacher Sydow.[195] He even maintained that the Protestant Church must frankly be constructed so as to tolerate heterodoxy. Not to mention the obviousness of its own founding principle, the Protestant Church in principle ought not deny the possibility that it could be mistaken. It must acknowledge that even the Reformation did not find the full expression, completely adequate for all times, of the infinite depth that is in Christ. To the contrary, Christ's vitally prominent place in [human] existence and knowledge is continually developing, and the goal of perfection will only be increasingly attained by free, collective activity in which no individual ought, from the outset, to be prevented from participating.

The outcome of the lengthy debate was that the majority of the assembly consented to the committee's proposals in their essentials. Accordingly, there should no longer be any commitment to the older traditional creeds or symbols, neither the three creeds of the ecumenical councils nor

---

194. Friedrich Julius Stahl (1802–61), convert from Judaism to orthodox Lutheranism, professor of church law and polity in Berlin. On August Twesten, see n. 107. On Friedrich Strauss, see p. 214, n. 91.

195. Victor Graf von Schwerin (1814–1903); Karl Leopold Adolf Sydow (1800–82), a student of Schleiermacher.

the old Protestant symbols. Instead these symbols were just something to be referred to. The formula for a real confession is that it should consist of the wording of scripture as the actual object of one's commitment.

What is this outcome of the general synod worth? If we assess it from a broader standpoint we can simply say that each of the three factions—the conservatives, the liberals, and the centrists—got caught up in inconsistencies and contradictions.

The conservatives knew how to hold firmly to the old Protestant statements of faith, and yet they did not wish to abandon the Union. How are these two aims compatible? To have both at the same time, they had to regard the confessional differences as not so essential that a union of the cultus and the governance system—a fellowship of the church as such in practice—cannot coexist with these statements. But how can they regard the confessional differences as nonessential if they once take their stance with the old Protestant statements of faith? These symbols surely ought to be retained, and so one must also share the view they themselves have about the enduring differences between the two confessions. Accordingly, how can one look upon the confessional differences as nonessential, when one recalls that in fact, owing to dogmatic differences, the Lutheran confession declares outright that a real church fellowship with the Reformed confession is not possible?

In this case it is also of no avail to set aside the Formula of Concord and maintain, as Twesten did at the general synod, that the Formula is actually no such confessional statement and cannot be viewed as a symbol. No one who knows the history of the Lutheran theological framework can deny that the basic ideas of the Lutheran confession have left their fullest imprint on the Formula of Concord, and that it is in actuality the seal and crowning achievement of Lutheran Protestantism's creedal development. Therefore, if the confessional status of various symbols is supposedly upheld, so that in ordination, based on confessional differences, some are committed to Lutheran symbols and some to the Reformed symbols, then doing so breaks up the Union; it is impossible to maintain it in the cultus and in church governance if it is abandoned in a person's confessional statement.

However, if one wanted to hold firmly to the old or traditional symbols of the faith, only as holding to what they have in common, and not in points where they differ, then this shared content had to be regarded as the actual substance of the symbols, and by doing so one takes up a centrist position. Yet the centrist position itself is completely incorrect in not wanting to recognize that the formula of commitment the committee established is looked upon as a new symbol. To be sure, the centrist position is not completely divorced from the old symbols; it is in principle correlated with them. But why should it not also be allowable to describe a broader advance in the development of something new? Yet after the antithesis between the two Protestant confessions is established, is not the characteristic and essential nature of each one simply what sets them apart and not what they still have in common? However, the centrists then say that what is essential and substantial is not what sets each one apart, but rather the common elements; and so that is the reason for taking a stand based on one of the two essentially different kinds of old symbols. This point cannot be expressed more clearly than it is in the synod's contention that the confessional separation was a mistake corrected by the Union.

Yet the authors and the adherents of the old symbols could not have thought this separation is mistaken. So viewing the separation as a mistake is just expressing how far we have come beyond their standpoint; there is not even resistance to recognizing that this [contemporary] standpoint with regard to the old symbols is an essentially new one. The question is simply whether this new standpoint is also tenable. Our answer to this question is simply "no," because the new standpoint is just half-hearted, is ambiguous and dishonest. People no longer want to hear about the old symbols, because they take offense at the special dogmatic stipulations contained in them. However, the new symbol is in turn also a dogmatic symbol that just sets itself apart from the old ones by its vagueness, as well as by the fact that it does not even truly have confidence in the dogmatic specification that it makes. The new symbol reverts from the specific contents of the old symbols to the vagueness of scriptural expressions. But what justifies this reverting from what is specific to what is vague? The synod declared the separation on which the confessional symbols rest to be a mistake that the Union would rectify. In saying this the synod deprives the confessional antitheses of their historical justification, meaning that the Protestant Church ought never to have separated into these opposing groups.

But what entitles the synod to make this contention? The confessional antitheses, as necessary moments of the development, were so embedded in the nature of things that Protestantism would have had to lack the inner impetus for its development if it had not made its meaning clear in these antitheses. Thus if the Union wishes to revoke the separation as being a mistake, in doing so it will undo the course of history; it will regard what lies before our eyes, in its full historical reality, as something that did not happen. For historical antitheses will not be overcome by diminishing them and, as it were, ignoring them; for one can only get beyond them and, by demonstrating the one-sidedness they inherently involve, resolve them into their higher unity.

Of course owing to this vagueness, and in contrast to the specificity of the old symbol, the new symbol cannot be satisfactory. But it is just as unsatisfactory in its material contents, which are both too much and too little. There is too much content, because the new symbol still occupies the same standpoint as the old ones; for when it proclaims belief in an only-begotten Son of God, who "emptied himself, taking the form of a slave" [Philippians 2:7], we have here largely the same dogmatic conception of the Son of God that is fundamental to the old symbols. But the question is why, if the new symbol cannot rid itself of the old affirmation, it cannot express this conception with the same specificity. Why does it either skip over the Trinity, the divinity of Christ, and all those dogmas the older symbols took to be so important, in complete silence, or else express them in such a vague and indecisive way? The obvious answer is because it wants to not merely express the view of the supernaturalists, but also to hold out something to the rationalists, something they can have a pretext for accepting. Thus the synod itself has no proper confidence in its own dogmatic view. It even wants to not exclude those opposed to it, and so that calls for dogmatic ambiguity and taking no stand. Were the Union none other than what the synod took it to be, it would therefore also be just something untenable and to be dismissed; simply a proof of the powerlessness of a time that is in just as little position to hold fast to the old ways as it is to bring about something new.

But the Union has indeed became a force in our time, one that must be recognized by those who still occupy the standpoint abrogated by the Union. Even those faithful to the old symbols, people such as Stahl and Twesten, have not dared to contravene the fact that the Union meets a need today, and is something that cannot be undone. It is the fruit of a conviction that came to maturity in the general consciousness of our day, the conviction that, in the process of development the confessional antitheses have undergone in the course of history, these antithetical positions have outlived their usefulness, have taken a toll on each other. Given the widespread education and enlightenment of people today, it is no longer fitting for the Lutherans and the Reformed churchmen to mutually accuse each other of heresy, to condemn each other, in the way they did at the time of the Formula of Concord and the older Protestant dogmaticians. Now each must concede that there is historical justification for the other's theological framework. But if each of them has an equally good entitlement, then they of course continue on side-by-side, but are also mutually exclusive. So there is as such no theological framework that would have had to make an unconditional claim to truth. Each dogmatic contention always positions itself in turn over against another one that it negates. So people ultimately acquire the conviction that the essence of Christianity does not, on the whole, consist of a theological framework that is fixed and systematized in a symbolic or confessional form.

This standpoint is of necessity the Union's standpoint. However, the work the Union believed it had accomplished at the Berlin meeting of the general synod, by adopting this standpoint, did not firmly establish that the synod also posited this standpoint in a unitary confessional document. They constantly circled around the issue. In order to escape from the antitheses of the old symbols, they declared themselves in favor of the Union. Yet they had scarcely proclaimed loyalty to the Union when they set up a new symbol that is also once again subject to the same antithesis. If we just ponder the Berlin synod's formula for ordination, is it not also a dogmatic symbol? With the proposition that Christ is the sole basis for all salvation, the synod believes it has expressed the essence of Christianity in a universally valid way, one beyond all disagreement. But is this not a dogmatic proposition too, one that, as such, can in no way claim to be universally acknowledged? One cannot demand faith in Christ as the sole basis for all salvation without presupposing, with this belief, the doctrine of Christ's divinity in a way that gets directly involved in all the conflicting dogmatic differences and controversies. No matter how flexible and nonspecific this formulation sounds, it still just leaves us with a purely dogmatic standpoint. Even those who declare themselves opposed to any commitment to a specific formulation are left with the same standpoint.

Suppose we ask how doctrinal unity and purity are said to be maintained. Sydow's answer is: By letting the Christian spirit freely prevail, the unifying and holy divine Spirit of the gospel of Jesus Christ, liberating for the salvation and life of the world, the Spirit that lives in him and is active in his church. One must then ask: Where is the free prevalence of the Christian spirit here, if a concept of Jesus Christ as the salvation of the world is presupposed, a concept that must be challenged dogmatically? In the Protestant Church, must tolerance for heterodoxy be built right into its structure, as the speaker says? If so, then the church is also tolerant of the heterodox view that Christianity is thinkable without the divinity of Christ, without his person being of absolute significance. If from the gospel story itself one is justified in understanding Christianity's founder as a purely human phenomenon, and in assigning the teaching about his divinity to a gospel whose origins already lie in the time when Christianity's dogmatics are taking shape, how completely different must be the form taken by the whole basic intuition of the essence of Christianity? So even the doctrine of Christ's divinity is a dogmatic concept that the Union must set aside, based on its own standpoint, because the Union can only be indifferent to everything dogmatic in nature. If we remove everything dogmatic, we are just left with the ethical aspect, with moral conviction as the essential thing. Then the Union is the expressed conviction that, despite whatever the dogmatic antitheses may be that pit them against one another, Christians of all confessions belong to one and the same Christian fellowship, provided that they simply stand on the foundation of a Christian moral consciousness.

Hence all attempts—like that of the Berlin general synod to consummate the Union dogmatically but utterly failing to do so—always face the same dilemma. They can only be either dogmatic in the sense of the old symbols, or else not dogmatic at all. If undogmatic, then they turn away from everything dogmatic and resort to the ethical aspect of moral conviction. So long as they dare not apprehend the Union in this sense, everything done to achieve this purpose remains half-heartedness that leads to no goal, as was also the case with the Berlin general synod. Although the orthodox faction was a minority in the synod, it nevertheless accomplished its objective, because it could not be confuted dogmatically. The overall result was simply that nothing was done. With all the consensus about church governance and in favor of urgently declared resolutions, so far nothing has actually materialized.

Although the Union had its own expert advisor (J. Müller[196] from Halle), the whole thing hinged on the issue of the confessional statement. According to him, it and its principles have been dealt with, so there is nothing more in particular to say about it. Stahl was the expert advisor on the matter of governance. Here too a brief remark sufficed: that a plan of governance was discussed, under which the church will be released from the previous system of regional control, by making the fundamental principle a governance system combining the consistories and presbyteries. The essential components of this system were the presbyteries, the district and provincial synods, the general superintendent of the province, the state synod, and the supreme consistory. The Berlin synod decided that this governance system should be called into being as soon as that was possible and feasible. Yet the arrangement for just a single supreme consistory put it in a very isolated position, because the orthodox faction continued to oppose it and decried the synod as a "robber synod" and a denial of Christ. Also, in January 1848 things reached a point at which events occurred that completely changed the state of affairs, and cast the whole issue of state-church relations in an entirely new light.

---

196. See n. 115.

From the outset there was due concern that Eichhorn[197] the president of the [Berlin] synod, who as the minister for spiritual affairs, paid attention only to those ones, out of the great majority of participants, who echoed his own views and favored his principles. However, lively the debate in the synod and the statements made from different sides in a series of the most verbose speeches about every point, there was basically no essential difference of opinion. The three discernible factions ultimately always shared the same ground, the supernaturalist view held by the church. The only difference was in the degree to which the strictly orthodox faction ultimately must be conceded to be more consistently in the right. The minister himself was simply the faithful instrument of the royal will, both at the synod and also otherwise. His intention was to make positive, ecclesiastical belief in revelation—what the king set down as the essence of Christianity—the supreme norm in church governance. So people called that "letting the church shape itself on its own." As often as the king found a new occasion for reiterating his catchphrase about the church's autonomy and a church governance resting on this principle, the king's lackeys and admirers could not be more amazed at the marvelous and enlightened turn for the better in the nature of the church under the rule of such a king.

How things stood with this "turn for the better" can best be seen from the pronouncement the minister made in the sixth session of the general synod, about the principles according to which he had previously handled the administration of the church. The occasion for it was a petition from several inhabitants of Mühlhausen, who had complained about oppression in the church and mistakes made by the church administration. The minister said that the church administration would have to act on behalf of shared concerns; but within these shared concerns it would also want to leave scope for the element of further development. The church administration has acknowledged the right to development but does not wish to bring about the development by itself, out of respect for the church, which should shape itself. So the precept of church administration was to be: upholding the existing order and at the same time actively working to keep open the path to further development. The ultimate goal was not stasis, but rather clearing the way for reform. The church administration must protect what currently exists until reform in an orderly way would become possible. It has sought to be most indulgent and considerate with respect to persons when it comes to protecting what currently exists, yet to proceed most decisively where the situation merits it.[198]

---

197. See n. 92.

198. [Baur, in the text] Acten der Generalsynode, 1:41.

The reason why the church administration has not managed so far to resolve, in a more satisfactory way, the discords that hinder and disturb the harmony of the church's consciousness today, the minister sought, most superficially and one-sidedly, to locate simply in the limited comprehension, in the misunderstandings and different conceptions, that for most people are said to be due to their neglecting to grasp the true nature of the Protestant Church in a deep and fundamental way. However, if people do not wish to go back in this way to the deeper basis for the conflicts that beset the life of the church today, and to recognize the historical justification for them, then they are adopting a standpoint that, going forward, makes it impossible to resolve the antitheses present today.

The program of church administration the minister put in place made its task the upholding of what endures every bit as much as it was the striving for reform. If indeed the one task can only limit the other, then special emphasis still falls on how decisively he said the existing order ought to be upheld. Yet before one makes it the task to most decisively hold fast to what exists now, one ought first to have answered the question whether the so-called existing order is actually something enduring; that is, whether it is sustained by the overall culture and moral consciousness of today, or else is divorced from it and only has the appearance of something enduring. Therefore it all turns on what the enduring order is that one wishes to protect. By recognizing the need for reform, people certainly already concede that what persists in present-day life no longer has an adequate basis, and must give way to something new. And if this existing order, which people also concede is untenable in virtue of the demand for reform, should nevertheless be most decisively upheld, then, in a time agitated by severe antitheses, the process of fermentation just becomes all the more violent, and the character of the movement all the more negative, when the old orders, powerless and inept, [seek] to maintain themselves, to remain in place via external support, to impede and restrict free development. In times when a new epoch of development breaks in upon the ruin of the old system, the future-directed people are those who look forward instead of backward and let the chips fall where they may, because there is no longer any validity in keeping things as they are. In the chaos of the new, incipient cultural stages, people of the future, with their intuitive minds, already foresee the direction in which things will evolve.

The pervasive view taking shape in the Eichhorn ministry was that church administration, principally a theological-political way of thinking, would serve as the foothold for very decisively suppressing contemporary currents of thought. Dr. Eilers,[199] a member of the government ministry, made the attempt, in *Zur Beurtheilung des Ministeriums Eichhorn* (1849), to justify the ministry's so quickly giving in at the first confrontation, and to blame the previous Altenstein ministry[200] for the basis of the complaint. This text is an apologue that simple proves how well-grounded is that verdict about the ministry.

The Protestant Friends

The zeal of the previous government in promoting the matter of the Union had called forth opposition from the traditional Lutherans. Now the entire spirit in which the current government dealt with the administering of the church, and pressed for ecclesiastical orthodoxy, resulted in an opposition movement, the so-called "Friends of the Light" or, as they called themselves, the "Protestant Friends."

The Protestant Friends were led by rationalists who had received their theological education in the Wegscheider[201] school of thinking, which was widespread in that region [i.e., Saxony]. The feature of that school is rationalism in a popularized form also accessible to the non-theological public, a rationalism that became a matter of partisan agitation. This form of rationalism first appeared at a time when the ecclesiastical reaction under the new government took on a more definite character and one could no longer be deceived as to what might be expected from the new regime.

Thus a conference of pastors in the Prussian province of Saxony, on 29 June 1841, decided to hold a second gathering in Halle, to also include schoolteachers and non-clerics, public officials and citizens. The number of participants from the two social classes grew, and interest in these gatherings of the Protestant Friends spread ever wider. In addition to the regular, general gatherings in Köthen for Pentecost and for harvest time, they now also held district gatherings, and the meetings in Köthen itself enlarged, with the 1844 meeting, into truly people's assemblies. Pastor Uhlich[202] of Pömmelte presided. His prominent personal attributes also especially included the talent for leading such a mass of people, for producing strange political concoctions and religious extravaganzas, and for cutting short discussion of their ominous extremes. The conference topics were contempo-

199. Gerd Eilers (1788–1863). The book was published in Berlin.
200. On the Altenstein ministry, see n. 79.
201. On Wegscheider, see p. 167, n. 34.
202. Johann Jacob Markus Leberecht Uhlich (1799–1872), founder of the Protestant Friends, later a pastor of the Free Community in Magdeburg.

rary religious matters, originally supposed to be scientific theological issues; but the general discussion deviated from this plan, for the assemblies took on a popular character.

At the 1844 Pentecost conference of the Protestant Friends, held in Köthen, Pastor Wislicenus,[203] from the Neumarktkirche in Halle, made a presentation about the so-called formal principle of the Protestant Church. The highlight of his talk, which occasioned lively discussions, was the formulation of the issue as to whether the principle be scripture or the spirit. He said the norm of faith was supposed to be the spirit, not scripture. In *Ob Schrift, ob Geist? Verantwortung gegen meine Ankläger* (1845), Wislicenus explained in more detail the meaning of his contention. The contrast others make within scripture, between the letter and the spirit, Wislicenus understood in such a way as to directly separate scripture from the spirit and to identify scripture with the letter. The spirit that produced scripture presented itself in scripture in the way spirit was. The way the biblical books speak is exactly how their authors thought. Thus we need say no more than that the spirit of scripture is in no way distinct from the letter of scripture. However, if one nevertheless wants to distinguish spirit from letter, then one is supposing that scripture contains both essential and nonessential features. But whoever would make this distinction, if not scripture itself? In putting the issue this way one has cast aside scripture as the objective norm of faith. But what then is the spirit, as distinguished from scripture in this fashion? There is the Holy Spirit that freely wafts or moves within humankind; is begotten from the eternal divine knowing, itself divine; has its law within itself and moves further on within this law; is not bound, in faith and knowledge, to an outwardly written law, but instead issued scripture only from itself. Scripture is the relic of a form of life, of a great deed and a great knowledge. It is an impelling force, but not fetters preventing further knowledge and learning.

According to this statement it seems that what a rationalist elsewhere called "reason," gets also called "spirit" here by its exponents among the Friends of the Light, and that seems to be an echo of the Hegelian philosophy. The Protestant Church originates from the joyous tidings of the freedom of God's children through the Holy Spirit [cf. Romans 8:21]. This freedom also enables it to recognize that the scriptures certainly bear splendid witness to the faith of the first Christian era, but they are not a law for

---

203. Gustav Adolf Wislicenus (1803–75) studied under Wegscheider in Halle and became a pastor in Halle. He was dismissed from his position, and later, after publication of a second book, was imprisoned for two years. He fled to the United States, but in 1856 returned to Europe and settled near Zürich, where he published his major work, *Die Bibel für denkende Leser betrachtet* (Leipzig, 1863–64).

subsequent times, since Christ sets the Christian communion free from the outward law and elevates it to the inner law of freedom [cf. Romans 8:2, James 1:25].

Since Wislicenus seems to have completely upended the Protestant scripture principle by drawing this distinction, Guericke, writing in the *Evangelische Kirchenzeitung*, called attention to the situation in order to protest against this position in the strongest terms, and to do battle against the Friends of the Light generally, as those who have totally renounced Christianity. Since the public became increasingly sympathetic toward the cause of the Friends of the Light, and since the gatherings that Uhlich arranged for now and then had the look of a public disturbance, the government therefore intervened. In July 1845, the government of Saxony banned all gatherings that called into question the confessional status of matters related to the Augsburg Confession. As the result of an order of its cabinet on 5 August, the Prussian government banned any public gathering of the Protestant Friends as well as their also forming closed societies, whatever they may call them. This ban was announced to the collective clergy and to affected teachers, and was enforced by the police when the occasion arose to do so.

Discussion of the Matter in Print; The Protesting Theologians and the *Evangelische Kirchenzeitung*

The mass gatherings then ceased, but a lively controversy now ensued in print. Following the appearance in 1844 of a large number of pamphlets related to this current issue,[204] the feud in print took on a new form.

Not long after Guericke became aware of the presentation by Wislicenus and sounded the alarm, protests against Wislicenus from all sides, by orthodox pastors, appeared in the *Evangelische Kirchenzeitung*, with the majority of them cast in very strong terms. Many declared straight out that they could no longer consider Wislicenus to be a Protestant pastor and a Christian, and they excluded him from the fellowship of the church. Following these individual protests, there was a further protest that several hundred people joined, even some from foreign lands, which confined itself to defending the Protestant scripture principle in opposition to Wislicenus.

---

204. [*Baur*] See the *Bruns'sche Reportorium* 4.1 (Oct. 1845) 26ff., where thirty-one of them are mentioned, the principal one being by Bernhard König, pastor at Anderbeck: "Der rechte Standpunkt: Ein ruhiges Wort in Sachen der protestantische Freunde zu Köthen gegen die Verunglimpfung derselben durch die sog. *Evangelische Kirchenzeitung* und ihren Anhang. Mit dem Motto: Vorwärts, nicht Luther, nicht Papst. Evangelische Freiheit!"

This protest [against Wislicenus] ought to have been especially important because of the number of signatories to it, although it just resulted in thousands of people responding to several hundred signatories. The latter responses came from all social classes, drawn from the main cities in the eastern provinces of Prussia, namely, from Magdeburg, Halle, Berlin, Breslau, and Königsberg. The largest number were from Breslau. Already in the first month, those who endorsed the response came from 52 cities, towns, and villages, and they included: 3 docents of Protestant theology, 124 holders of clerical positions, 46 clerical candidates, 35 university students of Protestant theology, 59 teachers in gymnasia, 300 other teachers, 13 university teachers, 72 university students, 142 lawyers, 175 physicians and pharmacists, 35 members of the highest corporate bodies of the land, 700 state public officials, 600 merchants, 400 owners of land in the state, 80 owners of nobility estates, 119 commissioned officers, and 2,000 factory workers. Thus the concern to respond was widespread, and the targets of the response were Hengstenberg and his *Evangelische Kirchenzeitung*. People saw this periodical as the sum and substance, as well as the vehicle, of all the reactionary tendencies that currently provoked such great dissatisfaction. In fact people were contesting against the whole system of governance that since 1840 was subservient to the concerns of the church.

A third faction took its stance between the other two contesting factions. It believed it could not keep silent when, from all directions, the Protestant Church was in danger of breaking up. It came forward in a declaration of 15 August 1845, which was published in the first issue of the *Monatsschrift für die unirte evangelische Kirche*, and signed by 87 men of various professions. The leaders of the group were a few well-known students of Schleiermacher, as well as Bishops Dräseke and Eylert.[205] The declaration stated that one influential faction in the Protestant Church holds rigidly to the understanding of Christianity it has inherited from the beginnings of the Reformation. This formulation is its "pope," and it counts all those who do not want to acquiesce in that formulation as irreligious, even politically suspect. The men of this faction are zealous, but not wisely so; they aspire to dominance in the church. They come forward principally in their associated organ, the *Evangelische Kirchenzeitung*. They utilized excommunication, thus harming the order of the church by endangering Protestant freedom of belief and freedom of conscience, and sought to dominate by their numbers. Their opponents likewise gather to confront them, pitting numbers against their numbers, and that has brought about the most extreme confessional confrontations, by giving the most heterogeneous elements room

---

205. Bernhard Dräseke (1774–1849); Rulemann Eylert (1770–1852).

and opportunity to get involved in the most provocative way. The result is that in the Protestant Church, on both sides here, the spirit of brotherly understanding increasingly threatens to give way to an ominous, tumultuous condition, posing the danger of fragmenting the church. Those who strive for dominance in the church bear the blame for this state of affairs.

Instead of lodging a moral protest against them, the undersigned persons expressed their own understanding of Christianity. They said that Christ is the sole ground of our salvation, but the doctrinal formulation of the free development onward from Christ is a matter for Christ. Based on this conviction, they further declared that they regarded a salutary solution to the conflict as possible only if there are not any capricious expulsions from the church; if each party gains the right to develop [its position] without impediments; and if a system of church governance comes about that assists the church in shaping itself, by the grace of the Lord, with renewed energy and with the active participation of the parishioners.

This declaration gave rise to a new flurry of written materials. The *Bruns'sche Reportorium* (April 1846), vol. 6, no. 1, enumerated no less than 57 pamphlets related to it, the last of which, Neander's "Worte des Friedens unter den Gegensätzen" (1845), is quite inconsequential. The most remarkable thing is the behavior of Hengstenberg himself. Since he took the 87 who signed the 1845 declaration as all being Schleiermacherians, his opposition to it in the *Evangelische Kirchenzeitung*, no. 84, of 15 August 1845, was wholly aimed at breaking completely with this faction, and with this goal in mind, now also publicly accusing Schleiermacher's teaching of heresy. Church-minded people had always been most carefully respectful of Schleiermacher himself. The only piece opposing him in the *Evangelische Kirchenzeitung* had been repelled by Schleiermacher's harsh offensive in the *Sendschreiben* concerning his *Glaubenslehre*, in *Studien und Kritiken*, 1829, p. 490. There he writes that "the soil lifts up right under our feet where this ominous larva wants to crawl out from the self-enclosed religious circles that declare all research outside the entrenchments of an age-old literalism to be satanic."[206]

It was very timely for Hengstenberg himself to remind us of these truly prophetic words of Schleiermacher. [He said] the chief cause for the Schleiermacherians becoming increasingly agitated is that they beheld in the ecclesiastically-minded folk the representatives of their own conscience, which in today's advances called out to them, ever more loudly, to make their confessional statement about Christ in complete seriousness. They did not wish to hear in these voices that those folk found the stalk of the

---

206. See p. 217.

ecclesiastical mind flourishing, the sap risen and producing sheaves, while their own stalk remains emaciated. In times when the Lord's death should be reiterated in his church, those who believe as such in the Lord, are bearing especially loud witness to him.

However, Hengstenberg's declaration of 15 August is just focused entirely on calling for the excommunication of the Schleiermacherians as a thoroughly debased faction. In speaking about the issue itself, Hengstenberg declares that it is worthwhile to see it directly acknowledged that the chief difference is in the realm of doctrine, and not in the realm of life [i.e., practice] as is the case in the differences between the Jesuits and their opponents in the Catholic Church. Here the difference does not involve certain dogmatic formulations established at the time of the Reformation; rather it involves the substance of the facts of the sacred history and the truths of the faith. It lies not on the soil of theology but instead on that of belief or faith; not on the soil of dogmatics but instead on that of the catechism. It begins not just with the Augsburg Confession, but instead with the Holy Scriptures and the confessional statements of the ancient church.

Hengstenberg then spells out the individual heresies of Schleiermacher and his followers. They concern: first, the doctrine of Holy Scripture; second, the ancient symbols or creeds—that is, the Schleiermacherians denying the Trinity and the creation of the world, and passing over all the parts of the creed from "conceived by the Holy Spirit" up to the ascension, together with the last judgment and final resurrection; third, the Athanasian Creed, to which they are spiritually opposed; fourth, the Augsburg Confession, for they shatter its substance, as Schleiermacher's doctrine of sin, together with its consequences, proves for christology and for passing judgment on the circumstances of one's life. These are the chief contents of Hengstenberg's declaration, presented with all the pomposity of a papal brief and composed in the tenor of the Old Testament theocratic perspective, abundantly interlaced with Old Testament passages—the tenor especially characteristic of articles in the *Evangelische Kirchenzeitung*.

One must concede that Hengstenberg has some justification when, in opposing the Schleiermacherians, he insists on specificity and decisiveness. The same half-hearted and ambiguous standpoint is evident in their case too. This faction took the same stance at the general synod, in constantly supposing that, with their Schleiermacherian Christ as the sole basis for salvation, they could unite the two sides, the traditionalist one and the modernist one. However, it was very apparent that people simply had to choose either to go beyond Schleiermacher, or to not resist those who insist on returning to the standpoint of the old symbols.

As the protests continued, the magistrates of Berlin, Breslau, and Königsberg turned directly to the king, addressing him with the request to give assurances of Protestant doctrinal freedom to the extent that it is not contrary to public morality and the security of the state; of freedom from encroachment by a faction having the intention of deploying the ecclesiastical authorities entirely contrary to the religious consciousness of the large majority of educated people and to the matter of the Union. These representations to the king were, for the most part, very unwelcome. The king rebuked them and warned, in a very clear statement, that he regards the faction of the *Evangelische Kirchenzeitung* as the sole staunch support of the church and the state.

Free Congregations

On one side, the traditional orthodoxy of the *Evangelische Kirchenzeitung* was said to be the norm for the state church. On the other side, because of this reactionary situation, the rationalistic movement stayed constantly active. Given this extraordinary state of affairs, it is not surprising that unusual things happened in many places.

In Königsberg, because Dr. Rupp,[207] the district pastor, had attacked the Athanasian Creed from the pulpit and declared the anathemas it contains to be un-Christian, he was dismissed from his position by the local consistory in December 1845. This gave rise to the formation in Königsberg of a Protestant congregation breaking free from the consistorial church. In a document dated 19 January 1846, the congregation declared that the obvious endeavor of the consistory and other authorities to make the ecclesiastical symbols of the sixteenth century, and their dogmatic foundations, strictly binding upon the faith of members of the Protestant state church, is in direct contradiction to the congregation's innermost religious convictions. Thus the congregation established the following principal tenets. This free Protestant congregation recognizes the Holy Scriptures as the basis for its belief in the oneness of God. It finds the supreme ethical norms for relationships to one's fellow human beings in scripture. By investigating the truth contained in scripture, it repudiates constraint by any creed or any

---

207. Julius Friedrich Leopold Rupp (1809–84). In 1849 Rupp was elected a member from Königsberg in the Lower Prussian Chamber. Two years later he was imprisoned by the government for several months. His granddaughter was the artist Käthe Kollwitz, who made a bronze statue of him installed by the *Freie evangelische Gemeinde* in Königsberg in 1909, with the inscription, "He who fails to live by the truth he believes is the most dangerous enemy of truth itself." This monument was destroyed during the Second World War but later rebuilt.

other authority; and in doing so it makes its own foundation the progressive ethical and rational consciousness of the congregation. It adheres to baptism and holy communion. Its members acknowledge that in all civic affairs they are subject to the laws of the state; that in their own affairs they are exclusively self-directed.

Rupp became the pastor of this congregation. But soon such radical elements appeared that Rupp's position became much more precarious, since, with all his inspiration, he was not suited to be the leader of a reforming movement. He succeeded only by the most extreme efforts, in that he had the freedom to permit use of the apostolic baptismal formula in the way a member of the congregation wished him to. He himself modernized it to read: "I baptize thee according to the ancient apostolic baptism, that Jesus is the Christ. I sprinkle thy head with water as the sign that thy soul will remain as the spring flowing from the mountains. As the water climbs heavenwards and again flows back to earth, so may thee always be mindful of thy heavenly homeland ." This amorphous character, which calls into question the baptism's validity, was the cause of new conflicts with the authorities. The whole status of the congregation remained entirely vague.

A similar congregation gathered around Wislicenus after the Magdeburg consistory, in April 1846, deposed him as a pastor in Halle "on account of gross violation of the existing rules for the liturgy and doctrine." The members of this congregation differed from the Friends of the Light in wanting to have nothing to do with a confession of faith. They only wanted to form an ethical association in which each person would remain free to believe what he or she wishes to, a free human fellowship of those who are free in their belief in an ever more complete revelation of truth, profession of faith, and doctrine, as well as simply free in their ethical practices. In a document addressed to the free Protestant congregation in Königsberg, Wislicenus even expressed the inclination to unite with the German-Catholics.[208] Associations of this kind, treating everything ecclesiastical as a matter of free ethics, letting Christianity be merged into the universal idea of humanity and also even calling into question its continuing to bear the name "Christian," also spread here and there, to Marburg, Nordhausen, and Halberstadt.

The Charter of 30 March 1847

The Charter of 30 March 1847 was issued in order to remedy the predicaments the government had to face in relation to the aforementioned kind

---

208. On the "German-Catholics," see p. 272, n. 50.

of associations, especially with regard to their authorization to operate as churches. Because of the current movements occurring in the ecclesiastical sphere, the king himself stated that he wanted to express in the Charter his principles concerning the permission for, and structure of, new religious societies.

The stipulations of the common law were compiled for this purpose, and the fundamental principle established that the specific rights of citizens are not to be restricted by particular official religious actions of a state-sanctioned religious society. The members of all the religious societies existing in the state, both societies officially recognized and those merely tolerated, are citizens with completely equal standing. For this purpose there will be introduced a merely civic verification system for births, marriages, and deaths. In accord with the stipulations of common law, the Charter distinguishes officially accepted churches and sects from those that are merely tolerated. The merely tolerated group breaks down into two classes. Thus the whole group of religious societies forms a series consisting of three levels. The highest level consists of the churches preferred by the government. At the lowest level are all the congregations whose principles are not at odds with reverence for the deity, obedience to the laws, loyalty to the state, and general morality. The middle level churches are entitled to have their clergy perform official legal acts, ones only certified as civil rights for the third level. The middle level comprises the societies whose confessional statements essentially agree with one of the two major Protestant churches—thus, all the orthodox sects that are largely just separable based on their historical points of departure from the state church.

One particular qualification even sets aside the distinction of these three classes, in that it makes possible a multitude of gradations and still leaves it to the king's discretion to grant particular rights to such societies, and thus to make them more or less equal to the church. The enlightened nature of the edict tolerating them met with widespread approval. However, the orthodox faction, without whose assent it certainly never would have been issued, sought in principle simply to gain from it a better pretext for expelling the rationalists from the fellowship of the church. This was clearly evident from the proceedings involving Uhlich.

The Dismissal of Uhlich

Since October 1845 Uhlich had been the preacher at the Church of St. Katherine in Magdeburg.[209] When he was challenged by the Magdeburg

209. See n. 202.

consistory for his deviations from the prescribed liturgy, his congregation interceded very energetically on his behalf.

After multiple deliberations, on 19 July 1847, the consistory put the following questions to Uhlich. First, has he decided to faithfully and conscientiously obey, in all his religious ceremonies from now on, the rules governing the ritual according to the church regulations? Second, has he ever, and in any way, sought to contravene the confessional statement of the Protestant Church as it is jointly affirmed by the Lutheran and Reformed Churches, specifically also the Apostles' Creed? If, based on his own subjective convictions, he was supposedly unable to agree to this, then the further question is whether he wishes to freely resign from his teaching office in the Protestant Church and take refuge under the Charter of 30 March.

Uhlich gave no unqualified answer to these questions. Instead he asserted his right to his own standpoint. Previous to this he had stated his position in a declaration to the consistory. He asked: How could one reckon, as sin on his part, the rationalism that the state church had instilled in him by its theological faculty in Halle, that he had openly acknowledged upon assuming his post, and that was still expounded today in Halle by Wegscheider, his teacher? What should one say about a consistory expressing itself in its proclamation so as to eliminate sixty years of development forthwith from the annals of the German Protestant Church, as though it had not happened? The consistory surely ought to ponder the consequences of arbitrarily intruding upon the fermentation process of the church in our day. It should look closely at his own impact. Uhlich is referring not merely to the full pews in his church, but also to the fruits in the spheres of life he has had the opportunity to impact up to now. One should look closely at the spiritual condition of Magdeburg, of the region, the province, and Protestant Germany. There is no concealing the fact that countless contemporaries only take offense at the preaching of what the consistory calls the basic facts and basic truths of Christianity; that they do not find them edifying and cannot do so in the present state of things. Rather, as things stand, they say: if only that which is offered to us counts as Christianity, then we may not want Christianity at all.

All this and more was of no avail. In September 1847, Uhlich was suspended in order to carry through with his dismissal in the proper way, through a disciplinary investigation. The consistory declared as erroneous the opinion that Uhlich's opposition to the consistory was a matter of differences in dogmatic views. The differences did not involve developments in dogmatic concepts where not everyone would have understood whether they are compatible with scripture. Instead they involved the most sacred and basic facts of Christianity, namely, facts about the person of our Lord

Jesus Christ, about his true death, his real resurrection, and his actual ascension. If this does not concern dogmatics, then nothing does! This single contention suffices to give us a notion as to the spiritual loftiness of such a consistory. What is the point of charters and religious edicts, when everything still ultimately depends on the caprice and dogmatic scriptural interpretation of a consistory, or on a sovereign's frame of mind? Is it not clear that church governance of this kind can take no steps without setting itself most decidedly into contradiction with the general culture of the time? Is it not clear, even where it thinks of itself as broad-minded, that it takes this stance only in order to freely allow to the one side what it all the more rigidly limits for the other side?

The Growth and the Suppression of the Free Congregations

The aforementioned Charter, and the action taken against Uhlich, of course took place at a time when one should have thought that the staff of authority was broken forever, in the absolutism of church governance as well. Uhlich was spared from being formally dismissed from office by the consistory, for he left the state church. His followers joined together in a public announcement of 29 November 1847, constituting themselves as a new Christian religious fellowship called the Christian Congregation.

In a printed text, "Declaration of Protestant Christians in Magdeburg," they described the congregation's guiding principles and the system they adopted for governing it. In conformity with that system, they chose twelve members of the congregation to be its elders, and they decided unanimously to call Preacher Uhlich to be their pastor. Since, by taking these steps, they assumed that their formation of the Christian congregation under that name was complete, they sought the approval of the state, and it was granted on 25 January 1848. Of the free congregations that formed based on the 30 March 1847 edict of tolerance, this one had the most members. At the height of its flourishing it was said to have about 5,000 members. It was certified as taking an authentically Protestant direction, yet it was hardly able to maintain itself for an extended period, as one of the remaining congregations of this kind.

The political movement that had its inception in 1848, soon after the congregation's founding, became just as hazardous for it as did the reaction that followed. While the congregation had taken a freer direction in the years of this movement, as soon as the opportunity arose people were all the more ready to take steps against it. As a political association, it came under the strictest oversight by the police. The disciplinary steps the government took against the congregation seemed to have assumed such a general and hostile character that, in 1852, a resolution was presented in the chamber to appoint a special commission to investigate government regulations not in harmony with the existing principles of the state's constitutional charter, that is, regulations with reference to dissident congregations, in particular the free congregations and the German-Catholic congregations. According to the resolution, both the Charter of 30 March 1847, and the specifications of the general common law as well as the constitutional guarantees of complete freedom of belief and conscience for Prussian subjects, would at present be curtailed indirectly for the dissident congregations, by the following measures: local expulsion of their clergy; limiting the right of assembly, in addition to withholding the resources for religious construction and for performing acts of public worship; the provision that, contrary to article 12 of the constitutional charter, the enjoyment of civil rights and the rights of citizenship be made dependent on one's religious confession; denial of corporate rights; requiring personal services and contributions for those serving the Protestant Church; not carrying out article 19 of the constitutional charter on account of the introduction of civil marriage; and so forth.

Yet this resolution got no further support in the chamber. The government openly expressed the intention to use every legal means to eradicate the whole dissident system. The high consistory issued an order excommunicating the free congregations, and the police closed them down for being political associations. Thus about forty congregations of this kind in Prussia and Saxony were almost entirely wiped out, leaving no evidence of their very energetic religious orientation. In February 1856 the appellate court in Magdeburg issued its verdict about the free congregation there, the same verdict as the one the city court issued three months before: that the congregation must close and its leaders be subject to punishment, because they aimed to discuss political topics in their gatherings, under the cloak of religion. Also in 1856, the supreme tribunal incontrovertibly put an end to the free congregations, stating that, as political associations, they are dissolved. A complaint lodged with the king in 1857 was just as futile; [the response was] that the police regulations should be kept intact. As Uhlich said in the Magdeburg Sunday newspaper when that verdict was handed down, the Magdeburg dissidents are just legitimate dissidents; the family affairs in which the church takes part, such as baptism, matrimony, and burial, fall legally under the citizen records system. Only at the beginning of 1859 did the ministry of the interior decree that all of the regulations posing obstacles to the free congregations be disregarded.

Deliberations about a Synodal System of Governance

From these phenomena that I juxtaposed here because they are interconnected, we do indeed see the general course taken by church affairs in Prussia since 1848.

The first consequence for the church, from the events of March 1848, was the collapse of the previous ministry for spiritual affairs. The concessions made on 19 March also included the appointment of a new minister, one of the most respected and broad-minded members of the general synod and the provincial diet, Count von Schwerin.[210] He proceeded directly to declare that he was thoroughly convinced the controversy most vigorously carried on in the Protestant Church for a long time could best be settled, and peace be restored in the simplest way, if people would, for the sake of the church's continuance and thriving development, just utilize the power of its inner truth, and would trust the gospel's living, and life-giving, spirit. He said he has already taken steps to see that the presbyterial and synodal system of governance, long desired by the Protestant co-religionists in the eastern provinces of the monarchy, can become a reality as soon as possible. He has appointed a commission to accomplish this.

The supreme consistory established in January, but not yet actually operational, was in turn dissolved on 18 April, and on 26 April the plan of an ordinance concerning the calling of a Protestant state synod was announced. In this announcement the king made known anew his conviction that the state's Protestant Church must not receive its system of governance via a regulation from the existing government; instead it must construct this system on its own. The time has come for completing this task, since continuing the current organization of the church unaltered would not be compatible with the change in the state's governance system.

Hence a state synod should have been convened to deliberate and decide on the future governance system for the Protestant Church, one in which the individual provinces would have been represented by elected delegates. The church's representatives were supposed to have come from those chosen by the district and provincial synods, and all the independent and irreproachable members of the Protestant Church were supposed to be voters and eligible to be elected. As the minister remarked in his order on 24 April, until the foundation of the Protestant Church's new system of governance shall have been established, the consistory's previous sphere of activity will undergo no changes. However, at the same time he also forcefully recommended that, prior to issuing particular legal regulations for this

---

210. See n. 195.

important area of concern under its stewardship, the consistory should let the principles of religious freedom, and the free practice of religion, serve as its guidelines. Also, it should carefully avoid anything that could seem incompatible with these principles, and that would include preferential treatment on the part of the state for any one dogmatic-theological orientation. Instead, freedom of instruction is to be allowed everywhere, and supervision of clergy and instructors is to stick just to requiring that everywhere, in the spirit of genuinely Protestant love and tolerance, Christian truth is to be based on the Word of God. By all these means, and under the pressure of the moment, the ministry heeded the loud call at that time for convening, as expeditiously as possible, a constituent state synod.

However, this synod never came about. Not only had the revolution been suppressed in the meantime; also, the public's views about the plan for its enactment called forth serious misgivings about calling a state synod. The *Evangelische Kirchenzeitung* faction even labeled the cry for a synodal governance system forthwith as a poorly-concealed hostility to Christ, and the arrangement for choosing electors as virtual atheism. In order to learn the opinion of the church about such a synod and the governance issue as such, in January 1849 the collective consistories of the monarchy called upon the Protestant theological faculties of the six state universities, and a few professors of canon law, to give their expert views. The expert views they received, and which were published in that same year, declared themselves almost unanimously opposed to the calling of such a synod, inasmuch as it was supposed to be composed, as to its non-clerical members, by choosing electors from the current membership of the congregations. They advised beginning an independent governance system for the church by creating official positions in the congregations. Several of these expert opinions furthermore declared most definitely that, on the whole, there ought never be a constituent synod, in the sense of a body enacting its majority decisions as to the confession, the cultus, and the governance system, for the entire membership to date of the Protestant Church of Prussia.

The Protestant High Consistory in Berlin

In 1848, the wish was expressed, from several quarters, for there to be a higher ecclesiastical authority dealing with the provisional status of the Protestant Church of Prussia, an authority that, in keeping with the interests of the church, provided more security for the church's transition into the new arrangements than did the office of the state minister for spiritual affairs, which so often changed its position during this period. Therefore this need was satisfied by establishing a special division of the ministry for spiritual affairs, a division for matters internal to the Protestant Church.

This new authority, in concert with the minister, then abandoned the route of a constituent synod, and believed that the ecclesiastical organization, first and foremost, had to take the lead, by officers of the congregations taking on the role of the congregation's representatives for all further connections formed within the body of the church. The plan for an organization of congregations that was worked up for this purpose got approved by royal decree on 29 June 1850, and the aforementioned Protestant division within the ministry was converted into a Protestant high consistory. The essential feature of a congregation's organization was the establishing of a congregation's consistory, made up of the pastor at its head, and at least four lay members, irreproachable family men more than thirty years of age, communicants in the church, who have become trustworthy in virtue of their antecedent moral conduct.

This new organization of the church largely met with a very unfavorable reception. Indeed there were two mutually incompatible kinds of objections to it. One side faulted it for being an accommodation in part to the democratic tendencies of the times and the collegial notions of a rationalistic canon law, and in part to territorial autonomy. Objectors in the other group sought to take it as the expression of hierarchical views and intentions. This latter objection was registered in the memorandum (simultaneously published) that the Berlin *Comité der Unionsvereine* presented to the minister for spiritual affairs and the high consistory, as signed by Jonas, Sydow, Pischon, and others. As the *Comité* understood things, for the high consistory the real church, as a divine institution, was said to be in part the organized government office of spiritual affairs, and in part the sovereign of the land as its foremost member; and the congregations are only said to be the spheres that these entities govern.

In any event the major issue was how, under these new arrangements, the right of the Protestant Church, a right enunciated in the Prussian state constitution of January 1850, to independently organize and supervise its own affairs, had in fact been acknowledged. The government maintained that this right was already in effect by the church having been completely made separate from the state, and therefore being independently governed, according to its traditional system of governance, by the sovereign as its most prominent member. Based on this perspective, all objections raised in the chamber out of respect for the Protestant Church's independence, objections alleging violation of the pertinent articles of the state's fundamental laws, could be turned aside. In fact it was solely the high consistory that ruled the church, in the king's name.

The Union and Lutheranism in Prussia

The strictly ecclesiastical and orthodox orientation supported by the political reaction held the upper hand to such a great extent that the Union came into question. Ever more obvious efforts to suppress the Union emerged from various quarters, efforts to authorize no other form of the church than a strictly Lutheran one.

In 1848 in Leipzig, an association of clergy from various state churches formed for the purpose of keeping the Lutheran confessional statements intact. The association regarded the modern Union doctrine, a basic teaching combining the two confessional positions, as syncretism. It then established provincial associations in several provinces, in Brandenburg, Pomerania, Saxony, Silesia, and Posen. These held a general assembly annually in Wittenberg. They did not wish to belong to a separate Lutheran church and initially did not exit from the state church, although in September 1849 they did collaborate for enforcing the Lutheran confessional position also in the liturgy, in the organization of the congregation, and in the government control of the state church.

Much that the high consistory did in the interest of this Lutheran faction could only be seen as detrimental to the Union. The outcome of all this was an order of the cabinet on 6 March 1852, in which the king declared it indubitably the case that the Union was not supposed to entail one confession converting to the other one, nor even less so the formation of a new, third confession. However, he said it should certainly result from the calls to eliminate the sorrowful barriers that currently forbid, from both sides, the uniting of members of both confessions at the Lord's table for all those who, having a lively sense of their fellowship in Christ, long for this fellowship, and to unite the two confessions in one Protestant state church. The Protestant high consistory has already been seriously endeavoring to clarify the views, and to prepare a proper understanding, of the true principles of the Union. But at this stage it is time to express these principles in the form of church authorities that are self-regulating, and by doing so to provide the guarantee that, in the governmental control of the Protestant state church, the combined fellowship of the two Protestant confessions should, with the grace of God, be securely upheld in the Union every bit as much as the independence of the two confessions.

These principles are as follows. First, the Protestant high consistory pledges equally: to supervise and represent the Protestant state church in its totality, and to protect and nurture the rights of the different confessions and the orientations on which they are based. Second, the Protestant high consistory consists of members from both confessions. But it can only accept as members those persons who can, in good conscience, accept the collaboration of members from both confessions in exercising its authority. Third, in circumstances calling for its decision, the Protestant high consistory decides them in collegial fashion, by a majority vote of its membership. However, when the business at hand is the kind in which the decision can only be handled based on one of the two confessions, then the preliminary confessional action shall be decided not according to all the members' votes, but only according to the votes of members of the confession involved, and this decision then shall serve as the basis for the resolution by the entire body.

Given the stance they took within the Protestant Church, the friends of the Union had to have felt very offended by this order of the cabinet. If the Protestant high consistory was supposed to be made up of members from the two confessions, then the only ones who could have a seat and vote were those devoted to one or the other of the two confessions. And in the event of a confessional split in the government control of the church, the motive can only be to implement this split via the pastorate and the congregation. So the Union seemed endangered in principle, and to be tolerated only inasmuch as it was secured by order of the cabinet. This gave adherents of the Union cause to assert their rights too.

Therefore in Halle, in 1852, the collective members of the theological faculty, a number of clergy, and professors from other faculties all signed a petition. It urged, first of all, that the Union, which rests purely on the consensus of the two Protestant confessions, be afforded the same official protection, and the same official nurturing and support, as those groups of the Protestant Church that take one side or the other in their confessional dissent. In the second place, it urged that the justification for the Union be acknowledged not merely where it has been authentically achieved, but rather everywhere where it has been actually introduced in congregations by adopting the Union regulations in worship, and in the appointing of clergy without regard to confessional differences within the Protestant Church—and not subsequently renounced in turn by the express declaration of the congregation in question. [The petition stated that] the Protestant high consistory, together with the king, should have arranged for the announcement of an authoritative interpretation of the order of 6 March along these lines.

These protests led to a new royal announcement, made on 12 July 1853 to the Protestant high consistory, which complained anew about the earlier announcement having been misconstrued. It objected to the assumption that the earlier announcement had intended to interfere with the Union of the two Protestant church communities, or indeed to completely nullify it and thereby produce a split in the state church. It said that the church authorities have conscientiously stuck to the position that departures from the regulations of the Protestant state church in individual congregations may only be introduced for consideration with the consent of their clergy and congregants; and departures may only occur after all precautions have been taken and this serious responsibility has been most fully set before the Lord, for any splits in his church will be on the shoulders of those who originate, or take part in, them.

This announcement seemed to be going back on the concessions made, about the rights of the two confessions, in the order of 6 March 1852. Alarmed about this, a conference of Lutheran clergy, meeting in Wittenberg in September 1853, delivered a protest. The king responded to it on 27 October 1853, by stating that it saddens him, and is proof of the disconcerting impact that distrust has on authority. He reminded them of what he had done in his thirteen-year reign to protect the separate confessions. But at the same time he warned about the effort to gain standing for a separate confession to such a degree that it would make unity in the church and in authority an impossibility. After such different and mutually contradictory declarations, what was the intention supposed to be?

At the present time,[211] the status quo can only be described as follows. The Union exists only to the extent that it constructs a confessional form of its own alongside the affirmations of the separate confessions. Yet what seems to matter now is just identifying, outwardly and accurately, which congregations are Lutheran, which are Reformed, and which are United. Opponents of the Union (such as Dr. Scheurl,[212] in the *Erlanger Zeitschrift*, vol. 27, p. 362) contend that only when the Lutheran confession, the Reformed confession, and the Union have each maintained its own distinct sphere, precisely demarcated spatially and in terms of persons, will there be an actually united Protestant state church existing in Prussia, one that would outwardly form a compact, robust unity. Then it would truly and outwardly form a church fellowship with the name "Protestant Church," under a single highest church authority, a fellowship that would be split up only for any special confessional functions and having its subdivisions based on its actual components, the existing Lutheran, Reformed, and United congregations.[213]

---

211. [*Zeller*] That is, 1856.

212. See n. 187.

213. [*Baur*] On this position, see also J. Müller, *Die evangelische Union, ihr Wesen und göttliches Recht* (Berlin, 1854). Opposing it is Kliefoth in *Kirchliche Zeitschrift* 2 (1855) 1ff., "Hat Dr. J. Müller das Recht der Union wirklich erwiesen?" On Müller, see Dorner, "Ueber den theologischen Begriff der Union und sein Verhältniss zur Confession," *Theologische Studien und Kritiken* 29 (1856) nos. 1–2. In the same issue [no. 2],

Stahl on the Union[214]

Stahl, the main lay leader of the conservative Lutheran faction in Prussia, authored *Die lutherische Kirche und die Union, eine wissenschaftliche Erörterung der Zeitfrage* (Berlin, 1859). This is the main book for getting our bearings as to how things now stand regarding the issue of the Union, and in particular how the Lutheran faction positions itself on this issue.

Stahl sees the most recent version of the Union as having a nonchalant attitude toward the differences between the respective teachings of the Lutheran and the Reformed churches. He sees this nonchalance and indifference as being linked with unbelief; he thinks that the Union is a work of unbelief. For him the Union is the direct opposite of the creed and the confessional church; it is their abolition and negation. Hence it would be impossible to hold simultaneously to the creed or confession, and to the Union. Stahl places major emphasis on the confessional stance, on the teaching, on dogma. Hence the true concept of the Union is said to be first and foremost the demand for the unification of the confessions. But how can the confessions unite if one neither declares all their differences to be inconsequential, nor absorbs one of the two theological frameworks into the framework of the other one? The former alternative would just be what Stahl found fault with as a spurious concept of a union, and the latter would no longer be called "union," but instead would be "absorption." So Stahl's actual thesis is that the Union is something inherently impossible, since it could only have been achieved within the confessional stance or theological framework of the Lutherans, for in no case can it provide something on its own. Instead the Union must hold firmly to the Lutheran confession as the absolute truth.

The question then can only be: what is the basis for the claim that the Lutheran theological framework is the absolute truth? In order to prove this contention, Stahl compares the two theological frameworks with each other. In doing so he sticks primarily with Zwingli[215] and counter poses him

---

see Müller, "Das Verhältniss zwischen der Wirksamkeit des heiligen Geistes und dem Gnadenmittel des göttlichen Worts." See also my own essay on the Protestant principle in *Theologische Jahrbücher* 14 (1855) 1–137. [*Ed.*] On Müller, see n. 52; on Kliefoth, n. 139; on Dorner, n. 178.

214. [*Zeller*]. This section was composed in 1859. [*Ed.*] On Stahl, see n. 194.

215. Huldrych (Ulrich) Zwingli (1481–1531). See the multiple references to the Swiss Reformer in Baur's *History of Christian Dogma* (n. 122), 272, 280, 284, 297, 301, 306–7, 311, 319–20, 321n. In discussing the confessional differences over the Lord's Supper, Baur writes (320): "Zwingli contended, on good grounds, that it is neither necessary nor conceivable to accept a real partaking of the body and blood of Christ; and he showed that, instead of a bodily presence and bodily partaking, only a spiritual

to Luther as much as he can, thus portraying Zwingli as merely a "humanist" and "naturalist"[216] who had no authentically Protestant interest in the Reformation. For Zwingli, who sees everything happening without mediation or intercession and [just] through God, the basic spiritual stance of the Swiss Reformation and the Reformed Church resides in the axiom: nothing salvific shall, or is allowed to, take place apart from (*praeter*) God. His reason for this does not lie in the doctrine of predestination. Zwingli's doctrine of predestination is instead just the high point of his negative Reformation and its basic idea: that nothing shall be salvific apart from God himself. This basic idea soars above all of God's creatures, institutions, and mediations as it does above all free life—right up to the empty heights where there is nothing but God alone. There, where there is nothing other than him, God is left to decide about salvation and damnation. With this teaching Zwingli nullifies not merely Lutheranism, but Christianity too.

It is obvious that [Stahl] brings up the doctrine of predestination here not only for referring to the central dogma of the Reformed Church, but also simply to relate predestination to secondary matters, so as to make it into the central dogma over against the doctrine of Holy Communion. For when he also calls the doctrine of predestination the absolute obstacle, and repeatedly states that the Lutheran Church cannot accept in any way the Reformed principle that God is the sole cause (see pp. 233, 413), this statement always just has in mind the doctrine of Holy Communion. Everything Stahl says in opposition to the doctrine of predestination is supposedly just being said in favor of the Lutheran doctrine of Holy Communion. Hence the axiom of the Reformed Church—that there shall not be anything salvific apart from God—amounts to saying that there shall not be any instrumental dispensing of grace; that created beings are not bearers and conduits of God's operations. What this view sets down from the outset is that there shall be no sacraments in the sense of "means of grace"; that sacraments shall only be symbols of grace. All the arguments, to the effect that "is" often has the meaning "signifies" and that Christ's body is in heaven, and any others, are just sought out after the fact in order to prove what already counts

---

presence and spiritual partaking could occur. Following him, Calvin specified this spiritual partaking more precisely as one in which, through the mediation of the substance of the flesh of Christ, the spiritual life passing over to us is imparted by a mysterious efficacy of the Holy Spirit.... Just as the irresolvable difference between the Calvinist representation and the Lutheran rests on the impossibility [for Calvin] of the participation of the unfaithful in such a partaking, so the closeness of the two positions to each other seems to rest on the concrete language employed by Calvin [about the body and blood of Christ]."

216. "Naturalist" (*Naturalisten*) presumably means here "non-sacramentalist" or "anti-sacramentalist."

as unmistakable prior to any proof (p. 142). It is as though that thesis could have been propounded in such general terms without it being grounded in the doctrine of predestination!

When everything is aimed at basing Stahl's claim, which makes Lutheran doctrine the absolute truth, on the Lutheran doctrine of Holy Communion, then we must look into the basis for this claim. However, in a scientific discussion of the kind Stahl wants to provide in his text, we can only be astonished at finding nothing at all for that purpose except the old and most trivial observation that, in Christ's words instituting the sacrament [Matt 26:26], ἐστὶ would not mean "signify" but instead mean "is." All Stahl knows how to say directly about the main point on which everything depends here is that the Lutheran understanding is nevertheless the simple way to understand it; that, even though there is supposedly no issue of an unbending rule here, such that the strict or precise understanding be preferred to the symbolic one, yet in any event there is no basis in this passage for departing from the precise one.

What rational person, then, can deny that the most customary usage takes ἐστὶ to be equivalent to "signifies"? Whoever can find it so natural to depart from the most customary usage in a case where one cannot do so without positing, for a passage so clear on its own, something at odds with all rational thinking? Only when one so completely disregards all that is natural and rational—and of course it cannot be otherwise in the Lutheran theological framework—is it in the end of no consequence whether one accepts such a transcendent procedure in Holy Communion as is the case in this particular Lutheran doctrine. But since such a denial of rational thinking is far too unnatural for any scientifically educated person, we must certainly also presume that, for Stahl, the actual motivation is something other than simply that ἐστὶ.

The motivation is to make the difference between the Lutheran and the Reformed theological frameworks as great as possible, in order to be able to combine Catholic hierarchical concepts, which cannot be cast aside, all the better with the Lutheran theological framework. For an example we only need read what Stahl says about the power of the keys.[217] Lutheran magisterial power is not said to be like the Catholic power of the keys, and is also not invested in the clergy apart from the rest of the church. However,

---

217. According to Matt 16:19, Jesus gave Peter "the keys to the kingdom of heaven, and whatever you bind on earth will be bound in heaven, and whatever you loose on earth will be loosed in heaven." The Catholic Church believes that this power (to forgive sins, to administer the sacraments, to teach, to rule authoritatively, etc.) is handed down to Peter's successors, the popes and his representatives. Some Lutherans claim the power of the keys for the Lutheran Church and its ministers.

it is said to be a divine fullness of grace, which is not the same thing as the preaching of the gospel; rather, this power is instead the gospel's application. Its application is of course said to be invested in the whole congregation, and yet is to be exercised in an orderly way by the priest as the one whose pronouncements are to be believed as God's own pronouncements. In the Reformed Church the power of the keys does not mean the gospel's application, but only its proclamation; that is, there is no power of the keys there, but merely the mission of preaching, and there is no absolution, but only counsel and guidance as to how absolution is to be sought. The Reformed clergy are therefore only teachers, and unlike the Lutheran clergy they are not God's instruments and servants; that is, they are not priests.

From what Stahl says about the doctrine of the universal priesthood we see, more specifically, how we are to understand the role of the Lutheran priest. The universal priesthood is not the principle for the governance system of the Lutheran Church. That principle is instead the religious callings or vocations of the ranks within the church. The principle is that the church is an organic body of three different ranks, each of which has a special calling for the exercise of authority in the church. The government authority, the *magistratus*, has external authority and control; the teaching office, the *ministerium*, has influence over the contents of the regulations, and its function is to preside over the church; the role of the congregation, the *populus*, is that of assenting or dissenting. In the governance of the Lutheran Church great emphasis is given in particular to the significance of the teaching role. While this role is of course designated conceptually as just the serving of the divine Word, that is, of preaching and administering the sacraments, in practice, and indeed based on divine authority, the essential power of exercising control over the church is ascribed to this role. The fundamental task of the teaching role is to be cognizant of doctrine and to repudiate erroneous teachings and, under the ecclesiastical authority of the sovereign, its counsel and approval regarding the compatibility of regulations with scripture is indispensable. Its tasks involve ordination, the power of the keys as conceived more narrowly, absolution, and excommunication. In the consistory, where the clerical and the secular elements work together, the clerical element is still always the focal point. Thus the church is also concentrated in the central, clerical point, and the God-fearing prince rules the church in that he proceeds in conformity with the counsel of its inspired teachers (p. 253).

One cannot state more clearly than Stahl has done here that, in the Lutheran Church, there is a priesthood, in a hierarchical sense, comparable to that in the Catholic Church. What significance has the congregation, or the government authorities or the prince, when the supreme and sole decision regarding all issues of ecclesiastical authority is in the hands of the teaching office? Hence the reproach addressed to the Reformed Church is that its defining idea is the right of the congregation; that the lay element would be the bearer of ecclesiastical authority over the teaching office. The Lutheran Church suffers great harm from the Union, because the Union results in a presbyterial system of governance. It is by no means merely for the sake of Holy Communion that the Lutheran Church does not want to hear anything about a union with the Reformed Church. It is very much the hierarchical, priestly spirit that dominates these so-called Lutherans. However, the one issue is entirely analogous to the other; the one draws support from the other, and the two together just constitute the true character of this Lutheran Church. There must be a priesthood standing as mediator between God and the people of the congregation, because otherwise there would surely be no divinely ordained ecclesiastical authority; and there must be an objective mystery of faith, such as the Holy Communion of the Lutheran Church, otherwise there would surely be no specific way in which the Lutheran Church has an advantage over the Reformed Church.

Hence [Stahl says] it all goes back to the matter of God as the sole cause, with this being the principle of the Reformed Church, a principle making a Lutheran union with that church absolutely impossible. The entire Reformed dissent from Lutheranism rests on the principle that God does not bring about salvation via means and instruments; and this point itself rests in turn on the philosophical idea of God as the sole cause. This Reformed principle in itself would be an interference that restricts and prescribes God's methods, which lessens his granting of grace. It is the basis for that current of abstraction and sorry state of ecclesiastical authority, that resistance to mystery, that brand of republican obstinacy in face of any earthly grandeur and sanctity (and from which the Zwinglian principle of the people's sovereignty is also said to stem). It is entirely beyond measure what an impact this principle would have on our entire way of understanding things, both ecclesiastical matters and even political affairs, and accordingly on the entire human condition—what world-shaping power resides in this principle, and how wholly significant such a power would be for the contemporary process of fermentation in all the religious-political and social attitudes and circumstances.

In order to convince ourselves what a vacuous recitation this is, and how little is in any way tenable in all of it, we need only make clear how the so-called Reformed principle of God's sole causality is actually to be understood. In this case one naturally thinks, first of all, of the doctrine of predestination, although this principle by no means involves just predestination. Also, where the Reformed Church would have formally disavowed predestination, the principle of the Reformed Church is said to be the same, for it is certainly also expressly stated that the doctrine of predestination is not the central dogma of the Reformed Church. But, when one separates the issue from the doctrine of predestination, how can one then still speak of sole causality as the principle of the Reformed Church? If, in Holy Communion, the bread and wine are not the body and blood of Christ, is it not pointless to maintain that there is no operative cause of salvation apart from God? Is not the word, the scripture, also such a cause? And, if the bread and wine are considered to be symbols of the body and blood, how can one say they are not also something operating salvifically? And does not the church itself also come into the picture here? Yet Stahl speaks about Zwingli as though he had regarded the church and all ecclesiastical means as counting for nothing. In sum, here we have none other than a series of the most vacuous and capricious contentions that have nothing to do with Holy Communion as such, but just involve the foothold they are believed to provide for Stahl's Catholic, hierarchical concepts.

What then remains as the essential difference if one does not presuppose these conceptions throughout? What is the power of the keys, what is absolution in the Lutheran sense, if one is not thinking here of the clergyman as having the character of an officer of God, as only a priest has it? In the end there would just be the little word ἐστὶ that is said to establish the huge divide between Lutheran and Reformed. However, the contention that here alone "is" cannot mean "signify" is so much a pure absurdity, remote from any proof, that we can simply infer a different and underlying motive for saying this, a motive one may not therefore state directly and candidly. In order to disguise this motive, one hides behind the word ἐστὶ, as though there were no getting beyond it. Thus the true salvific power resides in the Lutheran ἐστὶ. And yet it is not in the least said to be denied that someone can become blessed in terms of the Reformed doctrine of the sacraments. So what basis remains for being so exclusively opposed to the Reformed Church, when it must nevertheless be conceded that each person can become blessed in terms of his or her own confession? Is not this also just a new demonstration of what self-seeking motives and interests are the foundation here?[218]

Schweizer has rightly remarked that ecclesiastical and theological issues of this kind are never handled more poorly than when they fall into the hands of lawyers, and especially those who are Jewish by nature. It is in fact the truest service to the letter of the law when the entire theological

---

218. [*Baur, in the text*]. See Schweizer, *Protestantische Kirchenzeitung* (1859) nos. 27, 28, 29. [*Ed.*] Alexander Schweizer (1808–88), Swiss Reformed theologian and professor at Zürich.

and ecclesiastical system hinges on ἐστί being taken in its most literal sense. If one concedes, what no rational man can deny, that ἐστί can also mean "signify," then the whole system, together with all the distinctions it draws between the Lutheran and Reformed theological frameworks, collapses internally, and there is no Lutheran concept of the sacrament, no Lutheran power of the keys and absolution, and also no Lutheran hierarchy. We can only be amazed that such a theology has not already long been so refuted, and exposed as invalid, that it can no longer dare to appear so brazenly and even pass itself off as authentically scientific. (On p. 533 Stahl speaks of the forceful and thought-provoking rehabilitation of confessionalism, that is, of this neo-Lutheran theology, in science.) However, for the most part the Union theology itself is none other than mere literal theology that cannot get away from the basis of the old symbols, and yet undermines them in the most arbitrary way, by its distinction between *consensus* or unanimity, and *dissensus* or disagreement.[219]

We find the Protestant Church in Prussia, and in Germany on the whole, in this vacillating condition. There is a constant, indecisive vacillation between one's own confession and the Union. On the confessional side, in the strictest and narrowest sense, stands Lutheranism, with all the hierarchical interests and tendencies it associates with confessionalism. On the Union side there is of course a freer and more liberal outlook, although it also has an attachment to symbols that makes its resistance to confessional and hierarchical interference quite insipid and feeble. This outlook wants to affirm a consensus on those symbols that, going by their theological frameworks, are mutually exclusive—a consensus that is in fact nonexistent.

More on the History of Ecclesiastical Conditions[220]

Hengstenberg has been relieved of his position as a member of the scholarly examinations commission (he had been examining the candidates for secondary school positions in religion and Hebrew). Stahl has obtained his requested discharge from the Protestant high consistory.

The 1859 *Evangelische Kirchenzeitung*, no. 27, contains, under the heading "Protestation" (Solemn Declaration), an article in which the latest actions and announcements, by the ministry for religious affairs, with reference to marriage, dissident status, and so forth, are regarded as an abandoning of the Protestant state church. Following a cautionary reminder about

---

219. [Baur] In the *Deutsche Zeitschrift für christliche Wissenschaft* (October, 1859), Stier too has pointed out Stahl's contradictions. [*Ed.*] Ewald Rudolf Stier (1800–72).

220. This section contains supplementary information, apparently added in 1859.

Peter's denial [of Christ] and Judas' betrayal of him, the article concluded with the confident expectation that, everywhere where there is still fidelity to the Protestant Church, a solemn declaration in harmony with this one will follow. Instead of doing so, the high consistory issued a cautionary announcement to the collective consistories, since if such a provocation had incurred consequences, it could have provided the occasion for a serious disciplinary intervention. In numbers 42 and 43, Hengstenberg expressed great amazement at this. He had always so faithfully stood by the high consistory, and now this action had to be taken against him, whereas never is there a censoring of the *Protestantische Kirchenzeitung* and the *Neue Evangelische Kirchenzeitung*. Eight church patrons from the "Duchy of Magdeburg" protested in the same cause; see "Die revolutionäre Rechtglaubigkeit" in the *Protestantische Kirchenzeitung* (1859) no. 16. The article concluded with the following words. "This undisciplined, inflammatory conduct once again painfully reminds us that a system of church governance is lacking. If we had a system of church governance that the congregations, the districts, and the whole church could have articulated, how would it have been possible for a very few audacious and cunning partisans to have produced such alarm and disorder in the church by their rabble-rousing? How would they have instead appeared, in their vulnerability and their vanity, before the prodigious power of the Protestant public spirit?"[221]

The Union in the Palatinate

What took place in the Rhine province of Bavaria also pertains in this connection to the Union cause. Here too the affair took a course similar to that in Prussia. The occasion for it was provided by the tercentenary of the Reformation in 1817.

Soon after the celebration, congregations in Speier, Kirchheimbolanden, Bergzabern, Zweibrücken, and several other places, declared themselves in favor of uniting and set forth their declaration in special public announcements of their union. The royal administration, in its role as the Protestant consistory, took an active part in the matter. In January 1818, its decision was that it was especially pleased to accept the declaration of the congregations. Without intervening in any coercive or persuasive way, the consistory should try to discover the opinions and wishes of the individual

---

221. At this point Zeller adds a lengthy footnote, providing extensive detail about contests between advocates of local or regional church self-governance in various parts of Germany, and the forces of reaction that mandated centralized, authoritative control and management of Protestant church affairs.

congregations. If the outcome of this general inquiry were that the majority of the Protestants were in favor of uniting, then a general synod should be convened. In order to avoid all future missteps, the general synod should determine the manner of their union by mutual agreement. To this end the consistory would have to take into consideration the church doctrines, the rites, the liturgy, school instruction, church property, and church governance. In all these matters it would have to accept the collective decisions and give them its fullest approval.

Several general synods in Kaiserslautern deliberated about the matter, publicly announced a union, and the government assented to it in 1822. The confessional statement issued by the congregations said that the sole norm of their faith and life would be the gospel of Jesus Christ as it is clearly and plainly articulated, in how its meaning would appear to sound, unbiased reason; and that those who deviated from this norm in their teaching and their life would no longer be the church's teachers. The original wording of the relevant paragraph in the document of union read as follows. "The United Protestant, Evangelical-Christian Church recognizes nothing other than, or in addition to, the New Testament as the norm of its faith. In addition, it declares that all the creedal books or documents heretofore extant in the Protestant-Christian congregations and confessions, or held to be normative by them, shall no longer be retained." To the contrary, the high consistory wanted the general symbols and the creedal documents the two confessions had in common—excepting just those points in them about which the two confessions had previously been at loggerheads—made known as being the norm for teaching. However, the general synod, in 1821, had persisted with the following formulation (subsequently approved) of this section. "The Protestant Evangelical-Christian Church has proper respect for the general symbols and the creedal documents in use by the separate Protestant confessions, while nevertheless recognizing no other basis for faith and norm for teaching than Holy Scripture alone."

At that time this union already came to be suspected of religious indifference; yet until 1831 no attempt was made to interfere with the constraints imposed on creeds in the unified church. But in 1832 and 1833, the supreme Protestant ecclesiastical authority in the Palatinate had three of its members dismissed, and vacancies were filled, at the specific suggestion of the government, by Siess and Dr. Rust,[222] who was preacher and professor at Erlangen. What Rust did was to continually counteract the sense in which the Union had been concluded, and his doing so produced a most troublesome rift in the unified church. An official order of September 1835 from

---

222. Philipp Siess (n.d.); Isaac Rust (1796–1862).

the consistory stated that the doctrine of justifying and salvific faith in Jesus Christ must be declared the focal point for organizing all the other basic and distinctive teachings of the church. The order called upon the deanery to encourage and direct the clergy under it to explain and commend that doctrine to their congregants.

This order, as well as a pastoral letter written by Rust and issued by the Protestant consistory of the Rhine region in January 1836, provoked great dissatisfaction; and in July 1836 the high consistory was prompted to dispatch two of its counselors as commissioners in the Palatinate, in order to hear the complaint of the church members. Since nothing was done to relieve the situation, despite the promises of the commission, at the 1837 assembly of the chamber of deputies, the clergy, in association with the lay membership of the diocesan synod, presented a petition stating the complaint against the majority view in the consistory, a petition signed by 204 persons. The collective Protestant delegates from the Palatinate had endorsed this petition and submitted it to the chamber. The complaint was acknowledged to have both a formal and a material basis. Yet the chamber knew how to drag out the matter in such a way that it was not dealt with and resolved. The cleavage between the consistory and the unified church continued, and on every occasion, like that of the liturgy plan composed by Rust, it was evident how little the consistory was able to count on the agreement of the general synod.

The affair took a turn in which the unified church increasingly sought to disengage itself from the high consistory, that is, from its previous ties with the counterpart state church. This effort made concessions to the movement of 1848. A special general synod was summoned, and it was supposed to draw up a new election method for the presbyteries and synods, to give its view on the issue of separation, and to select a commission for the revision of church governance. The government approved the decisions of this general synod. The unified church of the Palatinate separated from the counterpart state church, and the consistory in Speier took over for it all the rights of the high consistory in matters of governance. In accord with the new method of election, transferred from the political domain to the ecclesiastical domain, the collective presbyteries and diocesan synods were supposed to be reestablished, and a commission was supposed to be seated for implementing a plan of governance, a plan the diocesan synod of 1849 had already sent to it, a plan to be sent to the next general synod for its deliberation and final decision.[223]

223. At this point Zeller adds a very lengthy footnote about the implementation of these election procedures, which he describes in great detail, including the historical background for them. He then adds to this a very extensive account of parallel concerns

A Further Attempt at Union: The Gustavus Adolphus Foundation

The goal of the Union was to smooth over the still-existing differences between the Lutheran Church and the Reformed Church, and to allow their differences to continue only to the extent that, alongside them, the unity of the Protestant Church, transcending their separation, once again was fully justified. Thus people also sought to establish unions that, without regard to the diversity within the state church, should arouse their consciousness of a single Protestant Church and heighten their interest in it in various ways.

The first union from this perspective is that of the Gustavus Adolphus Foundation.[224] In fact this union had a twofold origin. During the bicentennial celebration of the Battle of Lützen, in 1832, in addition to the desire to erect on the battlefield a monument to the heroic king, people also thought to found an association bearing his name. The purpose of the association was to support existing Protestant congregations in Catholic surroundings that are having to make do without the resources for church life and are at risk of gradually dying out. Grossmann,[225] the superintendent in Leipzig, was from the beginning the leading figure active in this endeavor. The cause first got a greater boost when Court Preacher Zimmermann,[226] who—still without knowing anything about the Leipzig foundation, which had existed for some years—issued from Darmstadt, in October 1841 in the *Allgemeine Kirchenzeitung*, an appeal to the whole Protestant Church for the very same purpose. A mutual understanding was then reached, and in 1843 the Protestant association of the Gustavus Adolphus Foundation got organized at a gathering in Frankfurt am Main.

Under the leadership of the central governing body in Leipzig, smaller local associations formed almost everywhere, and their delegates held a general gathering annually at a pre-designated site. These gatherings mainly aroused popular interest in the association, but governments could not avoid cooperating with them. The association was banned only in Bavaria because its name was antagonistic to the Catholic Church, for Gustavus Adolphus had of course defeated Tilly the Bavarian in battle. In Prussia they just wanted to have a Prussian association under the auspices of the king. Nevertheless the government in Prussia, giving way to the popular mood, relinquished its other interests, and when Prussian delegates too appeared

---

and events in Baden.

224. Gustavus Adolphus (1594–1632) was king of Sweden from 1611 until his death and led Sweden to military supremacy during the Thirty Years' War.

225. Christian Gottlob Grossmann (1783–1857).

226. Karl Zimmermann (1803–77).

at the 1844 conference in Göttingen, the cry went up, "the Prussians are here!" There was such joyous enthusiasm that at the Göttingen conference Dr. Lücke[227] looked toward a second conference at Waterloo.

The association was said to have its religious significance in its being a sacred, neutral zone for all the factions in the Protestant Church, one in turn presenting itself here, for the first time, as a united force. That is also why, in deliberations on the articles of association in Göttingen, they rejected the demand that what the association could support be defined more narrowly, rather than in general terms, as harmony with the Protestant Church. The next year, 1845, the association met in Stuttgart. This was indisputably the association's shining hour.

When the main meeting was held in Berlin in 1846, dark clouds had already formed over the association, and they now began to produce a heavy downpour. The main association in Königsberg sent Dr. Rupp,[228] who had resigned from the consistorial church. This posed the difficult question as to whether he was to be admitted or excluded. After very lively discussions, the decision, by a narrow majority vote, was to exclude him. This decision in Berlin aroused protests throughout almost all of Protestant Germany. People declared it to be a verdict on belief that is wholly in conflict with the purpose of the association, and most local associations registered protests against it in various ways. Nevertheless this situation just led to a much more decided fracture in the association, for in many of the local associations there was in turn a disaffected minority that threatened to leave and form a separate group had the association forfeited its ecclesiastical basis by rescinding its decision.

This exodus could easily have taken place at the gathering in Darmstadt in 1847, as the result of a new vote. But since Rupp had withdrawn in the meantime, the matter was settled in Darmstadt without revisiting the Berlin decision. In Darmstadt they decided that the judgment about excluding a delegate because of his failure to belong to the Protestant Church ought of course, where it should be necessary, be left to the main assembly. However, it should be done in proper form, free from the passions of the moment, and should give the true majority time to make its case. After this, the association continued its meetings and its effectiveness without any disruptions.[229]

---

227. See n. 52.

228. See n. 207.

229. Zeller adds a footnote here in which he gives the numbers of members and of congregations from 1847 to 1860.

The Eisenach Conferences

The more specific intention of the aforementioned Protestant conference was to establish closer ties among the various Protestant state churches in Germany. Related to it is the Protestant *Kirchentag*, which has already been meeting annually in Eisenach for a number of years.

This organization consists of delegates from most of the Protestant church governing bodies, who of course just wish to confer about church issues in a free, nonbinding way, but because of their standing form a very influential association. Its leaders are such men as Grüneisen, Nitzsch, Harless, Kliefoth, Vilmar, and others. The public does not have a very favorable opinion of such semi-official talks, and naturally so, for it does not place much trust in men who wish to throw their weight around in the church in this fashion.[230] At the 1857 *Kirchentag*, the conference sent its thanks to the German church governing body for having recommended a return to reformed principles in divorce cases, and for having recognized the full rights of Protestant church discipline. The 1859 assembly resolved to request the church governing authority to adopt the practice of intercessory prayers for the entire German homeland in addition to prayers for the provincial homeland.[231] It also brought up the issues of educational requirements for clergy in the filling of clerical positions, and the confidentiality of the confessional for Protestant clergy with regard to its concept, its worth, its standards,[232] and other factors.

---

230. [*Zeller*] One of the first things this organization did was to compile 150 Protestant "key hymns" in 1853, ones it recommended be universally adopted in all the state churches. Since then just a few places have actually adopted this set of hymns. It met with disapproval except in strictly orthodox circles, owing to the dogmatic illiberality and theological antiquarianism with which it excluded the most beloved and most beautiful hymns of the past hundred years, and stuck with the most unassimilable conceptions, the stalest turns of phrase, and the most antiquated forms of speech.

231. [*Zeller*] This practice then occurred in all lands represented by the conference except for Bavaria and Hesse-Homberg, and except for the cities of Frankfurt and Bremen.

232. [*Zeller*] The Dresden conferences were an offshoot of the Eisenach conferences. They were charged with a request originating with Eisenach in 1852, and coming from the royal governing authorities of Saxony, Hanover, Bavaria, Württemberg, and the two Mecklenburgs, to first of all bring about a liturgical consensus in the purely Lutheran state churches. The third and last of these Dresden conferences, held in 1856, caused a great stir because of its decision favoring the introduction of the private confessional, since it at the same time declared that the clergy would have not merely to proclaim absolution, but instead have to confer it by an act also valid in the eyes of God. In addition, the clergy would have to refuse absolution to unrepentant sinners, including, among other factors, those who impudently adhere to teaching that subverts and mocks the gospel. In the meantime the only perceptible effect of this decision has been

The Protestant Church Congress

However, the main association of this kind is the Protestant *Kirchentag* (Church Congress), which has existed since 1848. The great movement of 1848 provided the occasion for its inception.

With the political and social order then in peril, people sought their well-being in the church so as to counter the disintegrating and destructive tendency of the day by the unifying power of ecclesiastical consciousness. At that time several church-minded men, in different places and independently of one another, expressed the idea of such an alliance. The first to come forward was Bethmann-Hollweg in Bonn,[233] a senior government official. In April 1848, in a manuscript printed for friends, he disclosed the proposal for a Protestant church assembly in the course of 1848. This was said to be what occasioned the calling of all Protestant Christians of the German nation to an assembly portraying them as a whole. A number of Protestant men trusted by the church were supposed to assume the leadership, and the invitation to do so was to be issued to those who are in agreement as members of Jesus Christ, the head of the invisible church.

A conference held in Bonn in May 1848 made a similar proposal. It expressed the wish that the Protestant conference held in Berlin, in 1846, be enlarged into a universal, German general synod. In connection with this proposal, Dr. Dorner[234] in Bonn came forward with the plan for a centralized German Protestant national church. Independently of Dorner, Dr. Wackernagel[235] in Wiesbaden, together with two like-minded clergy in Odenwald, took the further step, in April 1848, of discussing a Protestant confessional church embracing the entire German people. The spring conference in Sandhof near Frankfurt am Main, where every six months the brethren of the region were accustomed to gather for joint deliberations, provided the occasion to bring up this matter.

At a new Sandhof conference on 21 June 1848, also attended by Bethmann-Hollweg, Dorner, and others, the decision was to arrange for a general, independent assembly of members of the clergy and laity of the Protestant Church of Germany, in order to discuss making arrangements for the Protestant Church of Germany under the current circumstances.

---

the heightening mistrust shown toward the efforts prevailing in the circles of government church authorities.

233. August von Bethmann-Hollweg (1795–1877), jurist and politician, who in 1845 was appointed to the Prussian council of state. He was active in Protestant affairs and later served as Prussian minister of culture and education.

234. See n. 128.

235. Philipp Karl Eduard Wackernagel (1800–77).

On the same day a congress of pastors also met in Berlin. The issue it took up was what might be done so that, at this decisive moment in time, the church could rise above its fragmentation. Stahl,[236] the privy councilor for justice [in Berlin] proposed a confederation said to include not merely the Lutheran and Reformed churches, but also the United Protestants. So, after the matter had been introduced in this way, and all sides had issued their invited documents, the first German Protestant *Kirchentag* met in September 1848, in Wittenberg, Luther's city. At the second Sandhof conference Wittenberg had been chosen unanimously as the place to assemble.

The principal decision at this meeting was to set up a Protestant alliance of churches to cultivate and promote all the shared interests of the church congregations belonging to it. The Protestant Church Alliance was not supposed to be a union doing away with confessional churches, but instead a confederation of churches, and embracing all church congregations that based themselves on the Reformation confessional statements—namely, the Lutherans, the Reformed, the United Church, and the Congregation of the Brethren. When eligibility to join the alliance was in doubt, the alliance determined that, instead of assurances given by the communion in question, the confederation should decide. For the further promotion of its goals, the assembly chose two committees, for narrower and broader goals respectively. The realization of the Church Alliance was only supposed to take place in an orderly way, namely with the legitimate representatives of the affected church communities being the right ones to set it up. In the event this were unsuccessful, the Wittenberg assembly would of course not found the church alliance on its own, but the assembly would meet regularly each year in order to nurture a properly-constituted unity of the Protestant confessions. If it were not possible to establish this unity outwardly, it would at least be nurtured inwardly, in the church's consciousness and as a voluntary enterprise. The assembly accordingly intended to constitute itself in a church alliance with official standing, and to place in its hands the governance of the church in all of Protestant Germany.

There seemed to be a very special motive for founding such an alliance of churches, one based on the circumstances at that time, namely, the national and societal conditions threatened by an altered mindset pervading people's attitudes and resulting from the decline of confidence [in institutions]. Although it was not the church's role to meddle in political and social issues, it would still have to stand up for the timeless, fundamental truths of religion and morality in this setting too. From the outset, an alliance of churches in this sense was a completely misguided idea, the realization

---

236. See n. 194.

of which would have resulted in none other than religious intolerance or compulsory belief, and oft-repeated inroads on general and individual freedoms. So it cannot be surprising that nowhere were people very inclined to accede to higher authorities.

At the third *Kirchentag* in Stuttgart, in September 1850, a report was presented about the results of efforts to establish the alliance of churches. But the report of these results was not very well received, and the goal itself, the realization of the alliance of churches, seemed to be more distant than it was previously thought to be. Nevertheless, the idea of an alliance of churches remains non-negotiable, and this assembly, as a free association, would have to work persistently toward its realization. Thus the church congresses became large conferences of pastors, which, like the gatherings of the Gustavus Adolphus Association, and chiefly because of the attention-getting publicity with which they are held, now here and now there, seek to influence ecclesial consciousness and, because of its strong impact, to react against everything in current endeavors that seems to be out of step with this consciousness. Together with the issues that are articulated, there is always the tendency—not unexpected from these gatherings and one for which men such as Bethmann-Hollweg, Stahl, Hengstenberg, and others are the main spokespersons—to safeguard ecclesiastical interests in the strictest sense.

Since the fundamental rights of Germans expressly favor the separation of church and state, and declare the concept of a state church null and void, inasmuch as the separation leaves it up to each religious society to organize and govern its own affairs independently, the second *Kirchentag*, in Wittenberg in 1849, made the topic of its deliberations the question: What is the church's assessment of the state's disassociation from Christianity, and what is the church's relation to the state? The answer then was: The Christian Church must retain recognition as a national institution in its two main confessions, with all this recognition entails. Special weight was nevertheless placed on retaining the Christian form of the oath prescribed by the state and regularly administered, on avoiding any provocation from an introduction of civil marriage, and on church weddings supplementing marriages already contracted and performed prior to, and independently of, church weddings.

It is not in fact apparent why separation of church and state should go so far as disassociating the state from Christianity; only the church is particularly concerned to present the issue in this way. When the state itself leaves matters to the church, it simply declares that, in doing so, it acts without regard to the difference between the confessions, inasmuch as it allows the various forms of Christianity, or even different religious societies, to co-exist with equal rights. From that it is self-evident that the religious character of the state is determined by those forms of religion or of Christianity that are the prevalent and vastly predominant ones in the state. The state is therefore Christian, Protestant, Lutheran or Reformed, according to which one or other of these forms of religion has the most members. One should have thought this would be the main issue, because religion is certainly a matter of individual freedom.

The church is not satisfied with this. As it actually thinks, the church always starts out from the assumption that there is no other Christianity than the very one it professes; and the church requires the state's cooperation to make this form of Christianity the one and only valid form. However much the church insists on becoming free from the state, it is still not confident enough to stand on its own feet. The church also demands that the state sustain and support it; that is, as church it also wants to be the state church, to have the state support, and give privileged status to, all that the church declares to be Christian. Hence when the state does not fall in line with the will of the church, then, to the church, the state seems to be un-Christian, and the church accuses the state of disassociating itself from, or renouncing, Christianity.

Hengstenberg's address to the Stuttgart *Kirchentag*, about the de-Christianizing of the oath, is an evident example of how far this can go, and how pronounced the tendency of a *Kirchentag* also is to simply validate, as Christianity, exclusively what it declares to be Christian in its own strictly ecclesiastical sense. The congress portrayed the wording of the oath, "So help me God," established as the exclusively legal form by the Frankfurt National Assembly, as being a denial of the specifically Christian profession of faith in the living God and Father of Jesus Christ, as an expression of deist consciousness. It said there ought to have been solemn protests against this oath; that a believing Christian could not approve of this formula. This was the proposal made in Stuttgart, whereas right there in Württemberg that formula was used for many years without anyone previously having thought to regard it as a profession of faith in deism. It is as though this oath would have prevented a Christian from considering the God in whose presence he took the oath to be also the living God and Father of Jesus Christ; as though one would not have presupposed this automatically of each Christian, and for that very reason this formula would have to have been just as sacred for that person as another specifically Christian formula would have put it. While people claimed to preserve a Christian's freedom of conscience by such proposals, they just foster an empty formalism owing to the supposition that true Christianity consists, first and foremost, of Christian-sounding formulas. Instead, conscience is led astray simply because of the suspicion of those whose unselfconscious Christian awareness does not give any thought to such consequences. In accord with the decision reached at the Stuttgart *Kirchentag*, the subcommittee sent to the government authorities the proposal that the Christian form of the oath be used again everywhere as the normal rule, albeit those who find it troubling for their conscience would be allowed to deviate from the ordinary system by confining themselves simply to the formula expressing general awareness of God.

Previous church congresses, the first two in Wittenberg, and the subsequent ones in Stuttgart, Elberfeld, Bremen, and Berlin, dealt with various topics from the same, strictly confessional, perspective. These topics were: religious observance of Sunday; the preservation of church property; the hymnal; the right of each Protestant congregation to use its own original catechism; the conduct of the clergy in relation to political matters; Protestant church affairs in the Rhenish Palatinate; the maintenance of Christian primary schools; Christian high school education; the situation of candidates [for the ministry] in the Protestant Church; the Catholic issue; and so forth. Particular proposals and representations were pertinent to a few governments—those of Oldenburg, Denmark, Baden, Lippe,[237] Nassau—but they were largely disregarded. However, in such cases too the *Kirchentag* took solace in the consciousness of having registered its Protestant confessional stance.

Yet such gatherings always have their greatest import by their bringing like-minded people together in brotherly and sisterly fashion. This mutual interaction, especially being together with those of such great repute in the church, not only strengthens one's own ecclesial consciousness but also provides entrée to circles where the interests of the church are most especially taken to heart. The discussions and deliberations about contemporary issues, the resolutions passed about them, and the speeches that can be made before a larger public audience in a more significant location, all provide a very opportune occasion for influencing public opinion in a more or less commanding way.

The proviso is that here too, as happened with the Gustavus Adolphus Association, interest gradually wanes when this scene is frequently repeated and, given all the inwardness of the faith community, issues also crop up that are not very propitious for the goal of the association. One of them is the resolution adopted in 1853 at the Berlin *Kirchentag*, by which the members of the German Protestant *Kirchentag* declared that they professed their

---

237. Lippe was a separate state of Germany until 1947, when it became a district of North Rhine-Westphalia.

allegiance to the Augsburg Confession of 1530, as being the oldest, most basic, joint attestation of publicly recognized Protestant doctrine in Germany. With this testimonial they conjoined the declaration that they hold firmly to every particular concerning the special confessional documents of their churches, and the United Protestants hold firmly to their consensus statement; and that the differing stances of the Lutherans, the Reformed, and the United Protestants on Article Ten of the Augsburg Confession,[238] and the distinctive circumstances of the Reformed congregations that have never accorded confessional status to the Augustana, ought not to detract from this declaration.

Theologians from Erlangen, Leipzig, and Rostock lodged a protest against this declaration, as being a harm inflicted on the Lutheran Church. When the Reformed are supposed to hold firmly to the confessional documents of the Reformed Church, and the United Protestants to hold firmly to their consensus statement, then the previous and allegedly unanimous testimonial is in turn annulled. The Reformed maintain for their part that what is taught differently and at variance in the confessional documents of their church *is* different and at variance, whereas the United Protestants believe and teach divergence from both Lutheran and Reformed doctrines where they are in conflict. Thus both the Reformed and the United Protestants in part repudiate what the Augsburg Confession affirms, and in part affirm what it repudiates. The Lutheran Church is not a subcategory within the church that is grounded in the Augsburg Confession; instead it is this very church itself, a church whose reach extends only to where the teachings of its confessional documents are valid. Its remaining confessional documents are not extraneous Lutheran confessions just related to the Augsburg Confession in the same way as are the confessional documents of the Reformed Church. For these other Lutheran confessions reiterate and reinforce those teachings of the Augsburg Confession that the Reformed in part contest. Accordingly the Berlin *Kirchentag* has sinned against both the Lutheran Church and the Augsburg Confession.

It is entirely natural for the committed Lutherans to look at things this way, and one cannot object to their doing so. Hence J. Müller's retort to that protest, in the foreword to the 1854 *Deutsche Zeitschrift*, is also completely vacuous, and skirts the main issue. Put succinctly, this same controversy occupying the Union—whether there could be a confessional statement in

---

238. Article Ten states that Christ's body and blood are truly present in, with, and under the bread and wine of the sacrament.

common for the Lutherans and the Reformed—is now transplanted in the soil of the *Kirchentag* as well.[239]

The Home Mission

Closely related to the *Kirchentag* is the Home Mission (*innere Mission*). Wichern, director of the Rauhes Haus[240] in Horn near Hamburg, an institution (since 1833) for rescuing neglected children, was a participant at the first Wittenberg *Kirchentag*. With considerable effort he got the Home Mission included on the congress agenda. He depicted most pathetically the God-forsaken misery of people and the lack of assistance from the church. It is finally time [he said] to pave the way for the Protestant Church to answer the summons by being a faithful alliance for loving deliverance.

In response to Wichern's motion, the allied churches expressly acknowledged, as one of their tasks, the fostering of Christian social purposes, associations, and institutions, most especially the Home Mission. The decision was to form a separate central committee for the Home Mission of the German Protestant Church, a committee linked organically to the other work of the *Kirchentag*. Thus the proceedings at the *Kirchentag* were divided into the Protestant conference on the first day and the congress for the Home Mission on the following day. There are nine departments for dealing with topics pertinent to the Home Mission, the departments for: recovery houses; prison conditions; itinerant preaching and distribution of religious tracts; voluntary poor relief and care of the sick; participation by primary school teachers in the Home Mission; city missions; the state of popular publications; keeping the Sabbath; emigration. From this we see

---

239. [Zeller] The final paragraph must have been written in 1854 or 1855, although what precedes it is from 1853. In a final revision of his manuscript, Baur wrote the following. "No *Kirchentag* has been held in the past two years. In 1859 that was because of differences within the committee, in that one faction sought to deal with marriage and the issue of dissidents, while the other faction was dubious about doing so. The main reason was that Bethmann-Hollweg, the president of the *Kirchentag* until then, had in the meantime become the Prussian minister for worship, and it is not very suitable for him, in this capacity, to continue presiding over the *Kirchentag*. According to the latest reports, no *Kirchentag* will be held in 1860. The two close friends, Hengstenberg and Stahl, who are always the major spokesmen, have of course made their views known in opposition to this decision, and General Superintendent Hoffmann agrees with them." [*Ed.*] Zeller continues with some additional recent information.

240. Johann Hinrich Wichern (1808–81). He studied theology at Göttingen and Berlin, then settled in Hamburg where he devoted himself to missionary work among the poor. He founded Rauhes Haus ("Rough House"), which continues to this day as a mission of the German Protestant Church.

how many things the Home Mission includes in its sphere of activities, and what different elements of social circumstances it keeps in view, in order to have influence on them.

Despite all this, sentiment about the Home Mission is still quite divided. Since it goes hand-in-hand with the *Kirchentag*, the considered view is that, because of this linkage, favorable public opinion about the Home Mission is on the decline. People of course oppose the name "Home Mission," which equates the pagans living among Christians with the pagans outside of Christendom. The name is indicative of a standpoint from which the crimes and evils of social life, which have such varied underlying causes, are considered, first and foremost, to be works of pagan unbelief and the doings of Satanism. The Home Mission has many opponents even among church-minded folk. There are those who wish to see the free activity of an association, such as that carried out by the Home Mission, as being detrimental to the orderly functions of the Protestant Church.

In any event when one considers the matter quite impartially, it is unmistakable that, because of how people so far have sought to be active on its behalf, and to claim that it is in the public interest, the Home Mission has become a pious, fashionable cause. People are indeed pleased with the name. They suppose that the name is indeed a great accomplishment, and hold the view that this name would have inaugurated a wholly new, and heretofore totally unnoticed, sphere of Christian-moral activity. One speaks of the God-forsaken misery of people, of the church's failure to aid them. Now, finally, as Wichern expressed it at the initial *Kirchentag*, the church must proclaim throughout the land, and bear witness, that: Love is mine; love befits me as does faith.[241] As though the same love would not also indeed have been previously recognized as a Christian duty and been practiced, just not as noisily and ostentatiously! The only proper norm for judging, in this case too, thus remains the simple saying, "You will know them by their fruits" [Matt 7:17].

The Protestant Alliance

In this context we finally also mention the Protestant Alliance.[242] It arose from demands expressed here and there for Christians of different confessions to unite in brotherly fashion.

---

241. An allusion to 1 Corinthians, chap. 13.

242. The Protestant Alliance still exists. It has a website, which states that it was founded by Anthony Ashley-Cooper, the 7th Earl of Shaftesbury, as a reaction to alleged Catholic hegemony.

The alliance had its beginnings when representatives from seven larger communities in Scotland sent a circular letter to the churches of England, Wales, and Ireland, inviting them to a gathering at Liverpool at which the call to a second large gathering was to be proposed. The preliminary gathering took place in Liverpool on 1 October 1845. It was very well attended, and the attendees agreed on a summary confession of faith as the basis of their union. This consisted of all doctrines held by the church to be biblical. The name "Protestant Alliance" was adopted at the assembly held in London on 19 August 1846. Some eight hundred of the faithful from various orientations attended: Episcopalians, Methodists, Presbyterians, independents, Baptists, Moravian Brethren. The main intention was declared to be fostering the union of believing Christians in view of the splits in the church, and warding off what, in the papacy and other manifestations of error and godlessness, worked counter to evangelical Protestantism. The alliance was also said to apply to brothers in the faith who are persecuted on account of their religion, without asking disturbingly about their confession of faith. In general the alliance is supposed to provide assistance wherever Jesus Christ might suffer in the members of his church. For this purpose it aims to gather reports from all quarters about religious and ecclesial conditions.

The Alliance first came to prominence at the assembly in London in 1851, at the time of the great London Exhibition. Almost two thousand persons were present at the sessions. There were lectures about Great Britain, Ireland, France, Belgium, Holland, Germany, Switzerland, the Piedmont, Algiers, and North America, and these lectures were subsequently published. There was a similar assembly in Paris in August 1855, contemporaneous with the Industrial Exhibition. Such assemblies were held now here, now there, in order to get a firm foothold in the different major countries of the Protestant confession, and to expand more widely by forming branches of the main association's operations.

The general assembly of the organization was held in Berlin in 1857. This meeting provided the occasion for also addressing the organization's position on ecclesiastical trends in Germany. Opponents of the Union like Hengstenberg and Stahl do not want to hear of an association aimed at uniting Protestants in a much broader compass, and their reaction is not unexpected. However, it can strike us as odd that there are also friends of the Union who speak out against this organization.

The Committee of the Union Association in Berlin issued such a statement in the *Protestantische Kirchenzeitung* of 18 July 1857, no. 29. This faction takes offense at the basic principles the organization affirms in the nine theses of its confession of faith. These are said to express only the quintessence of traditional, orthodox church doctrine. Hence, although the men of the organization do not presume to set the boundaries to Christianity and to the Christian brotherhood by this confession, they always seek out, as members of their organization, only those whose confession of faith holds to these traditional, orthodox ways of looking at things. Accordingly they limit the circle of their fellowship to a small segment of Protestant Christendom, indeed to those whose outlooks inherently bear the stamp of what is bygone and obsolete; whereas they exclude by far the larger part of the Protestants, precisely those in whom the force and focus of world history currently would seem to lie. This organization sticks too strictly in principle to its confession, and would split all the confessions; whereas any union would rest on surmounting the confession. On the latter point these opponents are quite correct. Thus the organization is as broad-minded on the one hand as it is narrow-minded on the other. While it is not established in Germany, it sets out from a way of looking at things that is, at least in Germany, an antiquated way of doing so.

The Current State of the Protestant Church; High Church Attitudes and Science

There is no question that the phenomena I have just described are especially characteristics of most recent times. There seems to be a great stirring within the church. Active within it is the impulse to step out into the public arena, to actively engage in present-day life, and to bear witness to its existence and importance by its activity on behalf of various goals it pursues in a very specific way. As harsh as the antitheses are, the church nevertheless always seeks out points of contact now here, now there, so as to bring about from them a more general understanding. It establishes associations, holds assemblies, enacts programs, and casts its nets in all directions, in order to attract like-minded people to a shared, large-scale course of action.

From all this, however, it is clear how very much the church is aware of its power today, and how very much this is a matter of enhancing and expanding this power. The church comes forward ever more decidedly and hostilely in opposition to all that appears to stand opposed to its own purposes. After the affair of the Straussian *Leben Jesu* had given people clearer insight into what a break with the church science could bring about, scientific theology above all had to suffer, because of the intensified zeal for ecclesial orthodoxy and the church's distrust of all that did not pass muster as devout theology. The horrifying phrase used to describe the external danger facing the church is "a science unleashed from faith." In a time when the course of science's development leads, of its own accord, to the task of coming to gain an understanding of general principles and going back to the ultimate grounds of belief and knowing, this could not of course have been without errors and extreme positions of various sorts. However, instead of paying attention to the inevitable differences, the extreme case was intentionally just made the norm or representative of all else that had any sort of relation to it, and science itself came under suspicion, so as to be able to express the same utterly condemnatory verdict about either one, the scientific and the unscientific positions.

There are few eras in which any freer scientific endeavor has been judged so harshly and unfavorably, in such a one-sided and partisan way, as has been the case for a number of years now. Although there are only a few who actually adopted a heresy-hunting tone, speaking scornfully of all science, the unscientific mentality of our era is all the more evident in the large number of people who allowed such fanatics to intimidate them into being completely silent or at least to influence them. They said the same things, only more decorously, and criticized, in a less vindictive way, all that was not in line with the dominant orientation. Younger theologians in particular believed they could not attain the goal of their efforts more assuredly than by certifying, as visibly as possible, their orthodox fervor.

This hostile attitude and stance of the church toward science has continued unchanged, although the state of play has altered somewhat because of it. The church is now striving toward an even loftier goal. After the experiences of 1848 brought home to people what overall dangers threatened the existing order of things, and how necessary it is to strengthen the positive foundations on which the existing order rests by using all the means at one's command, the church in this situation positioned itself wholly on the side of the state, in order to constitute itself as a power ruling with divine authority and in the same interests. The very men who defended most fervidly the principles of thoroughgoing reaction in the political domain also drew their main support from the church in doing so, and considered the church to be an essential component in the system of their conservative, divine arrangements.

However, the more the church had interests in common with politics, setting itself up, so to speak, as a political power, the more the hierarchical tendency grew within the church. This tendency is mainly what is characteristic of the most recent ecclesiastical phenomena. Not only is the church aware of its temporal power; also already quite clearly evident is the fact that the church cannot maintain the power it claims for itself without also pursuing hierarchical interests. In no other era than the most recent one has so much been written about the church, its concept and essential nature, its rights and authoritative powers, its functions and regulations. A series of writings is dedicated, with markedly heightened interest, to this most important issue of the day.[243] Most of the recent theological periodicals have an ecclesiastical intent, some exclusively and some predominantly so.

Since the currently predominant ecclesiastical orientation mainly arises from opposition to the Union, the Lutheran Church is therefore in fact the advocate for this position. However, from how far the orientation developing from that opposition has progressed in most recent times, one can of course see that, in its newest form as Neo-Lutheranism, it is different from traditional Lutheranism. Traditional Lutheranism was only involved in standing apart from the dominating state church so as to protect itself from the encroaching power of the Union, and to be allowed to exist as an ecclesial fellowship of its own. Apart from that, and in contrast to it, Neo-Lutheranism itself comes on the scene with the full power of a dominant church. Today it is no longer a matter of turning back, from the neology and unbelief of the previous century, to the pious faith of former times, or of the validation of a superficial Union as opposed to the rights of the confessional theological framework. Today one reaches back ever more decidedly to a past in which the Lutheran Church presented, within itself, the hierarchical character it was also internally structured to have. The Lutheran Church of the sixteenth and seventeenth centuries is the ideal people look back to. Renewing it is the goal toward which they strive, the foundation on which they want to build going forward. Just as the Lutheran theologians of the sixteenth and seventeenth centuries exercised their dominance by considering themselves to be the authentic interpreters of orthodox church teaching, so too today the main weight rests once more on the purity of doctrine as it is to be standardized according to the strict letter of the creeds or symbols. Thus the church now boldly comes forward, supported by its creedal confession and in opposition to science, so that pastors faithful to the symbols venture openly to prescribe, for university theology teachers, what and how they ought to teach.

The most noteworthy example of this kind was provided by the church conference of Stade in autumn 1853. At the conference in Stade, pastors from the duchies of Bremen and Verden also included the Göttingen theological faculty as a topic of their deliberations, and made the decision to term the faculty's ecclesiastical stance a flagrant incongruity. The conference sent its complaint about the faculty to the supreme ministry after a petition had previously been circulated for the signatures of all the pastors of these

---

243. [*Baur, in the text*] A few of the most notable examples, chosen from so many, are: Löhe, *Drei Bücher von der Kirche* (1845); Delitzsch, *Vier Bücher von der Kirche* (1847); Kliefoth, *Acht Bücher von der Kirche* (1843). [*Ed.*] On Löhe see n. 251; Franz Delitzsch (1813–90); Theodor Kliefoth (1810–95).

duchies. The Lutheran Church of Hanover would go so far as to mandate that the affirmation of faith and the teaching, including in the university, be purely Lutheran. Most notably this reminded one of precedents, such as that in the sixteenth century, when the Crypto-Calvinist professors in Wittenberg were pursued with relentless severity, and banished. The Göttingen faculty took this occasion to compose a statement in 1854: "Ueber die gegenwärtige Krisis des kirchlichen Lebens, insbesondere das Verhältniss der evangelischen theologischen Facultäten zur Wissenschaft und Kirche. Zur Wahrung der evangelischen Lehrfreiheit wider neuerlichst erhobene Angriffe."[244]

The Göttingen faculty made reference to the value and significance of theological science in Protestantism; to the task of the theological faculty as being not merely an institute for passing on church doctrine, but also one for keeping the salutary growth of the church on course by serving as a purifying and active ferment within it. The faculty also referred to the absence of constraints on faculty duties, and to the statutes of the University of Göttingen. In conclusion, they referred to the significance of symbols for the Protestant Church generally, and therefore then called attention to the mental indolence, the disputatiousness and domineering nature, as well as the traditional legality of this latest orthodoxy by which the Protestant Church, as it once did in the seventeenth century, would threaten to rigidify into a new legalistic church, since a new route to salvation would be established, not the route via faith, but rather one through professing the pure doctrine.

All this was quite timely, and so was also greeted with the approval of those not themselves belonging to the strict ecclesiastical faction. This just lessened the impression that the same men, who now saw themselves obliged [to support] this resistance, had previously always come far more to the aid of ecclesiastical interests than to what could serve the interests of science—as had in fact been the case with Lücke and Dorner. They now in part just reaped the harvest from what they had sown. The opponents were so little deterred by the response they got from the faculty's statement, that, to the contrary, they now sought to make public the full significance of their attack. Dr. Petri,[245] the spokesperson for the Stade pastors, right away published an elucidation of the Göttingen statement on the preservation of Protestant freedom of instruction, in which he asserted the rights

---

244. "Concerning the Current Crisis in the Life of the Church, especially the Relation of the Protestant Theological Faculties to Science and to the Church. On Preserving Protestant Freedom of Instruction in Face of the Most Recent Attacks Made Against It."

245. Ludwig Adolf Petri (1803–73), *Beleuchtung der Göttinger Denkschrift zur Wahrung der evangelischen Lehrfreiheit* (Hanover, 1854).

of the state church itself when there is the danger of an open break with it. The troublemakers are not the ones who defend the undeniably substantial rights of the church, but those who oppose us by disposing of our heritage or home, and seemingly with the inherent right to do so.

In the *Kirchliche Zeitschrift* he edited together with O. Mejer, Kliefoth[246] published an open letter to the theological faculty in Göttingen that took an even more pretentious and arrogant tone. He maliciously derided the faculty for how much it would lag behind the vitality of the church, in seeing itself no longer in a position to form a school to determine, and have enduring control over, the orientation of the younger generation of the clergy as they go forth from the lecture hall into practical life, with the majority of them going on into the camp of Lutheranism. It is all a question of the actual facts of life, and of the strengths that hold good there. In the same periodical,[247] Kliefoth once again expressed himself in the same tone, about the further clarification the theological faculty in Göttingen had issued in 1854 following their initial statement, in order to respond to what Petri, Kliefoth, and others had said in opposition to it. [He said] the faculty also has to pay attention in this case to the many points in which this ecclesiastical faction has fully expressed its self-consciousness, a consciousness that, harsh as it comes across, nevertheless also embodies truths, one the faculty could have at least not been hostile to. Meanwhile, the Hanover ministry had still not followed up on the demands of the pastors and the complaints against the faculty.

In this controversy, how the pastors spoke in opposing the professors was wholly reminiscent of how the sixteenth and seventeenth century theologians spoke, with just one difference. Back then, particularly in the seventeenth century, the university teachers were considered to be the authentic interpreters of Lutheran orthodoxy and ruled the church. Today, however, the churchmen and the men of science are set over against each other. Therefore when, in earlier times at least, one supposed that the whole apparatus of theological erudition was needed in order to be able to have the very most decisive authority in matters of faith and of orthodoxy, today things are different. Today science is indeed so far apart from the church that someone is then also capable of governing the church if he just stands most steadfastly on the bedrock of the symbols, and knows how to validate these symbols, as literally written and as originally sanctioned theological frameworks, and with all their consequences, as alone being the unadulterated, authorized doctrine.

---

246. On Mejer and Kliefoth, see n. 139.
247. [*Baur*, in the text] 1855, no. 2, 95ff.

Orthodoxy and Pietism

A novel example of how today, following this principle, people revert once again to the standpoint of the older Lutheran theology, we also see in the stance the ruling ecclesiastical faction takes toward pietism.

A short time ago people still saw pietism as a major opponent of free science. At the time of the Straussian movement, people still believed they must come to an understanding with pietism regarding the essence of Christianity, as we see in Märklin's publication, *Darstellung und Kritik der modernen Pietismus* (1839),[248] and in further deliberations occasioned by it. But today pietism shares the same fate as science. The church sets itself above both, with the same absolute authority, and imposes on pietism too the same norm of pure doctrine, namely, Lutheran orthodoxy.

This break between pietism and the strict ecclesiastical orientation came about because of the manifesto Hengstenberg issued against pietism, in the foreword to the 1840 volume of his *Evangelische Kirchenzeitung*. In a very trenchant criticism there, he charged pietism with its shortcomings: covert righteousness by works; disdain for doctrine, for the role of preaching, and for the wider ecclesial fellowship; subjectivist and separatist inclinations; in short, the preponderance of practical piety over dogmatic devoutness.

But the "Johnny-come-lately" churchmen delivered a quite different verdict about pietism. In an open letter to the Göttingen theological faculty,[249] Kliefoth accused the Spener orientation of having undermined and eviscerated the historical vitality of the Lutheran Church. He likened Spener to an alien outgrowth on the Lutheran Church. The fact that Spener sticks very carefully in doctrine to the specified Lutheran teachings does not count for much. Lutheranism [said Kliefoth] is not merely doctrine or a dogmatic orientation, but is specifically a church structure; yet Spener's concept of the church and all his views of church life, church institutions, church functions and actions are essential alien, and contrary, to the Lutheran ways of looking at things—they are essentially Reformed concepts. The Reformed Church's great war of conquest over the Lutheran Church begins with Spener, an assault that has proceeded over time with various names on its banner—first piety, then tolerance, then the Union, then confederation—but a war continuing right up to the present day.

---

248. Christian Märklin (1807–49) was one of Baur's and Strauss's close friends, with whom they had a lively correspondence.

249. [*Baur, in the text*] *Kirchliche Zeitschrift* 1, pt. 1, 22. [*Ed.*] Philipp Spener (1635–1705) was the founder of German pietism.

[Kliefoth continues that] Spenerian pietism has been outstandingly successful in its undermining activity. However, it has not been victorious on the church's behalf, and not even on its own behalf. Instead it has been victorious on behalf of an ally that it has not spurned from the outset, the rationalism or phase of anti-Christianity standing over against Protestantism. Pietism has made its alliance with rationalism, and in this alliance it has gained civil rights in Germany when the compromise between the two of them founded the University of Halle. There have always been subjectivistic Christianity and the un-Christian stance of Herod and Pilate—and these two stances become friends in the name of tolerance when that involves opposition to the objective church. Rationalism also put an end to orthodoxy. Then came the first blossoming of the theologians' church, in which the Herr Professors of Theology researched and imparted what is universally valid and true—naturally each one imparting something different—and in which their students, when they become pastors, have no notion that they received their office from the Lord Jesus Christ, but instead see their calling in considering themselves students of one or another great theologian; and what this theologian has imparted to them, they are in turn to impart from their chancels to their unfortunate congregations. Here then comes the split, because what the teaching profession offers to Protestant folk is not pious. The result is that almost none of God's congregation would remain unless those with theoretical knowledge would first of all disclose from the chancel their natural propensity to talk over people's heads.

In itself it makes no difference whether the theologians' church is structured by pastors or by professors. The main issue is that the church has the same stance toward pietism as it had in the seventeenth century. The natural reason for this is that today all the weight is put on dogma, on pure doctrine. Doctrine is the crowning achievement, the inalienable holy object, the Lutheran Church's heavenly glory, and not merely in the so-called "fundamental articles" of the faith, for everything in the true system is equally fundamental. Pure doctrine alone constitutes the essential nature of the legitimate church.

The Neo-Lutheran Concept of the Sacraments

After people had once begun to place such great weight on the church and pure church doctrine, on the domain of the church, it was a natural thing to keep on the same track. The concept of the church led on to the concept of the sacraments. They found it a shame that, in the Reformers' doctrine of the church, the doctrine of the sacraments had not attained its rightful influence on the church; that the sacraments certainly counted as the *notae ecclesiae* (marks of the church), but not as the foundation of its life; that the sacraments, these visible bearers of grace, recognizable as such to all, had not been made the bonds of the church; that instead these bonds were the workings of the Word, the invisible faith revealed only to those knowing the heart.

Hyper-Lutherans such as Delitzsch, in the *Vier Bücher von der Kirche*, and Münchmeyer, in *Das Dogma von der unsichtbaren und sichtbaren Kirche* (1854),[250] pressed for a sacramental concept of the church. The stance befitting the faith should embrace the sacraments. The distinction between an invisible church and a visible church got discarded, for there is no twofold church, only the One, Holy, Universal Church, and in this One Church, everything hinges on the sacrament of baptism. The church is not the fellowship of the faithful, but is rather the fellowship of the baptized, or rather, the totality of all those who, via the sacrament of baptism and by partaking of Holy Communion, therefore have, as such, become members of the body of Christ via the fellowship of the sacraments.

This sacramental Neo-Lutheranism therefore no longer wants to hear anything about an invisible church. Just as this sounds sufficiently Catholic, it even more strikingly has an affinity with Catholicism via its teaching about the clerical office. This is a major theme of the Neo-Lutherans, one indeed treated in a series of publications.[251]

In their doctrine of the church, just as they have thrust aside the Protestant concept of faith by their concept of the sacraments, so too they sacrifice the Protestant concept of preaching to the sacramental concept. They have also put a purely external objectivity in place of free, vital subjectivity as an essential feature of Protestantism's character. In order to subordinate preaching to the sacrament and to deprive preaching of its specific character, the preaching office becomes understood as a means of grace, and the preacher is made into merely an instrumental vehicle for the divine substance of grace. The main factor here is their giving to the divine act,

---

250. On Delitzsch's book, see n. 243. August Friedrich Otto Münchmeyer (1807–82). The title according to the online Tübingen catalogue reads *Das Dogma von der sichtbaren und unsichtbaren Kirche* (Göttingen, 1854).

251. [*Baur, in the text*] See the following: Löhe, *Kirche und Amt, neue Aphorismen*; Münchmeyer, *Das Amt des Neuen Testaments nach der Lehre der Schrift und nach dem lutherischen Bekenntniss*; Wucherer, *Ausführlicher Nachweis aus Schrift und Symbol, dass das evangelisch-lutherische Pfarramt das apostolische Hirten- und Lehramt und darum göttlicher Stiftung sei*; Kliefoth, *Acht Bücher von der Kirche*. [*Ed.*] Wilhelm Löhe (1808–72); Johann Friedrich Wucherer (1803–81). The Münchmeyer title differs slightly in the Tübingen catalogue. See Eric H. Heintzen, "Wilhelm Loehe and the Missouri Synod, 1841–1853" (diss., University of Illinois, 1964).

as conveyed via the human act, a form securing it from being marred by human sin and error. It all is said to take form from above, not from here below. This view counterpoises a church taking shape objectively, from above, to one doing so from below, proceeding from the subject. The church is an organism constructed and put together in divinely established ranks and institutes; it is an objective institution, implanted within humanity from the Holy Trinity. Hence, according to these Neo-Lutherans, the fundamental error of our time is said to be that people grasp the concept of the church from its subjective side, proceeding from faith and defining the church as the fellowship of the faithful, making it into a human product. This is said to be the source of all the wrongheadedness of the Reformed, the followers of Spener, the collegialists, right down to the most extreme forms of ecclesial democracy.

Here everything just points toward procuring a halo of divine glory for the clergy. The clerical office is said to be divinely instituted, and what they contend, first of all, about this office then carries over to those who hold this office, since the office in itself is sheerly an abstraction and cannot be separated from those persons who hold it. So they too are put in place by God. God first provides, by his spiritual gifts and guidance in one's life, the inner call or drive to the office. Then God is the one who orchestrates the preparation and readiness of the one called in this way, and in the end installs in the office the person thus made qualified to hold it.

However, if we ask what assurance there is that human influences are not also at work here—since of course all this must take place via human beings and human activity—then they are at a loss as to how to reply. For they do not venture to adopt, straight away, the Catholic concept of ordination with all it entails. The senseless and thoughtless character of this theory, one in fact rooted simply in the hierarchical interests of these ecclesiastical zealots, therefore resides in the fact that, whatever its catholicizing tendency, it is still not sufficiently Catholic so as to also have Catholicism's consistency. Catholicism is consistent in affirming that the church's institutions and offices rest on a tradition going back to Christ and the Apostles, and in linking this installation of individuals in the church's offices to an act the divine character of which is recognizable from specific, external signs. However, the Protestant ecclesiastical system does not rest on all these assumptions. Such idle talk about objective, divine ranks and institutions of the church would just be called laughable if it were not such a grave sign of the times.[252]

252. Zeller adds a footnote here about developments in September 1860, a few months before Baur's death. Protestant officials and representatives of Ultramontane Catholicism together issued the statement: "Protestants and Roman Catholics have joined hands in opposition to revolution and to anti-Christianity."

But what is the basis for the fact that it is precisely the Lutheran Church where this catholicizing tendency has such a widespread hold and where there is such a great inclination in this direction? Should we not conclude that too many Catholic elements have remained in the Lutheran Church from its beginnings, ones to which such a tendency can always attach itself once more, elements from which it accordingly must first be cleansed so as not to be exposed, again and again, to such a danger?

The "Theology of Established Facts"

The latest ecclesiastical phenomena are wholly suited for clarifying and understanding this tendency. Even apart from doing so, it is apparent how to get a taste of the most extreme thing that can happen to undermine, and make a mockery of, Protestantism. Up to now, no one has surpassed Dr. Vilmar in that regard.[253]

After Vilmar, in his position as consistorial counsel in Cassel, and as the most energetic assistant of the Hassenpflug government, had, for the goal of ecclesiastical-political reaction, done all he could to make the Reformed Church of Electoral Hesse into a Lutheran Church, and to give this church a properly Catholic hierarchical organization based on the sacramental concept of church offices, his splendid plan, to install himself as spiritual leader at the head of the church, foundered when he was already quite close to carrying out this plan, because the Elector of Hesse refused to allow it. Instead of ascending the "papal seat" of his Hesse church, Vilmar found himself transferred, all at once, to the theological faculty in Marburg. In order partly to recoup his losses from the miscarried plan, and partly to make the case that he was qualified for this position as teacher of theology, he then published *Die Theologie der Thatsachen, wider die Theologie der Rhetorik, als Bekenntnis und Abwehr* (1856).

The central idea of this theology is the almighty power of the church, that is, of the clergy. The teacher of theology has to show the members of his audience: that the church of Jesus Christ is the sovereign mistress in the spiritual world; that this sovereignty is exercised by those serving the church and by them alone; that in our day, when support by worldly powers has crumbled and positively threatens to collapse, when our forefathers' legacy of natural decency and order is manifestly on its final way down and in a few generations will be completely exhausted—in our own day, which

---

253. [Baur] See Gildemeister, *Das Gutachten der theologischen Facultät zu Marburg über die hessische Bekenntnisfrage und seine Bestreiter* (1859). [*Ed.*] Wilhelm Vilmar (1804–84); Johannes Gustav Gildemeister (1812–90).

doubtless points to the end of our people and of course to a terrifying end—that in these times his auditors, and they alone, can halt this collapse; and that, if this collapse nevertheless occurs, they are supposed to emerge from the general ruin unharmed, and to stand on the debris of the contemporary system, as the ones who gather together a new people.

Here too, in truly Catholic fashion, everything is built upon the concept of the sacrament, on the magical notion of the sacrament as a mysterious, physical act of God in which something wholly unique is bestowed. In baptism it is rebirth; in Holy Communion, it is Christ's bodily presence. Here everything is based on the contention that the clergy have not merely to announce the forgiveness of sins but also to impart it, and on the introduction of church discipline and excommunication, the horror of which intensifies as the blessings of grace are bound to the sacrament. This theology calls itself the "theology of established facts" (*Theologie der Tatsachen*) so as to make contemptible and derisory the truly scientific theology, as the "theology of rhetoric"; whereas a truly scientific theology surely neither needs, nor makes anything of, such a theology of "facts." These "established facts" are none other than the dogmatic, authoritative decrees, the fanciful, imaginative constructs, the hierarchical presumptions, of a system whose most dangerous enemy has always been untrammeled theological, historical, and philosophical research.

The Pneumatic Interpretation of Scripture

Thus, again and again, the church manifests the most hostile opposition to science. It is clear what painful circumstances scientific theology finds itself in when it is assailed from both sides by orientations that are in mutual agreement when what counts is opposition to science, notwithstanding how far apart these two outlooks stand from each other.

There is an outlook that wants nothing of what is called "church" and turns its back on the ecclesial community because of its aversion to the church of the multitudes. Instead it would rather adopt the position of a sectarian, separatist association. Instead of making its signpost the pure doctrines contained in the symbols, it wants only to stick to the sacred words of scripture. However, in taking this stance it isolates itself by the same harsh one-sidedness as we find correspondingly in the strict ecclesiastical faction with its doctrine of the church.

What help are the words of scripture if one does not understand them correctly? What help are they when one even intentionally disregards everything making for their correct understanding? When, instead of looking into the ages and origins of the canonical scriptures, and interpreting them based on the historical circumstances of their beginnings, one just opines that their being in the canon suffices, for these books would not be there if they did not in fact belong there? By making such issues superfluous, one also makes no essential distinctions either between the Old and the New Testaments, or among the individual books of the entire canon. This position treats the entire contents of the Bible as one absolutely identical whole. Thus it does not matter at all where one finds one's proofs. Everything one can in some way claim to be a biblical position has the same probative force and importance.

Adherents of this orientation hardly trouble themselves with shedding historical light on the past in which Christianity has its roots. They immerse themselves in the eschatological and apocalyptic ways of contemplating the near future as their facing the imminent end of the world. No books in the entire Bible are as important for them as those of the prophet Daniel and the Johannine Apocalypse. These books alone provide the key for the correct understanding of Christian truth. However, if we give some thought to how these two biblical books interpret that Christian truth, what misconceptions and obvious errors underlie their grasp of it, we can simply be convinced as to the overall basis on which their whole respective worldviews rest, and what value there is in a system whose fallacious principle only serves to provide a deceptive appearance of Christian truth, in a web of the most capricious and bizarre notions.[254]

Concluding Thoughts

On the whole, the phenomena in the most recent history of the church have not presented an encouraging picture. In the period since 1830 the antitheses have become ever sharper, although in the final analysis the balance still favors the side just aiming for hierarchical power and unconditioned acceptance of the authority of the church, of dogma, and of the letter. Whereas what the other side lacks are energy and decisiveness; and although it has agreement in principle, in any event it fails to hold consistently to this principle. We can only take comfort in the fact that the current state of theology and of the church, as well as the political conditions, belong to merely a

---

254. [*Baur, in the text*] One publication belonging to this category is: Auberlen, *Der Prophet Daniel und die Offenbarung Johannis* (Basel, 1854; 2nd ed. 1857). See also: Baur, "Die reichsgeschichtliche Auffasung der Apocalypse," *Theologische Jahrbücher* 14 (1855) 283–314; and Bleek, "Die messianische Weissagungen im Buch Daniel," *Jahrbücher für deutsche Theologie* 5 (1860) 45–101. [*Ed.*] Karl August Auberlen (1824–64); Friedrich Bleek (1793–1859).

transitional period and, at least indirectly, also work together to increasingly pave the way for a freer and more rational outlook.

Appendix

Up to now we have followed the main course of the action taking place in the history of Protestantism's development, principally in Germany. But there are a few phenomena outside this sphere, in addition to those within it, that we should look at briefly here. First we will look briefly at Protestantism's history in the German Catholic states and in foreign countries as a whole, Catholic and Protestant ones. Then we will also consider the sects existing in most recent times.[1]

1. Protestantism in the German Catholic States and in Countries Other Than Germany

In Bavaria

In looking into how Protestantism and Catholicism are related with regard to the legal status of the two confessions, in Germany itself, even in most recent times, we might not get very far before we run into Protestant religious complaints lodged against Catholic regimes.

In Bavaria the military had not been required to genuflect before the host since 1803, but by order of the war ministry the requirement was reinstated in 1838. The king decreed that, in Catholic worship services in the military, one is supposed to kneel down during the transubstantiation and at the blessing. Since the order applied to both Protestant and Catholic soldiers, the Protestant camp protested against it, not merely individual Protestant bodies but also the high consistory in Munich and two provincial consistories, those in Ansbach and Bayreuth. Also, the Protestant members of the Chamber of Deputies turned to petitioning the king directly as a group, in 1840, so as to circumvent, for the time being, making a formal complaint in the Estates Assembly. When the chamber took up the matter

---

1. The Appendix is attached to Part Three as Section 3C. But it is more appropriately regarded as an Appendix to the entire work because it includes some events that transpired prior to 1830 and also some non-Protestant movements.

in 1843, the war minister wholly dismissed the issue, saying that there was no middle road between keeping and canceling the order. Of course they then sought to placate the Protestants by various modifications of the order, first in the territorial reserves and then also in the active military forces. Yet however the order might be modified, matters essentially remained unchanged because it was an issue of principle as to whether Protestants could be required to participate in a Catholic cultic act.

There could be no doubt that genuflecting is a Catholic act Protestants cannot participate in without it weighing on their Protestant conscience. Yet people wanted to contest this very point, simply and solely on the grounds that it was impossible to justify the matter [of the king's order] from canon law. They said[2] that, for the Catholic, genuflection is adoration, the visible sign of inward worship; but for the Protestant it remains merely a form of courtesy. Of course if genuflecting were quite exclusively a religious act, then one would rightly wish that Protestants not be expected to do it, even in a military setting. However, since this physical position does not have a specific, universally valid religious meaning, but is quite another matter in a hundred instances, there could be nothing inappropriate for Protestants in genuflection required as a courtesy.

However, certainly from this very point it simply follows that the meaning of genuflecting depends, at the particular time, on the object before which it is done. But in the case before us this object is the deity believed to be present in the outward shape of the host. Therefore, because genuflecting has this specific religious meaning, the Protestant cannot carry out the act just as the Catholic does. Thiersch has correctly established that the main point here involves the essential difference in dogmatic specifications on each side, as he especially shows in his *Drei Sendschreiben an Döllinger über Protestantismus und Kniebeugung im Königreich Baiern* (Marburg, 1844).[3] This difference makes it impossible for any church refusing to accept transubstantiation to participate in some way or other in the form of cultus resting on that belief, so long as it maintains a lively awareness of this divisive difference. Hence there can be no doubt about the fact that the aforementioned order involves a violation, in principle, of the Protestant Church's rights and dogma.

The Bavarian government did of course appeal to the fact that genuflection as a form of courtesy, which the order reinstated, had existed unchallenged in the Bavarian Palatinate, as well as for all troops of Catholic

---

2. [*Baur, in the text*] See Döllinger, *Der Protestantismus in Baiern und die Kniebeugung. Sendschreiben an Professor Harless von Döllinger* (Regensburg, 1843). [*Ed.*] The author is Johann Joseph Ignaz von Döllinger (1799–1890).

3. Friedrich Wilhelm von Thiersch (1784–1860).

governments of Germany, right up until 1803 for all military personnel without distinction as to their faith, and that today it is still in place in the Austrian army. But this argument is wholly inadmissible, because the Bavaria of today, as a constitutional state, ought not be identified with Bavaria prior to 1803. Indeed the Bavarian constitutional document accords complete freedom of conscience to every inhabitant of the kingdom. The Bavarian government finally saw itself prevailed upon to decree that the display of respect before the Sacred Host should in future be performed once again according to the form prescribed prior to the order of 1838. With this, the 1838 order was withdrawn.

In Austria

What took place in the Ziller Valley, in Tyrol, reminds us even more of well-known scenes from the previous century.

In the Salzburg region there were, even now, Protestant elements that also influenced the neighboring Tyrolean countryside. In particular, Joseph Schaitberger's *Evangelische Sendbrief* was a popular religious publication much in demand.[4] A Protestant faith community formed in the Ziller Valley, owing both to such publications and other communications, and also to the acquaintance Tyroleans made with Protestants on their foreign travels. For many, their ties to the [Catholic] Church, having long become less heart-felt, also increasingly loosened outwardly. They felt the need to press for allowing free expression for the Protestant confession.

In 1826 several families made the decision to initiate their legal withdrawal from the Catholic Church. They registered with the local pastor for the six weeks of instruction prescribed for this purpose. The government and the clergy were set against instituting a non-Catholic public worship, appealing in this case to the fact that the Edict of Tolerance had not been promulgated in Tyrol. Finally, in 1834, the Protestant-minded group, whose membership had meanwhile grown significantly, received from Vienna the ruling that the government could not agree to its request; that if they wish to leave the Catholic Church, then they would have to emigrate to another province of the empire, one that already has non-Catholic congregations. Most of them had no desire to do that. Instead, in the course of 1836 they decided to depart from their valley and seek refuge in foreign lands. When they announced this decision to the authorities, they were instructed to leave the land. They were permitted just a four-month window of time to

---

4. Joseph Schaitberger (1658–1733), a Protestant evangelist. Apparently his *Sendbrief* was published well into the nineteenth century.

arrange their affairs. They then chose a representative from their midst who was supposed to look around, on the group's behalf, for assistance and acceptance in foreign lands. In May of 1837 this representative went to Berlin and presented to the king a letter of request, which was favorably received. Dr. Strauss[5] of the high consistory was dispatched to Vienna to handle the details there, and to arrange for a longer time allowed for the group's emigration. In September of that same year, the group arrived in Silesia on several trains, for it was decided that the new immigrants would, for the time being, make the city of Schmiedeberg its initial place of residence. There they found a very welcoming reception both from the inhabitants and from the government, and they gained permanent residence in Silesia.

In France

In France, the Protestants' equal standing with Catholics had made further progress as a result of the July Revolution, because the revised charter no longer singled out the Catholic religion as the state religion. This gave them the courage to also now contemplate an enlightened legislation and a more integral organization for their church.

First of all they sought a reform of the structural article of April 1802, which did indeed reinstate the older representative system of consistories and synods. However, then a synod was supposed to consist just of one clergyman and one layman from each individual consistorial church, thus in its entirety of just ten members (for five consistories made up one synod). A synod was allowed to meet only with the advance approval of the government, and under its oversight. So there were only very restricted provincial synods, and there was no mention at all of the general synod in which the older system had its democratic focal point.

Different factions initiated a reform of this system, and in 1840 the government believed it had to get involved in the business. Since the government's involvement in initiating the reform seemed to be ongoing, nothing was accomplished for the Reformed, or for the Lutherans in Alsace who were likewise attempting to draw up a constitution. Religious freedom was even threatened by the laws governing associations. Article 291 of the penal code states that, without the approval of the government, no association of more than twenty persons shall be permitted that regularly join forces with a religious or political or literary cause. Article 294 adds that it is forbidden for any premises to be rented for such associations, even permitted ones, unless prior permission to do so was granted by the local authorities. These

---

5. See p. 214, n. 91.

two articles of the 1810 penal code carried over unchanged into that of 1832. This issue became more acute in the associations law of 1834, which stated that article 291 is applicable to all associations, even if they do not normally assemble at regular times, and if they split into subgroups of fewer than twenty persons each. Since many law courts also applied the articles of the penal code to religious gatherings, that led to many legal proceedings, and a large number of petitions were submitted in the chamber to put an end to a legislation that made the Protestants' religious freedom dependent on the caprice of provincial authorities and law courts, in contradiction to the charter. The government ultimately found itself required to recognize the rights of Protestants.

There were also clashes between Catholics and Protestants, especially in Alsace. In 1842, Catholics in Strasbourg had published a falsified selection of passages from Luther's writings, under the title, *Die lodernde Fakel oder Dr. Martin Luther als Religions- und Sittenbesserer*,[6] and handed it out to the Protestant laity, in order to portray the Reformer as an embodiment of all that is abominable. This action prompted the pastors of the Augsburg Confession in Strasbourg to issue a letter to the members of their congregations, in which they spoke out very forcefully about the violent infringement by Catholics of the rights of other churches. In newspapers and pamphlets written by Catholic priests and laity the Protestants were accused of effrontery and madness, which had to amaze them as much as it distressed them. There was no concealing the intention to muster the Catholic populace against the Protestants, and in doing so to strip the Protestants of their duly acquired rights. Distorting the truth and seeking to slander them—the usual weapons of the Jesuits—once again served the Roman Church in the newly-initiated struggle. The Catholics threatened with reprisals based on the papal history, and admonished them to be peaceful, vigilant, and true to the faith.

The activity of the Methodist faction, which has the same significance in France as the pietist faction does in Germany, is an especially characteristic phenomenon in Protestant church history in France. Its main institution is the Protestant Society founded in Paris in 1833. The text circulated to advertise its presence stated that the Society has the sole purpose of disseminating Protestant truths in France with all the God-given means at its disposal. It is clear that such a society ought not lack the marks of catholicity in the true sense of the term. It must be no more and no less than a Christian society, so that, by avoiding secondary issues, Christians of all confessions will find in it the unity of the spirit through the bonds of peace.

6. "The Flaming Bundle or Dr. Martin Luther as a Reformer of Religion and Ethics."

All of them must worship the Lord Jesus as their Redeemer and their God, and must be able to affirm the fundamental truths of the universal church, namely, the fall and damnation of human beings, justification by faith, and so forth. What typically makes the Methodists effective is that their chapels are adjacent to the national churches and they administer the sacrament in them; that they maintain a special institute in Geneva for educating their clergy, and a special establishment in Paris for educating their missionaries, school teachers, and publishing house personnel; that their followers have set up a second Bible Society in addition to the one in Paris, to distribute the Holy Scriptures more to Catholics; that they involve themselves in the affairs of the Catholic Church as much as they do in those of the Protestant Church; and that they consider anyone who does not side with them to be an adversary, and only embrace those who are unconditional devotees. This society soon came to be distrusted because of its own zeal and its opposition to the national church.

The liberal faction, which also sought to get a boost by directing its attention to the needs of the time, founded the Society for Evangelizing Scattered Protestants. The first society of this kind started in 1838, in Nîmes. Since there are a number of Protestants scattered in towns and villages in southern France, but not enough anywhere to maintain a pastor paid by the government, the society sought to have instruction, edification, and partaking of the sacrament, provided via regular, ordained clergy under the supervision of the consistory. Since 1841 a Society for Evangelizing Protestants Dispersed in Eastern France has existed in Strasbourg. In 1842 the desire arose to constitute a society in Paris, under the auspices of Count Agenor de Gasparin,[7] a very pious churchman with quite eccentric plans. Its purpose was to see to the interests of the Protestant Church of France, although the leadership of its operations was to be entrusted solely to members of the lawfully constituted church. There was lively opposition to the exclusive orientation of this society, which based itself entirely on orthodoxy, and made the unity of the faith the first condition for collaboration with it. So there is an exclusively orthodox, pietistic faction in France too, one that does everything to promote the church's controlling authority.

Athanase Coquerel,[8] a quick-witted polemicist who had also written in opposition to Strauss's *Life of Jesus* in 1841, appeared on the liberal side, mainly advancing the cause of rationalism. Nevertheless he called his own

---

7. Count Agenor de Gasparin (1810–71), a French statesman and psychical researcher with an interest in spiritualism.

8. Athanase Laurent Charles Coquerel (1795–1868), a French Protestant theologian, pastor of the l'Oratoire de Louvre and a member of the National Assembly after 1848.

brand of rationalism "modern orthodoxy." In any event it is a very devout form of rationalism.⁹ Coquerel came out, with special emphasis, against obligatory confessions of faith because, by violating people's conscience, they lead to separatism. That is because they presume to improve, by impermissible human means, the unity of the church, a role the Lord has necessarily vested in the gospel, and because it is a Christian duty to pray, and be in communion, with all those who call upon the Lord with a pure heart.

Under the Restoration there was of course a faction that commended confessions of faith, and some also did so following the July Revolution. For this purpose the old symbol of the Reformed Church of France was inserted into the *Archives du christianisme* in 1839, in order to point in a timely way to this monument of the faith and piety of the forefathers. Exclusive journals repeated Stapfer's contention that the Reformed Church of France would have no legal standing without the La Rochelle Confession of Faith.¹⁰ A few consistories, namely those of Bolbec and Caen, decided forthwith to reintroduce the commitment to the symbolic documents, and in future to choose no pastor until he had subscribed to the La Rochelle Confession of Faith along with the church's disciplinary rules. However, this action also did not lead to a favorable outcome for the orthodox faction. Those opposing it were not only the liberals but also the orthodox, who had not yet completely cut their ties with the religion of the heart, and who knew the value of a faith freely growing from one's own experience. The orthodox declared themselves unreservedly in favor of the exclusive authority of the Bible, apart from any restrictive creeds or symbols. Indeed many who favored confessional statements averred that they would never accept the La Rochelle Confession in its unaltered form.

With these partisan efforts going on, one gratifying occurrence was the bicentennial celebration of Spener's birth,¹¹ organized in 1835 in Strasbourg and Rappoltsweiler by the efforts of the rationalists. In the name of the "Spener Foundation," and based on the expendable interest from a jointly-managed fund, a stipend was given every three years to a theologian

---

9. [*Baur, in the text*] See Pressel, *Zustände des Protestantismus in Frankreich* (1848), 78. [*Ed.*] Theodor Pressel (1819–77), a pastor in Swabia and a Reformation church historian. We cannot confirm this title in online catalogues, but it is cited under Pressel's entry in the *Allgemeine Deutsche Biographie*.

10. Philipp Albert Stapfer (1766–1840), Swiss statesman and scholar. The La Rochelle Confession of Faith, otherwise known as the French or Gallic Confession, was adopted in 1559 for the Reformed Church of France and included articles written by Calvin.

11. Philipp Jakob Spener (1635–1705), the founder of pietism, born in Rappoltsweiler in upper Alsace, and preacher in Strasbourg.

who, in a competition, delivered the prize-winning answer, and who had distinguished himself by his diligence and his irreproachable conduct.

Further evidence of the fact that, despite Protestant France's division into factions, it was disposed toward practical Christianity, is that several institutions were first established in recent times, namely the clearly Protestant hospitals in Avignon, Marseille, Montpellier, Nîmes, Paris, and elsewhere. They took their model from the Catholic Church, where one could actually find no fault with the charitable sisters in the public hospitals, other than their eager proselytizing. They wanted to have comparable attendants in the new hospitals, and regretted the fact that the Reformation had indiscriminately done away with all religious orders. That is how there came to be deaconesses, with a pious Protestant spirit viewed as the essential qualification for the office. Without making a vow [of celibacy], they devoted themselves to works of public charity, care for the sick, instruction of youngsters, rehabilitation of repentant prostitutes, and supervision of female prisoners. So far the institution of deaconesses has met with the full approval of all the factions.

An institute belonging in the same category is the colony in Sainte-Foy,[12] founded with the help of the government, by the Society for the General Interests of French Protestantism. There some twenty to thirty Protestant prisoners, and a few of their parents (those whose sons are subject to strict discipline because they are unruly), are confined for shorter or longer periods, and are said to be snatched from utter destruction. Associations for Protestants are also active in Algeria, where the government has set up four Protestant pastorates, three Reformed ones in Algiers, Oran, and Philippeville, and a Lutheran pastorate in Dély Ibrahim. These particular associations are the Strasbourg Bible Society and the Society for Evangelizing the Protestants in Eastern France.

We still have to say something about Protestant scholarly conditions in France. During the years 1835–38 there was repeated talk, in the Chamber of Deputies too, about setting up a third Protestant faculty of theology in Paris. Minister Guizot[13] took an interest in the matter, but the project was in turn cancelled since not only did the Strasbourg pastoral conference authoritatively declare its opposition, fearing it would be much to the detriment of the Strasbourg faculty, but the Methodist faction also was unhappy, on assuming it would be a liberal faculty. The Strasbourg faculty still continues to be the most significant Protestant institution in France that stands

---

12. Named for a young woman martyred in the fourth century, Sainte-Foy, in Conques, has a famous abbey church.

13. François Guizot (1787–1874), a French statesman.

on a foundation of German science. In a land where public opinion counts so much, the journals provide the best statistics about the standing of the factions. Since 1832, the journals of the Methodist faction are the *Archives du christianisme* and the *Semeur* [the Sower]. The organ of Count Gasparin is *Espérance* [Hope]. Most recently, it is dogmatically tolerant, and it adheres to the national church.[14]

In Switzerland

The Reformed Church of France is most closely related to the church in Geneva. Since 1813 the Methodist form of piety has also established itself in Geneva, and has spread from there. Under its influence, separatist associations arose in opposition to the state church, holding it responsible for the decline of true Christianity. These associations combined into a society calling itself "The New Church" and professing its allegiance to the old orthodox Protestant teaching. People elsewhere called them "Methodists," but in Geneva they called them "old fogies," "those wearing masks," that is, hypocrites, sanctimonious people.

In 1831 a Protestant society formed in Geneva. In 1832 it gave rise to a theological education establishment, supported by voluntary contributions and designed to educate orthodox theologians. In the canton of Vaud, Methodism made inroads into the state church itself. The clergy held so-called *Oratoires* (private chapel services), edifying evening gatherings in addition to the public worship services. After the collapse of the aristocratic regime in February 1845, the people's government forbade the clergy from participating in the *Oratoires*, which were threatened by the mob, and suspended a few clergy who disobeyed it. When the government then sent the clergy a proclamation commending the new democratic system of governance, together with the instruction to read it aloud from the pulpit, about forty clergy refused to do so. They appealed to a law according to which the government was only entitled to use the pulpit for edicts having to do with religion. The government punished these clergy with one-month suspensions. However, they largely believed that, under such a government, they had to resign from their clerical offices. They believed that by doing so, the ongoing needs of the church would cause great difficulties for the new

---

14. Baur lists in the text several organs of opposition to Methodism, giving the titles in German. Zeller adds a footnote on the more recent rise of a freer form of Protestant theology in France, one beginning with students from the Strasbourg faculty, but expanding to become cognizant of the Tübingen School as well as developing links with Dutch and Swiss Protestantism.

government. Indeed in many other places, those who otherwise preached unconditional obedience to the authorities, issued their call to undergo this new martyrdom inflicted by the democratic government. But the regime nevertheless carried through with its regulations, without giving thought to the consequences for the state church.

The multiple conflicts that occurred between the state and the church, in Vaud and other cantons of Switzerland, provided the incentive for Vinet,[15] professor of theology in Lausanne, to set forth a theory upholding the complete independence of the church [from the state]. Vinet deduced the freedom of the church from freedom of belief. He declared the coupling of church and state in the unity of the national church, to be inherently a falsehood, a doctrinal heresy, an adulterous morality, a sacrilege on the state's part, an unspeakable horror. The main elements of his theory are as follows. First, the national church adversely affects the initiative of religious conviction. Second, the individual ceases to have conviction as soon as the right or capability of having conviction is granted to the state. Third, the state is more detrimental to the church when it protects it than it is when it persecutes it. Fourth, secular and clerical authorities are so essentially different that they can never be conjoined. In France, the Catholic priest Abbé Lamennais[16] preached this same theory of the separation of church and state.[17]

In England: Puseyism (The Oxford Movement)

The most significant phenomenon of recent times in the English church has been called "Puseyism." It is all the more remarkable since it arose wholly from the distinctive character of Protestantism in England. It can only be explained and comprehended from the course the Reformation generally took in England; from the half-heartedness to which people stuck; from the concern they had from the outset to bring conflicting elements together as much as possible. When religious life as such regained more depth and inwardness, by following in step with the general political revolution, the English church too could not remain inhospitable to this movement. However, the church could not involve itself more deeply in it without stirring up the antitheses embedded in it and becoming more clearly aware of them.

---

15. Alexandre Vinet (1797–1847), a Swiss Protestant theologian. His theory is set forth in a series of books, starting with *Mémoire en faveur de la liberté des cultes* (1826).

16. See p. 142, n. 58.

17. Zeller adds a note about developments in Italy

The typically Protestant element expressed itself in Methodism. Under the influence of Methodism, a faction formed that people customarily call "evangelical." This faction held strictly to fundamental Protestant teaching. However, as it hardly wanted to make any concessions to the episcopal system, the democratic outlook of the lower clergy strongly pressed it toward restricting the supremacy of the episcopal aristocracy. Its demands led by various stages to the radicalism of the Protestant dissenters.

When the Whigs were in power for thirty years, as political allies of the Evangelicals, they sought to enact the Evangelicals' moderate principles. But the vigorous opposition of the High Church faction prevented anything significant from being accomplished, since the entire organization of the Episcopal Church had become too closely intertwined with the aristocratic basis of the English system of governance. Nevertheless the Protestant element had already been so strongly at work in the self-consciousness of the English church that there ought not have been a reaction called forth from the side of the church inclined toward Catholicism.

Puseyism, named after Pusey,[18] professor of theology at Oxford, came about in this setting. Pusey himself rightfully protested about this label, because the movement was neither a personal one nor a novel one. Before this people might have at least associated the name of Dr. Newman[19] with what was in fact an Anglo-Catholic movement. Newman was a more important spokesperson for this faction, which first came about in 1833, when teachers at Oxford University gathered to discuss the state of the church and the ways to remedy its shortcomings. They fully agreed that the Church of England has strayed from its own distinctive ecclesiastical consciousness; in other words, it has strayed from its catholicity because of the divisive consciousness of the dissenters.

The membership of those gatherings included, in addition to Newman, most notably Drs. Pusey, Hook, Keble, and Palmer.[20] They banded

---

18. Edward Bouverie Pusey (1800–82), Regius professor of Hebrew and canon of Christ Church at Oxford. In the 1830s he became acquainted with John Henry Newman and John Keble and sympathized with the Tractarians. When Newman left the Church of England for the Roman Catholic Church in 1845, Pusey became the leader of the Oxford Movement.

19. John Henry Newman (1801–90), an Anglican priest, poet, and theologian, and later a Catholic cardinal. He started out as an evangelical Christian, then moved to high-church Anglicanism, and finally converted to Catholicism. The Oxford Movement wanted to return to the Church of England many Catholic beliefs and liturgical rituals from before the English Reformation.

20. Walter Farquhar Hook (1798–1875), vicar of Leeds and dean of Chichester; John Keble (1792–1866), churchman and poet; William Palmer (1803–65), theologian and liturgical scholar.

together to support doctrines appearing so important to them—those involving communion and apostolic succession, and other points connected with them—by regaining more general and more emphatic recognition of these doctrines via the dissemination of their own publications. In addition, they pledged to oppose all changes in the liturgy and to return the cultus as much as possible to that of the ancient church. Their *Tracts for the Times* [1833–41] directly carried out this plan, for they began and continued their publication with great enthusiasm. However, after the appearance of *Tract 90*, which contained a new interpretation of the Thirty-Nine Articles, written by Newman, the series ended at the request of the bishop of Oxford.[21] From these *Tracts*, and also from consulting a few of Pusey's sermons and his open letter to the archbishop of Canterbury, we see the main points of their tenets.

For the Puseyites, everything depends on the doctrine of the church. They affirm that, in its interpretation of the apostolic symbols, the liturgy of the Church of England has not withdrawn from the Catholic Church. First and foremost, the church is said to be catholic, not merely in the idea of the church but in reality, as the Anglo-Catholic Church. The concept of the church is not an abstract idea, but rather the concept derived from the actuality of the existing church. The contrast between clergy and laity is a direct given of the church. The clergy are the actual representatives of the Holy Spirit, which comes upon them in ordination. Within the clergy, the episcopacy forms in turn the focal point from which the rays of the Spirit go forth. The gifts of the Holy Spirit have been preserved within the world solely by the episcopal succession. Striving for fellowship with Christ by some other route [than this church] is said to be attempting the impossible.

For the Puseyites, the doctrine of the tradition is connected with the doctrine of apostolic succession. It is only together with the tradition that the scriptures constitute the norm of faith. The church or the clergy has the absolute right to authentically interpret scripture. Individuals with their private judgment do not have this right. Yet absolutely infallible authority resides only with the general councils. However, this thesis clashed directly with the Thirty-Nine Articles.[22] For the twenty-first article states that the general councils can err, because they consist of human beings not all of

---

21. [*Baur, in the margin*] When Newman was sharply attacked for writing this, Pusey came forward to defend him in a brief document seeking to show that the views Newman expressed were by no means Roman, but were instead ancient catholic views. For that reason they are not to be ruled out by the English Reformation. This 1841 text by Pusey is the most significant thing he wrote.

22. The Thirty-Nine Articles were finalized in 1571 and define the doctrine of the Church of England as opposed to Calvinist and Roman Catholic views.

whom are governed by God's Spirit and God's Word, and those can sometimes err even in matters concerning God. The simple remedy [for the Puseyites] then comes from interpreting this article as meaning that, while the council members are of course fallible, they would be subject to higher guidance; that in fact the premise is that in all cases where they convene in the name of Jesus Christ, they are then of a heavenly nature, are catholic councils.

As for other doctrines, the Puseyites place the same importance on the sacraments as the Catholics do. Newman says that baptism, not faith, is the principal means of justification. The Puseyites hold the crass view that the Spirit is magically linked with the water. Their doctrine of Holy Communion stands in conflict with the Thirty-Nine Articles, for article twenty-eight denies transubstantiation. The Puseyites then maintain at least a real and nonlocal presence in the sacrament; also that the article does not rule out the Mass as such, in saying it is a sacrifice of remembrance. The Puseyites likewise approve of the remaining sacraments and celibacy, and therefore propose the restoration of the cloisters. As for the veneration of saints, their icons and relics, as well as for indulgences and purgatory, Newman only takes a stance against their misuse. This is the general position toward Roman Catholicism: that Romanism ought only be cleansed of its distortions; that, apart from these nonessentials, it is genuine catholicity. Newman even finds the Thirty-Nine Articles in turn in the decrees of the Council of Trent.

The only doctrine Anglo-Catholicism cannot accommodate is papal supremacy. Newman reckons it among the things that, having been brought about by providence, are also terminated by providence. This termination took place via the English Reformation. But one must ask: By what right do the Anglo-Catholics claim this, when in all other matters they adopt a Catholic standpoint? Puseyism is resolute only in its opposition to Protestantism. For it, Protestantism is essentially just the religion of the depraved human heart, and Luther, the head Protestant, is the Antichrist. Hence Puseyism's effort must now be to de-Protestantize the national church. Puseyism itself is only Protestant so far as it must be in order not to relapse into Roman Catholicism. The entire phenomenon is evidently explainable from Catholic elements still remaining in the Church of England.

This is the very reason why this Anglo-Catholicism was able to gain numerous adherents. Many adopt it, especially younger members from Oxford University, and from the clergy both in England and in Scotland. More than a few of them have taken the further step of crossing over to the Catholic Church, as Newman himself did at the end of 1845. On the other hand, people did not view Puseyism's progress with indifference. Right from the outset the cry to tear down popery (papalism) resounded throughout England. Pamphlets appeared in opposition to the Tractarians, the modern papists, the Jesuits. The bishops issued edicts against the new movement, and a number of petitions, bearing thousands of signatures, were submitted to demand that the secular authorities be vigilant. Pusey was declared suspended because he caused a stir by his preaching about Holy Communion.

In other matters the English church retained its familiar character.[23] There is nothing else of significance to mention from more recent English church history, apart from the regulations put in place to limit to some extent the vast incomes of the bishops, the sinecures and amassed benefices; and in contrast to assist the lower clergy by better endowments and an increase of pastorates. Lord Russell's church reform bill in 1834 addressed these goals.[24]

In Scotland, a puritanically-minded Protestant faction took particular offense at the right of clergy to a living, by which communities could also be saddled with unacceptable clergy. In 1834 the General Assembly granted communities the right of refusal, and in consequence the defenders of the freedom of the church, the "Non-Intrusionists,"[25] split off from the dominant church, in solemn protest against the moral constraint exercised by the secular power. Since 1843 a Free Presbyterian Church, through voluntary gifts, has established itself as the authentically Scottish national church.

---

23. Zeller adds a footnote in which he summarizes more liberal tendencies such as those found in *Essays and Reviews* (1860), a collection of seven essays that opposed Anglo-Catholicism and dealt with biblical criticism, evolution, evidences of Christianity, and other sensitive matters. He also refers to the American Unitarians William Channing and Theodore Parker, who were influenced by rationalism and familiar with German criticism. Neither Baur nor Zeller mention Samuel Taylor Coleridge (1772–1834), who had a major influence on more liberal forms of Anglican theology and was the most original English thinker of his time, a brilliant poet, and a student of German philosophy.

24. Lord John Russell (1792–1878) was the principal architect of the Reform Act of 1832. In 1834 the Poor Law Amendment Act was passed, but not a "church reform bill."

25. The Non-Intrusionists were opposed to "intrusive" demands for livings by the clergy. After ten years of conflict, they were defeated in the civil courts of England. Led by Thomas Chalmers, the Non-Intrusionists formed a separate Free Church of Scotland.

2. The Sects of Most Recent Times within the Catholic Church and within the Protestant Church

The New French Church

After the July Revolution, several Catholic priests in France, with Abbé Châtel[26] as their leader, sought to break loose from the authority of the See of Rome and to establish a French Catholic Church, one not state-supported but instead supposed to be supported by its adherents.

This church adopted the following ten principles. 1. The Word of God is our only rule of faith. 2. We accept three creeds, the Apostles' Creed, the Nicene Creed, and the Athanasian Creed. 3. We recognize as canonical all the books of the Old and New Testaments, books the Reformed Church recognizes as such, and regard their teachings as necessarily indispensable. 4. We believe that two sacraments, baptism and Holy Communion, are divinely ordained, and we allow the remaining sacraments, as pious practices that have existed since the earliest times of the church. 5. Worship services shall be conducted no longer in the Latin language, but instead, according to the ritual of the church, in the congregation's mother tongue. 6. Auricular confession is not commanded by God and we require it of no one, although before the faithful approach the Lord's Table, they ought to prepare themselves to receive general absolution. 7. We discontinue days of fasting, and entrust fasting to the piety of the faithful. 8. We accept a hierarchy in the church, consisting of bishops, priests, and deacons. 9. Our veneration of saints consists in thanking God for the grace bestowed on them. 10. Since religious instruction is one of the primary things people need, we regard it as our most important duty to abundantly scatter the seeds of God's Word.

This so-called New French Church was in fact just a product of the French liberalism that expressed itself in an overarching way in this case too. It was unable to thrive, and after several years of meager existence it was ultimately terminated by the police, in 1842.

The Saint-Simonians

The founder of this sect was Count Saint-Simon, who died in 1825.[27] Ever since his youth his lively imagination was occupied with lofty ideas. The

---

26. François Ferdinand Châtel (1795–1857). The French Catholic Church was a schismatic movement lasting from 1831 to 1842.

27. Henri de Saint-Simon (1760–1825), a French political, economic, and religious theorist who influenced nineteenth-century utopian socialism. He wrote a number of books, the last one being *Le Nouveau Christianisme* (1825).

general anarchy ensuing from the French Revolution, the disorder and disruption of all public circumstances, made a deep impression on him. Because of this he arrived at the idea of a general improvement of societal conditions, a perfecting of civilization. A new realm of prosperous peace was supposed to be established on the earth, a realm of love, of freedom and equality, of happiness for all people—everyone coming together in a single great and godly family. Moses has promised a universal brotherhood, Christ prepares the way for it, and Saint-Simon realizes it.

The major objection the Saint-Simonians had to Christianity is that it is too spiritualistic; that it sees in God just a pure spirit, and it spurns the material world, relinquishing it to Satan. As pure spirit, the God of Christianity points away from the material world and, in constant opposition to humankind, this God forces human beings to cut themselves off ever more from all material ties. In taking this view of the material world, Christianity has contempt for physical labor and disparages physical pleasures.

Catholicism gets praised for having realized all that, in the gospel, is realizable anywhere. The Catholic Church was the fullest societal actualization of Christianity, the most extensive uniting of human beings through love. By its hierarchy, it was a restraint on the despotism of secular powers. Via the antithesis of church and state, Catholicism proved to be the religion of spirit. Here Catholicism simply reverts to its main principle, that God is pure spirit, and God and world must be kept apart.

The importance of Protestantism is simply that it points toward the world, whereas Catholicism's importance lies in its aforementioned feature. The Protestantism that just wants a literal gospel until finally this literalism is fatal to it—the Protestantism that, in constant contradiction with itself, begets nothing but sectarian conflicts, metaphysical subtleties, imperial repression of the church, servile and spiteful scholarship, and muddled mysticism—must itself be nullified by the collapse of Catholicism.

A new order of things must rise up on the ruins of Catholicism and Protestantism, via the truth brought to light by Saint-Simon, the truth that God is the oneness of spirit and matter, is universal life. Christian dualism, with God as pure spirit set over against matter, must resolve itself into the absolute, living unity of a God who is love and who mediates spirit and matter in love. The supreme religion is the most perfect love, and of course love for the universe. But this love is not possible as long as antagonism exists anywhere, as long as fear or distress afflicts humanity anywhere, as long as there is anywhere a disharmony between humanity and the world. Only those who feel within themselves the needs and the suffering of all classes of people, and who incarnate all of humanity within themselves by a miracle of sympathy, can bring the true religion. This was the religious inspiration of Saint-Simon, of the greatest of all prophets who related to Christ as Christ did to Moses.

Since Saint-Simon saw that the most numerous social class loves the material world just as much as it does spirit, the main tendency of his teaching went toward sanctifying the material world spurned and cursed by Christianity. He sought to help those poor in body, most of whom were materially disadvantaged. The means for doing this, and on which the well-being of humanity depends, is industry [i.e., work, or employment]. Of all the social institutions, industry is the primary one for improving the physical, moral, and intellectual condition of the poorest and most numerous of human social classes. Realizing this goal on the one hand called for an arrangement of things in which every previous distinction in social relationships vanishes, so that one of the first principles of the Saint-Simonians is that all privileges of birth must be abolished without exception, first and foremost the right of inheritance. Thus the family would no longer inherit all one's wealth. Instead the state would come to own the entire basis of production. On the other hand, however, it was also acknowledged in turn that there can be no organization of societal life without a distinction as to people's circumstances, and this led directly to another major principle of the Saint-Simonians: to each according to his ability, and each ability according to its achievements.

All human beings, without exception, of course have an equal claim to life's pleasures and activities, although each one's claim is proportional to one's ability and one's achievements. This latter principle is what principally makes Saint-Simonism into a system that rearranges the entire social order. In order to place each one in society properly, according to his or her ability, there must be: a societal authority whose paternalism extends over everyone and all things; a central bank that has all the material means at its disposal and manages all the working poor; a civic education that is the essential foundation of the new structure; and an all-embracing hierarchy at the head of the whole system.

Since the principle and character of Saint-Simonism is said to be along the lines of a religious system, the new state, in which the whole of societal life is supposed to be reconfigured according to this principle and character, can therefore also simply be a hierarchy. Those ruling over the whole are priests whose dominion extends to all of life's circumstances, to spiritual ones as well as material ones. Under them are the three classes into which the whole society is divided: the learned, the artists, and the industrialists. These correspond to the three main capacities of human nature—understanding, feeling, and enterprise; in other words, the intellectual, sympathetic, and material activities—and their operations and results form the triad of science, art, and industry.

The hierarchy of the priests also has various levels itself. There is not merely a preparatory level, but instead also three stages, in proportion to one's insight, love, and strength. Only a few belong to the first level, the highest class, and these actually make up the college of priests. The highest fathers are chosen from them, one of whom is chosen as the high priest, as the priest-king of humankind, as pope, as the spiritual and secular leader of the entire society; the center of all powers and endeavors; the supreme authority, supreme love, and supreme intelligence of the entire society; the living image of God on earth.

These are the essential and basic features of a system that undeniably has a certain originality. It is a distinctive combination of a medieval hierarchy with the modern ideas of freedom and equality, humanitarianism and universal brotherhood. It is constructed on an analogy with Catholicism, only differing in that it rests on a pantheistic foundation and also incorporates political and material interests. The spirit from which it has in fact arisen is most definitively expressed in the very thing it teaches about abolishing the dualism of spirit and matter, and sanctifying matter; in other words, what has come to be called "the rehabilitation of the flesh," a move that is simply the further consequence of this materialism, and which, as communism and socialism, has become a theory both feared and infamous in our time. In one way, the Saint-Simonians exposed themselves to ridicule because of how fanciful they appear; in another way, they invite the justifiable accusation of spreading morally dangerous principles by putting forward a very free view of marriage and proclaiming the emancipation of women. The result of these latter points is that their society was banned as injurious to public morality and sound ethics, and an end was put to their gatherings. In fact Enfantin,[28] as head of the sect and its supreme father, played a role in both of these [socially liberal] positions.

Moreover, because of the scandalous direction Saint-Simonism took, and which led to its collapse, soon after its condemnation in 1832, not much more was heard of it. Nevertheless these people played their part in bringing into general circulation, and giving significance to, the principles of communism and socialism, the ideas of labor's general proprietary rights [i.e., ownership of the means of production] and of organizing laborers. Since then these ideas have had an even great impact.

---

28. Barthélemy Prosper Enfantin (1796–1864).

Irvingism

Irving,[29] the son of a well-to-do tanner, was born in Annan, in County Dumfries, Scotland, in 1792. In 1822 he emerged as a preacher in the Caledonian Church in London, and soon aroused quite a stir. His impressive figure, lively presentations, and whole style of preaching were attractive because he had a novelty and appeal all his own.

People compared Irving with a Knox, with a Luther. His prophetic, fiery zeal, his bold confrontation of this whole state of affairs, specifically all worldly greatness and grandeur, his most decided political freedom linked to the strictest Christian discipline and Old Testament legalism, recalled for them the old puritan times. With much eloquence he laid bare the misery of the lower classes in England. His preaching met with growing approval from audiences of all social classes, and that made him increasingly bolder in his public appearances. The crowds became ever larger.

Apart from his distinctive style of preaching, there was at that time only one dogmatic contention that made Irving well-known also in other places, his teaching about the accursed flesh of Christ. He said that, in becoming man, Christ had received this accursed flesh from Mary, since no other flesh was available and God had not created any new flesh after creating the world. As a result of this flesh, sin had its essence within Christ's inner self, in each possible form it can take here. All simply imaginable, impure thoughts and drives assailed him inwardly and tempted him to sinful acts. However, Christ has conquered them all in the power of God indwelling him and effected by the Holy Spirit within him. On account of this flesh Christ had to die. But through his death he eradicated the sin and reconciled God since, despite all the burden of the flesh, he, God in the flesh, completely healed our fallen nature. In the flesh he has borne the curse, which as God he could bear, and presented the sacrifice. At the same time, through his mode of life he has also become an example for us, a mode of life in which, as human and with a human soul, he had to do what he did in faith. When he was resurrected by the Father's omnipotence, because he had lived a saintly life in the days of his fleshly existence, he received a new flesh in place of his previous flesh, and now first became a perfect Son of Man. Having entered into heaven as the Son of Man, only now is he the prophet like unto Moses who saw God face to face, one who speaks to the

---

29. Edward Irving (1792–1834). Irvingism is also known as the Catholic Apostolic Church. The movement spread around the world, and at the beginning of the twentieth century there were an estimated 200,000 members in nearly a thousand congregations, most of them in England and Germany, but also scattered in other parts of Europe as well as North America and Australia.

church through his ordinances and through them makes known all of God's decrees. Only now is he God's priest, whose sacrificial offering, carried out daily in heaven, is the cause for God's grace abiding with the church. Now he has come into possession of the honor and might that he reveals through his servants, and that is the main foundation of the solace with which he consoles the church, as the current steward of his house during his absence.

As head of the sect, Irving made into distinctive phenomena the so-called "gifts of the Spirit" that were said to have been exhibited in his congregation in a way similar to how this occurred in Corinth at the time of the Apostles. In fact these gifts first emerged not among Irving's immediate acquaintances, but instead in the so-called "prayer societies" that made it their task to beseech God for a new and abundant outpouring of the Holy Spirit. In one Scottish society of this kind ecstatic phenomena were manifested, and members of a group sent to observe them declared them to be the gift of speaking in tongues and the gift of prophecy. About three years afterward, in 1830, the same phenomena occurred within a small circle in Irving's own house. What happened is that, while Irving was offering a prayer, one of those present suddenly interrupted the praying by uttering a few quite strange and inherently unintelligible sounds, albeit sounds blurted out in a powerful voice and sharply enunciated, sounds causing the others to shudder and be horrified.

An eyewitness who frequently observed this speaking in tongues[30] described the phenomenon as follows:

> Prior to the outbreak of the speaking, the affected person was perceived to be completely internally focused and absorbed, which was recognizable from the closing of the eyes and shading them with the hands. All at once, as though receiving an electric shock, there was a spasmodic convulsion that shook the whole body, and a fiery outburst of strange, Hebrew-sounding emphatic words streaming forth from the quivering mouth, words usually repeated three times and spewed out with unbelievable intensity and sharpness. After this initial flurry of strange sounds, which principally served to prove the authenticity of the inspiration, there always followed a shorter or longer deliverance in English, also repeated and in the form of words or sentences, and consisting at one moment of very strict and

---

30. [*Baur, in the text*] Hohl, *Brückstücke aus dem Leben und den Schriften Irving's* (1849); cf. *Studien und Kritiken* (1849) 197. [*Ed.*] This book, by Michael Hohl, published in St. Gallen, 1839 (not 1849), is cited by Georg Reich, "Der Irvingismus und sein religiöser Charakter," *Theologische Studien und Kritiken* 22 (1849) 193–242, quotation from 198.

earnest admonitions, at another of terrifying warnings, but also of fulsome words of comfort. Following this outpouring, the inspired person lapsed into total silence for an extended period, and only gradually regained composure.

Such persons describe their inner state as being overcome, suddenly and irresistibly, by the Holy Spirit; as having had no clear consciousness of what they felt compelled to express, and not even understanding what they uttered in a strange tongue.

A further point, the basis for Irving becoming the leader of a sect, was that he formally authorized such ecstatic phenomena. In October 1831, during the morning worship service Irving was conducting, for the first time in public an ecstatic young woman suddenly stood up and emitted the usual expressions of such ecstasy. Not only did Irving do nothing to put a stop to such a disturbance; he also instead took care to see that, in the future, such manifestations of the Holy Spirit in his congregation's worship services would be regarded as appropriate. Opposition and multiple attacks drove him to become increasingly persistent and unbending, and soon he began to preach exclusively about the gifts of the Spirit and their expressions. Ultimately, after lengthy proceedings, in 1832, the trustees removed him from his position, and a year later the presbytery at Annan, which had ordained him, defrocked him. In London, the reason for his dismissal was the disruption of orderly worship services; in Annan, it was his erroneous teaching about Christ's human nature. The London trustees demonstrated, from witness accounts, that for five years Irving had convened a society of his own in order to beseech God for the gift of speaking in tongues, and that he had demanded and driven the individual members of the congregation to do so themselves.

Irving then separated himself, and his army of followers, from the "Babylonian confusion" of the church and took his stance under the guidance of the Holy Spirit and under the great head of the church [Christ], by looking forward to its future, organizing no schism but just acting as a servant who affirms that his Master will soon appear. Irving now became so unbending as to boast, in a letter to his congregation, that, upon the last attempt at an amicable reconciliation, God has given him the grace to refuse extending his hand to the presbyters of Annan as a sign of brotherhood—indeed never again to partake of the bread and wine with them. Irving died not longer after this, on 6 December 1834.

After his followers, who had been expelled with him, constituted themselves as a community of their own, another element got added to what Irvingism originally was: the ceremonial, liturgical, hierarchical, or high church community that could not exist in Irving's way of thinking or that of the Scottish Presbyterians. The men of the Episcopal Church who had attached themselves to Irving, and on whom he depended since they supported his congregation, took his work into their own hands. Doubtless the inducement came from this side to bestow the title of "angel" on the clergy of the community, to reinstitute the entire organization of the ancient church, the elders, assistants, and deacons, and ultimately to give leadership authority to a college of apostles. The apostles stand at the pinnacle of the universal church. The prophets, who are at their side but subordinate to them, are the inspired ones who make known the mysteries of God that the apostles place in their hands, so that these mysteries come to the congregations according to the specifications and spiritual decisions of the prophets. An additional office of the universal church is that of the evangelists whose calling is to proclaim the gospel of Irvingism, i.e., its missionaries. A fourth office is that of the shepherds and teachers, who do not have a specific status.

In 1835 the apostles were separated [from the local congregations], the whole of Christendom was divided into twelve tribes, and the apostles were first sent out to them in 1836. To their view that the Christian Church is wholly corrupt, the Irvingites linked the assumption that the church existed in a perfect form, one corresponding to its essential nature, only at the time of the [original] apostles. That is why the church can only be reestablished via apostles. This reestablishment is under way today. It consists in there being once more an integral apostolate in Christendom, one that has to complete the task of the first apostolate and is fully authorized to do so. Today's apostolate in fact possesses all that is needed to lead the church to completion as soon as the church will just accept the apostolate.

While Irvingism very loudly bewailed the profound corruption of the church, it had a very lofty conception of the children of God on earth having the possibility of complete holiness. The baptized are summoned to be completely holy, of course while in their mortal flesh, for we cannot merely be halfway like unto Christ. Instead we are supposed to do, in the flesh, the works of holiness that Christ also did. Those works are the rebirth, but rebirth is not one with the gifts of the Spirit, which are first gained through the apostolic laying on of hands, if in fact one believes in them. If the Irvingite church is supposed to be the renewal of the apostolic church, then its members must also be able to have perfect holiness ascribed to them.

The Irvingites identify so strongly with the apostolic church that they also share with it faith in the imminence of the Parousia. Irvingism anticipates that the Last Things will commence in the very near future. In its very extensive liturgy, which encompasses these events in the most detailed way, only one heading is not represented, that of the grave. It believes it no longer must be concerned about the grave. Irvingites are explicitly assured that the future coming of Christ will occur in this generation. They make a threefold distinction: the ἀποκάλυψις or revelation of Christ as continually drawing near; the ἐπιφάνεια or epiphany, Christ's coming to his church in order to take it unto himself; the παρουσία or final return of Christ, visible to everyone, for the judgment and consummation of the world.

Thus according to Irvingism the historical basis for the entire development of the Christian church would have extended from the apostolic age right on up to Irvingism. During this time the church ceased being what it ought to be, for the entire church had become a sink of iniquity, a Babylon, and outwardly just synagogues of the Antichrist. Accordingly, one simply has to return to the standpoint of the apostles' consciousness, indeed directly to the standpoint that the facts indisputably show was merely illusory, the belief in Christ's Parousia. But if the Parousia was a mere illusion back then, for the same reason nothing has changed today. Can there be a greater denial of historical consciousness than this one?

In England and Scotland, interest in Irvingism very soon declined. About 1834 it supposedly consisted of seven congregations, but a short time later few were to be found. Irvingism directed more of its attention to Germany, although here too it was mainly just in Berlin that it found soil receptive to its aims. Apostles and evangelists came from England. It even won over such men as: C. Rothe, curate at the Church of St. Elizabeth; Rathmann, of the supreme privy council; General von Rudloff, author of a well-known history of the Scottish church; Assessor Wagenor, the editor of the *Neue Preussische Zeitung*; and others. At the beginning of 1848 the number of the faithful had grown to 30–40 persons. Then the congregation was supposed to become organized, but it lacked the necessary personnel. In fact there were no prophets in Berlin, for none of those there who had received the laying on of hands felt impelled to give "utterances." Hence they were assigned a prophet from England. Representatives of the four offices included, among others: Carlyle the apostle, Smith the prophet, Böhn the evangelist, Clayton the angel—all of them Englishmen. The available presbyters were Rothe, Rathmann, and Dr. Thiersch, the Marburg professor of theology.[31]

These two phenomena, Saint-Simonism and Irvingism, are characteristic of France and England respectively. In France the way of thinking expressing itself in Saint-Simonism passed over into a pantheistic materialism

---

31. [*Baur, in the text*] See *Reuter Repertoire* (July 1849) 36. The same information is found in communications about the cultus, namely, *Die Liturgie der Irvingisten*, 69 ff. [*Ed.*] We are unable to provide further information about these citations. On Thiersch, see n. 3.

with a Catholic hue to it. Similarly in England, the Presbyterian-Protestant Irvingism had a spiritual, ethically earnest tendency, but also an outwardly fanciful or visionary character. In each of these countries, the adherents were content with a hierarchical formalism.[32]

The Plymouth Brethren

The Plymouth Brethren[33] form another English sect that we can mention here alongside the Irvingites.

An Irishman by the name of Darby, previously a clergyman in the Anglican Church, had doubts concerning the doctrine of the apostolic succession of bishops. Driven to the opposite extreme from the Irvingite position, he ultimately denied that there are any ordained offices in the church. Declaring all churches since the apostles passed away to be defective, he taught that individuals alone could be rescued from the universal shipwreck. That rescue will take place when they distance themselves from the church, and shun public worship services and receipt of Holy Communion with the crowds. As a substitute for this, he offered himself as one directly called and endowed by the Holy Spirit.

About 1840 Darby went to the French-speaking region of Switzerland and caused considerable disorder for a few years there in Geneva, but even more among the dissident congregations in the Canton of Vaud that had separated from the state church. That went on until people finally resisted his authority and he had to leave the area. What ended there was now shifted to neighboring Württemberg by emissaries from Switzerland. In Württemberg an ecclesial radicalism seeks to make new converts, mainly

---

32. [Baur] See Professor [J. L.] Jacobi's "Heidenthum, Judenthum und Irvingianismus," *Deutsche Zeitschrift für christliche Wissenschaft und christliches Leben* 1 (1850) 39–46. Aristocratic sacerdotalism in ecclesial offices, and externality in performing the rites, are singled out as principal features of Irvingism. The excessive formalism from which English worship services suffer is present here to a heightened degree, and carries over to the minutest differences in vestments suited to the various offices. The liturgical and symbolic features are so completely set apart from the element of the teaching, that the Irvingites maintain that preaching is not in fact part of the cultus. The entire cultus goes back to the concept of a sacrificial offering, so that not only is Holy Communion designated as the focal point of the cultus, but also all emphasis rests on its meaning as a sacrificial offering. Communion is said to be the reproduction or re-presentation of what Christ, the high priest, does in heaven—a continuation of it on earth so far as that can be done by Christ's creaturely representative.

33. This is a low church, nonconformist, evangelical Christian movement originating from Anglicanism and starting in Ireland in the 1820s. John Nelson Darby (1800–82) was an influential early leader.

among the lower social classes, although so far with little success, while the Irvingites in northern Germany recruit among the aristocracy with their hierarchical forms. Darby's sect, called the Plymouth Brethren from the place it originated, gets its leverage from the same points Irvingism does: despair about the present, and proclaiming the imminent, extraordinary judgment, should bring the terrified ones to convert when the only means for standing before the Lord upon his return are at hand.[34]

The Württemberg Sects: The Harmonists, the Michelians, the Pregizerians, and the Adult Baptizers

Since other material that belongs to the history of German sectarianism is of too bizarre and too immoral a kind—for instance the sect of the so-called "self-righteous ones" in Königsberg in 1835, and that of the traditionalist Lutheran pastor Stephan in Dresden in 1830—when it comes to Germany we will just cast a glance here at the sects of our own region.

In Württemberg, the more deep-seated religiosity of the Swabians also is variously receptive to separatist, pietist, and apocalyptic elements, ones that were motivated all the more by the events of the time since the French Revolution. Georg Rapp,[35] a townsman and weaver from Iptingen, was the leader of the Württemberg separatists beginning in 1785. He gathered about him an ever-expanding circle. He spoke to these people about the necessity for a radical work of penitence, for apprehending grace in a tangible way, and being constantly aware of the internal witness of the Spirit. But at the same time he also spoke about the depravity of the church and the decline of church discipline, of the perversity of the teaching concerning the office of preacher and the administration of the sacraments. In doing so, he created the demand for a religious community in which none but the awakened ones stuck together as, so to speak, the remnant bodily corps of the Redeemer, in looking toward the coming of the Lord promised in the Book of Revelation.

When Rapp was questioned before the high court of the community, he stated that he professes no religion in the way that people do so today. He

---

34. [*Baur, in the text*] See the *Allgemeine Zeitung*, 8 March 1850, no. 67 supplement, 1082.

35. Johann Georg Rapp (1757–1847) was influenced by Boehme, Spener, and Swedenborg. His followers left the Lutheran Church in 1785 and because of persecution emigrated to the United States in 1803. Rapp settled in western Pennsylvania and started his first commune, called Harmony. He founded another Harmony in Indiana (which later became New Harmony when it was sold to Robert Owen). Ten years later he returned to Pennsylvania and started the town of Economy.

said his religion is that he loves whoever loves Jesus. The external church is of no consequence. But because abuses are present in worship services, and people indeed call themselves "Christian" but live as heathens, he could no longer participate in the church. His pastor preaches well enough for others, but does not go deep enough for him. The pastor does not make the road to blessedness narrow enough. God's Spirit does not let itself be imprisoned within any circle, for the church of Christ must let itself be impelled and moved solely by its bridegroom.

Rapp's followers also included the type of people who rejected infant baptism, holding that baptism must be postponed until individuals are able to examine and evaluate themselves, as to whether the separation of the kingdom of God from the Devil's kingdom has taken place within them. Others of them affirmed celibacy as one of their tenets, and Rapp himself also refused to take an oath.

At the beginning of the nineteenth century chiliastic hopes became heightened, and the preacher responsible for this was Pastor Friederich in Winzerhausen. In 1801, a caravan of twenty-one people set out to seek the Holy Land. In 1803, Rapp went to America, and soon after many followed him. As Harmonists, they founded a settlement near Pittsburgh, one whose patriarchal rule had Rapp as its leader until 1847. The separatist stance of those remaining behind in Germany had deteriorated into fanatical excess and recalcitrance in several different places. In 1816, from dissatisfaction with the ecclesial establishment, a large number of them, even those less ill-disposed, emigrated to southern Russia and neighboring provinces in Asia. To forestall further emigration, the government gave its approval to the colony of the congregation at Korntal, which, in holding fast to the church's theological framework, retained the older liturgy and ordered its ecclesiastical arrangements, independently of the state church's authorities, on the model of the Herrnhuters [Moravians].

The two principal founders of sects, in addition to Rapp, were Hahn and Pregizer. Johann Michael Hahn,[36] from Altdorf near Böblingen, was just two years younger than Rapp. Hahn differed from Rapp mainly because he was not so extreme a separatist; he always still adhered to the state church. For him the main issue was rebirth as an inner process proceeding by stages, via the spirit of Christ acting upon the heart of the believer. In this process, all that Christ once struggled with, suffered and accomplished in history for our salvation, Christ must now also struggle with, suffer and accomplish in each of us, inwardly and personally, in order to prepare us for being his

---

36. Michael Hahn (1758–1819). His alleged first name does not appear on his birth certificate. His followers were called Michelians (*Michelianer*).

children and receiving perfect bliss. This of course echoes Jacob Boehme. Hahn was certainly familiar with the ideas and writings of Boehme and Oetinger,[37] and from them he constructed a distinctive theory of creation and redemption. His followers, the Michelians, are very widespread in the land. Especially since the chiliastic events they expected to happen in 1836 did not come to pass, they stick more to the ethical emphasis of their master than to his mystical aspect, and in doing so they signify their moral seriousness. Because of this their opponents sometimes call them legalists or those who sigh (*Seufzende*), because they make a righteous life their strict task for the sake of the faith, and because their seriousness in carrying out this task often gives the appearance of somber melancholy.

The Pregizerians[38] differ from the Michelians by the joyous cheerfulness that is the basic tenor of their piety. They call their profession of faith a "confession of grace and gladness," in which they delight in being forgiven and blessed. Conscious of their consummate condition, they take pleasure in looking down on ordinary pietism and on the Michelians, as the sort who still laboriously take pains with the things the Pregizerians have long put behind themselves. They were very mildly counseled about their erroneous idea—as Süskind[39] put it in 1808, in an opinion of the consistory about them—that the reborn Christian would be without any sin or imperfection; that of course in someone reborn and considered as flesh, there would be sin, but that this sin would not belong to that person's actual self and could not be imputed to him or her; and therefore that even gross acts of debauchery have no import for piety. Also, the name of this faction with many members comes from Pregizer, the town pastor in Haiterbach, who died in 1824.

Lastly, we might briefly mention here the Adult Baptizers (*Taufgesinnten*), who appeared a few years ago in Stuttgart. They formed a small fellowship of craftsmen from Stuttgart and a few neighboring villages, who called themselves the "Friends of Christian Truth." The leading member was Schaufler, the toolmaker. In 1837 he refused baptism for a child he fathered because, by researching the Holy Scriptures, he came to the unshakable conviction that infant baptism would be contrary to everything Christ and the apostles had to say about baptism. Baptism is a bond with God that must be made with faith on the part of the human side. Hence baptism could only be performed with the human party's full self-consciousness. Other members

37. Jacob Boehme (1575–1624), a mystic and theologian born in Bohemia; Friedrich Christoph Oetinger (1702–82), a theologian and theosopher born in Württemberg.

38. Named for Christian Gottlob Pregizer (1751–1824), an influential figure in Württemberg pietism.

39. Friedrich Gottlieb Süskind (1767–1829), a professor and preacher in Tübingen and member of the Old Tübingen School.

of the fellowship concurred in refusing infant baptism. They appealed to Matthew 28:19 and Acts 2:38 and 41.

They were peaceful, retiring, upright and hard-working citizens. Only Schaufler acted eccentrically. He thought it requisite that one must sense the moment of rebirth; that one must, so to speak, be agitated, otherwise one has no certainty of being blessed. Also, he held the idea of unconditional election, a view otherwise unusual for the Swabian pietists and separatists. After the fellowship had made its view of infant baptism the rule in practice, it then also decided to adopt proper baptism for itself. It sought to connect up with Baptist congregations in northern Germany, in England and America. Onken, the Baptist preacher in Hamburg, accepted an invitation to Stuttgart, and there made presentations about the basic Baptist principles. As a result, Onken baptized twenty-two persons by immersion in the Neckar River on different days in October 1838. Schaufler undertook a second baptism by immersion of several persons in December of the same year.

As for Holy Communion, they maintained that only those who are believers and are reborn may take part, and that, in conformity with scripture, the rite must be performed with the breaking of the bread. They are treated very fairly by the church and by the state, but their movement is not growing significantly.

INDEX OF PERSONS

Achterfeld (Professor), 266
Adam (Biblical Figure), 382
Adolphus, Gustavus (King of
    Sweden), 445
Agricius (Saint), 272
Alexander I (Tsar of Russia), 115
Alexander the Great, 348
Altenstein, Karl von, 352, 357, 417
Ammon, Christoph F., 88, 156–57,
    163, 343
Angolême (Duchess of), 123
Angolême (Duke of), 126
Anton (King of Saxony), 120
Aquaviva, Claudius, 117
Aristotle (Greek Philosopher), 271
Arnoldi (Bishop), 273–75
Artois (Count of), 122
Ashley-Cooper, Anthony, 455
Auberlen, Karl A., 468
Augusti, Johann C., 88, 151

Baader, Franz von, 376
Bahrdt, Carl F., 45
Balaam (Biblical Figure), 391
Baltzer (Professor), 271
Barral, Louis M., 29
Barrot, Odilon, 128
Barth, Karl, 362
Basedow, Johann B., 45
Bauer, Bruno, 317, 344–45, 355–59,
    364, 399
Baumgarten, Michael, 383–84
Baumgarten-Crusius, Ludwig F., 216
Baur, Ferdinand C. xiii-xix, 4, 12,
    42, 46, 65, 89, 146, 206,
    212, 290–91, 293, 316–17,

328, 338, 346, 363–68, 371,
    374–75, 388–89, 395–96,
    435–76, 468
Bautain, Louis E., 268–70
Beethoven, Ludwig van, 43
Benedict XIV (Pope), 253
Bengel, Ernst G., 89, 212
Bethmann-Hollweg, August von,
    448, 450, 454
Bismarck, Otto E. (Statesman), 12
Bittner (Professor), 271
Bleek, Friedrich, 386–87, 468
Blucher, Gebhard von (General),
    104
Blum, Robert, 278
Boehme, Jacob, 377, 495, 497
Böhn (Irvingite Evangelist), 493
Bonaparte, Joseph, 21
Bonaparte, Napoleon (Emperor), 4,
    9–15, 18–19, 21–22, 24–25,
    27–35, 102, 104, 121, 240,
    273
Bonhoeffer, Dietrich, 371
Bordeaux (Duke of), 128
Braun (Professor), 266
Bretschneider, Karl G., 88, 170, 178,
    207–8, 216
Broglie (Duke of), 128
Broglie, Maurice de, 130
Broglie, Prince de, 32
Bruno (Archbishop), 274
Brzozowski, Tadeusz, 115–16
Bunsen, Karl J., 256, 406

Caesar, Julius, 348
Calixtus (George Callison), 155

INDEX OF PERSONS

Calvin, John, 162, 436
Carlos, Don (Spanish Pretender), 312
Carlstadt (Andreas Bodenstein), 156
Carlyle (Irvingite Apostle), 493
Carové, Friedrich W., 141, 272
Catherine II (The Great; Empress of Russia), 115
Catiline, Lucius S., 28
Chalmers, Thomas, 484
Channing, William E., 484
Charlemagne (Emperor), 27–28, 33
Charles III (King of Spain), 109
Charles X (King of France), 101, 122–23, 127–28, 221–22, 226, 242
Charles Martel (King of the Franks), 27
Chatel, François F., 485
Christina (Queen of Spain), 312
Cicero, Marcus T., 28
Clausen, Henrik N., 214
Clayton (Irvingite Angel), 493
Clement XI (Pope), 132, 296
Clement XIV (Pope), 108
Clement of Alexandria, 59
Coleridge, Samuel T., 484
Conradi, Casimir, 328, 332, 346
Consalvi, Ercole (Cardinal), 21, 109, 111, 113, 139
Constantine (Roman Emperor), 272
Copernicus, Nicolaus, 54–55
Coquerel, Athanase L., 476–67
Cousin, Victor, 244, 268
Creuzer, Georg F., 97, 213
Cuvier, Georges, 127
Czerski, Johannes, 275–76, 278–80

Dalberg, Karl T., 18, 26, 139
Darby, John N., 494–95
Daub, Karl, 89–90, 97, 328, 371
Delitzsch, Franz J., 381, 384, 459, 464
Descartes, René, 206
Dessole (Bishop), 30
De Wette, Wilhelm M., 198–202, 204, 369, 386–88
Dieckhoff (Editor), 398

Döllinger, Johann J., 242, 472
Donna Maria (Queen of Portugal), 313
Dorner, Isaac A., 375–76, 378, 395, 434, 448, 460
Dräseke, Bernhard, 420
Drey, Johann S., 292
Droste-Vischering, Clemens A., 255–56, 259, 265
Droste-Vischering (Countess von), 274
Dunin, Martin von, 257–58
Duvoisin, Jean B. 29–31

Eckermann, Jacob C., 88
Eichhorn, Friedrich, 357, 415–17
Eichhorn, Johann G., 94–95, 207–8
Eilers, Gerd, 417
Eliot, George (Mary Ann Evans), 328, 331, 362
Elvenich (Professor), 266
Enfantin, Barthélemy P., 488
Eschenmayer, Carl A., 335, 346–47
Esparto, Baldomero, 312
Evans, Richard J. 234
Ewald, Heinrich, 307, 393
Eylert, Rulemann, 420

Faust (Literary Character), 345
Ferdinand I (King of the Two Sicilies), 109, 115, 117
Ferdinand II (King of Naples and Sicily), 117, 250
Ferdinand II (King of Spain), 118
Ferdinand VII (King of Spain), 109, 132, 312
Ferdinand, Charles (Duc du Berry), 126
Fesch (Cardinal), 31–32, 121
Feuerbach, Ludwig, 325, 359–63
Fichte, Immanuel H., 325–26, 375, 378
Fichte, Johann G., 36, 38, 48–9, 51–2, 60–70, 73, 78–9, 316–17
Fischer, Kuno, 325
Flatt, Johann F., 88–89, 197
Flatt, Karl C., 88–89
Fock, Otto, 342

INDEX OF PERSONS 501

Forberg, Friedrich K., 61
Fortis, Luigi, 116
Francis II (Holy Roman Emperor), 10, 13
Frederick I (King of Prussia), 160
Frederick II (King of Prussia; The Great), 160, 253
Frederick William (of Brandenburg; The Great Elector), 147, 159
Frederick William II (King of Prussia), 160
Frederick William III (King of Prussia) 13, 62, 120, 158–59, 161, 258
Frederick William IV (King of Prussia), 224, 258, 352, 404–5
Friederich (Pastor), 496
Friedrich August (King of Saxony), 120
Friedrich Ferdinand (Duke), 121
Friedrich Wilhelm (King of Württemberg), 25

Gabler, Johann P., 97
Garibaldi, Giuseppe de, 238
Gasparin, Agenor de, 476, 479
Gass, Wilhelm, 384
Geiger, Franz, 141
George IV (King of England), 126
Gervinus, Georg G., 285–86
Gesenius, Wilhelm, 214–15
Gieseler, Johann C., 3, 6, 207–8, 210–11
Giessel, Johann von, 259
Gildemeister, Johannes G., 274, 466
Gizzi (Cardinal), 231
Gneisenau, Neithardt von, 104
Goethe, Johann W., 36, 38–39, 42–50, 335
Görres, Johann J., 257, 273
Göschel, Karl F., 325, 328, 346, 376, 392
Gregory VII (Pope), 110
Gregory XV (Pope), 296
Gregory XVI (Pope), 227–30
Grossmann, Christian Z., 445
Grüneisen, Carl, 407, 447

Grunow, Eleanore C., 50
Guericke, Ferdinand, 401–2, 419
Guizot, Francois P., 110, 478
Gunther, Anton, 270–72

Hahn, August, 213–14, 401
Hahn, Michael, 496–97
Hamann, Johann G., 38
Harlesss, Gottlieb C., 335–36, 447
Harms, Claus, 155–6
Harnack, Adolf, 381
Harnack, Theodosius, 381, 383
Hase, Karl, 266, 371
Hecker (Herr von), 282
Hegel, Georg W., 43, 51–53, 55, 68–69, 76, 89, 105, 135, 153, 172, 205–6, 316–28, 332, 334, 344–46, 352–55, 359–64, 371, 376, 378
Heinroth (in Leipzig), 214
Heintzen, Eric C., 464
Helena (Saint), 272–74
Hengstenberg, Ernst W., 214, 334, 336, 354, 389–92, 396–98, 402, 420–22, 441–2, 450–51, 454, 456, 462
Herder, Johann G., 38–42
Hermes, Georg, 263–68, 271
Herod (King of the Jews), 463
Hettner, Hermann T., 49, 52
Heubner (in Wittenberg), 214
Hilgenfeld, Adolf, 396
Hirscher, J. B., 307
Hodgson, Peter C., xviii, 326
Hofacker (Author), 309–10
Hofmann, Johann C., 381–84
Hoffmann, Ludwig F., 335–56, 454
Hohl, Michael, 490
Holborn, Hojo, 159–60
Hölderlin, Johann C., 68
Homer, 48, 348
Hook, Farquhar, 481
Hug, Johann L., 26, 95
Humboldt, Karl W., 104
Hundeshagen, Karl B., 15, 406
Huschke, Philipp E., 400
Hüsgen, Johann, 256

502 INDEX OF PERSONS

Ignatius of Loyola (Saint), 108, 117, 243–44
Irving, Edward, 489–93
Isabella II (Queen of Spain), 312

Jacobi, Friedrich H., 38, 52, 73
Jacobi, J. L., 494
Jahn, Johann, 26
Jansen, Cornelius O., 113
Jephthah (Biblical Figure), 391
Jeremiah (Prophet), 335
Jesus of Nazareth, 63–64, 86, 94, 96, 166, 172–73, 176–77, 181, 200–2, 269, 329, 339, 340–43, 357, 496 (*see also* "Jesus Christ" in the Subject Index)
Johann (Archbishop), 272–74
Johann (Archduke), 251
John V (King of Portugal), 132
John VI (King of Portugal), 118
Jonas, 431
Joseph (Biblical Figure), 340
Joseph II (Holy Roman Emperor), 300
Josephine (Empress of France), 11
Judas (Biblical Figure), 341
Julian (Roman Emperor), 209
Julianus (Saint), 113
Jung-Stilling, Johann H., 45

Kahnis, Karl F., 381
Kaiser (Bishop), 262
Kampe, Friedrich F., 284
Kant, Immanuel, 26, 36, 38–39, 44, 52–60, 65, 67–68, 70, 73, 76, 87–89, 143, 155, 183, 202, 212, 263, 268, 316–17
Kareu, Franciszek, 115
Keble, John, 481
Keller (Bishop), 262
Kellner (Pastor), 401
Kerber (Chaplain), 278
Kern, Friedrich H., 338
Ketteler (Professor), 304
Kierkegaard, Søren, 376
Kliefoth, Theodor F., 381, 398, 434, 447, 459, 461–63

Klüpfel, K., 350, 371, 385
Knox, John, 489
Kollwitz, Käthe, 423
König, Bernhard, 419
Köpf, Ulrich, xv, 329, 373
Kotzebue, August von, 104
Krabbe, Otto C., 384, 403
Krug, Wilhelm T., 212,
Kutusow-Smolenskoi (Prince), 102

Lambruschini (Cardinal), 230
Lamenais, Abbé, 142, 480
Lange, Johann P., 343, 375–76
Lavater, Johann K., 45–46, 92
Leo X (Pope), 273
Leo XII (Pope), 113–14, 116, 124, 305
Lessing, Gotthold E., 72
Leu, Joseph, 247–48
Liebing, Heinz, xiv, 6
Liebner, Karl A., 375–76, 395
Liguori, Alfonso (Saint), 119
Linde (Herr von), 282
Löhe, Wilhelm, 459, 464
Louis XVI (King of France), 4, 101
Louis XVIII (King of France), 101–2, 121–23, 127
Louis Napoleon (Napoleon III: Emperor of France), 225, 240–41
Louis-Philippe (King of France), 221–23, 226, 234, 242–43, 246, 249
Lücke, Friedrich, 212, 217, 338, 351, 375, 378, 386–87, 446, 460
Ludwig I (King of Bavaria), 120, 135–36
Luther, Martin, 24, 142, 155, 168, 230, 275, 279–80, 284, 383–84, 436, 449, 475, 483, 489

Mack, Martin J., 262
Mamiami, Terenzo, 236
Mannay, Charles, 29
Manteuffel, von (Minister), 303
Marheineke, Philipp K., 95, 153, 205–7, 290, 317, 320, 327–

INDEX OF PERSONS 503

28, 332, 346, 354, 357–58, 368, 371, 375
Maria Anna (Archduchess), 115
Marie Louise (Archduchess), 11
Märklin, Christian, 462
Martensen, Hans L., 375–77
Martignac, Vicomte de, 124–25, 127
Mary, the Virgin, 123, 230, 239, 272, 296–98, 337, 339, 345, 489
Marx, Karl, 51, 358
Maximilian (Holy Roman Emperor), 273
Maximilian Joseph I (King of Bavaria), 135
Mazzini, Giuseppe, 233–34, 238
Mejer, Otto, 309–10, 381, 398, 461
Menzel, Wolfgang, 347
Metternich, Clemens (Prince), 104, 119–20, 234, 249
Meyer, Heinrich W., 388
Michelet, Jules, 243–44
Miguel I (King of Portugal), 118–19, 133, 312
Möhler, Johann A., 269, 287–92, 295
Molè de Salvandy (Count), 128
Montgelas, Maximilian, 135
Montlosier, Comte de, 124
Moses (Biblical Figure), 209, 269, 348, 486–87
Mozart, Wolfgang A., 348
Muhammad (Prophet), 209, 348
Mühler, Heinrich von, 148
Müller, Julius, 298, 338, 371, 378–79, 395, 414, 434–45, 453
Münchmeyer, August F., 464

Neander, August, 209–11, 214–16, 338–44, 350–52, 354–55, 364, 371, 395, 421
Newman, John H., 481–83
Nicolai, Friedrich, 45
Niebuhr, H. Richard, 362
Nitzsch, Karl I., 212, 290, 368–70, 375, 378–79, 395, 408, 447
Novalis (Georg von Hardenberg), 48, 51

Oetinger, Friedrich C., 377, 497

Oliviera (Countess), 119
Olshausen, Hermann, 214, 386, 401
Onken (Baptist Preacher), 498
Origen, 59
Orpheus, 348
Owen, Robert, 495

Paca, Bartolomeo, 112
Palmer, William, 481
Parker, Theodore, 484
Paul, the Apostle, 66, 96, 338, 364–65
Paul I (Emperor of Russia), 115
Paul III (Pope), 244
Paulus, Heinrich E., 91–94, 96, 212–13, 353
Pedro I (King of Portugal), 133, 312
Pepin the Short (King of the Franks), 27
Perrone (Jesuit), 265, 297
Peter (Saint), 34, 107–9, 235, 241, 272–73, 287, 295, 297, 364–65, 437
Petri, Ludwig A., 460–61
Peyronnet (Duke of), 128
Philipp II (King of Spain), 132
Philippi, Friedrich A., 381–83
Pilate, Pontius, 463
Pischon, 431
Pius VI (Pope), 26, 115
Pius VII (Pope; Luigi Chiaramonti), 26–35, 107–113, 120, 136, 140, 254, 305
Pius VIII (Pope; Francesca Castiglioni), 114, 139, 226, 255, 259
Pius IX (Pope; Mastai Feretti), 230–41, 249, 270–71, 296–99
Planck, Gottlieb J., 20, 95–97
Polignac, Auguste, 125
Pombal, Marquis de, 118–19
Portalis, Jean E., 21
Portalis the Younger (Count), 124
Pregizer, Christian G., 497
Pressel, Theodor, 477
Preux, de (Bishop), 248
Pusey, Edward B., 481–44

Quinet, Edgar, 243–4

Raphael (Artist), 348
Rapp, Johann G., 495–96
Rathmann (Supreme Privy
    Councilor), 493
Ravignan, Xavier de, 242–43
Regenbrecht, Eduard, 277
Reich, Georg, 490
Reinhard, Franz V., 88, 170
Reinhold, Karl L., 74
Reisach, Count von, 120
Reyscher, A. L., 309
Richter, Friedrich, 325
Richter, Herr von, 282
Röhr, Johann F., 166, 212
Romberg (Councilor), 279
Ronge, Johannes, 274–78, 280, 284
Ronsin (Father), 123
Roothaan, Johannes, 116–17, 246,
    250–52
Rosenkranz, Karl, 332, 346, 359
Rossi, Pellegrino, 236, 246
Rothe, C. (Curate), 493
Rothe, Richard, 371, 375, 377–78
Rückert, Leopold I., 388–89
Rudelbach, A. G., 402
Rudloff (General von), 493
Ruge, Arnold, 51, 358
Rupp, Julius F., 423–24, 446
Russell, (Lord) John, 484
Rust, Isaac, 443–4

Sailer, Johann M., 26
Saint-Simon, Henri, 485–88
Sand, Karl L., 104
Schaitberger, Joseph, 473
Schaller, Julius, 346, 359
Schaufler (Adult Baptizer), 497–98
Scheibel, Johann C., 400–2
Schelling (Schlegel), Caroline, 48, 68
Schelling, Friedrich W., 26, 36, 38,
    51–52, 68–76, 79, 89, 135,
    205, 316–17, 324–5, 352–4,
    406
Schiller, Johann C., 36, 38, 42–44,
    46–50, 375, 398
Schlegel, August W., 48–50

Schlegel, Friedrich, 38, 48–51
Schleiermacher, Friedrich, 38,
    47, 50–51, 74, 76–87, 95,
    146, 149–53, 156–58, 163,
    172–99, 203–7, 210–12,
    215, 217, 288, 319–24, 331,
    338, 340, 368–71, 374–76,
    378–80, 382, 387, 393, 395,
    409, 420–22
Schlözer, Dorothea, 24
Schmid, Heinrich F., 185, 304, 381
Schneckenburger, Matthias, 406
Scholder, Klaus, xiv
Schott, C. F., 212
Schott, Heinrich A., 88, 171, 216
Scheuerl, Adolf von, 384, 403, 434
Schulz, David, 216
Schwarz, Carl, 2, 377
Schweitzer, Albert, 353
Schweizer, Alexander, 440
Schwenkfeld, Kaspar, 163
Schwerin, Victor von, 409, 429
Siccardi (Justice Minister), 313
Siess, Philipp, 443
Sigismund, Johann, 159
Sigwart, Christoph, 203
Sigwart-Müller, Constantin, 249
Sixtus IV (Pope), 296
Smith (Irvingite Prophet), 493
Snethlage, Karl W., 407
Spaur (Bavarian Ambassador), 237
Spener, Philipp J., 160, 462, 465,
    477, 495
Spiegel, Count (Archbishop),
    254–55
Spiegel, Ferdinand A., 264
Spinoza, Benedict, 73, 75, 79–80,
    174, 203
Stahl, Frederick J., 409, 412, 414,
    435–41, 449–50, 454, 456
Stapfer, Philipp A., 142–43, 477
Staudlin, Karl F., 88
Steffens, Heinrich, 400
Stein, Heinrich F., 104
Stephan (Pastor), 495
Steudel, Johann C., 212, 214, 333–
    34, 347, 370–71, 395
Stier, Ewald R., 441

Stolberg, Friedrich L., 212–13
Storr, Gottlieb C., 89, 91–2, 97
Strauss, David F., 3, 46, 67, 93, 212,
    247, 291, 326, 328–37, 339,
    341, 343–52, 355–56, 359,
    363–65, 368, 371–74, 385,
    387–88, 394, 457, 476
Strauss, Friedrich S., 214, 409, 474
Süskind, Friedrich G., 76, 89, 97,
    497
Swedenborg, Emanuel, 377, 495
Sybel, H. von, 274
Sydow, Karl L., 409, 413

Talleyrand, Charles M. de, 18
Tetzel, Johann, 275
Theiner, Anton, 280
Thiers, Louis A., 245
Thiersch, Friedrich, 472, 493
Tholuck, Friedrich A., 214, 336–39,
    386
Thomasius, Christian, 151
Thomasius, Gottfried, 381, 383
Tieck, Johann L., 48
Tittmann, Johann A., 169
Twesten, August D., 368–70, 375,
    409–10, 412
Tzschirner, Heinrich G., 170–71

Uhlhorn, Gerhard, 96
Uhlich, Johann J., 417, 419, 425–27
Ullmann, Carl, 210, 212, 216, 338–
    39, 375, 393–95, 398
Umbreit, F. W., 212, 375, 393

Vatke, Wilhelm, 359, 371, 392
Venturini, Karl H., 91
Victor Emmanuel I (King of
    Sardinia), 117

Villèle, Joseph de, 123–24
Villers, Charles de, 24
Vilmar, Wilhelm, 398, 447, 466
Vincent, Jacques, 142–43
Vinet, Alexandre, 480
Voss, Johann H., 48–49, 212–13

Wackernagel, Philipp K., 448
Wagenor (Assessor), 493
Wangemann, H. T., 399
Warnkönig, L. A., 307
Wegscheider, Julius A., 166–68, 212,
    214–15, 417–18, 426
Weisse, Christian H., 325, 343–44,
    357, 375, 378–79
Welch, Claude, 375, 381
Wendte, Martin, 364
Werkmeister, Benedict M., 26
Wessenberg, Ignaz H., 26, 134,
    139–40
Wichern, Johann H., 454–55
Wilke, Christian G., 357
Willem Frederick (King of the
    Netherlands), 130
Wislicenus, Gustav A., 418–21, 424
Wöllner, Johann C., 160
Wucherer, Johann F., 464

Zeller, Eduard, 6, 60, 69, 73, 75, 103,
    190, 192, 225, 241–42, 271,
    282, 284, 298, 302, 311–12,
    314–15, 336, 355, 379, 385,
    395, 397–98, 442, 444, 446–
    47, 454, 465, 479–80
Ziegler, Thomas, 141
Zimmermann, Ernst, 213
Zimmermann, Karl, 445
Zwingli, Huldrych, 203, 280, 435–
    36, 439–40

INDEX OF SUBJECTS

absolute spirit, 76n, 90, 293n, 318–20, 322, 326n, 337, 362
absolute, the, 57, 62, 69–70
absolutism, enlightened, 13n, 15
Adult Baptizers, 497–98
aesthetic ideas, 199–201
aesthetic sensibility, 42–43, 48
Anabaptists, 156
Anglicanism (Anglo-Catholicism), 405–6, 481–83
anthropology, 361, 363
antitheses, cannot be diminished or ignored but must be resolved into their higher unity, 411, 416
archbishop of Canterbury, 405
atheism, 22, 27, 60–62, 73, 75, 142, 169, 217, 283, 285, 358–63
Augsburg Confession, 127, 154, 157, 159, 161, 164, 453
Austria, 10–11, 12n, 101–102n, 119–20, 299–303, 473–74
autonomy, 37, 225, 291, 293n

Baden, 20, 111, 137–39, 143, 161–62, 240, 304–7, 310
baptism, 135, 277, 424, 464, 467, 483, 485, 496–98
Baptists, 456
Battle of Austerlitz, 10
Battle of Jena, 10
Battle of Lützen, 445
Battle of Marengo, 10
Battle of Waterloo, 12
Bauer, Bruno
  his critique of the gospels and turn to atheism, 355–58
  his early, orthodox Hegelianism, 344–45
  his teaching license revoked, 357–58
  on the Union, 399
Baur, Ferdinand Christian
  as a center-left Hegelian, 364n
  his christology, 46n
  his contribution to historical theology, 385
  controversy with Möhler, 288n, 290–91
  his criticism more methodical and more conservative than Strauss's, 368
  discouraged by current state of theology and the church, 468–69
  on the Gospel of John, 366–67
  his neglect of most English-speaking theologians, 484n
  on the opposition between Gentile and Jewish Christianity, 364–65
  on the Pauline, deutero-Pauline, and non-Pauline epistles, 365
  his reconstruction of the history of early Christianity, 364–67
  stands between Schleiermacher and Hegel, 324n
  on the Synoptic Gospels, 366–67
  tendency criticism of, 367

Baur, Ferdinand Christian (*cont.*)
    and the Tübingen School,
        363–68
    his view of the connection
        between metaphysical truth
        and historical mediation,
        64–65
Bavaria, 134–36, 148, 471–73
becoming (*Werden*), 75
Belgium, 129–31, 243
Bible Societies, 112, 114, 142, 232
Bible, as the most human of all
    books, 40–41
Bourbon restoration, 4n, 101, 125
Brandenburg, 145n, 147, 432
Brethren, Moravian, 449, 456

Carlsbad Decrees, 104–5
Catholic Church
    accuses Prussia of destroying the
        Catholic Church, 258
    in Austria, 299–303
    in Baden, 304–7
    in Bavaria, 134–36
    becomes more Protestant with
        divestment of external
        power, 19–20, 241
    becomes reactionary during the
        period 1815–1830, 107–43
    in Belgium, 129–31
    blocks meaningful progress in
        science, 295–96
    clashes with Protestants in
        France, 475–76
    condition of in Germany during
        Napoleonic era, 24–26
    conflicts with Germany, 252–87
    conflicts with state governments,
        298–311
    controversy over mixed
        marriages, 253–55, 257,
        259–62
    in France, 313–14
    frees itself from state control
        in Germany, 134, 139, 261,
        298–99, 302–11
    in Germany, 110–11, 134–39
    in Ireland, 133
    in Italy, Spain, France, 109–10,
        131–33
    loses its temporal power under
        Napoleon, 26–35
    the only saving church, 272
    orthodoxy and absolutism
        prevail after 1830, 260,
        263–68, 271, 295
    in Portugal, 312–13
    in Prussia, 136–37
    secularization of in Germany,
        17–20
    in Spain (after 1848), 312
    in Switzerland, 140, 314–15
    in the Upper Rhine, 137–39
    in Württemberg (after 1848),
        307–11
Catholicism
    accuses Protestantism of
        subjective free will and
        caprice, 292–93
    authoritarianism of, 295
    bad relations with Protestantism
        during the Restoration era,
        125–29
    its basis in the papacy and
        dogma, 141–42
    cannot exist without its popes
        and Jesuits, 252
    Catholic theologians required
        to submit to papal decrees,
        271, 295
    its critique of indifferentism,
        141–42
    disregards its actually
        existing relationship with
        Protestantism, 260–61, 294,
        310
    efforts by liberals to abolish
        celibacy in Germany, 143
    good relations with
        Protestantism during the
        Napoleonic era, 24, 26
    its polemic against
        Protestantism, 141–42,
        260–61
    as a subordinate stage in relation
        to Protestantism, 294

see also German-Catholicism
celibacy, 143
Charter of 1814, 102
Charter of 30 March 1847, 424–25, 428
Christ, *see* Jesus Christ
Christianity
    as the absolute, consummate religion (Hegel), 324
    as a moment of the divine life-process (Schelling), 71–72
    moral interpretation of (Kant), 58–59
    as the purest humanity on the purest path (Herder), 40–41
    purified of eudaemonism by Kant, 57
    speculative view of (Schelling), 72
    transcendent, miraculous character removed in favor of a more liberal comprehension (Goethe), 47
church, *see* Catholic Church, Protestant Church, Lutheran Church, Reformed Church, etc.
church history
    Baur's, 364n, 366n, 385n
    Neander's contribution to (focus on prominent personalities), 209–11, 354
    three periods of in the nineteenth century (1800–1815, 1815–1830, 1830–1860), 4–6
    what does "most recent" mean?, 2–3
    when does the most recent period begin (in 1835, 1830, 1814, 1800?), 3–6
Church of England, 482–83
church-state relations, 145–54, 261, 450–51, 480
communism, 363
concept (*Begriff*), 323, 327
concordat between Napoleon and Pope Pius VII, 21–22

concordat politics, 20, 27, 34, 109–11, 127, 134–37, 239–40, 300–2, 307–11
Confederation of the Rhine, 10, 19, 20, 25
Congress of Rastatt, 17
Congress of Vienna, 12, 19
consciousness
    and being, reality, 54–55, 317
    collective, communal, 197–98
    as finite, subjective, 53–54
    finite and infinite, 320, 362
    Christian, as a modification of religious consciousness, 195
    God in the form of, 187
    immediate, 84, 172
    phenomenology of, 318
    as the power that overarches everything, 195–96
    as reflection into self, 63
    revolution of, 2
    shapes of (Hegel), 318
    unity of, 191
    universe as objective ground of, 79
    see also self-consciousness
consistorial system, 152–53
Copernican worldview (shift from realism to idealism), 54–55

Daub, Karl, *Theologumena*, 89–90
de Wette, Wilhelm Martin Leberecht
    his biblical exegesis, 386–88
    compared with Schleiermacher, 202–4
    his philosophy of religion and dogmatics, 198–202
democratic (popular) principle vs. monarchical principle, 105, 165, 173, 222
Deutsche Jahbücher (*Hallische Jahrbücher*), 358–59
divinity
    as divine-human unity, 40–41, 63
    handles resistance of the finite, 85
    light of, 78

divinity (*continued*)
    not an isolated, individual
        subject, 190
    not something finite, 201
    philosophy as science of the
        divine, 69
dogmatism, political and
    philosophical, 53, 263

Edict of Nantes, 127
Eisenach conferences, 447
England, 480–84, 489, 493
Enlightenment
    actualized in the Union of
        Churches, 399
    destroyed the old faith, 82
    philosophers of, 45
    and science, 168
    shallow rationalism of, 45, 51
Episcopal Church, 456, 481
Erlangen theologians, 381–84
eschatology, 193
Eschenmayer, Carl August, his
    attack on Strauss, 335
eudaemonism, 57
Evangelische Kirchenzeitung, 214–17,
    396–98
exegesis
    biblical, 386–89
    critical (Eichhorn,
        Schleiermacher), 94–95
    rationalistic (Venturini, Paulus),
        90–94
    see also Baur *and* Strauss

faith
    Fichte on, 60–61
    as free self-consciousness related
        to God, 293–294n
    Jacobi on, 74
    progression from institutional to
        rational (Kant), 58–59
    and knowledge, 74
    rational, 168, 170–72, 213
    and reason, 268–69
    Schelling on, 72
    Schleiermacher on, 82, 86, 87,
        172

    and science, 375n
    Strauss on, 331, 371–72
Fathers of the Faith, 114–15, 121–22
Feast of Corpus Christi, 128
feeling (*Gefühl*)
    Feuerbach on, 361
    Hegel's interpretation of, 320–21
    the third to knowing and doing
        (Schleiermacher), 81, 83–84
    of utter dependence
        (Schleiermacher), 86, 179,
        319
Feuerbach, Ludwig
    The Essence of Christianity, 362
    on the essence of religion,
        360–62
    God-consciousness none other
        than species-consciousness,
        360
    Hegel's theological holism
        reduced to egoistic monism,
        362–63
    opposed to the Hegelian school,
        360–61
    on personal immortality, 325
    theology reduced to
        anthropology by, 361, 363
Fichte, Immanuel Hermann,
    defends the personality of
    God and opposes Hegel,
    325–26, 378
Fichte, Johann Gottlieb
    his alleged atheism, 60–62
    favors the Gospel of John, 65
    God as the absolute unity of
        being and life, the in-itself
        (*Ansich*), 62–63
    on God's love, 63
    goes beyond Kant by
        emphasizing religion
        (religious teaching), not just
        morals, 65
    his idealism as the consequence
        and consummation of
        Kantian philosophy, 60
    opposes Pauline Christianity,
        65–66

on the place of theology in the university, 66–67
posits as an immediate unity what first should be mediated by speculation, 62–63
separates the metaphysical and the historical, 63–64
significance of as national educator, 67–68
substitutes the idea of a moral world order for the idea of God, 60–62
fideism, 268–69
Final Recess (*Reichsdeputationrecess*), 18–19
France, 109–110, 121–25, 221–25, 313–14, 474–79
Frankfurt National Assembly, 224
Free Catholic Church, 275–76 (*see also* German-Catholicism)
Free Congregations, 423–24, 427–28
freedom
comes to awareness of itself in early nineteenth century, 37, 53
contemplation of the self by the self (Schleiermacher), 78
and dependence, inward reciprocity of, 86, 179
it principle as the moral law, 55–56
in Protestantism, 293–94
Schelling on, 72, 73n, 353
ultimate axis about which the human being pivots, 56
world history as progress of consciousness of, 52n
French Empire, 10–11
French Revolution, 9, 12, 14

Gallican Articles, 22, 32
genuflection, 471–72
German-Catholicism (*Deutschkatholicismus*)
assessment of, 284–87
criticisms of, 283
German government response to, 281–82
manifesto of May 1849, 282–83
not condemned by Rome because of fear of a new reformation in Germany, 287
its opposition to Roman Catholicism, 272, 277–87
and Protestantism, 283, 285–87
German Confederation, 12n, 101, 103–4, 224
German Empire, 12n
German philosophy (Kant, Fichte, Schelling, Jacobi, Hegel), 52
Germany
Catholic Church in during 1815–1830, 110–11
conflicts with Rome prior to, 1848, 252–87
German people had to awaken from their doldrums and become aware of their national identity and self-consciousness, 13–16, 52, 68
Irvingism in, 493
Jesuit activities in, 120–21
political conditions in after 1830, 224–25
political conditions in from 1815 to 1830, 101–5
sectarianism in is extensive and bizarre, 495
wars of liberation from French domination, 12–16
Gieseler, Johann Carl Ludwig
on the gospels, 207
on the most recent period of church history, 3, 6n, 211
God
as absolute unity of all being and life (Fichte), 62–63
attributes of, 190–91
becoming through distinctions and mediations, 75–76

God (*continued*)
    concrete identity of subjective and objective, knowing and being, infinite and finite, one and many (Schelling), 70
    essential being of not grasped by Schleiermacher, 197
    exists essentially in thinking (Hegel), 321
    and humanity are one (Fichte), 63
    as Kantian postulate, 56
    as living process of self-mediation (Hegel), 318–20
    personhood of, 74, 76n, 190, 192, 325–26
    self-revelation of (Schelling), 70–71
    trinitarian nature of rejected by Schleiermacher, 190–91
    vitality and totality of (Schelling), 70–71
    see also Trinity
God-consciousness
    belongs to the perfection of human nature (Schleiermacher), 180–89, 194
    and sensible consciousness (Schleiermacher), 180–83, 187
    as species-consciousness (Feuerbach), 360
Goethe, Johann Wolfgang
    as a free-thinking "non-Christian", 44n, 45
    God's revelation transcends the Bible, 46
    opposes both orthodox Christianity and Enlightenment rationalism, 45
Gospel of John
    Baur on, 366–67
    defense of its authenticity, 208–9
grace, 168, 173, 178, 269, 436, 438, 464, 485, 491, 495, 497

Gregory XVI, his reactionary stance, 227, 229–30
Günther, philosophy of, condemned by the Vatican, 270–72
Gustavus Adolphus Foundation, 445–46

Hanover, 62, 111, 137, 460–61
Harmonists, 495–96
Harms, Claus, on Luther's 95 Theses, 155–56
Hegel, Georg Wilhelm Friedrich
    essential element is thinking, reason, 322
    on feeling, 320–21
    general character of his system, 316–19
    his interpretation of Christianity, 324, 327
    Lectures on the Philosophy of Religion, 319–24
    on modern Germany philosophy, 52–53
    modern German philosophy reaches its culmination in him, 317
    on the movement of absolute spirit, 318–19
    as necessary advance beyond Schleiermacher, 324
    philosophy and religion have different forms but the same content, 322–23, 327
    philosophy as a process of consciousness, 318
    his philosophy both idealistic and pantheistic, 317–18
    religion as both finite spirit's knowing its oneness with the absolute and absolute spirit's own knowing of itself, 320
    religion as the explication of the idea of God, the self-consciousness of absolute spirit, 319–20
    remained hostile to Romanticism, 51

on the Trinity and the God-man,
   327–28
Hegelian School
   B. Bauer, Göschel, Conradi,
      Rosenkranz, Schaller,
      344–46
   right wing attempt to go beyond
      Hegelian philosophy to
      Christian theism, 324–28
Heidelberg Catechism, 161–62
Hengstenberg, Ernst Wilhelm
   his attack on Schleiermacher,
      421–22
   his attack on Strauss, 334–36
   founder/editor of the
      Evangelische Kirchenzeitung,
      214, 396–97
   his Old Testament theology,
      389–92
   his reactionary theology, 389–
      92, 397
   his sense of betrayal by the high
      consistory, 441–42
Herder, Johann Gottfried
   assimilated and expressed the
      ideas of his age, 39
   his impact on his time, 41
   as a multifaceted,
      comprehensive, innovative
      thinker, 38–39
   as a priest of "humanity", 39–40
Hermesianism, a form of
   Catholicism with affinities
   to Protestantism and
   condemned by the Vatican,
   262–68
heteronomy
   both Catholic and
      Protestant orthodoxy are
      heteronomous (Strauss), 291
   vs. autonomy, 37n, 291
   the will determined by
      something other than its
      own purposes, 55
historical theology, 95–97, 385
historiography
   challenge of writing about recent
      events, 1
   internal causes as the ground of
      external effects, 1–2
   pragmatic, 92–94, 95–97
history
   and metaphysics, 63–65, 67
   as self-actualization of the idea
      (Schelling), 71
Holy Communion, 162–63, 435–37,
   440–41, 467, 483
Holy Roman Empire, dissolution
   of, 10
Holy Spirit, 80, 196–98, 297, 326n,
   397, 418, 436n, 482, 490–91,
   494
Home Mission, 454–55
human being (*Mensch*)
   as essentially free and moral,
      55–56
   Feuerbach's view of, 360–63
   Hegel's view of, 319, 321
   as highly gifted, 47
   human love of God is God's own
      love of himself (Fichte), 63
   rationalism's view of, 166,
      263–64
   orthodox view of, 173
   Protestant view of, 294
   Romantic view of, 49
   Schleiermacher's view of, 83–84,
      178–84, 188–89, 197–98
   Strauss's view of, 332
   in unity with God, 64, 68
   as universal theme, 45–46
humanity (*Humanität, Menschheit*)
   as divine-human unity, 39–41
   Feuerbach's view of, 361
   Fichte's view of, 63–66
   as the highest achievement to
      which human beings can
      aspire, 40
   idea of must actualize itself, 46n
   Kant's view of, 57–59
   rationalism's view of, 96, 166
   religion of, 283
   Schelling's view of, 72–73, 353
   Schiller's view of, 47
   Schleiermacher's view of, 81–82,
      186, 188–89, 197–98

514   INDEX OF SUBJECTS

humanity (*continued*)
   Strauss's view of, 332
   utopian view of, 486–87
Hungary, 302
Hyper-Lutheranism, 459, 463–67

idealism
   its creation of a new ideal reality through the deepening of spirit within itself, 48
   everything for it emanates from consciousness, 53
   Hegelian, 317–18
   and nature, 69
   the other side of pantheism, 79–80
   the philosophical consciousness of the new age, 48
imagination (*Phantasie*), 49, 79, 185, 189, 193, 333
immaculate conception of the Virgin Mary, 239, 296–98
immortality, 56, 75, 193–94, 325, 348, 373
incarnation, 72–73, 197, 207, 327, 362
infinite, the true infinite embodied in the finite (Schelling), 71
intuition (*Anschauung*), 72, 80, 84–85, 202, 323, 413
Ireland, 133, 456, 494
Irvingism (Catholic Apostolic Church), 489–94
Italy, 109, 117–18, 226–29, 230–41,

Jacobi, Friedrich Heinrich
   his conflict with Schelling, 74–75
   faith as the immediate knowledge of God, 74
   his relation to Christianity, 74
   similar to Kant, 73
Jansenism, 113
Jerusalem bishopric (Anglo-Prussian), 404–6
Jesuitism, the natural consequence of Catholicism, 252
Jesuits (Society of Jesus)

   activities after 1830, 242–52
   activities between 1814 and 1830, 117–25
   activities during suspension (1773–1814), 114–16
   in Belgium, 130
   controversy over their teaching, 243–46
   in France, 121–125, 242–246
   their generals since reinstatement, 116–17
   in Germany, 120–21
   influence of, 122–23
   their instruction stifles individualism by rote learning, 243
   opposition to, 124, 250–52
   proselytizing activity of, 116, 121, 252
   reinstatement of in 1814, 108
   in Switzerland, 247–49
   Ultramontane convictions of, 123, 247
Jesus Christ
   his absolutely full strength of God–consciousness (Schleiermacher), 181
   his alleged sinlessness (Schleiermacher), 184–85
   embellishment of the tradition about him (Strauss), 331
   equally archetypal and historical (Schleiermacher), 173, 183–89
   as an example of the archetype of humanity well-pleasing to God (Kant), 58–59
   fullest realization of the divine idea possible for an individual, but not the absolute identity of the God-man (Baur), 46n, 186
   gulf between the God-man for speculation and for the church (Baur), 327–28
   as humanity in itself, the universal human being

(early Schleiermacher),
197–98
not simply a single individual
but universal humanity
(Schelling), 73
not simply an individual but the
idea of humanity (Strauss),
332
resurrection, ascension, second
coming as "prophetic"
doctrines (Schleiermacher),
176, 193
separation of the historical
Christ from the ideal Christ
by Schleiermacher, 185–86
Judaism, Kant's view of, 58
July Revolution of 1830, 5n, 221–23

Kant, Immanuel
his categorical imperative, 57
comparable to Copernicus, 54
his critical philosophy, 53
his focus on consciousness,
53–55
his moral interpretation
analogous to the allegorical
interpretation of the
Alexandrines, 59
no theoretical cognition of the
supersensible, 53–54
postulates of freedom,
immortality, and God, 56
practical reason becomes aware
of its unconditional and
absolute nature, 55–56
on radical evil, 59
on religion within the limits of
reason alone, 57–59
Son of God as personified
principle of the good, 59
Kurmark, 145

La Rochelle Confession of
Faith (French or Gallic
Confession), 477
liturgical reform, 149–51, 163

Lutheran Church
its opposition to science, 459,
467
in Prussia, 432–34
reactionary, zealous views in,
155–56, 160, 435–41, 459
retains too many Catholic
elements, 466–67
some congregations emigrated
to America, 401
Lutheran confessional (orthodox)
theology, 381–84, 399–404
Lutheranism, 161, 260n, 395, 399–
401, 404, 432, 436, 439, 441,
459, 461–62

Marheineke, Philipp
on the unity of church and state,
153–54
argues for the orthodox God-
man on Hegelian grounds,
327
his system of speculative
theology, 207
theology as a science
(*Wissenschaft*), 205–7
marriages, mixed, 253–55, 257,
259–62
mediating theology (post-
Schleiermacher factions),
338–43, 368–70, 374–77,
375n
metaphysics, and history, 63–65, 67
Methodists, 456, 475–476, 479, 481
Michelians, 496–97
miracle, 172, 174–77, 273–74, 330
moderate faction, 338–43 (*see*
mediating theology)
Möhler, Johann Adam
his controversy with Baur, 288n,
291
his misrepresentation of
Protestantism in Baur's view,
289–90
strengthens and heightens
Catholic self-consciousness,
287–88

Möhler, Johann Adam (*continued*)
  his *Symbolik* (on the doctrinal differences between Catholics and Protestants), 288–90

Napoleon Bonaparte
  abdication of, 11
  becomes despotic, 14, 027
  his conflict with Pope Pius VII, 26–35
  distinctive qualities of, 9
  his imitation of Charlemagne, 27–28
  invasion of Russia by, 11
  reappearance and final defeat of, 12
  recognizes importance of religion, 21–24, 27
nature
  Schelling's philosophy of nature as atheism (Jacobi), 75
  as a system of the rational (Schelling), 69–70
Neander, August
  his contribution to church history (focus on prominent personalities), 209–11
  enthusiastic admirer and devotee of the late Schelling, 354
  his *Life of Jesus Christ* as response to Strauss, 339–43
  opposed to banning Strauss's book but regarded it as completely reprehensible, 350–51
  his partisan, intolerant spirit, 354–55
New French Church, 485
New Testament criticism, 207–9, 328 (*see also* Baur *and* Strauss)
Nîmes, persecution of Protestants in, 125–26

Oxford Movement, 480–84

pantheism
  Hengstenberg's critique of, 335, 390
  the move beyond to a new theism, 324
  the One is all and the All is one, 70
  the other side of idealism, 79–80, 318
  as panentheism, 76n
  Schleiermacher's, 174, 190–91
  Spinoza's, 80
papacy
  Anglo-Catholicism does not accept papal supremacy, 483–84
  history of after 1830, 226–41
  liberal Catholics subordinated it to the church, 141
  orthodox Catholics regarded it as the foundation of the church, 140
  and the separation of spiritual from secular power, 33, 241
Papal States, 27–28, 112, 226–29, 233, 235–36, 240–41
parousia, imminence of, 492–93
Paulus, Heinrich Eberhard Gottlob, rationalistic exegesis of, 91–94
Peace of Lunéville, 9–10, 17, 20, 25
Peace of Westphalia, 17, 20, 25, 135, 260
personhood, comprises internal distinctions in the unity of consciousness, 191
philosophy
  indifferent to the absolute content of religion, 42
  and religion, 322–23
  remarkable growth of in early nineteenth century, 36–37
pietism, 462–63
Pius VII
  his condemnation of Bible Societies, 112
  human weakness of (not a saint), 27n, 35

INDEX OF SUBJECTS 517

his papacy under Napoleon,
  26–35
restoration politics of, 107–08,
  112–13
Pius IX
  despite efforts at reform, a
    defender of absolutism and
    Catholic orthodoxy, 230–34
  dogma of immaculate
    conception (1854), 296–97
  his efforts to suppress
    revolution, 235–39, 241
Plymouth Brethren, 494–95
pneumatic interpretation of
  scripture, 467–68
poetry
  ideal world created by it
    substitutes for religion, 43
  new classical age of in early
    nineteenth century, 36
political conditions, linked to
  ecclesiastical conditions,
  144–45
Portugal, 118–19, 132, 312–13
power of the keys, 437–38
predestination, 178–79, 436, 439–40
Pregizerians, 497
presbyterial system, 147, 153
Presbyterian Church, 456, 484
priesthood, 438–39
Proclamation of Kalisch, 102
progress, both gradual and
  revolutionary, 13
Protestant Alliance, 455–57
Protestant Church
  in Austria, 473–74
  in Bavaria, 471–73
  constant vacillation between
    one's own confession and the
    Union of Churches, 441
  during the period 1800–1815,
    36–38
  during the period 1815–1830,
    144–45
  during the period 1830–1860,
    392–469
  ecclesiastical conditions in
    Prussia, 145–48

ecclesiastical system in southern
  Germany, 148–49
in England, 480–84
in France, 125–30, 474–79
governance of in Prussia after
  1830, 407–17
its growing hierarchical power,
  458–59
its high consistory in Berlin,
  430–33
its later hostility toward science,
  458, 461, 467
opposed to pietism, 462–63
in Switzerland, 479–80
its theological faculties in
  France, 23, 478
Protestant Church Congress
  (*Kirchentag*), 448–55
Protestant Friends (Friends of the
  Light), 417–19
Protestant principle, 37, 51–52, 165,
  286, 288n, 293, 435n
Protestantism
  bad relations with Catholicism
    during the Restoration era,
    125–29
  based on spirit's essential nature,
    293
  its essence evident in scientific
    knowledge (*Wissenschaft*),
    206
  good relations with Catholicism
    during the Napoleonic era,
    24, 26
  as an intellectual movement in
    Germany, 36–38
  nothing intermediate between it
    and Catholicism, 286
  people treated as adults in, 294
  its situation under Napoleon,
    22–24
  its subjectivity is not subjective
    caprice but subjective
    freedom, 293–94
Prussia, 10–11, 12n, 13, 62, 104,
  136–37, 145–49, 158–61,
  398–404, 407, 429–34
Puseyism, 480–84

rationalism
  its chief defenders are Röhr and
    Wegscheider, 166–68
  de Wette's, 202–03
  for it faith's content is simply
    given historically, 195
  lacks historical sensibility, 374n
  vs. supernaturalism, 91, 165–71
rationalism and supernaturalism,
  inner mediation impossible,
  yet each needs the other,
  169–71
Rauhes Haus, 454
reason
  and faith, 268–69
  Hegel on, 322
  practical and theoretical, 55
redemption, 178–83
Redemptorists (Liguorians), 119
Reformed Church, 158–59, 162,
  164, 260n, 403, 426, 434–36,
  438–40, 445, 453, 477
Regensburg, Reichstag in, 17–18
religion
  and community, 84, 196–97
  its essential element in thinking,
    not feeling (Hegel), 321–22
  as explication of the idea of
    God, self-consciousness
    of absolute spirit (Hegel),
    319–20
  as feeling of utter dependence
    (Schleiermacher), 86, 179,
    319
  as both finite spirit's knowing its
    oneness with the absolute
    and absolute spirit's knowing
    of itself (Hegel), 320
  Feuerbach on, 360–61
  as intelligible contact of the self
    with the universe (early
    Schleiermacher), 85–86
  once belonged to the very
    substance of life, 82
  and philosophy, 322–23
  rooted in the deepest inwardness
    of human beings: feeling,
    83–84

  its substantial center restored by
    Schleiermacher's *Speeches*
    but in a new form, 82–84
representation (*Vorstellung*), 323,
  327
Restoration period (1815–1830),
  4–6, 101–5
restoration vs. resistance in the
  period 1815–1830, 105–6
Revolutions of 1848, 223–24,
  234–39
Roman Curia, 295
Roman Republic, 238–39
Romanticism
  its critique of morality and
    ethical life, 50
  its ideals of beauty and nobility
    to be sought not in classical
    antiquity but in the spiritual
    life of the Romance and
    Germanic peoples of the
    Middle Ages and later times,
    48
  includes the two Schlegels,
    Tieck, and Novalis, 48
  originates from an essentially
    Protestant principle, 51
  its political views, 51
  its preference for Catholic
    Christianity, 50
  its use of imagination and
    fantasy, 49
  its use of irony, 49
Rosenkranz, Karl
  author of *Hegel's Leben*, 332n
  idea of humanity united with
    God must be realized in a
    single absolute appearance,
    346
Rothe, Richard, his ethics and
  speculative theism, 377–78

sacred tunic of Trier, veneration of,
  272–75
Sainte-Foy, colony in, 478
Saint-Simonians, 485–88
Saxony, 10, 61–62, 120–21, 281, 417,
  419, 428, 432

INDEX OF SUBJECTS 519

Schelling, Friedrich Wilhelm Joseph
   his critique of Fichte, 69
   his early genius and later rivalry
      with Hegel, 68n
   God as becoming, 75–76
   on human freedom, 73n
   identity of spirit and nature,
      subjective and objective,
      69–70
   late views, in Berlin, 352–54
   his negative philosophy, 353
   philosophy becomes the science
      of the divine, 69
   his philosophy of revelation,
      352–53
   his positive philosophy, 325, 353
   speculatively retrieves the
      classical doctrines of
      Christianity, 72–73
   his view of Christianity
      (speculative, not empirical),
      71–72
   his view of God as vital unity,
      absolute totality, 70–71, 75
Schiller, Johann Christoph Friedrich
   Baur's encomium on the
      centennial of his birth, 47
   elevates the theater to a moral-
      religious institution, 43
   enriching one person beyond all
      others is inappropriate, 46
   opposes not Christianity but its
      soulless, abstract theology,
      44
Schleiermacher, Friedrich
   Christ as humanity in itself (*der Mensch an sich*), 197–98
   Christmas Eve shows how varied
      ways of understanding
      Christianity may peacefully
      coexist, 87
   on church organization in
      Prussia, 146, 151
   his critique of Harms and
      Ammon, 156–57
   defends authenticity of the
      Gospel of John, 208–9
   his distinctive sphere is religion,
      not philosophy, 77
   dogma of Christ as postulate of
      Christian experience, 87,
      186–87
   early work contains all the
      essential elements of his
      thought, 77
   on freedom, 78
   Glaubenslehre (*Christian Faith*), see Schleiermacher's *Glaubenslehre*
   historical Christ does not play a
      redemptive role in the early
      writings of, 86
   on the holy, rejected Spinoza,
      79–80
   influenced by Schlegel's
      Romanticism, 50
   inward reciprocity of freedom
      and dependence in the
      Speeches essentially
      different from the feeling
      of utter dependence of the
      Glaubenslehre, 86
   on liturgical reform in Prussia,
      149–50
   on religious feeling, 81, 83
   Soliloquies as subjective
      idealism, 78
   Speeches on Religion as objective
      idealism, 79
   Speeches on Religion directed
      to the cultured among its
      despisers, 81–82
   view of Christianity in the
      Speeches: redemption of the
      finite from its resistance to
      divinity, 84–86
Schleiermacher's *Glaubenslehre*
(*Christian Faith*)
   acquires an increasingly
      speculative character
      (subjective and objective
      consciousness), 196–97
   antithesis of God-consciousness
      and sensible consciousness,
      180–82

Schleiermacher's *Glaubenslehre* (cont.)
  argues from efficacy of
    redemption to cause in
    Christ, 186–87
  Christ realized in an endless
    diversity of individuals,
    188–89
  Christ's resurrection, ascension,
    and second coming as
    "prophetic" doctrines, 176,
    193
  claims to put an end to the
    rationalism-supernaturalism
    controversy, 172–73
  compared to Kant's *Religion
    Within the Limits of Reason
    Alone*, 183
  its critique of immortality,
    193–94
  as deterministic system, 179
  develops entire content of
    Christian faith from the
    testimony of immediate
    Christian consciousness,
    172, 195–96
  on the divine attributes and
    Trinity, 190–91
  God-consciousness belongs to
    the perfection of human
    nature, 187–89
  Holy Spirit as shared spirit of
    the collective consciousness,
    superseding Christ, 196–98
  internal coherence and historical
    significance of, 194–98
  lacks any object concept of God's
    essence, 197
  necessary progression from it to
    Hegel, 324
  no place for miracle in its
    system, 172, 176
  pantheism of, 174, 190–91
  person of Christ as equally
    historical and archetypal,
    173, 183–189
  person of the redeemer replaces
    the concept of redemption,
    180–83
  philosophy everywhere evident
    in it, 323
  position on belief in miracles,
    174–77
  rejects divine personhood, 190,
    192
  its relation to church teaching,
    191–94
  religion based on the facts of
    self-consciousness, 180
  separation of the historical
    Christ from the ideal Christ,
    185–86
  sophistical-dialectical and
    deceptive ingenuity of, 176–
    77, 181, 183, 189, 192
  its teaching about sin and
    redemption, 178–83
  its treatment of eschatology, 193
  underlying dualism between
    faith and reason in, 203–4
  unites democratic principle of
    reason and monarchical
    rights of Christianity, 173
  what appears to be the
    redeemer's act is really the
    immanent act of the subject
    itself, 182–83, 187
Scotland, 484, 489, 493
sects, 485–98
self
  free and self-determining vs.
    conditioned and dependent,
    79
  original unity with the universe
    (Schleiermacher), 78, 80–81
self-consciousness, 54–55,
  78–79, 180, 182, 187, 190,
  195–96, 198, 225n, 293, 317,
  319–20, 322n, 323, 348,
  356–57, 362–63
Silesia, 253, 282, 400–1, 432, 474
Son of God
  disciples recognized Christ as
    without resurrection and
    ascension, 176
  empties himself, 412
  as the finite in itself, 72

not paid as a ransom to God's wrath, 382
as personified principle of the good (Kant), 59
Sonderbund War, 248–49
Spain, 109, 118, 131–32, 312
speaking in tongues, 490–91
species-consciousness, 360, 363
speculative philosophy, 68n, 205n, 206
speculative theology, 46, 97, 207, 293, 324, 377–78
spirit
and the community of spirits, 79, 84
gifts of the, 490–91
knows itself as the free, self-determining, absolute subject, 77–78
supreme principle of, 293
see also absolute spirit, Holy Spirit
Stahl, Friedrich Julius, leader of orthodox Lutheranism, 409n, 414, 435–41
Steudel, Johann Christian Friedrich, his attack on Strauss, 333
Strauss, David Friedrich
Christ as "religious genius", 348
Die christliche Glaubenslehre, 371–73
claims core of Christian faith is independent of critical investigations, 331–32
compiles already existing materials, holds a mirror up to his own era, 349–50
conflict between Christian faith and modern science, 371–72
controversy over his appointment in Zürich, 247, 351
ecclesiastical reaction to, 350–52
on the embellishment of the tradition about Jesus, 331
history of dogma as its critique, 372–74
his incendiary impact, 333, 350–51
key to christology: Christ as a real idea in humanity, 332
The Life of Jesus Critically Examined, 328–33
mythical interpretation replaces supernatural and rational interpretations, 329–31
his negative vs. positive criticism, 330–31
negativity of his results, 363–64, 373
not the nature of the idea to pour out its entire fullness into a single individual, 46, 332
opponents of, 333–37
his rationalism lacks historical sensibility, 374n
his response to Bruno Bauer, 345
his response to I. H. Fichte, 326
Streitschriften (defense of his *Leben Jesu*), 347
"Vergängliches und Bleibendes im Christentum", 347–48
subjectivity, principle of, 51–52, 77–78, 294
supernaturalism, 89–90, 96, 165–74, 205–7, 212, 331, 333–34, 343, 347–48, 370, 374–76, 386, 394, 395
Switzerland, 140, 247–49, 314–15, 479–80, 494
synodal system, 145–47, 429–30

Test Act of 1673, 133
theism, 73, 75–76, 174, 190, 324, 325n, 326, 378, 390
theological journals, 97, 212–17, 393–98
Theologische Jahrbücher, 395–96
Theologische Studien und Kritiken, 212, 393–94

522 INDEX OF SUBJECTS

theology
    centrist, conservative, and liberal in the Union of Churches, 409–11
    and church, 2
    dogmatics after Schleiermacher strives to mediate faith and reason, 204–5, 211–12
    dogmatics during the period 1800–1815, 87–89
    opposition to critical, scientific theology grows in response to Strauss, 351–52, 457–58
    Protestant, after 1830, 316–98
    return of younger theologians to the old orthodoxy, 388, 458
    revolution in theological consciousness (1750–1815), 4–5
    as a science (*Wissenschaft*), inwardly unifying reason and revelation, 205–7
    study of has recently been discredited, 398
    as a university science, 66–67
thing-in-itself (*Ding an sich*), 54–55
Thirty-Nine Articles, 482–83
Tholuck, Friedrich August Gottreu, his attack on Strauss, 336
Tractarians, 482
Treaty of Schönbrunn, 11
Trinity
    Daub on, 89
    doctrine of, 327, 370, 412, 465
    as inclusive or holistic (Hegel), 326n
    Schelling on, 72
    Schleiermacher on, 191
    Schleiermacherian vs. Hegelian versions of, 319
Tübingen School
    new, 367–68, 371n
    old, 88–89, 333n, 497n
Tübinger Zeitschrift für Theologie, 212, 395

Uhlich, Johann
    dismissal of, 425–28
    founder of Protestant Friends, pastor of Free Congregation in Magdeburg, 417–19, 427
Ullmann, Carl
    influential editor of *Theologische Studien und Kritiken*, 210n, 212, 393–95
    as mediating theologian, 338, 375
Ultramontanism, 32, 123, 130–31, 141, 247–48, 295
Union of the Lutheran and Reformed Churches (Prussian Union of Churches)
    its antecedents, 159–61
    in Baden, the Palatinate, and Nassau, 161–62
    conflict between rationalism and supernaturalism in, 165
    created through celebration of the 300th anniversary of the Reformation in 1817, 146, 154–55, 158
    critique of by Stahl, 435–41
    disagreements about, 162–64, 398–404
    endorsed by Schleiermacher, 157–58, 163
    government efforts to enforce, 401–4
    introduced in Prussia, 158–61
    Lutheran resistance to, 399–404, 435–41
    and Lutheranism in Prussia, 432–34
    opposition to the Union liturgy, 400–401
    in the Palatinate, 442–44
    situation of in Prussia after 1830, 407–17
    status at the present time (1856), 434
    theological issues in, 379–81, 408–14
    union in ritual, not doctrine, 163–64
universe, and the self, 78, 80–81

universities
    controlled by the government or the Catholic Church, 267–68, 311
    demands for Lutheran orthodoxy in, 383–84, 398, 459–61
    efforts to purge them of critical elements, 352, 357–58
Upper Rhine (Württemberg, Baden, Electorate of Hesse, Grand Duchy of Hesse, Nassau, Frankfurt), 137–39

Waldensian communities, 131

Weisse, Christian Hermann
    advances a speculative theism, 325, 378–79
    advocates the priority of Mark, 325n, 344
    seeks to surpass Strauss positively, 343–44
world history, as the progress of the consciousness of freedom, 52n
Württemberg, 25, 262, 307–11, 494–98

Zwingli, Huldrych, critique of by Stahl, 435–36

www.ingramcontent.com/pod-product-compliance
Lightning Source LLC
Chambersburg PA
CBHW021229300426
44111CB00007B/483